THE LAST ORATOR FOR THE MILLHANDS

MERCER UNIVERSITY

MERCER UNIVERSITY PRESS

Endowed by

TOM WATSON BROWN

and

THE WATSON-BROWN FOUNDATION, INC.

THE LAST ORATOR FOR THE MILLHANDS

William Jennings Bryan Dorn

1916–2005

John Herbert Roper Sr.

MERCER UNIVERSITY PRESS
Macon, Georgia
1979–2019
40 Years of Publishing Excellence

MUP/ H966

Published by Mercer University Press
1501 Mercer University Drive
Macon, Georgia 31207

9 8 7 6 5 4 3 2 1

Books published by Mercer University Press are printed on acid-free paper that meets the requirements of the American National Standard for Information Sciences—Permanence of Paper for Printed Library Materials.

Printed and bound in the United States.

This book is set in Adobe Caslon.

ISBN 978-0-88146-690-4
Cataloging-in-Publication Data is available from the Library of Congress

Contents

To the hash man:

The speechifier bears watching

Note about Words

Words change over the years, especially for those whose profession is oratory. In the era from World War I to 1968, the words *black* and *African American* were simply not employed by many people in speech and writing. Both polite people and scholars used the word *Negro*, conspicuously capitalized, as the proper term for the race. An occasional synonym was *colored*, although it always had connotations that were problematical. Even the matchless Martin Luther King Jr. used Negro in most of his speeches and writings, with black and African American as seldom-used synonyms. King's mentor (and Dorn's beloved one-time neighbor and long-time friend) Dr. Benjamin Elijah Mays used Negro exclusively until a vanishing point in 1968 (after King's assassination), and then Dr. Mays changed his own language. Congressman Dorn self-consciously followed the lead of Dr. Mays and after 1968 began to use African American and black in his speeches and writings.

As a biographer, I hate putting words into people's mouths, especially those of serious-minded orators. Great orators need to have the chance to say what they said the way they said it, and the biographer needs to get out of the way. Dr. King intended to say Negro in the 1950s and early 1960s, and so did Congressman Dorn. Other people, including, memorably, Dorn's famous cousin Strom Thurmond, often pointedly used the word "nigger" or its cousin "nigrah," and they meant something Jim Crow in that usage. In quoting Dorn, I have put Negro into quotes because that is what such people in such context actually said. As for the Dorn patriarch, Eb Dorn, he sometimes used "colored" in official speeches, and I have quoted him as he so spoke. I have also shown in context how limited Eb Dorn's view of black people was; even in the speeches he was making early in the Great Depression days, "colored schools" could be improved but never become the equal of white. For anything after 1968, I have used standard language, especially since Congressman Dorn after 1968 used standard language and abandoned Negro. I have used black and African American even when referring to people in the nineteenth or early twentieth centuries. On an occasion in the text, it is necessary to quote the congressman, and at such times, I have quoted exactly what he said as he said it.

As noted in the text, the Dorn family, including the extended family of the First Baptist Church of Greenwood, had no patience with racist language. In all those boxes of his correspondence over the decades from the Great Depression to the twenty-first century, I found only one instance of William Jennings Bryan Dorn using the word "nigger." It was in a letter to his mother,

Pearl, while he was training in the Army Air Corps. It was a letter she shared with her Sunday school class, and members of the class promptly wrote to the cadet trainee with vehement scolding, shaming him by reminding him of "good Negroes" and "good Colored" people in his town. He was properly humbled, properly contrite, and properly apologetic, and he did not us the "n-word" again. He carefully preserved the record of his error, which he regarded as a great sin for which he needed forgiveness.

Acknowledgments

My debts are many. I name the people most prominently responsible. Once, Vann Woodward noted that he had never footnoted Charles Austin Beard but that he obviously owed much to Beard's thinking, and so he thanked Beard, who was then long dead—and who had never actually instructed Woodward (although he did inherit an office from him that included a remarkable collection of liquor bottles). In similar vein, I note that Karl Marx, St. Thomas Aquinas, and my mother, Dorothy Louise Watson Roper, all now long gone, made great impact on my thinking and need to be thanked, especially where the political way of life for William Jennings Bryan Dorn is concerned. Mother noted Congressman Dorn's help for education and his struggles (and they were *struggles*) for racial Liberalization, two connected passions. Marx, he hated, but Dorn studied him, and the Red Prussian surely gave the congressman his fascination with analysis based on class and classism, with attention to the masses who voted for the congressman and the classes who maintained the structures of the textile industry. Thomas Aquinas "baptized" Aristotle—and Bryan Dorn certainly approved full-immersion baptism—and developed a close study of the interplay of character and practice based on habit and discipline, which proved vital to the congressman's career.

Alexander Moore, sensitive and steady, working too hard and patient to a fault, inspired me to dream up this biography and has always been as much a "blue pencil" editor and creative consultant as the acquisitions editor in his title. When Alex left the University of South Carolina Press, I turned to Dr. Marc Jolley of the Department of Religion and Mercer University Press. Marc and I have done four major publishing projects over as many decades, and it has been delightful to work with him yet again.

Dr. Constance Schulz, superb historian of the colonial and revolutionary periods of South Carolina (and Maryland and other places), threw open her home, once residence of Rex Enright, and in processes introduced me to wonderful visiting scholars and to her own remarkable insights as a grand Puritan and Congregationalist preacher's kid; she was counterweight to my twin heritage of Cavalier and redneck. The Ernest Frederick Hollings Library at the University of South Carolina provides a remarkable treasure, housing both the Irwin Rare Book Collection (the congressman was a reader, and the Irwin collection allows one to read the same edition of what he read, especially in World War II and early Cold War days) and the South Carolina Political Collections, depository of the primary papers including correspondence, speech outlines, telephone logs, and other matter, such as especially superb interviews, particularly those conducted by director Herbert Hartsook. In a staff of hard-working professionals, Kate Moore stands out as one who consistently went far beyond reasonable expectations—or even unreasonable expectations.

The South Caroliniana Library is in the architecturally fascinating and historically significant building designed by Robert Mills and reorganized and recatalogued by Richard T. Greener, Harvard-trained scholar and black political activist of Reconstruction whose work was first pointed out to me by Thomas E. Terrill when I was new to the study of history and he was new to the practice of teaching. The SCL, heroically maintained by Henry Fulmer and Allen Stokes, has all the newspapers, especially the *Greenwood Index* and *Greenwood Index Journal*, plus the papers and daybooks of the family of the "bravest journalist of South Carolina," Harry LeGare Watson. The nonpareil John Hammond Moore has usefully developed a guide to all the newspapers that ever were in my own native state, especially the more obscure small-town and rural presses. The Thomas Cooper Library, its staff directed ably by Dean Thomas McNally, provides the *Congressional Record* serial set plus government documents plus the *Charlotte Observer* and the *New York Times*, which are so vital to modern political search work. Among many there, Bill Sudduth stands out for special favors and kindnesses.

For the congressman, politics, as for Pericles, was not only a business, but the only business. As such, the worthy opposition was noted as well for worthiness and for their opposition. Again, if Dorn's nemesis/mentor Marx is right, opposition is necessary to one's being and doing. The worthy opponent Dr. James Burrows Edwards was generous with time to review the interesting race of 1974 and other events shared in common with Dorn. Also, Charles "Pug" Ravenel, somewhat like Dorn in another era, invented new processes and techniques in campaigning for office, and the Charleston financier has placed his papers and left reminiscences at the SCPC, while his campaign advisor Bud Ferillo has been generous with time and valuable insights.

Research costs money and involves travel, even and especially in the days of wonderful online services, and my research and travel were helped mightily by the Institute for Southern Studies created by Walter Edgar and administered wisely by Bob Ellis, a fellow aficionado of Walker Percy. Still more research money was provided by the Division of Social Sciences at Emory & Henry College, and the wizards who found me money where there seemed to be none were Dean Chris Qualls and chair of Division of Social Sciences, John T. Morgan. By far the greatest sums of money came from the William Jennings Bryan Dorn Fund established to help scholars who are studying modern South Carolina politics, periods of time that inevitably crisscross the congressman's personal and political party papers. Besides the costs of doing research, Herb Hartsook and Steve Griffith and others of the Dorn Fund found money for defraying the high cost of publishing. There was also a generous grant from the South Caroliniana Society to help with such expenses of publishing.

Researchers are often lonely but never truly work alone. The reference librarians at Emory & Henry College, Jane Caldwell and Patty Greany and Jody Hanshew and Jan Kirby, all helped out with searches and book and periodical loans, and also were kind to listen to various ramblings about sources and their uses. The congressman had associates everywhere, and his good friends Arkansas Congressman Brooks Hays and Bob Jones University founder Bob Jones Sr. left documents at Emory & Henry College, documents and observations that the college archivist, Robert Vejnar, located and helped me interpret.

My mentors at the University of South Carolina History Department included the already mentioned Thomas E. Terrill but also Edward H. Beardsley (who brought me into the discipline, became my academic advisor, and stood witness to the marriage of his two students, Rita Roper and me), Robert Weir, and the late John Scott Wilson and John Duffy. Too, in the long ago when I first collected data on Congressman Dorn, there was the superb journalism mentor Harold Crutchfield, who put me in the governor's office with then-Governor Robert E. McNair, and above all with the late Wayne Seal, fine public servant who fed me information about those yeasty days of Lyndon Johnson and Richard Nixon. More important, Professor Crutchfield persuaded me to leave newspaper work and become an historian, being kind enough to see where my real talents lay (and also candid enough to tell me what talents I in no way possessed). Also from those days, the late Philip Grose, press secretary to Governor McNair and Governor West (and later their political biographer) assisted me with insights and reminiscences about the actors on stage then. I met Phil while both of us were fellows of the Institute for Southern Studies.

The congressman's large and sprawling family members have opened their homes to me and have opened their memories, all narrated with the best of red hills raconteuring, especially cousin Steve Griffith Jr., onetime judge and later counsel for Duke Power, and Dorn brother Watson, decorated navy hero and rising star in postwar military who left a promising "military industrial complex" career to help Bryan Dorn run for office.

History students at Emory & Henry College came with me on research trips, helping to do research in the 1974 gubernatorial campaign and providing me useful insights with their good questions and sharp insights: Anna Blydenburgh, Mark Robertson, Matthew Wilkinson, Carter Aylor, and

Aaron Gillespie. My son, the historian of Germany John Herbert Roper Jr., has been a wise and sharp-eyed critic. After one failed retirement at Emory & Henry College, I reemerged at Coastal Carolina University, and there, too, colleagues and students have helped me. Eldred E. ("Wink") Prince, John Navin, and above all chairperson Amanda Bryan have been generous in listening to me—and they arranged a forum for presentation of an early draft of the chapter on the election of 1974. Too, Dr. Bryan has been kind, along with administrative genius Stephanie Freeman, in helping me with travel expenses for research and presentations. Also at Coastal Carolina University, students Kiersten Camby, Brandon Stone, Kaitlyn Wood, Marie Romano, Sarah Mulready, and Jarrett Zissett have been energetic and kind in helping with research, especially with finding photographs and other images.

My wife, Rita Roper, long ago agreed to manage and maintain the life of an academic family in small teaching colleges and has figured out budgets and kept me on task, bucking me up and bringing me down as needed. I would never have paid attention to the civil rights movement happening under my nose if not for her and her moral commitments and broad vision.

The superb journalist Jack Bass, surely the best journalist of Dorn's era, would probably rather be called historian today. Whether it is the on-the-scene reportage he gave in another era or his reflective books or his continuing kindnesses to other scholars, Jack Bass is the best and does honor to North, South Carolina, which he notes is east and south of Due West.

There are still others I could name but will not, and all, all share responsibility for what is good. For the inevitable errors, I stand heroically responsible and uniquely guilty.

—John Herbert Roper Sr.

Prelude

"Please Help Us"
Please help us, for we have helped you.[1]

The letters were there as usual, and his secretary was answering them. They all said the same thing. A plant manager had given his millhands a mimeographed sheet that said to write to Congressman Dorn about fair trade and cheap-labor competition from abroad. It was orchestrated. Many workers sent in the sheet and signed it on the bottom.

But it was not completely orchestrated. Many, many others, especially women millworkers, wrote on lined paper in their own words and signed with care on the bottom. *Please help us for we have helped you. Please help us if you can and I will always help you. We worked six days a week, then five, now four, and they say soon, three. The plant may close. Don't forget us.*

Many of the women added something the plant manager had not thought to suggest to them: *P.S. I want you to answer me.* And most touching, in the careful, cursive writing of a onetime schoolgirl who dreamed now of Clemson College for her boys: *We trust in you. Please ans[wer].*[2]

It was 1958.

Congressman William Jennings Bryan Dorn sat in his stuffed-leather chair in his offices in the nation's capital. His dark hair was thinning now, and no blue-black forelock tumbled down into his eyes as it once did. In fact, his hair had receded, laying bare his broad forehead. He had picked up weight amidships, and he nowadays disliked being photographed without his jacket and tie.

Once, he was a boy wonder from the red hills and cotton fields of the Greenwood, South Carolina, countryside, and the state capital in Columbia had been daunting to him. Then, he was only twenty-three years old, and he was often in his shirt sleeves—in the piedmont style of short-sleeved, bleached white, cotton shirt manufactured in the red-clay and pine-tree re-

---

[1] Quoted, Faye Paige to William Jennings Bryan Dorn (hereinafter WJBD) 28 May 1958, William Jennings Bryan Dorn Papers, South Carolina Political Collections, Ernest Frederick Hollings Library of the University of South Carolina (hereinafter WJBD/SCPC); other millworker letters, May 1958, WJBD/SCPC.

[2] Ibid.

gion—and he had waved his powerful farmer's hands and pumped his muscled forearms up and down vigorously with the orator's flourishes that he thought Cicero had used in the old and innocent republic of Rome. Then, he had tossed his head to move the forelock out of his eyes so that he could look into the eyes of the people—his people, the middling class of the small-time farmer in Ninety-Six, the millworker couple who were spinners at Belton Yarn, the independent car dealer from Abbeville, the Anderson savings-and-loan guy, the Baptist minister from Honea Path.

The twenty-three-year-old called back the echoes of his namesake, William Jennings Bryan, the boy orator of the Nebraska prairie who had thrown thunderbolts with his voice, the orator who could be heard clear and firm anywhere in the little piedmont towns and village crossroads where he visited in 1898. Farm children T. E. "Eb" Dorn and his wife, Pearl Griffith Dorn, later proudly school teachers in the county schools, knew about the boy orator and admired him. Bryan had spoken in the town of Greenwood when the Dorns were teenagers, and newspaper accounts had it that 5,000 people—more people than the town population—came to hear the "Greatest man in America." They never forgot Bryan, champion of the common man, and the couple named their sixth child William Jennings Bryan Dorn. They always called him Bryan.[3]

Eb and Pearl Griffith Dorn reminded Bryan often and loudly that he was one of the people, a Christian brother to everyone, as good as anyone but not better than anyone else, a servant of the people. He was not chosen by God to lead, but God had chosen him to serve in office. To serve in office was not to lord it over anyone. There was only one Lord, and no man should pretend to be a king and certainly not a lord. The people, his neighbors, sent Bryan to the state General Assembly when he was only twenty-three years old, and then when World War II came in 1941, they sent him to the Army Air Corps, and they prayed for him in their white-washed, clapboard Baptist sanctuaries while he was fighting in Europe for more than eighteen months. When he got back from Europe, the people sent him to the US House of Representatives, at age thirty-one, and they told him to represent the commoners of South Carolina's Third District.[4]

---

[3] Interview: Steve Griffith and Watson Dorn with John Herbert Roper (28 February 2012), William Jennings Bryan Dorn Papers, South Carolina Political Collections, Ernest Frederick Hollings Library of the University of South Carolina, hereinafter JHR/SCPC; cite 1926 in WJBD/SCPC.

[4] WJBD/SCPC. Especially 1926.

He never forgot a name or a face, and he actually remembered all of them when he was a young congressman. He served alongside other recently discharged veterans who came to the House of Representatives in 1947: Dick Nixon, Carl Albert, and Jack Kennedy. All of those young congressmen remembered the folk back home who sent them to *Dee Cee*, and they palled around with each other and reminded each other that it was a miracle to be free and an honor to serve the common people. The handsome Kennedy was lace-curtain Irish and rich, and he joshed Bryan Dorn about his twangy accent, as Dorn joshed Kennedy about his sharp Brookline Irishisms, but they respected each other, and they reminded each other that there were working-class folk back home who were counting on them.

And now it was 1958. He took off his jacket and rolled up his long-sleeved dress shirt, sliding its expensive poplin up his still-powerful forearms. The face was broad and fleshly now, but the blue eyes still shined as intensely as they had in his youth. His people, the people—rednecks, lintheads, hicks, country bumpkins; his people, the people—salt of the earth, most of them Scotch-Irish, some German, all of them plain folk, jes' folks. They took their religion and their football and their politics the way they took their liquor—hard and strong and straight. They needed him. They were crying to him. He was the orator of the people. It was time to *do* for them.

What *did* Bryan Dorn do after he rolled up his monogrammed poplin sleeves? He did what he had always done before and what he would do again and again until he left the US Congress in the vain effort to become the governor of South Carolina.

He did things at two levels, one for the classes who owned the cotton mills and another for the masses who worked in the mills. For the classes, he remade existing laws and called on trade-commission regulators. The lawmaking and the personal persuasion with regulators was to ensure corporate tax breaks, protective tariffs and protective quotas, and above all the "right" interpretation of Japanese and other foreign "dumping" of subsidized textile goods onto American markets. He met with the informal Textile Group, both as a group that he convened as its secretary and individually one-on-one as major negotiator. In the group and in the one-on-one sessions, he pushed the classes to tell him just what they needed in order to keep the plants running in the red hills that stretched from Virginia's Dan River across both Carolinas and into the red clay of Georgia. In pursuit of Textile Group agenda, he log rolled and horse traded and otherwise bargained with congressmen from all regions and across all shades of the political spectrum, agreeing to support some things they wanted in order to get some things he wanted, the classic pork-barrel politics as some saw it, the craftsman-like "slow boring through hardwood" to build what constituents needed, as he read his Max Weber.

The classes were the actual power in the towns and villages of his Third District, and he was beholden to them. His expensive shirts were gifts from them, and they sponsored the famous barbeque political get-togethers at the mills, at the Baptist church grounds, and, most memorably, at his family's Barratt house in Greenwood on the road to Callison. Yes, he was in the classes, and he owed them and he served them.

Yet he was not of the classes. He was *of the people*, his Lincolnian phrase for his memoirs and his signature self-descriptor. If the people—the millhands, the scratch-ankle farmers, the Baptist ministers, the used-car dealers, the railroad workers, the forestry and agricultural extension guys, and above all the veterans and the school teachers—again turned away from him, as they had turned from his predecessor and as they had turned away from him in 1948, then he would not only be out of Congress, but he would also be out of his professed identity and his chosen role.

For the masses, he had a long-term goal to establish solid secondary schools to include an improved Clemson College, where their youth could be trained for high-skilled, high-value-added jobs in technical work. Child of teachers, he was something of a failed teacher himself, and he eagerly sought their company to talk about how to communicate the mysteries of chemistry and history by making even the least informed into an eager student. His other long-term goal was dramatically improved roads—not roads *out of* the Third District, such as the tourists took on their hurried way to the golden seashore, but roads *into* the Third District that connected good schools with good places to work and connected clean mill villages with a host of opportunities. He knew how economists could demonstrate that textiles were a "start-up industry," always primitive and always to be discarded when the larger society around the mills evolved and matured, but he did not want his people to be discarded like so many worn-out looms and spindles. He wanted a good future for them, and he did not think those processes could be rushed, for it would take a full generation, at least twenty-five years, of road building and school building to prepare the children of the millhands for the good jobs of the late twentieth century.

But in the meantime, his people needed their jobs in the mills, needed the paycheck even as they needed FDR's safety net of Social Security pension funds and unemployment insurance and New Deal regulations of the work environment and the other governmental interferences in business and markets that eased and ameliorated conditions of their short and hard lives. And above all, his people, his constituents in the mill villages, needed attention. They needed *him*. They needed to know that they could talk to him and that he would talk to them. They needed to know that he would use Congressman Dorn's power and authority to help their elder Paw, still traumatized from the Normandy invasion, at the intimidating Veterans Administration hospital. They needed to know that he would use Congressman Dorn's power and authority to help MaMaw get her tiny Social Security cheque delivered on time. They needed to know that they could count on him to give a personal *talking to* to their rebellious oldest son about career possibilities in the army or to their scared daughter about the opportunities if she would only stay in Lander College and get her degree. They even needed to know that he would call on the telephone and personally plead for a new job at one of Leon Lowenstein's mills or at Brother Abney's mills if they lost a job in the 1958 recession.

He called such works Liberalism with a capital *L*, and so this biography uses Dorn's own term in the same way. His Liberalism was the same as that of many Southern congressmen in this period, especially those in the piedmont mill districts. Robert McMath has aptly called their political agenda and their attitudes neo-Populist New Deal progressives. It was no accident Dorn was named for the Populist orator William Jennings Bryan, or that a brother was named for Tom Watson of nearby Thomson, Georgia, or that the prized family donkey was named FDR and exhibited with pride to the masses at the Labor Day barbeque. He and his piedmont textile colleagues invoked the name of Jefferson about small government, but they practiced the politics of Abraham Lincoln, and Bryan Dorn was open and honest in his admiration for Lincoln, even accepting with gratitude honorary membership in the Sons of the Union Army from his good friend Ulysses S. Grant III. His Liberalism, then, was hardly liberalism as understood in other eras and other places.

With heroes and guides like Brooks Hays and Sam Rayburn and with his own personal limited horizon, Bryan Dorn could never pass muster as a Southern version of Hubert Horatio Humphrey, the Midwestern liberal whom he liked. He could not even match up to the best standards of social justice in Lyndon Baines Johnson, the Texas liberal whom he profoundly disliked. To some degree, Dorn must also be described as a *progressive manqué*, one who followed progressive instincts a long way but ultimately failed to attain a genuinely progressive identity, the description C. Vann Woodward gave for both Dorn's hero Tom Watson and the description Woodward gave for Dorn's nemesis LBJ.

Introduction

Of the Millhands

William Jennings Bryan Dorn was the last orator for the millhands.

No one before him spoke so eloquently or so passionately about their hopes and dreams—and nightmares—and no one before or after did so much for them in terms of lawmaking and constituent service. As the folk of the mill villages themselves evolved and progressed, he evolved and progressed as well. He was never better than they at their best. As for the undeniably dark times and slow days, he shared their flaws but he was never worse than they at their worst. In all eras, he tried to call up the best that was in them and in him.

There was economic development in South Carolina's Third District long before the Civil War—a very healthy cotton economy, dairy-cattle raising, timber and related industries, and even a gold-mining operation. The textile industry and commerce could have developed in his piedmont hills naturally enough over time. His own family offered some proof of that in the Dornville experiment of Fool Billy Dorn, perhaps the richest man in the antebellum up-country and one who had abandoned cotton planting for gold mining. But the Civil War had intervened, and the coming of industry was long delayed. When it came, it focused on textiles in the piedmont countryside rather than in established cities. And it was initially white, rather self-consciously Scotch-Irish and Baptist white. Yet Bryan Dorn liked to note his own German and Welsh ancestry, and he was proud to say that by 1974 textile manufacturing employed many black people. He claimed there were more black people in the textiles than any other enterprise.

Like all modern manufacturing, especially during and after World War II, the textile firms had established professional organizations that gathered data concerning production, set standards for quality, and provided guidelines for managing personnel (that is, how to treat people). Like other such concerns, these professional organizations fetched up in New York in order to seek financing and to communicate with each other. Furthermore, they set up communication and publicity sites and lobbied in Washington, DC, and in Southern state capitals, and especially in Charlotte, not a state capital but the financial capital for textiles in the Carolinas and Georgia.

Regardless of political rhetoric about free trade or tariffs or quotas, there were always opportunities for highly specific legislated exemptions and exceptions concerning large established patterns in the increasingly complex and detailed rules of trade and commerce organic to the global textile industry. Much of the lobbying efforts were not really about free trade or fair trade but rather highly specific efforts to protect manufacturers of a grade and condition of cloth or dye or compound. Apparently inconsistent, it was in fact quite logical: grades of cotton from India needed to come into the US regardless of what cotton farmers said, and grades and conditions of cloth or dye must not come in from India, regardless of what consumers might say. Free trade for the former, tariffs and quota for the latter. Consistency in trade policy was not the issue: the specific needs of specific textile firms in the Southern piedmont were the issue.

Like all modern congressmen, regional representatives (and sometimes more localized subregional representatives) worked with the professional organizations on legislation. Early, Georgians and Carolinians formed a casual caucus, certainly by 1948, declaring in 1960 that it was an Informal Textile Group and a few years later the Congressional Textile Caucus. Business and economics historians have looked at the latter group with something like awe, especially its success after 1974, when the mill villages were shuttered and all the jobs had been "offshored" or otherwise exported. Thus Bryan Dorn as a very young congressman in 1951 had become part of a well-organized caucus, at the time without a name. It included the venerable Georgians Carl Vinson, Henderson Lanham, and James C. Davis and West Virginia's Cleveland M. Bailey, but also Kansas's Wint Smith and Pennsylvania's James E. Van Zandt, the latter both Republicans who needed tariff support for local special interests and who "log rolled" and "horse traded" with the textile folk.

Dorn was early and often in this group, and no less than Roger "Red" Milliken perhaps the most thoughtful and certainly the most articulate of the piedmont textile figures, credited him for leadership in the group. Indeed, when it became the Informal Textile Group, it was Dorn who was named its secretary and who organized the meetings with trade groups and lobbyists and negotiated with the congressional leadership for legislation. Interestingly, the important piedmont North Carolina textile interests (especially in Gastonia and Kannapolis) were a little slow in developing liaisons with their own congressmen, but they always counted on Bryan Dorn.

Dorn was a reader who all but ate books, and he read plenty of economics studies, especially economics history studies, that told him that textile industry was a "start-up" or "pace-car" industry, that it could only develop so far in terms of opportunities for its workers, and that the region must be transformed from the primitive textile industry into more sophisticated, high-wage, high-skill forms of production. To that end, he supported schools, not only primary and secondary, but also technical colleges and training institutes. Above all was his beloved Clemson College, and he was thrilled in 1964 when his favorite college became officially Clemson University. As will be developed at some length, he was a militarist, and he defended economic development through road building and dam building and school building as part of a military strategy, broadly cast. He collected and cited "hard" data showing clear correlations between textile production, textile profits, and full textile employment (with a marked improvement in wages and working conditions) and an aggressive military spending.

He longed to see the mill villages themselves transformed in place, with the mills gone but high-wage, high-skill, good-paying industries replacing them—still in the rural red hills country and still small town and neighborly. For all that, he dedicated his political career to the textile industry, and it seems poetically rounded that his failed bid for the governorship and his last session in Congress came at the moment of the 1974 Recession that all but destroyed textile employment in his region. He left office convinced that the right legislation could have saved textiles—and its mill workers—one more time, exactly as in the three Eisenhower recessions and in the years of Kennedy/Johnson growth.

William Jennings Bryan Dorn was largely defined by the textile industry. Himself a small-time farmer and child of educators who also farmed, Dorn understood that his career almost perfectly paralleled the path of the post-World War II textile industry, taking off in 1946, reaching a peak in 1974, and declining thereafter.

While the Dorns lived on farms, the farms were closely linked with the nearby textile mill villages in commercial and familial terms. He early came to understand that he would never get elected unless he built a foundational base of support in the nearby mill villages of the red hills. Like most politicians, Dorn wanted to be liked, fed off of the energy of a crowd, and was an expert at telling people what they wanted to hear, especially after listening to them intently. He may well have sought office for his own emotional well-being. Quickly, he realized that it was the mill villagers—the lintheads and woolhat boys and the frecklebellies and the transplanted crackers and peckerwoods—who were his political base. It was they whom he studied closely and worked for most ardently. He insisted he was *of them* and credited Lincoln for that phrase. He found in his King James Bible words of Jesus that one could be *in* but not *of*, and he determined never to be such a politician or such a person. Between 1946 and 1974 he really was *of them,* so completely of them that when he died in 2005, his popular successor, Butler Carson Derrick, could say then and repeat later that no one was ever so loved by his people.

The last orator for the millhands was *of the people* in all possible senses of his own Lincolnian phrase.

For the period 1916 to 2005, this is his—and their—story.

Chapter 1

Son of the Red Hills
1916–1941

William Jennings Bryan Dorn was son of Thomas Elbert and Pearl Griffith Dorn.

This was a Baptist family. It was in a Baptist community. All around in the red hills and cotton fields the neighbors were Baptists, and even the wayfaring transients were Baptists. There were more Baptists than sparrows, and the Good Lord had surely populated the hills and valleys with sparrows aplenty. Nor were these American Baptists with a capital *A*. These were Southern Baptists with a capital *S*.

Like good Southern Baptists, these two, called Eb and Pearl, believed in the biblical "quiverful of children," and they produced ten arrows of their own.[1] Each child was very much a child of both parents, but most especially Bryan Dorn. He was his father Eb's son in politics and his mother Pearl's son in personality, and so it is necessary to know what is recorded about his father's principles and about his mother's personality. The distinction between politics and personality is obviously artificial, since Pearl was intensely political and Eb had a strong and memorable personality. But the distinction does highlight significant differences, for Eb had developed a full-blown political philosophy before Pearl was born, and Pearl readily adapted his politics to her own skills, which were remarkable in terms of writing, speaking, and above all coaching writers and speakers. For his part, Eb lacked Pearl's communication talents, and he was less coach in any specific technique than he was inspiring about the policies of Tom Watson and William Jennings Bryan (his *version* of Watson's and Bryan's politics, another distinction with a difference). Finally, Eb as a personality was like most people, that is, *pale tea* compared to the dominating personality of Pearl. Congressman Bryan Dorn's politics and personality, then, are a glorious mess of intertwined in-

---

[1] Psalm 127:5, RSV (and all versions); Coleman family, 1910 US Census, Saluda Co.; Dorn family, 1920 and 1930 US Census, Greenwood Co., South Carolina Department of Archives and History, Columbia, hereinafter SCDAH.

fluences, with Eb laying out a Populist political agenda and Pearl articulating Populist goals through the personality that was called *Spunky* by harried daughters Lillian and Gracie, *Baby* by the favored Bryan, and *Nana* by the other children and the neighbors' children, in the sprawling "extended family."

Both the politics and the personality start with the unique nature of Southern Baptists in the hills that rolled alongside the waterways in the valley of the Saluda. Peculiar interactions between church, family, land, and water comprised much of what became a distinctive personality and even more distinctive politics.

What were these Southern Baptists? They seemed to be Calvinist in their assumptions about innate depravity, Lutheran in their talk about the absolutist quality of grace and the impossibility of saving oneself through human good works, as powerfully judgmental as any Muslim *imam*, and as organized on task as Pope Gregory. And all of it with tragic eloquence in their singing, storytelling, speechifying, cotton farming, cattle- and chicken-raising, fighting, and lovemaking.

These were Baptists before there were people called Baptists. In the eighteenth century days of "backcountry settlements" in the western high hills on the Allegheny slopes, New Light Presbyterians had preached a strong message of "moral depravity in man." Theirs was an unshakable conviction beyond the reach of mere reason that people left to their own devices would sin. And even with divine guidance and miracles, the elect, the chosen, those selected out ahead of time by Providence's predestination, even *they* could not save themselves or anybody else but could only keep Hellfire itself at bay by heroic action until the sudden moment arrived, with its completely undeserved and completely unreserved grace of God's forgiveness. There was then, from frontier days but all through all days, an awareness of the most powerful of passions, now demonic, now divine. There was also a need to remind themselves of their tragic inclinations, inclinations pulling one to Hell unless tempered and hedged in by confession and brotherly (and above all motherly) intercession. Natural inclinations by profound osmotic forces swept a person toward Hellfire and damnation unless one admitted everything and accepted the personal relationship with Jesus, the One who, although divine and part of the very Godhead, had stretched out his arms on the Roman cross because there was nothing else *even He* could do to save us from ourselves.[2]

Intense as the New Light Presbyterians were in the manifestation of their 1801 Cane Ridge Revival in Kentucky, such stirring evangelicals were yet *not emotional enough* for the folk of the red hills, who lived and moved and had their being in the most searing crucible of their own evil inclinations. St. Paul confessing the mysterious pain in his side that he thanked God for giving him was not more aware of his own drive to destroy himself than were the backwoods settlers, whether frontiersmen clearing the native American forests or engineers redirecting the rivers to create electricity.[3] Ferociously independent, cantankerous (especially about the trivial), and willing to kill you for looking at them wrong, these red-hills Baptists were yet sorrowful, wildly mirthful, preposterously generous, and equally happy to kick your ass or to share their barbeque, collards, and their sour mash.

No people so convinced of the evil of drink and dance ever drank or danced with as much determination—and skill!—and exactly because it was all evil.

And it was all good.

Indeed, because it was all evil and it was all good, they had to take all men as brothers. Their Bible told them that women were not equal and thus by definition were not brothers, and so women could run the farm and run the family and run the church, but they could not be brothers, and this was understood implicitly—and preached loudly to those who did not get it implicitly. So they had figured out brotherhood in a neighborhood that had women at the center of things, except a few things that mattered. These brothers would serve and sing and pray and above all confess their manifold sins and wickedness. Their generosity among a rural people who had little but food and land was astounding. And their tenacity in the face of an argument of whatever kind was also astounding.

Yet there was one circle they could not square. The American Baptists amongst them, the black folk who comprised the very large "minority" of the population in the valley of the Saluda, were these not brothers? Southern Baptists searched but could not really find a good biblical justification for segregating the black folk. Finally, it was decided that that did not matter—

---

[2] Robertson, *Red Hills and Cotton*, 7–15 and passim; Wright, *South Carolina*; Boles, *The Great Revival*; Sweet, *The Baptists*; Conkin, *Cane Ridge*.

[3] Conkin, *Cane Ridge*; Robertson, *Red Hills and Cotton*, 14 and ch. 6; exemplum, GHA, GHA/CU/SC.

not yet. The black brothers were seeking and saving themselves and traveling to the same Lord in the same Heaven, sometimes being baptized once and for all at the right moment in the same rivers, but they were *not* equal and that's how it was. Eb and Pearl often pondered this unsquared circle, and so their children often pondered it too. One thing they did decide: God had made these black folk and they too were children of God. The Ku Klux Klan and Pitchfork Ben Tillman and Cotton Ed Smith and many others were simply wrong about treating them violently. Eb and Pearl, and their children made right angles in that circle: violence against the black people, especially like that in Greenwood's Phoenix neighborhood in 1898, was flat wrong. It was even more wrong than the claim that the black men were brothers and therefore equal: inequality was the part of their circle that remained perfectly round. Eb and Pearl lived with that troubling contradiction and raised their children with that troubling contradiction without resolving it at all. For race relations, this place in this time produced a bad lot of white racists. But Eb and Pearl were the *best of that bad lot*, and at least they and their children were intensely aware of the evil of negrophobic violence, something with quite a history in the valley of the Saluda.

In terms of politics, Eb and Pearl Dorn lived idiosyncratically in a unique corner of the western piedmont. Their politics, as practiced by Eb and as preached by Pearl, the speechwriter and the great coach of male speakers, had everything to do with the land where they lived. In their lifetime, the old place had gotten a new name. Greenwood the county was established in 1897, boundary lines carved out of the ancient Edgefield District and the slightly newer Abbeville and Saluda counties. Their land lay in the up-country north and west of the fall line. The fall line was less a line than a band or zone stretching southwestward from Cheraw on the Pee Dee River through Columbia on the Congaree River down to the ghost town of Hamburg (*in but not of* today's Augusta) on the Savannah River. South and east of the fall line were slow-moving inland rivers that could be navigated from the tidewater through the low country up to the trading centers of Columbia and Cheraw and, once, Hamburg. North and west of the fall line, streams rolled down from the North Carolina Blue Ridge with too much force for a low-country boat to advance northward or westward beyond the river trading centers. But that disadvantage in transportation was an advantage in another way. The mountain-sprung streams moved with enough force to turn the wheels on a gristmill or any number of other producing mills. When the Civil War ended, these piedmont villages would build industrial centers, originally in textiles, alongside those swift running rivers. Too, engineers would dam up some rivers and rearrange things to create still more water power and make the piedmont the literal and metaphorical engines of economic progress in the self-proclaimed New South.[4]

Much was thus "man-made" or otherwise altered by humans. The forests had been clear-cut, but then timber men had replanted other trees, and so the beautiful and much commented-on woods in the hills took different shapes and shone forth different visages according to the passage of time and the work of people. Even those red hill elevations of some 600 to 1,200 feet had not always been *red*. Men raising cotton had gradually eroded the fertile brown soil, scraping down into the red clay substratum. The exposed red clay, now the topsoil of another era, was itself good for cotton and corn, but its brilliant appearance was a blood mark of man's abuse of the goodly earth, as it was no less a legitimate mark of progress.[5]

The Dorns were Germans in a part of the world thought to be Scotch-Irish. Their own people and thousands of other Germans had actually gotten into the Old Edgefield District, the original backcountry of South Carolina, before the Scotch-Irish. Landing in Charleston in 1764, Palatinate Germans received help from England's King George III and some English businessmen and moved into the piedmont, settling on Hard Labor Creek, where today's McCormick and Edgefield counties interconnect. Most were farmers rather than planters, but one of them, William Dorn, was a planter who in 1847 put more than a hundred slaves to work looking for gold. Thus establishing a gold-mining operation along Hard Labor Creek at Barite Hill, he for some years endured the jibes of neighbors who called him "Fool Billy" for abandoning lucrative cotton culture, but by 1857 he grossed somewhere between $900,000 and $2 million (in 2016 US money, between $22 million and $50 million) and was certainly the wealthiest man in the antebellum upcountry (though the low country's Joshua John Ward of Georgetown County claimed wealth in slaves alone that was more than $33 million, and Ward's rice lands were surely worth at least half that amount again, giving a conservative estimate of well over $50 million in today's currency).

This successful Fool Billy Dorn was collaterally related to William Jennings Bryan Dorn; his Dorns Gold Mine community became Dornsville. After the Civil War, in 1871 this country slicker Dorn sold out the depleted mine to none other than entrepreneur Cyrus Hall McCormick, who renamed the place for himself but had no luck finding gold. In 1882 a county was formed and named for the famous inventor of the reaper and other farm

---

[4] Edgar, *South Carolina*, 7–8; Carlton, *Mill and Town*; Wright, *South Carolina*, ch. 1.

[5] Edgar, 7–8; Wright, ch. 1.

machinery who had failed in this piedmont venture. In the fullness of time, Bryan Dorn bought tracts of timber and cotton land in McCormick County exactly to retain connection to Fool Billy and his idiosyncratic ways of politics and economics taught him by his parents.[6]

Also descending from those Palatinate expatriates who transshipped from Old Charleston were Strom Thurmond, the Durst family bankers, and the Outz political family. These were Protestant Germans who believed with Martin Luther that church should be a "priesthood of all believers" and that grace came for the sincere asking from *the* God, the real Lord, who was uninterested in who claimed to be "lord of the land" and who bowed as a peasant. As Carl Bridenbaugh notes, Germans in the backcountry "had come to stay," setting up crop rotation and wise stewardship over husbandry of animals on grazing land, in contrast with the slash-and-burn-and-move farming and husbandry that characterized other farmers of the same raw frontier.[7]

These Germans in the valley of the Saluda comprised barely 5 percent of the piedmont population, but they were related to and in intimate contact with majority German communities to their south and east such as Dutch Fork, Little Mountain, and Saxe-Gothe. In any case, the larger identity for the white ethnic groups in the piedmont was their Baptist worship ways. Most were convinced that God had a plan and that they must preach from the Bible and spread God's word and spirit. They were uniformly committed to governance in church and community that was horizontal and face-to-face. Again, the real Lord did not care for distinctions between lord and

---

[6] WJBD, *OTP*, 7–25; William Jennings Bryan Dorn Papers, 1916–1920; WJBD to Harold W. Dorn, 12 October 1951; WJBD to Annie Moore Morris, 1 October 1963, South Carolina Political Collections of the Ernest F. Hollings Library of the University of South Carolina, hereinafter, WJBD/SCPC; interview: Watson Dorn with Steve Griffith and Roper (28 February 2012), John Herbert Roper Papers, South Carolina Political Collection, hereinafter JHR/SCPC; Cantey Haile, "Gold Mining," *South Carolina Encyclopedia*, ed. Edgar, s.v. (380–81); Stephen C. Kenney, "McCormick," ibid., s.v.; Bobby F. Edmonds, *The Making of McCormick County* (McCormick, SC: Cedar Hill, 1999); inflation calculation, Morgan Friedman calculator of Consumer Price Index, pre-1975 statistics from Historical Statistics of the United States (USGPO, 1975); all data since then are from the annual Statistical Abstracts of the United States, hereinafter calculations listed as Friedman Calculator, with dates; WJBD/SCPC; Bridenbaugh, *Myths and Realities*, 141.

[7] Haile, "Gold Mining," 380–81; WJBD to Harold W. Dorn, 12 October 1951 and interview: Watson Dorn with Griffith and Roper (28 February 2012), JHR/SCPC; Sweet, *The Baptists*; idem., *The Presbyterians*; Bridenbaugh, *Myths and Realities*, 141.

peasant, and no such distinctions were brooked in governance of church or school or county council. Whether they adopted convictions or came already converted, the Dorns and the other Germans shared many folkways thought to be Scotch-Irish—not only worship ways but also music ways and food ways and speech ways. Despite the Scotch-Irish dominance of population and of many practices, the Dorns, like the other Germans, were by no means displaced. Indeed, the name *Dorn* means *thorn*, and the family stuck in place and was tough and hard to dislodge—and would stick *you* if you tried to displace them from land or anything else.[8]

Eb and Pearl were also Populists, although they never joined the Populist Party and did not vote for the dominant South Carolina Populist Benjamin Ryan Tillman (a virulent and violent negrophobe who supported Populist legislation on railroads, banks, and education but never left the Democratic Party). For all that, Eb and Pearl were devotees of Tom Watson, intrepid Populist of nearby Thomson, Georgia, and they were evergreen supporters of William Jennings Bryan, four-time Populistic Democratic nominee for president. One who has studied the self-named Populists of the 1890s in great detail, Robert McMath, has decided that some of their ideas and attitudes persist, even unto this day. McMath thus describes a "populistic New Deal progressive" as a Southern farmer who wanted federal intervention to protect against corporate abuses by railroads, telephone, and telegraph operators, and above all international investment bankers (the "financial managerial bourgeoisie" personified by J. P. Morgan).

Whether in the 1890s or the 1930s, these Populistic New Deal progressives imposed ceilings on interest rates charged on loans (which had climbed to levels between 50 and 75 percent at the turn of the century in the rural piedmont, according to the two careful economists Ransom and Sutch), regulated freight charges by railroad haulers, and demanded a much expanded postal service system to offer rural free delivery into the most remote and most neglected piedmont interior. Whether reeling from the Panic of 1893 or from the Great Depression of 1929, they powerfully mistrusted international banking firms and demanded oversight of their activities as well as protection against deflation, defined for them as steadily falling cotton and other commodity producer prices. As McMath notes, whatever era they existed—and Eb existed as a loud and active political spokesperson *throughout* the eras from 1893 to 1947—Populistic New Deal progressives

[8] Table, Edgar, op cit., 50; Bridenbaugh, *Myths and Realities*, 132–35.

were upset by the monopoly power of corporations and eagerly sought a countervailing power from federal regulations.[9]

Populistic New Deal progressives wanted an educational system to improve rural life by means of applied farming science, and Eb and Pearl wanted such educational improvements above all other reforms. The couple's lifelong commitment to education was thus as political as it was religious. The early Populists of the 1890s sought to develop an agricultural and mechanical college with educational extension services, including extension agents to advise the small-time cotton farmers and timber growers and dairymen. The Populistic New Deal progressives of the 1930s thus disposed what their political grandfathers had proposed. Clemson College (in those days Clemson Agricultural and Mechanical College) was created by the gathering forces of agricultural reform at the turn of the century and traced its genesis to that earliest phase of Populism. Under FDR and his various "alphabet agencies" of federal programs, Clemson expanded its assistance to the state's farmers exponentially. In fact, Clemson's Rural Studies professor George Hubert Aull in time became Bryan Dorn's mentor for the applied economics of political programs as well as personal tutor for all aspects of "the dismal science" of economics.[10]

All of Eb and Bryan Dorn's Populist goals had been advanced and most were realized successfully by Benjamin Ryan Tillman, known as Pitchfork Ben, the Edgefield farmer who bearded the lion General Wade Hampton and supplanted the old Bourbon cavalier in the US Senate. To some degree, Pitchfork Ben was himself less plain folk or commoner than landed gentry, having been raised on a plantation of some size in a landed antebellum family of prominence in Edgefield, the "county of Governors and Senators." For all that, Ben Tillman had mastered the plain folk language of the old Populists, and, in fact, on the stump was not only past master of Populist speechi-

---

[9] Thomas Ebert Dorn corr., 1898–1947; "Representing the People" (1984), WJBD/SCPC; "The Greatest Man in America," *Greenwood Index*, 12 March 1898, 1; McMath, "The History of the Present," 80, 90; interview: Watson Dorn with Steve Griffith and Roper (28 February 2012), JHR/SCPC; on TED and populistic New Deal progressives, WJBD, *OTP*, 146–47; Woodward, *Tom Watson: Agrarian Rebel*; Ransom and Sutch, *One Kind of Freedom*; Woodward, *Origins of the New South*; Tindall, *Emergence of the New South*.

[10] McMath, "The History of the Present"; George Hubert Aull Papers, 1937–1974, Special Collections of Clemson University, hereinafter GHA/SC/CU; Clemson folders, pamphlets, newspaper clippings, esp. corr. with GHA, Robert Jones, and Robert Cook Edwards, 1926–1946, WJBD/SCPC.

fying, but likely the forensic equal of the most famous Populists Tom Watson of Georgia and William Jennings Bryan of Nebraska. However, as noted, Pitchfork Ben had done everything *within* the Democratic Party, and he had not supported Bryan in his presidential runs. In the US Senate, Pitchfork Ben had demonstrated political acumen by working across party lines, especially with President Theodore Roosevelt, to gain Populist objectives, and in cooperation with T. R., who had famously pilloried Bryan and the Populists in presidential and other campaigns (saying that they should all be lined up against a wall and shot). Nor did Tillman experiment, as had Tom Watson, with any appeal to black voters. In fact, it was quite the opposite, for Tillman had developed a murderously intensive rhetoric of race-baiting. It was because of that negrophobic language (and rumors of personally sponsored actions of violence) that Eb Dorn never voted for Ben Tillman and Pearl Dorn could not celebrate him in her fulsome speeches. Indeed, Eb voted against Tillman and spoke loudly in favor of Tom Watson and Bryan, whom he contrasted with Pitchfork Ben on the issues of racial violence, if not full racial justice.[11]

To some degree, Eb, the political figure, and Pearl, the writing and speaking coach, had created a Populism that may not have existed outside their heads, especially as they described Tom Watson and William Jennings Bryan. The Georgian was one thing in the campaigns of 1894 and 1895 and 1896, when he sought black votes and when his Thomson farm served as a safe haven for at least one black man sought by a lynching mob. However, after 1897, Watson became as murderously negrophobic as Tillman or anybody else—and unlike Tillman, he was in bed with the railroad interests against whom he once had campaigned. As for Bryan, he in 1924 fulminated against the teaching of evolution in the public schools, going so far as to defend in court a Tennessee law against teaching the theory in public schools (and thereby personally attacking a Dayton science teacher defended memorably by Clarence Darrow). That episode was well known to school teachers Eb and Pearl, even and especially as they themselves taught the latest scientific lessons to their own charges, with particular emphasis on the correctness of Darwinian evolution through natural selection (a teaching that in that day and in Congressman Dorn's long career was *never* opposed by the Baptist Dorns, *nor* by the ministers of their Greenwood Baptist church). Indeed, the

---

[11] "Representing the People" (1984); Kantrowitz, *Ben Tillman and the Reconstruction of White Supremacy*; Blum, *The Republican Roosevelt*; Williamson, *The Crucible of Race*, 116–17; 130–39; WJBD, *OTP*, 26–30; 185.

Dorn family eventually occupied the very home built by regional evolutionist/scientist John Perkins Barratt, and they labored to get that home registered as an historic site (accomplished by son Bryan Dorn in 1985) *exactly because* of Barratt's studies in evolution. Like most of us, Eb and Pearl were thus quite selective in their memories of characters in their past; but the interesting thing is less their faulty history than their unswerving opposition to Pitchfork Ben's "orgy of extreme racism" during the "nadir of race relations."[12]

In any case, Eb and Pearl proudly named their seventh child, born 14 April 1916, for William Jennings Bryan and their tenth child, Watson Lee Dorn, for Senator Watson, and they pointedly taught all of their children that there were evils in Benjamin Ryan Tillman and glories in the Populism of Watson and Bryan. Where others, especially modern scholars, can find little difference in the policies of Watson and Bryan and Tillman, Eb and Pearl found a world of distinction.[13]

Thus, in the fall of 1934, when Bryan was barely eighteen years old, but already contemplating a political career, he listened to his father fulminating against Woodrow Wilson. The patriarch and political advisor was on that occasion looking back with great anger at the Progressive President because of Senator Gerald Prentice Nye's Special Committee of Investigation of the Munitions Industry. The North Dakota senator, very much a Populist Bryanite, although a Republican, was never reconciled to US entry into World War I, and Eb agreed with Nye fully. Eb, like Senator Nye, admired Bryan's "cooling off" negotiations when Bryan was secretary of state for Wilson, and he liked Bryan's opposition to imperialist expansion or any other expansion of US military commitments. When Bryan left the Wilson Cabinet in June of 1915, Eb had been proudly supportive, as he was of Tom Watson's *Jeffersonian* newspaper criticisms of US entry into World War I. After the US

---

[12] Woodward, *Tom Watson*; Barratt House, National Historical Register, SCDAH. Actually Perkins, while a dedicated scientist fascinated with natural selection and attempting an explanation of evolution, was hardly the equal of Darwin or Wallace in such studies and in no way their prototype, despite the family enthusiasm for him and his work: Lester D. Stephens, "Centers of Creation: John Perkins Barratt's Biogeological Theory of Racial Origins," *Journal of Southern History*, 80/2 (May 2014). "Representing the People" (1984); "orgy" phrase, Genovese, *The World the Slaveholders Made*, 111; "nadir" phrase, Logan, *The Negro in American Life and Thought*; WJBD, *OTP*, 26–30; 185.

[13] "Watson Lee Dorn Sr." (obit.), *Greenwood Index Journal*, 1 May 2017, 1; William Jennings Bryan Dorn, standard certificate of birth, 14 April 1916, Bureau of Vital Statistics, Greenwood Co., SC, SCDAH.

suffered more than 300,000 casualties, Eb considered that Bryan and Watson were vindicated in their opposition to American entry, especially when the League of Nations, absent US participation, appeared to be feckless and when the old colonial possessions remained unchanged for the victorious Allies.

In September of 1934, Eb announced that Senator Nye's investigations showed narrowly self-serving economic reasons to enter the Great War in order to help certain munitions makers rather than Wilson's declared reasons about a "world made safe for Democracy." Before that specific memory in 1934, the teenaged Bryan, when barely self-conscious politically, heard his father, Eb, and his erudite mother, Pearl, declare their fervent isolationism and anti-war and anti-imperialism just as clearly as they declared their objections to violence against black people.[14]

As Bryan Dorn further remembered it, there was plenty of opposition to World War I in his region, and the family's US congressional representative, Fred Dominick (a distant relative), spoke for many in the Third District in opposition to the Great War, as did Dominick's law partner (and still another relative on Pearl's father's side) Coleman Livingston Blease, who had famously become US senator after infamy as South Carolina's governor. Blease was known otherwise for racist demagoguery, but Eb and Pearl regarded Senator Blease's anti-war protest as something decidedly Populist, because his parents—following the speeches and the writings of Blease, Dominick, Bryan, and Watson—blamed the "rich man's war" on the ultimate rich men, specifically J. P. Morgan and John D. Rockefeller in the US and the Rothschild family abroad.[15]

Anti-bank and suspicious of the freight haulers and the telephone/telegraph agencies, Eb and Pearl Dorn expected diligent federal regulation of the much-distrusted international corporations. They expected robust federal assistance to those in threatened economic station (especially the honored elderly) and were reliant on Clemson College for lifelong practical learning and agricultural counsel. Outspoken in opposition to the Ku Klux Klan and other agents of negrophobic violence, Eb and Pearl were as well anti-imperialist and anti-interventionist. While proud of heroic military service by family members, the couple was opposed to militaristic adventurism.

---

[14] "Representing the People" (1984); *Congressional Investigations: A Documentary History*, ed. Schlesinger and Burns; Woodward, *Tom Watson*; Kazin, *A Godly Hero*; Cole, *Senator Gerald P. Nye*.

[15] WJBD, *OTP*, 5.

Such were the politics of this very political family into which Bryan Dorn was born. All family members were expected to know and practice politics, and it was decreed that some would serve in office, at least in local offices. Furthermore, it was a Baptist family accustomed to reaching decisions in group discussions organized around prayer, preaching, and the family Bible. Any change, however slight or subtle, from the Bryanesque Populism must be discussed in detail in full meeting, and after discussion and reaching of decision, all would advance together as a twenty-four footed political animal speaking with one voice. This family called it Populism, and Populism it was, though a strand found more in the upper Midwest than in South Carolina.

As for Bryan Dorn's personality, it is necessary to look at his beautiful and extroverted, often theatrical, mother, Pearl—especially looking at her own extended family before she met Eb and then marking the Griffith and Coleman relationships with her after she met him—as well as looking at her parents' relationship with their favored suitor and beloved son-in-law, Eb.

Pearl Griffith was from a Welsh family that comported itself along clannish lines, especially with common property in dairy farming and tree harvesting in a community called Zoar in Saluda County, a portion of the piedmont county called Old Saluda. Not only would the Griffiths and their kin the Colemans readily accept Thomas Ebert, but they would bring him literally and physically into the fold. He was resident on the farm of Richard Coleman and Mary Campbell Griffith between 1905 and 1910. Indeed, Eb and Pearl's first children, Thomas Elbert Jr., Lillian, and Gracie, were born on the Griffith farm in Zoar of Old Saluda.

These Griffiths, in that feckless red-hills way, were casual about spelling; their surname was spelled variously in official church and government records as *Griffith, Griffeth*, and *Griffitts*, and even the ancestral matriarch Dicy Griffith allowed her name to be rendered *Dicie, Dicey*, or *Dicy.* But in the same piedmont way, the Griffiths were quite emphatic to loudly and proudly pronounce their names and attach surname and Christian name to their place in the family: Richard Coleman Griffith was patriarch of the extended Griffith clan, Mary Campbell Griffith was matriarch of the "selfsame clan," and the two together were major forces in the kirk/church for the clan's community, Bethel Baptist Church, with its worship space and cemetery that were at once family and community.[16]

There was a big spread in age between suitor Thomas Elbert and the eligible Pearl Griffith, he being already thirty-five years old and she only twenty-one. This Dorn, called T. E. by school and church officials and Eb by older family members, was ever Mr. Dorn to the young, including the strikingly beautiful Pearl (who would call him Mr. Dorn throughout five decades of marriage). Yet this difference in age troubled none of the "marine fire band" of Griffiths and Colemans in Old Saluda. If anything, Eb's demonstrated maturity increased his standing as a potential husband. That and his size and legendary strength. In fact, in his memoirs, Bryan Dorn recounts a charming tale of bonnie Welsh lass and a strapping German peasant.[17]

Early in the new century, Eb Dorn had arrived to teach at Zoar Hill Academy in Old Saluda. This was a private school supported in part by Bethel Baptist Church; it was a one-room affair that aspired to prepare local boys for economic opportunity in the straitened but striving piedmont. The private school prepared some of the young men for entry into Clemson College so that they could "scientifically manage" the regional agriculture; others they prepared for a more immediate scientific management of their own farms. Standing over six feet tall and weighing more than 175 pounds with size 11 shoes, Eb was much larger than most piedmont farm boys in that impoverished era. More to the point, he was legendarily powerful. For his schoolteacher interview, he was not asked about his educational background (baccalaureate degree from Furman University with summer study of foreign languages at the University of Tennessee, Mercer College, and the University of Chicago). Instead, he was quizzed about his exact size and then asked if he could throw a 200-pound sack of guano fertilizer over his shoulder and walk smartly across a plowed field of forty acres. He replied that he could throw one such sack under *each* arm and walk quite smartly across such a field. And he backed up his bravura by "establish[ing] a physical force sufficient to maintain order." In October of that first year of teaching, restless

[16] Marriage license, Thomas Elbert Dorn and Pearl Griffeth (*sic*) Dorn, 5 September 1905, Bureau of Vital Statistics, Saluda Co., SC; US Census, Pop., 1910, Saluda Co., 1920, Greenwood Co., SCDAH; Sweet, *The Baptists*; on names, Thomas Elbert Dorn correspondence, Pearl Griffith Dorn correspondence, 1905–1947, WJBD/SCPC .

[17] WJBD, *OTP*, 1; "marine fire band," Webb, *Born Fighting*.

[18] WJBD, *OTP*, 9.

boys attempted to "run off" yet another teacher during rabbit-hunting season; T. E. picked up three of them to administer a whipping and prevented their escape by squeezing one between his thighs and clamping the other two under his German-farmer's arms.[18]

Yet as the years went by, T. E. Dorn established himself as a schoolmaster who was more than a strict disciplinarian. Over his tenure, Zoar Hill Academy not only prepared some for Clemson, but presented other graduates each year for entry into local sectarian colleges such as Lander and Erskine and Newberry, from whence could come community preachers and teachers. His extensive graduate studies in language and linguistics paid off for him, and for his charges. He instructed in classical and modern languages in a thorough way, and thereby taught a discipline of the mind as well as discipline of the body. The state colleges, both private and public, began to accept his graduates as freshmen, sometimes as sophomores, whereas most preparatory schools were embarrassed to find their graduates "set back" into "subfreshman" or other probational status until they could pass an examination on higher mathematics and on a foreign language. Even Wofford College, in the first quarter of the twentieth century surely the most demanding of the institutions in the piedmont, accepted his graduates as sophomores, primarily because they were already conversant in classical languages and mathematics.[19]

Such derring-do impressed the people thereabouts, and especially Richard Coleman and Mary Campbell Griffith. In fact, the Griffith paterfamilias, one generation before Richard Coleman, had built this first real school in Old Saluda, this Zoar Hill Academy, and the clan and neighbors were proud of its good work and happy to see that T. E. Dorn could carry on that work successfully. They admired the schoolteacher who could master any conflict with his strength but who also could master with his mind, and with his eloquence, something famously admired among the piedmont folk, who loved a good speech almost as deeply as a good fistfight.

The comely Pearl Griffith, in her late teen years of blossom, was one of dozens of students of all ages and sizes crowded into the one-room school. Afterward, she attended Lander College, then a church-affiliated teacher

---

[19] Ibid., 9; interview: Watson Dorn with Griffith and Roper (28 February 2012), JHR/SCPC; College Archives, 1900–1914, Wofford College, Spartanburg; quote, Samuel Childs Mitchell, WJBD, *OTP*, 9–10; Mitchell, "Aftermath of Appomattox," Samuel Chiles Mitchell Papers, South Carolina Library, USC, hereinafter SCL/USC; Hollis, *The University of South Carolina*, vol. 2, 114–18.

preparatory school in the town of Greenwood. Watson Dorn, youngest of the Dorn children born to T. E. and Pearl Griffith, recounted family stories that the attractive Pearl was herself attracting plenty of interest among the young townsmen who came onto the all-girl campus. Watson Dorn opined that about 1904, the jealous and concerned T. E. Dorn arranged to have her come to teach at the Zoar Hill Academy before she had earned her baccalaureate degree or any other teacher certification, something Eb could only have accomplished with the collaboration of Richard Coleman Griffith, who was both patriarch of the Colemans and Griffiths and guardian of the Zoar Hill Academy, not to mention benefactor of Mr. Dorn, the academy's supervisor and principal.[20]

With Pearl Griffith safely removed from the competition of Lander College's male visitors, T. E. Dorn pressed his own case aggressively, in the style of the high old Victorian lovemaking. He asked her to go with him to pose for a portrait in front of a photographer, a suggestion she thought improper. He persisted, and she asked her parents, presuming they would emphatically decline his "forward" suggestion. Instead, the admiring parents encouraged the courtship in all of its phases. Thus overwhelmed, the bonnie lass succumbed to the German giant, and there was passion aplenty in their lovemaking, but the onetime student always called her husband/teacher "Mr. Dorn" in the presence of all their children and all their friends. Always there would persist in the beautiful Pearl conflicting impulses—to attract and to please but also to be left alone and liberated from the demands of others. Loving Eb dutifully and quite deferential to him, Pearl yet demanded chances to go away ("visiting in Saluda"); as soon as Eb had any kind of resources, she insisted he buy her an automobile that she could use for herself, not a demand made by many wives of rural schoolmasters.[21]

Still more complicating were the reactions and relationships in the families that produced Eb and Pearl. Where Richard Coleman and Mary Campbell Griffith embraced the educational mission of the newlywed couple (in fact were themselves heir to such a mission), Eb's own parents, George Elbert and Elizabeth Byrd Dorn, did not accept it at all. George Dorn, successful plain folks farmer, was a cavalry veteran of the Civil War

---

[20] WJBD, *OTP*, 9; interview: Watson Dorn with Griffith and Roper (28 February 2012), JHR/SCPC.

[21] Interview: Steve Griffith with Herbert Hartsook and John Herbert Roper (31 January 2012), JHR/SCPC; Theodore Ebert Dorn to Angel (Pearl), 31 July 1927; see corr., WJBD and Grace Dorn, esp. Grace Dorn to WJBD, 26 July 1943, WJBD/SCPC.

who, in Reconstruction, had ridden before the black flag of his old general Martin Witherspoon Gary to fight in most literal sense against black people trying to vote or hold office. After those two fighting forays, 1863 to 1865 and 1876 to 1877, George had settled down to his farm in Edgefield and vowed to fight no more. He took for his bride Elizabeth Byrd, whose Edgefield family claimed descent from the Byrds of Virginia (as many throughout the South named Byrd did, although the connection was never definitively proved by her hardworking grandson genealogist, Bryan Dorn). At any rate, the lovely Elizabeth Byrd Dorn often "put on airs" in front of her "more country" neighbors and relatives, especially the Dorns. She had been uninterested in George before the Civil War and had only married the war hero after the war because the available "husband material" was much diminished by deaths in the fighting. On the Edgefield farm, George produced a rude plenty, and he trained up his son Eb to be a good, strong, productive cotton farmer. Plainly put, to George Dorn, his son Eb's interest in "book learning" was "sissy stuff"; to Elizabeth Byrd Dorn, it was déclassé.[22]

Thus it was that Eb and Pearl lived in the Coleman community and ran the Zoar Hill Academy with the full support of Colemans and Griffiths—and with the smoky disdain of the Dorns and the Edgefield Byrds. In 1920, after fifteen years of living with Pearl's folks, the couple at last went off on their own, departing the matriarchal farm and church and school in order to fetch themselves up in Greenwood County, where T. E. attained the highly political prize of district school superintendent after losing the race once before, in 1916. Pearl Dorn became a high school teacher in a mill school in Greenwood County, where she taught for a total of more than thirty years. The couple joined the First Baptist Church in the county seat. Nevertheless, Dorns and Griffiths remained close and congenial, enough so that the first child born away from the old farm was named Griffith to honor the nurturing red-hills Welsh family, and the interconnected extended families often worshiped together at Bethel Church, especially for occasions of thanksgiving or grief.[23]

---

[22] Brown, *Strain of Violence*; Cf. Burton, *In My Father's House*; US Census, Pop., George Elbert and Elizabeth Byrd Dorn, Edgefield, 1880; WJBD, *OTP*, 10–12.

[23] US Census, Pop., Richard Coleman and Mary Campbell Griffith, Saluda, 1910; T. O. (*sic*) and Pearl Griffith Dorn, Greenwood, 1920; school careers, WJBD, *OTP*, 8, 10.

T. E. enjoyed the Griffith blessing (and risked his own father's curse) for still another task: he wanted to school all the children in the community, and especially the black folk who had descended from slaves. More than one in three souls in the county were black, and the Dorns and the Griffiths were committed to schooling the people they called "the colored," albeit these commitments were executed within the Jim Crow and segregated setting wherein the children were kept separated by color. Too, the "worser part" of the district's school purse, less than one in ten of the funds, was dedicated to the sizeable population of black children. T. E.'s mission, progressive in its day, had its severe limits: he arranged to teach black children primarily in one-room structures housing old and worn books—and with black instructors who themselves had come up the ranks through such Jim Crow schools. Recall that T. E. was the best of a bad lot in the nadir of race relations, and that calibrated context certainly extended also into his educational mission.[24]

For all that, Superintendent Dorn was understandably proud of the hard work he did on behalf of what he called "the colored," for it was not popular work among his neighbors. In fact, it was some grateful black teachers and parents who had given him his seriocomic nickname *Supremetendent*. But, of course, even a potentially well-meaning white soul like T. E. Dorn did far less than what black children needed. For instance, he helped to consolidate white schools so that precious resources of teachers and buildings and books could be centrally located and available rather than scattered all over the sprawling county. The superintendent's efforts got the white children out of the one-room schools and into grade-appropriate schools with enough student population and large enough staffs to improve the public-school experiences, especially by differentiating between elementary and high school. And to get the children to the right schools, T. E. Dorn worked with officials to use public money for buses to transport the children. But all of that was strictly for the white children. As for black children, there finally were some consolidated high schools, though of lower quality than white schools and with teachers paid—by state law—less than white high school teachers.

Furthermore, a woman in the DeLaine family who remembers the instruction of the Jim Crow era has written:

---

[24] Quotation, Bible, KJV trans. used by WJBD; DC#013198, 5 October 1948, US Census, Pop., Greenwood, 1920, SCDAH; data on SC school spending, Harlan, *Separate but Unequal*, 205 and 205n; US Census, HS, Greenwood, 1900, 1910, 1920; US CR, 1900, 1910, 1920, Tables, "Sex, Gender, Nativity, and Color"; Logan, op. cit.

> It wasn't just the conditions of school buildings and teachers' salaries.... Transportation was a major problem. Often the rural students couldn't get to school to take advantage of the meager learning opportunities. Black students who graduated from [elementary school] could continue that education only by attending a distant high school, one perhaps as much as ten miles away. With no means of transportation, students needed to board in town. Most families couldn't afford that expense. Some young people tried walking to high school, finishing their chores before dawn, then taking the straightest route to the school, cutting across fields along the way. On days when the fields were too muddy, they walked along the road. School buses carrying white children splashed mud on them as they passed. Then, adding insult to injury, the young riders—filled with scorn learned from their parents (and perhaps bored with the monotonous, bumpy rides)—diverted themselves by trying to hit the walking black children with spit or soda-bottle caps while yelling the most degrading epithets they knew. By the time the black students got to school, after as much as an hour and a half of walking, they were late, dirty, tired, and angry.[25]

Thus were the conditions for black students in rural South Carolina, and such conditions were those praised by T. E. Dorn—and recalled favorably by his son Congressman Dorn. The Dorn family notions about helping black children were quite limited notions, as recorded by members of the DeLaine family, who became pioneers in litigating for integration in South Carolina. In their lawsuit and activism, the large DeLaine family recalled and cited exactly the quotation above. Once in office in the 1950s, Congressman Dorn would consistently resist integration by claiming that good things were happening for black children in the state schools. He said he knew about these good things from personal experience and from observations of his piedmont youth, with special emphasis on what father Eb had wrought. The members of the DeLaine family and of the NAACP legal team experienced very different rural black education in Jim Crow days, and the congressman until late in his career—until 1968—would reflect favorably on his parents' half-hearted efforts to help black children. There were limits to father Eb's racial progressivism and limits to the congressman's racial progressivism until dramatic "sea changes" (and lots of black voters) pulled Wil-

[25] Gona, *Dawn of Desegregation*, 10–11.

liam Jennings Bryan Dorn into a different stance on racial integration of schools.[26]

Life for the Dorn family in Greenwood was better than in Old Saluda, but far from idyllic. The age difference between Eb and Pearl, the many children, the challenges of teaching, the grinding poverty in the red hills after the 1925 cotton-price collapse, the biblical seasons of drought and flood, the way Eb had to tend to many matters in addition to and generally *before* seeing to his "Angel," the way Pearl had to tend to many matters in addition to and generally *before* seeing to her "Mr. Dorn," all contributed to marital problems. In the dog days of summer in 1927, Pearl Griffith Dorn announced that she doubted Mr. Dorn loved her, and she left the home, probably to stay with her parents and the extended family back in Saluda. It was a season, both for a teacher and a farmer—and for a mother whose youngest child was safely out of diapers and feeding himself—when a Lady could leave the farmland house and the schoolhouse for a few weeks to visit for a long stay with kinfolk down the road without such a visit fretting the neighbors. And she had taken such "visits" before. But this time, Angel told Mr. Dorn before she left that she doubted he loved her, and she made him "so miserable" with words and actions before leaving that this little vacation was qualitatively different, more threatening, than previous ones.[27]

Bryan Dorn saved the letter in a safe place, and it is marked "envelope addressed to Mrs. T. E. Dorn, Saluda, SC." It happened that Pearl was back on the job at the farm and in the schoolhouse and presumably in Mr. Dorn's bed within weeks, as was fitting for her assigned roles. In 1929, Eb and Pearl Dorn relocated the tribe of twelve over to the spacious John Perkins Barratt House, with its fertile soil on a small farm in Greenwood County. In that cash-strapped and creditless time of bank failures, Eb was able to get cash from his wealthy neighbor, Brother (John S.) Abney of the local Abney Mills. Eb reminded Brother Abney that "some jackass" might find money and buy the few dozen acres and build an ugly shack next to the handsome Abney mansion. When Brother came across with $500 in hard cash, the Eb Dorns took it, bought the small farm and Barrett House, and moved. The new place, with its gently rolling hills, was fertile for cotton and corn, but in

---

[26] Cf. Ibid. WJBD, *OTP*, 10–12; WJBD to A. C. Ware, 8 June 1961; Jesse T. Anderson (state superintendent of education), data enclosure to WJBD, 26 September 1961; WJBD to Anderson, (28?) September 1961, WJBD/SCPC.

[27] TED to Angel, 31 July 1927; retrospective on teacher poverty, WJBD to A. C. Ware, 8 June 1961WJBD/SCPC.

the German way also featured pine trees for timber sales and both beef and dairy cattle. The home itself sat astride a prominent elevation locally called Chinkapin Ridge and was landscaped with wax myrtles and crape myrtles and so many rose bushes of such vibrant colors that young Bryan, the school child, named the place "Myrtle Manor" and eventually wrote a poem in celebration of the estate. The shrewd Germans privately estimated the estate's value at some $50,000, or about $7,687,000 in twenty-first century money, at a time and in a season when a comfortable estate fetched $5,000. Bryan Dorn thereafter made Barratt House and its farmlands, pasturage, and timber stands his home place until he needed to be cared for in a nursing home after a traumatic car crash in his eighth decade.[28]

With half of the tribe out of the house—a girl married, a boy at West Point, another boy in Kentucky attempting to become an army officer—things must have been better for Pearl Dorn in the lovely new home than when she had walked out of the overcrowded former home place. But tension must have remained, for son George, the West Pointer, noted years later in a letter to Bryan: "It is a pleasure to learn that a certain amount of improvement has been negotiated around home." This cadet seeking an officer's commission from the US Military Academy often wrote formally and guardedly, but he dropped his guard sufficiently to reveal his worries about his younger brothers and about his parents' marital problems that had to be "negotiated"—and doubtless renegotiated often. It is significant that Cadet George avoided coming home for the holidays even though he had finally earned leave-time by rank and age and scholar's accomplishments without demerits. Too, the most sharply observant of the children, Grace, marked it that her mother, Pearl—whom Bryan called Baby and other kids called Spunky—often had "mad spells" and went for "long rides" in the fine car Eb bought her. Many of those "motoring trips" eventuated in her spending time with the Griffiths in Old Saluda, and, indeed, "spells" and "riding" and "long rides" became family code for times when Pearl was in "nervous exhaustion" and left Barratt House in order to be attended to by her Griffith family.[29]

---

[28] WJBD to TED, 27 July 1942; "Myrtle Manor," n.d. (1943–1945); "jackass quote" concerning land sale, interview: Steve Griffith and Watson Dorn with Roper (28 February 2012), WJBD/SCPC; Friedman Calculations, CPI, *Hist. Stat. of US*, 1942–1975, *Stat. Abstracts of US*, 1976–2010.

[29] George Dorn to WJBD, 14 October 1931; Grace Dorn to WJBD, 26 July 1943, WJBD/SCPC.

For all that, Eb still loved Pearl and Pearl still loved Eb. If the nature of that love had changed, the love itself had by no means gone away. And there were still the many duties for the matriarch and the "helpmeet" of the Supreme-tendent, now at handsome Barratt House, for a reduced but still sprawling family that remained "land poor"—that is, with illiquid wealth tied up in land and real property—during the lingering national Depression.

Something to remember about Bryan Dorn is that he was only eleven years old when Pearl dramatically walked out and only thirteen when the family moved to Barratt House. Like the other children, Bryan Dorn was strong in the physical and the mental image of their father, Eb. Watson was tallest, over six feet, and built most like Eb and also judged "handsomest" and with "best prospects." Unlike his brothers, Bryan did not grow as tall as the Dorn men, for he stood less than six feet tall, although at five feet and ten inches he was still taller than the average in that poor land in that poor era. And as for conditioning, the farm work—whether chopping cotton, stacking sawn timber, plowing behind a mule, weaning calves, or butchering hogs—made him powerful physically and tough mentally. For most of the period between 1925 and 1950, he self-consciously kept his waist size at thirty-two inches and kept his weight at 175 pounds, the same as father, Eb, in his prime. More important, he ensured through exercise and diet that he kept the 175 pounds muscular and not flabby.[30]

If he stood a little shorter than the other Dorn men, Bryan Dorn also stood a little shorter academically at the consolidated high school where he matriculated in 1929. His passion for speechmaking did not fuel the careful study of history or biology or mathematics. Yet, like his brothers and sisters, Bryan showed excellence in one carefully graded field of endeavor: public speaking. Nana Pearl, "Baby," as Bryan called her, was a fine writer and wrote speeches for all ten children to recite at oratorical contests. Too, she was a shrewd critic, and she had a good sense for what speeches would be appealing to both schoolteachers and to the captive audiences of school children. Bryan Dorn liked to tell stories and to give speeches in any case, and he flourished under his mother's tutelage.

In his memoirs, Bryan sometimes makes it sound as if he took his mother's writings and recited behind mules as he plowed, or to locust trees in the fields adjoining James Cuthbert Self's huge Greenwood Mill. In fact,

---

[30] Interview: Watson Dorn with Griffith and Roper (28 February 2012), JHR/SCPC.

Bryan, like his siblings, benefited not only from Nana's drills but also from some relatively expensive professional training in speech. He discovered the Leopold Schepp Foundation, a New York eleemosynary run by Protestant benefactors who wanted to help "boys and their problems" in impoverished areas. The foundation enriched public school instruction for its Fellows in a three-year program of mail-order training in elocution and declamation, all of its expenses "sponsored" by a local agent, Emma Andrews, who visited Bryan Dorn often and quizzed him and then reported on his doings. There was some money for materials, including practice speeches and manuals about public speaking, and there was a step-by-step certification process complete with bronze-colored, silver-colored, and gold-colored buttons to show achievement.[31]

Attaining highest certification from the Schepp Foundation in 1933, Bryan also graduated from the consolidated county high school in the same year. Along that way, using foundation training manuals plus debating tips and practice orations sent by mail from Cadet George at West Point and speeches mailed to him by oldest brother T. E. Jr., then in Kentucky, Bryan won declamation awards at church and at school and in the community. Encouraged by sponsor Emma Andrews, he applied for the foundation's cash prize of $200—some $3,143.28 in twenty-first century buying power. He won that prize. In other words, his charming recollections of giving perorations to the back side of a mule and orating in the cotton field behind Mr. James C. Self's textile-factory are true, but less than half the story. He was formally trained and drilled and critically evaluated in his public speaking.[32]

Thus doubly certified from secondary institutions in 1933, he was the first of the children not to talk about college—and the first child the educationist couple did not push toward college immediately after public high school graduation. Instead, Bryan Dorn agreed to stay on the farm, working for $10 a month (often computed as a share of the cotton crop) and continuing to take his meals free at Barratt House's board. After Bryan had settled

---

[31] Ibid. Cf. WJBD, *OTP,* 6–7; J. Harold Johnston to WJBD, 29 February 1932, 15 August 1932; Roger H. Williams to WJBD, 9 January 1934; Roger H. Williams to WJBD n.d.; (1934/1935); George Dorn to WJBD, 14 October 1931; T. E. D., Jr. to WJBD, (date?) 1929, WJBD/SCPC.

[32] Interview: Watson Dorn with Griffith and Roper (28 February 2012), JHR/SCPC; Friedman calculator 1929–2010, *Historical Statistics of the US*, 1929–1975, *Statistical Abstracts of the US*, 1975–2010; Roger H. Williams to WJBD, 9 January 1934; Williams to WJBD, n.d. (1934/1935); George Dorn to WJBD, 14 October 1931; TED Jr. to WJBD (date?), 1929, WJBD/SCPC; Cf. WJBD, *OTP*, 6–7, 10.

into this routine and set aside some of the earnings, Eb raised the prospect of his own alma mater, Furman University, perhaps by 1936. By 1936, however, his ambitious sixth son was planning a political career instead of planning a college career.

At that point, there was likely some tension between father and son. College to the Dorns was less privilege than responsibility. Eb and Pearl Dorn had been delighted to see the teenaged Bryan Dorn excel in public speaking. They were even more pleased to see him, or rather to hear him, declaiming, giving emphatic and articulate addresses at church gatherings and for his schoolfellows. And they were delighted that he taught Sunday school to the local children, discussing Baptist tracts that disproved Charles Darwin and that proved salvation by grace alone. They knew he believed in Darwinian evolution, that he believed in salvation by grace alone, and that he saw no contradiction between the former and the latter beliefs. They knew and he knew that he was demonstrating his ability to defend any point of view.[33]

In the mind of Eb Dorn, all that reasoned elocution was prelude to serious scholarship, especially now that the New Deal had developed some National Youth Administration (NYA) and other funding sources to help a cash-strapped son of a farmer attend Clemson College. However, to the focused and driven son, reasoned elocution was prelude to career. And the political career in those days needed no college, but it did need respect from fellow farmers who appreciated speaking skills. Indeed, Bryan Dorn insisted that his basic plan was shaped in his head "while still a child" and finally put forward for the Dorn family in 1936:

*1938, age 22, the South Carolina House of Representatives

*1940, age 24, the South Carolina Senate

*1942, age 26 (leaving state senate), US House of Representatives

*1946, age 30, Governor of South Carolina

*1951, age 35, US Senate[34]

Although Bryan kept these ambitions to himself until 1936, when he announced them, no one in the Dorn or the Griffith or the neighboring

---

[33] Pilgrim Society Study Tracts, n.d., (1929–1933); retrospective, WJBD to A. C. Ware, 8 June 1961; WJBD/SCPC; Cf. WJBD, *OTP*, 36–38.

[34] Phrase and list, WJBD, *OTP*, 6–7.

families blanched at the boldness of the plans, for after all, "young men dream that way on the farm."[35] This young man, inveterate reader, impassioned speaker, true Jeffersonian son of true Jeffersonian father, intended to be a politico after the fashion of the Sage of Monticello. But Eb Dorn was bemused if not actively irate that son Bryan was not taking a few years at Clemson or Furman to best prepare himself for Jeffersonian political roles. After all, the young Thomas Jefferson had spent time reading and declaiming under George Wythe and others at the College of William & Mary. Yet it seems that Bryan Dorn was able to offer Jeffersonian logic to win his case. He said as much in a speech long years later, but the lines of logic flow quite naturally from everything father and son already knew about Thomas Jefferson and Jeffersonian education in 1936. The logic is worth a brief look, for it reveals much about his congressional career and why he sought, however fecklessly, to be governor.

They knew that Jefferson was meritocratic, and their Calvinist persuasions could accept and even celebrate that the Virginian possessed a sense of mission. They knew that Jefferson's passion for equal opportunity was in no way egalitarian in terms of expected outcome. In fact, Jefferson was quite clear that many would fail in schools and then do other things. Despite their own "Puritan Jeffersonianism," the entire Dorn clan knew that Jefferson could never pass muster as a Baptist since he disbelieved the divinity of Jesus and had no truck with miracles. In spite of all that, Jefferson, at least to the Dorns, was a man with a mission, and that mission entailed a life of service by leaders called by some supernatural force to serve others. They ascribed to Jefferson a fondness for Jesus's parables, especially the one about the tares and the wheat, or the chaff and the grain.[36]

The Dorn clan preferred the images of tares and wheat since they understood that in early growth, tares could not be distinguished from wheat. The farmer's job, then, was to grow both crop and weed, wheat and tares; and then, at the fitting time just before harvest, he could winnow the tares. So they understood school, at least where higher education was concerned. It was a grand opportunity to which only some would respond while others in the fullness of a long season would reveal themselves to be tares, and at that point—but *not before that point*—they would be winnowed. No one, then,

---

[35] WJBD, *OTP,* 3, 6–7.

[36] Robertson term "Jeffersonian Puritanism," Idem., *Red Hills and Cotton*; WJBD, "Are We Educating...?", n.d. (1950s?), WJBD/SCPC.

should be dismissed prematurely as a tare, since each demonstrates his nature, wheat or tare, by his own growth and development.

The Dorns looked closely at Jefferson's 1784 pamphlet "Report of the Committee of Revisors Appointed by the General Assembly," his proposal (never adopted) for college preparation and college training by building methodically upward from a publicly supported foundational base in primary education. The Dorns found that Jefferson wanted the "boy of best genius" from each ward school, all told twenty in Virginia, to be chosen for at least one year of college preparation at public expense. Of these twenty "raked from the rubbish annually"—Bryan Dorn quoted Jefferson with pointed if not malicious emphasis—"the best half should be sent to William and Mary College [*sic*]; the other half were not fit for higher education at public expense. There was nothing equalitarian in this system."[37]

Bryan Dorn was declaring himself not to be in the "segment of that segment" that was "equipped to handle that kind of fare." But good Calvinist and good man-with-a-mission, he did not wallow in the mud of that self-evaluation. He could be a state senator and someday governor, and as such, he could make such meritocratic schools possible for other bright and deserving, and cash-strapped, "striving young men" in the red hills. He could, as mature adult politico, learn from scholars, and he could, as mature adult politico, share practical wisdom with the masters and the mentors at the universities. He was still in love with education and with lifelong learning, but his own moment for university study had passed, and now was his time for greater service. He could be no more ready for the General Assembly after seasons at Furman than he was right now. And Furman and Clemson College and other schools would be better served the sooner he got into political office, where he could help them with appropriations. That much, Eb Dorn accepted fully—long years later. For this moment, he took it as the best resolution possible with a determined and driven young man during the hard times of the Great Depression.

Besides working hard on the farm, Bryan became active at First Baptist Church in Greenwood, and indeed at other churches in the subregion. About a dozen Baptist churches were organized as Abbeville Conference for purposes of coordinating youth and adult education, and he worked with the

---

[37] WJBD, "Are We Educating...?"; source: Jefferson, "Report of the Committee of Revisors...," 1784 pamphlet, Rare Books and Special Collections, L/C.

youth Baptist Training Unions and also with the adult Sunday school, taking courses on how to teach youth and also courses on how to organize Bible lessons for adults. In time, he became supervisor of Abbeville Conference Sunday Schools, and he often traveled to observe Sunday school instruction in the dozen or so churches of Abbeville, Greenwood, and Saluda counties. He was not purely engaged in farm work and church service, not purely a Baptist ascetic, however, for he happily joined in the music parties organized by Eb for neighbors and others at Barratt House. Eb and Pearl would roll back the living-room carpet and move the furniture and arrange for local musicians to play traditional dance music, primarily Scotch-Irish ballads, while local grocer John C. Miller brought over "fancy foods," neighbors brought still more food, and regardless of teachings elsewhere, the Baptists danced fervently—and slipped away to drink locally made liquor generally called Hard Labor Creek Spirits.

Bryan loved dancing, and he was popular with the local girls. As he confided to mother Baby, none had eyes as "pretty blue" as hers, and none were really worthy of marriage, at least not yet. Doting mother and wary Dada and even matronly aunts at First Baptist Church such as Mrs. Page were very indulgent of the courtships of young Bryan, who drank hard, danced harder, told tall tales, and generally showed off at least two "country gals" at his sides on Saturday evenings—and then the next Sunday morning appeared at First Baptist Church or at a neighboring Abbeville Conference Baptist Church to be sure some of the same dance partners and drinking partners were in attendance at Sunday school. As novelist Reynolds Price, President Jimmy Carter, journalist Ben Robertson—and certainly the aspirant politician William Jennings Bryan Dorn—could testify, there was nothing staid or boring about the country people on Saturday night. And Sunday mornings were spent on hard benches while the minister reviewed the sins of drinking, dancing, and premarital fornicating (speaking strictly for the young men, the infamous double standard in gender that presumed that only young ladies from *other clans* might be the guilty partners, since the requirements for ladies in the local clan were strictest virginity in youth and devoted motherhood in maturity). The Saturday night hell-raising might end only hours before the church bells tolled for Sunday repentance, but all was taken as a seamlessly woven tapestry of hard work, good times, and guilty worship of a long and loud weekend.[38]

---

[38] Baptist Training Union pamphlets and Abbeville Baptist Conference Sunday Schools brochures, 1936–1940; Samuel M. Smith to WJBD, 21 August 1941, and

Bryan Dorn's Greenwood political homeland was inside South Carolina's Third Congressional District. The Third had almost no cities of size in those days, but it featured disparate geological regions that stretched from the Blue Ridge on the northwest boundary with Georgia and North Carolina, came down along the Savannah River through the piedmont into Edgefield and the new Aiken County that included sand hills, where its boundary line then swung northward again, out of sand hills and back up through more red hills of the piedmont, and then closed off its ellipsis in the eastern Blue Ridge. All of these places lay westward of the relatively populated Greenville and Spartanburg counties. Incorporated cities Greenwood, Anderson, North Augusta, Walhalla, Seneca, Edgefield, and Aiken were in those days more like towns than cities. People typically lived in villages formed by crossroads for farming communities or they lived and worked in man-made centers such as Ware Shoals, Graniteville, Langley, and Pelzer, which were designed as mill towns, where the real government and the churches and the schools—even the "scrip" money and the company-store credit for much of the twentieth century—were beholden to, if not actually property of, the "small-town rich man" who owned the textile mill.

Although the mills and the mill villages proper were overwhelmingly white, African Americans were still very present as farmers and in nearby communities. For instance, McCormick and Edgefield counties were majority black, and the Dorns' own Greenwood was more than 30 percent black. As in so much else, there was segregation, but black people were seen and heard every day, whether on the Dorns' own farm or in the black side of town. This kind of rural and small-town life was Bryan Dorn's upbringing and would define his life and career. Even the modest-sized Greenville and Spartanburg, to say nothing of Charlotte or Atlanta, were cities different in kind and degree from Third District towns.

There were certain resources that Bryan Dorn noted and celebrated from an early age: there were waterways, especially the Savannah River and the Saluda River watersheds, which could be dammed up and redirected and reformed into hydroelectric power and into recreational areas; and there was Clemson Agricultural and Mechanical College, which was not only a school but a major research center dedicated equally to scientific farming and to

---

WJBD to Baby (Pearl Dorn), 2 July 1943, John C. Miller to WJBD, 24 June 1943, and Mrs. Page to BD, 23 June 1943, BD/SCPC; *Greenwood Index-Journal*, church section, 31 January 1936; Robertson, *Red Hills and Cotton*, passim; Price, interview with Gross, 19 June 2006; Carter, *An Hour Before Daylight*, passim.

textile engineering, both of which relied heavily on sophisticated applications of biology and chemistry. Bryan Dorn carefully preserved an address by Clemson president E. W. Sikes in which he delivered a "charge" to the student body of 1936, which could have been the piedmont boy's own entering class. President Sikes drew on Charles Dickens's *Tale of Two Cities* to see the opportunity in the Great Depression, to see that the "worst of times" were also the "best of times," and that the sun was not setting but rising. The Clemson freshmen, all boys in those days, were reminded that "you men are at the dawn" and were told further that this "dynamic, mobile, volatile...age believes that everything that is being done can be done better." They were also scolded for thinking that anything could come easily, or that they would enjoy "soft living." At almost the same time, once-favored brother George, having failed socially and academically at West Point but still aspiring to officer status in the army, was saying almost the same things, quoting the same novelist Dickens.[39]

For good measure, Bryan Dorn as a farmer asked for help from Clemson specialist E. H. Rawl, writing to find out about cold frames and the raising of early-season tomatoes on piedmont farms. And more important, he clipped and studied a printed address by Clemson economics professor Hubert Aull, who explained some of the New Deal "alphabet soup" of farming programs in simple and effective language, and did so with a shrewd and practical-minded approach that disdained theory and accepted only the applications that were producing useful results for piedmont and Blue Ridge farmers. Bryan Dorn made it a point to introduce himself to Dr. Aull, and they became correspondents from 1937 onward, with Aull consistently providing accessible lecture notes about monetary and fiscal policies. Bryan Dorn was not going to get a baccalaureate degree, but he certainly was going to get a Clemson College education that would be pursued vigorously over a long career.[40]

And he would apply a goodly portion of that Clemson College education at once to 1936 political economics. FDR's New Deal had stalled out for several reasons: the Supreme Court had invalidated Roosevelt's programs in farming and industry, Republicans demanded government spending be reduced—and the Dorns thought that the president himself nursed doubts

---

[39] Sikes, "Charge to Class of 1936"; George Dorn to WJBD, n.d. (1937).

[40] E. H. Rawl to WJ BD, 25 January 1937; clipping, (1936), Aull; corr., Aull and WJBD, WJBD/SCPC, 1937–1974; Corr., Aull, SC/CU; Agricultural Economics and Rural Sociology, 1942–1960, UA/CU.

about what he had started. Whether calling things First New Deal and emphasizing practical efforts to put people to work or whether calling things Second New Deal and attempting broader social reform, in 1936 all the FDR programs were underfunded, understaffed, and thereby underserving, as Bryan Dorn understood the political economy. He studied the 1936 Democratic Convention program from Philadelphia, and the farmer politician marked it with sharp criticism that unemployment, after improving, was suddenly back up, reaching more than 19 percent by government measures. And Hubert Aull told him unemployment was likely much worse than the officially measured 19 percent. He also noted that certain Southern politicians, especially in the US Senate, were no longer working alongside FDR and were, in fact, now opponents of the New Deal. Lastly, he marked it that Missouri's anti-New Dealer congressman Champ Clark was pushing delegates in St. Louis to unite successfully behind FDR in the presidential campaign—but was simultaneously working vigorously *against* Roosevelt's programs.[41]

This was the convention when South Carolina's redoubtable US senator Ellison Durant Smith—Cotton Ed Smith—angrily walked out of the building merely because an African American minister delivered a benediction at one of the sessions. Subsequently, Cotton Ed Smith joined other conservative Democrats to stymie FDR's New Deal plans in 1937 and 1938 by blocking legislation concerning wages and hours, housing, and a federal anti-lynching law. For 1938, President Franklin Delano Roosevelt planned action against his most vigorous opponents in the Southern wing of the Democratic Party, taking aim especially at Georgia's Eugene Talmadge and Walter George as well as Cotton Ed Smith.

All three of these racist obstructionists were, in fact, quite important to the Dorn family. The young farmer Bryan Dorn, preparing for the 1938 run for the General Assembly, chose to avoid these fights, which among other things set the "Barnwell Ring" of wily state senator Edgar Brown against the still-vigorous Cotton Ed Smith and also against the New Deal mainline governor Olin Dewitt Talmadge Johnston, thereby creating a three-way brawl in 1938, whose nastiness left problems that lingered for the state Democratic Party. Since the Democratic Party was then the only game in

---

[41] E. H. Rawl to WJBD, 25 January 1937; clipping (1936), Aull; corr., Aull and WJBD, WJBD/SCPC, 1937–1974; corr., Aull, SC/CU; Agricultural Economics and Rural Sociology, 1942–1960, UA/CU; "Democratic National Convention Rules and Committees," 1936, WJBD/SCPC.

the state, the party's problems affected all aspiring young politicians at all levels. Despite FDR's continuing popularity among local millworkers, his attempted "purge" failed abysmally, and all the Southern anti-New Dealers were reelected, joined by a host of anti-New Deal Republicans in the US House and Senate. Nevertheless, as noted, there was still important support for and from FDR in people around Olin Johnston, and also James F. Byrnes and Charleston mayor Burnet Maybank. Thus, resistance to the New Deal was in the very air even as highly personalized support was in the very air, and both support and resistance were often focused on President Roosevelt himself. As the twenty-two-year-old candidate noted, the nasty and wild race for US Senate was the 1938 news in the state, and *not his own efforts* to gain entry into the South Carolina House. Fortunately for him, then, he could avoid specifics on the fights about personalities—and policies—while emphasizing his Populism and self-styled Liberalism and above all his youth and vigor.[42]

For the first phase, which was the 1938 run for the South Carolina lower house of the General Assembly, Bryan Dorn had a mentor who had long been teaching by example, none other than his father, T. E., the Supremetendent who had mastered running for local educational office. Now Dada helped his favored son to master the county politicking that T. E. himself knew so well. This race was truly local, and a kind of frantic "musical chairs" game emerged, with ten candidates vying for three seats to represent Greenwood County. Bryan Dorn considered that colonial Virginians had created the system for seeking and holding office: it was the barbeque dinner hosted by the politician, something Eb had long ago perfected in his own campaigns for educational office. Bryan Dorn, for his part, was always respectful (if not in awe) of Virginia, and always sincerely Calvinist and evangelical in religious practice, as well as deferential to Dada's deep and hard-won wisdom. Thus, Bryan learned how to host a party for everyone, and he learned how to provide "constituent service" for everyone. He knew the importance of putting one's feet under the same table as the feet of all voters, especially if the voters were situated beneath one in the socioeconomic order. He knew the importance of the avuncular touch and the breezy familiarity that the plain-folk farmer and the millworker expected in his politics. He knew the danger of "putting on airs" like his own maternal ancestor Bettie

[42] Dunn, *Roosevelt's Purge*; "Primaries," *Time,* 29 August 1938; interview with Romine (22 January 1987), WJBD/SCPC.

Byrd, and he would never put on airs. He also knew the vital importance of taking seriously the declared needs of voters. He especially knew the vital importance of making sure the voters actually got what they declared to be their "just desserts."

Such "swilling the planters with bumbo" worked for the colonial and early national Virginians, it still worked for Virginians of the Harry Flood Byrd decades, and it worked for his very political father T. E., who, like his model George Washington, often overawed with physical strength and courage, but more consistently won and kept respect by giving what the neighbor voters needed in the way of the smallest of favors and kindnesses. Bryan Dorn studied his father's actions and words, even his physical gestures; and he studied his neighbor's food preferences, not to exclude chitterlings and greens—chitlin' and collards—and made those his own preferences and then shared the fare at his place when he ran for office. He had learned at the ancestral Bethel Church and at the family's First Baptist Church and he had learned from watching Eb Dorn that some are called to serve some ways and others called to serve other ways. Those called to lead must never pretend to be *the* leader, but rather make it clear that they were serving at the call of the people. The believing office holder must needs be properly humble, and the voting crowds at barbeques were on the lookout for the *humble brag* and other affectations of office seekers.[43]

Within Eb's family, there were negative examples that instructed just as well as the positive examples of the Virginia barbeque and other models of the personal touch. In 1908, Eb's father, George Elbert Dorn, had run and lost against William H. Nicholson for state senate. At an early barbeque event, George Elbert simply forgot his speech, "blanked out" on everything he had intended to say. He stood awkwardly for a while, and the crowd yelled for the "Old Gray Mare" to pull out the speech "his wife had written for him"—or sit down. Afraid to reach into his pocket for his prepared remarks, George Elbert eventually sat down and later withdrew his name from the list of contestants. Not long thereafter, in still another such Edgefield race for an Assembly seat, Eb's brother Herbert Dorn ran into unexpected opposition from his own wife, who spread word that *her Bert* wanted to be elected only in order to drink in Columbia and chase after pretty girls there. This Dorn, *her* Bert Dorn, stayed in the race, but he lost disastrously. These particular Dorn family examples reminded Bryan Dorn about strong

---

[43] Sydnor, *Gentleman Freeholders*, passim; WJBD, *OTP*, ch. 2.

speechmaking and about getting the entire family on one's side in the contests.[44]

In this 1938 campaign, as in subsequent ones, Bryan Dorn was fully capable of bombast and theatricality, but in the middle of his most striking performances, he was careful and indeed self-conscious to make clear that he was only one among the folk, something he, in fact, believed with all his heart. One particular gesture captured in a photograph involved a self-deprecating little joke about himself, followed by extending his arms outward and comically smiling at his own foolish fallings-down, the way someone's maid had overheard him giving a speech to the cotton field, the way he had misquoted a Bible verse at the recent supper-snack, the way chitlin' and collards and cornbread threatened to thicken his middle, even the way his Chevrolet had broken down at a rally and he was compelled to "bum rides" from neighbors and church folk. And then he would stand there, having shared proof that he really was *jes' folks* and that he was open about the flaws in himself and in others. He encouraged the crowd to laugh at him, confident that they would also be *laughing with him* when he pressed onward to describe the foolish fallings-down of his opponents.

Like family heroes and namesakes Thomas E. Watson and William Jennings Bryan, this Bryan Dorn really was "of the people." Of course, his approach was not much like that of the wealthy patricians Thomas Jefferson or Robert Y. Hayne or Franklin Delano Roosevelt, and this *jes' folks* candidate of Populists had to be carefully selective in timing his references to political heroes. Indeed, there may have been no member of Congress that ever served who was less spontaneous in his speechmaking than Bryan Dorn. What he said, he had practiced saying. What he practiced, he believed. There were exceptions, moments when he blurted out something without thinking it through and practicing its delivery beforehand. Such moments he always regretted. It was best for the servant to study with the greatest care, know his facts, follow his cues, and then orate like Cicero with the fire of genuine belief checked by the icy restraint of doing one's homework thoroughly before the address. The man worked damned hard to make it look easy.

---

[44] WJBD, *OTP*, 38; US Census, Pop., Edgefield, 1880.

In this 1938 Greenwood County field of ten, one candidate, George Preston Callison, was a friend and, in fact, Bryan's cousin, the son of Clarissa Dorn Callison, who was Aunt Clara, the daughter of George Dorn and the sister of Eb Dorn. George Callison gave him pointers and helped him along the way. That gave him an ally (with one who would soon be a fellow in the same large army in the war) and reduced his number of opponents to nine. There were seriocomic helps too: at the first Greenwood barbeque stump, one candidate slipped into the nearby woods to drink liquor, overdid it, and subsequently passed out, falling off the stage when he returned from his tippling. He was quietly moved to a shaded area to sleep it off and withdrew the next day, reducing the field to nine, and Bryan Dorn's rivals to eight. Another candidate chose to sing, something often popular among the Scotch-Irish musicians of the hills; but this fellow was no singer, and he sang so off-key and so weakly that he, too, was eliminated from contention. That left eight in the field, and it left Bryan Dorn with only seven actual rivals.[45]

When it came his turn to speak, Bryan Dorn marched up confidently and began by "smiting the Philistine hip and thigh," much as he did in Baptist circle discussions. He had found a bromide from Thomas E. Watson, and he announced it carefully and loudly from memory: "Democratic institutions exist by reason of their virtue. If ever they fall, it will be when we have forgotten the past, become indifferent to the present, and utterly reckless as to the future. Ladies and gentlemen, with those words of Senator Thomas E. Watson, I come before you today."[46]

With no other prelude, this engaging newcomer soon had that first crowd with him. He kept that crowd that day, and subsequently spoke at every barbeque he could find, especially the ones sponsored at the mill villages. He gave all of them the same stump speech, always starting with the Watson quote, never using notes, always alternating between folksy raconteuring and formal Ciceronian "speechifying." Although radio was readily available, he wanted people to see him, to note his youth (he was the youngest candidate ever to run for the lower house, at least in Greenwood), and to appreciate at first hand and in person his passion and simplicity. Besides speaking formally at orchestrated events, he walked all over the county, talking informally with farmers and millworkers. He recalled that he often

[45] WJBD, *OTP*, ch. 2; on Callison in War, WJBD to Parents, 17 March 1945, WJBD/SCPC.

[46] WJBD, op. cit, 40.

walked some sixteen hours in a day and that he bore up well under the exertion because of his years of plowing fields of cotton and corn; a Clemson extension agent reckoned that a plowman often walked thirty miles in a long day. If someone was not at home, he left his calling card: "A Dirt Farmer and a Friend of the Working Man." In those peregrinations, he was especially careful to meet and greet the local sheriff, in South Carolina the main organizing agent for local politics.[47]

The combination of old Virginia ways and his own personal freshness, even innocence, combined with meeting thousands of people, worked well, and Bryan Dorn polled more votes than anyone that year in Greenwood County, more votes than anyone ever gained again in Greenwood County. He joined his seasoned cousin George P. Callison, also elected easily on the first round. Yet another friend with a long political tenure, Claude H. Gresham, needed a second round of voting to gain his own seat alongside Dorn and Callison.[48]

From this campaign Bryan Dorn drew still broader lessons, borne out in all his subsequent political behavior. First, he must work with his party's national leaders, especially if one of them was president. Yet he could never get as far away from his roots in the red hills and cotton fields and textile mill villages as Governor Olin D. Johnston had gotten in 1936. Early, Olin Johnston had recognized what an art it was to cooperate with the president and the US Congress to get things done, especially in a poor state like South Carolina, where precious little could be accomplished with state resources alone. Clearly, Governor Johnston understood that part of the political art. Yet he could not serve all South Carolinians, especially in the red hills. His overwhelming appeal was to his beloved "linthead" millhand—but not the many remaining farmers and the many small-scale business folk. Indeed, to defend progressive legislation on behalf of a subset of the white working class, he often fell back on the most awful race-baiting and negrophobic rhetoric, some of it verging on hysteria. At one extreme, then, was Governor Johnston, who in 1936 was yet another progressive manqué: much of his antiblack rhetoric wrought injustice, and much of his tightly focused class appeal eliminated chances for constructive legislation because it set a tone that eliminated the possibilities of compromise, especially in a state where

---

[47] Ibid., 39.

[48] *Greenwood Index-Journal*, 11 Nov. 1938, 1; "Dorn," South Carolina Legislative Manual of 1939, 83d General Assembly Sess., ed., James E. Hunter, 93, 148.

the legislature had the real power, and the governor must further his agenda by suasion and courtship of the assemblymen.[49]

By contrast, Cotton Ed Smith had done a far better job than Johnston of staying close to all the locals—but then Cotton Ed Smith had little intent to get things done, certainly not in the sense of improving the welfare of average South Carolinians by diversifying the economy, to say nothing of providing some basic services in roads and schools for those of any class or race in great need. In his rhetorical flights and his melodramatic actions—such as walking out on the 1936 Democratic presidential nominating convention because a black preacher was going to pray in public, and thereafter making a face and waving his hands as if to remove a stench whenever New Deal proposals were mentioned—Cotton Ed Smith set a standard for intimate but reactionary lawmaking that captivated a voting plurality of sandlappers. Like Johnston, Cotton Ed Smith could indulge some extreme antiblack rhetoric that defied his actual behavior and probably did not define his actual beliefs. In fact, watching these extremes of the entertaining and intimate reactionary Cotton Ed and the overly loyal New Dealer Olin D., Dorn was most taken aback by the way race-baiting and antiblack rhetoric could become political lives of their own as well as useful rhetoric. He had, of course, seen as much in distant relatives and warm friends in the Blease family. His parents, his Sunday school, his own conscience would not allow Bryan Dorn to flay black people in rhetoric, whatever the grander cause.[50]

For all these reasons, Dorn's actual model for finding and holding the correct balance was Edgar Allan Brown, "the Bishop of Barnwell," who earlier had served in the South Carolina Senate and who was now planning a return. Some journalists and historians from the Roosevelt days and later described Brown as anti-New Deal, yet, then and today, still others describe him as pro-New Deal, at least in state and county economics. He was, in fact, artfully *both at the same time*, and never got so close to the New Deal intellectuals and reformists that he angered the locals, just as he never so stymied New Deal initiatives that he became an enemy of the mainline Democratic Party. Above all, Brown never stepped out boldly as some kind

---

[49] WJBD, *OTP*, ch. 2 and WJBD/SCPC, 1936–1938; Olin Dewitt Talmadge Johnston Papers, SCPC, 1936–1938, hereinafter ODTJ/SCPC; Miller, "Piedmont Politician" (PhD diss., University of North Carolina, 1976); Carpenter, "Olin D. Johnston" (PhD diss., Emory University, 1987); Huss, *Senator for the South*.

[50] Ellison DuRant Smith Papers, 1932–1938, SCL; Hollis, "Cotton Ed Smith" (1970): 235–56; "Ellison DuRant Smith," *BDUSC*, s.v.

of liberal on things racial, but yet he generally avoided the extreme race-baiting that marked his fellow South Carolina politicos from Pitchfork Ben Tillman through Cole Blease to Cotton Ed Smith and Olin D. Johnston. In confidence, Dorn marked it that Edgar Brown could be a little dull and uninspiring, but his careful balancing between duty to national Democrats and responsibilities to local Democrats was Bryan Dorn's model for how to live a political life, albeit in Dorn's special case, with grander rhetorical flourishes worthy of a child of Nana's.[51]

In the 1939 to 1941 House sessions, Bryan Dorn joined the efforts to build schools and roads, about all his impoverished state had revenues to do. Despite the slowing down of the New Deal, South Carolina actually was getting more from the federal government than its citizens paid in taxes, a fact Bryan Dorn noted and stored away for use in the future races for political seats at other levels. There was also money from sales taxes dedicated to Clemson College and from other sums dedicated for the state secondary roads, and so a House assemblyman could see some tangible improvements in the red hills. Dorn thus enjoyed this legislative time in the lower house, but he was almost immediately preparing himself to run for the upper house, the state senate, where his prototype Edgar A. Brown intended to rejoin—and to direct.[52]

Young as Bryan was, family and personal history sat astride his broad shoulders, for the seat was still held by William H. Nicholson. The latter was the selfsame state senator against whom his grandfather George Dorn had foundered disastrously more than thirty years earlier. In fact, Nicholson, whose political acumen Dorn admired and learned from, was now a matured New Dealer who got important things done for farmers and schoolteachers—again, within the considerable constraints of a poor state's meager resources. Indeed, Dorn later admitted, there was little difference between Nicholson's policies that he had practiced and the policies that the young

---

[51] WJBD, *OTP*, ch. 2; Weber, "Vocation of Politics"; WJBD, "Extension of Remarks," Congressional Record Appendix, 25 October 1972, E8952; "Edgar Allan Brown," *Biographical Directory of Senate of State of South Carolina*, 1776–1964 (1964), 187; W. D. Workman, *The Bishop of Barnwell*; "Mr. Sound Government—Senator Edgar A. Brown," *South Carolina Magazine* (February 1958).

[52] "Dorn," *South Carolina Legislative Manual of 1941, 83d General Assembly Sess.*, ed. Hunter, 93, 148; WJBD, "Hon. Edgar A. Brown," Congressional Record, 92d Cong., 2d Sess., vol. 118, pt. 28, 18 October 1972, 37456; "Edgar Allan Brown," *Biographical Directory of Senate of State of South Carolina, 1776–1964* (1964), 187.

aspirant was planning. But the state senator was an old family foe, and he was in the seat that the striving young assemblyman wanted. Dorn learned quickly that Nicholson had made a real enemy out of Edgar Brown, who, as noted, was carefully balancing support for FDR's national party with his own closeness to the state electorate. In parochial terms, then, Nicholson was "too much" in the camp of Olin Johnston and possibly distanced from the plain folk—or at least *he could be made to appear distant* from the plain folk.[53]

There were other complexities involving Senator Nicholson. Once quite a successful attorney, Nicholson had invested unfortunately, perhaps recklessly, and lost a fortune in the early days of the Great Depression. Moreover, he apparently speculated in real estate and other property affairs in improper ways, for he had lost his license to practice law. Thus disbarred, he had suffered some local disgrace in the eyes of the mill owners, especially Self and Abney, and in the eyes of the regional bar, especially the Blease and the Griffith family lawyers. All of these friends and family members confided their fears about Nicholson's character and judgment to the Dorns, first to Eb Dorn, then to the much younger Bryan and Watson. For all that, Nicholson was a fine speaker and active thinker, and he had roared back, rising from his personal trough to win state senate election in 1933 by grasping the coattails of Franklin Delano Roosevelt. During the first governorship of Olin D. Johnston, he had become New Deal champion of the small-time farmer and millhand, establishing a winning coalition of voters in Greenwood. Once holding senate office, he applied for and was again granted his license to practice law in South Carolina.[54]

For this 1938 Greenwood County contest for the state senate, none other than James Cuthbert Self provided both an opportunity and a threat for Bryan Dorn. Self had sent attorneys and other agents to try to get Eb Dorn to run against Nicholson in the coming campaign. Eb Dorn had declined, citing his advancing age, but he did suggest that his bright and ambitious son Bryan Dorn could be the right candidate. However, Eb Dorn could certainly read the direction of political winds, and he extracted a promise from Jim Self to keep his support of Bryan secret—else the strong antibusiness sentiments of the time and place would work against the young

---

[53] WJBD, *OTP*, 48–51. Interview: Watson Dorn with Griffith and Roper (28 February 2012), JHR/SCPC.

[54] Interview: Watson Dorn with Griffith and Roper (28 February 2012), JHR/SCPC.

candidate and for the New Dealer Nicholson. Self and his people could read the same political winds just as well and agreed to stay out of sight. They provided some money, perhaps a thousand dollars, but kept it quite quiet. Judge Jeff Griffith, of the extended family, was himself providing approximately $500, and his means were far more limited than those of the mill-owning elite.[55]

In any case, this campaign would not turn on money, but on the personal appeal to the voters, something done by hard work over time rather than by expending funds. More important, Jim Self and Brother Abney accepted that Bryan Dorn would run a Populist campaign largely sympathetic to the New Deal and publicly unsympathetic to corporate leaders, whether corporate leaders were mill owners or otherwise. Watson Dorn, young as he was, mastered these details and incorporated them into his own understanding of state politics, lessons he would implement on behalf of his adored brother in the future. For the nonce, Watson watched and remembered everything, Dada watched and directed, Nana watched and wrote speeches, and all family members, especially the attractive Gracie, walked and walked and talked and talked about their candidate. Bryan Dorn implemented a campaign based on powerful appeal person by person, with absolutely no personal criticism of his opponent Nicholson, for whom he would express what he actually felt, namely, respect for any elder and deep professional appreciation for his expertise in lawmaking and politicking.[56]

In preparing for the race, Bryan Dorn deployed a fact about demographics in his red hills county. Rural, it still was, but textile proceeds now outpaced farming revenues. More to the point, population and voting were two different things: most people were still farmers, but most voters were not most people. Black people, most of whom were farmers, constituted one in three of the population but could not vote. And many white small-time farmers had come to the mills even though retaining their small farms. Thus, the most typical *voter* was now a rural millworker rather than a farmer; and the millworker village population was greater than the five wards of the smallish town of Greenwood. Fastest growing, and a place relatively unfamiliar to Senator Nicholson, was Ware Shoals. But there were also mills

---

[55] Corr., Self, Abney, and Griffith, 1936, WJBD/SCPC; interview: Watson Dorn with Griffith and Roper (28 February 2012), JHR/SCPC.

[56] "More Voters Now at Mills Than in the City," *Greenwood Index-Journal*, 24 July 1940, 8; "Many Enroll at Mill Boxes," *Greenwood Index-Journal*, 21 July 1940, 8; interview: Watson Dorn with Griffith and Roper (28 February 2012), JHR/SCPC.

at Grendel and 96 as well as Jim Self's mills and Brother Abney's mills. Not only were they the predominant face of his home county, but these millhands, men and women, registered to vote and were increasingly vocal in their talk about issues such as their schools, their roads, and their much-needed Social Security paychecks. Always comfortable with farming folk, Dorn bent to the more important task of making himself comfortable with the mill folk, the men and the women of the looms and the spindles.[57]

Everything was a challenge. Even to run against Nicholson, Bryan Dorn would have to campaign cleverly in order to be declared eligible to run when only twenty-four. If elected, he would become twenty-five in April of the sessions; but he would be only twenty-four during the campaign, at swearing-in, and for the first 100 days of legislating. It seemed he might well be ineligible to run because of his youth. He went to work with dispatch and cleverness, drawing on the specific wording of the state constitution as reaffirmed by the State Supreme Court in a 1933 case called by laypeople the Kemper Cooke Case: "The Senate shall be the sole judge of election returns and qualifications of its own members." First, he talked to brother George, commissioned despite his failure at West Point but temporarily not needed by the army in this brief season before the build-up of the "Arsenal for Democracy." He persuaded George to register for the state senate primary race. According to family tales, it was early morning after a long night of partying and George did not really comprehend what he was doing when he filed. Even so, George's filing held a place for one Dorn to run against the ancient foe Nicholson while Bryan arranged his unique campaign for eligibility. George, for his part, caught on quickly and "made a statement to the newspaper saying he had heard rumors to the effect his brother, Bryan Dorn, might be voted off the ballot."[58]

The executive committee met to consider the recommendation of county chairman Calhoun Mays, who advised the group that Dorn was too young, adding that, "If we permit him to remain on the ballot, then Shirley Temple could file as a candidate for the Senate." Standing before the committee, Dorn presented letters from Joseph L. Nettles, president of the Bar

---

[57] "More Voters Now at Mills Than in the City," *Greenwood Index-Journal*, 24 July 1940, 8; "Many Enroll at Mill Boxes," *Greenwood Index-Journal*, 21 July 1940, 8; "Greenwood," *Historical Statistics*, 1940.

[58] Anderson v. Blackwell, 168 SC Rep. 137, 167 SE 30, 4 January 1933; "Statement by Candidate W. J. Bryan Dorn," *Greenwood Index-Journal*, 3 July 1940, 1 and "County Executive Committee Votes to Place Bryan Dorn's Name on Senate Ticket," also, 1. "J. Bryan Dorn Candidate for State Senate," *Greenwood Index-Journal*, 3 May 1940, 8.

Association of South Carolina, Eugene Blease, once chief justice of the Supreme Court of South Carolina, and prominent Columbia attorney Clint Graydon. These letters testified to Dorn's good personal qualities and also stated that the law was not precise about the minimum age for filing, swearing-in, or starting to serve. The *Greenwood Index-Journal* records that Bryan Dorn next said: "In order to walk up and pay a fee to file as a candidate, you didn't have to tell your age; you didn't have to tell your race; you didn't have to tell anything. You just filed. Thus the only thing this Committee can judge is whether or not I had paid the filing fee, whether I had signed the pledge not to use whiskey or money to buy votes, and so on."[59]

To this statement, Dorn added the examples of Henry Clay, Andrew Jackson, and John Caldwell Calhoun, all of whom began careers young and each of whom, he claimed, filed for office before reaching the stated minimum age. Apparently, this meeting of the executive committee had drawn a crowd, most of whom were listening with interest to the discussion, and he said that he "could feel the tension," but also that he liked the way all were "looking me over good." He concluded with a Populist flourish directed to the gathered crowd more than to the executive members: "I cannot believe that a committee, whose numbers are so small, will undertake to tell more than 8,000 voters who they shall be allowed to vote for."[60]

The committee approved readily enough, at which point George Dorn withdrew his own name, and Bryan Dorn's race for Greenwood's senate seat of incumbent William H. Nicholson was on.

As the Democratic committee formalized its arrangements for debates, the size and scope of the undertaking came fully home to him. Not only was it personal and familial—"Senator Nicholson had beaten my grandfather, but I resolved that he would not beat me"—but also stakes were high at a professional level, for in that day the state senate had greater authority and significance than it wields today. Political scientists Valdimer Orlando Key and Alexander Heard had noted that of all states, South Carolina in this period had the most "localistic" politics, with state senators establishing "fiefdoms" in locales and with Edgar Brown a kind of prime minister negotiating between a structurally weak governor, a cabinet whose members were inde-

---

[59] WJBD, *OTP*, 48–51; "Democratic Committee Is Called to Meet," *Greenwood Index-Journal*, 24 June 1940, 8.

[60] "51 Pay Fees as Candidates for County Offices," *Greenwood Index-Journal*, 2 July 1940, 8; "Democratic Committee Is Called to Meet," 8.

pendent of the governor, and locally powerful senators who had baronial powers over small sections of friends and neighbors. As Bryan Dorn recounts in his memoirs:

> Back then a state senator was very powerful. He had a major role in matters regarding the courthouse and the tax structure and he practically controlled the entire county budget. The state highway department would not improve a road or cut a new one without the recommendation of the senator. The senator would recommend people for the highway patrol, set the salary of all county officials, and control appointments. All in all it constituted a little kingdom for the senator. A senator could do just about anything he wanted. They elected judges, too, so when a state Senator walked into a courtroom of one of the judges he helped elect, the judge usually rapped the gavel and welcomed the senator into the court. It was a far more powerful position than it is today.[61]

To secure these ends, he again put the extended clan of relatives and friends to work on the kind of walking and talking campaign he had waged for the lower house. Now, the stakes were higher and the competition more intense since it was head-to-head against a sitting legislator who enjoyed his own "little kingdom." Eb and Pearl Dorn, together as proud parents or individually, traveled the byways. So too did brothers George and Charlie and the doting in-laws, the Griffiths. As in the lower house race, Bryan Dorn himself walked everywhere, shaking hands when he found people, leaving his "Dirt Farmer" calling card when he missed them. He listened, too. They wanted roads, they wanted schools, and they wanted to remain farmers, but existing New Deal programs were not sufficient to buck up the increasingly difficult business of growing and harvesting and trading cotton and raising and selling hogs and mules and cows and chickens. Others in the mill villages worried about sufficient work hours and overtime and working conditions. Senator Nicholson, as part of the progressive or New Deal wing of the state Democrats, worked hard to support exactly such programs, but he did so ineffectively, since he had angered Edgar Brown, who sometimes eliminated some Greenwood County sugarplums from the larder. To complicate things, the distinguished looking sixty-two-year-old began to attack Bryan Dorn for his youth and inexperience, often saying condescendingly that "Bryan is a

---

[61] Key with Heard, "South Carolina: The Politics of Color," *Southern Politics,* 130–55; WJBD, quoted, *OTP*, 52, 48.

fine boy," but sometimes turning vicious and shouting, "The boy lacks judgment!"[62]

Several family members and friends urged on their champion, calling for an equally hard rebuttal and an equally hard attack. Instead, he took youth as an advantage. He had virtually no record, and he was in many ways innocent, if not ignorant, of some of the shadier aspects of state politics. Consciously, he became "Mama's boy" to every female in the crowd and "Little Brother" to every man there. Too, he shamelessly appropriated—stole, really—the Nicholson platform of New Deal support for farmers and factory workers. He genuinely loved farmers and millhands, and his compassion was fully legitimate, but until 1940 he had only vaguely supported roads and schools, and until this campaign had by no means actually thought through *which* New Deal programs he supported. He also borrowed from St. Paul the technique of "burning"—even metaphorically killing—one's foes with kindnesses. After each speech was concluded, he hurried over to shake hands with Senator Nicholson and with a third opponent, J. D. Thompson. In shaking hands, he would always say very loudly, in full Shepp Foundation stage voice, "That was great!" And he ran an advertisement in the *Greenwood Index-Journal* and other newspapers: "My only promise is to endeavor to keep my feet on the ground and tune my ear to the heart-beat of all the people." Lastly, he was careful to include in print and in face-to-face meetings and in formal speeches references to Pearl Griffith Dorn and to what "my mother taught me, at her knees."[63]

Actually, Eb and Pearl did not agree with each other on the tactics, and Eb, the man who knew muscle power and *force majeure* as well as intellectual persuasion, brought his favorite roughnecks and tough guys to some of the barbeque stump speeches, and these folks glowered ominously and murmured in their own stage whispers whenever Senator Nicholson criticized his young challenger. At the final session, before a crowd of some 2,000 in Ware Shoals, when Senator Nicholson made a snide remark about "this boy here," a number of Eb's rowdies went beyond stage whispers. They began to

---

[62] "Vocal Fireworks are Touched Off at Grendel Mill Speaking," *Greenwood Index-Journal*, 11 August 1940, 1; "Largest Crowd Hears Candidates at Ware Shoals," *Greenwood Index-Journal*, 17 August 1940, 1, 5.

[63] WJBD, *OTP*, ch. 2; "Variety of Subjects Given Attention," *Greenwood Index-Journal*, 28 July 1940, 1, 8; on Nicholson: Robert Cranford, "Educational Legislation Main Issue in Assembly," *Greenwood Index-Journal,* 8 February 1936, 1, and Pearl Griffith Dorn to WJBD, 10 November 1943, WJBD/SCPC; St Paul quoted, Rom. 12:20, KJV and most trans.

scream and yell and ball up their fists and gesture violently. Eventually the senator left the stage. In his memoirs, Bryan Dorn recalls that Will DeLoach, onetime bodyguard for the always controversial and always provocative Cole Blease, "asked Daddy when the shooting was going to start." And the mature politician, looking back, affirmed that "the only thing that prevented bloodshed was the other side was not prepared for this and hadn't come to the meeting armed. The tension was so high that if one gun had been fired, twenty-five people might have been shot." Given the bloody recent past of his "postage stamp of territory," the memoirist was guilty of no more exaggeration than was the hyperventilating bodyguard DeLoach.[64]

It worked at more than one level. Eb's tough guys enforced respect for Bryan in the crowd and Pearl's sweet reason seemed to make Senator Nicholson the ill-tempered bad man—and the young dirt farmer almost a victim. Above all, Bryan Dorn never tried to defend himself against the attacks of his opponent, but instead kept proclaiming his genuine roots in the red hills and his support of New Deal programs for farmers and factory workers. Defense, *sometimes against straw men*, was provided by family members. On the final day before voting, the family produced a carefully and cleverly worded handbill defending Bryan Dorn against accusations that he was "self-made," that is, the chosen stooge of mill owner James Self in Greenwood—a charge that was, of course, true to some degree. Quite cleverly, still honestly, but quite cleverly, the Dorns produced a handbill that warned voters to beware of other "accusations" and "tricks." The entire extended family distributed these handbills in person to voters coming to the polling places: his articulate and eloquent brothers George and Charlie gave speeches, and his womenfolk assured other womenfolk that this was a Good Boy who deserved this chance.[65]

For all this careful preparation and shrewd execution, the race was quite close. As votes were being counted, the Dorns and the Griffiths and their friends congregated in front of the *Greenwood Index-Journal* offices. The memoirist remembers that at least 1,000 people were there. The mill villages of Ware Shoals and 96 Mill gave "the boy here" a winning margin of some

---

[64] WJBD, *OTP,* 54; "Largest Campaign Crowd Hears Candidates at Ware Shoals," *Greenwood Index-Journal*, 17 August 1940, 1, 5; "County Campaign Ends in Display of Verbal Fireworks," *Greenwood Index-Journal*, 25 August 1940, 1, 7; interview: Watson Dorn with Griffith and Roper (28 February 2012), JHR/SCPC.

[65] WJBD, *OTP*, ch. 2; "All Sorts of Topics Given Airing," *Greenwood Index-Journal*, 4 August 1940, 1; "1200 Hear Candidates," *Greenwood Index-Journal*, 28 July 1940, 8.

683 votes over Nicholson, after subtracting the smattering of votes for Thompson. Had Dorn lost either Ware Shoals or 96 Mill, then Nicholson would have continued as state senator. The five districts of the Town of Greenwood were split evenly, and surprisingly Nicholson won a close race in little Grendel Mill, where crowd reaction had been especially raucous in favor of Dorn. In any case, both Senator Nicholson and J. D. Thompson promptly and graciously conceded defeat and pledged full support for the people's choice.[66]

Although this campaign worked, the family knew that he might be challenged on the floor of the senate itself, since the upper chamber was by specific constitutional declaration "sole judge of election returns and qualifications of its own members." As he prepared for the possible appeal and hearing, he initially missed the fact that "Tieless Joe" Tolbert had again registered a few candidates to run as Republican in the November election, something the irrepressible Tolbert had been doing futilely since 1898. This Tolbert, from a political family that fascinated Bryan Dorn, never earned enough votes to win in November, and the Democratic primary was the important political contest. In this case, W. Jeff Nickles had been registered as candidate for the Republicans in November. When the general election came in November, FDR won overwhelmingly, and all county Democratic candidates won a perfect 2,698 votes of 2,698 cast, with the exception of Dorn, who received 2,697 votes to one for W. Jeff Nickles. It was then that Dorn belatedly realized a new problem. If his election was disallowed, there was a legitimate candidate, Nickles, who was "still standing and still available." Indeed, Nickles promptly filed a protest about Dorn's age, and thus a living Republican in the red hills bid fair to be elected to the state senate, something surprising even for the redoubtable and colorful Tieless Tolbert—he who vowed to "avoid anything [like ties] that annoy[ed] him." It took away one of Bryan Dorn's arguing points, that is, that the people voted for him and there was no one else available. The people had voted for him, but there was a registered November-election and vote-getting candidate eligible to be seated if the dirt farmer were ruled to be too young. The first week of the new year of 1941 would feature some excitement in Columbia concerning this election when the state senate convened itself.[67] The issues—youth

---

[66] WJBD, *OTP*, ch. 2; more precise data, Cf "Precincts Tables," *Greenwood Index-Journal*, 28 August 1941, 3.

[67] "Bryan Dorn Is Nominated Senator," *Greenwood Index-Journal*, 28 August 1941, 1, 3, 8; "Republican Committee Denies Tolbert Group Seat," *Greenwood Index-Journal*,

and inexperience, eligibility and popularity, legitimate support and legal support—were with Bryan Dorn this year and would be with him again five decades later. Those issues helped him famously in 1940 and hurt him infamously in 1974.

These senators in session in Columbia were not exactly the same as the farmers and millhands who crowded in to hear what the committee in Greenwood would decide. But they were only a few degrees removed from such folks, and they were accustomed to and appreciative of the theatrics of a good show. According to his memoirs, corroborated by the *Index-Journal*, Bryan Dorn gave them exactly that. Quietly remaining in his seat, as instructed by Lieutenant Governor and Senate President Joseph Emile Harley, while the other elected senators were sworn in, Bryan Dorn waited for his moment. Ray Robinson Williams of Greenville, himself only recently sworn in, made the motion that his friend Bryan Dorn be seated. Williams was blind, and he spoke with Homeric eloquence about Dorn's service in the House and reminded the other senators that the people of Greenwood knew his age during the election campaign. Williams next borrowed some of Dorn's own language to ask in rolling cadences: "Who are we to challenge this honest election[?] Each of you better look into your own heart and examine your own background before you dare refuse admission to this august body to one who had the approval of the people, the sovereign people, who elected him and represent democracy."[68]

Then none other than Edgar A. Brown, "the power of the South Carolina Senate," rose to second the motion. Because Nicholson had plenty of friends left in the senate, Dorn had arranged for Chesterfield County's George K. Laney to follow Senator Brown's seconding speech. Laney, known to be personal friends with Nicholson, said, "Even Senator Nicholson would never suggest that the will of the people be thwarted. The people have spoken; let their will be done." The combination of sidebar arrangements and well-of-the-senate theatrics was more than enough to do the job,

---

21 June 1940, 1, 8; "County Votes Overwhelmingly for Roosevelt," *Greenwood Index-Journal*, 6 November 1940, 1, Precinct Tables, 2.

[68] Quoted, WJBD, *OTP*, 55–56; Williams quoted, "Bryan Dorn Seated as Senator," *Greenwood Index-Journal*, 14 January 1941, 1, 7.

and Bryan Dorn recorded that he "was seated in that great body, the youngest man in the history of the state to hold the office."[69]

By the time he actually turned twenty-five, Bryan Dorn was essentially a veteran senator, one who knew how to serve constituents back home in the red hills, but also one who knew his place as a junior in the tall totem pole of privilege and prestige that was the South Carolina Senate in 1940. He enjoyed the way judges in courthouse session held up proceedings in order to recognize his attendance, and he reveled in the smiles on the worn faces of millworkers and farmhands when a handsome new blacktop road with solid and wide shoulders was completed in their corner of the county, and the gratitude on the equally worn faces of female millworkers when a top-notch new school building was set up for the children in the mill village. Much as he enjoyed the pleasures of such prerogatives, Dorn retained his simplicity and his humility, and he was scrupulous in sharing credit for each constituent service rendered. More to the point, he took great pains to show deference to his elders in the senate, and, of course, *every* one of them was his elder that first winter. He studied at the feet of Edgar Brown and learned how to bide his time patiently and respectfully while other senators mulled some proposal for long days and even weeks. He came to feel in his country bones the full meaning of Max Weber's words when the sociologist said that lawmaking was the most difficult of carpentry, a "slow boring through hardwood." He lay into that painstaking process with equal parts determination and patience, going back and forth between contesting committee members, each of whom had some sort of objection or concern about some bit of legislation. Following the tutelage of Senator Brown, he remembered to work as hard on the details of some other senator's prized bill as he did on his own.[70]

Dorn learned of an expensive dredging project and general improvement proposed for the Port of Charleston in order to make the Holy City of the low country more of a player in modern trade and commerce. Not only was Charleston well beyond his own district, but the old capital was problematical for a piedmont senator. The city's people took pride in English traditions, including a High Anglican conceit in their own Pinckneys and Rutledges among an elite that seemed arrogant to a piedmont countryman.

---

[69] Quotations, WJBD, *OTP* 56; full quotations, "Bryan Dorn Seated," 1, 7; interview: Watson Dorn with Griffith and Roper (28 February 2012), JHR/SCPC.

[70] WJBD, *OTP*, ch. 2; Weber, "Vocation of Politics"; "Dorn," *South Carolina Legislative Manual of 1941, 84th General Assembly*, ed., Hunter, 23.

Too, the sizeable working class was Irish—not Scotch-Irish but *Catholic* Irish who had decades of rivalry with and even hatred of the Ulster Irish and the up-country Calvinists. The black majority, the big African American presence downtown, were oppressed, and yet they, too, still celebrated their own long years of traditions and unique Gullah culture in a way that was indecipherable for red-hills folk. In fact, Charlestonians—whether working-class Catholic Irishmen, Gullah-speaking African Americans, or the old-wealth Episcopalians of St. Michaels and St. Philips—collectively looked down low-country noses at the backwoods Baptists and their fundamentalist verities in Greenwood.[71]

For all that, a man who wanted to be governor must keep statewide needs in his vision, and so Dorn served low-country senators not only where it was quid pro quo legislative "boring through hardwood," but also where substantive service to the Mouth of the Savannah was integrally tied to development of the river's source in the headwaters of the Blue Ridge. Thus, looking ambitiously to the governorship, Bryan Dorn eagerly supported the Port of Charleston projects. He became one of the coauthors of the successful bill that established the South Carolina State Ports Authority. This work, too, he relished with an almost classic deontological pride in the craftsmanship and the artisanry of lawmaking—any lawmaking—that served some senator's constituents somewhere in South Carolina. With full support of Brown's "Barnwell Ring," with cooperation from the Olin Johnston New Dealers, but retaining the full affection of Cotton Ed Smith's naysaying traditionalists, Senator Dorn saw to it that roads were put through, schools erected, salaries advanced to appropriate officials, and grateful county judges reappointed. Too, despite some misgivings, he worked hard for Burnet Maybank as the elegant Charlestonian, sworn enemy of his family friends Cole and Eugene Blease, competed in two consecutive summer primaries before winning election to the US Senate.[72]

In addition, Bryan Dorn was selected for the senate's Board of Visitors to Clemson College, which chose him as secretary for their visit to the institution most important to him in his piedmont region. Taking leadership in the group for which he took notes, he urged that Clemson increase salaries for its professors, improve its chemistry laboratories, expand its much-

---

[71] Edgar, op. cit., 289–90; Duffy, "Charleston—the People & the Place."

[72] WJBD, *OTP*, ch. 2; notebook of legislation, WJBD/SCPC; Sam M. Smith to WJBD, 21 August 1941; Burnet R. Maybank to WJBD, 8 September 1941; Board of Visitors Secretary Report to Clemson College Board of Trustees, 13 May 1941.

appreciated extension services for farmers—and, marking it with special urgency, build some restrooms for visiting ladies. He further proposed that these outlays could be paid for by an increase of a nickel on a bag of fertilizer. Despite his busy schedule as youngest senator, he established an insurance agency for fire hazards back in Greenwood and completed basic training and some advanced training in artillery for the South Carolina Army National Guard, earning a certificate of service and honorable discharge with commendation. Dorn also joined the South Carolina Defense Forces, which trained on certain weekends in case of military emergency. Nor did he give up a social life, albeit one built largely around the Abbeville Conference of Baptist Church Sunday Schools, wherein he took charge of Sunday school and Training Union programs in some dozen churches in Greenwood, including a handsome new one established by mill magnate Jim Self in honor of his late mother, Callie Self. Bryan's sisters and his female buddies at teaching colleges, plus the Sunday school teachers, made sure that he had a gracious plenty of womanly companionship, and he brought at least one lady home to meet his Nana and Dada. He was, however, determined not to be indiscreet, not to boast, and above all not to rush into marriage, and so he confined activities to wholesome Baptist picnics and gatherings. There were, then, the happiest of auguries for one who planned to bid farewell to his senator colleagues and enter the 1942 US House of Representatives race for the Third Congressional District.[73]

These were good times along the Congaree River in the modern capital. But they could not go on without international interruptions. There were foreign complications more overwhelming than anything emanating from Charleston for the piedmont senator to conjure. Adolph Hitler's Nazi troops, after overwhelming Poland, astonished the world by rolling through France in a blitzkrieg followed by a fierce aerial pounding of England. At the same time, Josef Stalin in post-Leninist Communist Russia was establishing a regime terrifying to a believing Baptist. The up-country people of fundamentalist

---

[73] WJBD, *OTP*, ch. 2; notebook of legislation; "Dorn," *South Carolina Legislative Manual of 1942, 84th General Assembly Sess.*, ed., Hunter, 23, 45; Statement of Service, South Carolina National Guard, HQ Battery, 263 Coast Artillery, 5 December 1939–14 July 940; Enlistment Record, South Carolina Defense Forces, Co. K, 2d Reg., 23 June 941; Dinky Epting to WJBD, 4 September 1941; WJBD to Baby (Pearl Dorn), 10 August 1942; J. William Mindnich to WJBD c/o Dorn Fire Insurance Agency, 17 June 1941, WJBD/SCPC.

faith hated and despised Stalin's regime long before revealed facts fully documented the wretched abuses of the Gulag Archipelago and the Moscow show trials. Most powerfully, there was the heritage of William Jennings Bryan as it continued in the fervently isolationist and passionately anti-war Dada and Nana Dorn. As Bryan recalls in his memoirs, "I was opposed to America's entrance into that war because I had an equal distrust of Russian Communists...and German Nazis." *And because his hearth and home at Myrtle Manor was set four-square against involvement in another world war.*[73] Even in the eleventh hour of 1941 European hostilities, the isolationist rhetoric of Watson and Bryan ran strong for and from the state senator, both on the Callison Road farm and in the general assembly.

But on 7 December 1941, Bryan Dorn was at home with Dada and Nana, having attended church. He remembered it being cold for the red-hills December, and wet, with cloudy skies and a persisting drizzle. The Dorns had just sat down to Sunday dinner in the early afternoon, listening to the radio rather idly, when the announcer interrupted programming to tell of the stunning air attack on Pearl Harbor by the Japanese. Decades later, in 1966, Bryan Dorn remembered details about that day, especially "that we were at war and the men in my family would have to go." Later, it became hard to remember but Americans in many places beyond the red hills were also opposed to entering a European conflict, even after the attack on the Hawaiian naval base. Of course, there was no question about responding to the Japanese, and FDR readily attained a declaration of war against Japan on 8 December 1941. However, for many voting citizens and their lawmakers, the military conflict with Japan was strictly separate from joining the fight in Europe.[74]

On 11 December, as FDR searched for some way to persuade Americans to fight Fascism both in Asia and in Europe, Hitler provided yet another stunning surprise by declaring war on the US. That unexpected declaration ended the dispute for most Americans, and it was understood that World War II was now a global fight against international Fascism. Even so, this was not the case in every house in the red hills, and especially not in the Dorn and Griffith families. Eb Dorn, always favored in both families, and long the patriarch for the neighborhood around Myrtle Manor, was having none of this "internationalism" and "monopoly interest." He continued to

---

[73] WJBD, *OTP*, 57. See also, corr., 1939–1941, Personal Papers, WJBD/SCPC.

[74] Retrospective, WJBD to Edward Hymoff (*Pageant* magazine), 26 July 1966, WJBD/SCPC.

insist that the Old World's fight on the European continent was of no concern to Americans. As far as he was concerned, Americans might end up fighting in Asia but not in Europe, and in any case, he did not want his politician son going into the army or the navy, where two sons already held commissions and commitments and where the youngest sons still at Barratt House were chaffing to enlist.[75]

Old Testament leaders in the Dorn family Bible had seen disputes between fathers and sons before this one between Bryan and Dada. There was the especially poignant father-son dispute between King David and his beautiful and ill-begotten son Absalom, a dispute that produced Absalom's armed rebellion and sent the king into exile in a cave; and a dispute that eventuated in civil war and the execution of the once-favored and ever-loved Absalom; and the dispute whose postlude featured remorseful mourning from the restored king, mourning so morbid that his lieutenants had to upbraid King David. Bryan Dorn the Sunday school leader certainly knew about still other biblical disputes between fathers and sons. Too, there were such father-son disputes for leaders in America in other ages, and members of the Dorn and Griffith families. Indeed, it was not even the first fight between Bryan and Dada.

And so it was that this father-son dispute was nothing new, but no less painful for that. Like the many personal, biblical, and historical sons before him, Bryan Dorn defied his father—and the fathers of Eb before him. He left the state senate and enlisted in the armed forces.

---

[75] Ibid.

Chapter 2

The Good War 1942–1945

Folk called it the Good War, and so it has been taught to schoolboys and schoolgirls of both races and all classes, especially in South Carolina, even by the anti-war and isolationist Populist Eb Dorn. In his public role as T. E. Dorn, the superintendent was obliged to celebrate the goodness of the American cause in contrast with the obvious evil of the variegated fascists and their allies. The no-less anti-war and isolationist schoolteacher Pearl Griffith Dorn built her own lesson plans around such expressions of belief. The Rev. James E. Bowers at the First Baptist Church, always Populist and previously isolationist, preached and taught that there was a "time" and "a season" for all things, including war, as the preacher in Ecclesiastes said—and even the Prophet Joel said that there was a time to "beat ploughshares into swords and fight."[1]

In any case, the red-hills folk always sent a goodly portion, indeed a disproportionate number, of their young men into any war, whether it was the War of Independence, the War of 1812, the Civil War, the paramilitary wars that ended Reconstruction, or two world wars. And Eb and Pearl, Mr. and Mrs. T. E. Dorn of the Greenwood public schools, sent their boys T. E. Jr. [Tom], Griffith, George, Charlie, Jackson, Watson, and Bryan; in fact, sent so many from one family that Governor Olin D. Johnston brought Pearl Griffith Dorn to Columbia to recognize her for sending the largest number of sons from one mother to the Good War, at least in South Carolina.[2]

---

[1] Eccl. 3:1–8 and Joel 4:10, KJV; Brown, *Strain of Violence*; Robertson, *Red Hills and Cotton*; the Rev. James E. Bowers of Darlington, SC, accepted the call to First Baptist Church on 23 June 1943 and immediately began communication with WJBD, Mrs. S. W. Page to WJBD, 23 June 1943, and other corr., personal folders, 1939–1942, WJBD/SCPC.

[2] WJBD, "Seven Sons," with Ron Romine, 22 January 1981, audio-visual coll., WJBD/SCPC; *Acts and Joint Resolutions*, Regular and Extra Session of the General Assembly of South Carolina, 1944, vol. 43, 2d Part, 14 March 1944; "Pearl Dorn and T. E.

Political as he was, Bryan Dorn often talked this way, but he actually had no truck with some notion of a good or a bad war. He considered some wars necessary, and this one against the fascists he deemed necessary—as he did preparedness for another, later, one against the foe he *really* detested, the Russian Communists. Nor was he an internationalist who might talk about One World or a United Nations or a "soft" campaign to "win friends and influence people" or even, in some language, "win hearts and minds." Instead, Bryan Dorn wanted a "hard" readiness in a toughened military that was always prepared to go into action and apply force. And that standing army, with its large back-up reserves of part-time soldiers, would be supported by a powerful domestic economy that focused on jobs and savings and opportunities in a practical New Deal "make it work" sense. Like his father, he was Populistic and progressive in the New Deal frame of mind. Unlike his father, he was militaristic, something that started in 1942 and continually grew in force thereafter. Because of his commitments to such beliefs, he himself had joined the South Carolina National Guard and subsequently established himself as a part-time soldier in the South Carolina Defense Forces. He had taken these actions before the bombing of Pearl Harbor and at a time when he still hoped that the US could avoid European entanglements and the morass in the Pacific.[3]

As December wore itself out and the new year of 1942 came on, the reality of World War II settled in. Bryan Dorn remained very much the power-conscious state senator in the V.O. Key mold, using localistic influence to get the favored brother Watson into reserve officers training for the navy at the University of South Carolina, hoping that perhaps the training would take so long that the war might be over before Watson attained his commission. The entire family was troubled about Jackson, who despite his naming for *the* Stonewall Jackson, was slight of frame and seemed miscast mentally and physically for war. The senator from Greenwood pushed Jackson to get out and get exercise and otherwise toughen up. He also schemed to get Jackson admitted to the cadet corps at Clemson College, again with the half

---

Dorn and the 7 Servicemen," *Greenwood Index-Journal*, 14 November 1944, enclosure, WJBD to William Russell Carter, 26 July 1943, and WJBD to Folks (T. E. and Pearl Griffith Dorn), 28 February 1943, WJBD/SCPC.

[3] WJBD, *OTP*, ch. 2 and passim; "In His Own Words"; Enlistment Record, South Carolina Defense Forces, 23 June 1941; see bitter sarcasm on "Santa Claus" foreign aid "for the whole world," WJBD to Folks, 11 October 1944, WJBD/SCPC.

hope that perhaps the war would be over before the cadet could earn his commission. Jackson did not adapt any physical regime and avoided Clemson, and so eventually was brought into the army as an infantry "grunt." Meanwhile, Charles, who had failed at Annapolis, and George, who had failed at West Point, redeemed themselves during the war as officers in their respective services by coming all the way back up through the ranks to earn commissions. And Tom, true to his father's legacy, became an instructor for cadet students for a season established at Washington and Lee College in Lexington, Virginia, and the Dorns and Griffiths proudly called him Proff. Dorn.[4]

As for the senator himself, he resigned his post to join the fight, but not before efforts to find a suitable successor for his seat. Bryan attempted futilely to get his father Eb to run in a special election to finish out his term, but Eb had more sense than to attempt that. Instead, the family was happy to support Greenwood attorney and World War I veteran Calhoun Allen Mays, who won the special election of 8 December 1942. Once out of the senate, Bryan longed to be in the thick of the European fighting, but he intended to go in not only as an officer but as an officer in the elite air corps of the army.

Few aspects of military service were as romanticized in 1942 as the air corps, and Bryan and even isolationist Eb were both fascinated by the prospects, Eb by the technical training and education required and Bryan by the glamour attached. Even the different training facilities, in succession Biloxi, Mississippi; Louisville, Kentucky; Fort Benning near Columbus, Georgia; and San Antonio, Texas, fascinated him, as he wrote to Eb about the history and the geography of each new posting. Bryan was recommended for the officer cadet training by Greenwood mayor J. M. Marshall Sr., city school superintendent William Ernest Black, and Dr. John Marvin Rast, president of Lander College, the women's teacher training center in town where Nana had once matriculated. For its part, the Army Air Corps found the idea of a state senator becoming an air corps pilot newsworthy, and he was featured in *American Pilot Magazine*.[5]

---

[4] WJBD to Baby (Pearl Dorn), 25 January 1943, and WJBD to Daddy, 27 July 1942, WJBD/SCPC.

[5] WJBD to Daddy, 27 July 1942; "Mays," *South Carolina Legislative Manual of 1943, 85th General Assembly Sess.*, ed. Inez Watson, 28; WJBD to Baby (Pearl Dorn), 10 August 1942; reference letters, John Marvin Rast to Whom It May Concern, 15 August 1942; W. E. Black to Whom It May Concern, 14 August 1942; J. M. Marshall to

By late summer of 1942, Bryan was an ex-senator and full-time air corps corporal, but he avidly followed political doings back in the valley of the Saluda, subscribing to the *Greenwood Index-Journal* and corresponding with the Blease family, with friends of Georgia's US senator Eugene Talmadge, and with other politicos. He instructed his father to keep him in good standing with US senator Ellison Durant Smith (*the* Cotton Ed Smith), Judge Eugene S. Blease, US senator Eugene Talmadge, and "even Burnet Maybank," newly elected US senator. In fact, he and the family detested Maybank, partly for being Charlestonian but mostly for being the bitter enemy of (the recently deceased) Cole and Eugene Blease, brothers who were not only heroes and friends but also distant relatives of the Colemans and the Griffiths in Pearl's family, and their Newberry law firm included cousin Steve Griffith, assemblyman and judge. For all that, Dorn was shrewd enough to appreciate Maybank's "magic," and he took pains to stay on the very best of terms with the distinguished junior senator from South Carolina.[6]

Even though the air corps cadet and state senator Dorn liked the New Deal programs, especially for piedmont farmers, he reveled in the way Cotton Ed Smith and Gene Talmadge defied Franklin Roosevelt. He was unsympathetic when a reported 10,000 students and educators massed at the University of Georgia to protest the way Talmadge men in the state General Assembly slashed the university budget and slung insults at their scholars. In 1942 in both Athens and Atlanta, disparate groups united by hatred of Gene Talmadge—supporters of the university, those who protested extreme racism and lynchings, progressives seeking other societal reforms—joined together by the hundreds to march in protest against the governor. But Talmadge "race-baited" the "wool-hat boys" against the demonstrators and made the complex of issues into a racial struggle, easily weathering the protest, and even gaining popular support *because of* the protests. Despite the racial moderation preached by Dada and Nana and despite his own better inclinations, Dorn celebrated Talmadge's victory, exulting that "the wool-hat boys carried Gene away on their shoulders." Worse, in the only recorded instance in all

---

Whom It May Concern, 15 August 1942; "Dorn," *American Pilot Magazine*, 1943, WJBD/SCPC.

[6] WJBD to Baby (Pearl Dorn), 10 August 1942; WJBD to Daddy, 27 July 1942; (Chief Justice) Eugene S. Blease to T. E. Dorn, discussing Coleman Livingston Blease, himself, and the much-admired "young Bryan," Eugene S. Blease to T. E. Dorn, 17 March 1942, and Steve Griffith to WJBD, 5 July 1940, WJBD/SCPC.

his decades of correspondence, he descended far down into racist diatribe, scoffing that "nigger organizations" were no match for Talmadge.[7]

In these heady days in South Central Texas, Bryan Dorn was for a moment oblivious of his black neighbors and friends back in the red hills. He was not even meeting the eyes of his mother, Pearl, or of his Baptist Sunday school teachers that he once supervised. Scheduled for a solo flight, he was literally riding high, indeed flying high. He played in the heavens with the Valkyries, and he flew with Gene Talmadge amongst the race-baiters—at least in his head for a few days. He thumped his chest to show off for admiring ladies, including his absent mother.[8]

But Nana was unimpressed. He forgot that his mother and his Abbeville Conference Sunday school teachers, and certainly the Welsh Griffith clan, believed and taught that anyone, especially when indulging passions and neglecting upbringing, could "backslide" from the state of earthly bliss and material comfort into damnation and distance from God. He himself had often taught that a man could work and work and work to climb a height and then lose it in one misspent evening, especially if the "divil's likker" was involved in backsliding. On Christmas Day of 1942, he had liberty to go to Old San Antonio, and he declared that he had earned a break from his labors and indeed merited a real celebration befitting a modern hero. He found the Buckhorn Saloon, said to be the onetime playground for Judge Roy Bean, Wild Bill Hickok, and Jesse James. Shoving through its storied doors, he swaggered among its denizens, most of whom were airmen cadets or repairmen. Flexing muscles and otherwise showing off, he took a dare from men in the bar and slugged down a powerful eggnog—one with "more nog than egg." Although quite accustomed to wine, women, and song—boasting of his capacity for "Hard Labor Creek corn likker" and his success with girls from the hills—he was coming off of months of focused study of higher mathematics, intense physical training, an army diet, and "being couped [*sic*] up with a bunch of boys."[9]

Thrilling to the sensations in the Buckhorn, he drank hard and fast, and soon he was demonstrating the "one-legged dance" for delighted par-

---

[7] WJBD to Baby, 10 August 1942; it is the singular instance of using the "n" word in his voluminous correspondence, personal and official, WJBD/SCPC. Anderson, *Wild Man from Sugar Creek*.

[8] WJBD to Baby (Pearl Dorn), 2 January 1943, WJBD/SCPC.

[9] Ibid.

tiers. Then he was taking up a band member's fiddle and "calling" the steps and otherwise directing the Babylonians.

Given over to the emotions of the moment, he fell to earth when his commanding officer suddenly appeared, with military police in tow. Despite tears all around—he claimed even from the commanding officer—he was hauled away to the brig. Now, he actually did need reference letters to get "out of the clapper," as he had sarcastically said to his mother months earlier when he had sought such letters to enter cadet training. Letters or no, sympathetic tears of a supervisor or no, he stayed in jail more than a week, being released before dawn on the second day of the year 1943. He left jail in dirty and rumpled clothing, no longer hungover but looking desultory, if not completely wasted. He had no assurance that he would in fact become a pilot, might not get to fly his scheduled solo flight, might not even remain in the cadet corps. He suspected he might get no closer to the wonderful flying machines than their engines and their tires. He even worried if his newfound rank and compensation as corporal were in jeopardy.[10]

Yet all trained cadets were needed, and Dorn was hardly the only "flyboy" cadet who got drunk during the Christmas holidays. At the end of January, he was reinstated with demerits and warnings and was shipped out for Arledge Field in Stamford, Texas, where he joined the 308th training force. Soon, he was again flying with his instructors, and a solo flight was rescheduled. He wrote, "I am thrilled in spite of the fact that I get sick every day...with all these acrobatic stunts in the air such as stalls and spins with your head down and everything." His letters home, especially to his mother, but also to surrogate sisters at Winthrop College and his blood sister Grace, are filled with equal portions of anxiety that he would "wash out" and willful determination to excel. "I am just not satisfied to do things that the average man can do," he wrote to mother Baby.[11]

On 4 February, he at last made the solo flight and proudly sent home one set of cadet lapel wings each to Baby, to sister Kadell, and to surrogate sister Monkie (Mary Dalton Bell of Callison) at Winthrop College. He also had at least one set of wings stolen by a late-night female partner. In any case, he also sent home his "certificate," which sported a flying angel and the notice:

[10] Ibid.
[11] WJBD to Baby (Pearl Dorn), 25 January 1943, WJBD/SCPC.

Let it hereby be known that on the date of February 4, 1943
Aviation Cadet Dorn did depart from and return to this earth,
Alone and Unassisted, at Stamford, Arledge Field, Texas
Thereby making his first solo flight.
[signed] Doyle, Flight Instructor, Stamford Flying School
308th AAFFTD[12]

Next he went for advanced training to Enid Army Flying School in Oklahoma. There, the training was more intense, but cadets could get drunk and "cut a hog" during leave without worry of penalties as long as they showed up on time for morning exercises. Cadet Dorn reported, "I still tell lies to women" (generally using the name Bill rather than Bryan) near the base because he did not find any to trust, and he boasted of "hell-raising devilment" befitting a successful romantic flyboy. But in April he wrote despondently that he was "in the horse pistol" (an Appalachian pronunciation that he liked and adapted, much like *warsh* for wash and *darter* for daughter), quarantined because of infectious trench mouth. Chafing under the seclusion and kept from his companions and from the physical training he thrived on, he was also put back into another flight training cycle, and everything in his wartime career as fighter pilot was again delayed a full month. He worried that he would grow rusty both physically and mentally, and indeed on 7 June 1943, he reported dejectedly that he had in fact "washed out" of flight school and was scheduled to join enlisted men as a radio trainee in Sheppard Field, Texas.[13]

As usual, the Sunday school superintendent diagnosed himself by consulting the Bible, concluding with the observation of the Prophet Isaiah that even the "mighty will fall" if they become prideful and get into wrong relationship with the One God. He also quoted Jesus that the last shall be first and the first last, and that it was time for "shirt tails" and "wool hats" and "lintheads" among millworkers and farmers to rise up, while sons of the prosperous were to fall if "puffed up"—as he had let himself become. "Proud and arrogant," he had thought he would succeed as an officer when Charlie and George had failed on first try. Now, he found himself again among "the last," back at a basic-training facility despite his corporal rank and full year of

---

[12] Certificate, 4 February 1943, WJBD/SCPC.

[13] WJBD to Folks (Eb and Pearl Dorn), 19 April 1943, WJBD to Pearl Dorn, 9 May 1943, WJBD to Etta Dorn, 4 April 1943, and WJBD to Folks (Eb and Pearl Dorn), 7 June 1943; Certificate of Elimination from Army Air Force Pilot School with Flying Hours Credit, (signed) J. H. H. Bradford, 19 October 1943, WJBD/SCPC.

service, "with first class privates and corporals cussing me out and marching me around before daylight." But he resolved firmly to Daddy, Baby, and sisters, and to himself: "My brothers are doing well in the service.... They have redeemed themselves and now it remains to be seen if I too can follow in their footsteps."[14]

Bryan Dorn's extended family of blood relatives, distant relatives, and church "cousins" bucked him up with correspondence of encouragement and good cheer as effectively as they had in his two political campaigns. Watson, who knew he was himself the favored son, wrote, "Only real men can face defeat and smile." And he added bluntly, "I know how you feel, being Senator here at home and being a naturally proud person, to be humiliated by losing out." But Watson also told him, "[a] burning ambition and a will to overcome all will conquer all in the end." Then Watson passed along words their mother dictated: "George thinks his disappointment [at the US Military Academy] was for the best...and probably Charlie's [at the US Naval Academy]. Anyway, I know you are man enough to take it! Country will need men like you when war is over. Association with common man might be beneficial to you"—and she reminded him of the prerogative of campaigning as a common man and a workingman. For his part, he carefully reread Arthur Meier Schlesinger's *Age of Jackson*, with its emphasis on the Democratic Party's appeal to the laboring men of the Brooklyn and Philadelphia docks and streets as well as to the Tennessee men of the backwoods. Likely, Schlesinger overdid his theme; and even more likely, the corporal read more Populistic exuberance into the Pulitzer Prize-winning book than was there, but all of it, encouraging correspondence and bracing interpretation, bucked him up.[15]

Nor did his First Baptist Church family fail him. They reliably provided warm support—and tough love. The elder Mrs. S. W. Page, erstwhile choir leader and Sunday school enthusiast, wrote to praise him, "not because of your signal success or rapid rise in the material world, but because I feel you are one of God's humble servants." And the man who in pride and arrogance had used the word "nigger" and belittled the black race in one letter was told of her love and respect for "colored" Baptist Charles Marshall, who

---

[14] WJBD to Folks (Eb and Pearl Dorn), 7 June 1943, WJBD/SCPC.

[15] Watson Dorn and Spunkie (Pearl Dorn) to WJBD, 12 June 1943; WJBD to Mother, 1 January 1945, WJBD/SCPC; Schlesinger, *Age of Jackson*. Cf. Nevins, "At the Roots of Democracy," (review of *Age of Jackson*), *New York Times Book Review*, 16 September 1945, 1, book review section.

was fighting bravely in North Africa, and who, unlike her old Sunday school superintendent and senator, never forgot to write, and was proof that there was one Lord for all, and proof that we are all equal at the foot of the cross. Mrs. Page closed with a firm reminder that First Baptist Church sponsored "Colored Relief" and that former senator Bryan had yet to pay his portion of the fund to help Greenwood County black people (something he did at once, with profound apologies, and something he faithfully did thereafter).[16]

Possessor of an officer's dress uniform that he could not wear, the army air corpsman was cut deep by that kind remark from a lady who had no patience for extreme racism, even and especially in language. Instead, Mrs. Page, much as did his mother, reminded him of God's plan to use him in humble service to the "common man," indeed, "even the colored." "Greatness," Mrs. Page concluded, "comes from character." At least five letters from relatives and surrogate sister Mary Dalton Bell combined to remind him yet again that he had been "reared" better than to be bitter about defeats, arrogant about successes, disdainful about the less fortunate—or forgetful that God's black people stood ever vigilant in the shadows at the barbeque and in the glare of the cotton fields, unseen by other white men but looking fixedly into the eyes of Bryan Dorn. And those black men and those white lintheads and those scratch-ankle farmers of both races all stood ready to look and listen whenever the Last Orator found his voice once again. Considerably chastened until his fleshy cheeks burned red, he got the message and vowed to straighten up and do right without whining and without using hurtful words, certainly never again racist words.[17]

Transferred next to an Illinois base near St. Louis, Bryan entered training as a radio operator who had to master complex codes, and after that he entered a long period of such training in Sioux Falls, South Dakota. Although he had been denied an officer's commission, airmen were still paid better than other grunts and gobs in the army and navy. After a few months at $30 per month, his pay had doubled, and with party time curtailed, he began to save money. True to German-Carolinian parsimony, Bryan Dorn took full advantage of the chow and the board provided, spent very little, and thus "saved virtually all of it," that is, at least $1,800 during his three-and-a-

---

[16] Mrs. S. W. Page to WJBD, 27 June 1943, and WJBD to Mother, 6 December 1944, WJBD/SCPC.

[17] Ibid.; Grace Dorn to WJBD, 3 July 1943; Marguerite Dorn to WJBD, 24 July 1943; Watson Dorn and Spunkie (Pearl Dorn) to WJBD, 12 June 1943, Monkie (Mary Dalton Bell) to WJBD, 3 August 1943, WJBD, SCPC.

half-year tour of six states and as many European countries. Mother Pearl, otherwise the Baby caricatured for being beautiful but ditzy and prone to "mad spells," sold a rusted and malfunctioning old vehicle owned by Bryan for the unheard of price of $100 and created a savings account for him. Family members were astounded at the price she got for the old car, none more so than its owner. Pearl bought savings bonds with the money he sent home, and she presented him with some savings bonds she had bought with her own money. All told, she presided over a savings account for him that was in twenty-first-century money worth more than $25,000.[18]

Smarting from some of the scoldings (and from some of the misguided and unknowing praise), Dorn entered a physical regime in order to play army football and to box in army championship matches. To play the line in football, he bulked up to 184 pounds, but to box at light-heavyweight, he reduced himself to 174 pounds; sometimes he had to lose or gain ten pounds in a single week, depending on the sports schedule. In addition, he began doing voluntary farm work at nearby Dakota farms, one memorable weekend helping a septuagenarian German-American couple get in the last of a crop just ahead of a sleet storm. The farm work "prospered him," his football team won more than it lost, and he won his boxing matches, eventually becoming light-heavyweight champion of the 9th Army Air Wing (some 15,000 men).[19]

Dorn eagerly took on other responsibilities, and he took the opportunities to learn things, especially about the machinery of the airplanes, but he did not again seek an officer's commission. He was quite conscious of the vertical nature of military command, and he was carefully deferential to the officers in their presence; but the larger portion of his work he conducted far from their scrutiny. Most of the time, he was in the company of noncommissioned corpsmen, and among them he shared in the jolly horsing around that enlisted men indulged in while doing their assigned tasks, and he and they maintained the complex machinery of the aircraft with twinned regard for safety and efficiency.

Bryan thought often about Chinkapin Ridge and "Myrtle Manor" perched on it, and he wrote down a completed version of his poem that he had apparently started years before:

---

[18] Nana (Pearl Dorn) to WJBD, 16 October 1943, WJBD/SCPC; *OTP*, 59; Friedman calculation, CPI, *Hist. Stats. of US to 1975*, *Stat. Abstracts of US, 1976–2010*.

[19] WJBD to Daddy, 27 December 1943, WJBD/SCPC; *prosper* as transitive verb often in KJV translation, especially in farming context: Gen. 24:40, 42, and 56 .

"Myrtle Manor"
In the last hundred years,
"Myrtle Manor" has known happiness, love and tears.
Silhouetted against the sky high on a hill;
While the winds blow balmy, warm and chill.
It is reminiscent of the Ante-Bellum South and its ladies fair;
Of peafowls and white pigeons fluttering in the golden air.
Of the day of Stuart, Hampton, Jackson and Lee.
With its high balconies and columns of white
And fragrant gardenias like perfume in the night.
Myrtle and boxwood everywhere.
Laurel? ah yes, over there.

Magnolias, roses and skies of azure,
Fleecy cotton with crooning darkies
and air that is pure.
We are on the ramparts of the world;
Our glorious flag to unfurl.
We trust in our arms and a Power Divine.
To make our nation victorious and sublime.

History is filled with the victories of man,
But it is in the home where peace will stand.
You who are in charge of the homes of our men
Forget not that freedom is preserved therein
So toast to you "Myrtle Manor,"

On Chinkapin Ridge in the State of Carolina.
Though I roam the seas and sail in the blue,
Someday I will come back to you.[20]

---

[20] "Myrtle Manor," March 1943; although he named the estate "Myrtle Manor" while in high school and apparently wrote a few verses as early as 1936, this version is dated March 1943, and he proudly sent it to Pearl Griffith Dorn, WJBD to Spooky, 25 April 1943, and to surrogate sister Mary Dalton Bell, WJBD to Monk, 25 April 1943; undated letter from sister Grace acknowledges her own receipt, n.d. (April 1943), WJBND, SCPC.

This tangle of observations is hardly good poetry, but it catches his state of mind, both his optimism about winning the war and his determination to return to a better condition in "the State of Carolina"—albeit that condition would also reflect some necessary changes that he saluted a little begrudgingly. Most poignant is that oft-repeated desire that the black people show him their happiness in old roles, first slavery, then Jim Crow subjugation; *but these were the very roles that he also announced had to disappear soon.* About the same time, mother Baby sent him a postal card featuring an aged "Darky" in a cotton field, his own beard as fleecy as the cotton around him; and in response Bryan thanked her profusely and confessed that even seeing the "Darky" in that pose made him emotional. Always conflicted about race, he was in this moment more of a racist than either parent but in no way a hater of color (in fact, still pained by his onetime use of the phrase *nigger*). He truly loved the "Darky" *in a particular role* and he truly wanted more for those sable brothers—even and especially as he was truly afraid of the rapid changes in racial roles going on all around him in the armed forces.[21]

This last phase of stateside training passed by in a blur of happiness, nostalgia, optimism, and anxiety. He was certified as a crypt analyst, one who had to transmit directions and orders in secret codes, and sometimes one called upon to listen to enemy transmissions in an effort to "crack" their code. He was transshipped with the 6th Tactical Air Command (TAC) to New York on 16 February 1944, acutely conscious of a grand and dramatic assault that was in the works, even as he was too far down the high chain of command to know many details at all. Scarcely one month later, his TAC unit was in England, and he knew that very soon he would be somewhere on the continent behind the lines of combat forces—behind the lines but quite close to front lines in the early phases of his deployment across the channel. This 6th TAC was part of the 9th Air Corps led by Hoyt Sanford Vandenburg, redoubtable and aggressive commander. Corporal Dorn and friends still knew nothing in particular, but they were assured that something really big was in the offing, and with Vandenburg in the lead, it would be risk-taking and outsized and unprecedented, whatever it was.[22]

---

[21] Ibid.; Nana to Bryan, postal card, "Old Black Joe in a Southern Cotton Field," 26 November 1943; and WJBD to Folks, 30 November 1943, WJBD/SCPC.

[22] Certified copy of honorable discharge, William Jennings Bryan Dorn, 10 October 1945; overseas 26 February 1944 to 26 September 1945; Battles and Campaigns: Normandy, Northern France; Rhineland; Central Europe; Corporal Crypt Analysis, 6th

Given a few days off in the late spring, he left his temporary base and went to see nearby London. Near Buckingham Palace, he found Etta Dorn's cousins, the Llewellyn Lloyds. This Welsh family were distant relatives to father-in-law Richard Coleman Griffith and Judge Steve Griffith. Most interesting to Bryan, their oldest son, Richard Dafydd Vivian Llewellyn Lloyd (under pen name Richard Llewellyn), was author of a novel that he adored. *How Green Was My Valley* was an affecting narrative about abuse of coal miners in Wales and also a fetching description of Welsh hills that called to mind his own piedmont hills. He had read the novel in its Armed Services edition by borrowing it from the base library at Sioux Falls. "The house was full of noise and laughing, and the smell of the cooking made you so hungry you would have pains inside." That line could describe any of dozens of neighborhood events at Myrtle Manor. Fittingly, the novelist was himself an enlisted soldier on duty in Italy at that moment, and the family was feeling his absence sharply. The Llewellyn Lloyds were gracious to Bryan, and their little girls climbed all over him, reminding him of nieces and nephews from home, some of whom he had never seen at all.[23]

"How things come back if you start to think of one and become tangled up in memory." That line applied for him in the moment and again later, not only about Chinkapin Ridge in Greenwood County. A few days after returning to base, he read that the Llewellyn Lloyd home was struck by a "robot bomb." He reported to his mother and father that the "two sweet little girls whom I had just visited were killed." Although by now he was learning each week about hometown friends and service friends perishing in battles, and he had seen the destruction rained down on London and its citizens, the killing of the two girls cut more deeply. "I have thought about them a lot," he confided to his parents.[24]

On 6 June 1944, he at last understood at least a part of the plans and execution of the huge campaign he had entered. The Normandy Invasion began before dawn on that overcast day amongst days and days of rain and fog.

TAC Squadron, Good Conduct Medal, 1945, WJBD/SCPC; Meilinger, *Hoyt S. Vandenberg*; *Time* cover, 15 January 1945.

[23] Richard Dafyyd Vivian Llewellyn Lloyd (hereinafter Llewellyn), *How Green Was My Valley* (Armed Services ed., 1940), 10, Irvin Rare Book Collections of Ernest Frederick Hollings Library, University of South Carolina, Columbia; WJBD to Folks (T. E. and Pearl Dorn), 20 August 1944, WJBD/SCPC.

[24] Llewellyn, *How Green Was My Valley*, 14; WJBD to Folks (T. E. and Pearl Dorn), 20 August 1944, WJBD/SCPC.

Allied troops, more than 150,000 of them on some 5,000 vessels that also carried some 30,000 army vehicles, crossed a stormy English Channel to be met by German troops who had long been dug in and who had long ago established artillery positions in occupied northwestern France. Bryan Dorn in the Army Air Corps busily "humped ammo" and otherwise helped load ordnance onto some of the 800 planes that took flight from nine English air bases. Some planes bombed forward positions on the coastline before the landing, but many more carried more than 13,000 airborne troops, six full regiments of parachuting infantrymen, who were dropped onto the Nazi-occupied northern littoral of France. One wing of daring glider planes drifted silently through the morass of artillery and "ack-ack flak" bearing infantrymen who crashed their planes into farm fields and forests and then jumped out and began shooting; and one of those unlikely pilots was Bryan's fellow German piedmont resident J. Strom Thurmond, who also had left the state senate to join the war.[25]

On the day itself, the corporal was too busy to contemplate the magnitude of D-Day, the name he was taught later to call the land, air, and sea assault that General Dwight David Eisenhower (styled Overlord commander for this mission) coordinated for American, British, and French Resistance forces. Instead, he was focused and methodical in his physical labors of loading men and materiel onto planes, many of which were flown by his old cadet mates in Texas; and then he was even more focused as he performed his cryptanalysis for the many disparate communications captured from Germans and received from American and British radio operators.

This cryptanalysis of transmissions from radio operators on the airplanes told him among other things that many pilots flew to the wrong sites, dropping paratroopers into death traps. It told him that some bombardiers were bombing the wrong targets. It told him that a frightening number of planes were shot down or were lost and presumed downed somewhere. But it also told him that the German defenders were underprepared and received no support from the terrifying Panzer tanks that stayed well back of the bloody beaches instead of coming forward when landing forces were most vulnerable. Furthermore, members of the TAC benefited from "code cracking," in which the German cryptic codes were demystified by the crypt analysts. Bryan and his fellows had "cheat sheets" that showed them what the

---

[25] WJBD to Folks (T. E. and Pearl Dorn), 25 September 1944; P. M. "Archie" Archibald to WJBD, 21 November 1945, WJBD/SCPC; Bass and Thompson, *Ol' Strom*, 73–74.

German messages really meant to say. As a result, Overlord commander General Eisenhower knew of changes in German positions and strength at those positions as quickly as two hours after the forces began to make their changes. For once, Bryan realized, the men doing cryptanalysis were contributing in a very substantive and not purely metaphorical way to the day's effort.

Allied casualties from D-Day were high, frighteningly high, and it was terrifying, even at an English air base, to see the return of the wounded, knowing as he did that far worse cases were being treated back on the site in Normandy, to say nothing of those who had to be buried there. Surely 9,000 or more American forces died on that first day, but just as surely 100,000 got into forward position beyond the beaches where they came ashore. Dorn's Populist spirit was at the forefront as he wrote his folks about the grand, bloody channel crossing:

> The generals get most of the publicity in the papers and will get nearly all the credit on the pages of future history but it is the common soldier that makes possible great victories and triumphs. It is also the common man that builds great countries and maintains civilization. As time goes on I can appreciate more and more the enlisted men of our Army. They are drawn from the common people of America.[26]

By July, the 6th TAC were themselves shipped over, and Bryan found himself in Brittany, just inland from the famed Celtic coastland that was said to be the cultural hearth for the North Britons back in his own piedmont hills. He and his fellows were setting up communications and supply lines. Although well behind the lines of the boldly advancing Allied infantry, Bryan and the 6th TAC were in that month officially in combat, and as he told his folks in censored V-mail, "winning" now. His own work was not only important for maintaining communications and for setting up supply lines for the forward troops, but it was also important for establishing a line of retreat if the vaunted Nazi forces should suddenly reverse the Allied tide of advance. Most intriguingly, because the German cryptic codes were now "solved" by the Allied TAC units, he and other crypt analyst technicians

---

[26] WJBD to Baby (Pearl Dorn), 2 January 1943; quoted, WJBD to Folks (T. E. and Pearl Dorn), 14 January 1945, WJBD/SCPC.

were finding out and revealing exactly what the German leaders were attempting to do with their troops.[27]

Dorn pushed himself to do well, and he was proud of the teamwork in his hardworking unit. Nevertheless, there were days of some considerable frustration, and on one such miserable July day in Rennes in Brittany, an officer, one Watters, fixed his own personal anxieties directly on Bryan. New England enlisted man Paul M. "Archie" Archibald recalled, "Watters used language to you that was a discredit to any man who wore the uniform of our country." Archibald also recalled that his friend Dorn was reigning boxing champion, and he could tell that the corporal was quite ready to strike back at the offending officer Watters. "Modestly," continued Archibald in his reminiscence, "I take a little pride in the fact that I was able to talk you out of some of your anger." Bryan accepted his cussing-out with bitter resentment, but neither he nor Archibald "talked back" to Watters, and the moment, and the entire difficult day, finally passed. Things got better for all concerned, and Watters focused his attentions on other personnel. Soon the 6th TAC was stringing communication wire and humping materiel into Paris itself. To Bryan, it was "the most beautiful city in the world" even in its wartime occupation. In fact, the city had been spared the extreme devastation visited on other places, and he thrilled to the charms of its history and culture. All the same, he and Archie Archibald continued to speak often, and always hotly, about the "abuse from officers during the war."[28]

As duties in France became more routine, Bryan played still more football, boxed still more, and, with Archie Archibald and others, organized an Enlisted Man's Club with its own constitution, club room with equipment, and paid attendants (who had to be the rank of corporal). He scheduled events, mostly boxing matches and football games, for the Noncommissioned Officers (NCO) Athletics Clubs. Some of these activities were conducted within earshot of artillery fire, and all of them involved men who lived in simple tents pitched in French, Belgian, or Dutch forests. Ever the

---

[27] WJBD to T. E. and Pearl Dorn, VE mail, 4 September 1944; WJBD to T. E. and Pearl Dorn, VE mail, 25 September 1944; WJBD to Folks (T. E. and Pearl Dorn), 25 September 1944, regular mail; certified copy of honorable discharge, William Jennings Bryan Dorn, 10 October 1945; overseas 26 February 1944 to 26 September 1945; Battles and Campaigns: Normandy, Northern France; Rhineland; Central Europe; Corporal Crypt Analysis, 6th TAC Squadron, Good Conduct Medal, 1945, WJBD/SCPC.

[28] Paul M. "Archie" Archibald to WJBD, 21 November 1945; WJBD to Folks (T. E. and Pearl Dorn), 20 August 1944 and 25 September 1944; and quotation, Archibald to WJBD, 21 November 1945, WJBD/SCPC.

politician, Dorn made friends in all places, but especially among the infantrymen, artillerists, medics, and the many cooks and bottlewashers who supported the forward troops. As he continued to box, he strung out more victories and took more trophies, becoming light-heavyweight champion of the French NCO Athletics Clubs and the Dutch NCO Athletics Clubs, as well as retaining his 9th Air Corps crown.[29]

Dorn observed a black fighter who was a professional boxer from Detroit often compared favorably with the matchless Brown Bomber Joe Louis. Bryan spoke and wrote with admiration about the skills and prowess of this unnamed boxer, and he attempted to arrange a bout with him. Although Bryan expected to lose, he was anxious to test himself against such daunting talent. There were complexities, for once not racial but rather legal technicalities, about how a professional could box against an amateur, even in the armed forces in France. The match never happened, and eventually he lost track of the boxer airman, apparently even forgetting his name. He came away from his experiences in the ring and at the ring with a strong sense that all sports should be racially integrated—and indeed that all endeavors should be racially integrated. Nevertheless, even in the safety of letters to intimates, he always said that such integration would have to proceed slowly back in his native red hills. In that day, his racial progressivism was there, but he kept it carefully out of public sight—at least in South Carolina politics.[30]

Along these racial lines, one friendship that he formed became a political touchstone for this most political of men. It informed much of his political thinking about race and racism, and it demonstrated his public stance of moderate segregation and his private and personal stance of integrationism. W. Bryan ("Bill") Drane of Elizabethtown, Kentucky, was one of tens of thousands of black soldiers serving in Europe. Although the air corps TAC units were essentially segregated by squadrons, it was inevitable that black and white corpsmen would encounter one another, as Bryan had encountered the professional boxer. Dorn talked often, and sometimes at exasperating length, about the black people he knew back in Greenwood, but he was talking about cotton farmers, Baptist ministers, musicians, cooks, and day laborers, all denizens of the racially ordered and orchestrated piedmont South Carolina. In those cases, he was talking about people who played roles carefully calibrated and who were in no sense at all equal friends with him.

---

[29] "Constitution of the Enlisted Man's Club HQ 6th TAC," 27 December 1944; WJBD to Dad (n.d., fall) 1944, WJBD/SCPC.

[30] WJBD to Dad, (n.d., fall) 1944, WJBD/SCPC.

Bill Drane was different. He was an educated man, an intellectual, *likely also named for William Jennings Bryan*, and thus someone who shared concerns—and Populist heroes—with his white friend. Drane talked straight-up to Dorn, one Bryan to another. He boldly and sometimes bitterly contrasted the good treatment of black men in Europe with the Jim Crow mistreatment back in his native horse country in Kentucky's northern bluegrass region. He also complained about the Ku Klux Klan violence in Elizabethtown, and Bryan Dorn had to confess for his own Greenwood a similar racist violence. Indeed, much of his own home's violence, especially the Phoenix Riot of 1898, was fully equal to and often greater than the extremist violence of Elizabethtown. Bill expected, and got, an equal friendship with Bryan, and that equal friendship spread to other members of the Drane family in Elizabethtown's bluegrass hills and to other members of the Dorn family in Greenwood's red hills. The two talked candidly about Klan and other violence, including the fact that negrophobic language legitimated such physical violence. Bill Drane thus reinforced the ancient Sunday school command that the word *nigger* must never be used under any circumstances. Lastly, the two talked about the rightness of integration and the fact that it must come during their own lifetimes.[31]

The Dranes and the Dorns kept up with each other during the Good War and thereafter. For his part, Bill Drane kept telling Bryan to be a Thomas Jefferson and "give up a few home votes for justice," a message delivered face-to-face and repeated in writing. At first, the two used Jefferson's name differently, almost oppositely. For Bryan, invoking Jefferson gave a politician the protection afforded by state rights, local rule, limited government, and other aspects of "going slow" in pursuit of justice for the Dranes and other black people in all regions of the US. In fact, during the war and thereafter, Bryan invoked every one of those comfortably qualifying conditions to civil rights. However, Bill Drane invoked Jefferson the writer of the first draft of the Declaration of Independence, the one who declared slavery to be wrong—and a wrong worthy of revolution. Scholars have never reached consensus on a legitimate way to invoke Jefferson, and the soldiers both thought that the Sage of Monticello had declared that "a foolish consistency is the hobgoblin of little minds." But these two in their conversa-

---

[31] W(illiam) Bryan Drane to WJBD, 6 May 1963 (retrospective) and WJBD to Drane, 13 May 1963 (retrospective), WJBD/SCPC; Raitz and O'Malley, "The Nineteenth-Century Evolution of Local-Scale Roads in Kentucky's Bluegrass," *Geographical Review*, 94 (Oct. 2005), 415–39.

tions used the contrasting images, Bill Drane's purist revolutionist and egalitarian, Bryan Dorn's purist on local and limited government.[32]

After many discussions, the white Bryan vowed to the black Bryan that he would "practice fair play" in race relations. He vowed that he would practice Jeffersonian local rule, limited government, and state rights without opposing civil rights and Christian responsibilities. And he agreed in writing with another member of the Drane family who said, "A Negro who has been pushed off onto 'God's Little Acre' in America cannot get much of what is his Birthright." Dorn had to agree that Erskine Caldwell's *Tobacco Road* novels captured farming poverty for both races—and he had to agree that the black farmers' fate looked even more forlorn than the white farmers'. Furthermore, Drane and family members would call Bryan out if he strayed from "the right track" in pursuit of justice or "fair play." The Dranes' reminders goaded him in 1944 and all through the next decades, always making him think and arguably helping to make him change after 1964.[33]

As he reported to "The Folks," Bryan intended to "keep the boys stirred up" and in hopeful spirits, to encourage the "common man" and provide healthy structures as well as many incremental rewards since "the brass" were not providing structure, were almost obsessed with verbal abuse, and showed little interest in worthwhile entertainment for the grunts, who did the real work in the war. He appreciated the role played by his successor, state senator Calhoun Mays, in arranging for Governor Olin D. Johnston to honor Pearl Dorn for sending seven sons into the war, and he wrote appreciatively to Mays and gave his mother tips on how to deliver her speech, successfully persuading her to make it a paean to the Common Man. He also forbad her from crying, and despite family worries that Pearl Dorn was somewhat unstable, Baby acquitted herself with a quiet and powerful womanly dignity. He was especially pleased that Field Adams, a black neighboring farmer, wrote to declare his own appreciation for the appropriate words that Pearl Dorn had spoken about sacrifices made by *all* piedmont farming and mill

---

[32] W(illiam) Bryan Drane to WJBD, 6 May 1963 (retrospective), and WJBD to Drane, 13 May 1963 (retrospective), WJBD/SCPC; TJ attributed, but Emerson, "Self Reliance," 1841. On the way that Americans use and misuse Jefferson, see Peterson, *The Jefferson Image in the American Mind* (1960 ed.), passim.

[33] W(illiam) Bryan Drane to WJBD, 6 May 1963 (retrospective), WJBD/SCPC; Caldwell, *God's Little Acre*; Mixon, *The People's Writer*; dramatizations of Caldwell's Tobacco Road novels were WJBD's favorite plays, WJBD to Folks, 27 January 1945, WJBD/SCPC.

village families. Adams understood her words to include black troops as well.[34]

By late autumn, the 6th TAC was in Belgium and then Holland, and the German lines were shifting steadily backward. As for his own air corps, the fighter planes that he once trained on now escorted B-17s engaged in saturation bombing: "The great air fleet is giving Germany a terrific pounding night and day." He added almost maliciously, "the better the weather, the more medicine [the Germans] get." For security purposes, his letters usually were labeled with a date only instead of with a dateline that would reveal a tactical location. In fact, even the pridefully prepared souvenir Easter and Christmas menus he sent home were embossed "Somewhere in Holland or Somewhere in Germany."[35]

Dorn learned in some detail from brothers Charlie, Watson, and Tom, now all three assigned to the South Pacific, about the bloody "island hopping" waged against the Japanese-occupied fortifications in that theater. He learned from *Stars and Stripes* military newspaper and from unauthorized sources that the Russians were rolling the Nazis backward out of Central Europe and toward the Allies. As he began to talk with civilians, including Germans, he also heard enough about the conduct of Russian troops, and he heard enough about Stalin's treatment of his own people, that he was confirmed in his preexisting hatred of Communism in general and of Soviet Communism in particular—indeed, confirmed in a preexisting distrust of *Russian people* as an ethnic group.[36]

Withal he harbored a numbing dread that the powerful German infantry, with its almost irresistible Panzer tank division, might suddenly reverse the Allied advance and come rolling back against the hard-won forward positions. On 16 December 1944, Field Marshal Gerd von Rundstedt sent the 5th and 6th Panzer divisions of Hasso von Manteuffel and Josef "Sepp" Dietrich on a fearsome blitzkrieg, creating the infamous "Bulge" in the Allied forward lines. Dietrich was bound for Antwerp, Manteuffel for Brussels. This Ardennes Offensive was much worse than Bryan dreaded, and for ten

---

[34] Adams quoted, WJBD to Folks (T. E. and Pearl Dorn), 1 November 1944; WJBD to Folks (T. E. and Pearl Dorn), 24 October 1944; WJBD to Mother, 16 January 1944, WJBD/SCPC.

[35] WJBD to Folks, 24 March 1945; WJBD to Folks, 1 November 1944; WJBD to Folks, with enclosure menu, 28 November 1944, WJBD/SCPC.

[36] Charles Dorn to WJBD, 5 March 1945; T. E. Dorn Jr. to WJBD, 31 October 1946; interview: WJBD with Ron Romine (4 February 1981), WJBD/SCPC; and WJBD, *OTP*, 78.

days the mighty Panzer tanks and some half million of the world's most efficient infantrymen inflicted almost 100,000 casualties on the American and British troops trapped in the frozen woods.

Worried as he was, Bryan was one of many who thrilled to the bold retort "Nuts!" given by General Anthony McAuliffe when his encircled 101st Airborne unit was asked to surrender. And for all his disdain for "the brass," he was delighted to learn how George Patton had force-marched the Third Army through the snow and ice to save the trapped 101st men. The advance was broken on the day after Christmas, the "Bulge" was erased by the third week of the year of 1945, and Bryan and the others in the 6th TAC were on the scene in combat during the bitterest cold, stringing *commo wire* and *humping ammo*—but above all analyzing the desperate and fatally important crypt messages they picked up on their radio equipment. All told, casualties totaled some 89,500 American forces, some 1,400 British forces, and an estimated 100,000 German forces. American deaths were more than 19,000. With the 28 January 1945 confirmation that the Panzers were all gone from the stage and the Germans in full retreat eastward, Bryan and his fellow 6th TAC NCOs posed in the snow for the photograph below, one taken more in exhausted relief and gratitude rather than in breast-beating exhortation.

Not long after their own picture was made, Bryan and other NCOs noted with bitter resentment that high-ranking officers, some of them clearly "desk jockeys" new to the front, were inspecting the battle site and filing their own reports, posing for photographs, and generally taking credit for the dearly bought triumph. One of those arrogant officers said that he was making important "observations." It did not spoil the moment, but Dorn never forgot this additional display of officers' arrogance. Nor would he forget that odd usage of the word observation to describe a highly paid desk jockey prancing around in the bloody snow seeking credit for sacrifices rendered by common men. Thereafter, he used the term observation in nonmilitary contexts as a smarmy reference to anyone, especially politicians, seeking personal aggrandizement. Sometimes the offender was the onetime corporal himself—and if someone "called him out" on such behavior, its truth always stung and he always apologized.[37]

---

[37] John Bolt Culbertson and Benjamin Elijah Mays called him out: "Bryan Dorn Representing the People" (1984) and interview: WJBD with Romine (4 February 1981), WJBD/SCPC; WJBD, *OTP*, 76.

By February, the advance of the Allies in the European theatre not only speeded up but began to look unstoppable. Making his way among civilians as the 6th TAC occupied more and more of Germany, Dorn enjoyed learning a little German and reveled in studying the crops. Among other things, he was pleased to see that his favorite piedmont food, collard greens, grew plentifully anywhere in Germany. He was dismayed, however, that no army cook in all of Europe could prepare them. Instead, he did so himself, cooking up a mess of collard greens and corn bread for some hitherto innocent Northern army mates, who hungrily sopped up the cornbread with the "collard likker" that Bryan poured onto their tin mess-kit standard-issue plates. They approved the fare, though approval may have been encouraged along by a different "likker," that is, the Kentucky sour mash that he also poured out for them into their tin mess-kit standard-issue mugs. It was quite a repast in the standard-issue army tents pitched in the snow.[38]

On 12 April 1945, FDR died. Back home, Dada and Nana were devastated, for they had lost a hero; but the corporal was ambivalent about FDR, supporting the New Deal enthusiastically but distrustful of the Roosevelt foreign policy people, whom he considered naïve in some cases, cowardly in worst cases. Knowing nothing about the new president, Harry S. Truman, Dorn was yet hopeful, especially if the relatively obscure Missourian was bringing in a new foreign-policy team. Talking with German civilians, he was confirmed in two beliefs that he had formed in combat. He doubted that FDR's team agreed with these beliefs, but he was hopeful that Truman and his advisors would grasp them. First, he was assured again that it was air power that had broken Germany, especially in its devastation of farms and factories and the townspeople. "They convinced me that it was the wave after wave of American bombers, day after day, that cracked their will to resist. The human body, brain, and nervous system can stand only so much of that. If you run in and out of your house in your shirttail night after night, week after week, and month after month, finally you will go nuts." Second, German folk reported in chilling and redundant detail about Russian troops out of control, raping women, beating elderly men, and stealing everywhere they went. He was by then completely convinced that the Russian Communists were not so much fierce allies as they were irresponsible and menacing forces despoiling Poland and Hungary and the rest of Central Europe. He also marked it that every G.I. he met "had a dislike of Russia; a fear of another

---

[38] WJBD to Folks, 10 April 1945, WJBD/SCPC.

dictatorship...[and never] forgot that Russia invaded Poland a few days after Hitler and was just as guilty as Hitler for the start of World War II."[39]

Plenty of more knowledgeable military strategists disagreed then and still disagree about the success of Allied bombing—or of any carpet-bombing.[40] And Dorn's exaggerated anti-Communism produced a disproportionate distrust of the Russian troops. The point is not whether he was finally right or wrong, but that wartime observations and discussions with people on the scene reaffirmed two of his dearest beliefs about foreign policy: Soviet Russia was an enemy as surely as the German Nazis had been, and the way to beat them was with air power. Since he would never play much of a role in foreign policy, the upshot of such belief in his congressional career was the militaristic Keynesianism so foreign to his father, Dada, but so central to his own identity. Dada had arrived at a policy of federal spending focused on farm needs by faithful adherence to William Jennings Bryan Populists. Bryan himself arrived at a related policy by abandoning the foreign policy of his namesake, and his father, and justifying massive expenditures by the needs of nonstop world conflict with totalitarian foes.

Such understanding as he had of air power and carpet-bombing was applied to the Pacific theater but with reservations more sanguinary than sanguine. Correspondence with brothers Watson, Charlie, and Tom convinced him that the Japanese could not be defeated by bloody island-hopping as the sole strategy. They told him that the European forces would have to move to the Pacific, bringing with them massive air power to defeat the Japanese, whose fierce resistance island by island presaged a like defense of their own homeland. In particular, Tom described for him work on the new bombers, but also noted for him that even carpet-bombing did not much affect the will of the Japanese military. The corporal then wrote to Nana and Dada to warn "the folks" that their sons and sons-in-law in the Pacific would soon be joined by their sons and sons-in-law currently in Europe, and that all of them would be engaged for long months, even years, in a bloody land and air assault on Japan.[41]

In the meantime, summer had arrived in Germany so cold and wet that it did not seem like summer, and there remained the major task of finishing

---

[39] First quoted line, WJBD, *OTP*, 74–75; second quoted phrase, WJBD, *OTP*, 78.

[40] Literature reviews: Meilinger, ed., *The Paths of Heaven* and Mueller, *Airwar*.

[41] Watson Dorn to WJBD, 5 March 1945, Tom to WJBD (retrospective), 31 October 1946; WJBD to Nana and Dada, 25 September 1944, WJBD/SCPC.

off Hitler's infantry before addressing the exhausting and indomitable Japanese. The 6th TAC pressed on and on, into Saxony, reaching Braunschweich, a once beautiful and cultured place now quite reduced and humbled; it had even lost its German name and was called by the conquering and the conquered Brunswick. Berlin lay only 125 miles away, and between the pincers of westward moving Russians and eastward moving Americans, the Third Reich shrank in size. Dorn's commanders told everyone that soon all would be transshipped again, this time to "Asiatic theatres." New codes in new cryptography would have to be learned. Archie Archibald and Bryan struggled with new codes, listened for old codes, and in the long, long dull spaces in their communication van or in their tent, they talked about Russian Communists and the infiltration of Soviet Communist agents into the American army and government. Both were convinced that there were many, many spies and many, many fifth-column Communists. Moreover, they hypothesized a dangerously "soft" policy toward the Soviets in the person of Henry Agard Wallace, who had just stepped aside as vice president in favor of Truman. To Archibald and Dorn, Wallace was not only *the* major force in the left wing of the Democrats but also a *naïf* who simply did not "get it"—*it* being the extreme danger of Russian Communism and its many adherents in the military and state department.[42]

In any case, honors came to the 6th TAC. The entire unit received the Presidential Citation from Commander-in-Chief Truman, and from Belgium came the *Fourragere*, a special commemorative shoulder strap awarded to those units recognized twice in the Order of the Day. Bryan Dorn himself had earned no fewer than four battle stars from the combat experiences. He knew too that Watson and young Jackson, about whom he had worried, had been just as honored, and more important were both living. Yet the awards, also given posthumously to dead comrades, were bittersweet, especially as there remained the awful next challenge, the "Asiatic" or Pacific assault vaguely but terrifyingly forecast by brothers Charlie and Tom.[43]

In such a frame of mind, the news of the atomic bombs dropped on Hiroshima on 6 August 1945 and on Nagasaki on 9 August 1945 completely astonished him. Barely comprehending what the terrible new weapon was, he did insist that the "nukes" had spared the lives of men already in the Pa-

[42] WJBD to John P. Oliver, 13 January 1948 (retrospective); Paul M. Archie Archibald to WJBD, 1 April 1948, WJBD/SCPC.

[43] Citations, certified copy of honorable discharge, 10 October 1945; displays, "Bryan Dorn Representing the People" (1984), WJBD/SCPC.

cific such as Tom and Charlie, and in a more indirect way, had possibly spared his own life. He, like many, became convinced that the bombings saved the lives of at least one million American fighting men (the widely predicted number of casualties from a land assault on Japan). To his plans to fight the Russian Communists with air power were now added *nuclear* air power, and again, an aggressive federal spending policy for domestic ills, with all of this justified by a nonstop totalitarian threat emanating from Moscow.[44]

The stunning attacks also told him that he was going to be discharged soon, transshipped with friends like Archie Archibald to New York and then to Camp Gordon, which was across the Savannah River from his native piedmont and very close to the home of his hero Senator Thomas E. Watson. Yet again, Dorn found a favored passage from novelist Llewellyn Lloyd: "Everybody was singing. Peace this was again." Honorably discharged on 10 October 1945, he weighed in at a career-low 161 pounds and made his way for several hours along country roads by hitchhiking, since the Army Air Corps provided no travel funds or transportation for men to get home once "detached."[45]

When he fetched up at Myrtle Manor, Dorn revealed to Nana and Dada that he planned to reenter politics at once. He had about two months to present himself to county nominating committees that were preparing for the Democratic primaries the summer of 1946. Nor was he going to challenge Calhoun Mays for his old seat in the state senate. Instead, he took aim at the Third District US Congressional seat held by Butler Black Hare, who haled from a distinguished elite landholding family from his Nana's own Saluda. Having served multiple terms from the Second District, Hare in 1932 had been "redistricted" into the Third District as South Carolina's declining population occasioned the elimination of one district so that the Palmetto State thereafter had five, not six, districts. Sitting out a few sessions, Hare had then won the Third District seat in 1938, compiling a record of serving schools, building roads, and resisting civil rights measures while also resisting brutal Klan aggression. Too, he was a careful student of

---

[44] WJBD to John P. Oliver, 13 January 1948; interview: Watson Dorn and Steve Griffith Jr. with Roper (28 February 2012), WJBD/SCPC.

[45] Llewellyn Lloyd, *How Green Was My Valley,* 19; certified copy of honorable discharge, 10 October 1945; interview: Watson Dorn and Steve Griffith Jr. with Roper (28 February 2012), WJBD/SCPC.

the economy, having written a graduate thesis concerning economic developments in South Carolina after the Civil War. Thoroughly dedicated to finding meaningful jobs for all his people, Hare was a fine congressman, and his political values and votes were essentially what Dorn would want them to be. For all these virtues, Butler Black Hare was guilty of a single vice: he occupied the seat that William Jennings Bryan Dorn intended to take.[46]

---

[46] WJBD, *OTP*, 59–60; "Butler Black Hare," *Congressional Biographical Directory*, s.v.; Congressional Record, 78th Cong., Sess. 1, Vol. 90, 29 May 1944; Sess. 2, Vol. 91, 26 May 1945, 12 June 1945.

Chapter 3

Starting Again 1946–1947

Bryan Dorn was comfortable back at Myrtle Manor on Chinkapin Ridge on the road to Callison. However, he was in no sense relaxed. Rather, he was comfortable like a boxer preparing in secret for a bout where he knew the rules and knew the opponent and knew the ring as well. He began almost at once, certainly by November, to pester his family about a run for the Third District seat in the US House of Representatives. The Dorns began a canvass, that is, they canvassed their own large family and the Griffiths and the First Baptist Church, neighboring farmers, and other acquaintances such as mill owners Jim Self and Brother Abney and grocer John C. Miller. Support from all of these would be necessary, if not sufficient, for such a campaign.

He told all of them that he had not voted in 1944. That decision he credited to a strong opinion pronounced by James Aloysius Farley, "the official political prophet" of the New Deal. For all that Farley had done to build up voting blocs for Franklin Delano Roosevelt, and for all of Farley's devotion to "tax and spend, tax and spend, elect and elect," the New York Irishman took complete exception to FDR's 1940 decision to run for more terms than George Washington. In protest, Farley permitted his name to be filed for presidential candidate in the Massachusetts primary of 1940, and Associated Press wire reporters speculated that Farley fully intended to run for president himself that year. At any rate, Farley withdrew his support from FDR in presidential campaigns from 1940 onward, thereby moving himself to the periphery of Democratic presidential campaigns. Bryan Dorn retained an affection for Jim Farley and kept up correspondence with him for the remainder of the Irishman's life. Thus, he cited Farley's opinion of FDR's second and third administrations as authoritative, prophetic, and personally transformative.[1]

---

[1] WJBD to Folks (T. E. and Pearl Dorn), 8 November 1944; "James Aloysius Farley," *Congressional Biographical Directory*, s.v.; "James Aloysius Farley," *Time* (cover), 20/18, 31 October 1932; Walter Edgar, "Olin DeWitt Talmage Johnston," *Encyclopedia of South Carolina History*, s.v.; "Farley Permits Filing," *Chicago Tribune*, 11 February

What Corporal Dorn said about the election was true but only part of the story. *Most* soldiers and sailors serving in World War II did not vote in 1944; that is, about 85,000 absentee ballots were counted, where more than sixteen million men and women were enlisted, with something over eleven million overseas. Unlike the Civil War and unlike the wars subsequent to World War II, there was no mechanism, no infrastructure, no rules and procedures, or any military or civilian officials who had set things up to let the millions of enlistees vote while serving overseas. The politics of that nondecision remain complex and hard to follow. It seems hard to imagine the commander in chief failing to win most of those votes and also hard to imagine a strong and increasingly resentful Republican opposition permitting some kind of machine delivery of eleven million votes for FDR. States' Rights Democrats and segregationists worried that black soldiers would vote in large numbers (setting up a precedent for black citizens voting in peacetime as well), and some vocal right-wing Republicans, led by the *Chicago Tribune*'s Colonel Robert Rutherford McCormick, complained that "FDR's machine" would all but compel the soldiers and sailors to vote for the commander in chief. Yet there were still other reasons for both FDR and his Republican opponent, Thomas E. Dewey, to avoid a fight over the issue and to walk away from those voters. Despite the efforts of Theodore Francis Green of Rhode Island and Scott W. Lucas of Illinois in the Senate and Eugene Worley of Texas in the House, only a much weakened soldier voter bill made its way to FDR, and it had many restrictions hampering soldier voting overseas. To keep his support among hard-edged Southern Democrats and to avoid further controversy with Republicans and for still other reasons, FDR allowed the weak bill to pass into law without his signature. That undigested story need not deter this story; it was simply the case that almost eleven million service personnel at war overseas were *effectively unable to vote* in national elections in 1944.[2]

1940, 12A; "Democratic Committee Is Called to Meet," *Greenwood Index-Journal*, 24 June 1940, 8; W. B. Ragsdale (AP wire), "Want Farley to Remain Chairman," *Greenwood Index-Journal*, 13 July 1940, 1. Cf. Farley, "Why I Broke with Roosevelt," *Collier's*, 31 June 1947, 1, 6i.

[2] Jordan, *FDR, Dewey, and the Election of 1944*, 210–15; 220–22; Burns, *Roosevelt: Soldier of Freedom*, 521–31; "US at War: The Nation," *Time*, 43/3, 17 January 1944, 17, and "GI Vote Snags," *Newsweek*, 17 January 1944, 36; newspaper clippings, 1944, Jonathan Worth Daniels Papers, Southern Historical Collection of the Library of UNC; Congressional Record, 17 January 1944; South Carolina repeal of military absentee vot-

Of course, Bryan Dorn, as a state senator who had voluntarily left office in order to join the Army Air Corps, could have worked out something in order to vote. As for his agreeing with Jim Farley, Dorn stated it loudly enough in 1944, but he apparently had missed Farley's *even louder* pronouncement in 1940. In the 1940 election that Farley sat out, Bryan Dorn not only voted for Roosevelt, but, as noted, for two full legislative sessions thereafter he had worked in the senate in cooperation with the master parliamentarian Edgar A. Brown and with New Dealer (and Farley protégé) Governor Olin DeWitt Talmadge Johnston. Indeed, in 1940, FDR was so popular in Greenwood, especially in the mill villages, that a county committee member's suggestion that a mild protest be recorded against a third term was heatedly shouted down—until the presiding committeeman (and Dorn family friend) Calhoun Mays noted that nobody was going to second the abortive motion and ruled that the matter be dropped.[3]

By 1944, however, Dorn had discovered Farley and his reasoning, and thereby began his long-lived correspondence with the prophet now on the periphery. As he had discussed with fellow corpsman Archie Archibald, Corporal Dorn had not been happy with FDR's state department or his military guidance, and remained particularly unhappy with the Henry A. Wallace left wing of the party: He said that Wallace and his people refused to acknowledge the dire threat posed by Stalin. When Harry S. Truman, a vice president largely unknown to Dorn, suddenly became president, the already disgruntled army airman was dubious and then disdainful. On the other hand, the Republicans' 1944 presidential nominee, Thomas E. Dewey, was too much the dandy, too much the Manhattanite, and too much the privileged businessman for a South Carolina politician of any era, and especially one from the Populistic mill villages and farming communities of the red hills.[4]

---

ing rights. 14 March 1944, *Acts and Joint Resolutions of the General Assembly of the State of South Carolina*, vol. 43, Part 2, 63 and 805.

[3] "16 Delegates for State Convention," *Greenwood Index-Journal*, 6 May 1940, 1; "County Votes Overwhelmingly for Roosevelt," *Greenwood Index-Journal*, 6 November 1940, 1, 2; "Farley Permits Filing," *Chicago Tribune*, 11 February 1940, 12A; W. B. Ragsdale (AP wire), "Want Farley to Remain Chairman," *Greenwood Index-Journal*, 13 July 1940, 1; WJBD and Farley: WJBD to Farley, 26 January 1953, Farley to WJBD, 18 December 1958, WJBD/SCPC.

[4] WJBD and Farley corr., 1944–1958, WJBD/SCPC. Cf Smith, *Thomas E. Dewey*; Dewey was not native to Manhattan and less of a New Yorker than his opponents or proponents claimed.

Thus, the last year of the Good War seemed to the soldier a good time not to vote at all, but instead to observe from afar, survive the combat, and only later reenter things political. By contrast, the first year of peace, 1946, seemed to him exactly the right time for a good enlisted man and good Populist to challenge the privileged elite Butler Black Hare, owner of a large and well-managed cotton and pine-tree estate in Saluda County and author of progressive legislation for autonomy in the Philippines. It was also time, he decided, to establish a Southern Democratic alternative to those he considered to be privileged Northern Republicans and to "One World" Henry Wallace Northern Democrats who downplayed the threat of Soviet Communism.

Bryan Dorn often noted that South Carolina politics were "always personal and always factional," and the factions largely rested on relationships between families in local areas. He was not metaphorical, but rather literal in observing his piedmont. In education, church, and politics, parents and siblings and friends, Dada and Nana Dorn's Greenwood farm family and Nana's Griffith relatives in Saluda, Walhalla, and Newberry, formed a loose and sprawling confederation of biblical tribes. Blood kin and distant kin and neighbors who might as well be blood kin, all these pitched in for the young veteran's run for US Congress. Years later, when Bryan Dorn worked for the JFK campaign for presidency, he jokingly claimed that the Kennedy clan and its family politics was a copy of the Dorn clan and its family politics. And JFK for his part jokingly claimed that his Southern Democrat supporters with their own family politics were copying *him.* More probable is that family politics dominated an era of intensely personalistic and localistic governance, which was also a time of simple and even straitened family finance with lingering traditions of sacrifice and voluntarism still redolent of the Good War. Where families were big and closely connected to place, whether it was rural piedmont farmland or urban lace-curtain Irish, the political ambitions and activities of a family's boy immediately became the political ambitions and activities of the extended family. As Jack Kennedy had said of his 1960 presidential campaign, why should he trust an "expert" who was only an expert at losing for other men when he could claim the undivided loyalties of his brothers?[5]

---

[5] Interview, WJBD with Romine (3 February 1981), interview: Watson Dorn and Steve Griffith with Roper (28 February 2012), WJBD/SCPC; Sorensen, *Kennedy*, 30–38; Kennedy, *True Compass*, 121–51.

For 1946, Dorn's family campaign would not only be the tactics for his own family and politics but for his opponent's as well. The large Hare farming family in Saluda and neighboring counties produced his competitor in the Democrats' contests—again, in contests where only Democrats' primaries "counted" because the Republicans led by Joseph Warren "Tieless Joe" Tolbert (1865 to 1946) so seldom mounted effective contests for US congressional seats. Not only was Butler Black Hare a distinguished patriarch beloved by his constituents, but he too was well served by his own large and sprawling extended family of blood kin and friends who might as well be blood kin. There was even some crossover in kith and kin amongst sitting congressman and challenger: during redistricting that had put political friends into the redrawn Third District, Butler Hare declined to run against the Dorns' friend Fred Dominick because of the close ties between Dominicks and Hares. To make the contest still more of a challenge, Congressman Hare took positions and professed beliefs that were much the same as Bryan Dorn's. Hare, too, thought that Olin D. Johnston went too far in his New Deal politics and that Cotton Ed Smith and Gene Talmadge went too far in strictly local politics. In Washington, Hare followed the lead of Texan Sam Rayburn, who reminded Dorn of South Carolina's own parliamentary master Edgar A. Brown.[6]

Following Rayburn's lead, Hare voted for a strong military, for public work projects involving waterways and state universities, a social security "welfare net" of retirement pensions and unemployment benefits for the common workingman, high taxes (approaching 90 percent of income reported beyond an arbitrarily proclaimed "middle class" level), and "fair trade" restrictions on goods coming from overseas while using the State Department to open up markets for American-made products to be exported. And following Rayburn, Hare fought against federal civil rights legislation concerning lynching and voting while resisting legislation that helped organized labor. Lastly, still true to Rayburn's well-worn pathways, Congressman Hare never used negrophobic terms, he avoided the Ku Klux Klan, and he spoke warmly and affectingly about a better future someday for all black people, although it appeared to be a future that was *quite far off* indeed. Butler Black Hare, too, was in favor of state rights and was not opposed to civil rights,

[6] Butler Black Hare Papers, SCPC, especially 1946–1947 and introductory essay.

although he did not have the Kentucky Drane family monitoring his speeches and votes.[7]

What distinguished Bryan Dorn from Butler Hare was a thought and a language that the orator was developing for his politics. He was taking the words of his family heroes and namesakes Jefferson, Jackson, Watson, and Bryan and applying them to new situations. None of those men had seen or heard of the foreign totalitarian threats that Corporal Dorn had fought. And none of those men had seen or heard of the gigantic industrial and financial corporations that could destroy life in a small village—and sometimes menaced life anywhere in the world. For all that, the terrible crises of financial collapse and massive unemployment and total war had, in fact, fired the foundry anew, had melted what had been, and had tempered it and given it a shape different than before. The Greenwood farmer was still a fighter, still a citizen soldier, still a farmer grunt. But he had been through the crucible of foreign combat, and the experiences there had taught searing lessons, lessons that changed the meaning of old words and even changed the direction of the forced-draft march. The lessons had been hurtful, and their knowledge was not so much "carried to the heart" as carried to the gut. It was the same words in the same old song, "but with a different meaning since you've been gone."[8] Although there is substance to commend and substance to condemn in his style of message, the first task is to know *what* he intended to say by certain phrases that he used all the time. These words have to be reviewed and explained his way in order to apprehend what he did and said in 1946 and thereafter.

One word was *money*. William Jennings Bryan was still right: *You shall not press this crown of thorns down on the head of the farmer, you shall not nail him to the Cross of Gold.* Dorn often quoted that sentence to crowds, and it always

---

[7] *South Carolina Legislative Manual*, ed. Watson, 1932; Hare, remarks (FEPC), Congressional Record, 79th Cong., 2d Sess., Vol. 92, Pt. 1, 28 January 1946, 484–85; Hare, remarks (trade), Congressional Record, 79th Cong., 2d Sess., Vol. 92, Pt. 1, 7 February 1946, 1073; Hare, remarks and vote (rural mail carriers and holidays), Congressional Record, 79th Cong., 2d Sess., Vol. 92, Pt. 2, 14 February 1946, 1328–29; Hare, remarks (veterans' benefits), Congressional Record, 79th Cong., 2d Sess., Vol. 92, Pt. 1, 24 January 1946, 363–64; Hare's votes on trade, lynching, poll taxes, and social security, Russell C. Carter to WJBD, November 23, 1945, WJBD/SCPC.

[8] "Knowledge carried to the heart," from Allan Tate, "Ode to the Confederate Dead 1937," *Collected Poems*, s.v.; Holland, Holland, Dozier, "It's the Same Old Song," *Motown in Love*, ed. and introd. Jordan, 155–56.

stirred a response. But both speaker and listener were talking a new language with the same words. Gold itself was not the devil. Rather, it was that gold was one more thing to trade. Like cotton, like rice, like a heifer, like a stand of timber, like a mule, like a pork belly. The government treasury printed notes of legal tender, no longer backed in the US by gold or silver or other specie, but now backed by the big battalions of armed grunts and behind them the bigger battalions of farmers and the even bigger battalions of millhands and factory workers, and behind those worker ranks, the rapidly growing ranks of salesmen and chemists and engineers and specialists who understood husbandry and textiles and cotton and soil and water. It was the muscle power of those armies—the ones who shot and got shot to protect you, but also the ones who answered the work clock before the cock crowed and, too, the ones who sat in laboratory coats and examined specimens of soil and meat and fibre, and above all there were teachers, mostly ladies (again, Nana was his living model), who taught everyone how to do any of these things—the muscle power of these massed armies that made a gross domestic product of goods and services. Money was only one sign, one signifier, another symbol for the exchange of all those goods and services.

But for peacetime trade to work, that sign and signifier had to be protected in its stated value by the agreements reached in the United Nations Monetary and Financial Conference (Bretton Woods Conference) of July 1944. One month after the Normandy invasion, forty-four Allied countries, but not the USSR, had met in a ski resort in New Hampshire to develop a stable but adjustable exchange rate for member currencies. Funds for postwar rebuilding were available, and the Bretton Woods Conference also attempted to ensure orderly trade among member partners. Within carefully calibrated limits, no member state could change the value of its currency unless it could demonstrate a "fundamental" problem in balance of payments. The different countries that had stood shoulder to shoulder in the Good War now stood together to declare that there were carefully calibrated ratios of value for the dollar and the pound and the franc and the krugerrand, and eventually even the German mark and the Japanese yen. The US dollar was the international standard, and it was pegged to—*gold!* Otherwise, a lot of sincere and hard work by armies of millhands and farmers and salesmen—and their teachers and for that matter the citizen grunts who shot and got shot at to protect them—could be valued at nothing at all, and we could descend again into the maelstrom of economic collapse.

Still heir to his namesake, Bryan Dorn defended gold as an international standard for the US dollar in world trade. At the same time, drawing more directly on his namesake, Bryan Dorn rejected gold as the *singular national standard* for the US dollar in strictly domestic trade. Indeed, for Dorn, there was now *no* singular national standard for the US dollar in strictly US domestic trade and commerce except the value declared for the dollar by the markets there. A student of international trade in this postwar world, Dorn was never as naïve as he might sound on occasion, and he was never a hypocrite. He was instead a Cold War Democrat in the world of Bretton Woods Conference agreements that created an International Monetary Fund (IMF) and any number of related international agreements about credit, currency, and finance. Those new agreements, among other things, made the US dollar the international currency and retained gold as the dollar's standard in world trade while at the same time allowing the dollar to rise and fall at home according to its demand and supply in strictly domestic markets.[9]

Then there was this word *trade* and its companion *competition*, for long years always pronounced *freetrade* and *freecompetiton*. It was as if each phrase was one word, and as if both of the otherwise singular words were one phrase: Freetrade and Freecompetiton. Indeed, Dorn's schoolteacher-parents told him these words set Yankees and their tariffs apart from Southerners as much as any other fighting words. But a lesson of this World War II was that trade and competition had to be fair more than free. He himself would come to intone *fairtrade* and *faircompetition* as joined phrases vital to his Modern South. And now it was just as vital to farmers—after all, Bryan Dorn was a farmer's farmer—as it was to millworkers and mill owners. Since Thomas Jefferson remained a guiding light, he sometimes forgot in the full flow of an impassioned speech and said "freetrade" when he intended to say "fairtrade." When that happened, he was neither hypocritical nor careless, but only speaking a language of a postbellum shorthand: For farmers and millhands to be free and for cotton and cloth and clothes to sell successfully, there had to be *fairtrade* and *faircompetition*. Bryan agreed with the old Populists that farmers of the late nineteenth-century had tried to play by old rules in a world where other farm products in other countries were helped by various government subsidies and assistances and then those selfsame farmers had tried to buy implements and fertilizer and machinery in a world where such manufactured products were protected by tariffs.[10]

---

[9] Keynes, address, Bretton Woods Conf., 22 July 1944, *Coll. Works of John Maynard Keynes*, vol. 26, 101; Hull, "Bretton Woods," *Memoirs of Cordell Hull*, s.v.; WJBD also consciously went to school to Clemson economist George Hubert Aull, corr. between WJBD and Aull, 1936–1946, WJBD/SCPC and corr. between Aull and WJBD, George Hubert Aull Papers, 1936–1946, University Archives, Clemson University Libraries.

[10] Keynes, address, Bretton Woods Conf., 22 July 1944, *Collected Works of John Maynard Keynes*, vol. 26, 101; Hull, "Bretton Woods," *Memoirs of Cordell Hull*, s.v.;, corr.

Now, in 1946, the old imperial colonies were either freed or on the way to independence, and these new nation-states subsidized their cotton production and built tariff barriers to protect their cloth and clothing products. The farmer Bryan Dorn wanted his own farm's fair chance in the piedmont, and he wanted his millhand supporters—finally—to be paid well. He considered that in the Asian and North African colonies and countries the farms were still basically unfree plantations and that the factories were dirty and unsafe, and he considered that the "cost advantage" of those new competitors was built on the backs of workers, unfree farmworkers and slave-wage factory workers. Until and unless the competitors actually paid their farm workers living wages and actually improved conditions for factory workers, there had to be tariff protection for products made by piedmont farmers and workers. Two who got their start in piedmont mill villages, US Senator Olin Johnston and Congressman Joseph Raleigh Bryson, demonstrated that millhand support could take a politician a long way. By contrast, the politician Dorn intended to take millhands in the Third District a long way, insisting that they were potential members of the middling class—that they would buy improved homes on mortgage, put Fords and Chevrolets into their garages, and in some cases send their boys to Clemson College to be engineers and managers and send their girls to Winthrop College to be schoolteachers.[11] The Populist words of another century may or may not have been bourgeois and capitalist, and the academic point of that debate was boring to him. The same Populist words of this century defined a people who were climbing into bourgeois capitalism. Bryan Dorn treated them as neighbors and family regardless of income and wealth partly because in many cases they *were* neighbors and family; but mostly he treated them as neighbors and family because he intended for them to join him in the new middle class of the modern piedmont.

Connected in all cases to fair trade and fair competition was *foreign aid*, a strictly bad word in Bryan Dorn's peacetime language. No longer an isolationist and anti-war man like his father and mother before him, Dorn was

---

between WJBD and Aull, 1936–1946, WJBD/SCPC and corr. between Aull and WJBD, George Hubert Aull Papers, 1936–1946, University Archives, Clemson University Libraries; Palmer, *"Man Over Money"*; Kazin, *A Godly Hero*.

[11] Corr., WJBD and Aull, 1936–1946, WJBD/SCPC and University Archives, Clemson University Libraries; Keynes, address, Bretton Woods Conf., 22 July 1944, *Collected Works of John Maynard Keynes*, vol. 26, 101; Hull, "Bretton Woods," Memoirs of Cordell Hull, s.v.; on tariffs, Terrill, *Tariffs*; "From Cotton Mill to Congress," handbill, 2 June 1954, Joseph Raleigh Bryson Papers, SCPC.

vigorously anti-Communist and thus vigorously internationalist and militarist. He concluded from the Good War that certain evils, bound up in totalitarianism, had to be fought with military might, and that there would be less blood if the military might was applied sooner rather than later. Sounding much like the Cold War philosopher Hannah Arendt (whom he read and cited), Dorn refused to parse the difference between Fascism and Communism: both were totalitarian, and both forgot fair means in order to attain their ends, and their ends were actually only about power in any case. Hitler, Stalin, Mussolini, Tojo, Mao Zedong—Bryan Dorn mixed the references as if there were no ethnic or ideological differences between the characters. The postwar US was the policeman for the world, and it must resist the totalitarian thugs and outlaws.[12]

To do so, the US would have to ally with "authoritarian," but not totalitarian, men in countries that might someday become democratic. These included Francisco Franco Bahamonde, Juan Peron, Rafael Leonidas Trujillo, and other allied and anti-Communist "strongmen." The national budget, then, must be a large one in order to fund a big and mobile military almost constantly on call. Bryan Dorn readily assented to the expenses in blood and treasure on the Korean peninsula and the expenses in treasure to keep Greece and Turkey free of Communism. But none of that was foreign aid, it was defense. Foreign aid, the expenditure of US funds in other lands to build schools and roads and other "infrastructure," Bryan Dorn rejected, whether it was the Marshall Plan or money for newly independent lands in Africa and Asia or money for Latin American governments. He considered foreign aid to be the cynical transfer of money from poor people in rich countries to rich people in poor countries, and he insisted that his South Carolina piedmont citizens were not, in fact, in a rich country themselves. Foreign aid was a phrase he consistently spoke with contempt. "Poor impoverished Southern farmers are made to pay taxes to support a Santa Claus deal for the whole world."[13]

By contradistinction, there were the honored words *land* and *jobs.* As to the former, the red-hills people—Welsh and Scotch-Irish and German—

---

[12] Best example, WJBD to Hal Kohn, 20 January 1948, detailing address before Rotary Club of Newberry, SC; WJBD to Folks, 11 October 1944, WJBD/SCPC. See Arendt, *Origins of Totalitarianism*

[13] Literature and corr., Franco Bahamonde, Juan Peron, Rafael Leonidas Trujillo; quote, WJBD to Folks, 11 October 1944, WJBD/SCPC. See Arendt, *Origins of Totalitarianism.*

had ever been drawn to and repelled by their own land, always hurrying away from it and always coming back to it. Always restive, always complaining about their bit of land and often taking their leave, but also coming back to the same patch of land. And always there was somebody, some old folks, who never left, the denizens, the constants, the plain folks that never forgot you, the ones who always welcomed you back—you, the prodigal son of the land—back into the fold, if not with a ring and robe and a fatted calf, then at least with pulled pork and potato salad and collards and "heavenly hash" dessert. And back in the shed, a long and strong pull on the bottle of liquor secreted from Mama's disapproving eyes. But now the land was a little less mystical, a little less magical. It, too, was a commodity, something that could be traded and swapped and borrowed against, something whose value had to be calculated in material terms. But yet it was still partly magical, something whose value was not exactly calculable, and still something you had to have, especially if you had decided to go off and work in one of the textile mills. If you did that, you had to be sure to hang on to your bit of land that you could always work—and hunt on and fish on and drink at—even and especially while fetching up in a home built by the mill owner and living a life regimented carefully by work whistles and safety bells and noon horns for dinner. When Bryan Dorn spoke of land, he would remain in the Populist traditions of mysticism and practicality, of coming and staying, of the most profound of identities, but those identities always and ever deeply conflicted, no less powerful for their doubled meanings and their thick and tangled and contradicting connotations.[14]

Not quite as talismanic but still powerful in its mysticism was the word *jobs*. The overwhelming shock of the Great Depression in which he grew up had demonstrated that good people could go a long time without a good job, almost no matter what they attempted to do. Nervous about big government and mistrustful of central government planners, Dorn was all the same a product of the lean days, for Southerners almost double the biblical seven lean years, that stretched from the agricultural collapse in 1925 until the preparations for World War II in 1939. It was scarifying. Local hero Tom Watson had developed Rural Free Delivery (the blessed RFD) for the mails, and in processes helped establish the local postal station with its rural carriers as valuable jobs for rural people. The twentieth-century RFD of the

[14] Fatted calf and ring, Parable of Lost Son, Luke 15:11–51, KJV, as used by WJBD; Robertson, *Red Hills and Cotton*, passim; WJBD, "Myrtle Manor," poem (n.d., 1943–1946), WJBD/SCPC.

mails was the one substantive Populist accomplishment of Senator Tom Watson, and it was a significant and transforming achievement recognized as such by Dada and Nana and their many kin and friends.[15]

Providing rural people with dependable and free mail delivery and with civil-service jobs were twin duties performed brilliantly after Senator Watson's death by Postmaster Jim Farley, who made such duties linchpins of his "tax and spend, tax and spend, elect and elect." Cooperating with Farley, and with his successor postmasters in turn, were US Senator Olin D. Johnston, state Senator Edgar A. Brown, and Congressman Butler Black Hare. Too, waterworks and various projects for roads of all kinds not only laid the basis for better jobs someday, but the construction gave good work in the building processes. That, too, had been mastered by Olin Johnston as both governor and US senator. And long term, jobs would be improved in quality and increased in number by good public schools, as T. E. and Pearl Dorn had shown, and by higher education, as the Clemson College of Presidents E. W. Sikes and Bob Poole and Economist Hubert Aull was showing. William Jennings Bryan Dorn inherited all of this from a young age, and he honored these duties until his final labored breaths. Few elected folk so self-consciously and so consistently worried and schemed and planned to find jobs for the people in all parts of his South Carolina as did Dada's child and the Nebraskan Great Commoner's namesake.[16]

Most complicated of words was *Negro*, now capitalized. Bryan Dorn tried to pronounce it carefully, and no one recalls him lapsing into the vile usage *nigger* after that one embittered slip in a letter to Nana. He and his family still liked and still used the word *colored* and always spoke it with a genuineness not always heard in the word *Negro.* Brother Watson and cousin Steve Griffith have recalled that once the three of them went looking for votes at a "fish fry" that turned out to be a Ku Klux Klan rally. Despite the extreme

---

[15] Woodward, *Tom Watson*, 210–12.

[16] WJBD, *OTP*, 6–12: on education and jobs, 6–12; on connections between jobs and race relations, 200–205. Almost weekly in correspondence, even in good times, WJBD made a pointed reference to the number of people unemployed, examples: J. W. Teague to WJBD, 3 June 1958 with enclosure, R. H. Swallow, Bigelow-Sanford Carpet, Inc., Belton, form letter to employees; Edith Cummings to WJBD, 31 May 1958; Faye Paige to WJBD, 28 May 1958; Ida Mae Lowe to WJBD, 25 May 1958; Joe Melton Martin to WJBD, 29 May 1958, Thelma Crawford to WJBD, 4 June 1958, WJBD/SCPC; interview, Watson Dorn and Steven Griffith with Roper (February 28, 2012), JHR/SCPC.

desire for all votes, Bryan Dorn and family left the scene quickly, and Griffith has marked it that "Bryan had many chances to join the Klan and never gave them the time of day." But that much was quite traditional and had been the case for the Dorn family before the revolutions brought by World War II. Negroes before World War II were farmhands, often renters and croppers on local farms, and they were not part of the factory workforce in the mills. A few were preachers—for their own dark flocks—and a few were schoolteachers—again, for their own colored folks. But in the Good War, Negroes had gone into combat with Bryan Dorn, and some had even become officers who could tell him what to do. And he had thrilled to the sight of the champion Negro boxer while paying serious attention to the critique of race relations by the Drane brothers. Too, the grateful French and Italians and Germans had treated the piedmont Negro soldiers the same as they treated the piedmont white soldiers. Things were changing, and Bryan Dorn realized that it would eventually be a great change, though he had precious little idea how rapidly much of that change would be starting.[17]

Dorn was already moderating his words and stance toward the Jim Crow institutions that defined his region, and in the most cautious way he was trying to get ready for a new world where black individuals were no longer the "mud sills" at the bottom of things. He was comfortable around black farmers and handymen, amiable and kind and sometimes even caring if their families were suffering, but he was less comfortable around the well-educated preachers and teachers in the black community. He followed the old formula: "Southerners do not care how close Negroes get as long as they stay low, and Northerners do not care how high Negroes climb as long as they stay away."[18] He was accustomed to and even enjoyed closeness and fellowship with black farmhands and day laborers and cooks and cleaners. He said he wanted a black middle class, but he did not want them rubbing shoulders in a familiar way, them and theirs equal with him and his. For all of his contradictory wants and wishes, Dorn was aware that history was bringing some racial integration whether he liked it or supported it or not. He was aware, too, that New Deal leveling and the Fair Deal tide that

---

[17] Two letters from Drane, WJBD/SCPC; interview, Watson Dorn and Steven Griffith with Roper (28 February 2012), JHR/SCPC; Myrdal et al., *An American Dilemma*, passim.

[18] Two letters from Drane, WJBD/SCPC; Myrdal et al., *An American Dilemma*; on propinquity Williamson and Woodward dialogue, *C. Vann Woodward, a Southern Historian*, 213.

"raised all boats" would eventually put the working class of both races in propinquity. Aware of the full implications of what he supported, he avoided discussion of eventualities partly because his base of support, both his millworkers and his farmers, could not handle such discussions. At least that is what he said. Millhand attitudes were, in fact, changing more rapidly than he acknowledged. In reality, he avoided discussion of eventualities because *he* could not handle it. Of all the words and all the signings and significations, "Negro" would be the most awkward for William Jennings Bryan Dorn. It would be the word most fraught with old traditions that comforted him and most fraught with new hopes and new dreams that troubled him.

With this particular vocabulary, Bryan Dorn assembled his team and prepared for the contest against the long-serving and confident Butler Hare. Perhaps the most remarkable recruit to his team was brother Watson Lee Dorn. The handsome and clever officer had become congressional staff liaison for the US Navy during 1946 discussions concerning the efforts to realign the armed services. As family members recollected, Watson, although only a junior officer, had his own chauffeur and "rode in style" from meetings amongst congressmen, the highest of officers in each service, and various concerned lobbyists. Working hours were not long, the ladies liked his uniform, and the world appeared to be his oyster. Bryan Dorn asked him to leave Washington, resign his commission, and enter law school at the University of South Carolina in order to serve as semiprofessional campaign manager—at a fee of no more than $500 to be paid *after the campaign*. It was not an easy sell, but Bryan convinced Watson that he had done enough in the military, would enjoy being a country lawyer, and would find excitement and fulfillment in the challenges of the political action. In quick order, Watson Dorn left the promising military life, enrolled in the School of Law at his alma mater, and began to draw up plans for the extended Dorn family to build "marine fire drill teams" of political volunteers in the courthouse and feed-store gathering spots in the red-hill countryside. He established an index file of names and offices held by local people, with notations as to their association with Congressman Hare and their political leanings.[19]

Sister Gracie Dorn, a bright student of economic development with a staff job in Columbia, was initially unhappy with her beloved brother's plans to run for Congress; she had pushed hard to have him offered a plum of a

[19] Interview, Watson Dorn and Steve Griffith with Roper (28 February 2012), JHR/SCPC; letter from Watson, WJBD/SCPC.

job in her own agency. Likewise, older brother Tom Dorn, ranking high in the air force and establishing standards for effective auditing of the armed forces' huge expenses, dyspeptically asked what plans his impulsive younger brother had in the likely case that the popular and redoubtable Congressman Hare won reelection. Nevertheless, Grace Dorn gave him $500—in an era when average per capita income in Greenwood County was $2,000—and Newberry cousin Judge Jeff Griffith also gave $500. Dada, still eloquent, though weakened by untreated heart problems, and Nana both gave speeches and leaned on church members and old students. The historic if dilapidated and drafty Myrtle Manor, with its spacious lawns, remained the place to gather for good music, good dancing, surreptitious Baptist drinking, great stories—and serious politicking. Brothers George, Watson, and even a rather grumpy Tom all pitched in to give speeches in different venues. In the highlands of Walhalla, cousin Russ Carter from the vantage points of his automobile garage and repair shop and the local chamber of commerce, spoke loud and often and spied on and reported about the doings of Congressman Hare's supporters. The Self and Abney families moved quietly in the hushed circles of the country textile elite, knowing that their man Bryan could be hurt by too public an embrace by the often-resented bosses.[20]

Congressman Hare was no fool, but he had trouble taking this challenge very seriously. He knew how solid his support was in his own Saluda, and it seemed that in the town of Greenwood his support was also solid. One odd feature of the contest is that surviving photographs of Butler Hare in 1947 make him look quite a great deal like surviving photographs of Bryan Dorn in 1974, and family members have sometimes wondered if young Bryan saw his own future in the face and the actions of his worthy opponent. At any rate, the Dorn family was all but conceding the five wards in their own town of Greenwood and were instead spending maximum time in the town of Anderson. Also, they remembered the vital importance of the textile communities in Ware Shoals and 96 Mill and Grendel, and they tried hard to make a personal contact at every textile mill. People in Grendel had not

---

[20] Interview, Watson Dorn and Steve Griffith with Roper (28 February 2012), JHR/SCPC; letter from Russ Carter; letter from Gracie, letter from Tom, (summer) 1946; "to the People of the Third District," (summer) 1946, flyer obviously paid for by Abney and Self but listed as "Friends of Bryan Dorn at Matthews and Greenwood Cotton Mills by People Who Know Him Well" and written in style as if spoken by millhands, WJBD/SCPC.

voted for Dorn for state senator and he had won anyway. This time, they could not afford to lose Grendel.[21]

Remembering wartime talk with fellow grunt Archie Archibald and their buddies at the NCO clubs, Dorn tried to make meaningful connection with the many, many returning veterans who had been overseas and who had come back with bitter memories of abuse by privileged officers. Hare was not an officer in that war, but perhaps he could be made to seem like them. Too, the returning veterans still bitterly resented the way that the mythical civilian *Jody*—he of acrid marching and drinking songs—had stolen a march on the girls and the jobs and the colleges in the four years that grunts and gobs had slogged through Europe and Asia. Whether angriest at *Jody*, Germans, Russian Soviets, or the cussed luck of the blood on the Carolina moon, perhaps these fellow veterans would resent Butler Black Hare—or trust Corporal Dorn.[22]

In speechifying, Hare was eloquent and respectful, if a little distant from, his opponent and members of his audience. Farming and textile crowds were not impressed with the good work he had done for Filipino governance. They worried about high costs for the things they had to have, and they chafed under rules that kept down prices for crops and wages for hourly labor. Although there were controls for wages *and* prices, to the war-weary folk, it seemed that their wages were uniquely held *down* while prices went *up*. And it seemed to many of them that wages for organized labor at the North, and above all wages for congressmen, were not only comfortable but excessive. Bryan was trim and bouncy while Butler was hefty and well-fed. Bryan had a mop of hair no longer trimmed for inspecting sergeants while Butler was losing hair in the front and had a high forehead that made him look either distinguished and intellectual or pompous, depending on one's political preferences. Butler was what he was, loyal public servant, distinguished lay leader in church, professorial student of agricultural land development, member of the landed gentry. Bryan was a fiery Baptist song leader and farmer and veteran, handsome enough to attract the ladies but not dashing enough and not incautious enough to make any husband jealous. In fact, having no steady girl, Bryan in these days often took Gracie as his escort, or sometimes Nana, and was assiduous that no one misunderstand

---

[21] Interview, Watson Dorn and Steve Griffith with Roper (28 February 2012), JHR/SCPC.

[22] Ibid.; Asa "Archie" Archibald to WJBD, 21 November 1945, WJBD/SCPC.

his bachelor status. Too, he was careful and cautious in his surreptitious drinking of spirits, sober but not prudish in the crowds.

In the stump speeches of that summer's Democratic primary, Butler Hare gave Bryan Dorn one unique opportunity in an otherwise unflawed campaign for reelection. He spoke proudly of making *observations* at the site of Battle of the Bulge long after the terrible fighting, establishing for his audience that he was a veteran member of Congress with important committee assignments and responsibilities. Bryan could sense in the crowd, mostly veterans and relatives of veterans, that same resentment he himself had felt so palpably when desk officers and congressmen had come around the battlefield after the worst of the suffering in the blood and ice were done with. Careful not to overplay it, Bryan Dorn looked at the plain folk in the surrounding crowd and said that he too had "made observations at the Battle of the Bulge"—and had counted himself darned lucky not to get killed in the observations as he relayed coded messages and humped ammo and helped take charge of prisoners, since his observations came as an active-duty corporal while the fighting was still going on. The crowd was appreciative, and the story of the exchange was retold by expert piddlers and fiddlers who liked to imitate the politicians at the feedstore and on the farm.[23]

Otherwise, Bryan Dorn emphasized the good things done by men of young age, trying to turn the weakness of inexperience into an asset. He celebrated Mozart's music, Thomas Jefferson's Declaration of Independence, William Cullen Bryant's "Thanatopsis," and William Pitt the Younger's service as prime minister, all examples where talent trumped age. For his part, Butler Hare wryly noted that Moses had written the Ten Commandments at age eighty, a good riposte in Bible Belt territory. But Bryan Dorn, the fundamentalist Baptist, dutifully noted that God Himself thought up and spoke the Ten Commandments, not Moses, and Moses had only received them. That much was more in good fun than in turning votes. Then Bryan Dorn went farther and said everyone could go look it up in Genesis. Somehow, among all that crowd of biblical literalists, it slipped that day, but an alert *Greenville News* reporter marked it that neither congressman nor candidate seemed to know that the story of the Ten Commandments was chronicled in Exodus, not Genesis.[24]

---

[23] WJBD, *OTP*, 66; see Asa "Archie" Archibald to WJBD, 21 November 1945, WJBD/SCPC.

[24] WJBD, *OTP*, 64–65; "Both Candidates Wrong about the Bible," *Greenville News*, 29 July 1946, 7; Griffith, "William Jennings Bryan Dorn: Eulogy," 18 August

Honest John Taylor of the far hills above Anderson came aboard to help in the remote villages of Oconee, Pickens, and Anderson counties, as well as the town of Anderson. Taylor had lost to Hare in a race wherein his marriage to a "Northern girl" was used against him, but Taylor's help had as much to do with fondness for young Dorn as resentment of the sitting congressman. More usefully, the Hall newspaper family in Anderson endorsed Bryan, with editor and publisher Wilton Hall, himself once a state assemblyman, energetically writing up stories of speeches and then editorializing about the virtues of the youngest candidate. The *Anderson Independent* noted Bryan Dorn's service to Clemson College when he was state senator, and the paper noted how Dorn intended to use the research of the Clemson professors to find better jobs and better opportunities for the folk of the red hills. The "postal patronage" sponsored by Tom Watson and Olin Johnston was promised, as if Butler Hare himself was not a proponent and past master of postal appointments, not only in the jobs for carriers but in the service of RFD to the far-flung denizens. The Soak the Rich taxing policy of Roosevelt and Truman was cited as a good thing, even as the aspirant officeholder and family supporters complained of taxes on working-class voters. And in advocating Hare's own policies, Bryan Dorn boldly and proudly used the word *Liberal* to describe Southerners such as he was. As had Tom Watson and William Jennings Bryan before he was born, Dorn invoked Thomas Jefferson as the original liberal and called on the Third District voters to follow him "on the road from Monticello."[25]

Many words were biblical, and specifically Baptist, while generally evangelical: God's Truth was to be spread as broadly and as rapidly as possible by the believers, and the public service of politics included activist ministers and politicized congregations. Throughout the century, evangelical language and biblical narratives were part of South Carolina politics, and especially so in the state's piedmont. Indeed, a cynical Charlestonian's map of the state labeled the entire area north and west of Columbia as Baptist, with cartoon figures depicted in single-gallused coveralls, wool hats, bare feet, and with impassioned and wild-eyed stares. Less comically, Dorn and other orators of the day presumed a certain predestination laid out by a

---

2005, Thomas Cooper Library, WJBD/SCPC; Ed Chaffin, "Hare, Dorn Blast at CIO's PAC in McCormick Meet," *Greenwood Index-Journal*, 29 July 29, 1946, 5; Manuel J. Rogers, "Pickens Voters Hear Hare, Dorn," *Greenwood Index-Journal*, 31 July 1946, 7.

[25] The speeches follow a pattern preserved for years, Dorn, "Brink of Ruin," Jefferson-Jackson Day Dinner, Charlottesville, VA, 23 May 1959, WJBD/SCPC.

judgmental God with a definite plan that included guidelines for right conduct by those chosen to lead. Brothers and Sisters and Beloved, as those words were written from Jesus Christ in His preaching, were forms of address used actively and naturally. So, too, were the sonorous hymning phrases *God Bless His Heart! Lord Willing and the Creek Don't Rise! Peace, Be Still,* and *Will You Come and Pray?* These words and phrases formed evangelical call and response in everyone's speech in an unaffected but very affecting way. Value, justice, right and wrong, and God's will were all words that suffused the politics and the speeches of the politicians, and ministers often chose sides in local and sometimes state and national political races. With the exception of some ugly anti-Catholic assaults on New Yorker Al Smith in 1928, however, South Carolina pulpits and Sunday school discussions and potlatch gatherings featured the language of evangelical Christianity as deployed on behalf of FDR's New Deal and Harry Truman's Square Deal, something markedly different from Northern evangelicals, who were heavily Republican in the period from 1929 to the 1970s. In fact, even in 1928, despite anti-Catholic talk launched at Smith, South Carolina's evangelicals including Cole Blease and T. E. Dorn had supported the New Yorker against Hoover and the Republicans. Too, as novelist Reynolds Price and President Jimmy Carter both noted in their different ways, the evangelicals of the backwoods were as often marked by forgiving and tolerance as by damning judgments, and the fervent prayers for forgiveness on Sunday mornings generally followed some serious hell-raising on the Saturday night before.[26]

To challenge the Hare family in 1946, Bryan Dorn and his family had to remember and practice the basics of country politics, which were really the basics of country church gatherings: the Bible quoted with authority but also an easy humor, loud and impressive oratory complete with theatrical gestures, and barbecue up front—with liquor out back. As noted, the Dorn family thought that the piedmont politicking followed old Virginia patterns of "treating" and feeding. Where Virginians, especially those in the tidewater and south side, featured shad roe and clambakes, piedmont Carolinians featured hog and hash communally cooked and communally consumed. As Bryan Dorn the youth had marked it, many of the farmers gathered for a

---

[26] Charlestonian's map of South Carolina, possession of Dorothy Anne Bowers; interview, Price with Gross, "Fresh Air," 19 June 2006; Carter, *An Hour Before Daylight*; Williams, *God's Own Party*.

political barbecue made their choices then, at a first meeting, early in campaign. Prodded by Dada and Nana, Bryan Dorn could see with his own eyes that a young politician only had one chance with many of the voters, and that chance came at the first political stump meeting, called *stump* because in the Lincoln-Douglas debates, the Little Giant Stephen Douglas had taken to climbing up on tree stumps in order to be seen alongside his extremely tall opponent. Long decades later, in South Carolina at Gallivants Ferry in the Pee Dee marshland, General Wade Hampton III (who was more than big enough to be seen anywhere) famously took to a stump in the fall of 1876.[27]

By 1946, the physical tree stumps were mostly gone and candidates spoke instead from platforms and other stages erected for the purpose. But the name *stump* remained, and the imperative to strike hard and fast and memorably at a stump meeting was at least as intense as it had been earlier. In late life, Dorn recalled:

> Stump meetings were scheduled all over the county. How well you spoke was critical. It was customary in those days for a lot of community leaders to make up their tickets right there at the meeting. Many is the time I've seen an old-timer sit up against a tree on a couple of croker sacks and mark up his entire ticket—all the people he was going to vote for and recommend to his friends—from congressman to game warden. He'd look the candidates over. He'd talk with friends and he would make up his mind right then whom he was going to vote for. That's why it was important to make a good impression. The meeting also was a social gathering. Farmers not only came to see the candidates, they came to talk. They talked about weather and crops and how many bales they expected to make. And they talked about barbecue.[28]

Dorn recalled the ritual of the barbecue with all the pride of a man who raised and slaughtered cattle and hogs and with all the pride of the candidate who unfailingly made the "hash man forget to be stirring." Some weeks after the hog-slaughtering crew killed and chopped up and cured the pig, the cooking crew dug a pit in the ground, and the cutting crew cut up green wood for the fire-building crew to set ablaze in a huge, very hot fire. When the fire died down and glowing coals remained, the coals were shoveled into the pit and chicken wire was laid across the coals. The ham, shoulders, rib,

---

[27] WJBD, *OTP*, 32–34.
[28] Ibid.

and backbone were laid on the coals with only the chicken wire between the meat and the coals, and Dorn recalled, "that smoke and heat would come up and cook the meat. It was a very slow, delicate process which would make delicious meat."[29]

All this time, a black man, apparently always a black man trusted to stir without ceasing, was stirring barbecue hash, which was the parts of the hog not being pit-cooked, plus some beef, onions, potatoes, red peppers, and butter, in a large iron pot. Like the pit-cooked hog, the barbecue hash had to cook all night, and if it was not stirred constantly, then some of the hash stuck to the bottom of the iron pot and burned and ruined the taste, at least for the discerning. While the pit crew could get drunk and ignore things for long moments, the trusted hash-stirrer had to stay sober, alert, and *had to keep stirring*. As Dada reminded his political sons, "the hash man... understands the game. He's seen 'em come and go more than anybody there." But if the political speaker spoke so loudly and so forcefully and so interestingly that even the veteran hash man stopped his stirring, then that candidate had a real chance of winning. Bryan Dorn had seen Pitchfork Ben Tillman and Cole Blease make black men quit stirring by race-baiting and demagoguing so frighteningly that the hash man had to listen from literal fear for his life. Dorn, by contrast, wanted the hash man to listen to happy possibilities—to be sure, possibilities of economic improvement and not social justice. In his best performances in 1946, it is remembered of Dorn that the hash man often "lay his stick down." And when that happened, as Dada preached it, "you got 'em all. If you got the hash man, you get everybody."[30]

Family legend and local lore has it that at most of those primary sessions in the dog days of summer 1946, Bryan Dorn got the hash man and Butler Hare did not. Perhaps more to the point was the way that the Dorn and Griffith family and friends energetically *met* everyone, especially at the mills as the shifts changed. When the first shift came on at 8:00 in the morning, Nana and Gracie were there with sample ballots and flyers; Nana was still a striking beauty and Gracie was pretty. Decades later, a mill manager recalled a "pretty cousin" being nice to everyone at the Alice Mill in Easley, and he said that her good looks and winning ways had won over that particular first shift of citizens. The "pretty cousin" was likely either Bryan's mother, Pearl, or his sister Gracie, but otherwise the official's recollection

---

[29] WJBD, *OTP*, 33.

[30] WJBD, *OTP*, 34; WJBD, "In His Own Words," with Romine (3 February 1981) re: 1946 campaign, WJBD/SCPC.

was more right than wrong. The second shift, which came on at 4:00 P.M., and the third shift, which commenced at 11:00 P.M., were more challenging. Tom and Watson and George and sometimes Dada or Uncle Russ were there for the oncoming second shift, but *Corporal Dorn himself* was there for the much-oppressed third shift, and he took time—and was permitted time by mill managers—to talk with the workers one-on-one. Despite Butler Hare's hard work for them, the distinguished congressman had never come around at 11:00 at night to shake hands and chitty chat, and the plain folk never forgot that the "young fellow" did.[31]

When it came time to vote, it was not even close. Although Butler Hare scored points and votes in several of the Greenwood wards, he was swamped in the mill villages and in the rural farming villages. The final tally stood at 31,164 for Dorn, 19,423 for Hare. The inexperienced corporal had won nearly 62 percent of the votes cast with his thousand-dollar budget and his nonstop family campaigning. True to form, Hare was shocked, but also true to form, he was classy, conceding his defeat to a worthy opponent and pledging to help make a smooth transition from the 79h Congress to the 80th. As for the off-year general election, Tieless Joe Tolbert once again attempted to rally Republicans to stand for office, but only a "scattering" of three votes were recorded for Dorn's November opponents, while some 3,527 faithful came out and voted to be sure that the Democratic would be the person serving the Third District in Dee Cee.[32]

1946 was a year of revolt against incumbents, perhaps something of a revolt against the New Deal. Republicans regained the House of Representatives and gained seats in the Senate. It appeared to be a sign of changing tide, as interpreted by many Republicans. It also appeared to be a sign of trouble for the inexperienced Harry S. Truman as he attempted to rally his party in the aftermath of a total war and in the strange new context of an emerging Cold War in which his every action was compared to actions that might have been taken by the increasingly mythic figure of FDR. At any rate, President Truman was quick to send personal congratulations to the

---

[31] Reminiscence of Easley mill official (1948), WJBD/SCPC; interview with Watson Dorn and Steve Griffith and Roper (28 February 2012), JHR/SCPC.

[32] "Supplemental Report of the Secretary of State to the General Assembly of South Carolina," *Reports and Resolutions of South Carolina to the General Assembly of the State of South Carolina, vol. 1* (Columbia, SC: General Assembly, 1947), 5–7; Clerk of the US House of Representatives, "South Carolina," *Statistics of the Congressional Election of 5 November 1946*, comp. William Graf (Washington, DC: US Government Printing Office, 1947), s.v.

newly elected Dorn, and the congressman was quick to join forces with him, speaking on behalf of Truman in his district throughout the winter before and immediately after taking office. More significantly, Texan Sam Rayburn, who had exercised much influence over Butler Hare, was also quick to welcome young Dorn to the new US Congress. Rayburn, reduced from majority leader to minority leader, was bent but not bowed and spoke with determination in welcoming Dorn to a Congress that was likely to be embattled and troubled.[33]

It was time to put aside the victory celebrations, get to Washington, and get to work.

[33] WJBD, "In His Own Words," with Romine (3 February 1981); Truman to WJBD, 22 November 1946, John W. McCormack to WJBD, 22 November 1946; Sam Rayburn to WJBD, 21 November 1946, WJBD/SCPC.

Chapter 4

Stepping Out—And Falling Down
1947–1949

The young congressman eagerly unpacked his belongings and set up his offices in the Cannon Building. On the walls he intended to place a picture of Newberry College, a portrait of Jim Self, a pastoral scene from Walhalla, another pastoral scene from the Pickens countryside, a picture of an antebellum mansion in Edgefield, a picture of Matthews Cotton Mill in Greenwood County, and a picture of some representative building on the Clemson College campus. Only a few of the pictures had arrived, and he was especially sorry that he did not have the Clemson College scene to be sent by President Robert F. Poole. He unwrapped the packing and hung the framed pictures that he did have. Then he hurried on to other tasks. First among tasks, he found, hired, and began working with his congressional assistant, Ruth Meacham. Together, they set up a routine for the Washington office and also began to discuss and plan a routine for the Greenwood offices to be established in the Federal Building back home.[1]

About Ruth Meacham, he had a lengthy communication from Nana Dorn, who described with some precision exactly what kind of secretary and assistants he would need for his offices in order to serve his constituents in Washington and in Greenwood. Nana Dorn was quite emphatic that he would need *A Man* to be the secretary, because constituents and other congressmen would expect to find a man in charge. However, he would need an efficient *Woman* to be the assistant and do the typing and the filing and to answer the telephone. The secretary and the assistant must be absolutely loyal and must always remember that they represented a congressman who himself represented the people. They must never try to make policy or claim responsibilities they did not have, but they must understand what Bryan

---

[1] James C. Self to WJBD, 27 January 1947; WJBD to Robert F. Poole, 27 January 1947, WJBD to Chamber of Commerce of Newberry, 27 January 1947, Arthur Brown to WJBD, 29 January 1947, WJBD to G. F. Rucker, 27 January 1947, WJBD to Carl Alexander, 27 January 1947, WJBD/SCPC; "On Capitol Hill," *Anderson Independent*, 1 January 1947, 1.

Dorn would do if he were there. Sometimes they must cover up a mess the congressman had made, and always they must ensure that the congressman got the full credit for large accomplishments and *none of the blame*, even for any small missteps. All inquiries by Third District citizens must be answered promptly and politely, as if addressed to a trusted friend of the Dorns, even if only to say that the congressman was out of the office for the nonce and would be in touch with them on his return.[2]

Ruth Meacham was all of these things. She warned him that her North Carolina identity might cause him problems and that some voters and even some in the South Carolina delegation might expect a sandlapper, might even expect someone from the red hills of the district. But the two put this concern aside and hurried to set up appointments and establish a routine, including the occasions when she would be able to work at the Federal Building in Greenwood. Despite sincere efforts, the congressman was unable to persuade Newberry's Charles Berkeley Fellers to be the Man, and he did not locate other comparable talent among male applicants. Instead, Meacham found a "second girl," Edna Burnett, who could be brought on as second assistant. Edna Burnett, red-hills native, newly wed to DC businessman (but Greenwood native) George Burnett, was all of the things Nana wanted. Since George and Edna were Greenwood folk, Edna was ideal for going to the Federal Building offices in Greenwood to help the congressman meet constituents on his travels back home; the Burnetts could even make trips to the Greenwood offices to represent Dorn when he was on the job in Washington. Edna Burnett enjoyed the return trips to see home folks, even though those home trips were more work than relaxation.[3]

Ruth Meacham and Edna Burnett got along famously, and each was eager to be the kind of congressional assistant that Dorn (really Nana) said that she should be. Before much time passed, Meacham and Burnett came to understand and to support Dorn's grander ambitions, and both worked self-consciously not only as the assistants to the congressman but as political staffers for someone who might seek the governorship once Strom Thurmond vacated it, or the US Senate seat held by "the man with the magic,"

---

[2] Pearl Dorn to WJBD, 9 January 1947, WJBD/SCPC.

[3] Ibid.; example of Meacham discretion, Meacham to WJBD, 9 October 1947, enclosure, Jean Crouch to WJBD, 9 October 1947, Crouch's confidential note about forthcoming marriage to Strom Thurmond; failed effort to lure "best man" available, Grace Dorn to Watson Dorn, 29 January 1947 re: Charles Berkeley Fellers of Newberry, Pearl Dorn to WJBD, 28 April 1947 re: approval and admiration of Meacham, WJBD/SCPC.

Burnet Maybank, or even the Senate seat held by Olin Dewitt Talmadge Johnston, the man who had bested both the powerful Cole Blease and Cotton Ed Smith. The Dorns and Griffiths preferred that he seek Maybank's Senate seat, something Meacham and Burnett quickly came to understand.

Staff members and very close friends came to realize that the Dorns resented Maybank for his Charleston uptown elite identity, for his Episcopalian identity in a land of Baptists, for his defeat of family friend and hero Judge Eugene Blease, but also for his abilities to redirect federal funds toward Charleston (and sometimes *away from* the red hills). At such moments, Congressman Dorn complained about Senator Maybank's tax-and-spend policies, but, in fact, he was himself a tax-and-spend New Dealer/Fair Dealer (the term was after all traceable back to Jim Farley, whom he much admired). Olin Johnston was also a tax-and-spend New Dealer, but he was so clearly true to his own region of "linthead" millhands that Dorn could fight the senior senator as a worthy opponent, issue by issue, always considering Johnston to be his kind of man. By contrast, he judged Maybank an elitist with no real interest in the state's poor. In other words, Maybank was "guilty" of being what all Charlestonians were, that is, the ancient elite who had lorded it over the red-hills folk, the perpetrators of the "evils of Egypt" who must be "whip[ped]...to a farewell and a frazzle." Exactly *because of* such strong feelings, Dorn kept himself in check, exercising something like mannered Victorian politesse around Charleston's Maybank, while unbending quite naturally with the piedmont's friendly rivals Thurmond and Johnston. Meacham and Burnett understood Dorn's true feelings, and they perfected the extreme politesse toward Senator Maybank themselves.[4]

Living in the Continental Hotel, Dorn was a bachelor who knew that he could not afford to live the bachelor's "high life in Dee Cee"—could not afford it because he was in debt and earned "only" $12,500 ($136,502 in 2017 money), but that was set against short-term demand notes equal to 15 percent of his salary. Too, the freshman congressman shared with his family long-term obligations that ran to several hundreds of thousands in current

[4] See correspondence among Meacham, Burnett, and WJBD for all of 1947–1948, but especially: Ruth Meacham to C. H. "Grits" Gresham, 20 February 1947; Meacham to Edna Burnett, 29 June 1948; Meacham to Andy Griffith, 12 March 1948; Meacham to Watson Dorn, 22 July 1948: "WJBD" (actually Edna Burnett) to J. Fred Buzhardt, 23 June 1948, about McCormick supporters in primary; Olin Johnston's preference for grits and biscuits and plain folk food, Johnston to WJBD, 25 February 1960, WJBD/SCPC; on up-country resentment of Charleston, see Robertson, *Red Hills and Cotton*, 81, 98–111; quoted, 100.

money. In the tradition of the red-hills folk, he was "land poor." More important than finances, he could not *afford* to compromise his most cherished Baptist and Populistic beliefs about "simple living." He met journalists, and he went to informal get-togethers with some of them, especially young Allen Drury, who had come to the Senate Press Gallery in 1943 for United Press International (UPI) when a severe back injury took him out of active military service. To Drury and to congressmen of all sorts and conditions, Dorn made it clear that he could share a few drinks with them on occasion, but they would never see him in the company of women who were not carefully screened ahead of time as suitable escorts for official occasions, and he even informed them that sometimes the escort might well be his mother or his sister. In fact, that very January, newly elected Congressman Dorn attended Governor Thurmond's reception for the South Carolina delegation, and he was all dressed up in black-tie finery with lovely sister Gracie on his arm as "date" for the special evening.[5]

As to matters more purely connected to any congressman's job, Bryan Dorn wanted badly to be a member of the Military Affairs Committee, but he knew that appointment was unlikely. The sweeping Legislative Reorganization Act, signed into law with a flourish by President Truman on 2 August 1946, had eliminated many subcommittees, even some entire committees, and otherwise attempted a streamlining of assignments held by members. There were simply fewer committee memberships to go around. Too, Democrats had lost the majority in the House, and Republicans would thereby get favorable appointments, with many newly elected representatives seeking the Military Affairs Committee.[6]

Even so, Dorn approached the redoubtable Robert Lee Doughton, "Farmer Bob" of North Carolina, who had served his congressional district since 1911, with a brief absence to fight in World War I. Congressman

---

[5] US Code Title 2, ch. 3, 31 (2); pre-1975 data are the Consumer Price Index statistics from *Historical Statistics of the United States* (USGPO, 1975). All data since 1975 are from the annual *Statistical Abstracts of the United States*, Morgan Friedman Inflation Calculator, hereinafter, Friedman Calculator. WJBD to C. M. Parker, 13 January 1947; on Drury and journalist friends, WJBD to Sarah Bailey, 24 February 1961; corr., WJBD and Gracie Dorn, 1946–1947; WJBD to George Dalton Ball, 2 February 1947 concerning genteel poverty and Baptist morality, WJBD/SCPC; Drury, *A Senate Journal, 1943–1945*, 1–5, and idem., *Anna Hastings*, Irving Dept. of Rare Books and Special Collections, Ernest Frederick Hollings Library of the University of South Carolina, hereinafter RBSC; "On Capitol Hill," *Anderson Independent*, 2 January 1947, 1.

[6] US Code Title 2, ch. 3, 31 (2).

Doughton had been born in Laurel Springs in the high hills of Allegheny County during the Civil War, and thus had survived cataclysmic wars both in his own Appalachia and in Europe. The committee chairman was polite, and he was impressed with the new fellow's bearing and countenance, but he made it clear as a bell ringing in the valley that his Military Affairs Committee had *no vacancy*.[7]

Instead, Minority Leader Sam Rayburn and Minority Whip John McCormack worked with South Carolina's senior ranking congressman, James Prioleau "Dick" Richards, and assigned "the new man" to Clare Hoffman's Committee on Expenditures in the executive departments. Hoffman, Republican from Michigan, fully intended to make this oversight committee as powerful as was suggested by James Madison's original plan for a select group that would keep tight rein on the purse strings. With that historical reference, Dorn was mollified by appointment to a lesser committee. Once fully apprised of Hoffman's plans, he was even attracted to the possibilities in such an assignment, given the huge debts left over from World War II and the continuing talk about still more congressional spending.[8]

Always admiring of the Virginians, Dorn was delighted when Senator Willis Robertson urged him to join the National Council on Christian Leadership (NCCL), a bipartisan group of evangelical Protestants who gathered to worship together. Shortly after arrival in DC, Dorn eagerly attended an NCCL retreat that featured men from both parties and all corners of the sprawling US. Many of the same number attended the huge Calvary Baptist Church in DC, where Bryan Dorn was pleased to find Ruth Meacham among the thousands of worshippers. The "Protestant Cathedral" in the old Penn Quarter on 755 8th Street Northwest was in the heart of town and convenient both to the Continental Hotel and to Capitol Hill. This impressive edifice, with its very large congregation, did in a religious way something that Bryan hoped to do in national politics. It united North and South. Pastor Clarence Cranford was American (that is, Northern) Baptist, and was on track to become president of the American Baptist Con-

---

[7] "Robert Lee Doughton," *Biographical Directory of US Congress*, s.v.; WJBD to Doughton, 17 December 1946, WJBD/SCPC.

[8] US Congress, *Minority Committee Assignments* (Washington: USGPO), 2; Congressional Record, Vol. 93, Pt. 1, 80th Cong., 1st Sess., 9 January 1947, 2; expansion of powers and scope, Hoffman Committee on Executive Expenditures, Congressional Record, vol. 93, Pt. 2, 80th Congress, 1st Sess., 4 March 1947, 1644–1649; "Dorn Lands Place on 'Hot' Committee," *Anderson Independent*, 21 January 1947, 4.

vention. Yet in his congregation was a very large number of Southern Baptists, most prominent being Brooks Hays, congressman from Arkansas, lawyer and "erstwhile social worker for Christ," and one who was on track to be president of the Southern Baptist Convention, one of the few laypersons so elected.[9]

There seems to be no other church that had in its membership at the same time men who were president of the American and president of the Southern Baptist conventions. Hays in particular was important to Dorn. The Arkansan believed that God had made us all, including black and white. Furthermore, Hays believed, as did Bryan Dorn, in "civil rights and states' rights," professing a confidence that Southerners working at the local level would bring political equality and social justice for black citizens in their own communities. They would do so out of Christian conviction in response to prophetic dream. And they would do so voluntarily and not in response to economic pressure and certainly not federal pressure from "outsiders." Above all, Brooks Hays was master politician, arguably a statesman, and was often called upon to mediate disputes, especially about race relations, inside Southern regions and between congressmen representing different sections of the US. Dorn quickly came to love this Calvary Baptist Church, enjoying and benefiting from the mediation of Brooks Hays while glorying in the sermons delivered by Clarence Cranford.[10]

Also at Calvary was the ancient Vaughn Bible Study Class that met in intimate setting each Sunday before congregational worship in the cavernous sanctuary. The class was named for the redoubtable American Baptist reformist and evangelist Francis William Vaughn, who had established the discussions in 1890. Loosely connected to NCCL and to the Vaughn Bible groups were prayer breakfasts early Thursday mornings. In those days, the breakfasts were truly interdenominational and strictly bipartisan. In the

---

[9] Corr., Willis Robertson and WJBD, 1947, Ruth Meacham and WJBD, 1947–1960; corr., Brooks Hays and WJBD, 1947–1959, WJBD/SCPC; "Brooks Hays," *Biographical Directory of US Congress*, s.v.; Baker, *Brooks Hays*, 108–16; Calvary Baptist Church website, accessed 22 May 2012; Brooks Hays, address, n.d. (1961?), Emory & Henry College, Earl Gladney Hunt Archives, Emory & Henry College, hereinafter EHC.

[10] Corr., Brooks Hays and WJBD, 1947–1959, WJBD/SCPC; "Brooks Hays," *Biographical Directory of US Congress*, s.v.; Calvary Baptist Church website, accessed 22 May 2012; Baker, *Brooks Hays*, 108–16; Hays, *A Southern Moderate Speaks*, 25–62; Hays, address and Earl Gladney Hunt notes, EHC; interview, EHC archivist Robert Vejnar (14 January 2010), in possession of JHR.

prayer breakfasts, Bryan became acquainted with rural Southern Democrats who were much like Dorn himself, but he also made friends with Republicans Wayne Morse of Oregon, Alexander Wiley of Wisconsin, and Walter Judd of Minnesota. Within weeks, Dorn was taking his own regular turns as discussion leader in the Vaughn Bible Study Class and as a fundraiser and rally force for NCCL and for prayer breakfast activities. In the red hills, being with close Baptist friends who remained friendly despite political rivalries was accepted as a matter of course, but he gradually came to see that in the nation's capital some church activities were quite political indeed, and sometimes partisan. Even so, for much of the time, Calvary and its Vaughn Bible Class, at least for Bryan Dorn, were neither political nor partisan.[11]

Dorn's congressional career coincided with a steady growth in the seats held by military veterans. Prior to the 80th Congress, most representatives had not served in the armed forces. The percentage jumped to nearly 50 percent with the 80th, and the percentage rose each year thereafter, reaching a high of 73 percent when Dorn began his final term. As he always noted thereafter, Dorn quickly made friends with fellow military veterans in the House. Richard Nixon, freshman Republican congressman from California, Jack Kennedy, freshman Democratic congressman from Massachusetts, and Carl Albert, freshman Democratic congressman from Oklahoma (who eventually married a sandlapper and showed withal a curiosity about, and even passion for, all things Carolinian). There were commonalities in attitude between Dorn and these three congressmen, who had all recently been in the Good War, and the commonalities had little to do with party identity. Each of these service veterans had become anti-Communist in the later years of the war, and none was having any truck with so-called Soviet Allies. Each was hopeful about a technologically advanced military, and each wanted to deploy resources into the missiles and jets of an independent air force and to use the fearsome atomic bomb as a defense shield against the distrusted Soviets. Each was nervous about any "sizing down" of the army and navy, especially given their presumptions that Stalin would soon be adventuring in

---

[11] Blake and Palmer, *The Vaughn Bible Class, Calvary Baptist Church, Washington, DC; a Fifty Year History* (Franklin Center, PA: The Franklin Press, 1940); flyer with WJBD caricature, Vaughn Bible Class, retrospective, Cranford to WJBD, 24 October 1962; Nathaniel Leversone (NCCL) to WJBD, 26 November 1946, with lists of members and duties; on January retreat planning, Abraham Vereide to WJBD, 26 November 1946; Cranford to WJBD, 24 October 1962, on Prayer Breakfast, cf. retrospective complaint of NCCL politicization, Russell B. Long to WJBD, 24 June 1959, WJBD/SCPC.

Central Europe, Central Asia, Southeastern Asia, perhaps all of Africa—really anywhere. Most important, each of these freshman congressmen agreed with Dorn that a strong and progressive Democratic Party must cooperate with like-minded Republicans to make sure that there were jobs for the returning veterans and jobs for everybody else, as well as schools and roads for a powerful "peacetime infrastructure."[12]

Dorn presented himself to the experienced members of the South Carolina congressional delegation already seated, especially Lucius Mendel Rivers of the First District. Rivers was on the Armed Services Committee, and he shared Dorn's concern for the enlisted man, for the rural workingman, and for a foreign policy that prepared for hot conflict with the hated USSR. Although a Charlestonian, Rivers was as country as Bryan Dorn in his style of life and set of assumptions. In office since 1941, he had originally gained election by campaigning *against* Charleston and *for* the rural man, whether farmer or factory worker. Over time, he made his own separate peace with the classes of the Holy City, but he took it as a matter of course that he was enemy of the large bloc of voting black citizens. He liked his liquor, perhaps a bit much, and this worried Dorn, who controlled his own drinking, and frankly used it primarily for political purposes in the Virginia countryman's style of "hosting and treating." Mainly, Bryan Dorn admired and trusted Rivers for his expertise on military affairs and things Democratic in DC. Also in the delegation was its senior and its organizing genius, Dick Richards of the Fifth District, one especially committed to foreign affairs and the military but one who remembered his relationship to the masses and the classes of the central piedmont textile mills of both Carolinas. Too, there was Greenville's Joseph Raleigh Bryson of the Fourth District, onetime millhand, who spoke as passionately, if not as eloquently, as Bryan Dorn and for the same causes. In contrast to Rivers, Bryson was a *tee-totaller* who decried the devastation of *likker* even as his delegation mate and good friend Mendy Rivers celebrated it. And there was the Second District's John L. (Johnny Mac) Macmillan of Florence and the Pee Dee, one who served to-

---

[12] Clever and Segal, "After Conscription," 5–16; Aaron Blake, "The Long Decline of Veterans in Congress in 4 Charts," *Washington Post*, 11 November 2013; WJBD, "In His Own Words," interview with Romine (3 February 1981), WJBD/SCPC; WJBD, *OTP*, 67–73; similar remembrance by Kennedy, Nixon, and Albert: Sorenson, *Kennedy*, 17, 25–26; Nixon, *The Memoirs*, and Ambrose, *Nixon*, Vol. 1: *The Education of a Politician*; and Albert, with Goble, *Little Giant: The Life and Times of Speaker Carl Albert*; (JFK) "Education and Labor," (Albert), "Post Office and Civil Service," *Minority Committee Assignments* (Washington: USGPO, 1947), 2.

bacco and cotton interests (the last truly large cotton holdings of the Palmetto State) as much as textiles, but one who knew the workings of small farms and small mills as did the Dorn family. More than the others in the delegation, Johnny Mac really knew how to negotiate the New Deal administrators and their programs to the benefit of his own people. All of the South Carolina congressmen were New Deal guys and anti-Communist folk, and all were completely dedicated to the study and practice of parliamentary procedure and constituent service. Bryan Dorn fit in with them at once. Congress was his institution, he was an institutionalist, and Macmillan, Rivers, Riley, and Richards were his teammates, as well as his superiors, in *the* institution.

The South Carolina delegation and the rest of the newly elected Democrats, along with the returning Democrats who had survived the difficult 1946 elections, were called together by President Truman for an early session council. At that moment, the president had seen popular support collapse on him. In the afterglow of V-J Day, Truman's personal-approval rating among voters had actually approached 90 percent, a number recalled by Dorn in later years with something like wonder. By the time of the called council, however, Truman was barely approved by one-third of the voting public who were polled. There was anger about labor unrest, marked by some work stoppages and some violence and rumors of corruption at a time when most mainline unions and most nonunion workers were simply going to work and bound by various agreements not to strike. These resentments against certain unions were exacerbated because prices seemed to rise despite price controls, and wages for most people were legally frozen. As Dorn had seen on the campaign trail, the plain folk were convinced that "only their own" wages were being "controlled" and that all costs were rising. Taxes were at an all-time high, and the full employment days of all-out war were over now, with fears of an economic slowdown and with perhaps ten million veterans returning immediately to prewar jobs, with most of those veterans having some kind of legal claim to their former jobs. All of these frictions affected all Southern congressmen, and especially the South Carolinians, and Bryan Dorn attended this meeting with considerable misgivings, despite his loyalty to the institutions of the Democratic Party and the US Congress.[13]

When he and the others met with Truman, however, Dorn was impressed with the chief executive's down-to-earth qualities, his practical-minded nature, his obvious anti-Communism, and some qualities of "feed-

---

[13] WJBD, "In His Own Words," interview with Romine (3 February 1981), WJBD/SCPC.

store/seed store" common sense from the Missouri border state and neighboring Midwest that made the Carolinian comfortable even as Northeastern and urban Democrats made him uncomfortable. An officer in World War I who had been through trench-war combat, Truman had also suffered financially because of the low rate of return on the war bonds he had been compelled to buy. Those experiences gave him something in common with the Populistic New Deal Southerners. Moreover, the president seemed to understand that there were military challenges from the Soviets, and he had already showed his willingness to use the newest and most terrifying weapon of the air force.

Truman seemed disinclined to overdo the demilitarization now that the United Nations was proclaimed in effect. As to jobs, he showed genuine compassion and shared the foreboding that the immediate return to the workforce of ten million discharged soldiers and sailors (and the more gradual return of an additional five to six million gobs and grunts) would displace some good workers and create a new employment crisis. Truman agreed that price controls should protect the country from a potentially ruinous inflation, a rise in the general level of prices that could devour the modest salaries and small savings purses of average citizens (much as he had suffered himself in the 1920s). Lastly, at this first meeting, Truman did not preach much about civil rights, or at least Dorn did not notice such preaching. Dorn, like the veterans of the South Carolina delegation, thought he had found a kindred spirit who believed in racial justice that could be arrived at gradually by local initiatives. These observations were reinforced by Sam Rayburn, who, in a special meeting of a baker's dozen of new Southern congressmen, provided "hot-cakes well-flavored with sage political advice" about getting things done with President Truman.[14]

So armed with such reassurance, Bryan Dorn returned home in early March to speak vigorously on behalf of Harry S. Truman before crowds in his own Third District, and also in Greenville. At the same time, he placed in the *Congressional Record* similar words of official praise for permanent recording. Noting that while Abraham Lincoln was nowhere the intellect of his secretary of the treasury, Samuel Portland Chase, we nevertheless forgot

---

[14] Pearl Dorn to WJBD, 11 March 1947, with enclosure, clipping on WJBD speech, *Greenville News,* 11 March 1947, WJBD/SCPC. Cf. insider Eric F. Goldman's very different view of Truman, *Rendezvous with Destiny*, passim; "On Capitol Hill," *Anderson Independent*, 26 January 1947, 1.

Chase and made Lincoln immortal "for the sole reason...that Abraham Lincoln had intellectual humility and a sense of humor." He also opined,

> We have a man in the White House today as President of the United States who is modest, who is humble, who springs from the American people, and one who has the same type of intellectual humility.
>
> [I] commend [Truman] for his great battle on behalf of all the American people rather than pressure groups.
>
> [This is my] first opportunity to publicly commend Harry S. Truman for his great work in closing days of World War II [that] saved thousands of American lives.[15]

He concluded these and a number of speeches in this spring season by saying that Truman was "growing, developing every hour with the job," and absolutely "need[ed] support" from all Americans in a period of "great crisis."[16]

Meanwhile, he entered into the work on Clare Hoffman's committee. He liked Hoffman at once, and the young piedmont Democrat quickly became good friends and good teammates with the experienced Republican Michigander. Two things Hoffman set about to investigate in full were labor racketeering and the costs and benefits associated with various proposed mergers of the branches of the armed forces. Not only was Dorn fascinated with the details in this work, but it threw him into cooperation with those fellow newcomer veterans Kennedy and Nixon, each of whom in his own way was breaking a lance over labor racketeering and duplication of services and operations in the military. Hoffman could survey issues of labor racketeering because the federal executive departments, through the Department of Justice and also through the National Labor Relations Board, had often expended funds on behalf of the rights of labor, but previously without much congressional advice and consent.

As for merging the army, navy, marines, and air force, or at least coordinating them more efficiently, there was much talk about saving money by eliminating duplication of effort. There were only "back of the napkin" estimates for the cost in blood and treasure from World War II, but Dorn and others guessed it was something more than twice the gross domestic product. During the exigencies of wartime, Congress had routinely accepted all such expenses. Now, Hoffman intended that his committee take a reasoned

---

[15] *Congressional Record*, Vol. 93, Pt. 1, 80th Cong., Sess. 1, 10 March 1947, 1870–71.

[16] Ibid.

look into peacetime expenses, which "surely" could be reduced by streamlining the structures of the armed services. Initially, Dorn agreed fully with his chairman, noting that there were "two armies," a separate air force for four branches, and "four girl forces" for each branch, in his mind wasteful duplication. He betrayed the outdated chauvinism about "four girl forces" in services that had already redundantly demonstrated their extreme need for women in the ranks; but he also failed to realize the futility of actually unifying and merging the military branches. Whether logical or not, four very distinct services (including "two armies") had emerged from World War II, each with its own flying machines. Clare Hoffman's committee was not going to reverse that, but the junior backbencher still made it a favorite talking point for this season.[17]

As to labor unions, particularly the highly politicized American Federation of Labor (AF of L), organized labor was vital to the Democratic Party and especially for the coalition of interest blocs that FDR had cobbled together, a coalition that Truman fully intended to keep in one piece. The more radicalized unions of the Congress of Industrial Organization (CIO) were part of the broad wartime Popular Front and supported the left wing of the party but often took very independent lines on issues such as wage and price controls, and above all on issues of racial policy. Hoffman had partisan reasons as a Midwest Republican to trim the sails of the AF of L, especially the powerful and actively Democratic automobile and steel workers in his Michigan. Dorn, as a Populist in a district where almost no mill or farm featured a union, was adamantly opposed to the various iterations of textile worker organizers and farm labor advocates, and indeed only a few millworkers or farmhands in his own district had ever dared to show interest in unionizing. As a matter of fact, he and every South Carolina congressman inevitably worked closely with the more bourgeois unions, such as postal employees and civil service employees or teachers' educational associations, as well as the well-organized railroad workers and teamsters, and he never complained about such organizations. Importantly, few of these bourgeois unions and associations were in any sense progressive on social issues, especially race relations. Dorn and most Southern congressmen voted to weaken rights to collective bargaining and to diminish the effectiveness of strike lines as recognized by "secondary boycott strikes" of sympathetic unions; and

[17] WJBD to Fletcher Jones, 25 April 1947; Bert Clarke, news release draft, Hoffman Committee, n.d. (April) 1947, WJBD/SCPC.

on such issues there was common cause across party lines of majority Republicans and minority Democrats on Hoffman's committee.

Committee members were energetic in the hunt, and some union leaders made themselves remarkably big and slow-moving targets, blatant in their unsavory actions, especially since newspaper and magazine journalists were eager to share in the splashy revelations of strong-arm tactics against opponents, graft and scandal of all kind, and anything that smacked of "racketeering," the term of the day for activities in restraint of free and fair trade and commerce. Besides some Communist Party USA (CPUSA) activity and some implanted CPUSA activists in some big-city unions, there was some involvement by organized crime. Only a few of the CIO union chapters were truly "Red" and even fewer of the AF of L were "mobbed up," but each discovery was a point against unions in the piedmont for Dorn, a point against Truman Democrats for Hoffman, and a point for the Republicans in the Midwest.

The most fertile investigative grounds seemed to be among certain unions that restrained trade with violence and bribery in the delivery of produce to grocers in large cities. J. Edgar Hoover's Federal Bureau of Investigation (FBI) was chasing CPUSA and rogue criminal components in some of the cases, and Dorn early made acquaintance with such "G-men," whom he happily involved in the investigations if any labor leader was slow to respond to his committee inquiries. Indeed, Dorn came to know Hoover himself, dealing with him always as a man to be feared more than loved. His new UPI friend Allen Drury sent him into laughter by paraphrasing Rudyard Kipling: there is a "universal tendency to walk wide o' J. Edgar Hoover, for ah o' creation he owns." Both men liked Kipling, and they knew of his *Barrack-Room Ballads*, one verse of which described Queen Victoria as the "Widow at Windsor" who must be walked carefully around, "for 'alf of Creation she owns." It seemed to the newspaperman and to the congressman that Hoover, in fact, claimed twice as much of Creation as did the Widow of Windsor—"*ah*' instead of only '*alf*."[18]

Hoffman's committee scored some publicity points in these cases, and young Dorn was given the chance for his own headlines in a news release in early spring:

---

[18] Corr. between Hoover and WJBD, esp. Hoover to WJBD, 15 November 1947, WJBD/SCPC; quote, Drury, *Anna Hastings*, 177, RBSC; Drury citing Kipling, "The Widow of Windsor," *Barrack-Room Ballads* (1892).

> Committee members making the investigation were flouted by local union officials," said Bryan Dorn, South Carolina Democrat, until they learned that agents of FBI and BIR were on hand, too delving into union books and finances, ...[during] on-the-ground investigations in Philadelphia.... "Rank and file members of the local unions appear to be in the grip of racketeers who have seized the union and [*sic*] squandering its funds," said Mr. Dorn. "There is no accounting of union funds. Only two alleged audits of the union's books have been done in six years. Union members who asked for accountings have been beaten and sent to hospital. Arthur Goldberg—secretary treasurer—drew union funds without apparent authority to do so. Merchants are forced to buy advertising.[19]

That much of Dorn's work with the Hoffman committee appealed to all Democrats who wanted fair and honest dealings in trade and commerce, especially those who honored unions and wanted the unions to be honorable. However, Dorn pressed far beyond such investigations and sought headlines concerning CPUSA influence and activities, especially for New York congressman Vito Marcantonio and his labor activists. The Italian Democrat from East Harlem represented blacks, Italians, and Puerto Ricans and deftly moved between the CPUSA, the Republican Party, and the Democratic Party, but he eventually declared himself to be the one and only congressman who was member of the American Labor Party (APL). Marcantonio delighted in the theatrics of the disputes and began to use "Dorn of South Carolina" as his own *bete noir* and designated Enemy of Organized Labor, linking all Southern congressmen to "the economic expansion of our monopoly capital," "warmongering," "Red-baiting," and "the imperialist program." For his part, Dorn enjoyed the theatrics and played his role for Marcantonio's constituents as faithfully as the Italian Harlemite did for the red-hills folk.[20]

Such press and publicity were good at home for each congressman, but it was not pure showmanship, despite the respect and affection each held for the other person. In the world of political ideas, each man honestly thought

---

[19] Bert Clarke, press release, n.d. (early spring 1947), packaged for distribution to SC newspapers by Ruth Meacham and Edna Burnett, WJBD/SCPC.

[20] FBI, Vito Marcantonio File # 1000-28126; Hoover to Matthew F. McGuire, custodial dossier, 28 July 1941: "high marks for character, courage, and honest...should be investigated for reprehensible speeches [heard by agents]...passed security clearance." US FBI Archives online 0721, J1.1412: vol. 83, Washington, DC.

the other represented an evil conspiracy. Marcantonio labeled the old Populists who hated large corporations and big investment banks "tools of capitalism," and Dorn labeled Marcantonio—who was closer to Trotskyite—"Stalinist." He proudly saved any clippings that noted Marcantonio's attacks on him and made sure they were available for consumption by his constituents. At the same time, he was pleased to see Jack Kennedy fighting similar fights against Communists and corruption in CIO unions on his own committee assignment, Education and Labor. Meanwhile Dick Nixon made even larger headlines investigating Communism and corruption as part of the House Un-American Activities Committee (the notorious HUAC). By contrast, their fellow freshman Carl Albert was content to do the quiet and tedious constituent service through the appointment of postal clerks and the extension of rural postal routes back in Oklahoma on his committee assignment, Postal and Civil Services. Only later did Dorn realize how much more faithfully the Oklahoman was following the mentor Jim Farley than he himself was (and only later did he realize the wisdom of Albert's actions in contrast with his own). Much as Dorn liked Albert, he thrilled to the virulent anti-Communism that linked him with the up-and-coming Nixon and Kennedy and that brought him newspaper and magazine copy space, especially with the *Washington Star* newspaper and David Lawrence's slick new weekly periodical *US News & World Report*.[21]

Anti-Communism was a way to connect some of the defense policy considerations with discussions about military branches and other issues in military affairs, and to do so on Hoffman's committee. Defense expenditures were the lion's share of executive discretionary spending, a lion's share now being carefully examined. It was hard to disentangle foreign aid, which might be humanitarian, from aid to foreign military forces; the efforts to disentangle the involved strands sometimes put Marcantonio and Dorn together in opposition to some funding, but for very different reasons. As civil war erupted in Greece and Turkey, Truman worried that Communists, allied with or at least partly funded by the Soviet Union, might overtake both countries. Rather than work through the United Nations to ensure humanitarian aid, Truman provided unilateral aid to Greece, thereby establishing

[21] Congressional Record, Vol. 93, Pt. 1, 80th Cong., Sess. 1, 11 December 1947, 1306–307; Shaffer, *Vito Marcantonio*, passim; Meyer, *Vito Marcantonio*, passim; Antonio, *I Vote My Conscience: Debates, Speeches, and Writings*, ed. Rubinstein, 227–71; US Congress, "Post Office and Civil Service (Carl Albert)," *Minority Committee Assignments*, 2; US Congress, *Majority Committee Assignments*, 2.

the Truman Doctrine, and much of that aid was always for the anti-Communist military forces. Marcantonio wanted strictly multilateral aid for humanitarian causes, all of it funneled carefully through the UN—and he was all but rooting for the Communists to win. Dorn opposed spending money abroad on foreign aid, and for a brief time he and Marcantonio opposed the aid to Greece. That brief cooperation ended abruptly when Dorn realized that the anti-Communist Greeks might well *lose* without serious aid for weapons. Quickly, he began to support the entire aid package, military and humanitarian, and thereby swung once again into a more forthright fight against the East Harlem radical on all fronts.[22]

An interesting feature of this first session in Congress is that Dorn focused so exclusively on Communism abroad and racketeers in labor unions in Philadelphia that he made only a handful of remarks about race relations despite the red-hot topics of the day, including disputes about fair housing, fair employment, voting rights, and lynching. He voted predictably enough with the Southern bloc, but seldom spoke to the points at issue. Even more interesting is the contrast between Dorn and his new friend Albert with regard to constituent service back home. While Dorn complained about the tedious nature of tasks such as the endless negotiations about extending rural postal routes or contracting some of the more remote ones, and while he grew weary of trying to facilitate appointments for postal officials in the tiny local offices his red hills, Albert delighted in doing such things. To Dorn, Albert looked a lot like a younger Olin Johnston. Some reflection might have told him that Albert also looked much like Dorn's hero and pen pal, Jim Farley, and quite a great deal like Dorn family hero and legend Thomas E. Watson. The latter had rightly claimed paternity over Rural Free Delivery, and the former had demonstrated how to make it the most salient feature of constituent service for the folks back home.[23]

Only some years later did Dorn realize that he was failing to provide the constituent service—reliable delivery of the mail, patronage appointments for friends and relatives of political friends, help with the complexities of USDA farm programs, and help with the complications of Social Security old-age and disability aid—that identified the Populist congressmen in the

---

[22] Vito Marcantonio File #100-28126, US. FBI. Archives online 0721, Jl.1412: vol. 83; Antonio, *I Vote My Conscience*, ed., Rubinstein, 227–71.

[23] Corr. WJBD and J. B. Hare, December 1948 and May 1949, esp. retrospective, Hare to WJBD, 13 May 1949, WJBD/SCPC; Woodward, *Tom Watson*, 210–12; "James Aloysius Farley," *Time* (cover), 20/18.

rural South. His mail was filled with notes from people who delighted in his anti-Communism, and he answered these notes excitedly. But he neglected a prompt and useful response to the many supplicants who worried about losing the community post office, who wanted a patronage appointment or reassignment, or who needed help with a government form. Many such a letter-writing constituent was hopelessly confused about state, county, and federal lines of authority, and in such cases Dorn and his staff in that first term made brief, almost curt replies. For Congressman Dorn in 1947, the detail-oriented, patient, tedious, and steady work of serving constituents on personal matters took second place to lambasting Reds and racketeers.[24]

For instance, on the grand issue of merging or otherwise restructuring the armed forces, Dorn threw himself into his studies and met as many air force experts as he could, being thrilled to sit and talk with and then correspond with his old Overlord commander, Hoyt Vandenberg. He was even more delighted to meet and come to know the legendary Russian expatriated jet pilot and theorist Alexander Nikolaievich Prokofiev de Seversky. The latter was a particularly romantic entrepreneur who had lost a leg in World War I but continued to fly (with permission from Czar Nicholas II himself). He helped develop jets both for military and commercial use and sought and gained asylum in the US following the assassination of Tsar Nicholas and family. Seversky founded Republic Air, a commercial manufacturer. Dorn talked strategy with his old commander Vandenberg, but with Seversky he talked about jets and he listened with awe to the most stirring stories (the most bizarre of which were true). It was his fascination with the new air force of jets and missiles in the context of a coming struggle with Russia—the point of view of another favorite he cultivated, Bonner Fellers—that put him into *Time* magazine and on the front page of the *Washington Post.* While arguing with Congressman Marcantonio on the House floor, Dorn excitedly made the point that the Russian Communists would leave Greece at once if they thought a wing of air force bombers not only would attack their mercenaries but might attack Russia itself. "What will stop Communism in the world?" he asked. "An air force right here in America...that

[24] Hare to WJBD, 13 May 1949; WJBD kept no file on post office appointments and postal stations at all for period 1947–1949, while he kept very full files on same issues, 1951–1975, Boxes 1–12, WJBD, SCPC; Weber, "Politics as a Vocation," 128.

can fly to any part of the world and return, [an air force] capable and willing to use the atomic bomb."[25]

Those words caught the attention of Andrei Vishinsky, Russian ambassador to the UN, who was in Lake Summit, New York, getting ready for a UN discussion of postwar arrangements. On September 18, Vishinsky was drawing up a speech in which he would compare Winston Churchill and Charles de Gaulle and South Carolina's own diplomat Jimmy Byrnes with Napoleon and Hitler and also connect various European and American leaders with Wall Street. Then he found Dorn's quote. Quickly, he pounced, calling Dorn a *podzhigateli voiny,* or warmonger. He also called him *neopytnyy*, that is, inexperienced or neophyte. That English label, "inexperienced warmonger," became a quoted label for pictures on the 21 September front page of *Washington Post* "above the fold," as the pressmen once said. It also became copy space in *Time* magazine when Vishinsky was featured on its cover the third week of September. Vishinsky went on to request that the UN consider action against the "war criminals" Churchill, de Gaulle, and Byrnes as well as some other action against the "inexperienced warmonger" Congressman Dorn. The Russian ambassador was playing to theater and expected no UN action, but he did succeed in raising the level of diplomatic anxiety during a particularly hot time of the Cold War.[26]

Dorn reveled in the attention, and on the House floor he asked rhetorically why he was singled out. He answered his own question by saying that the Russians really were afraid of our air force, associated him with that dreaded and unmatched force, and thus aimed to discredit him. He also all but crowed like a bantam rooster for friends and relatives, especially old 8th Air Corps buddy Charlie Donahue, now in the Midwest. However, he was prompt in assuring State Department people that he supported the Truman policies and intended no attack on George Marshall, Warren Austin, Eleanor Roosevelt, or any other officials. He even put it in writing for them that he had "utmost faith in the United Nations Conference," sincerely wanted "lasting peace," and had "great faith in our delegates" to the UN. Indeed, he wrote Austin, he reposed faith in the Russian people and their leaders be-

---

[25] Kuhn, "Russia Asks U.N. for Action Against 'War Propagandists;' Leading U.S. 'Warmongers,'" *Washington Post,* 19 September 1947, 1; WJBD, quoted, "National Affairs," *Time*, 51/13, 29 September 1947, 21–23; "Podzhigateli voiny!" *Time*, 50/18, 3 November 1947, 28; "Vishinsky Meets the Press," *Time,* 51/14, 6 October 1947, 83.

[26] AP, "Text of Vishinsky's UN Speech," *Washington Post*, 19 September 1947, 2; Jones, "Austin Charges Vishinsky Falsified," *New York Times*, 21 September 1947, 1, 45.

cause of their bravery during World War II and presumed that Vishinsky was speaking only for himself. Austin wrote back at once, apparently relieved, and a few days later both Marshall and Eleanor Roosevelt wrote personal notes, rather slyly recording in writing that he supported their policies, had faith in them as agents and diplomats, and intended no insult to Russian leaders. Furthermore, another of South Carolina's own diplomats, John E. Peurifoy of Walterboro, acting assistant secretary of state, assured State Department members that Dorn was no hothead and no maverick. Dorn was in these instances showing himself to be both very clever in playing to red-hills audiences and very measured in dealing with his own Democratic diplomats. For all that, the statements of reassurance by Eleanor Roosevelt, signed in her own shaking hand, rang more tinny than true, and members of the State Department were relieved to see Vishinsky turn his attentions away from Bryan Dorn the *neopytnyy* and the *podzhigatel voynoy* who might or might not be a warmonger but certainly was inexperienced—and completely without portfolio—in these discussions. He had made himself a conspicuous problem for diplomats for a brief moment—and then he again disappeared from their view.[27]

Otherwise, Dorn eagerly absorbed hard data and soft opinions from air force officials, hoping some day down the road to establish himself as a military expert with oversight power in the US Senate. Already, he was learning the painful lesson that congressmen made little impact on such issues as "the seventy-group air force" or the intercontinental ballistic missiles with nuclear warheads in bunkers in the Dakotas or on other remote underground launching sites. Even the House Committee on the Armed Forces, chaired by Farmer Bob Doughton and featuring his new friend, the redoubtable Lucius Mendel Rivers, even this standing committee with its purse strings made little impact on the military planners, at least with regard to these specific issues Dorn studied so assiduously. In fact, he saw that the US Navy fully intended to keep jets and missiles within their own service bailiwick, with jets launched from aircraft carriers and missiles launched from subma-

---

[27] WJBD, "Remarks," *Cong. Rec.*, vol. 93, pt. 1, 80th Cong., 1st Sess., 11 December 1947, 1306–1307; Jones, "Austin Charges," *New York Times*, 21 September 1947, 1, 45; Grace Kempton to WJBD, 22 September 1947; WJBD to Charlie Donahue, 18 December 1947; WJBD to Eleanor Roosevelt, 29 September 1947; WJBD to George Marshall, 29 September 1947; WJBD to Warren Austin, 29 September 1947; Austin to WJBD, 2 October 1947; Roosevelt to WJBD, 8 October 1947; Marshall to WJBD, 6 October 1947; corr., John Peurifoy and WJBD, November and December 1947, and Peurifoy to WJBD, retrospective, 25 June 1951, WJBD/SCPC, 1947.

rines, and both kinds of boats themselves nuclear powered. His actual preference, following Seversky, Fellers, and Vandenberg, was to base missiles and jets in the US and dramatically deemphasize the navy, especially its aircraft carriers, which the "fly boys" discounted as "things that only defend themselves." Instead, a long-distance bomber could fly at 30,000 feet over the North Pole in order to attack the Russians if the Soviets marched on Western Europe. Whatever he learned and however forcefully he spoke as a congressman on Clare Hoffman's committee, he could only decry wasteful spending because of duplication of weapons; he could not take much of a real hand in setting military policy at all. He was, then, more neophyte than Vishinsky had charged.[28]

In the meantime, there were some family concerns, concerns that again reminded him of his own observation that South Carolina politics was always factionalized, personalized, and family-connected. Cousin governor Strom Thurmond sent him an ambitious plan for waterways development in the state, made a point of sitting by him during discussions about regional graduate education (a plan to use one regional medical center for training black physicians in the South without having to integrate Deep South schools), and enthusiastically told him he would be nominating the congressman for Junior Chamber of Commerce (JAYCEE) Man of the Year. But Thurmond also asked Gracie to work in his offices and invited her to take a governor's business trip with him. All of this made Bryan Dorn anxious. Thurmond was rumored to be quite the lady-killer, and the congressman reacted as a Southern man nervous about his sister's honor. "Personally," he scolded Gracie, "I had rather you would stay out of Strom Thurmond's office, for your own good if for no other reason. His reputation and fastness concerning women is nation-wide, so do not kid yourself about that either." The concept of such "fastness" scared Gracie off readily enough, and the governor did not invite her again into his office or on trips. Dorn relievedly asked her to "destroy this letter," which, of course, she did not even think of doing. Otherwise, Gracie encouraged her brother in still another assumption that he articulated: "All of those fellows fear me as political opposition above anyone in South Carolina today." That assertion, unlike

---

[28] Col. Montgomery to WJBD, 1 July 1946, with enclosure, *US Strategic Bombing Survey, Summary Report, Pacific War* (Washington, DC: USGPO, 1946).

his strictures about Governor Thurmond's "romantic links," was unwarranted by any facts—and a poor starting point for serious political planning.[29]

Looking back at that fast-moving and complicated first year in Congress, Dorn recalled, "I was naïve enough to believe I could jump up and storm the people and turn them around as I always had. I didn't realize how much it would cost and the type of organization I needed.... I was in a hurry in 1948." In his hurry, he determined that it was Burnet Maybank who was vulnerable, and thus it was the Charlestonian's Senate seat he would seek. Timing was crucial and involved subtleties. To compete in and win the summer 1948 Democratic primary for the US Senate, he needed to inform the state Democratic party chairman William P. Baskin of Bishopville, and certainly the South Carolina delegation, that he would be challenging Burnet Maybank and would not be a candidate for the Third District congressional seat in the same primary. The party must find a suitable person to run for his barely warmed seat in the Cannon Office Building, and that could only happen in a contest among several candidates in the congressional primary to be held on the same summer's day. Thus, he informed the head of the South Carolina delegation, Congressman Dick Richards, and notified officials in Columbia that he would not seek the House seat in 1948 but instead would seek the Senate seat. That step, taken early in the spring of 1948, made the powerful and dangerous Maybank a competitor, and would make competitors of at least three other powerful and ambitious men back in South Carolina: Neville Bennett of Marlboro County, who had run for governor and lost in 1938; Alan Johnstone of Newberry County, who once had served as state senator from Richland County; and Florence County's Marcus A. Stone, who had run for governor in 1946 against Thurmond.[30]

Before taking this step, Bryan went to Myrtle Manor and visited friends and relatives and neighbors, traveling around the scenes of his triumphal victory over Butler Black Hare. Judge Griffith and wife, Bertie Griffith, gave him particular encouragement, and the couple would again give him $500, his biggest single campaign contribution. Another Newberry attorney, Frank C. Clarkson, canvassed county voters and found resentment of Maybank and a preference for Dorn over the sitting senator. Brother Watson at

---

[29] Thurmond to WJBD, 13 January 1948; Thurmond to WJBD with enclosure "Awake and Accomplish," 3 May 1947; WJBD to Grace Dorn, 25 July 1947, WJBD/SCPC; Bass and Thompson, *Ol' Strom*, ch. 6.

[30] WJBD, *OTP*, 88–89; Jordan, *The Primary State*, 78–79.

the law school of the University of South Carolina was clear-eyed and cautious, offering opportunities for the congressman to meet with ambitious young law students in Columbia, even to give a formal address—but Watson warned that losing could really set him back and that some voters would be unhappy that he had left his congressional seat so quickly. Oldest brother Tom, rapidly gaining rank in Bryan's adored air force, was characteristically more blunt, insisting that his younger brother have a serious plan for earning money should he lose this race. Russ Carter in Walhalla was enthusiastic about his prospects, but not for US Senate; the small-time businessman of the Blue Ridge wanted Dorn to run for governor. Friend and ally Thomas Harrington Pope Jr. of Newberry let the congressman know that he would defer to Dorn for governor *or* senate and only asked early notification so that he could run for the office that Dorn did *not* contest.[31]

At Myrtle Manor, however, he saw first-hand some family facts more troubling than his four or more potential opponents for Senate. He saw that Dada's heart problems, largely ignored and untreated by a big and tough man who tended to ignore medical authorities, were making the patriarch fade fast. This physical decline was hastened along because Dada still attempted hard physical labor on the farmland, even and especially in the heat and humidity of Greenwood's early-arriving and long-lingering summer. As Nana had warned, there was no talking to Dada about these issues. He was not seeking help or treatment, and it seemed unlikely he could last much longer. With that awful news, the man who would be senator learned too that he was losing connection with Dada's plain folks. They thrilled to his anti-Communism, but were agitated about Truman's civil rights proposals. Above all, the folks back home were feeling neglected on the constituent services, the mundane tasks of listening and helping when a rural mail route was cancelled, of helping out someone's son who was denied a postal clerkship or passed over for an appointment, or someone's grandmother who was denied her widow's benefits by the Social Security officials. There was not much time left for serious constituent service during the activities of the campaign against Senator Maybank and three other aspirants, but he might distract such otherwise unserved folk if he talked about race relations as well as the air force. He would need to stoke the Populist anger against Communists and black people and the allies of Reds and Feds and blacks in the

[31] WJBD to H. Klugh Purdy, 22 January 1948; Frank C. Clarkson to WJBD, 8 January 1948; WJBD to Bertie Griffith, 6 January 1948; about Pope and Maybank, Watson Dorn to WJBD, 24 June 1948, WJBD/SCPC.

Henry A. Wallace wing of the Democratic Party. He would have to give them rhetoric about Reds and Feds in the civil rights movement—Reds and racketeers were essentially moot for the stump in the Third District.[32]

Dorn went back to Washington deeply troubled about Dada. He was no less anxious about losing touch with the emotions of the millhands and farmers and small-time "bidness" people. He spoke movingly about Reds and Feds and stirred piedmont audiences with both themes. But he was coming to see that the larger fear for the home folks was Feds—and not just in the sense of powerful central authority threatening local Jeffersonian rule. Any federal help, however mild, for black people—even trying to prevent their beatings and killings—was utterly unacceptable in the Third District of 1947 and 1948. Calvary Baptist friend and congressional colleague Brooks Hays's idea about bringing racial justice gradually from the ground up at the local level appeared impossible in the counties of his district, and probably in all counties of the Palmetto State. At least it was impossible in this sour season. Back in Arkansas, Hays had worked to help some black people vote, and he had cooperated with a gradual integration of higher education for graduate and professional training in law and medicine at the University of Arkansas. Nothing remotely like that was possible in Dorn's district, he now understood. He even went through the motions of sending out a questionnaire to chosen constituents concerning civil rights, and the results were more spectacularly negative than he had expected. His home folk not only wanted metaphorical red meat about race relations—they sometimes wanted literal blood, as he would see in several telling instances in the year of 1948.[33]

Dorn also took account of the fact that attractive candidate Dr. James McLeod of Florence County had died suddenly of a heart attack, thereby removing a major contender and opening up the field considerably for those who would challenge Burnet Maybank for Senate in the forthcoming sum-

---

[32] T. E. Dorn health, retrospective, Grace Dorn to WJBD, 15 July 1947, and WJBD to Pearl Dorn, 24 March 1948, WJBD/SCPC.

[33] Cf. Baker, *Brooks Hays*, 108–16; Hays, *A Southern Moderate Speaks*, 25–62; on racial attitudes, see corr., 1946–1947, which virtually smokes with extreme negrobphobia—he is careful neither to disagree nor to use the crude language, but see exchange, M. E. (Tommie) Thomas and WJBD, 10 July 1950 and 12 July 1950 retrospective; questionnaire, WJBD to Bob Aldrich, 10 February 1948 (even lynching is unworthy of concern), WJBD/SCPC. See esp. wise admonition of brother Watson Dorn that WJBD may have to "be quiet" about his racially moderate attitudes and ideas, Watson Dorn to WJBD, 9 January 1948 and 24 June 1947, images, see WJBD, *OTP*, 78–80.

mer's Democratic primary. He found as well that he had some welcome journalistic support in the press gallery from one Mildred Johnson of the weekly *US News & World Report.* For instance, when Millie Johnson learned that the Third District representative was so dedicated to weight-training and working-out that his personal trainer declared Dorn to be "an Adonis," the reporter dropped that description into several ears and the "Adonis" label made its way into print in the Washington presses—but more importantly, it was picked up and used by Eleanor Mundy of the *Greenwood Index-Journal* and by Wilton Hall and L. C. Hembree of the *Anderson Independent* back home in the district.[34]

The always-reliable staff assistant Ruth Meacham was convinced that Millie Johnson fell in love with Bryan Dorn quite early, and UPI's Allen Drury may have had Millie Johnson in mind when he (with her help) wrote the fictitious character Anna Hastings, who told friends, "I'm going to marry [him]...he doesn't know it yet. But I've decided who it's going to be. And he will." The specific words, in Drury's novel *Anna Hastings*, appeared in print in 1977 but were spoken in 1948. That novelistic character, like Millie Johnson, dated Joe McCarthy and Jack Kennedy and other bachelor politicos and was clever and successful in her flirtatious approach to the already-married congressmen. Drury consulted with Millie Johnson about Anna Hastings and other of the novel's female reporters and emerged with the telling phrase: "the careful two-year campaign that had brought her gallant lover so unexpectantly yet insistently to answer—not pop—the question."[35]

Millie Johnson, like her friend Allen Drury, had professional training on the job in the press gallery during World War II. A native of the broad inner coastal plain of eastern North Carolina, Millie Johnson had been born and raised on a tobacco farm in Coats. Bright as a penny in school, she was encouraged by her parents to attend college, and she went off to the Baptist-supported Campbell College in nearby Buies Creek. There, she met Marvin Lucien Skaggs, chair of the social science department and a scholar trained at the University of North Carolina when that school was arguably the best at training social scientists, at least for regional studies. Skaggs produced an important monograph concerning the borderland of the Carolinas Blue

---

[34] On "Adonis," see WJBD, *OTP*, 79–80, and *Greenwood Index-Journal*, summer issues, 1947; "On Capitol Hill," *Anderson Independent*, 25 January 1947, 1; Mundy and Hembree identified, Moore, *South Carolina Newspapers*, 132.

[35] Ruth Meacham to WJBD, 1 November 1948; retrospective, WJBD to Sarah Bailey, 24 February 1961, WJBD/SCPC; Drury, *Anna Hastings*, 59, 73, RBSC.

Ridge, which the prestigious UNC Press published in its James Sprunt series in *History and Political Science*. It remained an important document for decades, and was reprinted often. Rather than merely note local-color stories about the mountain borderlands in the fabled Blue Ridge (which was a major swath of territory in North Carolina but occupied only a part of four counties in South Carolina), Skaggs probed racial and ethnic questions with an eye to economic justice. Skaggs pushed his young student Millie Johnson along, urging her to use her social-sciences skills in journalism, and he also pushed her to leave his own Campbell College and go to his beloved UNC, which in those days accepted a few hundred female students at the junior and graduate level. Millie Johnson went to Skagg's alma mater and earned her degree in journalism with the support of her farming parents. Then, like many aspiring journalists, she went off to Washington, DC, in search of newspaper and magazine work, a decidedly man's world, but one that had residential cubbyholes for the most dedicated female journalists.

Proud of the North Carolina journalists of the day, Millie Johnson befriended and learned from men such as Jonathan Worth Daniels, David Brinkley, and Samuel Talmadge Ragan. They led her to meticulous and detailed reading of each day's *Congressional Record* and they led her to careful research in the handsome leather-bound volumes of the *Record* and sometimes even the ancient *Globe*. At the same time, she took pride in standing toe-to-toe with journalists and politicians in a man's world of swagger and cigars and booze and raucous language about football and boxing. For all that, Millie Johnson was not above using her good looks and Southern-belle wiles to gain a scoop or an insight in a day when politicians as different as Jack Kennedy and Strom Thurmond expected—and famously got—sexual favors at the most, and serious flirting at the least, in their interactions with the overwhelmingly young and overwhelmingly female congressional administrative assistants and student interns. She used what was fair in love with the Cold Warrior. Regardless of how much Allen Drury's newswomen characters are like Millie Johnson, this much is so: she designed to gain his love long before Dorn realized it. This transforming love and relationship was vital to Millie Johnson many months, if not two full years, before it was apparent at all to Congressman Dorn. For the nonce, he was fixated on winning the Senate primary, and this "pretty one in the press gallery" had significant—but not the only and not even the most important—things to tell him in his campaign.[36]

To understand how far Bryan Dorn was willing to go to gain Maybank's Senate seat, it is necessary to backtrack a bit and mark some racial events that had so remarkably changed the atmosphere in the always racially charged, but not always violently negrophobic, South Carolina. Bryan Dorn in 1946 was not alone among white Southerners who sincerely liked Congressman Brooks Hays's Baptist and liberal states-rights solution to a Jim Crow system that seemed to be increasingly out of touch with modern US society—but also out of touch with important biblical pronouncements by Jesus Christ, whose personal relationship in salvation was more important for each Baptist believer than any single aspect of doctrine. As noted, Brooks Hays in Arkansas had worked with various church and communal groups to permit voting, and indeed, Orval Faubus, while campaigning for governor, consciously appealed to the "Negro bloc" of voters so empowered in Little Rock (understanding that other black citizens in the Arkansas Delta and in the cotton fields south of the Arkansas River would *not* be permitted to vote). Furthermore, Hays had cooperated with church and communal groups to see that graduate and professional training in law and medicine were available at the University of Arkansas in Fayetteville, and in Little Rock for certain aspects of university law and medical training. So impressed were Strom Thurmond and Bryan Dorn and other folk who in 1946 were calling themselves progressive in education and moderate in race relations that a number of Deep South governors and congressmen met to consider how to use the University of Arkansas medical training as the integrated setting for South Carolina and Alabama black people. In such a regional center, black scholars would pay in-state tuition and be eligible for scholarship help provided by South Carolina and Alabama, the money paid to the University of Arkansas. All of these things seemed to spring naturally from a position that Bryan Dorn called "states' rights civil rights," and sometimes "real" Liberalism (meaning the kind espoused by Thomas Jefferson before he became president).[37]

---

[36] Retrospective: Millie Johnson to WJBD, 5 January 1949; WJBD to Paul Wooten, 28 August 1959, WJBD/SCPC; Drury, *Anna Hastings*, 59, 73; Brinkley, *David Brinkley, a Memoir*, 48–65; Skaggs, *North Carolina Border Disputes*.

[37] Bass and Thompson, "The Liberal Governor," *Ol' Strom*, 79–88; retrospective, Mays, "Regional School Policy Is Wrong, Shows Helplessness of Negroes," *Pittsburgh*

However, there was a scarifying event during February of 1946 in Batesburg in South Carolina's rural mid-country, where fall line gave onto sand hills. It set in motion a series of other events that killed off any Brooks Hays-inspired states' rights civil rights, at least for South Carolina, whether such a moot program might be called liberal or progressive. In the second week of February 1946, Sergeant Isaac Woodard, a Goldsboro, North Carolina, native who had served in the US Army in the Pacific during the Good War, was mustered out of service at Fort Gordon, the place where Corporal Dorn himself had been mustered out of active duty the preceding fall. Sergeant Woodard had earned decorations for his courage under fire in a quartermaster unit during the bloody island-hopping of the final years of World War II. Boarding a Greyhound bus in his dress uniform and with medals affixed, Woodard carried his official discharge papers. Woodard declined to sit in the Jim Crow section of passenger seats, and he argued with the bus driver about permission to leave the bus to use a nearby restroom that was for whites only.

The bus driver reluctantly let him sit where he chose and allowed him to leave the bus to use the "white" restroom. However, the driver did make a note to himself to report the activist who was causing trouble, and thus by definition, "disorderly." On the morning of 12 February, the Greyhound pulled into Batesburg (today's Batesburg-Leesville) for a brief stop, and the driver exited the bus to report Woodard's presence to the chief of police, Lynwood Lanier Shull. Chief Shull, with several deputies, promptly came onto the bus and apprehended Sergeant Woodard, demanding to see his discharge papers, and then dragging him off the Greyhound for questioning about conduct. From that point on, testimony is murky, but Shull and his deputies and possibly civilian volunteers then used billysticks to pummel Woodard, being careful to aim for his eyes with their blows. These blows may have caused a concussion, as Woodard suffered amnesia that persisted for several weeks thereafter. Officer Shull and his assistants then took the blinded and bloodied G.I. to a prison cell to await a hearing before a local judge. When it was time for court to be in session that day, the judge fined Woodard fifty dollars for disorderly conduct, and the veteran paid with some of his discharge pay. Woodard recalled very little of what happened in the next week, and Chief Shull never told much, but Woodard asked for a doctor, and one arrived after at least two more days. For an indeterminate num-

---

Courier, 1 January 1949, 14; Baker, *Brooks Hays*, 108–16; Hays, *A Southern Moderate Speaks*, 25–62.

ber of days, perhaps a full week, Woodard languished in a hospital in nearby Aiken; at last his frantic family members figured out where he was and arranged for him to be transferred for treatment to a proper veteran's facility in Spartanburg in the piedmont. Doctors there were unable to do anything about his vision in either eye, but satisfied themselves that his amnesia was cleared up, and dismissed him. Returning home, he visited the local NAACP, whose members tried to get South Carolina officials to take action—including the self-styled progressive Governor Thurmond, who spoke proudly of a decrease in racial violence under his regime. After an incredible period of seven months passed with no action at all, the executive secretary of the NAACP, Walter Francis White, made an appointment for 9 September 1946 to see President Truman about the matter.[38]

In the White House, Harry S. Truman learned of this outrage and lost his famously losable temper. Already, he had been pushing the armed services to enforce FDR's Executive Order 8802, which was said to integrate the army and navy, but whose implementation took more executive energy, even enthusiasm, than Roosevelt ever had for civil rights. Truman was adamant in his insistence that the Cold War could never be won in a "colored" world of Asia, Africa, and Latin America by an America that put its most abusive features of Jim Crow into the faces of those former colonials trying to decide whether the Russians or the Americans had the best path to economic independence, as well as political independence. That a decorated veteran, in uniform, with papers in hand and medals on chest, could survive what the Japanese hit him with only to lose his eyes and nearly lose his life in Governor Thurmond's South Carolina was more than President Truman intended to put up with. He had been "going slow" on civil rights to appease the South Carolina delegation, but now he decided to move with full speed on these issues, specifically by creating a Civil Rights Commission, complete with mission statement, measurable objectives, and federal enforcement powers vouchsafed by officers serving the attorney general. From those speeded-up plans came *To Secure These Ends*—a powerful statement drawing its title from the preamble and its conception of natural rights from the US

---

[38] Andrew Myers, "The Blinding of Isaac Woodard," 63–73; Michael R. Gardner, "Harry Truman and Civil Rights: Moral Courage and Political Risks," University of Virginia Television News Homepage, 2003, accessed 5 June 2012; Bass with Thompson, *Ol'Strom*, 86n; Kari Frederickson, "'The Slowest State' and 'Most Backward Community': Racial Violence in South Carolina and Federal Civil Rights Legislation, 1946–1948," *South Carolina Historical Magazine*, (April 1997), 184.

Constitution—and a Civil Rights Commission, whose first order of business was to try Officer Shull and others from Batesburg on behalf of citizen Woodard, who was blinded because he was a black man and thus had "standing" in such a case.

Truman might be moving quickly in his mind, but the case came to trial slowly, landing on 5 November 1946 in the Eastern District of South Carolina Federal Court presided over by distinguished sandlapper Julius Waties Waring, who made his residence in a historic home on a fashionable section of Meeting Street below Broad in Charleston. The federal attorneys were poorly prepared, and the case was badly argued. The careerist federal attorney interviewed only the bus driver, who told him that Woodard was indeed disorderly, and Chief Shull swore that he used his billystick only in self-defense after being attacked. Although Judge Waring was enraged by what had happened to the uniformed Woodard, he found no error in proceedings and brought down the gavel on the jury's "not guilty" verdict for Officer Shull. The case quickly moved into liberal consciousness, becoming subject of a dramatization by Orson Welles and several folk songs, most famously by Woody Guthrie.[39]

As for Judge Waring, he was not only powerfully moved, but vowed to take action in some way because the incident clearly demonstrated how unconcerned native white South Carolinians were about protecting civil rights at the local level, despite all the talk from Dorn and Thurmond about states' rights civil rights. Dorn responded to the episode by declaring that local officials had to maintain order, essentially denying that any abuse had occurred. The aspiring senator was already enraged with Judge Waring, partly because he was double dipped in Charleston heritage, but mostly because of a scandal involving the elderly judge's ruined marriage. Waring, whose maternal and paternal ancestors came to Charleston eight generations before him, had once led a charmed career, being a favorite of both Cotton Ed Smith and Burnet Maybank; indeed, Waring was credited with working some of the magic that elected Maybank in a close race for governor, and when the narrowly defeated Wyndham Manning filed a protest, it had been Waring who successfully defended Maybank and the voting processes in Charleston.

---

[39] Roper, "The Negro and the New Deal: Franklin Delano Roosevelt's Policies on Race," passim; *To Secure These Ends*, ed. Brownell; Yarbrough, *A Passion for Justice*; USA v. Lynwood Lanier Shull, Case #16605, Eastern District Court of South Carolina (Columbia), 1946, National Archives and Records Administration, Southern Region, Atlanta; Myers, "The Blinding of Isaac Woodard," 63–73.

However, Waring in 1945 had thrown over his long-suffering wife, Anne, and compelled her to get a ninety-day Florida divorce—a demand that she followed dutifully, accepting a generous monthly payment, a fair sum of money, and a guaranteed bequest for their daughter, Annie. It was all so that the sixty-four-year-old could marry the striking New York beauty Elizabeth Avery Mills Hoffman, with whom he had begun an affair after several bridge-playing sessions with Elizabeth's devoted husband, Hoffman, and the judge's devoted wife, Annie Waring. Waties Waring, never before especially liberal in his rulings on racial matters, became quite the committed reformist, inviting black people to dinner at his fashionable home and speaking publicly on behalf of ending Jim Crow. He credited this transformation to the fetching young Elizabeth Waring.[40]

Bryan Dorn marked this impassioned confession in his reading and stored it away in his memory in case an attack was needed against a liberal district judge who bid fair to interfere in South Carolinians' treatment of black people. In the meantime, the senatorial candidate had already determined that white South Carolinians wanted more than his votes against federal anti-lynching laws—they wanted red-meat rhetoric denying that any such out-of-court physical violence ever occurred in any case, along with red-meat rhetoric that no one, not the NAACP, not the federal government, not Northern church folk, not some "Negro bloc" of Northeastern voters, no one, was going to impose protection of African Americans against depredations by white citizens defending segregated buses, segregated toilets, segregated schools, segregated hospitals, segregated cemeteries, and any other aspect of Jim Crow. Preparing for the stump, he was ready to forget all about Brooks Hays and use states' rights to defend the most wretched abuses.[41]

Dorn, Thurmond, Olin Johnston, and other state politicians were percipient in realizing that Waties Waring would soon be involved in affairs more immediately threatening than federal protection of African American lives and property: the whole political side of Jim Crow, that is, its ability to keep black people from voting, was under siege in the courts by the NAACP. Olin Johnston, while governor in a second term from 1942 to 1945, had surprised people by declaring that the Democratic Party primary

---

[40] Yarbrough, *A Passion for Justice,* viii, 3, 31. Cf. WJBD, *OTP*, 96–99.

[41] WJBD, *OTP*, 96–99; Yarbrough, *A Passion for Justice*, 31, 36–41 Gardner, "Harry Truman and Civil Rights"; corr., WJBD and Thomas, esp. WJBD to Thomas, retrospective, 12 July 1950, WJBD/SCPC.

was off-limits to black Democrats because the party was a private club and could exclude anyone from its ranks that it chose to exclude. This ruling was challenged by George Elmore, a black man who sued party official John Clay Rice for denying him the right to vote in the primary of 1947. This case, *Elmore v. Rice*, was heard in Waring's Eastern District Court on 12 July 1947, too late to help Elmore himself but in timely fashion for the 1948 primary of such importance to Congressman Dorn and other candidates for Maybank's seat in the Senate. Waring ruled that a political party, particularly the dominant Democratic Party in South Carolina, was in no way a private club and could not exclude black people or anyone else who was otherwise qualified to vote. Party leaders responded on two levels.

At the rhetorical level, Governor Thurmond spoke ringingly about the state's "customs and traditions" and declared a willingness to "resist all efforts to invalidate the practices, the customs, and the institutions, which we in South Carolina cherish." Moreover, Governor Thurmond vowed to do anything, *anything*, to defend those Jim Crow customs and traditions against any trespassers, federal, NAACP, Urban League, Yankee church, liberal press or otherwise. For his part, Congressman Dorn declared that Judge Waring should be impeached, partly for getting divorced, partly for marrying a New Yorker, but mostly for suggesting that Isaac Woodard enjoyed the right to his eyeballs and life and for suggesting that the Democratic "party of the people" was not an exclusive private club. Thurmond began to send out communications on letterhead that showed he was commander of the State National Guard, and Dorn attempted to get the House of Representatives to consider impeachment proceedings. Thurmond and Dorn were eye-catching in these actions, but William Baskin, working on behalf of leaders in the party, was more practical-minded. He accepted the fact that black citizens could not be excluded from joining his party, but said that all potential and current members must sign an oath—an oath to support Jim Crow for toilets, schools, hospital wings, cemetery plots, seating on public transportation, everything except actually voting in elections.[42]

---

[42] WJBD, "Criticism of Judge Waties Waring," *Congressional Record*, 80th Cong. 2d sess. Appendix, 27 July 1948, A4654; exchange of telegrams, Thurmond and WJBD, 5 February 1948, WJBD/SCPC; Bass and Thompson, *Ol' Strom*, 111–12; example of letterhead from Clemson; Yarbrough, *A Passion for Justice*, vi–viii; George Elmore v. Clay Rice, Case #1702, Eastern District Court of South Carolina, EDSC, 12 July 1947, National Archives and Records Administration, Southern Region, Atlanta (NARA).

Whether Baskin dreamed this up all by himself or not, it seemed nothing less than genius to Bryan Dorn, Olin Johnston, Strom Thurmond, Alan Johnstone Jr., and other leading state Democrats. There were precedents for test oaths of various kinds for joining clubs, even political parties calling themselves clubs, and segregationists were optimistic about a favorable ruling for Baskin's ploy of the Jim Crow oath despite *Elmore v. Rice.* One who demurred was David Brown, black resident in Beaufort since the late nineteenth century. Brown knew family members who had voted in Beaufort, usually for the Republican Party, and he intended to vote in the primary for his Democratic Party. When Brown attempted to register to vote for the upcoming 1948 primary, he was denied when he declined to swear the oath of allegiance to Jim Crow. He then sued Baskin, chair of the party. Like Elmore, Brown was a member of the NAACP, and he, too, was supported by NAACP lawyers when the case was scheduled on Judge Waring's docket for a 16 July 1948 hearing. Waring ruled that no political party could extract such an oath from those attempting to vote in primaries sponsored by the party. His ruling, like his earlier ruling in *Elmore v. Rice*, surprised no one, certainly not Congressman Dorn, but it gave senatorial candidates the chance to show off rhetorical skills in the final moments before the actual voting. This time, the NAACP had succeeded in getting a ruling *before* the party primary was actually held. In some places, such as Dorn's Third District, local officials could use clever tricks, backed up by Ku Klux Klan demonstrations, to discourage a large turnout of black voters. But in Maybank's First District, heavily black and marked also by a concentration of educated African Americans, it was obvious that as many as 33,000 black individuals were registered. Throughout the state, some 50,000 black men and women were registered—in contrast to a mere 3,000 in 1940. The increase in registration, from 3,000 to 50,000, was the most spectacular increase in percentage—1,566.7 percent—then or ever again for any state. Soon, the senatorial candidate had proof that they fully intended to stand in line and vote.[43]

That was that. Black citizens were going to vote in the primary within two weeks. The negrophobic white vote could be marshaled to telling effect, especially by Bryan Dorn and by Alan Johnstone Jr., who fell over each other

[43] Brown v. Baskin, 78 F, Suppl. 933, EDSC, 20 July 1948, NARA; Grofman and Davidson, ed., *Controversies in Minority Voting*, 7–34; Yarbrough, *A Passion for Justice*, iii, 31–41; data on "neophyte" black voting, Walton et al., "Woodward's New Intellectual Stream," 171.

trying to make the more outrageous response to the popular calls to punish Judge Waring. Dorn dropped his Victorian politesse in his speeches before Congress, actually showing a personal disdain for Judge Waring that he never showed foes such as Congressman Marcantonio. Even so, Alan Johnstone Jr. scored points with voters by stating that Dorn was slow to do anything about Waring's assaults on the segregated sanctity of toilets and bus seats. As for Governor Thurmond, his biographer, the journalist Jack Bass, notes that he was careful never to use the word *nigger*, but that otherwise he used a harsh racist language that was "stunning" to otherwise sympathetic young senatorial aides who in 1988 listened to recordings of his 1948 speeches. Whatever else, Bass also reported that "the crowd loved it," considering that Thurmond was more truly "with them" than Dorn, Alan Johnstone Jr., Olin Johnston, or anyone else who spoke in anger about Waties Waring. Furthermore, Thurmond declared that he was through with the national Democratic Party and was creating a States' Rights Party—popularly called Dixiecrat then and later—whose standard he would carry along with Virginia's Henry Fielding in the coming November presidential race. Rather than seek Maybank's Senate seat, Cousin Thurmond was seeking nothing less than the presidency.[44]

That left Burnet Maybank, who had long ago figured out how to have it both ways. In that era before instantaneous and universal coverage by electronic devices, a candidate could get away with saying one thing in one locality and then saying something the opposite in another. Thus, in the upcountry districts and even in the Pee Dee Fourth District, Maybank spoke against the integrationist Judge Waring and his ruling, but he cooperated with black people in his native Charleston and specifically asked that they vote for him—and *against* the segregationists Dorn, Alan Johnstone Jr., Marcus Stone, and Neville Bennett.[45]

There were other complications, for once not racial, in this contest. In November of 1947, Burnet Maybank had lost his wife, Elizabeth de Rousset Myers, to heart attack. Dorn had been quick to send heartfelt condolences. As the July primary approached, he "called off the dogs," refusing to criticize his grieving opponent in this campaign. The decent manners cost him time and space in this crowded and cramped race. In addition, he was given some

---

[44] Bass with Thompson, *Ol' Strom*, 86–88, 99–107.

[45] WJBD, "Criticism of Judge Waties Waring, (27 July 1948)" A4654; Bass and Thompson, *Ol' Strom*, 111–12; Edgar, *South Carolina*, 517–20.

documents that suggested the sitting US senator had failed to help Greenwood constituents buy surplus military property at the Coronoca section of town to be used for public housing or other public purposes. There was even some further evidence that perhaps Maybank himself worked some magic to make a personal fortune in buying and reselling the condemned federal property for private rather than public purposes. Dorn buried the evidence and never addressed that subject at all. Instead, Dorn produced flyers emphasizing his early and loud resistance to Truman's civil rights proposals, his plans for a merged army and navy, his support of a seventy-group air force, and his close ties with politicians in neighboring Georgia, especially the unique controversialist Herman E. Talmadge (at the time briefly out of office thanks to a Georgia Supreme Court ruling that he was in office unconstitutionally). Maybank exchanged kindly written expressions of gratitude with Dorn, and the final weeks of the primary campaign featured the senator being magic and majestic and the congressman focusing on issues concerning Reds and Feds—but with no hint that his worthy opponent was guilty of association with Reds or Feds.[46]

The photograph below shows one of the scenes from events that benefited Burnet Maybank and enraged his opponents, none more so than Bryan Dorn. Despite his opposition to voting by black citizens, Dorn resolutely declined chances to join the polite businessman's White Citizens Council, and he emphatically declined membership in the Ku Klux Klan, once even leaving an advertised country fish fry that was revealed to be a gathering of undraped Klansmen. Even so, Dorn benefited from the Klan and the Citizens Council since black people were hampered and often completely prevented from voting in districts two, three, four, and five. However, such machinations simply could not keep some 33,000 African Americans from voting in Charleston's downtown wards, and even in some more removed and rural wards of the heavily black First District.[47]

When votes were counted, Maybank had won 161,608 votes. His total was more than fifty percent of all votes, more than the combined votes for

---

[46] Corr., Maybank and WJBD, esp. Maybank to WJBD, 28 June 1948; flyer, re: GA, "Two Great Southerners," June 1948; flyer, Reds and Feds, "William Jennings Bryan Dorn, Candidate for US Senate, June 1948; Coronaca, Sam T. Reid to WJBD, 12 November 1947, enclosure, Maybank to J. M. Marshall, 14 December 1946; WJBD to Gary G. Pridgen, 6 April 1948; corr., H. E. Talmadge, esp., WJBD to Talmadge, 1 March 1948, WJBD/SCPC.

[47] Interview: Watson Dorn and Steve Griffith Jr. with Roper (28 February 2012), JHR/SCPC.

Bryan Dorn, Alan Johnstone Jr., Marcus Stone, and Neville Bennett. Dorn came in an admirable second, with 76,749 votes, the lead in five counties, and the majority in Edgefield and Greenwood counties. To the failed contender, the arithmetic was obvious. Subtract those 33,000 black votes, some of those very men depicted in the picture, and Maybank would have only 135,608 votes, less than fifty percent. Maybank's black vote, vouched safe by Judge Waring, gave the Charlestonian a majority and not a mere plurality. Dorn, "with no Negroes voting," would have finished second—135,608 to 76,749—but with enough votes to compel a two-candidate runoff against Maybank. Surely, Dorn reasoned of that hypothetical runoff, he could count on supporters of his opponents, giving him a victory, 142,410 to 135,608, over the detested Charlestonian. Thinking still farther ahead, beyond the arithmetic, and assuming a huge turnout with every single one of Johnstone's, Stone's, and Bennett's supporters coming to the polls and voting for him, Dorn concluded that he could have won that runoff, the one without black votes. Judge Waring, then, had "cost" Dorn his chance to become US senator, despite other talk elsewhere about his having been in a hurry and not understanding how to organize such a campaign. Others to blame were the black people such as Elizabeth Waring, NAACP plaintiff attorney Matthew Perry, as well as less specifically denominated Communists, outsiders, and troublemakers.[48]

Not only was Dorn infuriated with Judge Waring and his progressive young wife from New York and their supporters in the "Communist front" NAACP, but he also was infuriated with Burnet Maybank, the Charleston native who could drink and swap racist jokes with gusto around the white folk but the man who got African Americans to come and vote for him in huge numbers. Among other things, Dorn had a letter signed by James Myles Hinton, African American, who wrote on behalf of the Negro Citizens Committee of South Carolina, an arm of the NAACP (which also included Dorn's good friend, the white man John Bolt Culbertson, whom he never blamed for this or other pain brought by such "agitation"). Hinton, backed up by a baker's dozen of signatory district chairmen, claimed to represent tens of thousands of the state's black people. In the letter, he had assured Dorn that blacks will be voting and would do so knowing full well about his efforts to impeach J. Waties Waring, a man described in the Negro Committee manifest as a judge "who needs no defense from any person or racial group, for he stands upon the dignity of his Judgeship and manly char-

[48] Jordan, *The Primary state*, 78–79; WJBD, *OTP*, 87–90.

acter." And now these people had made good their threat. It reminded him of Maybank's 1942 defeat of Eugene S. Blease, who was onetime chief justice of the state Supreme Court, longtime law partner to cousin Judge Steve Griffith, and half-brother of distant relative and all-time Dorn and Griffith family hero Cole Blease. In that race, Maybank had drawn some up-country votes and Blease had drawn some low-country votes, but "magically" all 10,000 votes in Charleston had gone to Maybank, wiping out the judge's 5,000-vote lead once those Charleston wards were counted. Dorn was convinced that Maybank must have cheated to get all those Charlestonians to vote for him over Eugene S. Blease. And he always heard and used the "magic" term with the bitterest of irony in describing Maybank superhumanly effective City operatives. Whether the primary was all white, as in 1942, or integrated, as in 1948, the man with the "magic" always won.[49]

Dorn looked at Hinton's letter and showed it to others. The petition said plainly, "Negroes will vote in South Carolina, regardless of what you say and think." Nor would any of that race vote for him now that "the issues before the American Public are so clearly shown" after his congressional speeches lambasting Waring. These same black petitioners concluded, "Negroes PROTEST YOUR REMARKS AS UN-AMERICAN" (Hinton's capitalization). In that, and most other eras, Dorn took it as a fact that *he* was the expert on who was American and who was un-American—and no less an authority than J. Edgar Hoover had assured him that the NAACP was filled with Communists, fellow-travelers, and those "duped" by Communists. For all that, a number of petitioners were known to Dorn, especially the Rev. E. E. Gaulden, pastor of the Bethlehem Baptist Church in Newberry. The Rev. Gaulden was a particularly articulate man, and he had written a good history of the black congregation and its handsome church building, tracing the church's origin to 1868; in time, the building was placed on the National Historical Register. Yet here was this prominent Baptist African American—about as un-Communist as a believing Baptist could get—signing the Negro Committee of South Carolina's petition. Rhetoric aside, Congressman Dorn knew perfectly well that non-Communists were signing the petition; he probably suspected the truth, namely, that *none* of the black Baptist ministers were Communists.[50]

---

[49] Jordan, *The Primary State*, 76–77; WJBD *OTP*, 89.

[50] Negro Committee of South Carolina to WJBD, 22 June 1948; Hoover to WJBD, esp. 15 November 1947, WJBD/SCPC; *OTP* on Blease, 89; Key with Heard, "South Carolina: The Politics of Color," *Southern Politics*, ch.7.

Angry as he was about black support for Senator Maybank, the lame-duck congressman and failed senatorial candidate was still child of Nana and Dada. It is a mark of the sheer power of his childhood rearing that Dorn kept his public composure, congratulating Maybank in gentlemanly fashion and promising to help him and cooperate with him in all ways. In fact, Dada was not long for the South Carolina world, and he would die on 5 October 1948. His son was certainly true to Dada's memory, because Bryan Dorn convinced Maybank that he accepted the primary results as legitimate. The senator wrote that he was "deeply appreciative of your congratulations because I know your sincerity." Moreover, some five years later, Maybank's son would note in a letter to Dorn that the senator always regarded Dorn as a gentleman who was truly his friend, something hard to glean from private correspondence but easy to understand if one watched the gentleman of Myrtle Manor in his public behavior. Perhaps unrelated, Dorn became deathly ill during these events and entered himself into the Walter Reed Hospital for a thorough checkup to ensure that his "Adonis body" did not mask a heart or lung problem like Dada's. It was likely stress resulting from sheer physical exertion and money problems, although nothing is actually known from the correspondence or family memories. Among other things, Dorn realized he could never find the money to repay Judge and Bertie Griffith for the money they extended, to say nothing of expenses newly married brother Watson Dorn had incurred as campaign manager trusting that he would be reimbursed. Too, the congressman was dismayed to have his Chevrolet stolen from him on the campaign trail, a crime even the vaunted and terrifying J. Edgar Hoover could not solve, despite some personal exertions by *the* G-man of the FBI.[51]

Withal it was a thorough defeat. Black citizens had not *hypothetically* voted. As shown in the photograph, they *actually* voted—and in numbers large enough to give Burnet Maybank a majority in a field of five on the first voting. It was not particularly "magical" that 33,000 black people who had been loudly told that they should not vote by Dorn, Alan Johnstone Jr., Bennett, and Stone subsequently declined to vote for Dorn, Johnstone, Ben-

---

[51] Maybank to WJBD, 12 August 1948 telegram; retrospective, Burnet Rhett Maybank Jr. to WJBD, n.d. (August 1948?); WJBD health, Grace Dorn to WJBD, 15 July 1947, and Watson Dorn to WJBD (n.d.), "Tuesday night" (July 1947); TED and WJBD, esp. WJBD to TED, 18 November 1948, and TED to WJBD, 15 November 1948, WJBD/SCPC; Certificate of Death #013198 Thomas Elbert Dorn, 5 October 1948, SCDAH, Columbia.

nett, or Stone. As Vann Woodward noted memorably, "neophyte Negro voters" behaved with rational self-interest, no matter how short a period of time they had been able to vote. Such statewide offices from 1948 onward were going to involve African American voters, especially in the big cities.[52]

In any case, Dorn had problems beyond black voting in this campaign. He had borrowed money from a Greenwood bank, apparently some $1,500, and that debt (more than $15,000 today) was less metaphorical than what he owed Judge Griffith and Watson Dorn. The latter two, of course, would forgive his debt; but the former demanded payment when due. Finding the money to pay posed a problem for a lame duck whose only jobs had been cotton farmer, soldier, and politician. Not only was he not returning to the House of Representatives in the third week of January 1949, but, turn about being fair play, the Hare family had installed James Butler Hare as the Democrats' unopposed nominee for Congress in the November elections. James Hare often stated that he had only run because his worthy predecessor Bryan Dorn (worthy successor to his own father, Butler Black Hare) had chosen not to stand for election to the Third District House seat in 1948. Whatever was wrong with his heart or his lungs cleared up quickly, but a hole had opened in his soul. Balm for his pain came from the Baptists back home, especially Ada Griffith Cromley from Nana's people, who sent a verse from the hymn "A Charge to Keep I Have":

> A charge to keep I have
> A God to glorify
> A never dying soul to save
> And fit it for the sky
> To serve the present age
> My calling to fulfill
> Oh! may it all my powers engage
> To do my Master's will.[53]

---

[52] Jordan, *The Primary State*, 76–79; Woodward, *Burden of Southern History* (3d rev. ed.; 2008), 100; Walton et al., "Woodward's New Intellectual Stream," 153–88.

[53] Friedman Inflation Calculator; James Butler Hare to WJBD, 14 November 1949 and 7 January 1949, WJBD/SCPC; James Butler Hare Papers, 1948–1951, SCPC; Charles Wesley, "A Charge to Keep I Have," (Leviticus 8:35), *Short Hymns on Select Passages of Holy Scripture* (1762); Ada Griffith Cromley to WJBD, 15 August 1947, WJBD/SCPC.

There remained the presidential campaign, and Dorn owed personal favors to his cousin, Strom Thurmond. Too, he was genuinely angry with Harry S. Truman, although he was characteristically careful not to make it public how angry he was. Olin Johnston said he was for Truman *the man* but not for *his platform*. Dorn would not make that claim. However, he did not break completely with the national party. He campaigned vigorously for Thurmond and Fielding on what he always called the States' Rights Democrat, and not the Dixiecrat, ticket. At the same time, he made inquiries with the National Democratic Committee to see if the party could use him in some capacity, receiving important help in that inquiry from Sam Rayburn and Olin Johnston. And he negotiated, quite unsuccessfully, with several agents to see about professional speaking. He let it be known that he was available for work of almost any sort, and several friends rushed forward to suggest opportunities.[54]

G. Marshall Moore of Greenville proposed establishing a corporation that would buy up FHA loans to veterans and then resell the loans, and he wanted the former congressman as the president and figurehead. A more amorphous opportunity was with the state Grange, which was trying to set up Dorn as a full-time representative as well as part-time speaker. Fairly straightforward was the offer from Columbia's Carroll H. Jones to be a super-salesman of life insurance for Jones's Fidelity Mutual Life Insurance Company. For the good reasons that he was quite uninterested in these opportunities and quite unqualified to perform such tasks, Dorn graciously declined. In fact, in this period, he spent a large amount of his time writing personal letters to some thirty supporters thanking them for helping him in the failed campaign—and leaving the door open for a return in the near future.[55]

Because people genuinely admired his speeches, Dorn decided to write a book. He met Lambert Davis, lately editor of the *Virginia Quarterly Review* and the new director of the University of North Carolina Press. Davis was succeeding the wildly successful William Terry Couch, who had made the UNC Press a significant regional—and reformist—publisher of books supportive of the National Association for the Advancement of Colored

[54] Corr., November 1948, esp. WJBD to Grits Gresham (template for thirty political supporters), 5 November 1948, WJBD/SCPC.

[55] G. Marshall Moore to WJBD, 16 November 1948; Carroll H. Jones to WJBD, 15 September 1948; C.P. Key to Brother Dorn, 28 February 1949; WJBD to Grits Gresham (template for 30 political supporters), 5 November 1948, WJBD/SCPC.

People (NAACP) and other progressive causes. Without losing the regional focus, Davis wanted to "balance out" the press's list by offering some monographs with a "different point of view." Dorn proposed a book that critiqued the civil rights movement with its activism and power centered on federal activity and proposed in its stead states' rights civil rights, that is, "grassroots" reformism and progressivism voluntarily entered into one community at a time. His presentation was engaging, and Davis urged him to produce some 50,000 words and send it forward. Dorn was encouraged and began writing. Still, even as he made palaver with friends and associates about these and other projects and possibilities of work, he was unfocused and distracted. Older brother Tom, always tempted to scold in any case, was quite beside himself in lecturing about irresponsibility and lack of planning. Gracie, who could be something of a scold herself, spoke more in sorrow than anger about his lack of training to do anything other than serve in politics. Mother Pearl was by turns his Baby and his Nana, and sometimes both. Bryan knew he could return to farming. In fact, he was well aware that Myrtle Manor was in some decline because the recently deceased Dada had been unable to get out and supervise renters and managers of both races, none of whom seemed especially dedicated to scientific farming, as noted dyspeptically by neighbors, friends, and distant relations.[56]

It was the presidential campaign, especially the chance to speak and interact with people in Virginia, that gave Dorn most heart. Already friends with newly elected Commonwealth governor Lindsay Almond, he met and made friends with US Senators Carter Glass and Harry Flood Byrd and Congressman "Judge" Howard Worth Smith. When speaking for Thurmond, especially in the valley of the Shenandoah, Dorn always noted the geography and the history and the Civil War battles. With Harry Byrd's help, he gathered information about battles from local historians and newspapermen, and he listened eagerly to the many Civil War buffs, who told the most moving of war stories. In his memoirs, he describes himself winning over hostile crowds by talking about the Confederacy. No one in the valley remembers much support for Truman in 1948, and valley crowds were seldom hostile in any case. The first part of the memory seems flawed, even disingenuous. But the second part of the memory, that he won the crowds

---

[56] Interview: William Terry Couch (10–11 January 1980), JHR/SHC; Tom Dorn to WJBD, 15 November 1948, and WJBD to Tom Dorn, 18 November 1948; James B. Hare to WJBD, 14 November 1949; Lambert Davis to WJBD, retrospective, 16 January 1951, and WJBD to Davis, 20 January 1951, WJBD/SCPC.

over to him with the states' rights message based on Robert Edward Lee, Thomas Jonathan Jackson, and Thomas Jefferson, seems entirely plausible. He was, after all, a great orator, and the citizenry came to the events already in love with Stonewall Jackson, "Marse Bobby" Lee, and *the* Jefferson. Newspaper accounts describe crowds as entranced and enthusiastic. Voting records show that the valley went for Eisenhower, as did the entire Commonwealth, increasingly a Democratic state only in the local politics, where the Byrd Machine ruled. Otherwise, Virginia was Republican at the presidential level, and the party he loved was in power only in the local offices of the Commonwealth he loved.[57]

Bryan Dorn performed a real balancing act, and his distinction between States' Rights Democrat and Dixiecrat may seem strained today. However, in 1948 and 1949, it was likely a distinction with a difference. As South Carolina Democratic insider and analyst Frank E. Jordan put it, "Thurmond had been the leader of the group that believed in opposing the national party from the outside." Dorn never joined Thurmond's "outside" group but instead tried to function as deeply inside the national Democratic Party as a States' Rights Democrat could, following a model established by Edgar A. Brown and, to some extent, Cotton Ed Smith and before them Benjamin Ryan "Pitchfork" Tillman himself. In South Carolina, states' rights folk now made no bones about their opposition to *any* sort of civil rights—even the right to life and limb itself (as had been shown in the Woodard blinding in Batesburg and also in the 1947 Willie Earl lynching in Greenville). Dorn followed suit in South Carolina states' rights fashion with a cool disregard for the reality of the bloody lynchings and maimings. Brooks Hays was still Dorn's friend and still appealing, but the Baptist Arkansan was no South Carolinian. In the Palmetto State there was to be no states' rights civil rights but only states' rights. There was also no question that the state Democratic Party was largely given over to states' rights, with the notable exceptions of Senators Olin Johnston and Burnet Maybank. Mayo, South Carolina's Richter Herman Moore, then a student at the University of South Carolina, organized the school's Democratic Party around states' rights without civil rights, but he made it very clear the States' Rights Democrats were not Dixiecrats. Moore was himself engaged to Caroline Dabbs, daughter of James McBride Dabbs, the most influential liberal reformist in South Carolina,

---

[57] WJBD, *OTP*, 107–108; correspondence, Byrd, Glass, Almond, Judge Smith, November 1948, WJBD/SCPC; Tindall, *Disruption of the Solid South*, 40–42. 52.

and Moore was a great admirer of his future father-in-law. Correspondence between lame-duck congressman and student politicos makes it very clear that they were trying to build a locally oriented, anti-civil rights Democratic Party that was independent of the Dixiecrats—*and especially* independent of governor and presidential hopeful Strom Thurmond.[58]

There survive other pieces of evidence that his States' Right Democrat identity was accepted as valid in its day. President Truman kept his cool, and he and Dorn cooperated on various projects, much as if each considered himself still part of the same team. Even a lame duck was needed vote by vote on the complexities of the foreign-policy agenda, and Dorn was a dependable man in the goal of containment. Too, his compassion for the common grunt and gob was matched by the president, who had guided artillery in the field in World War I but had lost his soldier's savings in devalued bonds—and had seen desk officers bully the men doing the real fighting. Truman's wage- and price-control administrators might be doing something that Dorn rejected in the abstract, but he worked with them concerning the folk affected back in the red hills. As the State Department and FBI people could always attest, Congressman Dorn was personally polite, genuinely considerate, listened intently, and worked tirelessly for the team's declared ends. For instance, Joe Muliere of the Orangeburg Chamber of Commerce needed to talk with President Truman about an economic issue of great importance for his postage stamp of territory, and Dorn facilitated a personal and face-to-face meeting in which Muliere got what his townsmen wanted and Truman was assured of support in certain policies (obviously not having to do with civil rights). It seems most likely that Dorn regarded all presidents as deserving of respect and at least a hearing for their programs just because of the office that they held, and this concept was deepest in the grain for those chief executives who were Democrats. Long years later, when Americans began a fond reconsideration of Truman's years and the once-hated man became in golden memory a beloved figure, Dorn could truthfully say that he had always dealt honorably and affectionately with the man from Missouri. In such raconteuring, he could engage in some exaggeration

---

[58] Purdy to WJBD, 24 January 1948; WJBD to G. P. Callison, (n.d. February?) 1948; WJBD to Billy McGarrity, 11 February 1948; 1948 retrospective on civil rights and states rights, WJBD to John Temple Graves, 9 December 1949, WJBD/SCPC; Myers, "The Blinding of Isaac Woodard," 63–73; "Radio Station Officers," *Gamecock*, 1 October 1947, clipping; "Warren and Williams to Debate Here," *Gamecock*, 26 October 1948, clipping; L. Mell Glen to Richter H. Moore Jr., 29 October 1948 (loan to USC States Rights Democrat Club), Richter Herman Moore Jr. Papers, SCPC.

about how they agreed on broad policies, but he was absolutely straightforward in describing his personal attitude and behavior toward Truman—or any other figure who served as president.[59]

The autumn foliage in 1948 was beautiful in DC and in South Carolina's red hills, and especially so in the valley of the Shenandoah, where the outgoing congressman visited battlefields and spoke for Thurmond before appreciative crowds. For all that, it was a sad, even funereal season. In October, he returned home and buried Dada in the family's ancient Beulah cemetery. He continued, fuzzily, even aimlessly, to look for employment opportunities, and he tried to make his final speeches before Congress memorable for their historical research, eloquence, and reason. Also, he wrote notes to congressmen, especially Virginians and Georgians, expressing his pleasure in serving with them. And despite protestations about "giving up on politics," he also wrote in his own hand long and detailed notes to those who had voted for him and campaigned with him, working with brother Watson Dorn to keep careful records county by county on elected officials, party regulars, and others and how they had voted in recent months. In other words, he continued to behave much like a politician with plans for seeking office again. Otherwise, he tried hard to be an effective congressman, at this very late date (too late for election but just in time for anxious constituent neighbors) paying attention to the issues of postal routes and postal clerks and other details about the rural mail services so long supported by guides and mentors Tom Watson, Jim Farley, and the Blease family.[60]

---

[59] WJBD (Ruth Meacham) to Andy Griffith, 12 March 1948; WJBD to Griffith, 4 May 1948; Watson Dorn to WJBD, 17 March 1947; WJBD to Charlie Donahue, 18 December 1947; WJBD to Eleanor Roosevelt, 29 September 1947; WJBD to George Marshall, 29 September 1947; WJBD to Warren Austin, 29 September 1947; Austin to WJBD, 2 October 1947; Eleanor Roosevelt to WJBD, 8 October 1947; Marshall to WJBD, 6 October 1947; corr., John Peurifoy and WJBD, November and December 1947, and Peurifoy to WJBD, retrospective, 25 June 1951, WJBD/SCPC. 1947 WJBD, "Remarks," *Cong. Rec.*, vol. 93, pt. 1, 80th Cong., 1st Sess., 11 December 1947, 1306–307; WJBD, *OTP*, 68–77 and picture insert; and "In His Words (Truman)," SCPC.

[60] Marshall (surname missing) to WJBD with clipping re: Winchester, VA, 17 November 1948; Glass to WJBD, 12 November 1948; job offers, George Marshall Moore to WJBD, 16 November 1948, and Thomas Corcoran Jr. to WJBD, 6 January 1947; John C. Taylor to WJBD (fall "Sunday night") 1948; postal routes, corr., L. S. Griffith, Pee Wee Ellison, W. A. Gailey, 1948; Kenneth Crouch to WJBD, with clippings, *Bedford Democrat*, 28 October 1948, WJBD/SCPC.

Dorn also disappeared from time to time, especially when the House was out of session, and at least once even briefly when it was actually *in session*. Staff members and congressmen, especially Congressman-elect James Butler Hare, expressed their sympathy for him, but Jim Hare also declared bemusement that it was hard to find him and hard to get responses from him. Millie Johnson of *US News & World Report* often came by, as if to interview or to check facts on a quote, and staffers suggested to the lame-duck congressman that "the pretty one" might have set her hat for him. Millie Johnson also wrote *to* him, noting that virulent anti-Communist senator Joe McCarthy was spending a long weekend with her at her father's farm in Coats. She gave the South Carolinian details about what Southern foods the Wisconsinite liked and disliked and also noted for him that "Tail Gunner Joe" was a onetime boxer who, like Bryan Dorn, believed in an aggressive offensive strategy, sometimes even eschewing normal defensive tactics in seeking to land the "K.O." Even more provocatively, Millie Johnson wrote Dorn on election eve from a DC party for the Republican winners—for whom Joe McCarthy was recognized (at least in that gathering) as guru—and excitedly told him that Senator McCarthy wanted to help him in an election campaign for Congress or the Senate. Millie then handed the letter to the senator, and he scrawled a brief note of his own to the congressman, and the journalist packed up the liquor-stained document and sent it as a missive to the Myrtle Manor address.[61]

In terms of what Millie Johnson really knew about the infamous Tail Gunner Joe, it seems likely she knew exactly what another North Carolinian named Mary Brinkley Driscoll knew in that day. Mary Brinkley Driscoll, sister of journalist David Brinkley, was a skilled legal recorder who worked in Senator McCarthy's office. She reported that the Wisconsin veteran had returned from the war with one overwhelming goal, to "promote decent housing for veterans after the war." Another anti-Communist journalist known to all these people, and especially Mary Driscoll and Millie Johnson, noted that Senator McCarthy was primarily devoted to the real estate interests and their lobbyists. Mary Driscoll worked for this senator because it was her job, and while working for him, kept mum, even and especially around her brother David, the journalist. By contrast, Millie Johnson seemed to be

---

[61] James Butler Hare to WJBD, 14 November 1949; retrospective, WJBD to Sarah Bailey, 24 February 1961; Millie Johnson to WJBD, n.d. "Sunday night" (before 10 October) 1948; Millie Johnson to WJBD with McCarthy note, n.d. (November 1948); Millie Johnson to WJBD, retrospective, 5 January 1949, WJBD/SCPC.

"playing" him for information for her bosses at *US News& World Report* and also seemed to be playing him against the true object of her affections, the onetime congressman from South Carolina. As noted, she and Allen Drury had written a book about the female journalist Anna Hastings, a composite of several real people—and this Hastings had "played" the object of her affections in much the same way in order to marry the fellow she had chosen.[62]

If Millie Johnson were "playing" Bryan Dorn in this way, it worked. The mysteriously absent lame duck hurried back to DC and shared with Millie some serious reservations about Joe McCarthy's drinking, boxing strategies, and general behavior around politicians. He began to insist on more of her time without intrusion from the Tail Gunner or any other eligible bachelor. Without much fanfare and with little notice even to intimates, Bryan Dorn and Millie Johnson married, apparently in January 1949 at the end of Dorn's term, disengaging "the pretty one" from David Lawrence's magazine and from the Senate Press Gallery, though she would remain friends with unnamed female journalists and with UPI's Allen Drury, novelist and memoirist.[63]

When the 81st Congress convened and the 80th was thus completely over and done with, the newlyweds traveled to Coats to stay with her folks on the Johnson farm. Then they traveled to Myrtle Manor to stay with Nana, and then they disappeared. Apparently the couple headed "out West," where Dorn occasionally "hired out" for day work on farms, much as Air Cadet Dorn had done in the past. The couple also showed up all over the Palmetto and Old North states for brief periods, again with Bryan Dorn hiring out for day labor on farms. Millie Dorn became pregnant quickly, and the Dorns, Griffiths, Johnsons, and family were two parts joyous and five parts anxious about "what in the hell Bryan was doing"—or what he was going to do. Judge Griffith not surprisingly forgave the "loan," sending his cousin's check back in the mail and telling him to get back into politics, preferably as candidate for Third District congressman in 1950. Brother Watson, with a family of his own now and a law practice in Greenwood, forgave whatever money—probably $1,000—he was owed as campaign manager for the abortive senatorial race. The Rev. James Bowers, maturing

---

[62] Brinkley, *David Brinkley*, 112–14; retrospective, WJBD to Sarah Bailey, 24 February 1961, WJBD/SCPC; Drury (with Johnson), *Anna Hastings*.

[63] Corr., Millie Johnson, 1948–1949, especially Millie Johnson to WJBD, n.d., (November) 1949, WJBD/SCPC; WJBD, *OTP*, 109; interview: Steve Griffith with Watson Dorn and Roper (28 February 2012), JHR/SCPC.

as the patriarch of the First Baptist Church, counseled the newlyweds about political opportunities and churchly duties. Nana and her brother-in-law Russ Carter urged reentry into politics. Sibling army officer Thomas Dorn thundered from the Pacific that a family man ought to show some responsibility and some common sense—and ought to be quick about it. Even President Bob Poole of Clemson, who had canceled campus appearances for Dorn when the congressman began to campaign for States' Rights Democrats instead of Truman Democrats, encouraged his onetime and future mainline Democratic ally to get back into things political.[64]

For her part, Millie Johnson Dorn declared that she loved her man even more than before, but that he was demonstrably incompetent at anything other than politics. She wanted him back in, and back in at once, with herself as campaign manager and family members ready to do their parts—ever-faithful Judge Griffith willing to extend money one more time without much hope of repayment and even willing to lend out his son, Clemson College student Steve, as the promising scholar prepared himself for law school at the University of South Carolina. Bryan Dorn appeared unenthusiastic, and largely feckless, about nonpolitical jobs. Helping out rather desultorily around Myrtle Manor, tending his baby daughter, Brianna, and teaching Sunday school for the Rev. Bowers, he surprised only one person when he filed for candidacy in late winter 1950 for the congressional seat occupied by James Butler Hare.[65]

The surprised person, genuinely so in his correspondence, was Congressman Hare. If Bryan Dorn wanted to take the Third District seat from still another Hare, there would be a bitter fight over it. Above all, scholarly patriarch Butler Black Hare and dignified son and naval veteran James Butler Hare would remind everyone that William Jennings Bryan Dorn had been largely useless in constituent service and indeed had "barely warmed his seat" in the House office building during the 80th Congressional Session before *stepping out* for the Senate—and falling down. An oddly appropriate parallel in political career was with cousin Strom Thurmond, lame-duck governor and defeated Dixiecrat presidential candidate. Both red-hills men,

---

[64] Interview, Steve Griffith with Hartsook and Roper, 2 February 2012, JHR/SCPC; James Butler Hare to WJBD, 14 November 1949; job discussion, C. P. Key to WJBD, 28 February 1949; corr., the Rev. Bowers, Pearl Dorn, Russ Carter, and Thomas E. Dorn, esp. 18 November 1948, WJBD/SCPC; "Religion Must Be Appreciated Positively," (the Rev. James A. Bowers) *Anderson Independent,* 6 February 1949.

[65] Interview: Watson Dorn and Steve Griffith, with Roper (28 February 2012), JHR/SCPC; and WJBD, *OTP*, 111–13; Roper, "The Art of Political Biography."

once featured in magazines and newspapers, were now out of office, and neither had prospects for a private or government job. But neither Dorn nor Thurmond had by any means abandoned political ambitions despite their current status as rejected candidates.[66]

If Weber were right, then Bryan Dorn needed to accept the defeat, look for reasons rather than excuses, and find a strategy for the next campaign—one in which ethnic prejudice and other inflamed passions would likely play no small role. Avoiding racial prejudice in a campaign and offering real substance for voters were also preached him at the ethical level by the Rev. Bowers, his Sunday school classmates both in Greenwood and at Calvary Baptist, and the departed Dada and the still vibrant Nana—and were in his deepest held values.[67]

And so Bryan Dorn had been confirmed in the common wisdom that he was too young, too little known, and from too rural and obscure a place to win the US Senate. He also had been confirmed in the no-less-common wisdom that race-baiting was hardly passé. In fact, it was no less strong, in the day of Strom Thurmond Dixiecrats and Fair Deal Democrat Olin Johnston than in the days of Ben Tillman in the early 1900s, Cole Blease in the 1920s, or Cotton Ed Smith in the 1930s. To survive in politics, he must find his way, perhaps by tailoring racial messages to the color of the audiences and sidestepping principle as "magically" as Burnet Maybank. Perhaps he would bait the races as loudly and as adroitly as Olin Johnston—but let mainline political allies in DC know that it was all an act for local consumption and not a belief. What he could not do was to pretend that racial passions would be absent in any statewide contests; indeed they would be "very present" in purely district contests. Brother Watson Dorn had warned him thusly early in the Lost Cause of the senatorial campaign. After all, Tillman, Blease, Johnston, and Thurmond were each from the same red hills, and each had connections, familial, legal, and otherwise, in the Third District. Even to recapture the limited prize of the Third District congressional seat, Bryan Dorn must master the complexities of racial politics. When he spoke,

---

[66] Corr., 1948–1950, James Butler Hare Papers, SCPC; Bass with Thompson, *Ol' Strom*, 119–33.

[67] Weber, "Politics as a Vocation," 128; Baker, *Brooks Hays*, 108–16; Hays, *A Southern Moderate Speaks*, 25–62; on racial attitudes, see corr., 1946–1947, especially the way he deflects his correspondents' negrophobia; i.e., Watson Dorn to WJBD, 9 January 1948 and 24 June 1947; WJBD, *OTP*, 78–80.

he would still look beyond the white crowd into the eyes of the "hash man," the ubiquitous black man who would meet his gaze even as the white constituents had their backs to his stew pot and to him and his race. Church and family teaching would not let him attack black people, and he continued to believe with Brooks Hays (also out of elected political office) that racial justice must come, but come much more slowly than any black person would reasonably want.

Perhaps anti-Communism—both its perfectly legitimate expression in a Cold War that could become hot and its exaggerated and theatrical uses in contests that had little to do with international or military affairs—perhaps anti-Communism could be wielded as the pyrotechnic weapon in place of race and racism. And perhaps the passions of anti-Communism could be deployed in support of genuine economic reform, much as Harry Truman occasionally seemed to be doing. On the other hand, Joe McCarthy had demonstrated that there were limits to riding anti-Communism, and to a large degree, Bryan Dorn himself had demonstrated the limits. His people hated Communism, but they were desperate for the constituent services of Truman's Fair Deal. Even if Republicans took the White House in 1952, there must still be constituent service, of the kind performed by Mendel Rivers, Johnny Mac McMillan, Dick Richards—and James Butler Hare.

A congressman had to listen to his people, talk directly to them, and serve them. It was, finally, not Bryan Dorn's seat nor James Butler Hare's nor Butler Black Hare's: it was the people's congressional seat. Max Weber had also said, "Only he has the calling for politics who is sure that he shall not crumble when the world from his point of view is too stupid or too base for what he wants to offer."[69] So much could be said for Bryan Dorn. He had to promise to provide genuine constituent service if permitted back into the US House. And whatever he did or said about Reds and Feds would have to be secondary to a tight focus on the everyday needs of the people of his district. Whether they were farmers, like the Dorns and Hares, or millworkers, each citizen in the red hills had been suffering since the Great Depression, and each had genuine needs that the candidate must not himself be "too stupid or too base...to offer." And so he made ready to reenter the race for the seat that belonged to the people of the mill villages, small towns, and small farms of South Carolina's Third District. Only this time, Millie Johnson Dorn intended to be the campaign manager.

---

[69] Weber, "Politics as a Vocation," 128.

Chapter 5

A Fair Deal for Textiles
1950–1952

With Dada dead and gone, Bryan Dorn had to face the fact that his political compass was gone as well. He could and did disagree with Dada, but the discussions had been vital to him since the disagreements were about means and not ends. Now those discussions were impossible. His Bible psalm told him that "my times are in thy hands," that is, God was in charge of larger things, and he had to "get right" with the changing times as the real Lord unfolded them.[1] Surely, the times had changed. He was certainly what he always had been, that is, a Populistic New Deal progressive with an internationalist concern and a hard-edged anti-Communist perspective focused on dangers from the USSR. Much of that was Harry S. Truman, but there were things about Truman, especially his allegiances to organized labor and his commitments to civil rights, that were beyond the pale for Third District voters. Dorn still agreed with Brooks Hays that civil rights for black people had to come—and were best served by local initiative emerging after a long period of time. But Hays was out of Congress, and Bryan Dorn wanted to be back in Congress.

For all that, his people, especially in the mill villages, needed much of the New Deal/Fair Deal "safety net" legislation (as he noted often, most of his constituents would never live to collect Social Security: the laboring South Carolina classes of both races died at age sixty)—and they certainly needed some of the protections from the federal government for working conditions. Much as he needed financial and other support from Jim Self and Brother Abney, Bryan Dorn was not part of the class of managerial bourgeoisie and not part of the emerging textile elite. He could serve them, and he did serve them. *He was in them but he was not of them*, in the biblical phrase.[2] Whether a kid practicing speeches in the shade of trees at the far edge of Jim Self's property or a politician accepting Brother Abney's spon-

---

[1] Psalm 31:15, KJV.
[2] John 17:14–15, KJV source for adaptation.

sorship of a barbeque at the mill village community center, he understood their power and influence. And also their existence in another class that he could not (and did not want to) enter.

Dorn lived alongside the small-time farmers and went often into the mill villages and rubbed shoulders with the millhands. *He was not in them but he was of them.* He made them his people, and their concerns became his concerns. When he was out of office, Jim Self or Brother Abney did not pal around with him—and never would. Instead, he was sought out by the simple Baptist believers in the mill villages and the simple Baptist believers in the small farming communities. They needed an active and relatively *large* federal government—active not only with regard to tariffs and currency and aspects of trade and finance but also active to protect them in their work and lives. He needed to build his own version of a Southern Fair Deal, one tailored to the millhands but also acceptable to the textile elite. For this 1950 campaign, he set to work developing his own red-hills Third Congressional District mill village Fair Deal.

And he had to do it with only memories of Dada, albeit memories often whistled up by Nana, by Millie, and by other voices of conscience, some of them black, like his army mates the Drane brothers and like his fellow red-hills Baptist Benjamin Elijah Mays. The Selfs and the Abneys paid for the hash, and for that matter, paid for the hash man, the lone black man in the audience who stirred the hash during the speeches before everyone fell out, fell to, and ate. But it was not the Selfs or the Abneys who sat at picnic tables and ate alongside Bryan Dorn. It was millworkers. Before any sat down to eat, there were the speeches to the millworkers. And in those speeches he had to gain the attention of the hash man. As always, the millworker crowd could not see the hash man, for he was behind them and they were looking at and listening to speechifiers in front of the audience. But while speaking, Bryan Dorn could see the hash man, there in the shade beyond the straining crowd, and he had to look steady into his eyes.

What Dorn developed was not simple or elegant, but it bid fair to work in these times. Especially if he remembered that his times were in God's hands.

Having lost his congressional seat, Bryan Dorn developed and never lost a sharp sense of how it felt to lose power and authority, how he physically hungered to get back into the game, the only game that mattered. To do so, he must outtalk James Butler Hare, which was not hard to do for such a passionate speechifier. But he must also *serve* as well as Hare father and son had served—and that *was* hard to do, especially for one whose track record of constituent service was poor. Talking could defeat Jim Hare, especially since the Hare family was not noted for effective talking with the masses; but if elected, the congressman must then serve all constituents, and the most quotidian service (straightening out VA benefits or Social Security payments and above all postal appointments) were the things remembered. He had to proffer his program at different levels, and it must be sincere. Above all, as he now knew painfully well, all proposals, no matter how popular, must be spoken in the context of a solemn promise to serve the many little needs of the many voters. None of the *little guys* was little in his own mind, and none of his (or her) needs was little to them.

The Fair Deal for the textile people operated at two levels, reflecting the classes at the top, whose wealth dominated the Third District, and the masses at the bottom, whose hearts and minds were most like his own. Bryan Dorn's proposals must be his own, shaped by compromise between what the classes at the top would allow and what the masses at the bottom most needed. And it must be ratified at the ballot box in 1950, and thereafter ratified person by person in intimate transactions with the folk in mill villages like Pelzer and Ware Shoals and Slater-Marietta and Matthews. The proposals would be offered in boardrooms to Leon Lowenstein, Jim Self, Brother Abney, Charlie Daniel, and other members of the classes, that is, the managerial elite. The proposals must then be sold to plain-folk masses in Baptist picnics, for these were the fundamentalist believers who did the actual work in the textile mill and on the small-scale farms and at the small-scale mom-and-pop retail stores and local finance "bidnesses" of the Third District. There were not only the words of the Baptist Sunday school, but also and always important words of a very different source, Machiavelli. The secular Florentine had written that the politician "has to respect the nobles, but must not make himself hated by the populace."[3]

Nor did it end there, for once elected, he must then cooperate with congressmen in the Congressional Cloakroom—in that era a spacious sit-

[3] Quoted, *Essential Writings of Machiavelli*, ed. Constantine, 74. See reading by Erica Brenner, *Be Like the Fox*, for the intepretation offered herein.

ting- and smoking-lounge—working with Midwestern Republicans and with Dixiecrats from Georgia and Virginia to put enabling statutes into law that would help the political economy of the Southern textile industry and its related businesses. Unless he could help congressmen from other regions and from the other party with what other constituents needed and wanted, neither masses nor classes in his own red hills could gain a tithe of what they expected.[4]

By drawing on shrewd insights from Clemson economist George Hubert Aull and the deft political machinations of Clemson College vice president (and soon-to-be president) Robert Cook Edwards—*Bob Eddards* to his fans and to his detractors—Bryan Dorn spoke for a cohesive program largely based on Keynesian policies as developed by fellow Southern congressmen who largely ignored the elegance of Keynesian economic theory for the effective practice of a politics based on heavy federal support for one's district. It worked effectively from 1951 until its failures in 1974, when the congressman himself faltered politically in more than one place. In other words, he actually had something of substance to offer his people in his home. Yet he could only make this comprehensive Fair Deal for Textiles work if he got himself elected to the US Congress, and to do that he faced no easy fight.

It is propitious to see the particularities of this Fair Deal for Textiles as he drew it up while out of office in 1950 and then to see how he went about getting himself back into office in order to effect his program. He was convinced that Jim Hare could not effectively provide anything as good as this Fair Deal for Textiles.

It started with advice, really instruction, offered at Clemson College's School of Rural Economics. Their Dr. Aull was called Hubert by Clemson friends (and George by supplicants who pretended to know him), but he was Doc Aull or Proff Aull to the admiring "student" Bryan Dorn. Aull had graduated Clemson College in 1919, studied rural sociology and regional economics with the renowned Wilson Gee at the University of Virginia, earning a master's degree, and then in 1937 earned the PhD from the University of Wisconsin, along the way mastering quantitative analysis and macroeconomic

---

[4] Correspondence, WJBD, Ernest Frederick Hollings, and Earle E. Morris, especially 1949–1974; writings and files of editorials for *Anderson Independent*, 1964–1971, especially "Weasel Words," 6 August 1971, George Hubert Aull Papers, Special Collections, Clemson University, hereinafter GHA/SC/CU; correspondence, George Hubert Aull, especially 10 June 1953, 12 June 1953, and 17 March 1956, WJBD/SCPC.

theory. Because of his own seminar teachings, but also because of his own empirical observations, Aull discarded the classical models of economics.

A deeply believing Baptist, Dorn "baptized" Lord Keynes and tried to apply stimulative economics to rural communities and small towns. He focused on unfair taxation, especially regressive taxes such as sales taxes, and he called for improvements in education. In practice, his call was that the state (and each of its counties) spend resources equitably so that children in poor communities could be well educated. Prosperity was contingent on an improvement of conditions for the least and the lowest. Aull got to that concept through a combination of Lord Keynes's politics and the same impulses that caused Baptist churches to send busses out to get the poorest folk and open their basements for counseling for drinkers and other sinners. Folksy yet coolly analytical, Hubert Aull was happy to help the politicos, especially Bryan Dorn, and later Ernest Frederick Hollings and Earle Morris Jr. Kind and thoughtful, he was also quite willing to tell any public officials or office-holders or office seekers when they were wrong. And that included Clemson president Robert Poole, whom he disdained, and his successor Bob Edwards, whom he much admired.[5]

After much study and important correspondence with the long-serving and unblinking Dr. Aull, Bryan Dorn concluded two things about rural economics. One was that markets did not always "clear" for the reason that there was imperfect competition, and in some places monopoly control. To abandon the mom-and-pop store or the millworker to such monopoly markets in the name of free trade and perfect competition was unjust, even tyrannical. The second was that modern economists' belief in the "fine tuning" of regulated interest rates (the federal government buying and selling of debt and regulating prices and costs of scarce commodities and scarce labor resources) could do almost as much damage to consumers as leaving them to the vagaries of unrestrained monopoly.

Bryan Dorn was not even born when William Hope "Coin" Harvey and William Jennings Bryan first won over Nana and Dada to the original Populist programs. Indeed, there had been a full decade, an historian's era, since New Deal Southerners, the next generation of such Populists, had enacted legislation to protect local and small-town businesses and small farms and to protect the people who worked on those farms and in those factories.

---

[5] Correspondence, Robert Cook Edwards, especially 1949–1974; writings and files of editorials for *Anderson Independent*, 1964–1971; GHA/SC/CU; Aull to WJBD, 10 June 1953, 12 June 1953, and 17 March 1956, WJBD/SCPC.

But a group of second-generation New Deal legislators, the Populistic Southerners of the postbellum era of Harry Truman, were still present in the flesh in the South Carolina delegation. These were Joe Bryson, Mendel Rivers, Johnny Mac Macmillan, and Dick Richards, to say nothing of their boss, the Texan Sam Rayburn. In 1950, Bryan Dorn was out of Congress, but he was still fully in spirit with the Populistic Southerners. The essence of such second-generation New Deal legislation for the Southern Fair Dealers was to protect workers' factory and farm environments and to vouchsafe Social Security benefits for old age and disability. But equally of the essence was regulation of financial institutions that managed investments in stocks and bonds.

Bryan Dorn was suspicious of stock-market brokers and large-scale insurers (and reinsurers and their supporting derivatives traders). He was determined to keep banking local, confined within South Carolina's boundaries, and to keep banking carefully separated from insurance underwriters and far removed from investment brokers. The Fair Deal generation of South Carolina legislators in Columbia and in Washington regulated interest rates on loans and carefully monitored and even investigated insurance underwriters' fees and charges and premiums. Banking, insuring, investing, and lending were to be kept as strictly separate entities almost as autonomous in their spheres of influence as Congress, Supreme Court, and president.

The masses and the classes were united in preference for managed trade, for tariffs on foreign goods, and for quotas on imports. Eschewing classical economics with its elegant models of free trade and untrammeled markets, the South Carolina delegation, following the wishes of the classes and the masses, interfered constantly in trade and in other markets. Wages and prices were not allowed to "float" or otherwise adjust flexibly, and markets of all grades and conditions were assigned "whistle blowers" and "gate keepers." Capital was not permitted to flow freely in terms of farming or textile factory production, and there was no pretense that it should. Senator Elison Durant Smith ("Cotton Ed") might have been the quintessence of traditional racism and social retrogression, but he voted for legislation to protect small-time cotton farmers in their banking, marketing, and shipping operations. Virginia's Carter Glass—the lordly *Ky-ah-tah*—might have been the very marble bust of the Old Dominion patrician, but he authored and enforced legislation that kept banks firmly within the boundaries of state lines and kept banks away from involvement in activities of investing or underwriting insurance. And these two US senators, never to be confused in any way with progressive legislators, in these cases did the bidding of Populistic forces in the masses among voters. Such forces and such voters were especially predominant in the small South Carolina farms and in the compact South Carolina mill villages.

Such Populism had merged with the new economics of John Maynard Keynes, a thinker whom Dorn read and talked about with Hubert Aull. The candidate did not mention Keynes by name in 1950, and certainly never invoked the economist's name on any dais during his political career. But he absorbed and applied the lesson that the federal government must be the direct supplier of some goods and services, and he demanded that the federal government be the direct employer of certain workers, namely, the US military. Longtime congressman Barney Frank of Massachusetts, looking back at all this, labeled it accurately "militaristic Keynesianism," a propitious tag for the South Carolina delegation, with its insistence on heavy federal spending for a big army, a big navy, and (for Bryan Dorn) a seventy-unit air force with intercontinental missions. Not for nothing did candidate Dorn keep wide-angle-lens glossy photographs of troops massed for inspection at Fort Gordon, Fort Jackson, and his personal favorite, Donaldson Air Base. None of these bases were in the Third District, but each employed Third District folk in the ranks and each employed Third District suppliers of services to the military. Following Mendel Rivers, Dorn believed in aggressive resistance to Soviet and Maoist Communism, which necessitated a big military force. But, also like Mendel Rivers, he believed as fully in the stimulative effects of big-government spending in his district.[7]

Other important sources of his thoughts and actions came from the textile classes: James Cuthbert Self, Leon Lowenstein, Brother Abney, and Robert Stevens. The classes formed a power elite with a managerial and financial base in New York, and they formed a power elite that employed full-time lobbyists in Washington to oversee legislation about the textile trade, especially when powerful Republican congressmen and sometimes President Eisenhower's administrators talked loudly about free trade. At least in the 1950s and 1960s, the classes in South Carolina wanted banking to be local, separate from insurance underwriting, and separate from risky investing. Particularly significant for the classes was Lowenstein, an especially articulate Jewish entrepreneur who demanded toleration not only for Jews but also for all ethnic groups, to include "Negroes," a word he pronounced as carefully as did Candidate Dorn. These textile men, plus others, including Greenville construction figure Charles Daniel (who built the factories but also built all the buildings in service support) and *Greenville News* proprietor Roger

[7] Frank, "The New Mandate on Defense (2013)": 50–56.

Peace, had real concern for the red hills—and for the people of both races and all classes there.

Because of those concerns, the classes supported any number of market interferences, especially in trade, in order to preserve jobs and indeed communities down home—but only so long as such market interferences worked to their own profit as well. Dismantle the textile Fair Deal, and each was perfectly ready and able to do what the next generation did, which was to play the free-market game of global finance and global trade by moving their operations "offshore" with consummate skill and splendiferous success. Lowenstein was particularly blunt when he noted his willingness to leave South Carolina if the important incentives of tariffs and quotas were removed—and he included in those incentives the Populistic separation of banking, insurance, and investing. Indeed, Lowenstein was specific in talking with candidate Dorn: if tariffs and quotas and exchange rates were not maintained, he would have no choice but to take 17,000 South Carolina jobs *abroad*. By contrast, if the US Congress could raise tariffs and maintain exchange rates and retain the existing quotas on imports, Lowenstein could *add* 8,000 jobs to nine plants in the state. The septuagenarian did much charitable work for Dorn's district and seemed really to like Dorn, but he was just as willing to make his millions in Asia as in the red hills.[8]

Lowenstein, Self, Stevens, Abney, Daniel, and Peace, each relying often on Hubert Aull, were joined in future years by other figures, most prominently Benjamin Claude Inabinet, creator in 1955 of a specialty chemical company, Defender, and Roger Milliken, the entrepreneur of polymer fibers for Deering-Milliken Corporation, which by 1958 had built a remarkable research campus in Spartanburg. In 1949, Lowenstein and the Greenwood executives created the Informal Textile Group to meet in Washington with the South Carolina delegation—and sometimes the president of the US—to discuss legislation and regulation. Veteran piedmont Georgia congressman Carl Vinson (best known for his dominance of Veterans Affairs and other aspects of military budgets) was the original catalyst in the House of Representatives for this informally functioning group of businessmen, professors,

---

[8] On moving offshore, see WJBD, address (citing Lowenstein anonymously), *Congressional Record*, vol. 101, pt. 2, 84th Cong., 1st sess., 18 February 1955, 1766–67; Lowenstein and WJBD, 1950–1972, especially retrospective: Lowenstein to WJBD, 15 June 1962; Lowenstein to WJBD, 28 June 1963, with enclosures from clipping, *Anderson Daily Mail*, 13 June 1963, 1, and Lowenstein to Jacob K. Javits, 28 June 1963, and WJBD to Lowenstein, 5 July 1963; also note correspondence with others, Self, Inabinet, Abney, 1950–1961, WJBD/SCPC.

and office-holding politicians. Even before Bryan Dorn was elected, the Informal Group made him a member. When the men formalized their organization, calling it the Textile Group, Congressman Vinson named the elected Congressman Dorn the secretary of the group and expected him to conduct monthly meetings in DC, but also to be ready to facilitate impromptu meetings and conferences at any time. Officially dating to 1960, the Informal Group was actually on the scene and obviously effective throughout the era of the 1950s, and Bryan Dorn was present at its creation in the final moments of the 1940s before he regained elective office. Regardless of Congressman Jim Hare's beliefs or intentions, the distinguished "lord of the land" was bypassed by the onrushing Informal Group with its chosen candidate.[9]

There was also serious research that Bryan Dorn did, although much of it had already been done by none other than Butler Black Hare, distinguished landowner, patriach, and student of land and wealth. Taking census numbers, even working with friends and staff through a US Census Bureau series of printouts, Dorn found that his congressional predecessor was right: the large cotton farms were gone from the Third District, and the New Deal programs had been a boon to the large-scale and not to the small-scale cotton farmer. For farming, the implications were several, again all first noted by the elder Hare as a scholar who wrote about such things and as a farmer who practiced what he wrote about. For one, cotton farming wanted deemphasis in their part of South Carolina. Timber cultivation, cattle raising, and corn growing made more sense, as did more radical departures, such as damming up and otherwise redirecting the tributaries of the Savannah and Saluda rivers to provide electric power for the textile mills and for military installations—but also recreation and tourist opportunities for countless mom-and-pop services in small towns, some of those small towns actually brand new even if already in journalist Russell Baker's shrewd term "quainted." For another, since almost no voting constituencies in the district were large-scale cotton growers, Third District farmers would be unharmed if

[9] Retrospective, WJBD to GHA, 29 August 1972, GHA/SC/CU; Informal Textile Group, Textile Group, and Textile Consortium in WJBD corr., 1949–1979, especially retrospective, Lowenstein to WJBD, 15 June 1962; WJBD to Charles Daniel, 11 March 1952; Walter Montgomery to WJBD, 18 May 1962; J. A. Gallimore to WJBD, 7 June 1962; J. C. Self to WJBD, 18 September 1962; "In Response to (E. D. Lewis)" circular, 5 August 1960; Russell F. Taylor to WJBD, 5 December 1960; WJBD, "Bryan Dorn Representing the People," 1984 cassette, Greenwood District 50 South Carolina Educational Television, WJBD/SCPC; Cook, *Carl Vinson: Patriarch*.

Congressman Hare—or would-be Congressman Dorn—withdrew price and cost supports from local cotton in order to bring inexpensive (but superior quality) Indian percale cotton to the district's mills.[10]

More successfully than either Butler Hare or James Hare, Bryan Dorn had met, studied with, and was ready to work with the Clemson economists and engineers and the textile entrepreneurs. They knew that he stood ready to help build functioning coalitions across state lines, indeed beyond the Southern boundaries and into the Midwest, to retain and even expand a Fair Deal for Textiles by helping with Midwestern waterway projects and their regional farming projects. Too, Bryan Dorn still had "a double share of the spirit" of his namesake's matchless ability to speak to the masses, more so than Butler Hare or James Hare, both of whom were, by contrast, members of the agrarian elite and by no stretch plain folk, however Populist in some of their politics. Again, the Hares, father and son, understood exactly what Bryan Dorn understood, understood exactly what Hubert Aull understood, and certainly could talk with the classes, with the Selfs and the Peaces and the Abneys. For all that, Dorn had been much more intentional in cultivating Dr. Aull and the Clemson rural economists. Equally important, Dorn had been much more intentional in cultivating the textile classes in his own district and elsewhere. Aull's Keynesian analysis for textiles featured a common language built on common assumptions developed from the same data.[11]

One large issue was the source of inflation. It was understood as either cost-push or demand-pull, and sometimes both. In that day, cost-push came primarily from well-organized labor unions. Especially in something like the traditional small farm, the mom-and-pop store, or the textile industry, cost of labor was always more than two-thirds of all costs. The Hares and Dorn, all truly devoted to the people who made up that "resource" of labor, were convinced that an increase in wages would simply cause many millworkers and grocery clerks and service-station attendants to lose their jobs. All of the enterprises of the Third District were run on a tight pulley: costs had to be contained, and the largest and most easily controlled of those costs was wag-

---

[10] Printouts, US Census Bureau, 1950, WJBD/SCPC; "quainted," Baker, "Our Old European Relatives Find Us Quaint," *Chicago Tribune*, 19 July 1980, 11; idem., "Sunday Observer; the Taint of Quaint," *New York Times Magazine*, 2 August 1983, 1.

[11] "Double share," 2 K 2: 9; WJBD to GHA, 29 August 1972, GHA/SC/CU; Informal Textile Group, Textile Group, and Textile Consortium in WJBD corr., 1949–1979, especially retrospective, Lowenstein to WJBD, 15 June 1962, WJBD/SCPC.

es. Hold down wages, and the enterprises could compete while employing a full-sized force of workers. Let those labor costs (wages) rise, and laborers would have to be let go, the oldest, most worn-out and lowest skilled—that is, *the most vulnerable*—to be let go first. Dorn had absorbed from Keynes through Aull the concept that wages were "sticky downward," that a general salary level did not "float" or otherwise move up and down at all, but rather moved more like a ratchet, coming down or going up with some real effort—and an effort that reflected danger of a heavy load dropping on one if wages could actually move freely and quickly, as implied by the classicists, whose elegance and whose confidence about "optimality" Dorn completely mistrusted.[12]

There was also demand-pull, and it came from direct purchases by a government during time of war or crisis. Dramatic increases in demand for goods and services pulled prices up inexorably, and especially when a credible foreign threat militated against cautious buying and careful bargaining for the best price. To protect against the depredations of such demand-pull, there was no choice but to go to price-adjustment administrators like Eric Johnston, count on them being honorable and aboveboard, and arrange for price controls—even and especially knowing that a day of reckoning would come when it no longer made sense to protect with artificial ceilings, but that "floating ceilings" would rise disastrously high above the ratcheted wages of millworker, farm operator, retail used-car salesman, local independent grocer.[13]

From Professor Aull, from textile leader Leon Lowenstein, from various business publications, and from other reading, Dorn found words summed up in one thoughtful pamphlet that described the fiscal policy, writ small for his textile region: fiscal policies, of taxing and spending, could improve unemployment during slow times but could worsen inflation during times of rapid growth. Child of the Depression and then young assemblyman of the late New Deal, Bryan Dorn agreed that the national government had to intervene to make jobs during recession and certainly during depression. He also knew that in wartime, all hands could be employed, and his

[12] Keynes, *Collected Works*, vol. 29, especially J. T. Dunlop to Keynes, April (1938), reprint, 283–85; Heilbroner, *Worldly Philosophers*; Charles E. Daniel to GHA, 30 December 1954, retrospective, Robert F. Poole to GHA, 29 January 1955, GHA, SC/CU.

[13] Keynes, *Collected Works*, vol. 29, 64–65; see correspondence with Eric Johnson, especially years 1950–1951, WJBD/SCPC; see files, Aull columns, *Anderson Independent*, 1964–1971, GHA/SC/CU.

standard for national employment remained World War II; he never accepted the concept that some 4, 5, or 6 percent of people were "naturally" unemployed. He always knew how many unemployed people there were—in 1950 it was some five million—and he always cited that number with anger, especially during times when politicians of both parties might be scrambling to take credit for "full employment" that left "only" 5 percent of the labor force unemployed.[14]

The pamphlet that he preserved and used was reproduced many times and was actually from businessmen who were in cooperation with the Americans for Democratic Action (ADA), Hubert Horatio Humphrey's liberal activists whose ideas Dorn otherwise despised. But Aull and Lowenstein and Dorn himself accepted the central Keynesian belief that, *during recession* or other economic downturn, deficit spending, in which the federal government spent more money than it received in taxes, was necessary to stimulate the economy and drive toward full employment, which for Dorn was a minimum of some 97 percent. When the economy was not growing, that is, when the gross domestic product was stationary or even declining from one business quarter to another, there was so-called *slack*, and fiscal-deficit spending could "kick-start" the economy while improving employment. Most important, such fiscal-deficit spending during recession or other economic downturn would not start inflation, a general rise in price levels. The policy then must consider spending and taxing against a "full employment" and growing gross domestic economy before demand-pull inflation was created.[15]

Quoting William Brill from Eric Johnston's pamphlet,

> [Inflation] comes when more goods cannot quickly be produced to satisfy the *increased demand* [author's italics]. That is not the case when there is unemployment and idle plant capacity. Increased demand then simply means that more people will get work. Inflation only comes when there is money demand that cannot be met by the production of more goods. [In World War II] demand for goods in the form of means of destruction was practically unlimited, and labor and plant capacity were fully employed.[16]

---

[14] William W. Brill to WJBD, enclosure, 18 April 1961, retrospective, WJBD/SCPC.

[15] Keynes, *Collected Works*, vol. 29, 50–51; Brill, enclosure and remarks, retrospective, 18 April 1961, WJBD/SCPC.

[16] Brill to WJBD, enclosure, 18 April 1961, retrospective, WJBD/SCPC.

Obviously there was peacetime inflation, but Dorn accepted Brill's explanation; it was not because of spending and taxing, but because of "administrative prices" that created "cost-push," perhaps most tellingly in various awkward quotas and set prices for agricultural products at a time when American farmers did not need them at all—at least his constituent farmers in Third District did not.[17]

There was, as Keynes made clear, the danger of deficit spending when the economy was growing rapidly, something that "this administration" was guilty of, as far as Dorn could see. Quoting Brill again:

> If we do have during peace time a real inflation due to too much money chasing too few goods, the Federal Government should operate at a surplus. It would then take from the people more in taxes than it pays out in government expenditures. It would thereby sop up the excess spending power by taxation [demand-pull] and relieve inflationary pressures. This means that we should aim not at a balanced budget but at a budget which will balance our economy by a deficit in times of recession and a surplus in times of growth.[18]

Dorn was relieved to find that Keynes himself disdained long-term government hiring, especially in programs favored by "do good" and "one world" big government liberals. The candidate was a small government liberal and a Keynesian only in terms of the rule on using the budget to "balance our economy." Given his understanding of the need for military spending, he preferred cutting back most nonmilitary programs, allowing the military demand for hardware and services and workers—probably two noncombat workers for every combat soldier, sailor, or airman—to pull the country to truly full employment. Once relative quiet was created (certainly not the situation of the Cold War, with its expensive and edgy "containment" of an aggressive and adventuresome Communism) then the military could be sized down, general spending could be curtailed, and taxes, always hard to raise, could stay the same, since the balance between reduced spend-

---

[17] Ibid.

[18] Ibid.; WJBD to Eric Johnston, 6 December 1951, WJBD/SCPC.

ing and the same taxing would still produce a surplus in a growing economy.[19]

In some ways, it might seem that Dorn would have been better served in his arguments by Friedrich A. von Hayek, especially since Hayek's language about central government and centralized planning was so similar to the congressman's—always suspicious and dubious, occasionally approaching clinical hysteria. Hayek's disproof of optimality in all exchanges, especially for "clearing" labor markets, his almost pathologically negative instincts about government actions concerning markets, and his focus on the sensitivity of interest rates and availability of credit, all seem to fit Dorn's thinking. In fact, Dorn did know about Hayek and admired his rhetoric about planned economies of communistic states, but he was not Hayekian, partly because George Aull was not, and partly because Hayek showed too little concern for the lowest and least. It was mostly because William Jennings Bryn Dorn read widely and carefully without making himself a discerning or nuanced student of "the political economy." Whatever rhetorical perorations revealed about inherent inclinations, the demands to put people to work kept Bryan Dorn from serious absorption of Hayek's actual policies as opposed to his rhetoric. Noting that there is an inconsistency in Dorn's use of Keynes and noting some unplumbed and even undigested sources in Hayek for Dorn is about all a chronicler can do. His carefully constructed Fair Deal for Textiles was built on Keynesian sands that he suspected were shifting, but an alternate foundation in Hayek did not interest him. Nor did it interest the New Deal Populistic progressives already in the South Carolina delegation. That delegation generally voted for a militaristic Keynesianism, and their policies were very much the policies of Dr. Aull, the country Keynesian—and of his student, candidate Dorn.[20]

---

[19] Brill, enclosure and remarks, retrospective, 18 April 1961; Keynes, *Collected Works*, vol. 29; WJBD never said as much, but his votes reflect such views, "militaristic Keynesianism," WJBD/SCPC; Frank, "The New Mandate on Defense," 50–56; GHA to Will Lou Gray, n.d., 1951; GHA, "Report on Charleston Port Grain Storage Facilities," 3 August 1954; Economic Steering Group, retrospective, 1961, S. Ernie Wright to GHA, 26 May 1961, GHA/SC/CU.

[20] William W. Brill to WJBD, enclosure, 18 April 1961, retrospective; Hayek, *The Road to Serfdom*, rhetoric seems to inspire "Toward Socialism" by WJBD and elsewhere, and he speaks of Hayek's political language, WJBD to Edward Ball, 20 July 1964, WJBD/SCPC; however, Hayek, *The Collected Works* does not make the policy impact of Keynes, *Collected Work*, 1929–1971, GHA/SC/CU.

One thing was certain, the "mild" inflation of the Truman years was not mild for small-town and rural folk of either race or gender. As he noted often, Dorn's people lived physically demanding and relatively short lives. Those demanding and short lives featured wages that barely budged and almost always included periods of under-employment or even unemployment. Such savings as they had been able to put aside fetched rates of return even lower than the rate of "mild" inflation. Germans who lived through the 1920s hyperinflation left testimony that genuinely upset the farmer at Myrtle Manor about even the mildest inflation.

Defining inflation as a general rise in the level of prices, Bryan Dorn said it was the greatest enemy of small business and the deadliest threat to the many retired elders, disabled veterans, and disabled textile and farm workers. The causes of this deadly effect could come from two different directions, and congressmen had to pay close attention and "keep their eye on the ball" to discern which one was the culprit in a given set of circumstances. There was demand-pull and there was cost-push, and anyone who believed in an active and powerful military, as he did, had to "own the fact" that his military policies bore economic effects not only onto his beloved fellow soldiers and sailors but also onto the retired veterans and the civilian workforce back home. In Dorn's Keynesian world, high wages, especially union-scale wages, produced inflation by cost-push. Government purchases of goods and services, both direct purchases and those he thought would be indirectly "multiplied" by a factor of at least two, could make inflation by demand-pull. The disaster of inflation thus inhered in government macroeconomic policies. It was important to resist that disaster by reducing spending, but only when full-employment levels were attained.

For all that, federal spending to ensure jobs in the Third District was the Keynesian policy that trumped all other economic policies, even more than trying to reduce spending once full employment was attained nationwide. Dorn was painfully aware that there were many occasions when national employment outpaced employment in the valley of the Saluda or the on the slopes of the Blue Ridge. As long as employment lagged in his red hills, there must be government spending, most of it in so-styled earmarks specific to his district in larger legislation. The budget could be balanced by cutting other federal spending, but if that were impossible politically, then the country could suffer some inflation rather than have jobs disappear in his beloved district, where his blue-collar and farming friends lived so close to the edge of economic disaster.

So building his program, Dorn of course realized at once that it sounded like the Hares, both father and son. He conceded as much to his family and friends and remembered as much in his memoirs. The son, James Butler Hare, was a moderate segregationist who worried about and resisted the Ku Klux Klan but otherwise opposed every progressive piece of legislation concerning black people, usually on the grounds of states' rights. Too, Hare was dubious about farm support programs, and, like his scholarly father, was convinced that Third District farmers could function effectively in current international markets provided the government protect agricultural producers against the machinations and outright cheating of freight haulers, whether truck or rail, and protect against rate fixing among storm- and risk-insurers. That much was garden-variety New Deal Populistic progressivism as celebrated and enforced by South Carolina politicians, not to exclude "Cotton Ed" Smith. Although Hare disdained price controls as such, he (like Bryan Dorn) accepted many forms of price control. Because of old Populist legislation and New Deal laws and now Fair Deal laws, Third District farmers accepted plenty of government regulation—and *expected* federal help in production quotas, rules about processing, safety standards, subsidies and other help for transportation, communication, and help underwriting the insurance against the many risks in agriculture.[21]

As to the textile mills, Hare was essentially another Populistic New Dealer who expected government interference in the marketplace (tariffs and quotas), to provide cheap cotton from abroad, and to protect locally produced textiles from cheap import competition. Looking directly at the masses as well as the classes, Jim Hare saluted the South Carolina General Assembly push for a federal change in Social Security standards so that retirement with full pension benefits could begin at age sixty. Like Dorn, Jim Hare could be eloquent in support of this change in the federal law—and like everyone else he, too, knew that General Assembly resolutions carried no weight with the federal government—and he knew that he was only a backbencher with no ability to effect such a dramatic change in federal law. In the same Populistic New Deal way, Congressman Jim Hare supported federal subsidies for schools, so long as those subsidies did not bear "strings" concerning treatment of black children in education. On domestic issues, there was thus little daylight between the *Hare fils* and *Hare pere* and even less daylight between *Hare fils* and contender Dorn.[22]

---

[21] WJBD, *OTP*, 125–30; on Smith, see character Wint Smith (Cotton Ed Smith) in Drury (with Millie Johnson), *A Senate Journal* and idem., *Advise and Consent.*

[22] *Greenwood Index*, February through June 1950; *Anderson Independent*, February through June, 1950; Butler Black Hare Papers and James Butler Hare Papers, SCPC.

If there was precious little policy difference, there was personal difference at two levels. First, Dorn was allied with the emerging Informal Textile Group. Second, the Dorns and the Hares understood how close the race would be, and each candidate began to focus on the most minor of policy differences while emphasizing in grand scale personal differences. Thus, each man drank down the bitter gall and wormwood, some of which they themselves had brewed up and then believed. James Butler Hare was convinced that Bryan Dorn had abandoned the congressional seat never intending to return, as proven by his long period of absence without communication to or with constituents in the Third District. Dorn was convinced that James Butler Hare had made fun of the Dorn family, especially brother George, who had been arrested for a drunken spree that involved a group who robbed at gunpoint and then drove cars fast through at least three states fleeing law enforcement. In fact, these beliefs about each other were related.

Bryan Dorn's strange disappearance out West may have been connected to George's embarrassing troubles; that is, Bryan Dorn was "out of pocket" to give himself "deniability" about his brother George's doings and misdoings. Apparently, Congressman Hare in the House Cloakroom had made a cutting remark about George Dorn's troubles, a remark passed on from the congressional delegation members (or their pages) to Bryan Dorn. However, Congressman Hare immediately apologized when he realized the severity of the charges—armed robbery, resisting arrest—and also because he realized that George may have been a drunken and unwitting accomplice along for the ride rather than stick-up man or the "getaway" car driver. Too, Hare hastened to offer any legal or other support he could to George Dorn's defense. George had fallen a long, long way, but no one in the Hare or Dorn families thought the onetime military officer would commit armed robbery. All presumed he had gotten drunk again and participated unwittingly in a robbing spree orchestrated by stronger—and nastier—characters among his drinking associates. Nevertheless, these nuances were forgotten by both sides as soon as the Dorn family entered the lists against the Hare family. Come the winter primary filing day of 1950, no more apologies were proffered, no apologies were accepted, and the melodrama began. Each campaigning family proceeded as if dealing with dishonorable families in an otherwise honorable contest. The stakes were high, the gloves were off, and Bryan

Dorn reread Machiavelli to remind family and friends—and mostly himself—that *nothing* could be "left to chance."[23]

In the rural up-country, certain traits were the same whether in a textile mill, a lumberyard, a small-time cotton field, a mom-and-pop feedstore floor room, along a postal route, or at a Baptist barbeque. Tempers were famously short, fists were often balled up, and some group in any gathering was almost always ready for a fight. At the same time, memories were famously long, and nowhere lengthier than when a personal slight was recalled by master storytellers. Besides the friends and relatives of the Hares—no small number—there were the many voters who had expected Congressman Dorn to tend their constituent needs attentively, and to do so for a good, long time. Brother Watson, cousin Steve Griffith, and cousin Felder Dorn all recall more than one instance when citizens in the district yelled their displeasure and disdain for the congressman who had deserted them. Yet that was not the greatest cut. Yelling was at least one part of ongoing communication, and that might be addressed with pluck and humor, which all members of the Dorn and Griffith families possessed in abundance. Worse was the definitive snub, the exaggerated silence of the men and women who would cross the street and deliberately look away and avoid eye contact with family members who were campaigning. These cuts, Watson Dorn, Steve Griffith, and Felder Dorn remembered with anguished ache a full six decades later. The onetime and future congressman was going to take his lumps from a goodly portion of his district's voters because he had, in fact, quit them at a bad time. He could and did apologize profusely and promise sincerely to serve them as no one ever had served any folk ever before.[24]

Milllie Dorn had laid out the outlines for the way to campaign and was a constant critic in the best sense of the word. She strategized and advised, but the unblinking journalist could not go into the field on walking tours. After preparing her man to be a candidate and after getting him started, she had to withdraw from many aspects of the race. In June, she had presented Bryan with a baby girl, named Brianna to honor both the candidate and the

---

[23] Interviews: Watson Dorn and Steve Griffith, WJBD/SCPC; *Greenwood Index Journal*, 1950, and *Anderson Independent*, 1948–1950; James Butler Hare corr., 1950, JBH/SCPC; WJBD, *OTP*, 127; *Essential Writings of Machiavelli*, ed. Constantine, 68–69, 74, 84–87.

[24] Interviews: Watson Dorn and Steve Griffith, quoting Felder Dorn, WJBD/SCPC; WJBD, *OTP*, 118; *Essential Writings of Machiavelli*, ed. Constantine, 74.

great Populist namesake, and she stayed at the large and drafty Myrtle Manor raising the child with help from various white and black friends of the Dorns. As for Nana, she, too, was a guiding force in campaign rhetoric and for some tactics, but she occasionally fell into "major moods" and otherwise became distracted from the day-to-day needs of the campaign. Thus, Watson Dorn, the country lawyer, quickly became the actual campaign manager. Cousins Steve Griffith and Felder Dorn as well as a good baker's dozen of Dorns and Griffiths and Bleases were field troops who walked and walked and talked and talked.[25]

For his part, Watson Dorn had ascertained that majorities in the counties of Abbeville, Newberry, Oconee, and Saluda were hopelessly gone over to Jim Hare and therefore immune to appeals. Either because folk could not forgive Bryan Dorn for abandoning them, or because they sincerely loved Hare father or son, those four counties were in the column for James Butler Hare. With some effort, Watson persuaded the family and friends to gamble: ignore these lost-cause counties and instead double their efforts where the race remained close in Anderson, Edgefield, Greenwood, McCormick, and Pickens. It was risky strategy, since it literally involved abandoning some 48 percent of the Third District voting population with no assurance of winning the remaining portion (a bare majority) where James Butler Hare also enjoyed personal popularity and the advantages of incumbency. Complications with unknowable contingencies involved two additional primary candidates: the down-home Theo Vaughn of Anderson and S. T. Heyward of Clemson. These two would draw votes from Jim Hare and from Bryan Dorn in about equal measure, and in any case, a four-man race made it unlikely that any single candidate could get a majority on first ballot. Thus, the primary season could subdivide itself into two races, a four-way in late spring and a runoff in early summer.[26]

Fortunately, Watson Dorn had good relations in that day with the press in the district. The *Greenwood Index-Journal* was owned and edited by Harry Legare Watson, a dependable journalist for almost fifty years in the region, all but a few of those in Greenwood. Harry Watson was himself a thorough reporter fascinated by politics, and he staffed a good crew, especially the very political husband-and-wife team of Frank and Eleanor Mun-

---

[25] Interviews: Watson Dorn and Steve Griffith, JHR/SCPC; Grace Dorn to WJBD, 26 July 1943; "Dorn Representing the People (1984)," WJBD/SCPC; WJBD, *OTP*, 118.

[26] Interview: Watson Dorn, WJBD/SCPC; Jordan, *The Primary State*, 106–107.

dy. Somewhat more problematical was the *Anderson Independent*, especially the newspaper's volatile and unpredictable Wilton Hall. Editor and publisher Hall was member of the General Assembly, had once filled a vacancy in the US Senate, and remained very much an aspirant to higher office. Above all, Hall was intensely aware of the fact that his newspaper served the district's largest city, Anderson, and the district's largest public institution, Clemson College. Although more people actually read the dailies published in Greenville and Spartanburg and Columbia, Third District citizens found much more political information about their congressman and about the race in Hall's *Independen*t and in Watson's *Index-Journal*. Hall, an unreconstructed New Dealer, disdained Harry Truman's racial liberalism and was nervous about the foreign policy of containment, but he was loudly in favor of Truman's Fair Deal for domestic policies. In particular, Hall was proud of the involvement in the Fair Deal by South Carolina's own financier Bernard Baruch and economist Ludwig Lewissohn. Bryan Dorn himself, but also Doc Aull, Watson Dorn, and members of the family, made sure that Wilton Hall fully comprehended how much of Fair Deal economic policy their campaign understood and supported. It worked because it was true. In fact, it was no less true of James Butler Hare, but the sitting congressman and his family and friends were not effective in explaining as much to the journalist Harry Watson or to politician newspaperman Wilton Hall.[27]

Despite the disadvantage of being the man who abandoned the House of Representatives in order to run for the Senate, Bryan Dorn created certain advantages for himself in campaigning with the people of this district. The advantages had to do with his method of campaigning and also with his personality—and his method of campaigning was tightly interwoven with his personality. He was still the young air force veteran and former boxer, and he was still the onetime cotton farmer who now raised dairy cattle and marketed his own pine board. He was still Dada's boy who knew how to throw a barbeque picnic and who knew how to appeal to the roughnecks from the dirt farms and the textile mills. He was still the Baptist Sunday school leader. As noted by an astute student of Populist campaigners, the Populists in the 1890s and "populistic New Dealers" thereafter had "adapt[ed]...the Methodist circuit-riding system as an organizing tool." Baptist Sunday

---

[27] Ibid.; Moore, *South Carolina Newspapers*, 130–34; "*Index-Journal* Editor Dies This Morning [Harry Legare Watson]," *Greenwood Index-Journal*, 5 November 1956 obituary.

school organizers and their visiting speakers also "rode the circuit," establishing political linkages through personal relationships, and Bryan Dorn was past master of that "organizing tool."[28] Above all, he was still Nana's fine young man that the Third District's mothers and spinster aunts doted upon.

The campaign was based at Myrtle Manor, where locals had long been accustomed to huge gatherings hosted by Dada in school-board campaigns and other local political races. The Dorns, Griffiths, Colemans, and others brought in butchered pigs by the truckload and established the famous "hash man" under a guarding shade tree to stir the cauldron with the savory hash. They also brought in local bands to play. As in all such gatherings, social or political or familial, there was liquor aplenty carefully secreted in a barn or in the trunk of someone's Ford. At the same time there were entire families, with many children, and always ministers and Sunday school members, and as always no one drank openly from a container but many faces turned suspiciously red and voices grew loud and boisterous. Bryan Dorn added his own touches. He had several prized donkeys, one of which he named *FDR*. The late president remained by far the most popular figure in the Third District, and at the propitious moment the donkey would be trotted out and Bryan Dorn would loudly announce, "Here is FDR!" The crowd, rural people who still appreciated a good donkey, always "went wild" with enthusiasm, and some of that FDR enthusiasm was "psychologically" orchestrated to rub off on the candidate. Of course, talking about the late Tom Watson and the late FDR were good ways to avoid talking about the increasingly unpopular Harry Truman and his dreaded civil rights plank, subjects never mentioned on such occasions.[29]

Leaving Chinkapin Ridge, he and his cousin drivers drove the old 1937 Chevrolet as mercilessly as did Nana—and with little more sense of direction as to destination. It often broke down, but even the breakdowns became political moments, with Bryan and his fellow campaigners handing out flyers and buttonholing those who gave them rides or those who came to repair the beleaguered Chevy. In more organized fashion, Watson Dorn scheduled appearances at town squares in all the little towns of the five targeted counties. Watson generally arranged for cousin Steve Griffith to drive while the young attorney himself rented a flatbed truck and other relatives drove rental

---

[28] Interview: Watson Dorn, WJBD/SCPC; quotation and insight, McMath, "The History of the Present," 100.

[29] Interview: Watson Dorn, WJBD/SCPC; *OTP*, 119–23; interview: Steve Griffith, WJBD/SCPC.

cars. As a vehicle approached a town, a Dorn or a Griffith or a Blease would announce over a loudspeaker that Bryan Dorn would be speaking in twenty minuets at the town square. Then the flatbed truck would fetch up in the square and a country string band would perform on its "stage" until a crowd gathered. Then another relative would review Bryan Dorn's military record and his career. Finally, the candidate himself would hop lithely onto the flatbed.

Generally wearing an expensive suit, often white linen or seersucker, sometimes navy broadcloth, he always gestured as wildly as a circus barker. He was essentially an enthusiastic Sunday school teacher talking about the religion of politics. Always it seemed natural to him. Usually it moved his audiences.[30]

Brother Watson recalled with admiration and affection the "psychology" employed, for Bryan Dorn reached the people "who were ignored," and, in fact, "[he] exuded a knack for touching the spirit of the people." Sounding much like them, Bryan Dorn was both "down home" and scholarly. He said he wanted to be their voice in Congress, the "voice of the people." These were the people, textile mill workers and scratch-ankle farmers that the Hare family served nobly but scarcely *knew* in person. Not only did he drive great distances inside a small area, but he walked, sometimes ten or twelve miles in a day. Steve Griffith remembered that his cousin would walk across a plowed field and shake hands with a farmer sweating at his plow and ask him to think about voting for him. He would go into a country store and order a sandwich and crackers and talk with the owner/operator and hangers-on there, sometimes saying nothing more specific than "I just wanted to speak with you." It was face-to-face, eyeball-to-eyeball, and redneck sincere. Jim Hare could not physically compete with this candidate—and he was entirely too dignified even to attempt it. Looking back at such campaigns he had observed, Edgefield's Butler Carson Derrick, himself later congressman for the selfsame district, insisted that "probably no man was ever loved by his people like Bryan Dorn in those days."[31]

In Pelzer, Dorn talked about highways built in Iran and Iraq to serve herds of goats and donkeys, and then he asked rhetorically, *Where is the highway that ought to be here?* As he asked this question, a farmer grabbed Steve Griffith and said, "This is a great man! Who wouldn't vote for him?"

---

[30] Interviews: Watson Dorn, Steve Griffith," WJBD/SCPC.

[31] Ibid.; reminiscence, Butler Carson Derrick, "The Art of Political Biography," 22 January 2013, WJBD/SCPC; *Essential Writings of Machiavelli*, ed. Constantine, 74.

And Steve, not missing the moment, squeezed the man's arm and said, "Go get your family and your neighbors and vote for him!" Again, Jim Hare and his relatives could not campaign like that.[32]

All campaigners for Dorn, not least Bryan himself, pressed flyers into the hands of the people. These flyers were designed by Dorns and Griffiths and in their day conveyed a message in its way as country slick as anything conjured at greater expense by Madison Avenue ad men. There was a picture of Bryan Dorn and a picture of the tenant house where he was born in Greenwood. There were some brief phrases about his farming, his war service, and his church service. The flyers folded up into something easily held by hand, and the simple words and simple graphics were ideal for the hard-working textile and farming workers. Unlike Hare and others, the Dorns knew that most textile workers and most local farmers could read, and, in fact, were proud of their ability to read. Nana and Dada had helped the previous generation to learn to do so, and this generation of millhands was the beneficiary of that work. Millworkers had some vocabulary, they had colorful expressions, and they loved a good story, all features of any Baptist sermon and all features of Bryan Dorn speeches and the flyers. Steve and Watson and other family members would give a few dollars to some young fellows, and these teenagers would be driven around the mill villages handing out these flyers in neighborhoods. If the boys found no one home, they left the flyer in the door. The candidate himself mastered the technique of appearing at a mill as the midnight shift came to work, shaking hands, handing out flyers, and at least once giving a long campaign speech. Members of that 1950 campaign insist that they went to every textile mill and covered every street in every mill village, at least in the five chosen counties, and from the voter turnout in the mill villages, it seems entirely possible.[33]

The first primary ballot was close, as expected. What was unexpected was that Bryan Dorn polled the *most* votes, 24,010 to Jim Hare's 22,837. However, it was a plurality and not a majority. As feared, Theo Vaughn with 4,806 votes and S. T. Heyward with 1,923 votes had collected enough support to prevent a majority poll on first ballot. Hare seemed to be exhausted by the prospect of a runoff primary, but the Dorn clan and friends seemed to be wildly energized. Both candidates understood that many would fail to vote in a runoff, and thus their own vote totals would drop. That was why the veteran Jim Hare was disheartened, for he had the task of declining and

[32] Interview: Steve Griffith, WJBD/SCPC.

[33] Ibid.; WJBD, *OTP*, 119–25.

deteriorating *less* than his opponent. In the runoff, the Dorn team was able to retain 98 percent of their first ballot, polling 23,581. By contrast, the dispirited Hare family held only 87 percent of their first ballot, polling 19,840—and thereby exiting congressional politics.[34]

At once, with great patience and painstaking care, Bryan Dorn began a campaign to win back the Hare family as friends and allies. Part of that was practical and even disingenuous—he needed their support and the support of the 20,000 Hare partisans concentrated in four counties. Nevertheless, much of it, probably most of it, reflected Bryan Dorn's firm conviction that politics was important business and those who served always deserved respect and appreciation, especially as they took their exit from the only important stage he knew. Anyone who served, *even and especially opponents*, deserved his respect and thanks—and from this moment on, all such opponents got his respect. From this moment onward, victorious opponents, even Republicans, were warmly congratulated in person and in writing. Losers, even Republicans and especially Northern Republicans, were warmly thanked for their service in person and in writing.[35]

While making his preparations for the return to Congress, the nominee and everyone else learned on 25 June 1950 that the Communists of North Korea led by Kim Il Sung had attacked South Korea, led by the US-supported Syngman Rhee. Kim's troops crossed the 38th parallel that had been established as a boundary between the ideological rivals who dominated the peninsula in northeastern Asia. Details were few, and the attack was a shock.

What to do was a dilemma. As recently as 12 January 1949 Secretary of State Dean Acheson had told the National Press Club that nothing in the Korean Peninsula was of vital concern to US security, and one week later the House of Representatives had declined foreign aid of any kind to Syngman Rhee's authoritarian but decidedly anti-Communist Republic of Korea. Jim Hare, while serving, had voted against the aid and had paid little attention to the tensions in the peninsula, despite his own scholarly interest in foreign affairs, his hatred of Communism, and his father's own history of activism in Pacific Ocean affairs. As for Dorn, despite his vigorous anti-Communism,

---

[34] Jordan, *The Primary State*, 106–107.

[35] Roper, "The Art of Political Biography," 22 January 2013; idem., "Bryan Dorn," address, 15 May 2014, American Council of Special Collections, Columbia, SC, hereinafter ACSC.

he had made no issue at all about the votes concerning South Korea in the town-square debates and in other venues.[36]

Bryan Dorn had to catch up quick to learn the facts and familiarize himself with the issues. Not unexpectedly, the dedicated Cold Warrior concluded that Congress had missed the facts of dangerous aggression. No less than Red China's Mao Zedong was said to be helping Kim Il Sung, and that intelligence alone was enough to send Bryan Dorn into an aggressive support of Syngman Rhee. In that support, he was well behind the curve of the rapidly developing Truman policy, which sought United Nations support to stop North Korea and which quickly sent no less than Douglas MacArthur with two full army divisions into the fray. Thus lately in step with Truman, he was out of step with national popular opinion— and the folk in the red hills had not even heard any of these Korean issues discussed by any of the primary candidates, especially the winner.[37]

Back in Washington, Bryan Dorn had to make it up with Harry Truman and the national Democratic Party. At the personal level, it was easy to do, since he liked Truman and since he had been careful in the Dixiecrat campaign to speak *for* his cousin Thurmond rather than *against* his party's president. Nor had he ever accepted the term Dixiecrat for himself in that presidential race; while out of office he had volunteered to speak for mainline party regular Democrats in many different venues. Too, even by the early weeks of January 1951 the Korean War was a consuming liability for Truman, a bloody mess in a little understood quagmire that by then involved the huge ground forces of Mao's Red Army. Truman was happy to have Dorn's support for the increasingly unpopular war, and arranged a fact-finding trip to Japan and Korea for the congressman in late fall, concluding in Thanksgiving of 1951. The trip—the longest period of time he would spend away from Millie—put him with army, navy, and air force brass but also with common grunts and gobs. He saw plenty that was wrong but was profoundly reaffirmed in his anti-Communism, even and especially if one had to support an authoritarian like Syngman Rhee. Following philosopher Hannah Arendt, he concluded that anti-totalitarian authoritarians like Chiang Kai-Shek and Syngman Rhee could be persuaded to develop democratic social policies and free-market economies over time. He was pleased

---

[36] HR 53330, remarks, Cong. Rec. vol. 95, pt. 7, 81st Cong. 1st sess., 28 June 1949, 8534; *Congressional Record*, vol. 95, pt. 8, 81st Cong., 1st sess., 26 July 1949, 10255.

[37] WJBD, remarks, *Congressional Record*, vol. 95, pt. 11, 81st Cong., 1st sess., 12 October 1949, 14337–39.

to spend hours with Douglas MacArthur, and he concluded from these discussions on this trip that both military and political policies in South Korea were "on track."[38]

As for the Truman domestic policy, Dorn lined up often with Sam Rayburn and Jack Kennedy and Carl Albert, each of whom had befriended the red-hills man early and remained his ally if not benefactor. JFK was on the make, bound for the US Senate, while Rayburn was ever the House's brilliant schoolmaster, a grander version of Dada with his own board of education offices in the bowels of the House chamber where errant Democrats and youngish Republicans were quietly and privately shown the error of their ways. By contrast with the flashy JFK and the authoritarian Rayburn, Carl Albert became Dorn's model for quiet and patient and tireless constituent service, the politician's politician and the most loyal, most effective, and the least obvious among party insiders.[39]

One dramatic force abuilding was Lyndon Baines Johnson, like JFK on the make and rising toward the Senate, perhaps toward the presidency. LBJ was initially a friend, but he had shown such coldness toward his personal and political benefactor Sam Rayburn (apparently even scheming to convince FDR that Rayburn was not to be trusted), that Dorn moved around the giant Texan with an outward caution and inward distrust. Despite regional distinctions and differences in personalities, even differences in morality (JFK was famously a womanizer, LBJ famously a corner-cutter on his path from poverty to wealth), LBJ, Rayburn, Albert, and to some extent even the New Englander JFK were much the same, essentially Populistic New Dealers focused on pocketbook issues and all but obsessed about nagging unemployment and poor schools in their respective homelands. Each man, too, could see quite clearly that treatment of black people must change, both short term with regard to basic rights and long term with regard to structural changes in economic opportunities. Moreover, each of these men, with different accents and different time tables, conceded privately that Harry Truman was right about racial justice for the long run: racial integration

---

[38] Paul Mousel to WJBD, 8 May 1951; WJBD and Millie Dorn, October and November 1951; WJBD, "Bryan Dorn Representing the People," 1984 cassette, Greenwood District 50 South Carolina Educational Television, WJBD/SCPC, hereinafter "Bryan Dorn Representing the People," 1984; Arendt, *The Origins of Totalitarianism* (1951; 1966).

[39] WJBD, remarks, HR 53330; WJBD, "In His Own Words" and "Bryan Dorn Representing the People," 1984; Congressional Papers, especially VA folders, 1951–1956, WJBD/SCPC; Board of Education, Caro, *Means of Ascent*, 17.

and economic opportunities were bound to be the tasks for the next dozen Congresses and the next half dozen presidential administrations.[40]

As Dorn saw things, there was a greater sense of urgency about speeding up the arrival of economic opportunities than there was about speeding up arrival at that point of racial integration. If Greenwood's own Benjamin Mays at Morehouse College and his bright young students and A. Phillip Randolph and the leaders of the NAACP and Urban League and CORE could march with Truman and support his policies because of racial possibilities, then at some level cousin Strom Thurmond (then out of office and temporarily with few prospects in this year) and various reactionaries were right: Truman's economic Populism and his official policies were going to bring racial integration in the long run. Redoubtable Senator Olin Dewitt Talmadge Johnston, hero of the millhands, intended to postpone arrival at that interracial intersection as long as possible. In the meantime Senator Olin Johnston would offer his textile masses genuine and material service alongside a negrophobic rhetoric of scary intensity. The combination of racist demagoguery with substantive economic reform enabled Johnston to come close to the original William Jennings Bryan and Thomas A. Watson as a regional folk hero of the red hills—and it allowed him to defeat in one-on-one contests Cole Blease, Cotton Ed Smith, Strom Thurmond, and handsome young Fritz Hollings—South Carolina's political equivalent of striking out the heart of the 1927 New York Yankees batting order.[41]

With Olin Johnston, Truman had set to one side his own racial Liberalism in order to get needed support for the other parts of the Fair Deal. For all that, Dorn knew that he was not that kind of Olin Johnston genius: he neither supported such an expansive welfare state nor would he engage in race-baiting. Less adroit and more sincere than LBJ or Olin Johnston, William Jennings Bryan Dorn went into Congress in January 1951 as an aggressive Cold Warrior supporting an unpopular war (a picture of a Korean scene went up on the walls in his new offices alongside pictures of Brother J. S. Abney, Clemson College, Newberry College, and a pastoral scene from Walhalla). He was otherwise a moderate segregationist and a Fair Dealer

---

[40] LBJ betrayal of Rayburn, Caro, *Means of Ascent*, 17, 18, 23, 124; populistic New Deal progressives, McMath, "History of the Present," 80–100.

[41] Simon, *A Fabric of Defeat*; Huss, *Senator for the South*; Bass, *Ol' Strom*, 119–34; Bass, "Art of Political Biography," 22 January 2013; Olin DeWitt Talmadge Johnston Papers, 1923–1956, SCPC, hereinafter ODTJ/SCPC; WJBD and ODTJ, 1950–1956, WJBD/SCPC.

who focused government spending on the textile industry. He did so knowing that it was currently a season for extreme racist rhetoric. Yet he did so knowing as well that a new season was around the bend when racial language could not be harsh and hateful, when black people must be real citizens. He came back into office planning a political stance at once conciliatory with all sides and lonely, since the only person with whom he agreed completely about domestic policy, foreign policy, and civil rights was the Arkansan Brooks Hays, his beloved Vaughn Bible Class Sunday school mate now out of office although still active as lobbyist and facilitator for church justice causes.[42]

Dorn and others who genuinely liked Truman and wanted to bring economic Populism to their impoverished regions urged Truman and his people to go slow on confrontation with Jim Crow. In the newly formed Congress, Dorn was neither a freshman nor a returning letterman; in football parlance, he was like a player who had been quite active as a freshman and then took the so styled "redshirt" that kept him involved in team activities but not in actual contests. He was pleased to gain an assignment on the Veterans Administration Committee, on which he was quite junior, but he quickly reacquainted himself with Populistic New Dealer Texan Olin "Tiger" Teague, who was generous with his personal time and politically patient with the hard-charging redshirt sophomore on his committee.[43]

There was also the House Un-American Activities Committee (HUAC), which was still going strong. Bryan Dorn liked its members and agreed with most of its policies. He often spoke in their favor, but he did have two overwhelming problems with their focused anti-Communism. First was his own hard-won lesson from 1949: his constituents cheered Red-baiting and Fed-bashing, but they *voted* on pocketbook issues. Thus, his focus must always be trained on their district macro-economy and even their highly personal needs in his beautiful but impoverished Third District. Second, he had friends, one white and one black, who were subject to Red-baiting and to HUAC investigations. The first of these was John Bolt Culbertson, Greenville attorney and ally in many causes involving millhands; Culbertson was a dear friend but disagreed with Dorn about how fast to

---

[42] Hays, *A Southern Moderate Speaks*; WJBD to J. S. Abney, 25 January 1951; correspondence, WJBD and Hays, 1947–1956, and Vaughn Bible Class Pamphlet, 1951; WJBD and Drane brothers, 1945, 1946, and especially retrospective, William Bryan Drane to WJBD, 6 May 1963, WJBD/SCPC.

[43] VA folder, 1951 and Congressional folders, 1951–1953, WJBD/SCPC.

bring reform, with the congressman saying *Go slow* and Culbertson saying, *It has already been too long*. The second was Benjamin Elijah Mays, born to children of slaves in the onetime Greenwood community of Rambo. Now the distinguished Morehouse College president, Mays was known personally to Dorn and the congressman genuinely admired his work. Even better, Culbertson and Mays were in the Baptist reform tradition that Dada, Nana, and the Rev. Jim Bowers had taught, the self-same traditions of Brooks Hays and members of the Vaughn Bible Class in DC. Without giving Culbertson or Mays much support in specific social causes, Dorn at the same time was bound and determined that neither man would be swept up in some bogus congressional sweep of suspected Reds.[44]

In the meantime, Dorn stood at that frontier between core values in the party's ideology and practical lawmaking, that awkward place where generalized values met specific bills pending before members of Congress. No piece of legislation, Fair Deal or otherwise, was "actualized" in Aristotle's sense or otherwise "real" in anyone's meaning of the word until it could be paid for—and nothing could be paid for without advice and consent from the House of Representatives. Working with Sam Rayburn and Olin Teague and others—and adroitly rolling logs with Midwestern and Western Republicans—Bryan Dorn could help create strong protections for South Carolina textile manufacturing and better health care for veterans in the VA system. He could work with Populistic New Deal progressives to improve the protections of welfare capitalism, or the safety net, or whatever one wanted to call such constituent service for small-time farmers, small-time businessmen, and millhands. And all of that helped black people as well as white people. Too, he would continue to make personal gifts to black congregations and to help black veterans and the many black "constituents" (generally prevented from voting in the Third District, although quite a potent force in cities of size outside his district) on their pocketbook issues, if not on their social issues.

As for those social issues addressed frontally by Truman's strong civil rights platform, Dorn resisted. He cooperated with Sam Rayburn and Olin Teague and friends in the Virginia delegation who answered to the Byrd Machine. These shifting coalitions of folk were able to slow things down, to hang things up, to underfund and even defund certain Fair Deal initiatives, especially fair housing and equal employment. As a consequence, many of

---

[44] John Bolt Culbertson Papers, SCPC; Roper, *The Magnificent Mays*. 233, 240, 244–50; Herbert Hartsook, remarks, "Art of Political Biography," 22 January 2013.

Truman's civil rights provisions could not be actualized during the years of the Fair Deal. On the largest social issues, Dorn's Fair Deal for Textiles was for the white people.[45]

On one point in particular, Dorn abandoned parliamentary tricks and went loudly public rather than his more typical strategy of helping to bury things in subcommittees. The issue was fair employment, something that Dorn would endorse and loudly vote for in twenty more years. But in 1951, few things so concerned millhands as the concept of special compensatory treatment for the profoundly disadvantaged black workers pushed off the old cotton farms but denied entry into factories. Truman and racially liberal allies in Congress proposed a federally mandated Fair Employment Practices Commission (FEPC), making permanent and powerful FDR's wartime agency of the same name. Truman's FEPC was to enforce an end to discrimination against people of color in the competition for jobs. In fact, even then Dorn tolerated this much as far as the military went, and to lesser degree, with some more complaining, he tolerated it with regard to those civilian firms who contracted to do work for the military, namely, civilian contractors going onto Donaldson Air Base in Greenville, Fort Jackson in Columbia, or Fort Gordon in Augusta, should have integrated workforces. As noted, each of those large military installations lay outside the Third District, but each was close enough for constituent contractors to be directly affected. He and his people were genuine patriots, and many families in his countryside were like the Dorns, who had sent a family platoon to train at such military bases prior to service overseas.

But as for making all civilian workplaces fully integrated, the idea was beyond Bryan Dorn's comprehension. Beyond the textile mills, the mom-and-pop stores, and the small businesses in the medium-sized and small towns, these workplaces that featured a few dozen people "in propinquity," where laborers worked side by side in close quarters, for those sites (the majority of businesses in the Third District) Dorn supported traditional Jim Crow separation by color. He intended for the nonmilitary small and medium business, at least in his Third District, to stay segregated in the near term.[46]

---

[45] VA folder and general folder, 1951–1953, WJBD/SCPC; Aristotle, "Metaphysics," *Works,* vol. 8, ed. and trans., Ross.

[46] Congressional folders, 1951–1953, WJBD/SCPC; "propinquity," Woodward and Williamson, *C. Vann Woodward*, ed., Roper, 213.

Yet Truman not only had a goal of integrating the workforce, he established his FEPC to work in tandem with the Justice Department to ensure that all businesses engaged in interstate commerce gave men and women of color the chance to work for them. After some time attempting to demonstrate that some businesses were not interstate, Bryan Dorn faced the fact that that all businesses were: in the early days of FDR's New Deal, the Supreme Court considered that virtually all business was interstate commerce, since all roads connected to some road that left one state and entered another state, and since all businesses in the modern world used resources from other states. Thus, even those relatively isolated mom-and-pop stores in the rural piedmont were engaged in interstate commerce. That was especially the case in his homeland, where it was no long trip to Georgia or North Carolina, and indeed Millie's favorite professor had made a serious socioeconomic study of the fluid and permeable Carolinas and Georgia borderlands. Too, Bryan Dorn wanted businesses to grow and prosper, not as abusive monopolies, but far beyond what most were, and thus he wanted all businesses in the Third District to become interstate commerce. The FEPC, if fully funded and staffed with committed civil rights personnel, could compel integrated workforces even and especially in the segregated mom-and-pop businesses of Bryan Dorn's country.

One defense was states' rights civil rights, Brooks Hays's singular insistence that each state claimed a sphere of influence over affairs inside its borders. But unlike John C. Calhoun, in his own statements and restatements of states' rights, Bryan Dorn had always said that in case of conflict, the claims of the federal government, by fact if not by justice, inevitably took precedence. A fully funded and fully empowered FEPC in conflict with South Carolina's Jim Crow laws and practices in the workplace would finally win any dispute once the judiciary began a full and systematic review of such conflicts. Thus, he would talk about states' rights civil rights, but he would turn his greatest energies to destroying the FEPC, and in this practical fight, there were conservative Republicans who would join him. And, though he regretted it, there was the fact that it suited all Republicans to make Truman appear incompetent and unable to enforce his own policies. For a myriad of reasons, Truman's FEPC was a suitable target for the congressman; that is, it was a target he could not miss.[47]

---

[47] Hays, *A Southern Moderate Speaks*; Hays and Dorn correspondence, 1948–1958, WJBD/SCPC.

As for the practices of states' rights civil rights in South Carolina, James F. Byrnes had been elected governor in 1950 and thus was the enforcing officer as well as guiding light for whatever the Palmetto State used its sovereign rights to do about civil rights. Byrnes took office as the most distinguished living sandlapper and the only native son with a resume as long as John C. Calhoun's. Once very important in FDR's administration, Byrnes had served as senator, vice president, Supreme Court associate justice, and secretary of state. In Truman's administration, he specialized in foreign affairs, but in 1949 he left the State Department in tight-lipped but white-hot anger over some issue of foreign policy. Perhaps there were other things not expressed by Truman's people: liberal integrationism was part and parcel of Truman's foreign policy, and Byrnes represented moderate segregationism, hardly acceptable to Truman or his team. Perhaps, too, Byrnes was not respected for his foreign policy acumen as much as he thought he deserved. Byrnes, for his part, considered Truman and Dean Acheson insufficiently aggressive in the fight against Communism. For their part, the Cold Warriors may have doubted Byrnes's diplomatic skills.

As governor, Byrnes set his face firmly against any form of integration while also trying to end violence against the state's black population. He increased allocations for the State Law Enforcement Division (SLED) and gave firm orders to prosecute Klan or other violent negrophobes. He also vowed to make the school system truly separate BUT equal, and he spent heavily to improve salaries for black teachers, improve education courses at South Carolina State College, buy new books for the black schools, and build some impressive new school buildings. But the main part of his formula remained the word "separate," and Bryan Dorn knew there would be no gradual integration between 1951 and 1955 while Jimmy Byrnes held sway. That much, plus the firm commitments to protect the lives and persons of black people, Bryan Dorn saluted; but a problem for him was that Byrnes had completely disengaged himself from the national Democratic Party. Since Dorn, following Brooks Hays, fully intended to remain a Democrat, Governor Byrnes emerged as a powerful and prestigious problem for him. Byrnes must be accorded maximum respect, but Dorn could not follow him.[48]

---

[48] "James F. Byrnes," *New York Times* obituary, 10 April 1972; James F. Brynes Reading Room, Law Library of the University of South Carolina; Hays and Dorn correspondence, 1951–1955, WJBD/SCPC; *Essential Writings of Machiavelli*, ed. Constantine, 68–69, 74.

Dorn's congressional and personal correspondence files show his careful work to dismantle Truman's efforts at racial justice in the workplace, as they show his specific assurances to the small-town people who owned the little businesses in the Third District. He was emphatic in such correspondence, saying that Communists existing at every level of business and government were misleading local black people—he was meticulous to write *Colored* in correspondence and to say *Negro* in public address. He also portrayed the FEPC as a massive juggernaut of overwhelming threat to the small businesses back home. He knew full well he was exaggerating the intent and effect of FEPC. He was also emphatic that only he could protect the Third District from excesses of "One Worldism" and "Northern Liberalism." Withal he insisted that he was a liberal following the racial assumptions and practices of Thomas Jefferson, William Jennings Bryan, Woodrow Wilson, and Franklin Delano Roosevelt—claims that academics could uphold if and only if one presumed that no thinking man ever evolved beyond a particular perspective on a social issue.[49]

One address in particular caught up his full passions and full oratorical skills. He called it "Toward Socialism," and he delivered it in the nation's capital and nearby, memorably in Charlottesville, Virginia. He made sure that newspapermen and women and magazine men and women quoted it, and he made sure that constituents high and low got copies. In the speech, he celebrated Thomas Jefferson by name and Brooks Hays by inference. He defined Liberalism to mean small government, locally based, with a grass roots racial justice and a community's care and concern for the less fortunate citizens. Baptist community compassion and local community self-help were yoked with the younger Jefferson's Virginia states' rights (certainly not the president who bought the Mississippi River Valley and conducted economic warfare against the British—most of that by executive fiat). He talked about big government creating demand-pull inflation by direct purchases and goods and services, and he noted that such resultant inflation in an indirect and gradual way worked hardships on mom-and-pop businesses. He also complained that big government laid ruinous regulations on the backs of the same small firms, which created an immediate and direct hardship on the same firms. It was Populistic in tone but ignored the same Populistic reliance on government interference in imperfect markets and preference for regulations to protect the consumer and the small-time producer from mo-

---

[49] Congressional files, 1951–1953; personal files, 1951–1953; retrospective, WJBD to Grace Andrews, 21 April 1958, WJBC/SCPC.

nopoly suppliers. It was quite stirring but did not have a great deal to do with his actual political behavior, which was to support the Fair Deal on pocketbook issues in his district, and to continue supporting the remains of the Populistic New Deal, especially in veterans' benefits and in Social Security pensions for the elderly and the disabled—both of which came early and often for the denizens of his Third District, who lived short, care-worn, and hard lives. In later years, he would concede that when push came to shove, he supported welfare Liberalism as practiced by the Truman Democrats. The ideals of "Toward Socialism," like his preference for the rhetoric of Frederick A. Hayek, were sincere enough, but at the point of voting, he was and would always be a militaristic Keynesian with a Fair Deal for the textile classes and masses and with a sizeable protective safety net for service veterans.[50]

As Dorn perfected the delivery of this signature speech, he came to realize something important about his role and his reputation. The speech, deeply spiritualistic and emotionally stirring, yet had a rather academic tone as well. He could preserve copies of it and be proud of it decades later, even and especially if he changed his mind about the small-government policies prescribed therein. Yet "Toward Socialism" came from that 50,000-word manuscript that he had presented to editor Lambert Davis of the University of North Carolina Press. That manuscript itself was intensely time-bound, with a tone and a scope appropriate to a campaign in his congressional district alone. In future years, he might even be ashamed of it, especially if it sat on the shelves in book form. Davis told him as much, declaring "sympathy" for the intent and admiration for some of its suggestions (such as Dorn's proposal to spend $20 million, in twenty-first-century currency $177 million, to build a medical college for black students). On the other hand, Davis noted "factual inaccuracies" and logical "sloppiness" and urged a long and concentrated period of "digging up facts" and "thinking things through." The UNC Press was not going to publish the manuscript, and Davis implied that such a book published elsewhere could bring eventual him embarrassment. Dorn appreciated the counsel and never sent the manuscript and book proposal elsewhere, probably after talking with Millie Dorn, one quite wise in the ways of publishing. Furthermore, again probably with Millie Dorn's

---

[50] WJBD, "Toward Socialism"; correspondence with Grace Andrews, especially retrospective, Grace Andrews to WJBD, 21 April 1958, WJBD/SCPC.

help, he seems to have destroyed the manuscript, for nothing like it remains in the sizeable collection of Dorn papers.[51]

There was one issue, however, that was so personal and so principled that it made a breach between President Truman and Bryan Dorn. It was not, in fact, about any aspect of race relations. Indeed, this subject created a rift between Bryan Dorn and most of the Truman Democrats, even some in the Southern ranks. The issue was the Korean War, and the flashpoint was the personal nature of the dispute between General Douglas MacArthur and his commander in chief. Truman removed MacArthur for insubordination on 11 April 1951, replacing him with Matthew Bunker Ridgway and calling Mac home to stateside. Dorn remembered the event bitterly, pointedly noting that he had been with MacArthur "only 48 hours before" the firing. Not only was Dorn stunned by the surprise, but the general himself apparently was completely unprepared. Subsequently, MacArthur enjoyed a ticker-tape parade in New York, a memorable appearance before Congress, and enough popular acclaim even for his large ego. Not obvious in April, but obvious by the following November, was the way the war effort improved *after* Mac's removal.

On things military, Bryan Dorn, in retrospect, was never well informed on grand strategy, but only on specific tactics. While neither he nor his biographer were particularly qualified to analyze MacArthur's strategy in Korea, a host of carefully executed military studies now judge Mac wrong. The record shows clearly that the dramatic turnaround in the war effort can be traced directly and consequentially to MacArthur's removal and Ridgway's installation. As to constitutional issues, there are simply no records of any commander in chief allowing any of his field officers to defy direct orders on such large issues. The onetime air force man liked the idea of bold air attack on China, not to exclude nuclear weapons. But in the field of conflict as authorized by President Truman and supported by the UN international forces, MacArthur's infantry tactics resulted in disaster, while his successor Ridgway rolled the North Korean and Chinese forces back to the original 38th parallel, thereby achieving the stated mission of the conflict. In this instance, as with the civil rights disputes, Congressman Dorn at the time won the fight on the home turf of public opinion but he lost the war on the issues, and in retrospect he looks limited in vision and perception, however

---

[51] Lambert Davis to WJBD, 16 January 1951, and WJBD to Davis, 20 January 1951, WJBD/SCPC.

politically shrewd for the nonce. By contrast, Truman lost the fights in contemporaneous public opinion and yet won the foreign and domestic wars in all regards. For 1951, Truman's unpopularity, largely traceable to the Korean War and to his civil rights initiatives, sank as low as any recorded by modern polling techniques; by contrast, Bryan Dorn's regional popularity soared.[52]

For all his heady rhetoric on the grand issues of Reds and Feds, Bryan Dorn otherwise stuck to his legislative knitting for his constituents. There was the slow, patient, deliberate service to Third District citizens and the even slower and more patient development of cooperation and teamwork with the agencies of special interest and their officers, or, if you will, their lobbyists. Robert Schumacher joined his congressional staff, and for four sessions was the "Man" that Nana had wanted to run his offices on behalf of his people. Schumacher understood that it was less important to Congressman Dorn what some general wanted than was the issue of how grunts and gobs were actually treated on active duty—and even more important how veterans were treated in VA facilities long after their active duties were completed. Many government agencies at all levels of public affairs dealt with currently serving troops and with veterans, and several of those agencies were served by none other than Robert Hayne Hare from "that family" in the Third District. Officially, the onetime JAG-court legal officer was, by 1950, navy liaison to Congress, with special duties to show various appropriations committees why the navy and the marines needed something in particular funded. Brother Watson Dorn had left such a position in order to direct Bryan's 1950 campaign, and so the Dorns already knew much about this work that still another Hare was doing. Robert Hayne Hare took special pains to show the Veterans Affairs Committee why naval veterans needed particular services. The congressman always paid attention and saw to it that Tiger Teague and those who outranked him on Veterans Affairs heard the liaison officer out. Generally, Bryan Dorn was unfailingly polite to political opponents, especially when the contest was over, and he was so with Robert Hayne Hare. A naval commission had begun a study for a navy museum in Charleston, and then-Congressman Jim Hare had nominated his close kin

---

[52] Stueck, *The Korean War*; Casey, *Selling the Korean War*; WJBD, Eulogy on MacArthur, *Cong. Rec. vol. 110, pt. 3, 88th Cong., 2d sess.*, 5 April 1964, 6871; WJBD, "Bryan Dorn Representing the People" (1984), Greenwood District 50 South Carolina Educational Television, cassette, WJBD/SCPC; and Casey and Stueck, "Reflections on the McArthur Controversy."

to serve on that commission. Nothing was official until the elected congressman could affirm the nomination, but of course Bryan Dorn was quick to close the deal on the appointment. It was yet another example of the way families were the catalysts of South Carolina Democratic politics, not only in the contests for seats but in the operation of politically mandated functions. It was also one more example of Bryan Dorn's determination to make and keep political friends. Robert Hayne Hare in particular and the Hare clan in general were thereafter loyal political and personal friends, as Dorn intended.[53]

The first year back in the Old Congressional Offices thus ended with personal success against a backdrop of a failing presidency, a failing war, resurgent Republicans, and demoralized Democrats.

---

[53] Key, "South Carolina," *South in Politics*; correspondence, WJBD and Grace Andrews, 1951–1958; V.A. folder, 1951 and Congressional folders, 1951–1953; id est, retrospective, Robert Hayne Hare to WJBD, 23 March 1960, WJBD/SCPC; interview: Watson Dorn, JHR/SCPC; *Essential Writings of Machiavelli*, ed. Constantine, 68–74, foes; Aristotle, *Politics*, trans., Jowett, Bk 1, ch. 2 and 3, family.

Chapter 6

Sound the Horn
1952–1956

In many ways, Dwight David Eisenhower was Bryan Dorn's perfect answer to the contemporaneous failures in his country. Ike was the personification of a thoroughly remoralized two-party politics. He was a hero of modern war, that is, a great military engineer who identified problems within precise parameters and then deployed force in exactly the right amount to fix the stated problem. He could fulfill the mission as agreed beforehand. Ike was no dreamer, for who wants a dreamer for an engineer? Dorn considered FDR and Harry Truman to be great architects—and they had dreamed up grand plans, many of which Dorn liked. But Dorn wanted an engineer who could make things *work*. Someone needed to eliminate waste and instead focus carefully the use of scarce and expensive resources, especially human resources. Someone needed to eliminate the bad plans, or at least the unworkable plans, and thereby save the good plans. A chief executive, bucked up by cooperative legislators, needed to incorporate political compromise in the way that Dorn read about in John Stuart Mill's essays. President and congressmen and congresswomen had to regain an understanding of compromise, both for getting laws passed and for administering resultant services wisely and equably. Ike the military engineer knew how and when to compromise and knew how to prevent the perfect from becoming the enemy of the possible.[1]

By contradistinction, Harry Truman no longer inspired by the winter of 1952. As Dorn judged it, the president was worn out by the many challenges he had bravely faced—and also worn out from political wrangling to no good end, much of which was his own fault. If Truman stepped aside, Bryan Dorn would be happy to endorse and work for the election of Eisenhower. And when Eisenhower was elected president, Congressman Dorn

---

[1] Mill, *Collected Works*, ed. Robson, vol. 31; practicality, WJBD, *OTP*, 237–38; on Eisenhower, 152–55; 174–75.

would be happier still to work with him to move the country forward and "clean up the mess in Washington," as was said in the day.[2]

There was a problem. It was stunning to Bryan Dorn and to many. Eisenhower had no personal political history, that is, no experience working on behalf of either party. He had mastered the intensely political military during an extremely political world war, but those were gifts demonstrated in the military context of army, navy, and air corps, not the American political context of Democrat and Republican. That was the general problem, the one of inexperience, or rather experience in a military politics less relevant for civilian context. But there was a specific problem as well. Ike revealed that he was, at least in the Truman era, a Republican. Bryan Dorn would ever and always work *with* Republicans but never *for* them. His namesake had more than once remarked, if finding himself standing on a manure spreader in order to address a crowd, that he had never before stood on a Republican platform. Bryan Dorn also regarded Republican platforms as manure spreaders, and he was no more inclined to stand on one than William Jennings Bryan or Tom Watson or Andrew Jackson.[3]

On 29 March 1952, Truman announced that he would not seek reelection, and that announcement was followed on 11 April 1952 by Truman's public agreement to release Eisenhower from his military duties in order to pursue political office *as a Republican*. Bryan Dorn's Democrats then faced the daunting challenge of finding a good candidate for president to run against a good man who was standing on a manure spreader.

Adlai Ewing Stevenson emerged as leading candidate, and Bryan Dorn fully approved. Stevenson, the intellectual, was a self-proclaimed liberal, but in a professorial way, that is, detached and cool about commitments. Case by case, his practices and performance were perfectly in line with the Populistic New Deal progressives of the Southern states. In fact, Stevenson had North Carolina roots and branches in his family, and he could and did talk with Dorn and the other Southern members of Congress about vinegar-based or mustard-based barbeque, bright leaf or burley tobacco, whether any elec-

---

[2] On Truman, WJBD, "In His Own Words"; WJBD/SCPC; WJBD, *OTP*, 90–91; Eisenhower as Democrat, WJBD, *OTP*, 134; Eisenhower as politician, WJBD, "Statement on the Passing of President Eisenhower," 28 March 1969 press release, speeches, WJBD/SCPC.

[3] Bryan and Republicans, Cherny, *A Righteous Cause*; WJBD and Republicans, "Future of the Democratic Party," *Cong. Rec. vol. 110, pt 3, 88th Cong., 2d sess.*, 13 February–3 March 3,1964, 2965–66; and WJBD to LBJ, 10 January 1964, WJBD/SCPC.

tronic instrument could be properly involved in traditional country music, Scotch-Irish ways of establishing a family farm—and he knew most of the verses in "Amazing Grace." On the thorniest issue of the day, race relations, Stevenson assured Bryan Dorn and others that a new day of justice must come, but that it could come slowly, with all due deference to Southern reluctance to change social etiquette. Stevenson on race issues was thus no threat to the vision of Brooks Hays—or that of Bryan Dorn.[4]

Nor was there any question that a President Stevenson would work with Keynesian economic policies aimed at finding jobs and building roads and schools in loyal districts like Bryan Dorn's. There was likewise no worry that he would attempt anything at all as grand as Truman's plans for dramatically changing Social Security to include federal guarantees of medical care for all Americans. And, although no military hawk, Stevenson was sufficiently anti-Communist and sufficiently committed to the maintenance of Southern air bases, naval bases, and army training centers that Cold Warriors like Dorn among Southern delegations were comfortable. Too, Stevenson chose as his running mate Alabama's John Jackson Sparkman, the venerable Southern Democrat. This, then, was not 1948, and Bryan Dorn happily worked for Adlai Stevenson for president, confident that the Democrats remained safe again in the Third District.[5]

As for competition in the selfsame district for Congress, Bryan Dorn himself was safe from primary challenges in 1952. The Hares were at peace with the Dorns, the once-reluctant counties of Abbeville, Oconee, and Saluda were now filled with Dorn constituents who had been well served, and the locally based "Methodist circuits" (bands or cells of family and friends) were ready to go into action once again. In fact, between 1952 and 1956, Bryan Dorn was able to deploy Southern Populistic New Deal language and the Fair Deal for Textiles that made his Third District a "safe seat" for him.[6]

---

[4] WJBD to Frank Van der Linden, 21 November 1955; WJBD to A. S. Mike Monroney, 21 September 1952; retrospective, Estes Kefauver to WJBD, 14 November 1956, WJBD/SCPC; Martin, *Adlai Stevenson of Illinois*.

[5] Retrospective, Estes Kefauver to WJBD, 14 November 1956, WJBD/SCPC; Martin, *Adlai Stevenson of Illinois;* Steve Fraser, "Lettered Numbers Man," *Los Angeles Times*, 13 February 2005, bk. section 1; Parker, *John Kenneth Galbraith*.

[6] James Butler Hare corr., 1950, JBH/SCPC; WJBD, *OTP*, 127; "cells": American Legion Resolution #547 (Dorn coauthor), 30 August–2 September 1954 and WJBD to Miles D. Kennedy (director, American Legion), 16 February 1955; twenty-five form letters (coauthor WJBD) American Legion Posts to Congressmen and Assemblymen, 3 October 1956, and retrospective, WJBD to Wint Smith, 26 June 1956.

Careful student of Machiavelli as noted, Bryan Dorn understood well that no matter how astutely he practiced the art of politics, he could always be dislodged and even disgraced by a chance turn of Fortuna's wheel. He understood that good things came from very hard and very patient, very diligent work over years and years. He also ruefully acknowledged that one large error, or even one piece of bad luck, could undo the slow and patient building he had done. His insights were, in other words, one part Machiavelli in the Republic that had its princely—that is, autocratic—features. There was also one part Aristotle, especially the sharp focus on a certain family shape and size, a rural setting, a preserved place for farming, a protection of property—especially property in land, combined with the understanding that only by the most assiduous study of his constituency could he keep their favor. And there was a final and large part of the Fair Deal, both Harry Truman's "good lessons" about serving by faithfully meeting the needs of voting workers and Harry Truman's "bad lessons" about pushing too hard and too fast on a social agenda.[7]

Although there was some luck in his achievement, Bryan Dorn succeeded because of the most careful attention to certain issues that dominated the thoughts and feelings of his red-hills people. These issues dominated his own thoughts and feelings, because he was completely "of the people," as he liked to say. He was a cattleman or husbandman who had started as a cotton farmer, and farming was the traditional engine of his piedmont, albeit now faltering. He supported and pushed along the modernizing textile industry that was the current-day engine of growth, but he knew even then that the textile industry would live only so long, even in the Third District. Like his own Army Air Corps, these engines could fly—but not forever. For the future—for that next engine of growth for that new day when he intended to serve as the governor of South Carolina—there was needed a sophisticated, knowledge-based and value-added industry and service. Ever the child of schoolteachers, he had come to believe that constantly improving children's education plus continuing education for adults, much of it based at Clemson College, was the fuel for whatever new engine emerged in the red hills. From family, class, and personal experience, he knew where his interests lay, and he could convey those interests to people all over the Third District with the conviction of one who lived what he believed. There were specific issues

---

[7] "Bryan Dorn Representing the People," (1984), WJBD/SCPC parallels, Machiavelli, *The Discourses*, ed. and trans., Constantine, ch. 6 and 24; Aristotle, *Politics*, trans., Jowett, Bk 1, ch. 2 and 3, family; ch. 4, land and property.

he had to address as this people's congressman: veterans and their peacetime ailments; trade and aid and quotas for textile products; farming issues involving allotments, price supports, and quotas; and land-use issues, especially forests, waterways, "sustained growth," and "multiple use."[8]

Also and always there were the undying issues of race and racism, the threat posed to any program by negrophobic demagoguery, the impossibility of regional improvement without also improving the lot of black people, and the way racist demagoguery was the perpetual Gordian knot that must be untied to achieve general interracial economic progress. He addressed this tangle of issues in the general context of liberal Keynesian economics, with the Southern drawl of states' rights as enunciated by the Sam Rayburn Democrats in his Congress. 1952 bid fair to be a wonderful year for the congressman, and he wanted as well to be part of a reinvigorated national Democratic Party. Among other things, there was a chance to move up rapidly in the Veterans Affairs Committee, provided that Democrats again controlled the legislature in 1952.[9]

The home base for the Dorn family and the political base for Greenwood County remained Dada's venerable home that the romantic Army Air Corpsman Bryan Dorn had rechristened Myrtle Manor, complete with poem for the occasion. In June of 1952, the extended family, whose members included school officials, military officers, and attorneys, convened and agreed that the T. E. Dorn property, its well-built if drafty house, its several hundred acres of timberland, and its several hundred cattle, all of it should be deeded over to William Jennings Bryan Dorn, provided that he maintain it as a family, political, and social center of activities, as had Dada. Although friendly and familial, negotiations took some time, with Bryan Dorn eventually putting up some $22,500 (more than $206,000 in current money) to give to Nana so that she retained "lifetime interest" of unspecified portion in the home and farm and also retained a small farm and farmhouse on the property to rent out to people, with her keeping the rental income. It was a bargain for a working farm with an historic house (eventually placed on the National Register in 1985), but it came with plenty of responsibilities for Bryan and

---

[8] Corr., GHA and WJBD, 1952–1956; Pete Jarman to WJBD, 4 November 1952; WJBD to J. S. Mayson, 26 September 1952; J. P. Coates (SCEA) to WJBD, 5 August 1954, and WJBD to Coates, 6 August 1954, WJBD/SCPC; also WJBD, Earle Morris, and GHA corr., GHA/SC/CU.

[9] Pete Jarman to WJBD, 5 October 1952, WJBD/SCPC.

Millie Dorn. Not least of those responsibilities was dealing with Nana on problematical days when "mad spells" affected her behavior.[8]

Besides concerns about Nana running the farms and the houses, these negotiations reflected red-hills attitudes toward men, especially including the tradition of having a patriarch for the clan or extended family. In keeping with this increased sense of history—rather than poetry—Bryan Dorn began calling the home place Barratt House, as it was originally called in 1853 by its owner John Joseph Gail ("Jack") Barratt, the gentleman scholar who read widely and wrote about science and philosophy. Jack Barratt himself had received the handsome gothic structure, with its stuccoed walls and interior frescoed murals, as a gift from his father, the regionally prominent scientist Dr. John Perkins Barratt. The Dorns were always fascinated by local lore and local pastimes, and Bryan Dorn was in 1952 becoming more self-consciously a student of local history, compiling and keeping records about his relatives and friends and what their families had done in the valley of the Saluda. Among other things, he learned that Dr. Barratt had been an early admirer of Charles Darwin and had supported evolution as a hypothesis to explain things, especially about farm animals, and had advocated the teaching of evolution in the schools, especially with regard to agricultural education about raising cattle and crops. Perhaps surprisingly, in the 1950s in the Third District, Darwin was not especially controversial, and Bryan Dorn was thus comfortably at home with his Baptist identity, his Sunday school teaching, and his application of Barratt's and Darwin's evolutionary theories to the raising of prize cattle and hardy timber. He was proud that scientific discussions, literary discussions, and other expressions scholarly and intellectual once took place in the old Barratt House. Neighbors and friends shared the pride of local association. That William Jennings Bryan once had spoken with such passion against the teaching of evolution in a famous Tennessee trial of a schoolteacher was simply never mentioned in his namesake's correspondence—nor was it recalled by friends and relatives.[9]

---

[8] WJBD, "Myrtle Manor" poem, n.d. (1943–1945); Millie Dorn to WJBD, 25 November 1951, WJBD/SCPC; Morgan Friedman Inflation Calculator, *Historical Statistics of US, 1952–1975* and *Statistical Abstracts of the US, 1975–2012*, hereinafter Friedman calculator; WJBD to J. M. Lesesne, 24 March 1954; Pearl Dorn "spells," Grace Dorn to WJBD, 26 July 1943, WJBD/SCPC.

[9] Barratt House deed and notes, 10 June 1952; patriarchal duties and place, Grace Dorn to WJBD, 26 July 1943; WJBD to H. E. Freeland, 10 September 1952; WJBD to Lundy Coleman, 6 June 1952; WJBD to Andy Griffith, 11 June 1952; and WJBD to P. M. Garvin, 29 April 1952, WJBD/SCPC: "Barratt House," National Register Properties,

Although Barratt House was in transition both in name and deeded title, it continued to perform its same local political functions begun when Dada strode the grounds "in seven league boots." On Labor Day 1952, traditional kick-off date for state politicking, Bryan Dorn again hosted a marvelous barbeque with speechifying by local and county politicians, an appearance by the prized donkey *FDR*, string-band music from a local country group, and much raucous discussion, made the more raucous as visitors slipped away into the timberland or out to their trucks to take long and strong pulls on their secret caches of liquor. Following what he had studied of Virginia countryside politics, Bryan Dorn was doing constituent service, reminding the citizens that he was and always would be one of them, with his feet under the picnic tables with theirs, and his elbows rubbing theirs as they ate his food and listened to his stories. The congressman was everywhere. The onetime boxer shadowboxed with men of all ages, and the onetime football lineman practiced blocking techniques and yelled enthusiastically about Ware Shoals football, Greenwood football, and, of course, Clemson Tiger football. Adlai Stevenson and John Sparkman were mentioned as loudly and almost as often as FDR, Tom Watson, Andrew Jackson, and Coach Frank Howard, and generally to enthusiastic response. Bryan and Millie, Nana (who that day was "on," with happy and engaging avuncularity and full-bore genteel charm), Dorn siblings, Griffith cousins, and local candidates all closed down the festivities that evening confident that the Democrats were secure in their Third District.[10]

Beyond Chinkapin Ridge, however, the Eisenhower forces were gaining ground, especially among the college-educated and the business people of the cities. Ike was even gaining some support among the black people of the Charleston area who could and would vote. It seemed an actual possibility that South Carolina presidential electors could go Republican regardless of what the Third District did. Properly focused by fear, Bryan Dorn spoke often and traveled extensively outside his own district trying to pump up the crowds for Stevenson and Sparkman. His efforts, plus generous portions of tradition and good organizing at the state level, contributed to electoral votes for the Democrats in November. However, two Upper South states, the be-

---

SCDAH. On Bryan, Cf. Lawrence and Lee, *Inherit the Wind*, and on Barratt, Cf. Stephens, "Centers of Creation."

[10] "Seven league boots" folklore, Beard and Beard, *American Civilization,* also Murray, *Seven League Boots*; Sydnor, *Gentlemen Freeholders*; WJBD to Andy Griffith, 11 June 1952; "Bryan Dorn Representing the People," (1984), WJBD/SCPC.

loved exemplar Virginia of Harry Byrd and Andrew Jackson's Tennessee, went for Eisenhower. The South was no longer "solid" for Democrats.[11]

As often was the case, South Carolina was an exception—and in this case, an exception that did not much matter in the national election. It was by electoral vote a smashing 442 to 89, and by popular vote a daunting 54.9 percent to 44.4 percent. More ominously, Republicans captured a net of 22 congressional seats, sending Sam Rayburn packing as majority leader and installing in his place Massachusetts Republican Joseph Martin. And the US Senate became Republican, with Ohio's Robert Taft taking majority leadership away from Arizona's Ernest McFarland. Bryan Dorn would not be moving up in the Veterans Administration Committee, but instead merely hanging on as a minority party member. The House, the Senate, and the White House would be one Republican world for the first time since Herbert Clark Hoover. Bryan Dorn always said he could work effectively with farm-state Republicans and reasonable men and women of any party. In 1953, those claims were about to be tested.[12]

War and pocketbook issues were foremost for Bryan Dorn, and for him the two were entangled if not organically one. After all, he was a "militaristic Keynesian" who relied on defense spending for much government stimulus, especially for the unemployed and underemployed in his district who could find jobs at Fort Jackson, Fort Gordon, or Donaldson Air Base—or in a major war, at bases and at ports far beyond South Carolina. The Korean War directly employed his people, and military benefits for veterans offered the hope of better lives upon honorable discharge (subsidized mortgages, tuition for college or other job training, medical care if service related). If Ike actually ended the conflict at once and brought soldiers and sailors home quickly, there would be an immediate increase of several hundred thousand unemployed because of discharge from duty; there would also be loss of all the works that airbases and navy yards and training forts needed from civilians. He worried about unemployment increasing and also about a slow down, if not recession, for the entire economy.[13]

---

[11] Tindall, *Disruption of the Solid South*, 47–54, 72; Clerk of House of Representatives, *Congressional Quarterly Guide to US Elections* (4th ed., 2001).

[12] Tindall, *Disruption of the Solid South*, 47–54, 72; SC contentiousness and loss of national importance, Wright, *South Carolina*, 167–214.

[13] Frank, "The New Mandate," 50–56; Fraser, "A Lettered Numbers Man [Galbraith]," *Los Angeles Times*, 13 February 2005, bk. sect. 1; corr. Aull with WJBD, 1952–1962, WJBD/SCPC and 1952–1962, GHA/SC/CU.

Related to these job issues were the issues of fairness and protection for wounded and otherwise disabled veterans of this unpopular Korean War that Dorn supported so vigorously. The wounded were counted at 100,000 by 1953, and already the VA committee had fought with the Truman administration about skimping on health care and treatment benefits for these men and women. In particular, Dorn and other committee members were exercised about emotional and psychological disorders and disabilities (not then called post-traumatic stress syndrome), most of which were completely unfunded by the VA. Truman's people at least had their hearts in the right places. The Eisenhower people, especially Secretary of Commerce Sinclair Weeks, Secretary of Agriculture Ezra Taft Benson, and VA official Sumner Wells, were talking a language of cutting costs, and Dorn was convinced the costs would be cut by gutting benefits for the grunts and the gobs who were most vulnerable in this hot season of the Cold War.[14]

But there was also his white-hot anti-Communism. Dorn was still angry about MacArthur's dismissal, and he still favored saturation bombing, with the possibility of a nuclear bomb dropped on the peninsula and even somewhere in China. Truman's stepped-up bombing in summer of 1952 had somewhat placated him: North Korean power plants were bombed at the Yalu River during June, and the Communist capital Pyongyang was bombed thereafter on 11 July. But Eisenhower was talking about ending the war promptly and returning troops home soon. There were badly kept secrets that the president-elect had traveled to Korea for a fact-finding tour not long after his spectacular election. Third District folk wanted their boys home, but not without victory, and for Dorn victory seemed impossible without full deployment of the world's greatest air force. Worried about Truman, he was angry with the Eisenhower people and their talk of an early withdrawal from the peninsula. Of Ike, he suspected a lack of commitment to resist Communist aggression, whether Soviet adventurism or Chinese and Korean revolutionism.[15]

---

[14] James R. Mann to WJBD and WJBD to Mann, 22 January 1952; WJBD to P. G. Sherer, 30 January 1952; WJBD to Miles D. Kennedy, 26 June 1952; WJBD to William E. Bergin, 10 September 1952; WJBD to Bergin, 29 September 1952, WJBD to Robert S. Galloway Sr., 21 May 1953; Robert C. Schumacher (for WJBD) to Elmer R. Baker, 2 May 1953; VA folders, 1952, 1953, WJBD/SCPC.

[15] WJBD to Yon Chan Yang, 23 July 1954; Argyle R. Mackey to WJBD, 15 September 1954; WJBD to Martin Dies, 8 May 1953, WJBD/SCPC; WJBD, retrospective, "Douglass MacArthur," *Cong. Rec.vol. 110, pt. 3, 88th Cong., 2d sess.*, 6871; WJBD, *OTP*; and WJBD, "In His Own Words," WJBD/SCPC. Thomas, *Ike's Bluff.*

And those were the issues for the people of the masses. But yet the classes, at least the textile and textile-related elites, sensed a threat as well. There was as much talk about free trade as there had been since Adam Smith wrote *The Wealth of Nations*. Such talk threatened industrial industries in regions beyond the red hills. New Englanders Jack Kennedy and John McCormack were worried about industry in Massachusetts, and Midwesterners Hubert Humphrey and George McGovern were worried about industry, especially mining operations, in Minnesota and South Dakota. Union leaders for the automobile industries were concerned about trade issues too. For all their opposition to organized labor in textile mills, the classes of the as-yet-unnamed textile group (and the Carolina congressmen who served their interests) always worked closely with so-styled Big Labor on issues of trade regulations. A very important Reciprocal Trade Agreement that protected American industry against foreign competition, in that day, Japanese manufacturers, was to expire in early winter of 1954, and the Eisenhower Republicans were talking enthusiastically about consumer benefits from a completely free trade system liberated from the tariffs and quotas, the very things deemed essential to survival not only by textile elites, but also by automobile elites, mining elites, and others declared to be "special interests."[16]

Of course, each elite grouping, textiles in particular, was a special interest, as was each grouping of working-class people, millworkers in particular. From top to bottom in the complex class system of the red hills, the Eisenhower people with their enthusiasm for free trade threatened wealth and power at the top—and the nature of jobs at the bottom. However much Bryan Dorn admired Eisenhower the man, Ike's handlers were certainly talking about economic policies that threatened the very foundational structures of the Third District. In addition to his political misgivings, Bryan Dorn again absorbed scholarly forecasts from Hubert Aull that warned about "unfair trade," especially with Japan.[17]

By summertime of 1953, Eisenhower had arranged a truce in Korea and had begun sizing down the armed forces. Bryan Dorn was livid. He shared correspondence with Syngman Rhee, albeit holding his nose, since the doctor was

---

[16] WJBD to Marguerite Tolbert, 5 February 1951; WJBD to Walter W. Benson, 15 January 1952, and memorandum on congressional resolution concerning cotton grading and pricing, n.d., 1953, WJBD/SCPC; see also Sorensen, *Kennedy*, 45n, 55–59.

[17] GHA to WJBD, 10 June 1953, and WJBD to GHA, 12 June 1953, and GHA, "Weasel Words," retrospective, 6 August 1971, GHA/SC/CU.

a militaristic authoritarian. Yet he fully supported him against the opposition Kim Il Sung. The latter was a Maoist Communist, and the congressman judged Maoist Communism to be even more offensive than authoritarianism (a distinction between totalitarianism and authoritarianism that he read that very year in political philosopher Hannah Arendt's *Origins of Totalitarianism*). Too, by this season, Bryan Dorn had completely accepted the falling-dominoes hypothesis for Asian foreign affairs, and he judged that dominoes falling in Vietnam, Cambodia, Laos, and Thailand were direct threats to Taiwan, indirect threats to Japan and Indonesia and Australia, and indeed ultimate threats to American Pacific interests, not to exclude Hawaii. General Mark Wayne Clark, prominent in the World War II Mediterranean Campaign, had been elevated to commander in chief of the Far East Command and of the United Nations Command—just in time to be ordered to sign the truce. The brilliant, blunt, and egoistic New Yorker signed the documents on 27 July 1953 with the annoyed statement to the press that he was in the "unenviable position of being the first U.S. Army commander to sign an armistice without a victory." Most Americans were happy that the combat fatalities, some 29,000, were at last slowing down, if not completely over. But Bryan Dorn paid close attention to other words General Clark spoke on the selfsame day of armistice: "I must tell you as emphatically as I can that this does not mean immediate or even early withdrawal from Korea. The conflict will not be over until the Governments concerned have reached a firm political settlement." The congressman agreed completely and when the disgruntled General Clark resigned his two command posts and asked also to retire from his army commission, Bryan Dorn joined more powerful players who worked behind the scenes to get Clark into position to become president of the Citadel, South Carolina's military college in Charleston.[18]

Whether the falling-dominoes hypothesis could explain grand foreign policy or not, for Bryan Dorn falling dominoes surely fell into place for the macro-economy as soon as Ike arranged a truce and deemphasized military spending—and as soon as his people began talking about free trade as opposed to fair trade. In July, the very month of the truce, the National Bureau of Economic Research (NBER) measured a reversal in the growth of the

---

[18] Lindsey Parrott, "Truce Is Signed," *New York Times*, 27 July 1953, 1; correspondence, Syngman Rhee, 1948–1958; Mark Wayne Clark and the Citadel officials, 1953, WJBD/SCPC; Presidential Papers, 1953–1954, College Archives, the Citadel, Charleston, SC; WJBD, *OTP*; Arendt, *The Origins of Totalitarianism*; Thomas, *Ike's Bluff*; Stueck, *The Korean War*. Cf. Moyar, *Triumph Forsaken* for WJBD views.

gross domestic product and a decline in employment. By NBER's established standards, a serious recession was underway, and it would last from July 1953 until May 1954, with unemployment rising to 6.1 percent and economic growth a *negative* 2.6 percent. The Third District, improved under FDR and at least holding its own under Truman, slipped back down to the bottom of the tall and shaking American economic ladder. Bryan Dorn, listening as always at luncheon to the classes and at barbeques to the masses, was convinced that curtailment in defense spending and curtailment in other spending was hurting his own district more than others. Yet he was also convinced that it hurt all American districts. He was in broad agreement with Midwestern Republicans and Populistic Southern Democrats that stimulative spending was called for in such a recession. He was also convinced that the Democratic Party had a campaign issue for "off-year" congressional elections in November 1954: Ike, like Hoover before him, was bad medicine for the national economy, reversing economic growth and bringing inflation. As it always was for Bryan Dorn, the effective rhetoric was grounded in research-based study of economic realities. His own staff, led by Secretary Robert Schumacher, but also Clemson's Bob Edwards and Hubert Aull, Big Labor economists, piedmont bankers C. Douglas Wilson and W. W. "Mac" McEachern, and the Textile Group—especially Jim Self and Brother Abney—all condemned Ike's macroeconomic policies and called for retention of the threatened Fair Deal for Textiles. The textile classes and their professors and statisticians uniformly called for a return to militaristic Keynesianism.[19]

Machiavelli taught Bryan Dorn well that Fortuna always played a role in things political. To meet sudden turns of her wheel, the successful politician must adapt quickly to profound surprise. In such vital moments, one might need to respond as a lion and smite the opposition without much regard for what happened to those so smitten. But one might also need to respond as a clever fox, fleeing the conflict and fitting into the new scene in order to fight another day. There were immediate and long-term consequences for either

---

[19] NBER, *US Business Cycle Expansion and Contraction*, 20 September 2010; correspondence, C. Douglas Wilson, W. W. McEachern, James C. Self, John S. Abney, Erick Johnston, Robert Cook Edwards, George Hubert Aull, 1953–1956; WJBD to Walter V. Benson, 15 January 1952, and WJBD to Grace Andrews, WJBD to James C. Dozier, 3 May 1954, Robert Schumacher (for WJBD) to Newton G. Hardin, 28 October 1953, WJBD/SCPC.

choice made, and the successful politician made the choice right for the context. No successful politician always responded as lion, and none always responded as fox. Two such surprises spun Fortuna's wheel in 1954, and Dorn chose to respond to each as a fox. One was the monumental decision by the newly established Earl Warren Supreme Court concerning school desegregation. The other surprise related to the unique opportunities and threats presented by the sudden death of Burnet Maybank, senior US senator for South Carolina.[20]

On 17 May 1954, Earl Warren published the Supreme Court's unanimous decision in *Brown v. Board of Education.* As noted, the landmark case involved an earlier case heard in Clarendon County wherein Dorn's nemesis J. Waties Waring had announced that the mere fact of physically segregating children was a harmful discrimination that made such a segregated education inherently *unequal.* Given Bryan Dorn's close scrutiny of such judicial cases, and given the number of attorneys in his extended family, the decision itself was not the surprise. Rather, the surprise was the unanimity of the court, the emphasis in Earl Warren's pronouncement, and the insistence that redress must begin at once, "with all due deliberate speed." Among associates, Brooks Hays and the Kentucky Drane brothers and others had convinced Bryan Dorn that integration would come, and that Jimmy Byrnes's ostentatious spending on "Negro schools" was only a stopgap and no substantive remedy.[21]

Yet Hays and the Drane brothers and his own reading of unfolding events had also convinced the congressman that there was *plenty of time.* Eisenhower had assured many Southerners that they could vote Republican without voting neo-abolitionist and that any steps toward integration would come slowly and with judicious measure. Furthermore, the very appointment of career politician Earl Warren as chief justice was supposed to "protect" white Southerners from the much-feared William O. Douglas and other integrationist jurists on the court. After all, Warren, when governor of California, had presided over the wretched policy of interning thousands of Japanese American families who were loyal citizens—and had done so for no other reason than to placate the racists of the Golden State during World

[20] *Essential Writings of Machiavelli*, ed. Constantine, 58, 64–67, 68–69; 92–93; Fortuna and Ecclesiastes, WJBD, *OTP*, 102–103.

[21] Third District responses, Congressional Files, May 1954 to August 1956; corr., Howard Worth Smith, William H. Tuck, WJBD/SCPC; Branch, *Parting the Waters*, 113–140.

War II. And now here was the selfsame California politico writing major constitutional law as if he were John Marshall. And for purposes of governing South Carolina and every Southern state, Warren was at the moment fully as important as John Marshall.[22]

Realtor Earl Middleton, a black associate and later political ally of Dorn's in Orangeburg, has described the Brown decision as "the dividing point in my lifetime as far as blacks' freedoms were concerned." Since Middletown was a World War II veteran and a bright entrepreneur whom Dorn admired, his opinion could not be taken lightly. Knowing how many South Carolina blacks agreed with Middleton, and harboring long-term ambitions that someday would require black votes, Bryan Dorn wanted to proceed even more cautiously than he normally did in walking the pathways of race relations. By contrast, his millhand and *small bidness* constituents were not in the least constrained. They wanted to impeach Earl Warren, and they threatened any black children attempting to enter previously white schools. His constituents' letters dripped with racist acrimony, and he responded to each note with assurances that integration was not going to come any time soon and that he agreed with "much of what you say"—being especially careful and cautious not to specify *what* exactly he agreed with.[23]

Dorn cast about rather desperately, and again Brooks Hays gave him the response. The mercurial Strom Thurmond produced the Southern Manifesto—the Declaration of Constitutional Principles—a statement by Southern congressmen and senators rejecting the Brown decision by denying the authority of the judiciary to mandate integration in states, "a clear abuse of judicial power." Its important sentence read, "We commend the motives of those states which have declared the intention to resist forced integration by any lawful means." Despite worries about his cousin's immoderation, Dorn took solace from Hays himself, who praised the temperance and wisdom in Thurmond's wording. It took some time to develop the wording in such a way that seventeen senators and ninety-nine congressmen felt comfortable enough to sign; it also took some face-to-face persuasion. Dorn took a hand in editing, and played his role in the face-to-face persuading. Over the next

---

[22] Middleton and Barnes, *Knowing Who I Am*, 85–95; Branch, *Parting the Waters*, 21, 25 112, 124–25; Roper, *Magnificent Mays*, 244–47; Schwartz, ed. and introd., *Capturing the Future: Earl Warren*; Thomas, *Ike's Bluff*; Ambrose, *Eisenhower, Soldier and President*.

[23] Middleton and Barnes, *Knowing Who I Am*, 90; Congressional files, 1954, WJBD/SCPC.

twenty-two months, all members of the South Carolina delegation signed Thurmond's manifesto, as did all members of the Virginia and Georgia delegations. One good friend of Dorn's, Tennessee's leonine Albert Gore Sr., refused to sign, and Dorn respected that decision. Finally, in March of 1956, the manifesto was in shape for signing, and it was published in the *Congressional Record.* Congressman Dorn was proud of his small part in it, and sent tear sheets of the manifesto out to friends and constituents. Absent in it was any talk about integration coming by state action, and the vehemence of the objections to the Supreme Court could make a rational person wonder how "lawful" would be the resistance. Like the other signatories, Bryan Dorn considered that he had taken a principled action worthy of a Solon such as Henry Clay or perhaps even James Madison. Not until 1968 would he quit mentioning the manifesto altogether, seeing it for what it was—and hoping that others would forget (or tacitly forgive).[24]

At the same time, Dorn was quite aware of what his people could be like when riled over racial issues. He wanted the response to be like the one engineered by the Harry Byrd Machine in the beloved Old Dominion: set the greatest lawyers in the country to work slowing things to a crawl while keeping the mobs out of the streets. It was the boardroom, not the feedstore, where Bryan Dorn hoped to find and deploy the foxlike tactics of obfuscation and delay. But he knew how easily street mobs could be stirred in his district. He knew of the Phoenix Riot near his home in 1898, something that haunted Nana to the end of her days. And his own Dada had refused to vote for Pitchfork Ben Tillman because of the senator's wild and violence-encouraging negrophobia, much of which Nana and Dada connected directly to black deaths at the hands of mobs inspired by him. Of course, cousins included the fiercest race-baiter of all, Coleman Livingston Blease, a man Bryan Dorn both admired and feared for his control over the emotions of a crowd. He sought Brooks Hays's counsel not only as a moderate segregationist who wanted to go slow and let things develop gradually from the home base, but also as a believing Baptist who wanted racial peace. Dorn agreed with Hays that the manifesto was the right response, and he agreed with his Virginia exemplars William H. Tuck and Judge Howard Worth Smith that a foot-dragging, legalistic slowing down of all processes was the

---

[24] Fortuna, WJBD, *OTP*, 102–103; Brooks Hays to WJBD, 13 April 1953; The Southern Manifesto, *Cong. Rec., vol. 102, pt. 4, 84th Cong., 2d sess.*, 4459–60; tearsheets, 1956, WJBD/SCPC; Tindall, *Disruption*, 41; Bass and Thompson, *Ol' Strom*. Cf. WJBD, *OTP*, ch. 7 on civil rights in which the manifesto is *unmentioned.*

best modus operandi. Too, he retained some hope that Eisenhower would order his Department of Justice to move with a matching slowness. After all, Ike was telling people, albeit in private, that he was surprised by Earl Warren's behavior.[25]

If he really believed what he told the Drane brothers and Earl Middleton and Brooks Hays, he could have chosen to roar like a lion and behave like his admired friends, the white John Bolt Culbertson and the black Benjamin Elijah Mays. But Dorn concluded that "the better part of valor is discretion"—though he knew perfectly well those were the words of Shakespeare's cowardly and temporizing Sir John Falstaff. Yet Falstaff was quite accurate about one thing in that scene, as likely were the signatories of the manifesto: "In the which better part I have saved my life." Thus did the Solons of the Southland slip around like a fox, and thus did they live to fight another day. Bryan Dorn promised himself to be a lion in a future time. For this brief season in 1954, 1955, and 1956, the congressman's foxy strategy was just right for retaining power in his district. It was planned as well to set up Dorn's chances for being governor in another day in another era, a day when not only Earl Middleton and Bennie Mays but all black folk of age would be voting for gubernatorial candidates.[26]

When Labor Day rolled around in 1954, it was time again to host the Democratic barbeque at Barratt House. Since he was unopposed for his congressional seat, Bryan Dorn focused energies on listening to his neighbors and on the needs of Democratic candidates. Though not senior by age or service, Dorn was secretary of the South Carolina delegation in DC and important in the still unnamed but effective textile group of Carolinians and Georgians. Much like hosting a barbeque for poorer neighbors, his work for the delegation and for the textile group was decidedly tedious and had few immediately obvious benefits. But he reveled in it all the same, taking an intrinsic joy in arranging the business luncheons and the hurried and pointed discussions with lobbyists and corporation representatives and setting up press conferences and sending out press releases—just as he took an intrinsic

---

[25] Corr. South Carolina delegation, especially March 1956; corr., Howard Worth Smith, William H. Tuck, WJBD/SCPC; WJBD, *OTP*, 44; riot, 150; Tindall, *Disruption*, 49–54.

[26] Cf. corr., William and Bryan Drane, 1946, 1954, 1956, John Bolt Culbertson, 1956, WJBD/SCPC; Culbertson Papers, 1956, SCPC; Machiavelli, *The Essential Writings of Machiavelli*, ed. Constantine, 68–69; Shakespeare, *King Henry IV, Pt. 1*, Act V, Sc. 4.

joy in sharing country string-band music, the surreptitious drinking of liquor, the conspicuous displays of barbeque and New Deal speechifying, and the annual glory of FDR the donkey romping before the wildly enthusiastic crowd of Third District Democrats. He and Millie had another baby girl, Olivia, whom he had proudly showed off for congressmen and staffers living near him in McLean. Now he even more proudly showed her off at church events and at barbeques back home. For her part, daughter Brianna was becoming a good little Dorn Democrat with her own small-child speechifying and posturing at age four and a half. Much was wrong in Ike's world, but much was right in Bryan Dorn's world.[27]

Amidst the long weekend's general hell-raising and revelry, news came of a sudden death that changed South Carolina politics utterly. Burnet Maybank, the magic man, dropped dead of a heart attack at his mountain retreat in Flat Rock, North Carolina. It was said by some that he perished in a bordello that he favored, but Dorn never discussed such scandals. What he did have to discuss was that, in the few weeks until November, the pearl of great price, the US Senate, was again out there for the taking. Many ambitious men hurried forward, and that included Bryan Dorn. But wily Edgar Brown, he of the "Barnwell Ring," as described by political scientist V. O. Key, and he who was master of the upper House in the South Carolina General Assembly, won out over all claimants at a hurriedly convened convention of party regulars at Columbia's Jefferson Hotel. As always, Bryan Dorn hastened to give the convention's chosen nominee his full support. He told Edgar Brown the truth, that the "Bishop of Barnwell" remained his model for how to act as a Democrat in South Carolina. He did not reveal to Brown how much he had disliked Maybank and how *badly* he himself had wanted to be nominated. In fact, Maybank while still alive had betrayed no knowledge about Dorn's true feelings; and certainly his family had no clue. The senator had considered the congressman to be a friendly supporter, even an important ally, rather than nemesis. All of those perceptions, the feelings of Maybank's surviving family and the feelings of Edgar Brown, were exactly where Bryan Dorn wanted those feelings and opinions to be—not because people misunderstood, but because he was so careful in his public statements and in his formal presentations (and because he and a very few family members kept his actual feelings secret).[28]

---

[27] WJBD to Peter Oldham, 2 March 1954, WJBD/SCPC.

[28] WJBD to Sol Blatt, 20 October 1954, other correspondence, WJBD and Brown and Maybank, September 1954; Burnet Maybank III to WJBD, n.d., September 1954,

And then came still another surprise from Strom Thurmond, who was currently out of office, out of favor with the national Democratic Party, and disconnected from officials in the state Democratic Party. Yet he remained the master of racist appeals to the old Populists. He was still the man whose father had worked successfully for negrophobe nonpareil Ben Tillman—and still a man whose father would have been governor himself but "for an unfortunate killing [that he committed]." Thurmond baldly declared that he was write-in candidate for US Senate and that his wool-hat boys could go to the polls and show the "Barnwell Ring" that each of them could write—and would *write in* the name of the racially pure Dixiecrat. Despite the mid-state machinations of Sol Blatt and Edgar Brown, Thurmond largely overstated the power and reach of the "Barnwell Ring." It did make a perfect campaign pitch for a people who wanted someone more exciting than Edgar Brown. And Thurmond was definitely exciting, especially when he could appeal to South Carolina white assumptions about being "picked on" by some combination of Yankees, political insiders, and a phalanx of African Americans (most of whom still could not vote in the many rural precincts of the Palmetto State). As Thurmond's biographer the veteran journalist Jack Bass noted in three different books drawing on his close observations of the campaign, *Ol' Strom* was nothing if not an opportunist and a political genius who knew when to take the gamble and when to make the jump. Alienated from the Democrats in national and state party organizations, Thurmond simply ran a highly personal campaign as the South Carolina segregationist sui generis, a winning ticket, at least in 1954.[29]

As for Bryan Dorn, his own feelings about his cousin were "complicated up," as William Faulkner phrased it. There was something undeniably magnetic, charismatic, if you will, about Thurmond, even and especially when he was being reckless in his language about black people, his approach to the national Democratic Party, or his approach to the long-serving state Democrats. Or to women. While an up-and-coming educator Thurmond had famously "carried on" with Sue Logue, who was convicted of murder and executed (it was a badly kept secret that in 1943 that Thurmond ar-

---

WJBD/SCPC; Workman, *The Bishop of Barnwell*; Key, "South Carolina"; September 1954, Edgar Arthur Brown Papers, EAB/SC/CU.

[29] Bass and Thompson, *Ol' Strom* (rev. ed.; 2003); Bass and Poole, *The Palmetto State*; Bass and De Vries, *Transformation of Southern Politics*; Jordan, *South Carolina, a Primary State;* September 1954, Strom Thurmond Papers, ST/SC/CU; 1954 election pamphlets, SCPC/USC; Bass, "Art of Political Biography," 22 January 2013.

ranged to ride with Logue from the women's penitentiary to the very "death house," with its electric chair, "a-hugging and a-kissing the whole way," according to the car's driver). A long-rumored relationship with at least one black woman was constantly denied but decades later confirmed. And he had tried to put Bryan Dorn's own sister Gracie in a compromising position, had she not been warned from making a proposed road trip by her protective and angry brother. Worse, Dorn was unsure what Thurmond actually believed, since his actions and statements had in a few years bounced from progressive to reactionary, from big spending to "pay as you go," and from reasoned to racist.[30]

That hot autumn of 1954, Thurmond played the race card boldly and blatantly, avoiding the "N-word" itself but otherwise using all the code words for white supremacy and hatred of black humanity. It was so extreme that in later decades, younger friends and close associates emphatically denied it because they simply could not believe it, having seen nothing of the sort in the period 1970 to 2000. But Jack Bass and Bill Workman and Lee Bandy and Frank Van der Linden and other newsmen of the day had it in their notes and filed it in their accounts—and it is preserved quite memorably on film. Beyond the flaming Tillmanite rhetoric, Bryan Dorn worried if his cousin could provide constituent service in the way Maybank had. Of course he had no way of knowing, since Thurmond had been governor and judge and not congressman or senator—Thurmond was to that point untested in the quotidian tasks of helping out with postal routes and pension plans and other headaches of local service. At any rate, it did not matter. *Ol' Strom* had won the election and barreled into the Senate, borne there by Bryan Dorn's very own red-hills folk in the dramatic and unprecedented write-in campaign.[31]

And so it was that Strom Thurmond, who so recently seemed politically dead, was in the Senate, probably to stay. Adjusting himself to that new fact, Congressman Dorn had to recalculate the working relationships inside the South Carolina delegation. He intended to work as effectively with the mercurial Thurmond as he had with the much more predictable Maybank,

---

[30] William Faulkner to Jean Stein, *William Faulkner: Letters and Fiction*, ed. Watson, 54; Bass and Thompson, *Ol' Strom*; Bass, "Art of Political Biography," 22 January 2013; and WJBD to Grace Dorn, 25 July 1947, WJBD/SCPC.

[31] WJBD to Frank Van der Linden, November 21, 1955, WJBD/SCPC; Bass and Thompson, *Ol' Strom*; Bass, "The Art of Political Biography"; Tindall, *The Disruption of the Solid South*, 36–41; Black and Black, *Politics and Society in the South.*

and as he still did with Olin Johnston. In any case, the rhetoric of the stump was often disengaged from lawmaking in Washington. Johnston and the late Maybank sometimes talked about commitments to grand schemes, but in practice each man always painstakingly took care to meet the specific needs of his voting masses while tending to different but equally specific needs of the ruling classes. To be sure, Thurmond talked hotly about limited and local government and seemed to be in some defiance of the classes of his state. For all that, Dorn was relieved to find that Thurmond's rhetoric on race and rhetoric on states' rights had nothing to do with his behavior when it came to the Fair Deal for Textiles. Indeed, the newly seated US senator at once showed that he "got it." The Fair Deal for Textiles—its complex apparatus of tariffs and quotas and reciprocal agreements in fair trade—was essential to the fundamental structure of the South Carolina piedmont and to large degree to the entire piedmont that stretched from north Richmond to eastern Alabama. Almost seamlessly, Strom Thurmond took his own place inside the unnamed textile group and worked conscientiously on behalf of the Fair Deal for Textiles even as he ringingly denounced federal spending and federal regulations.[32]

In the earliest days of the recession, Eisenhower had proposed a genuinely Keynesian solution, what amounted to the largest and most ambitious of all the public works projects attempted by any administration. It was indeed militaristic Keynesianism of Bryan Dorn's kind, for it would directly employ tens of thousands of construction workers in building infrastructure for defense purposes while indirectly employing still more hundreds of thousands who provided services to the larger projects. Ike and his people initially proposed some $25 billion (currently more than $300 billion dollars), and Bryan Dorn calculated that the Keynesian multiplier would make that a total of some $62 or $63 billion added to the gross domestic product, which was itself barely $386 billion in this year of recession. Such a huge stimulus would cause the economy to pick up speed and grow and likely reduce unemployment to a point far below 3 percent. Had the proposal been purely for peacetime projects, Congressman Dorn might have been reserved and cautious, but since it was to establish a network of transportation and com-

---

[32] Bass and Thompson, *Ol' Strom*; Bass, "The Art of Political Biography," 22 January 2013.

munication for defense purposes in a hot war, he supported it enthusiastically.[33]

This proposal was Eisenhower's Federal Aid Highway Act to establish the "National System of Interstate and Defense Highways." Eisenhower had been inspired by German highways he had seen, and he said his network of highways would not only provide "speedy, safe transcontinental travel" on the "broad ribbons across the land" for civilians, but more significantly, it would guarantee "quick evacuation of target areas [for] escape in case of nuclear attack." Redoubtable Governor Jimmy Byrnes emerged from the July governors conference excited about what such a network of roads could do for South Carolina.[34]

Eisenhower himself could not attend the 12 July conference at Bolton's Landing in Lake George, New York. There was a death on Mamie's side of the family, and Ike wanted to support his wife properly. Instead, Vice President Nixon represented the administration, and he certainly carried the mail effectively. Speaking well, as he generally did for such a knowledgeable and bipartisan audience, Nixon found the governors and staffers and veteran journalists quite receptive. Not only Republican governors and not only Democrats like Byrnes, who were sympathetic to Nixon and Eisenhower, but also liberal Democrats as well were enthusiastic. Such was generally the case in the twentieth century, where there were proposals for "concrete and asphalt" construction projects largely paid for by the federal government—but much of that started with Ike. The magnitude of what Eisenhower proposed was far beyond anything FDR had done for road construction. Public opinion, while not sampled very scientifically, was also favorable, and the Republican-controlled House and Senate expected a relatively easy passage. Two Democrats, Al Gore Sr. of the Senate and George H. Fallon of the House, were quick to jump on board and began working on proposals in their respective Houses, with Sam Rayburn promising good support from his side of the aisle to Majority Leader Martin.[35]

---

[33] Lewis, *Divided Highways*; US Department of Commerce: Bureau of Economic Analysis: Gross Domestic Product, 1954; Morgan Friedman Inflation Calculator, *Historical Statistics of US, 1952–1975* and *Statistical Abstracts of the US, 1975–2016.*

[34] Lewis, *Divided Highways*; Frank, "New Mandate on Defense," 50–56; Parker, *Galbraith.*

[35] "Address of the Vice President," 12 July 1954, *Proceedings of the Governors Conference*, 1954; McClure, ed., *A Legacy of Leadership*, 90; Richard Weingroff, "Federal-Aid Highway Act of 1956: Creating the Interstate System," *Public Roads*, 60/1 (Summer 1996): sidebars; Rose, *Interstate Express Highway Politics.*

Despite bipartisan enthusiasm and despite much popularly expressed support, both bills for a Federal Highway Act soon foundered. There was the question of how to pay for a $25-billion expenditure. New Senator Thurmond jumped into the fray demanding that the roads be paid for by toll fees assessed on travelers—a remarkable demand from one supported by wool-hat boys who detested toll roads. The wool-hat boys themselves quickly let both Thurmond and the entire South Carolina delegation know that toll roads were unacceptable. A few Republicans suggested a bond issue, noting *a la* Keynes that deficit spending during a recession stimulated the economy for the nonce, and the bonds could be paid later during a time of full employment, when future expenditures would be cut back accordingly. That proposal, although perfectly consistent with what FDR had done and fully in line with Professor Hubert Aull's macroeconomics, was utterly unacceptable to most Midwestern Republicans and to almost all the Populistic New Dealers among Southern Democrats, including Bryan Dorn. Other proposals initially appealing to Dorn involved taxing the products, that is, the tires, the gasoline, the individual trucks themselves. Also, FDR's legacy, the twin traditions of "tax and spend, elect and elect" and "soak the rich," suggested a huge tax on the corporate industries involved in manufacturing and distributing tires, gasoline, and vehicles. Congressman Dorn, like all his fellows, quickly learned from well-organized lobbyists how unpopular were such proposed user-taxes.[36]

The House sponsor George Fallon, the Big Man from Baltimore, was caught flat-footed both by the speed and by the effectiveness with which his otherwise popular bill was stopped in its tracks. Fallon, over 6-feet 2-inches tall in a time when that was almost basketball-player size, was popular, and he thought he knew his way around Sam Rayburn's Board of Education, not to mention the milder manners of Majority Leader Joe Martin. But for a full year, Fallon's bill was essentially dead in the House Ways and Means Committee. Dorn was quite worried, since no stimulative spending was happening at all, and the recession was deepening disastrously in the no-growth business quarters that stretched out between July 1954 and May 1956. The classes back in his district, bankers McEachern and Wilson, textile men Self and Lowenstein, *Greenville News* magnate Roger Peace, and Spartanburg broadcast man Walter Brown, were in touch not only with the congressman, but also with Commerce Secretary Sinclair Weeks and with the advisory

---

[36] Lewis, *Divided Highways*; Rose, *Interstate Express Highway Politics*; Congressional files, 1954–1956, WJBD/SCPC; White, "Where are The Good Roads?"

committee for the project, especially General Lucius Dallum Clay. Clay in particular told the classes that the bill was quite dead, and that its death would stall if not prevent an economic recovery. Wise old Dr. Aull called for some way to pass the bill for macroeconomic reasons, and hard-charging construction man Charlie Daniel made the same call for his own microeconomic reasons—he was ready to pour concrete and hire men with picks and shovels.[37]

The congressman had been too clever by half. It had been great sport to score Republicans for high unemployment and high taxes, to tell the millhand constituents that they should not have to pay tolls or pay still higher income taxes, and at the same time to blast the Eisenhower administration for its budget deficit. But all of Sam Rayburn's boys, and especially Bryan Dorn, had also ballyhooed the wonders of an interstate highway system. For once, this most practical minded of lawmakers had no useful proposal for getting a piece of legislative work done. To complicate things, Harry Byrd made a ringing call for "pay as you go" and promised a bill in the Senate that would require Secretary Sinclair Weeks to withhold any spending until funds had been secured ahead of time. As usual, Bryan Dorn saluted his hero Harry Byrd, but the proposed Byrd amendment, if passed, might well prevent *any* roads from being built. Suddenly, there was no hope for a quick stimulus to pull out of recession. Indeed there was precious little hope that roads would be built at all. And it was none other than Bryan Dorn who had so effectively told his constituents that the US built roads for goatherds in Iraq and Iran and then asked loudly, "Where are your roads [in Greenwood]"? He did not mention roads in Germany or Italy, but such foreign aid as offered by the Marshall Plan was equally disdained among his constituents and in his own judgment.[38]

Despite the legislative mess and the bowdlerization in his arguments, Bryan Dorn knew that he and Southern Democrats had found a set of talking points for the 1954 off-year elections. Republicans could be blamed for Earl Warren and for unemployment and for big spending. He knew quite well that the campaigns in which he served the Virginians Tuck and Smith and the Georgian Paul Brown would go well with these tactics. When elec-

---

[37] Lewis, *Divided Highways*; Congressional Files, especially Self, Lowenstein, Peace, Walter Brown, Daniel, George Hubert Aull, and WJBD, 1954–1956, WJBD/SCPC; WJBD and GHA, GHA/SC/CU.

[38] Lewis, *Divided Highways*; interview: Steve Griffith and Watson Dorn with Roper (28 February 2012), WJBD/SCPC.

tions came in November, his friends for whom he campaigned won reelection. He knew quite well that Southern Democrats in this season could make it without his help, but he loved being in the crowds. Indeed, Democrats stormed back into the House, and Sam Rayburn was restored as majority leader. The off-year elections in US Senate were painfully close, essentially a tie, but Oregon's liberal Republican Wayne Morse voted consistently with Democrats, and his vote then and later made and kept Lyndon Baines Johnson majority leader of the senior assembly. Throughout the remainder of Bryan Dorn's long congressional career, his Democratic Party would be in charge of the House of Representatives and the US Senate.

But getting elected and taking control was not governing. In the bowels of the Board of Education room in the House, Sam Rayburn was blunt about duty and stern about how to fill it. Rayburn reminded his team that it was time to fix unemployment and that the Federal Highway Act was vitally needed as a part of that repair. Possibly there in the famous boardroom, or perhaps somewhere else, one of Bryan Dorn's favorite Populists, Hale Boggs of Louisiana, came forward with the solution. Boggs said to set up a fund like the one for Social Security. Relatively small taxes could be levied on the trucks using the roads, and relatively small taxes could be levied on tires and gasoline, and the huge volume of traffic would yield a huge revenue. By now, trucking companies and tire companies and petroleum corporations had come to realize that the proposed taxes were small indeed in comparison with the volume of revenues about to come their way. As those tax revenues came in, they were to be deposited in the highway trust fund, and it would be *Pay as You Go and a user tax*, but in Boggs's trust fund the tax burden on users would be small, and the funds so gathered would be dedicated to the highways and not mixed in with other government spending projects. Bryan Dorn and everyone else was quite relieved, especially Strom Thurmond, who was delighted that the federal government would pick up 90 percent of the costs for South Carolina with a minimum of taxes, and thus the new senator was liberated from his own immensely unpopular toll-roads proposal.[39]

Byrd slightly revised his proposal and passed his amendment in the Senate. It said that if collections fell below projections, then Secretary of Commerce Sinclair Weeks was to postpone new projects until revenues and expenditures were again in balance. That was not truly Pay as You Go, but it

---

[39] White, "Where Are the Good Roads?"; Morris, "Eisenhower Signs Roads Bill," *New York Times*, 29 June 1956, 1; Lewis, *Divided Highways;* Boggs: Weingoff, "Federal-Aid Highway Act" and Rose, *Interstate Express Highway Politics*.

was close. There was no contradiction in what Boggs wanted and what Byrd wanted, at least not in 1955. Rayburn and Al Gore Sr. met to reconcile the revised bills and offer one that both legislatures could sign. In late spring, the reconciled bill all but zipped through the two houses, with Bryan Dorn a most enthusiastic player in this game. Although a bit player in the early lawmaking, Dorn observed with appreciation Hale Boggs and Al Gore Sr. and learned from them concerning this kind of complicated, bipartisan legislation. Indeed from late spring 1956 on, he would be associated with the interstate system almost as much as he was associated with VA projects and military spending. And in time, he would be able to parlay his youthful lessons learned with his own evolving skills until he was truly a major player in the extending of the interstate system.[40]

Throughout this decade, Bryan Dorn insisted that interstate roads were essential to the civilian defense needs of evacuation from nuclear attack, and thus the huge system was very much part of his militaristic Keynesianism. On 29 June 1956, Eisenhower signed the public works project—too late to reverse the recession that had already played itself out in May but in plenty of time to alter quite dramatically many aspects of American life and society. In fact, Ike was stricken with ileitis, an inflammation of the ileus in the small intestine, and he could not perform the ritual of signing in the White House with special pens for relevant legislators. Instead, he signed in the Walter Reed Hospital in several subdued sessions; he did not actually complete signing all pieces of the complex legislation until 30 June. The shrewd engineer had effected a huge public works project and great structural change in his country, but as so often happened, Ike was so quiet and understated that it was some decades before historians and others realized the size and scope of his achievement. The initial spending was closer to $27 billion than the projected $25 billion, and the Boggs trust fund and the salutary effects on each state of such projects soon made the entire state delegation—and certainly every governor of South Carolina afterwards—enthusiasts for I-85, I-26, I-20, I-95, and the other "broad ribbons across the land" of palmettos and pine trees.[41]

---

[40] Rose, *Interstate Express Highway Politics*; Morris, "Eisenhower Signs"; WJBD, "In His Words," WJBD/SCPC; WJBD, *OTP*, 201, 213.

[41] Morris, "Eisenhower Signs"; Thomas, *Ike's Bluff*; Ambrose, *Eisenhower, Soldier and President;* WJBD, "In His Words," WJBD/SCPC; WJBD, *OTP*, 201, 213.

The Fair Deal for Textiles remained in some jeopardy. Eisenhower's men had not destroyed all the important policy provisions, but neither were they energetic about vigorous enforcement of specific practices. Nor did they talk frankly with the Japanese, whom Dorn blamed for subsidizing their own exports and closing their own markets. Of course, there was the Cold War dilemma for Dorn, the supreme Cold Warrior. Japan and Taiwan and other valued allies were permitted status as favored trade partners for diplomatic and strategic reasons. Dorn agreed that allies in the Cold War must be helped, but he believed that the Japanese in particular protected their own industries with tariffs and trade restrictions while they often "dumped" government subsidized products, including textiles, onto US markets. Generally, even as the recession lifted and growth resumed in the summer months of 1956, textile mills continued a sluggish performance, for textile products moved slowly, textile inventory backed up, and textile mill workers seldom gained overtime.[42]

For these reasons, Bryan Dorn was delighted with a handy monograph, Lewis E. Lloyd's *Tariffs: The Case for Protection*. Lloyd's study made a hash of free trade, much more so for solid political history than for macroeconomic theory, but Lloyd, like his reader Dorn, was no dummy about theory either. It was elegantly argued, and Bryan Dorn memorized passages and brought up Lloyd often; he proudly displayed an autographed copy of *Tariffs*. He especially liked a sentence about wealthy consumers who benefit from cheap imports: "He personally can buy cheaper, while it will be some other individual who will lose his job or have his weekly pay reduced." As for diplomacy and rewarding allies with special trading status, Lloyd said what Congressman Dorn always said; that is, the Russians were afraid of a great US air force, not of economically strong US allies. Lloyd offered proof that congressmen should take care of their own districts rather than career diplomats, who were experts in foreign trade as such but not experts in particular American regional products and employment. Dorn particularly liked to quote "the State Department through GATT [General Agreement on Tar-

---

[42] Remsen Bauknight, J. J. Norton and twenty-four general managers to WJBD, folder, August 1955; 200 letters from textile workers, Whitmire Plant of J. P. Stevens, October 1955; list of 400 millhand signatures, Abbot Worsted Mill, October 1955; Roger C. Peace to WJBD, 9 August 1955, with plan to meet in Greenville; Robert C. Johnson (J. P. Stevens and American Cotton Manufacturers Institute) to WJBD, 26 August 1955; correspondence, WJBD with Ed Baumel, 1956–1958, especially Baumel to WJBD retrospective, 19 April 1958, WJBD/SCPC; photograph essay, *Life*, 44/16, 19 April 1958, 32–33.

iffs and Trade], has bound the United States Congress to international commitments—a field which the Constitution delegated to Congress."[43]

That rhetoric not only played well in Ware Shoals and in Pacolet—Dorn considered it to be simply true. And his opinion was affirmed by some important young politicians. There was a fair trade protection piece written by Jack Kennedy as cover story for the *Atlantic*, and Dorn delighted to quote selectively from it, as he did a specialized piece of research about regional job losses and gains by W. H. Miernyk (who wrote for a Japanese-sponsored journal of economic geography). The congressman mastered these lines of scholarly and popular argument, passed the materials around the delegation of which he was secretary, urged the readings on the coalescing textile caucus, and mentioned them to many other people. By 1955, he was preaching to a converted choir in his regional part of the church, but only a new administration in the White House working in tandem with Sam Rayburn's team could successfully intervene on behalf of the textile industry. One thing prescient about Lloyd's little book had been forecast by none other than Leon Lowenstein, founder of the Lowenstein Corporation that had a baker's dozen mills in the Third and Fourth districts: eliminate fair trade, that is, remove all remaining tariff protections, and "industry could begin an exodus to low wage countries." Lowenstein had been clear that he was quite ready to leave South Carolina unless protected by the tariffs, import quotas, and other "interferences in classic free trade."[44]

One long-running issue emerged in this same period, initially only among the classes in boardrooms in late 1951. It involved a proposed federal dam at Trotters Shoals and a proposed Duke Power Plant at Middleton Point, both on the Savannah River. The controversies in these issues emerged on the public stage for the classes in 1952. By 1956, Trotters Shoals fully engaged Anderson politician and editor Wilton Hall, Clemson's Bob Edwards, Georgia's senator Richard Russell, and Strom Thurmond—not to mention

---

[43] Lloyd, *The Case for Protection*, 27, 46, 167; Terrill, *The Tariff.*

[44] Lloyd, op. cit., 45; WJBD to Eddie Kemp, 27 May 1954; WJBD to L. B. Adams, 29 April 1954; Thomas F. Young to WJBD, 18 January 1954; WJBD to Dan M. Zimmerman, 11 February 1954; correspondence with Lowenstein, WJBD/SCPC; Kennedy, "New England and the South," *Atlantic*, 97/1 (January 1945): 32–36 (cover story); Miernyk, "Labor Mobility and Regional Growth," 71–80. Kennedy was critical of Southern labor policy in the piece, describing it as an unfair trade policy in interstate policies and politics, and so WJBD was careful to select and quote the *international* Fair Trade and not the *interstate* Fair Trade aspects of the senator's essay.

the Olin Johnston, by this period arguably the most powerful politician in South Carolina. The words *Trotters Shoals* would be associated with Bryan Dorn thereafter, and generally in a negative context. Although his position was quite clear and quite consistent, it confused friends and foes then and has confused ever since—a sign that the great orator failed to get his message across as clearly as he should have.

Since his first arrival in the House in 1949, Dorn had "rolled logs" and otherwise traded votes on waterway projects, especially those of importance to Rocky Mountain Republicans Wayne Aspinall, Edgar Chenowith, and Henry C. Dworshak. The red-hills man, like the other Sam Rayburn congressmen, fully expected federal expenditures on waterways projects, especially on the Savannah River. After all, South Carolina had great potential for man-made power, and "an electrical spark has fired the South to build a new civilization," as a booster had put it when Bryan Dorn was very young. George Tindall noted,

> The Southern states as a whole had an estimated potential of 5,500,000 horsepower in their rivers, more than a third of the waterpower available 90 percent of the time east of the Rockies. The greatest potential was along the Appalachian slopes where mountain rivers flowed toward the Atlantic...through narrow valleys that could readily be dammed—all in proximity to coal that could be used for supplemental steam power.

If North Carolina provided the powerful slopes for the headwaters, it was South Carolina and Georgia that provided the narrow valleys, especially in the red hills of the Third Congressional District. And all of that was a short train haul away from the coalfields of Clinchfield in Virginia that gave their very name to an important freight line that served Dorn's district.[45]

However, the Duke Power Company had pioneered in harnessing that river power—in South Carolina's central piedmont and sand hills—and its officials in Charlotte fully expected to develop electrical power in the westernmost hills of Bryan Dorn's state. All such private-enterprise projects themselves involved complex legislation and multilayered permissions from governmental and private entities, and Dorn's family members were well acquainted with such cooperative work. The congressman calculated, along

[45] Tindall, *The Emergence of the New South*, 71–72; O. L. Fisher to WJBD, 5 August 1956; Wayne Aspinall, Edgar Chenowith, and Henry C. Dworshak, Water Projects Folders, 1956–1958; "Clinchfield Railroad" flyer with map, n.d. (1952–1958); J. E. Rankin to WJBD, 20 July 1951, WJBD/SCPC.

with the members of the informal textile coalition, that a private Duke Power Plant project would yield millions of tax dollars every year for years to come and would employ several thousand people in relatively high-wage jobs. Of course, there were attractive benefits in still another federal dam project, recreation lakes and suchlike, with power generated by the Tennessee Valley Authority or perhaps by some cooperative of South Carolina agricultural users. But yet none of that was as attractive to Dorn as the Duke Power Plant. Cousin and onetime campaign guru Steve Griffith eventually left a state judgeship to become general counsel for Duke Power in Charlotte, and both he and executives Norman A. Cocke and William McGuire provided Dorn quite a great deal of data. Too, Dorn was convinced he could persuade Mead Paper Company to set up a paper mill along the same shores of Middleton Point, and that proposed facility would mean sales for timber men like Dorn himself, as well as thousands of mill jobs that paid better than textile mill work or scratch-ankle farming.[46]

Unfortunately, officials at Duke Power and at Mead Paper both insisted that a federal dam on Trotters Shoals would be a "deal-killer," because Duke's engineers were convinced that the upriver dam there would alter the flow so completely that no downriver plant at Middleton Point could function properly. Wilton Hall of the *Anderson Independent* disagreed, and he intended to ride the Trotters Shoals project into state or national office, perhaps even taking Bryan Dorn's seat. Again, there were no scientific polls taken, but the congressman's mail ran heavily in favor of Trotters Shoals, and Bryan Dorn found his private-enterprise projects a "hard sell" in a region whose masses had grown quite fond of New Deal pubic works. Too, he had supported earlier Savannah River projects from the headwaters down to Charleston Harbor, and he was in the midst of congressional negotiations for the considerably more expensive public works project, the interstate highway system. For these days and many thereafter, the congressman was in public position of opposing a popular federal dam in Anderson County while helping Midwestern and Western Republicans build federal dams in

[46] W. C. Rhodes Jr. to WJBD, 9 April 1951; WJBD to John J. Rich, 19 February 1952; WJBD to J. K. Breedin, 18 February 1952; WJBD to John J. Riley, 19 February 1952; TVA folders, 1952–1958; WJBD to N. A. Cocke, 1 August 1958, WJBD/SCPC; *Charlotte City Directory*, 1930.

their respective regions. On Trotters Shoals, he won the classes to his side promptly but never entirely convinced his real people, the masses.[47]

By July 1956, Bryan Dorn could take stock of things and locate the battle lines for the next two decades. No matter how angry folk got about his opposition to the Trotters Shoals Dam, they trusted him overwhelmingly on the specific issues of constituent service and his work with the gradually emerging Informal Textile Group to save the mills—and their jobs and their overtime. He noted carefully the "pressure groups," and said that "this is an age of pressure groups based upon good public relations and membership." In particular, he noted the pressure group of the American Medical Association (AMA), and he became a warm correspondent with Dr. Thomas Parker of Greenville, a surgeon who was gaining national prominence in doctors' lobbying groups. Although quite right wing (even sympathetic to the John Birch Society), Dr. Parker tolerated progressive stands on many things but early extracted from Dorn—and insisted on retaining—ironclad promises not to support the liberal Democrat programs that became Medicare and Medicaid. As to things racial, not only Dr. Parker but also the masses favored Dorn's stance, no matter how awkward the future looked to the congressman himself. Someday Dorn would pivot from moderate segregationist to moderate integrationist, and that pivot would cost some votes among racist working-class whites while gaining many "neophyte" black votes. In the meantime, however, he followed Brooks Hays's religious and political strategy of moderation and caution and calls for peaceful discussion, and all of that played very well with his own people, the more so because he fully believed it all.[48]

Concerning the Cold War and "falling dominoes" in eastern Asia, Dorn was completely worked up over the issues, and occasionally almost apoplectic—but he also understood that only a new administration could bring a serious build-up of missiles and other weapons and restore a large standing army. For the nonce, he could feed his people's anti- Communism

[47] O. L. Fisher to WJBD, 5 August 1956; Aspinall, Chenowith, and Dworshak in Water Projects Folders; CF "In His Own Words" introductory matter, where archivists are unsympathetic with WJBD's reasoning on Trotters Shoals, WJBD/SCPC.

[48] WJBD to Alan Newcomb, 29 July 1952; WJBD to John S. Hoover, 4 November 1955; correspondence with Thomas Parker, especially, Thomas Parker to WJBD, 10 February 1953 and 12 March 1954 and WJBD to Parker, 12 March 1954; Congressional Files, 1956, WJBD/SCPC; Woodward, *Burden of Southern History* (3d rev. ed.), 100; Walton et al., "Woodward's New Intellectual Stream," 153–85.

without expending a lot of political capital attempting to build up the armed forces in a season when the commander in chief intended to fight no wars. For all these reasons, he reveled in the restoration of Sam Rayburn to speaker of the House and he could tolerate (without in the least trusting) LBJ as majority leader in the Senate. As for Strom Thurmond, the onetime Dixiecrat was showing himself to be a fine provider of genuine constituent service in the US Senate. Too, Senator Thurmond was completely on board with the congressional textile caucus abuilding—and he revealed more than once to his cousin that he, like the congressman, intended to make no public enemies and intended never to make permanent enemies of any legislators or executives, not even in private. Thurmond, like Dorn, "would bear no grudges." That would be important for the two kinsmen and their interconnected families as well as for South Carolina and regional politics.[49]

---

[49] Bass, "Strom Thurmond" and Roper, "Bennie Mays and Bryan Dorn," The Art of Political Biography," 22 January 2012.

Young congressional candidate Bryan Dorn—
still in fighting trim and still with a shock of hair.

Courtesy of South Carolina Political Collections

Bryan Dorn speaks for Dick Riley in Cayce during successful 1978 gubernatorial campaign. Far left is Democratic Party Chairman, the scholarly Don Fowler of the University of South Carolina.

Courtesy of South Carolina Political Collections

President Lyndon Baines Johnson gives the "laying on of hands treatment" after which the congressman loyally served the Great Society, ca 1968.

Courtesy of South Carolina Political Collections

Barratt House (called Myrtle Manor by the young poet Corporal Dorn) was host site for Labor Day campaign barbeques for Democrats from 1952 to 1980.

Courtesy of South Carolina Political Collections

A tall and powerful man Ebert "Eb" Dorn was active in public schools, "Supreme-intendent" of Education for Greenwood County to the school children and Dada to Bryan Dorn, ca. 1916

Courtesy of South Carolina Political Collections

Pearl Griffith Coleman Dorn—called "Baby" by son Bryan and "Spunky" by daughter Gracie—was a great speech coach who left the classroom to drill her children in speechifying, especially her favored child Bryan, ca. 1914

Courtesy of South Carolina Political Collections

President Kennedy speaking to Clemson Tiger Marching Band in meeting arranged by Bryan Dorn.

Courtesy of South Carolina Political Collections

"We can't stand any more Japanese goods here." Congressman Dorn meets with Chamber of Commerce manager Ed Baumel at Federal Building in Greenwood during depths of second Eisenhower recession, ca 1958.

Courtesy of South Carolina Political Collections

The Office Force in 1951. From left to right Julie Hendrick, Bob Schumacher, WJBD, and Dot Abbot. The force usually turned around letters from constituents the same day received.

Courtesy of South Carolina Political Collections

Congressman James C. Cleveland, R-NH, receives cotton (supplied by Cal Kinard of Epworth in Greenwood County) from Dorn. In all matters legislative, Bryan Dorn worked across the aisles and across the regions.

Bryan Dorn (right) with bull at Barratt House farm in newspaper photo for *Newberry Observer*.

Courtesy of South Carolina Political Collections

Bryan Dorn with Millie Johnston Dorn, ca. 1950. Briefly out of office, he traveled with his new bride, who realized he could only do politics. She directed his next successful campaign for U.S. House.

Courtesy of South Carolina Political Collections

Eb and Pearl pose—at Eb's insistence and with support of Pearl's Saluda family, ca. 1905.

Courtesy of South Carolina Political Collections

Young Congressman Dorn with millhands on site in Third District textile factory. Dorn's successor, the popular Congressman Butler Carson Derrick, claimed that no one was ever more loved by the District's millhands than Dorn, ca. 1951.

Courtesy of South Carolina Political Collections

The hometown paper *Greenwood Index-Journal* was always supportive of the Dorn family—and especially of the favored son Bryan, "Youngest [state] Senator" in the Army Air Corps.

Chapter 7

Hitting the Stride
1956–1960

The 1956 Labor Day barbeque at Barratt House again featured happy talk about large-scale plans for Southern Democrats in the White House and both houses of Congress. Adlai Ewing Stevenson was again the nominee for US president, and his running mate was again a Southerner, this time Senator Carey Estes Kefauver, a wise though hard drinking politician from Tennessee. Winning some support for president during early primary campaigns, the lantern-jawed Kefauver represented well the self-professed "Populistic New Deal progressives." Audaciously sporting a Davy Crockett coonskin hat, Estes Kefauver was proud of the Tennessee Valley Authority and Social Security and a strong national defense, especially the militaristic Keynesian focus on deployment of large forces of men in the services. While personally a professed liberal on many aspects of race relations, Kefauver, like Adlai Stevenson, was comfortable with states' rights civil rights and with policies of going slow on integration. He was Bryan Dorn's kind of man, as indeed was Adlai Stevenson.[1]

Fresh from the August nominating convention in Chicago, the Stevenson-Kefauver ticket had enjoyed the famous post-convention *bump*, as surveys measured public approval. The personally popular Eisenhower and his unpopular policies in August were marked by the George Gallup polling people at 45-percent support, unchanged by the Republican convention in San Francisco. By contrast, Stevenson-Kefauver had *bumped upward*, to 41-percent support from a summer starting point of 37 percent, and the folk gathered at Barratt House were hopeful of gaining at least four more points in the time remaining before November—and of course they were hopeful of knocking *down* some of that 45-percent support for Ike. Among other

---

[1] Martin, *Adlai Stevenson of Illinois*; picture of coonskin hat, Fortenay, *Estes Kefauver*; policies, Gorman, *Estes Kefauver; a Political Biography;* Ernest Frederick Hollings to WJBD, 25 July 1956; WJBD to Benmont Tench, Jr., 14 May 1956, WJBD/SCPC. Cf WJBD, *OTP*, 134, 147–48, 174: WJBD in retrospect changed his mind about Stevenson's candidacy.

things, the locals took pride in their Congressman Dorn, who had addressed the Chicago delegates concerning Japanese dumping of textile goods and the hurt it caused the local textile industry. On the beautiful sloping lawn, with happy traditional music and folk "well likkered up," the four-point gap between Eisenhower and Stevenson seemed small indeed and the White House appeared attainable.[2]

More to the point for sandlappers, the Democratic Party was especially strong in South Carolina in this Indian-summer season. And the congressman was confident of good working relationships between DC Democrats and the politicos in Columbia. As noted, the maverick Strom Thurmond seemed fully on board with both state and national party organizations and was emerging as an extremely effective legislator on behalf of Fair Trade for Textiles. In the office of the governor, up-country native but midlands-reared George Bell Timmerman Jr. was a successful proponent of economic development based on roads and schools. Timmerman was a late-arriving but suddenly very loud champion of segregation (who preserved two linear feet of correspondence celebrating his vigorous support of Jim Crow), and he had won election in 1954 in a "brutal" racist campaign in which he expressed his contempt for African Americans Bennie Mays, Earl Middleton, James Hinton, and Modjeska Simkins and declared that his gubernatorial opponent, progressive Columbia mayor Lester Bates, was nothing less than a "Communist agent." In his second annual report, Governor Timmerman had said, "A man's most priceless possession is his racial heritage" and earlier he had declared to state teachers meeting in conference in Columbia that "integrationism was always Communist"; "only an evil mind could conceive it...only a foolish man can accept it." This was scary stuff for Dorn, the moderate segregationist, who contemplated a future pivot to moderate integrationism and who counted each of those black people as his friend. Indeed, Governor Timmerman at times in 1956 could be scary even for Strom Thurmond folk.[3]

---

[2] Presidential poll, George Gallup, August 1956, Institute for Research in Social Sciences, University of North Carolina, hereinafter IRSS; WJBD, *OTP*, 209–10; WJBD to S[teve] C. Griffith, 2 November 1956, WJBD/SCPC.

[3] George Bell Timmerman Jr. Papers (hereinafter GBT/SCPC), 1950–1958, especially Segregation Folders: Mrs. George Kerr to Timmerman, 4 June 1954; audiotape, WIS television, 8 June 1954, SCPC. Modjeska Simkins, quoted, *Charles Wickenburg Reporting*, 3 May 1954; campaign files, 1954 and DNC files, 1956; Timmerman, "Second Inaugural (*sic*) Message to South Carolina General Assembly," 11 January 1956;

But yet Timmerman otherwise liked the highway proposals and other aspects of the national programs, and he had spent eight years as the lieutenant governor creating and then running a state development board that had lured industries into South Carolina by offering tax breaks but also by demonstrating substantive improvements in roads and schools. Unlike his famous predecessor Jimmy Byrnes, Governor Timmerman in early 1956 seemed unlikely to make some kind of grandstanding protest against the national party in a way that could damage congressional funding for South Carolina's roads and state universities. After all, roads and schools seemed to be the very stuff of Timmerman, the public servant; roads were largely federal in funding and South Carolina's colleges and universities needed assistance by federal funds. Regardless of wild rhetoric and race-baiting, Timmerman seemed to be ready to cooperate with the federal government on policies important to him.[4]

Temporarily, Bryan Dorn lay to one side any worries about the future beyond 1956. Instead, he could revel in yet another successful party gathering in this season. FDR the donkey was as popular as before, still evoking wild cheers. Mere mention of Herbert Hoover and even Thomas Dewey still drew jeers. Bryan Dorn moved among his friends and neighbors and found much continuing unhappiness with Eisenhower policies on trade, which were blamed for lingering textile doldrums and sluggish growth in textile employment. Furthermore, his new secretary, Robert Schumacher, seemed to be the kind of man Nana had wanted—and more important, Schumacher seemed to be the kind of man the locals wanted, whether encountering him in DC, the Federal Office Building in Greenwood, or at a barbeque.

As for the treacherous issues of race relations and integration, it was Eisenhower and the Republicans who were drawing the blame for the immensely unpopular Earl Warren court. In general, the political scientists then and later marked it with wry words. Eisenhower himself remained popular, but he had "no coattails for Republican candidates to ride on" in seeking their own offices. Very few among the masses gathered there understood why Bryan Dorn resisted the popular proposal for a dam at Trotters Shoals, but all of them liked the idea of Duke Power building a plant. The secretary of the South Carolina delegation and the workhorse of the de facto

---

address, South Carolina Education Association, Columbia conference, 17 March 1955, GBT/SCPC.

[4] GBT/SCPC, 1950–1958; Timmerman, "Second Inaugural (*sic*) Message to South Carolina General Assembly," 11 January 1956, GBT/SCPC.

textile group was resplendent at table at his barbeque and was justifiably hopeful about the coming political year.[5]

In the presidential campaign that fall, Dorn worked hard for Stevenson and Kefauver, campaigning in Florida for them. Robert Schumacher and the down-home staff took care of any constituents who came by Washington or the Greenwood offices. The Florida crowds who came out to hear Congressman Dorn were enthusiastic, and Democrats, especially the learned and articulate Stevenson, were convinced that Eisenhower could be bested in a face-to-face debate. They proposed one in Florida, a state that was Southern in its northern panhandle but heavily Northern, even transplanted New Yorker, in Miami and along the so-styled Gold Coast of its southeast. However, Eisenhower was much too shrewd to engage in a debate, and he declined. Soon, Bryan Dorn and everyone else learned that this race was much more about television than ever before. The carefully managed Ike, every gesture and word orchestrated brilliantly for television broadcast (and recorded in multiple closed sessions), was perfect for this medium—and neither Stevenson nor Kefauver were. Bryan Dorn had nothing to do with television in this instance, and Republican brilliance on the vacuum-tube devices was a troubling portent for his personal fortunes some day when South Carolina, too, would rely on televised campaigns. Indeed, the Florida race was a disaster for Democrats, with Eisenhower quickly gaining some 57-percent approval and never losing it. So, too, was the race a disaster outside the lower Southern states, increasingly called Deep South rather than Solid South. Not only Florida but also Virginia, Tennessee, Texas, and even Louisiana went Republican. When polls closed, the counting revealed that Ike's huge margin in Florida was his margin in the country as well. His 57 percent of the popular vote translated into a smashing 457 to 73 score in electoral votes.[6]

Furthermore, Bryan Dorn could see some troubling demographic trends brewing up, even in his solidly Democratic red hills. Republicans did

---

[5] Kaplowitz, "Using Aggregate Data to Measure Presidential Coat-tail Effect"; Gail Russell Chaddock, "History Shows 'Coattail' Effect Not So Crucial to President [Eisenhower]," *Christian Science Monitor*, 14 October 2012, 1; campaign files, 1956; Robert W. Hemphill to WJBD, 25 October 1956, WJBD/SCPC.

[6] WJBD to Ignatius Sterghos, 27 September 1956; Kefauver to WJBD, 9 November WJBD/SCPC; Tindall, *Disruption*, 49–55; Bass and DeVrites, *Transformation of Southern Politics*; Clerk of House of Representatives, *Congressional Quarterly Guide to US Elections* (4th ed., 2001).

very well in cities, especially among young professionals with college degrees. The blackest counties in his state supported Stevenson, as was generally the case in all Southern states, but that was because the blackest rural counties did not let black people vote. In Charleston, by contrast, Eisenhower had won impressive support among educated black people. They were at the moment a small group, but they were a rapidly growing group. Too, Dorn had to acknowledge that many rural black folk, especially in his own McCormick and Greenwood counties, had been prevented from voting by fraud—those might have been Republican votes. It was still the Charleston black wards, the old stomping grounds of the late Burnet Maybank, where black men and women voted, and many of them voted for Eisenhower. Too, in urban areas like Greenville, Spartanburg, and Columbia, educated and white-collar white folk had voted for Eisenhower. Such a class of white-collar voters did not yet exist in any size in the Third District, but Bryan Dorn wanted improved education, growing cities, and improved income for all his people. Looking down the road, if the Third District was transformed, as he fervently intended it to be, the Democratic Party could be left behind in a future when the entire state would be less poor, less rural, and better educated than in 1956. His friend, transplanted Northerner David Dows in Aiken, fully intended to build a Republican Party based on educated, white-collar white business people who would insist on much better roads and schools, and Dows warned Dorn that such a group would be less interested in the "safety net" and other federal interferences in the market than the millhands and farmers and rural business people who voted Populistic New Deal progressive.[7]

Meanwhile, in South Carolina, the General Assembly that fall completed its Segregation Session, enacting many laws designed to reaffirm Jim Crow, especially in public schools. It withdrew accreditation for private Baptist—and black—Allen University to train schoolteachers (leaving no black college, public or private, with the minimum number of PhD-holding faculty members to retain accreditation). The legislature had power greater than the governor, particularly as that lawmaking power was wielded by the "Bishop of Barnwell," Edgar Brown, and his allied state senators. Both legis-

---

[7] Tindall, *Disruption*, 48–55; Bass and DeVries, *Transformation*. Cf WJBD, *OTP*, 167, re: "new" Dorn; and Dows, 152–53; Dows, interview, Watson Dorn.

lative houses made a loud clamor on behalf of segregation, and Timmerman not only signed the acts into law, but claimed them loudly as his own.[8]

In fact, Timmerman so concentrated on segregation that he oftentimes neglected the economic development that first gained him acclaim. He delegated the recruitment of industry and the management of his selfsame development board to the vigorous lieutenant governor, Ernest Frederick "Fritz" Hollings (who emphasized economic development almost to the exclusion of race-baiting). Timmerman himself willingly took the name "Segregation Governor" and was content to identify himself with a hard-edged Jim Crow even to the exclusion of progressive economic development based on schools and industrial recruitment. Among other things, he proudly and loudly signed into law an act that no member of the National Association for the Advancement of Colored People (NAACP) could work in a public capacity at state pay at all. Everyone knew that the best black teachers and state college professors were members in good standing of the NAACP, not to mention a sizable group of white professionals, most prominently Bryan Dorn's warm personal friend John Bolt Culbertson. Governor Timmerman also successfully pressured University of South Carolina officials to fire Charles C. Travelstead, dean of education, who had called for a moderate response to the Brown decision so that schools could remain open. And, most stunningly, Timmerman forbade the highly respected and overwhelmingly popular evangelist Billy Graham to preach to his usual integrated crowd in a public space—so that the determined reformist moved his rally out to Fort Jackson, where he preached to tens of thousands in an integrated setting on the federal facility.[9]

Thus, South Carolina's state executive officers and legislators had done what Bryan Dorn most feared: they had focused on race to the exclusion of progressive reform, school support, and economic development. This Segregation Session also portended political obstacles for Bryan Dorn's hopes to become the governor in 1958. It was again affirmed, as had been the case in their turn for Olin Johnston, Strom Thurmond, Jimmy Byrnes, and now George Bell Timmerman, that family and race still counted the most in

---

[8] "Segregation Governor" and "Segregation Session," terms, William Douglas Workman, 1956–1958, William Douglas Workman Papers, SCPC, hereinafter WDW/SCPC. George Bell Timmerman, Governor's Papers, 1955–1959, SCDAH, hereinafter GBT/SCAH.

[9] Lesesne, *A History of the University of South Carolina*, 126–30; Governor's Statement (Billy Graham Rally), 22 October 1958, GBT/SCPC; Frady, *Billy Graham*, 409.

things political— so much so that otherwise progressive South Carolina governors since the 1930s gave up on school building, industry recruiting, health campaigns, and road construction in order to "get right with God." But that divinity was the god of Jim Crow. Dorn had to decide whether to seek substantive reform while only pretending to worship the false god, as Olin Johnston did—or to follow his successful cousin Strom Thurmond and pay full obeisance to the false god in this season, even and especially at the expense of substantive lawmaking.[10]

Jim Crow and economic development were not only *the* issues for Bryan Dorn, aspirant governor of South Carolina in the coming 1958 contests; they were also front and center for the sitting congressman as 1957 dawned. Still using his Baptist hero Brooks Hays as the *bonum exemplum*, Bryan Dorn wanted to delay integration peacefully through quiet lawyering—but he really did expect integration to come, for he honestly wanted *delay* and not *prevention*. Meantime, he wanted a serious address of economic issues, with vigorous attention to the Fair Deal for Textiles. Always connected to economic issues was military policy, all of it, including a powerful air force response to Russian military adventurism. He wanted large and well-trained armed forces, and he wanted those servicemen compensated during *and after* their years of active duty. There should be educational benefits for recently discharged veterans, and there must be dignified (and expensive) care for wounded veterans and for all veterans as they aged. If Brooks Hays showed him the Baptist approach to gradual integration, it was Jack Kennedy who showed him a "missile gap" between US and Russian weaponry, and it was Tiger Teague who showed him shameful neglect of emotionally wounded veterans and destitute elderly veterans. Hale Boggs showed him the vital importance of the interstate highway system to isolated rural Southern populations, and the Rocky Mountain and other Western Republicans showed him the importance of dam building and power generation. Fur-

---

[10] Segregation folders, especially Elmer G. Million (Allen University) to GBT, 17 March 1958; and Governor's Statement (Billy Graham Rally), 22 October 1958, GBT/SCPC; GBT, Governor's Papers, 1955–1959, SCDAH; Edgar, *South Carolina*, 527–28; Key with Heard, "The Politics of Color," ch. 16 and 17, *Southern Politics*; *South Carolina Legislative Manual of 1956, 98th General Assembly Sess.*, ed., Watson, James F. Byrnes Reading Room, Library of the South Carolina Law School, USC; Ballantyne, "Ernest Frederick Hollings," PhD diss., Cambridge University, 2014; idem., *New Politics in the Old South*; Bass, *Ol' Strom*; Huss, *Senator for the South*; and 1956–1958, ODTJ/SCPC; Johnston and race, Bass, "Art of Political Biography," 22 January 2013.

thermore, Colorado congressmen Wayne Norviel Aspinall and John Edgar Chenowith and other Westerners stood ready to help him with the Duke Power project, even if supporting Middleton Point entailed voting *against* the federal funding of Trotters Shoals (again, waterways and interstate highways and improvements in education were all part of defense spending in Dorn's thinking). And, as always, it was Sam Rayburn who showed Bryan Dorn how to get things done in Congress.[11]

The connections of defense to education and to economics had been especially tangled since May of 1957, when reports came that the Soviet Union had launched *Sputnik*, a satellite with spying capability (and also with the dreadful possibility of space-based missile launching). Militaristic Democrats, led by Jack Kennedy, leaped to attack the administration for the "missile gap" and began talking about a space race, whose loss portended losing no less than a space war. Eisenhower's public response was to keep a cool outward demeanor and to play down the news. His private response was to continue quiet and effective support for space exploration programs (what eventually became the National Aeronautics and Space Administration, or NASA) and to cooperate with Democrats like Dorn (and Kennedy) to build up preexisting federal space exploration. On 7 November 1957, Ike in a calculated way went public, very public, taking to the television to make a particularly effective speech describing the proposal for a new federal agency charged with exploring space.[12]

Although still angry about Soviet technology, Bryan Dorn was thrilled with this particular developing trend. After all, it was his air force and his Clemson College and related institutions that could cooperate in yet more militaristic Keynesian spending. As for the threat from Soviet expertise, Bryan Dorn was affirmed in his long-running hatred of the Soviet Russians, and he hoped that something like *Sputnik* at last could wake up other Americans. As things continued to develop, Professor James Rhyne Killian Jr. of Massachusetts Institute of Technology, the dominant player in NASA, loosened the space-exploration programs from their military moorings and eventually moved them into civilian control. This process of making NASA civilian

---

[11] Congressional files, 1957–1959, especially Wayne Norviel Aspinall, John Edgar Chenowith, and Sam Rayburn, WJBD/SCPC. Rayburn quoted, WJBD, *OTP*, 203.

[12] William Jorden, "Soviet Fires Earth Satellite into Space," *New York Times* Special Edition, 5 October 1957, 1; Glen P. Watson, "How the Space Act Came to Be," typescript, NASA Historical Reference Collection, NASA Headquarters, Washington, DC; Eisenhower, "Space," address, 7 November 1957, CBS Archives; "Democratic Leaders Attack Administration Sputnik Reaction," *Aviation Week*, 9 December 1957, 31–32.

rather than military took some time, and Bryan Dorn resisted it as best he could. He never really accepted the idea of civilian space exploration, and he was ever vigilant for creative and aggressive responses to Soviet adventurism in the Cold War. Militaristic Keynesianism was not some metaphor for him, but literal; and Dr. Killian's eventual success in putting NASA under civilian control was a personal defeat for Bryan Dorn.[13]

Nevertheless, the excitement about space exploration was soon dwarfed by yet another recession and by racial problems that made a moderate and gradual integration problematical, if not politically impossible. Congressman Dorn took it as a given that race relations always worsened during economic hard times, and his district had barely staggered to its feet after the first Eisenhower recession when a second and sharp one landed on the entire nation. To the Segregation Sessions of a hateful General Assembly was added an eight-month business downturn that once again clobbered the textile industry workforce. The gall and the wormwood is that on things racial it was none other than Brooks Hays who lost control of the political processes in his own Arkansas. The whole sorry story was so overwhelming that Brooks Hays's moderation strategies were discredited on all sides, right, left, and center. The man himself was soon driven from office—by a popular vote ringingly asserting itself against his once-powerful and effective political apparatus. In 1957 and thereafter, those who knew of Brooks Hays spoke with respect for his church work (he was elected president of the Southern Baptist Conference) but had little good to say about his racial policies or other aspects of his politics. For Congressman Dorn, who held tightly to friends and associates, it was doubly painful because he lost an ally in Congress and because it hurt to see Brooks Hays taunted in defeat. Even when South Carolinians publicly disavowed Brooks Hays's moderation on issues of segregation, Bryan Dorn took great pains to preserve the friendship, especially the deep brotherly relationship grounded in the Baptist faith. To understand why Brooks Hays fell from Arkansan grace while remaining dear to Bryan Dorn, one has to look at Hays and Arkansas the way that the South Carolina congressman did in 1957.[14]

---

[13] James Rhyne Killian Jr., "Memorandum on Organizational Alternatives for Space Research and Development," *Exploring the Unknown*, vol. 1, gen. ed. Logdson et al., 628–31; Eisenhower, "Space"; "Democratic Leaders Attack," 31–32.

[14] Hays, *A Southern Moderate Speaks*; Hays, address, Emory & Henry College, 7 October 1963; "Congressman Hays," *The White Topper Newspaper*, 14 October 1963, Emory & Henry College Archives, Emory, VA; Congressional Files, 1957–1958, especially Vaughn Bible Class, WJBD/SCPC.

Arkansas was where regionalist geographers located the Upper South, but in 1957 its political climate was not that of North Carolina or Virginia. Reversing the old Christian mystic's language, it was not *in* the Deep South, but it was *of it.* This was especially the case for certain farming communities beneath the Arkansas River that cut the state roughly into a northern half and a southern half. In the northeast corner, the delta of the Mississippi River established a culture and a politics dominated by Memphis, the capital of the Delta. By contrast, it happened that over in the northwestern corner, the state university had been established in Fayetteville, tucked away in the beautiful Ozarks where it was somewhat removed, if not protected, from the often-vitriolic racism of the Delta and of the farming south. Thus, the University of Arkansas integrated itself with remarkably little difficulty, and by 1948 had even established integrated training at its law school and at its medical center in the state capital at Little Rock. As noted, Strom Thurmond, in his progressive educationist phase of being governor, had explored some way to use state money to send South Carolina black students to the Arkansas Medical School, which could serve as a regional training center for physicians of all races. Other Southern governors explored such concepts as well.[15]

Meanwhile, black citizens since World War II had been able to vote in the wards of rapidly industrializing Little Rock, and most of these voted for Orval Faubus, originally a self-proclaimed racial moderate who had committed himself to a gradual integration of the public schools in exchange for significant black votes in the gubernatorial elections of 1954 and 1956. There was a respected cadre of black professionals in the state capital, and these had long worked with progressive industrial managers, economic development businessmen—and with Brooks Hays and Governor Orval Faubus. To Congressman Dorn, Faubus (a distinguished intelligence officer in World War II) had initially seemed fully dependable as a Populistic New Deal progressive who would continue to follow Hays's lead on gradual integration.[16]

---

[15] Interviews, James William Fulbright (21 March 1983) and Comer Vann Woodward (18 and 19 July 1978; 12 October 1980), JHR/SHC; Randolph, *Ozark Magic*; Cochran, *Vance Randolph*; Ashmore, *Arkansas*, States and Nation series, ed. Smith (1976); Goodspeed Brothers, *Biographical and Historical Memories*.

[16] Interview: James William Fulbright (21 March 1983), JHR/SHC; Roper, *Magnificent Mays*, 212, 237–38; Reed, *Faubus*, 108.

Faubus, again like Bryan Dorn, worked simultaneously with the masses and the classes. The classes wanted continuing industrial growth in Little Rock and continuing improvement in schools there; they did not want racial unrest, and they expected continuing peaceful, gradual integration of all things. The Little Rock School Board had determined to begin integration at the Central High School in fall of 1957, and initially it was Brooks Hays who counseled delay while Orval Faubus supported the progressive timetable. Rather suddenly, Governor Faubus switched positions, not only in terms of the timing of integration but in terms of preventing it for all time. In early September, Governor Faubus stunned the Little Rock mayor Woodrow Mann and the Little Rock Board of Education—to say nothing of President Eisenhower and Attorney General Herbert Brownell, each of whom was, as usual, working quietly and unobtrusively through back channels to facilitate the long-planned integration of Central High School.[17]

Governor Faubus called out the Arkansas National Guard to block entry of the nine black students, and he played melodramatically to the masses who gathered in town to protest integration. It became violent, and the violence was captured for a surprised and dismayed viewing public on national television news. Faubus had more surprises in store, including the complete withdrawal of the Arkansas National Guard forces, leaving the city and its Central High School in control of segregationist mobs. If Congressman Hays had been unprepared for Governor Faubus to be a convert to hard-edged Jim Crow, he was even more unprepared for the cool, almost professional demeanor of the Little Rock Nine. Assisted by officials in the NAACP, these students had been training themselves intellectually and emotionally for exactly these contingencies of violent resistance. Faubus played brilliantly to the masses on television in Arkansas, but the Little Rock Nine played even more brilliantly to the middle class watching television elsewhere in the US. As for Brooks Hays, he tried to facilitate, to mediate, to be in between Eisenhower's men and Faubus's men. He found to his embarrassment that nothing he could tell federal agents was of much use, since Faubus had no real reason to tell anything to Brooks Hays that he could not tell directly to President Eisenhower—or to the *CBS Evening News*.

Congressman Hays, to say nothing of Congressman Dorn, was then surprised still more when President Eisenhower reemerged as the tough Overlord commander, sending federal troops to integrate Central High

---

[17] Reed, *Faubus*; Branch, *Parting the Waters*, 222–25; Executive Order 10730, General Records of the US Government, Record Group 11, National Archives.

School and ingloriously standing down Governor Faubus while appearing to ignore Brooks Hays. More general than president, Ike commanded Attorney General Brownell: "Let's apply the best military principles to it and see that the force we send there is strong enough that it will not be challenged, and will not result in any clash." The force sent there was none other than the 101st Airborne Division, and the mobs did not challenge these real soldiers, these famed Screaming Eagles. Too, President Eisenhower announced his support of the 1957 civil rights bill, and began to work effectively with none other than the master of the Senate, Lyndon Baines Johnson, to get it passed.[18]

In the Vaughn Bible class at Calvary Baptist Church and in the prayer breakfast meetings of Congress, Brooks Hays and Bryan Dorn thus had much to pray over, not only that black and white Arkansas citizens would escape death and injury, but also that all concerned could make sense of the political currents in which they had until recently so placidly floated. Of course, Strom Thurmond demonstrated an effective response, giving a hard-edged defense of segregation in a famed filibuster against the proposed Civil Rights Act. Thurmond's filibuster lasted a full twenty-four hours and cemented his reputation as the man who "always does what he thinks is right even when he's wrong." Much as Thurmond's filibuster endeared him to the white folk of the red hills, LBJ's much quieter work among senators actually got a Civil Rights Act passed in 1957, albeit one with no "teeth" for meaningful enforcement. Governor Faubus for his part endured his licking from President Eisenhower in 1957 and then closed the Little Rock public schools for the academic year 1958 to 1959, an action that proved impossible for the federal government to overturn.[19]

Once, Congressman Dorn had deployed then-fashionable talk about states' rights civil rights and called for a gradual development of racial justice built up from the local level. Such words now seemed pale tea indeed compared to the heady brews concocted by Dorn's associates to his left, i.e., Jack Kennedy, LBJ, and even Estes Kefauver. By contrast, to his right, friends Faubus and Thurmond and the Harry Byrd were talking about "interposi-

---

[18] Reed, *Faubus,* 108; Branch, *Parting the Waters*, 222–25; Draft for Little Rock Speech (third draft), 24 September 1957, Papers of Dwight David Eisenhower, Ann Whitman File, National Archives; Caro, *The Years of Lyndon Johnson*, vol. 3: introd. and pt. 5 "The Great Cause."

[19] Hays, *A Southern Moderate*; idem., address, EHC; Thurmond supporter of Pacific Mills, Duncan, SC, quoted, Bass, "Political Biography," 22 January 2013; idem., *Ol' Strom*; Branch, *Parting the Waters*, 222–25.

tion" and "massive resistance." At home in his district the classes were sporting signs that said "Impeach Earl Warren." Meanwhile, if the ranks of the Ku Klux Klan did not actually swell in the valley of the Saluda, the hooded men were certainly more obviously on the scene with burning crosses and death-talking chants. When the members of the Byrd Machine actually closed some public schools in Southside Virginia to prevent integration, they thereby did violence to Dada's and Nana's most cherished institutions—and they did it in Thomas Jefferson's very Commonwealth.

Things seemed pretty crazy, too crazy to remain in the shrinking middle with the good Brooks Hays. Indeed, Hays perished politically: once banished from his congressional seat, he never regained it, even in quieter times. Calculatedly, Bryan Dorn stepped to the right and became aggressive in his defense of segregation, if not *segregation forever*, at least for the nonce. He even saluted his good friend, the Rev. Bob Jones Sr., who issued a pamphlet showing biblical justification for segregation—something that Dorn *completely disbelieved*. Despite his deep personal beliefs, he allowed Bob Jones Sr. to cite Dorn's support on the radio station WMUU (World's Most Unusual University). Television might have limited effect in the rural red hills, but the fundamentalist faithful did listen to WMUU and to Dr. Bob Jones Sr. Not only did Dorn welcome the radio support, but he happily joined the Cooperating Board of Trustees of Bob Jones, an honorific with no voting powers but a clear sign of who supported whom, especially on racial issues.[20]

It was unlike the congressman's performance and behavior in previous years, and the printed words and the surviving audiotapes were bound to haunt him some future day when black men and women actually gained statewide voting rights and statewide voting power. That day loomed on the near horizon, and Bryan Dorn recognized its inevitability, given legal and political trends that he knew perfectly well by careful study. He preserved a troubling letter from S. T. Shaw, a self-designated Colored Man from Cleburne, Texas, in the congressional district of Sam Rayburn. Shaw sent him a postal card written proudly and with precision in green ink: "I would like so much as to hear from you. Why are you against the Colored People in there [*sic*] right to vote in elections. Do you not believe in the Golden Rule? You do not have to clear everything with Rayburn."[21]

---

[20] Bob Jones Sr, "Is Segregation Spiritual?" (1957), corr., Bob Jones Sr., especially Annual Reports to Trustees, 1956–1967,WJBD/SCPC. Also a Cooperating Trustee was Senator Olin Dewitt Talmadge Johnston, as noted, one otherwise well to WJBD's left.

[21] Shaw to WJBD, 21 March 1959, WJBD/SCPC.

As he usually did with black correspondents, Dorn was careful to reply promptly and to thank Shaw for his "nice" note. As usual, he then said noncommittally, "I appreciate your taking the time to let me know how you feel about important legislation before the Congress." Then he uncharacteristically said something of substance, knowing that Shaw would likely share the note with other black people and also knowing that he would then be held accountable for what he said: "I am for every one voting who is an American citizen and who pays taxes and believes in the Constitution of the country." He concluded by "enclosing a little speech" that he had delivered in opposition to the 1957 Civil Rights Act. But he did not respond to the biblical question about Jesus's Golden Rule because he could not. He did *not* want black folk to treat him as they were being treated in the late 1950s, especially in the political processes that were his love. The congressman knew from bitter experience how it felt to be out of politics. To keep his own place in politics, Bryan Dorn would have to bring temporary harm to the "hash man" and the other black constituents among his people. Quietly, he worked to protect Benjamin E. Mays and John Bolt Culbertson from anti-Communist witch hunts that were actually anti-civil rights campaigns. But for other civil rights activists who were not personal friends, he either attacked or did nothing to help. In this season, he was, in fact, acting out of character and acting against Christian conviction. There was truth in the words of the Texan Shaw.[22] That truth hurt.

By the winter of 1958, it was time to focus on the coming gubernatorial primary. This time he said nothing in public about the governorship, and he certainly did not drop out of the race for US Congress. Instead, he worked with delegates and party regulars to be drafted or otherwise "called" to run for governor. He had thought he found a clever way to play the racial politics almost as successfully as cousin Strom Thurmond, but to do so in a way that could win votes in the late Burnet Maybank's black wards in Charleston County—and also in a way that the state's black citizens would trust him as he guided South Carolina into a new era of gradually emerging integration and gradually unfolding opportunities based on better (but temporarily segregated) schools for all. He expected party regulars as well as the masses and the classes to remember the compassion and the hard work of the Third District congressman during this second Eisenhower recession. No less than venerable Edgar A. Brown—rejected for US Senate but completely in com-

---

[22] Ibid.; WJBD to Charles G. Garrett, 19 January 1956, WJBD/SCPC; Golden Rule, Matt. 7:12, KJV trans. used by WJBD.

mand of the South Carolina Senate—sent Congressman Dorn a heartfelt note: "You have grown greatly in statue [*sic*]." Even the seriocomic misspelling of *stature* shows the very real goal in the unintended joke: Bryan Dorn very much aspired to a statue of himself, one befitting the governor who would work with the "Bishop of Barnwell" to build good roads and good schools and thereby bring good jobs directly to all five districts of their state.[23]

Brown was not alone in his raised estimate of Bryan Dorn. Indeed, the "Bishop of Barnwell" was only responding to what his keen political eye saw "among the legislative leaders in Congress." As a matter of fact, Bryan Dorn was likely the most loved congressman in the House in 1958, if the intensity of such a thing could be measured. In any case, he was surely the most loved congressman ever to serve in the Third District. He was in some ways perfect for the district of the rural red hills, with its waterways and its textile mills and its many small businesses and the rapidly evolving system of interstate highways and good farm-to-market roads and its Clemson College.[24] But Brown's kind assessment was actually too late to be useful. What made Dorn perfect in one place was not necessarily the most effective sale in the other four districts of the Palmetto State—especially those for whom the "Barnwell Ring" of Edgar Brown and Sol Blatt was tiresome or irrelevant, or both.

Among those voters beyond the Third District, the man who fascinated them was the figure with the face of a matinee star, Lieutenant Governor Fritz Hollings. This Hollings had learned and then mastered the mechanics of the development board built by George Bell Timmerman. He used his handsome visage and his baritone voice in person, much as young Dorn had once wowed constituents with his baritone voice and with his own handsome face—and with a body once built "like Adonis." But Fritz Hollings could do all of that for television, too. And like it or not, 1958 was not a contest featuring Bryan Dorn, the young air corps veteran of 1947. Instead, party folk now beheld Bryan Dorn, beloved congressman who had picked up weight amidships, whose hairline had receded, who now looked much like old Congressman Hare (either of them)—and much like the mature states-

---

[23] Brown to WJBD, 20 April 1959, WJBD/SCPC; Brown and WJBD, April 1959, EAB/SC/CU.

[24] Brown and WJBD, April 1959, EAB/SC/CU; Butler Derrick, remarks, "Art of Political Biography, 22 January 2013."

man William Jennings Bryan. In the "beauty contest" phase of nominating a man for the governor, Fritz Hollings had all the advantages.

Nor was Fritz Hollings mere show and flash. His development board had brought industries into South Carolina even during the depths of this frightful recession. Congressman Dorn had done yeomen work in the same labors, but it was *Hollings's* development board, especially after Governor Timmerman made segregation *the* main gubernatorial responsibility. Among other things, the lieutenant governor had deployed the very strategy of the Asian "state champion" industries, namely, to offer out-of-state corporations the lure of lower wages and lower taxes. The selfsame things complained about by Congressman Dorn and the classes in Washington—low wages, low taxes, few regulations—could be applied with smashing success to lure southward corporations from Ohio or Massachusetts or New Jersey looking for relief in costs, especially costs of labor. It all depended on whom you were talking to, where, and when, details that Hollings never fumbled.[25]

Moreover, Fritz Hollings also knew that captains of Northern industry did not want to bring their families into redneck trailer parks marked by lynch-mob violence and substandard schools. He assured the businessmen that South Carolina was a place of dramatically improving schools with good roads and plenty of good, clean water and dependable electricity. On these issues, Hollings worked magic as adroitly as ever did his Charleston predecessor Burnet Maybank. The lieutenant governor presided over sessions of the General Assembly, though the office had little effective power and the responsibilities were mostly ceremonial and procedural. Fritz Hollings had presided over the Segregation Session at its depths, sitting there with leonine dignity but seldom saying anything. In the minds of aggrieved white voters suffering a recession and newly angered by black aspirations, Lieutenant Governor Hollings had been associated with Jim Crow, especially the new legislation of 1957. Yet he had personally said nothing at all untoward about race, and consequently Hollings enjoyed a following in the black wards in his own Charleston. He had "pulled it off." Pivoting to racist whites, he reminded them of the Segregation Sessions; pivoting back to black voters, he assured them of his good will and his plans for a new day. No one called him out on the contradictions, as no one had ever called out Burnet Maybank on his contradictions. Hollings was, in fact, not unlike the "magic" man in his

---

[25] Ballantyne "Ernest Frederick Hollings," PhD diss., Cambridge University, 2014; idem., *New Politics in the Old South*; Bass and DeVries, *Transformation;* Rivoli, *The Travels of a T-Shirt.*

appeal to all sorts and conditions of political personhood. Ruefully, Bryan Dorn realized that 1958 was going to be the year of Governor Fritz Holllings.[26]

Dorn needed to drop the pursuit of the governorship in this season and instead make 1958 and the next four years thereafter great years for the Third District. Filing again that winter, he faced no opposition in the primary and would face none from Republicans in November. Only a few people knew that he had sought the governor's chair, and those few kept a dignified and very politic silence.

Fortunately, Dorn could talk *and legislate* true to his heart on issues economic, especially concerning his people who were millworkers and servicemen. Digging into his homework, the studious child of Dada and Nana examined what the National Bureau of Economic Research and Hubert Aull had to say about the current recession. NBER staff economists marked this recession's commencement in August 1957, and the reliable Dr. Aull once again assured him that NBER had competent and honest professional economists. Some experts thought this recession might end sooner rather than later, but the gross domestic product actually shrank 3.7 percent. This disastrous shrinkage was coming at a moment when folk needed growth at a *positive* 3 percent in order to repair the damage to employment from the first recession. Moreover, unemployment peaked at 7.5 percent, a level unacceptable for the Populistic New Deal progressive who still thought in terms of 97 or 98 percent employment as "full," even though economists warned him such a level seemed unlikely. Too, Tiger Teague's VA committee had reams of data showing the misery of Korean War veterans, not only the tens of thousands recovering from physical and mental wounds, but also the fully able-bodied and well-adjusted who simply could not find a job anywhere at all, and especially not in the red hills that they loved as deeply as the congressman did. Working under Teague, Dorn steadily gained seniority and since 1956 had been chair of the vital pensions subcommittee.[27]

---

[26] Jordan, *Primary State*; Ballantyne, "Ernest Frederick Hollings," and idem., *New Politics for the Old South*; Ernest Frederick Hollings Papers, 1957–1958, SCPC; Hollings to WJBD, 25 July 1956, WJBD/SCPC; George Bell Timmerman Jr. Papers, Governors Papers, 1955–1959 and Ernest Frederick Hollings, 1959–1963, Governors Papers, SCDAH.

[27] NBER, 3Q_1957-2Q_1958, US Business Cycle Expansion and Contraction, 20 September 2010; correspondence, Aull and WJBD, Congressional Files, 1958; L. Bates Gerald to WJBD, retrospective, 4 February 1963 (*sic*; 1964); Pamphlet Committee print,

Damage to textile-mill villages was especially severe, and the congressman's mail was filled with the most heartfelt correspondence, much of it sorrowful rather than angry. In his way, he actively busied himself trying to find individual jobs for particular constituents who were out of work. And in their way, the Abney and the Self and the B. C. Inabinet and other classes understood the desperate need to find places for at least some of these displaced workers. Together, Dorn and the classes could honestly tell the masses that they on occasion found jobs for some of them. Of course, he knew that these problems were structural, and Lewis Lloyd and Hubert Aull convinced him that only careful attention to the details of tariffs and quotas and rules of trade as well as the exchange rate could so shelter the American textile industry enough for it to grow—and thereby bring his people back to work on the lines at three full shifts. In other words, he knew that there were policy issues that must be resolved, and that these were macro forces that must be addressed. All the same, he also knew that every integer in the economist's statistics was, in fact, a woman of the red hills whose hours had been cut back and whose sons faced a dim future. Those quoted in the preface spoke at this very time. "Such as these" asked sincerely, "please help us." Speaking of the apparatus of quotas but also the government programs that gave money to the needy, a severely straitened veteran in Whitmire offered a telling phrase: "Please don't take this little bit of income from our people who are your people."[28]

Some of "our people who are your people" gave him what economics professors call "naïve Keynesianism." Officials in Whitmire noted that the various federal programs put cash into the hands of people who would spend it at once—and they also noted that such immediate spending was exactly the kind of stimulus called for in yet another recession. C. E. Lucas, an Indianapolis veteran who considered himself a constituent of Dorn's, expressed a

---

Ben Neufield to WJBD, 24 June 1957; "Statement of the American Legion, Dept. of SC," 1958; folder on VA, 1957–1958, VA. Controller of Medicine and Surgery, *Current and Projected Veteran Load through 1986,* 4 June 1958; HR Print #222, HR, 85 2d sess., 26 June 1958, corr., Jack Z. Anderson, O. E. Teague, WJBD /SCPC; corr., speeches, GHA/SC/CU.

[28] J. W. Teague to WJBD, 3 June 1958, with enclosure, R. H. Swallow, Bigelow-Sanford Carpet, Inc., Belton, form letter to employees; Edith Cummings to WJBD, 31 May 1958; Faye Paige to WJBD, 28 May 1958; Ida Mae Lowe to WJBD, 25 May 1958; Joe Melton Martin to WJBD, 29 May 1958, Thelma Crawford to WJBD, 4 June 1958, WJBD, Thomas E. Malone to WJBD, 16 January 1958, SCPC; "such as these," Jesus's words, Mark 10:14; Matt. 19:14, Luke 9:48, all trans; corr., speeches, GHA/SC/CU.

workingman's version of "naïve Keynesianism" that was also spoken in the red hills. "The veterans," Lucas said, "will keep their money in circulation in the United States and make business better for all." Such letters for Dorn were not proof that the average citizen grasped Keynes, even in a naïve way. They were instead proof that the average citizen expected the government to get in there and help when jobs were scarce, pay was low, and needs were overwhelming—and that help would come primarily through the federal government spending as well as regulating international markets.[29]

Because the problems were so intimate and so individual and specific, Dorn went home often to hear the pleas and petitions of the Third District folk. The popular *Life* magazine ran a spread of photojournalism concerning unemployment problems in the US. There was special attention to the piedmont textile mills. There on page 32 of the slick magazine is a picture of Bryan Dorn sitting at a table listening to Ed Baumel, manager of the Greenwood Chamber of Commerce. Baumel is caught in full action, gesturing with his hands in his congressman's face in protest about Japanese dumping of textile goods onto American markets. *Life* quotes him: "We can't stand any more Japanese goods here." Other men at the table lean forward, anxious to testify to Their Man. The way the photograph is cropped, it is obvious that still other men were there, equally as anxious, but not displayed in this picture because they—but not their passions—are scissored out of the graphic. The congressman's blue eyes, a pained pale grey in the magazine, glow intently as he listens to Baumel. He takes in what his people are saying. A caption notes that the chamber of commerce and other citizens in Greenwood demand that their congressman take action. It is in the category of the hurtfully honest. A few days after publication, Baumel wrote a note disclaiming the words of the caption and apologizing for the way the photograph shows that "I was giving you a bad time." Bryan Dorn wrote back that the photograph and the caption were good. They were honest. He was glad that the magazine publicized these real problems. He again vowed to work with Congress to discipline the Japanese for dumping subsidized products. He again vowed to restore textile manufacturing in the red hills.[30]

---

[29] C. E. Lucas to WJBD, 11 March 1957, WJBD/SCPC.

[30] *Life*, 44/16, 21 April 1958, 32–33; E. A. Baumel to WJBD, 19 April 1958, and WJBD to Baumel, 23 April 1958; C. R. Breazeale to WJBD, 7 June 1956; WJBD to Oriana Carter, 23 January 1957, WJBD/SCPC .

Dorn arranged with veteran Republican Pennsylvania congressman Richard Murray Simpson to hold special hearings on trade policies, and these hearings took up much time and space in 1958. He, Simpson, and three other congressmen sponsored a bill to hobble presidential authority in setting tariff rates and quotas through treaty negotiation. Of course, he would never make such an intensely political campaign partisan, because for Dorn the most political was always the most bipartisan. Simpson understood all of that too, as he understood that the great orator was in command of this committee. Also effective in testimony was Congresswoman Elizabeth Kee of Fifth District West Virginia, who scored the Eisenhower administration for lack of concern about four million unemployed workers, especially the hardships thus worked emotionally on their families. These Simpson-Dorn hearings on free trade problems gained attention in interrelationship with the many trips to hear testimony back in the red hills. Articles and pictures in the magazines and in the newspapers attracted attention from voters back home who came out to witness at the congressional offices in the Federal Building in Greenwood. But the people speaking, even yelling in the Greenwood offices, were themselves recorded in various media and then made their way back to the hearings in the chambers of the House of Representatives. Some of the millworkers themselves were even brought to Washington to witness in front of the congressmen and the press there gathered. For Simpson's Pennsylvania, it was not textiles and synthetic fibers but steel and aluminum and related heavy industry; for Representative Elizabeth Kee, it was coal, and for still others it was automobiles. But all together, they shut the door against free trade: the congressmen formed a "piece-bright paling," a fence or gate that could protect God's workers who cried out from their hearts in testimony as painful, as poignant, and as real as any witnessing in an austere Baptist tent during revival. Congressmen, even and especially those representing prosperous uptown *bidnesses* and suburban residential developments, heard it and responded. Eisenhower's hated Reciprocal Trade Agreement (actually Truman's treaty) remained in force, but individual representatives imposed special exceptions and hedged its provisions. They said that a Democratic president (and probably any Republican successor to Ike) would dismantle the damnable thing and pay intense attention to American manufacturing needs and interests.[31]

---

[31] Simpson Dorn 1958 Hearings, see *Congressional Record*, vol. 104, pt. 8, 85th Cong., 2d sess., 29 May–18 June 1958, 10697–772; *Congressional Record*, vol. 104, pt. 13, 85th Cong., 2d sess., 7 August 1958, 16542–47; WJBD, remarks, *Congressional Record*,

For his own part, Bryan Dorn made many personal interventions between constituents and officials at all levels of government. For instance, he arranged for telephone lines for forty people in the Tompkins Community of Edgefield County by putting personal pressure on the regulatory agency and on the local telephone supplier. He worked with Anderson attorney William L. Watkins on behalf of Shirtmaster Manufacturer to preserve, at least for the nonce, some 300 jobs by giving the nearly bankrupt firm a needed break from IRS pressure to pay what it owed in taxes. As always, he argued, unsuccessfully, with other congressman, about more generous benefits for Social Security recipients—again making the South Carolinian Populistic point that small-time farmers and millworkers did not generally *live* long enough to collect full Social Security benefits. On the selfsame day, he worked intimately with President Boyce M. Grier of private Lander College to get a federal loan for a college building project. He worked directly with his textile benefactor Jim Self alongside lobbyists and attorneys in the Pine Marketing Institute on issues of local train service for timbermen and textile manufacturers—in doing so, of course, helping his own personal interests as a timberman. Yet in the instant, his personal microeconomic involvement in timber was as nothing compared to the political stakes in the macroeconomic issues of his district's textile plants.[32]

The recession of 1957 to 1958 passed, its conclusion marked by the NBER in the second business quarter of 1958, specifically April. 1959 came on, but no millworkers forgot the pain wrought by two recessions in one presidency. Nor did they forget their congressman's willingness to listen to them and his efforts on their behalf.

Connected with textiles was the military, as it was connected with the citizenry. Millworkers were themselves veterans, and these millworker veterans sent their sons into the military of this day. Congressman Dorn knew the Army Air Corps of World War II, and he had paid close attention to the

---

vol. 104, pt. 10, 85th Cong., 2d sess., 27 June–14 July 1958, 13724; quoted phrases, Hopkins, "The Starlight Night"; Elizabeth Kee, "Keenotes," 10 February 1958, Elizabeth Kee Papers, West Virginia Archives and History, Charleston, WV; "Olin Teague"; Folders, Textiles, and Tariffs, 1955–1958, WJBD/SCPC.

[32] Visit Eisenhower and Nixon, WJBD to D. J. Gray (Riegel), 10 August 1956; WJBD to Jolly Owdom, 25 June 1958; WJBD to William L. Watkins, 25 June 1958; WJBD to B. M. Grier, 20 June 1958; WJBD to J. C. Self, 20 August 1958; W. C. Hammerle to WJBD, 19 June 1958; WJBD to B. M. Grier, 20 June 1958, WJBD/SCPC.

new army and new air force of the Korean War era. He had himself taken advantage of veterans' benefits for his own medical treatment, and he kept close tabs on the operations of the VA hospital at Walter Reed, but also and more importantly, the VA hospital in Columbia. Besides presiding over hearings about free trade and fair trade, Bryan Dorn also took an active role in the hearings chaired by Olin Teague. These hearings, conducted at the same time, had to do with appropriate levels of support for wounded soldiers and for veterans who years later became seriously ill from emotional wounds that the committee traced back to combat experiences. These issues were seen very differently by the Eisenhower men and by the congressmen. Much of the difference was by rank: Ike and Omar Bradley and others in command of the VA hospitals were field officers who were experts in budgets and were rightly suspicious of exaggerated claims leading to unwarranted expenditures. Tiger Teague, Bryan Dorn, Mendel Rivers, and other congressmen were grunts and gobs who had seen and had felt the pain of the cold and the heat and the bullets and the bombs—and they knew jolly well that World War II and the Korean War combat brought some wounds that manifested themselves much later for veterans.

But it was also political and partisan. Populistic New Deal progressives worried about the common man and especially the ailments of the common man, to include unnamed and little-studied emotional disorders and distresses that assailed the noncommissioned doughboys and jarheads. To their concerns about the common man were added the eloquent words spoken by Elizabeth Kee about the common woman, those who were themselves veterans and those who were married to, widows of, or daughters of troubled veterans. Like Bryan Dorn, Elizabeth Kee made the connection between the pain of the unemployed (in her case, mine workers) and the pain of the veteran, especially since they were often the same person. Like everyone on the VA committee, Congresswoman Kee made it clear that millions of people virulently disagreed with the bland assessments of veterans' health proffered by the Eisenhower men of rank.[33]

For the full VA committee, as well as Dorn's subcommittee on pensions, there were hearings in 1958, and these hearings were both substantive and theatrical. Teague was appropriately the tiger, the ancient wounded tiger who knew all about these jungles. Elizabeth Kee was equally as ferocious,

[33] VA Hearings, *Congressional Record*, vol. 104, pt. 1, 85th Cong., s.v.; see Elizabeth Kee, remarks to VA, ibid., 27 January 1958, 1129; Pearson, "Olin Earle Teague and the Veterans Administration," PhD diss., Texas A&M University, 1977.

fully aware of her status as the lone woman in this man's world. Dorn understood the timing involved in this theater, and he patiently let Teague and Kee take the lead. He tried to be scholarly, even intellectual, listening with intent and studied patience and then unloading volleys of facts as well as Baptist eloquence. Across the desk, Eisenhower's men Sumner Whittier and Henry Higley seemed fully equal to the task. Eisenhower was famously proud of his ability to force the army into a budget—he often said that he knew first-hand how generals exaggerated needs to justify expenses. Too, his "bigger bang for the buck" reliance on nuclear weapons offered chances to reduce the size of conventional forces dramatically, especially with the Korean peninsula in tenuous armistice and the bloody charges a painful memory rather than an ongoing series of battles. And the president was deeply suspicious of defense contractors and consultants and others whom he would eventually label a "military industrial complex" that was both fiscally wasteful and prone to recommend dangerous policies. Some of the president's budget cuts, Congressman Dorn and his fellow Southern Democrats supported; they, too, had seen field-grade officers in action, and they, too, knew about waste and risk as seen at ground level by an enlisted man. But what Eisenhower called military industrial complex was nothing less and nothing more than militaristic Keynesianism, the very stuff of Dorn's politics.[34]

However, as Eisenhower's men sought to combat recession and unemployment with deep peacetime reductions in expenditures (the exact opposite of the Keynesian fiscal policy recommended by Hubert Aull and prosecuted by Sam Rayburn), the relatively large VA budget hove into their view. Budget hawks Sumner Whittier and Henry Higley beheld a wasteful bureaucracy with its many hospital projects and entitlements expected by millions of veterans. In fact, Whittier claimed, no one before him had even succeeded in getting an actual count of veterans being served, to say nothing of the many more who expected to be served. In administrative language, there were SC, or service-connected disabilities incurred while on active duty, and these Whittier and Higley fully intended to treat in hospitals under VA auspices, especially in those cases where the veteran wounded or sickened during war now during peacetime found himself unable to pay for expensive

[34] VA Controller of Medicine and Surgery, *Current and Projected Veteran Load through 1986,* 4 June 1958; HR Print #222, HR, 85th, 2d sess., 26 June 1958, corr., Jack Z. Anderson, O. E. Teague, WJBD, DP/SCPC; Ambrose, *Eisenhower,* vol. 2; Thomas, *Ike's Bluff*; Eisenhower, address, 17 January 1961, Federal Register Publication Systems, Public Papers of the Presidents, 1960.

treatments and surgeries. On the other hand, Whittier and Higley were opposed to VA expenditures for treatment for NSC, that is non-service-connected disabilities, even for those severely stricken and even for those in great economic distress. They found that such NSC cases constituted nearly half of the beds in hospitals under VA auspices.[35]

Whittier and Higley focused in particular on treatment of tuberculosis, or TB. Once a terrifying scourge, TB was largely conquered by the middle of the twentieth century, and many thousands of beds once dedicated to both service-connected and non-service-connected tuberculosis patients were emptying out. Other chronic diseases, some requiring operations, were related to complications from TB, and these were filed in bureaucratese as GMS&N (general medical, surgical, and neurological), an awkward abbreviation designating treatments for noncombat-TB-related complications. Aging veterans from the two world wars were much more likely to develop such problems after active duty, sometimes long after discharge. As such, they were designated as non-service-connected; such victims could be treated by the VA, but they were far, far back in the queue behind the service-connected patient. There was growing demand for beds to treat such NSC sufferers of TB, even as there was less and less demand for beds to treat such diseases among the SC sufferers. Thus, Whittier and Higley marked for permanent removal 5,000 beds once dedicated to GMS&N. But if such beds were removed, then the NSC veterans who suffered related diseases could not be treated, including many cases where the veteran had no money to be treated in some other facility. No less than the People's General Omar Bradley himself headed a commission that saluted the budget cutting of Whittier and Higley; indeed, General Bradley proposed still more cuts. The VA committee thus confronted not only "faceless bureaucrats" and "pencil pushers" but also one of the most famed figures—and faces—of the Good War.[36]

Yet it was little contest. Around twenty million men and women had served in World War II and to that had been added another couple hundred thousand in the ongoing Korean conflict with its unsteady armistice. All those veterans had made sacrifices in career paths in order to serve at low pay for long seasons, sometimes a combat tour of three years in World War II,

[35] Folder on VA, 1957–1958: especially, J. J. Bullard to WJBD and WJBD to Bullard, 11 March 1958, WJBDP/SCPC

[36] Eisenhower, budget message, 8 March 1958; pamphlet committee print, Ben Neufield to WJBD, 24 June 1957; "Statement of the American Legion, Dept. of SC," 1958; folder on VA, 1957–1958, WJBD/SCPC.

with often the same drafted man then making a second combat tour in Korea as an activated reservist. All of them, and all of their loved ones, were profoundly skeptical of the NSC designation. To a person, those suffering were convinced that the actual origin point of their diseases *was, in fact, service-connected.* As Dorn quoted them, no one of them had ever split hairs or otherwise quibbled about service-connected duties during active duty, but rather did everything asked, and at once. The congressman never really conceded any veteran to have a malady that was NSC: Dorn considered that the sacrifices in service made all subsequent maladies SC. Famously, all seven of Nana and Dada's sons were veterans, and each of them used VA services, considering the care and treatment a just compensation for valuable service rendered. Indeed, eldest son Tom Dorn remained in the air force, auditing budgets professionally, and he was quite specific in warning about "blanket cuts" that would hurt the VA. Dorn and his relatives read and understood John Locke's concept of a social contract, and the congressman's constituents, if unfamiliar with Locke, nevertheless understood New Deal entitlements vouchsafed by the beloved FDR—the very entitlements resisted by Republicans. Olin Teague and Elizabeth Kee were well pleased with the testimony elicited by Bryan Dorn, and they were even more pleased by his own eloquence in personal testimony after hearing witnesses.[37]

Col. L. Bates Gerald, a Charleston lumberman and very active Republican, was himself an officer but from another era. Colonel Gerald praised Tiger Teague, Elizabeth Kee, and Bryan Dorn, thanking them all for helping "our less fortunate buddies"—and their often destitute widows. Nor were those three alone: the VA committee was militaristic Keynesian and demanded money for the armed services, and Tiger Teague's committee generally got what it demanded for the veterans. Indeed, it was never an easy visit to the committee, or to Dorn's subcommittee on pensions, for a field officer—and hell for a career bureaucrat. As their friend the lumberman put it, it was past time to address "the salary racket" for desk officers and their assistants. When budget administrators Sumner Whittier and Henry Higley made some missteps, the entire committee pounced. During the sessions,

---

[37] Folder on VA Committee, 1957–1958; folder on Subcommittee on Pensions, 1957–1958, especially correspondence, Olin Earle Teague and Elizabeth Kee; T. E. Dorn to WJBD, 1 November 1955, WJBD/SCPC.

Teague's committee rewrote policies in such a way that the designation NSC became less and less operative.[38]

Dorn was able to help his constituents in material terms while scoring rhetorical points for the Southern Democrats. This was partly political in the larger sense, because Populistic New Deal progressive Southerners enacted and enforced laws and policies aimed at the pocketbook needs of Southern citizens. As he noted in an interview, Southern Democrats chaired no fewer than fourteen of the twenty major congressional committees in a time, 1958 to 1974, when Democrats alone chaired the committees. As he also noted, few of the "pocketbook" committees were chaired by Northerners, and "it didn't really matter who was President." Looking back, he was to muse almost whimsically, "And people wonder why the South made such a great progress during that period." Democratic partisans of the New Deal and the Fair Deal, Southern congressmen working with Sam Rayburn, ensured that their working-class constituents, especially the military veterans among them, could retain their "safety net" stretched out for them as part of a social contract involving wartime sacrifice and peacetime challenges.[39]

Withal, Bryan Dorn spent most of his hours most of these days concentrating on minute details of constituent service at the personal level. All over South Carolina, veterans, and especially their widows, wrote directly to him for specific help with pension issues and with survival-benefit issues. Generally, he was able to help. He invariably responded to an inquiry with the phrase, "I am so glad you asked me," his signature acknowledgment that without such requests for constituent service, the congressman could not do his job—a distant but palpable echo of his period of service, 1947 to 1949, when he had *failed to render* full constituent service (and then had to go back to the farm for a congressional season, a correlation that he marked as a causation).[40]

Sometimes to respond to his people, he chose to dissemble and to be more disingenuous than his better nature wanted. For instance, in his hard

---

[38] Folder on VA Committee, 1957–1958; folder on Subcommittee on Pensions, 1957–1958; "Statement of the American Legion, Dept. of SC," 1958; folder on VA, 1957–1958; retrospective, Col. L. Bates Gerald to WJBD, 4 February 1964, WJBD/SCPC; Pearson, "Olin Earle Teague."

[39] Quotation, interview, WJBD with Joe Wider, (n.d., transcribed 1993, Colleen Bradley); Congressional Files, 1958–1975, WJBD/SCPC; Locke, "Second Treatise"; McMath, "The History of the Present."

[40] Congressional Files, 1957–1959; for tone, if not specifics, see interview, WJBD, with Wider (n.d., transcribed by Bradley, 1993), WJBD/SCPC.

work on behalf of veterans, he received much heartfelt and deeply racist correspondence from those who did not want their family's veterans to be compelled to share a hospital room with some black family's veterans. Yet the Truman policy and the policy carried out by Eisenhower was quite clear: the VA hospitals could not be segregated, and there had to be two beds per room and sometimes dozens of beds in some wing of such a hospital. Mississippi's Jamie Whitten sponsored bill HR 10547 to accept integration on the face of it but to guarantee that no veteran could be compelled to accept integration in his hospital room. The bill had little chance of passing, and Dorn did not even believe in it himself. But he could support it, knowing that his vote in committee and vote on the floor were meaningful to his millworker and veteran families while knowing that the legislation had no chance of passing. In this case, he supported something he *did not believe* in—voting for something *he hoped would not pass.* Most of the time, his bill-writing and committee work was more honest, no matter how practical or impractical. In this case, his practical vote-seeking got ahead of his practical committee work and a closer probing by journalists at the time or by political opponents could have shown a hypocrisy that bordered on the foolish. But in the same case, there were no such close probings by white journalists or by political opponents, and he could again postpone the showdown between belief and practice on Fair Deal liberalism and racial liberalism and what Dorn persisted in calling his own Liberalism.[41]

Closer to actual beliefs and values was still another issue that Bryan Dorn considered to be intimately and organically interconnected with the VA and with all constituents. He was convinced that still more war was likely, and he knew that future wars were going to bring future casualties of all sorts and conditions. He was thereby dismayed to find the Eisenhower men "projecting budgets" on an assumption of a long period of unbroken peace, in which there would be very few combat casualties. Indeed, Whittier and his associates were making thirty-year calculations as if no new wars would be fought. Unable to sway Whittier and his staff in committee hearings, Dorn con-

[41] WJBD to John J. Flynt, 28 January 1957; Jamie Whitten, especially 1958–1959; J. J .Bullard to WJBD, 14 March 1958, and WJBD to Bullard, 11 March 1958, Congressional Files; folder on VA, 1957–1958; Liberalism in Deep South context, compared to Byrd Machine Conservatives of Virginia, Wider interview (n.d., transcribed Bradley, 1993), WJBD/SCPC; also see WJBD, *OTP*, passim on Liberalism in context.

vinced his fellow congressmen, the journalists covering the hearings, and the constituents back home, to include competent historians.[42]

Complicating things still more were ancillary services, especially educational, counseling, and therapeutic services for rehabilitating wounded and sick veterans. Many physically disabled veterans were perfectly capable of holding full-time jobs if only educated and trained to that level; yet Omar Bradley's commission was recommending the elimination of many of those educational and counseling services for the NSC and even for some SC. Such budget policies struck at Bryan Dorn in the most intimate of emotional places: his parents, Eb and Pearl, had made education and counseling nothing less than family missions—and now bean counters were eliminating such services! It was a double blow, eliminating jobs during President Eisenhower's second recession and also taking away services that provided opportunities for brave heroes. Whittier and Higley, Bradley and Eisenhower could all talk about "economy policies" and "efficiency" and "trimming fat." Bryan Dorn was ready to talk about fulfilling societal obligations and earned rewards, as well as finding ways to educate veterans up and off the farm and up and out of the mill.[43]

One interesting aspect of these discussions was Eisenhower's own role. Normally above such specific political battles, the president on 8 March 1958 spoke before both houses with his budget message. An important portion of that message was pointedly aimed at veterans' entitlements, especially the educational and ancillary benefits that affected veterans with NSC ailments and afflictions. Ike was uncharacteristically plain and unusually specific in his endorsement of the Bradley Commission recommendation and in his enthusiasm for specific cuts to veteran entitlements even for the SC designees. He supported his budget hawks, who were carefully analyzing medical costs at VA hospitals, including the unpopular elimination of beds and even less popular delays in construction of authorized facilities. He planned to cut his military budget not only in direct military expenditures but also for veterans' entitlements and any extension of those entitlements to the spouses and dependents of veterans. Too, he followed the commission in its call to

---

[42] WJBD to J. J. Bullard, 11 March 1958, WJBD/SCPC.

[43] Folder on VA, 1957–1958, especially corr., J. J. Bullard with WJBD, 11 March 1958; Eisenhower, budget message, 8 March 1958; pamphlet committee print, Ben Neufield to WJBD, 24 June 1957; "Statement of the American Legion, Dept. of SC," 1958; WJBD to Carl Reynolds, 19 March 1956, WJBD/SCPC.

cut back growth of entitlement payments to widows, orphans, and other dependents of World War II and Korean War veterans.[44]

This complex man, Eisenhower, so often derided as bland and uninspiring, was almost left wing in his approach to the Korean conflict, having ended the "hot" phase of actual shooting quickly, in the first six months of his administration. On civil rights, he attempted quiet diplomacy behind the scenes, yet was forceful and effective when Orval Faubus chose to grandstand and thereby endanger the citizenry. Overall, he had labored with success to make New Deal and Fair Deal programs *work* rather than eliminate them. He was, in most things, what Congressman Dorn considered a good and effective engineer focused on making things work while others designed the architecture. Yet as he dealt with these veterans, Eisenhower's approach to the FDR safety net was less modulated than it had been for Social Security and related civilian entitlements. During a recession, disabled veterans and their families faced real suffering, and Eisenhower, Bradley, and their VA budget staffers did not seem to acknowledge that fact.[45]

Responding to the budget officials, Dorn let his correspondence from veterans back home do much of the speaking. He shared the specific examples in concrete and particular detail in the homespun language of his constituents. In terms of the VA, his constituency stretched from New England to the Florida Keys and from his own valley of the Saluda to the Hawaiian Islands. Moreover, since Eisenhower had been uncharacteristically bold and specific, Bryan Dorn changed how he referred to the president. In 1958, he began to describe Eisenhower and his people as "bitter" and "bitterly opposed to justice"; and he said that Eisenhower's "economy policies" brought microeconomic pain for individuals while exacerbating the macroeconomic pain for the entire country. He continued to "run against Hoover," and since Eisenhower had presided over two painful recessions with a third one brewing up, Dorn announced that the decorated general was no improvement over Herbert Hoover. Indeed, he even associated the Eisenhower administration with peace activists, with "One Worlders and Internationalists," phrases of opprobrium back home—and darned odd phrases to describe that administration.[46]

Dorn was in close contact with any number of organized veterans associations, specifically the local chapters or posts of the American Legion, Vet-

---

[44] Eisenhower, budget message, 8 March 1958.

[45] Ibid. Cf. Ambrose, *Eisenhower*, vol. 2 and Thomas, *Ike's Bluff*.

[46] WJBD to Lillie C. Moore, 22 July 1958, WJBD/SCPC.

erans of Foreign Wars, and Widows of World War I. These and other cells he mobilized as effectively as any Communist revolutionary or Methodist outreach committeeperson. The county service agents and sometimes entire town councils could and did work with him to stir up the Legionnaires and the VFWers and other groups to write to US Senators Johnston and Thurmond on behalf of Dorn's legislation. He kept leaders and followers well informed whenever local service agencies or fraternal groups gathered to talk about their problems. And he "did not neglect the ladies," that is, the Ladies Auxiliaries attached to American Legion Posts. Sometimes such auxiliaries counted more than 100 active members who voted in elections and pressured congressmen and senators. For instance, Mrs. H. W. Bradbury, Fannie B. Bartley, and Vivian Pruitt each personally arranged for more than 100 letters to go to relevant US senators and other lawmakers.[47]

He made clear to these activist cells of veterans and widows that he needed not only specific support for particular bills, but also that liberal Democrats (that is, militaristic Keynesians) needed support on relevant committees, to say nothing of electing a president who would listen to the plight of veterans. He reminded and reminded correspondents that it was imperative to vote in Democrat primaries in Southern states and then again in the subsequent fall general elections. And he pounded Eisenhower Republicans for becoming enemies of entitlements for veterans and their dependents. He pushed things farther, quoting North Augustan J. C. Cregar about Ike: "The common soldier made him what he is, but he is quick to forget."[48]

In working with these groups, Bryan Dorn began to reveal to selected cell-leaders some of the "inside ball" tactics of congressional committees. In summer 1958, he let trusted leaders know that Eisenhower would veto legislation for new hospitals and for increased entitlements for widows and orphans; he also reminded such constituents that the Democratic majority was not a "super majority"; it lacked the two-thirds voting strength that could override a veto, no matter how grave the documented need for the bill. He also emphasized to these activist veterans that the 86th Congress would be the place to pass legislation, provided that the 86th Congress had a veto-

[47] Folders, 1958, VA Pension Subcommittee, i.e., correspondence with J. F. Jeffries, Kenneth Copeland, Williams C. Pruitt; in May alone: Mrs. HW Bradbury, Fannie B. Bartley, and Vivian Pruit, WJBD/SCPC.

[48] J. C. Cregar to WJBD, 17 March 1958; statement of American Legion, Dept. of SC, flyer, VA folders, 1957–1958, WJBD/SCPC.

proof Democrat majority. Again, he reminded his large auxiliary groups that Southern primary states would decide the issues in spring and summer of 1958, and the ladies needed to find out for certain if Democrat candidates were "liberal" on veterans issues (especially concerning veterans' dependents, including widows and daughters).[49]

Of course, Bryan Dorn continued to work across the aisle with Republican lawmakers and with the Eisenhower administration for all manner of things. The way he talked about "pencil pushers" and "faceless bureaucrats" on the stump did not at all reflect the way the actual middle range of officials were treated; no doubt, each such official considered him their friend. Even the top drawer of bureaucracy, Higley and Whittier, understood the theatrical aspect of the various hearings, and even those two knew Dorn's warm and avuncular side. This behind-the-scenes treatment of middle-range bureaucrats was also obvious in a farming issue. Yet another farm bill emerged in 1958, one that made an impact on the ease of obtaining cotton for his textile mills—and one that affected the large-scale cotton growers who were still important in the low country, midlands, and Pee Dee districts of South Carolina, should Dorn seek the governorship. The whole process was one tough slog, but Dorn again demonstrated the lawmaking memorialized by Max Weber as "slow boring through hardwood"; that is, the work demanded strength applied constantly rather than all at once (and patience and perseverance more than overwhelming blows). Dorn won praise from both sides of the congressional aisles and from White House staffers for his work on the 1958 farm bill. The final version did less for farmers than a Populistic Democrat demanded but did more for them than Eisenhower's economists wanted. It cost more than Eisenhower wanted, and it paid out less than farmers wanted, there was more market interference than a classical economist wanted, and less actual government demand than Dr. Aull and like-minded economists wanted. Yet when it passed, Abbeville's George M. Wright spoke for many when he said, "You and others who have worked so hard for the best interests of the cotton farmer and the cotton manufacturer are certainly to be commended in getting the legislation through the

[49] WJBD to Lillie C. Moore, 27 June 1958; WJBD to Charlotte A. May, 14 May 1958; WJBD to L. K. Kirkey, 20 June 1958; WJBD to David MacBride, 2 May 1958, WJBD/SCPC.

House."[50]

As the final year of Eisenhower's administration began, Bryan Dorn turned his attentions to the candidates for the Democratic nomination for president. All frontrunners were agreeable to him, with Jack Kennedy being someone he genuinely liked and LBJ being someone he genuinely disliked. However, JFK seemed too much the Yankee liberal for election in the valley of the Saluda while LBJ appeared well suited to red-hills tastes. Stuart Symington of Missouri was his kind of man, as was Estes Kefauver, and so was Adlai Stevenson, but these were all a little bland compared to JFK or LBJ. The red-hills people would prefer LBJ, much as they preferred FDR, and Dorn would have to live with LBJ and even be publicly enthusiastic about the Texan as he had had to live with and be publicly enthusiastic about FDR. He realized then that LBJ would be most effective for Populistic New Deal progressives. If only the powerful and dangerous man could be persuaded to go much more slowly on civil rights.[51]

In any case, all Democratic contenders seemed superior for his purposes than the obvious Republican nominee, Richard Milhous Nixon. All Democrats with a real chance of nomination seemed fully amenable to, if not enthusiastic about, militaristic Keynesian policies and a hard line on the Cold War with emphasis on the air force and reliance on university-research spending for missiles and for militaristic aspects of space exploration. Oddly, he reflected, the militaristic Keynesian policies were also excellent descriptions of the Nixon that he knew and admired. For all that, Nixon stood on a Republican platform, and all those standing there must be opposed in elections (even and especially if they must be worked with in lawmaking).[52]

The congressman was not only named for William Jennings Bryan, he was looking more and more like him and sounding more and more like him, if the Nebraskan had developed a piedmont twang. When the 1960s primaries began, Bryan Dorn pushed his leaders of the masses and leaders in the classes to return his kind of liberal Democrat to the White House—and to create a powerful Democratic majority in both houses.

---

[50] George M. Wright to WJBD, 18 August 1958; Fisher to WJBD, 5 August 1956, WJBD/SCPC.

[51] WJBD to Paul Walker, 16 July and 19 July 1958; Congressional Files, 1959: Robert C. Edwards and George Hubert Aull, WJBD/SCPC; GHA/SC/CU.

[52] WJBD to Paul Walker, 16 July and 19 July 1958; Congressional Files, 1959: Robert C. Edwards and George Hubert Aull, WJBD/SCPC; GHA/SC/CU.

Chapter 8

The New Frontier
1960–1963

In April of 1960, the National Bureau of Economic Research (NBER) issued a report on the state of the nation's economy. This private "think tank," created in 1920 by a distinguished team of academic economists led by Wesley Clark Mitchell, was important to Dorn, primarily because Doc Aull recommended it highly. In this instant, the NBER confirmed what the classes Leon Lowenstein, Jim Self Jr., Charlie Daniel, and Gordon McCabe already knew quite well. The Eisenhower administration was suffering its third recession. More poignantly than the professors of the think tank, and more poignantly than the classes, the textile millhands knew this for a fact. After all, the classes were not issuing dividends or collecting many, and their profits had diminished. But the masses had lost overtime pay, the third shift had disappeared, and for some unfortunate mill villages, entire textile plants had completely shut down. The NBER and Doc Aull and statisticians for the classes thus gave official confirmation of what millhand constituents in the Third District reported in often desperate communications.[1]

Specifically, the NBER measured the change in the gross domestic product as *negative* 1.6 percent; that is, the economy was again shrinking, and at a time when the population was advancing rapidly, with still more Baby Boomers being born and with retired folk (excepting the millworkers and the black people in the Third District) living much beyond the age of sixty-five. The most important statistic for Congressman Dorn in this third Eisenhower recession was the official measure of unemployment, soaring to 7.6 percent. The congressman continued to insist that unemployment should not be above 3 percent, although NBER and even Doc Aull told him a "full" employment rate would be 95 percent, or 5 percent unemployment.

---

[1] NBER, *Annual Report of the Director of Research to the Board of Directors,* ed. Wesley Clark Mitchell, vol. 1 (February 1921): 1–18 re "Preface: Please Help Us" for corr., WJBD/SCPC, 1958–1961; WJBD, Robert Cook Edwards and Earle Morris, GHA/SC/CU.

However one measured it, unemployment was unacceptably high and economic growth unacceptably negative.[2]

Generally, such problematical economic news portended good things for Democratic candidates for office, especially in the Third District's rural communities, where the small farms, the small *bidnesses*, and the textile mills were. But in this recession, Dorn was shaken deep down. Past master at cooperating across the party aisle and across regional lines, the congressman had to concede how much more could be done with strong presidential leadership. He considered that it really was necessary to get these Republican economists out of the Cabinet and out of the White House staff. The US could not accept much more such economic damage in the teeth of the daunting military challenges from the Soviet Union. As he generally did, Congressman Dorn combined, if not conflated, strong military structures with strong economic structures. There was an "essentiality of the textile industry to national security," as he said on the floor of the House. As far as he was concerned, Eisenhower's men were weakening both sets of structures at the same time. Democrats needed to restore the right kind of Cold War economy with a self conscious militaristic Keynesianism. The next president must be committed to Populistic New Deal programs for the South, all of which must be connected in some way to national defense and military preparedness.[3]

But such a "militaristic Keynesian" must be *electable*—and therein lay the rub. From 1952 and especially 1956, Dorn had come to see that many such men he deeply admired, not least Estes Kefauver and Adlai Stevenson, were simply unelectable. Among 1960 contestants, he much preferred Stuart Symington of Missouri, one who had stood with him on issues of an expanded air force and an aggressive Cold War posture toward the Soviet Russians. Yet Dorn reluctantly concluded that a Symington nomination would finally do no better than had the Stevenson selection. Tangled up with the issue of electability was the complex of issues involved in civil rights, certainly hardest for Dorn to swallow, and hardest to explain. The right man had to

---

[2] NBER, 2Q 1960-1Q 1961, US Business Cycle Expansion and Contraction, 20 September 2010; GHA to WJBD, 10 June 1953; S. Ernie Wright to GHA, retrospective, 26 May 1961, GHA/SC/CU; corr., GHA and WJBD, 1960, WJBD/SCPC.

[3] WJBD to Ignatius Sterghos, 27 September 1956; WJBD to B. M. Barackman, 18 April 1961; J. K. Cauthen to WJBD, 31 August 1960, WJBD/SCPC; WJBD, "Textile Remarks," *Congressional Record*, vol. 107, pt. 5, 87th Cong., 1st sess., 18 April 1961, 6174–79; Hearings, *Congressional Record*, vol. 107, pt. 18, 87th Cong., 1st sess., 11 April–14 April 1961 *Daily Digest*.

be on the right side of history, that is, progressive with regard to unfolding civil rights for black citizens—while also sensitive to the needs of Southern congressmen to proceed slowly on civil rights. It was a distinction with a difference, for Dorn really wanted civil rights to proceed slowly, not to be blocked forever.[4]

To Dorn, there were three such electable candidates, all from the US Senate: Hubert Horatio Humphrey of Minnesota, John Fitzgerald Kennedy of Massachusetts, and Lyndon Baines Johnson of Texas. The congressman actually liked and admired Humphrey, "Horatio Hornblower," with his "Politics of Joy." But the mere mention of his name in South Carolina conjured up images of the 1948 Democratic convention when the Minneapolis mayor had stood so boldly for substantive civil rights, not to mention his early and continuing role in the neo-abolitionist Americans for Democratic Action (ADA). Humphrey's record was withal a civil rights identity impossible to defend for a sandlapper politician. That left LBJ and JFK. Regional loyalty and political practicality dictated support for LBJ, but Bryan Dorn mistrusted him more profoundly in 1960 and 1961 than ever before—he was still the man who "ratted out" his own benefactor, the late Sam Rayburn. And he had been too clever by half in his logrolling work for the 1957 Civil Rights Act, leaving senators on both sides of the act subsequently unconvinced of his sincerity. For his part, Bryan Dorn told a constituent that his own relations with Senator Johnson were "very strained."[5]

As to JFK, personal affection and personal trust in the Irishman's zeal for fighting Soviet Communism combined happily with personal agreement about militaristic Keynesianism that focused on assisting harried home industries. If only JFK could be persuaded to go slow on the civil rights movement, which both men agreed was moving forward inevitably if not ineluctably. But even if JFK could not be so persuaded, Bryan Dorn knew many ways to slow down presidential initiatives by horse trading in the congressional corridors—and he knew how to slow things down without forcing acrimonious confrontation (what he considered the Virginia way, not the

[4] WJBD to Ignatius Sterghos, 27 September 1956; Kefauver to WJBD, 9 November 1956, WJBD/SCPC; Eric Pace, "Stuart Symington, 4-Term Senator," *New York Times* obit., 15 December 1988; Tindall, *Disruption of Solid South*, 42, 55–60 ; Bass and DeVries, *Transformation of Southern Politics*.

[5] Brock, *Americans for Democratic Action*; Humphrey, *The Education of a Public Man*; Caro, *Years of Lyndon Johnson*, vol. 2, 17; correspondence, WJBD with Lyndon Baines Johnson, 1952–1960; see "very strained relations with Senator Johnson," WJBD to H. C. Jones, 7 March 1960, WJBD/SCPC.

Deep South tactics). As for the really big issues of putting everyone to work while fighting the Communists, the old navy skipper JFK understood the need for a powerful air force, as he understood the need for federal research at Clemson College. Even better, JFK "got it," that stimulative fiscal policy more often involved tax cuts rather than increases in nonmilitary spending. Significantly, some of the classes of the Third District, especially Leon Lowenstein, were early on the side of Jack Kennedy.[6]

The masses were suspicious of Yankee identity and hostile to Roman Catholicism, but Lowenstein insisted that economic progress was always coupled with social progress, an approach that Bryan Dorn was obliged to salute, given Lowenstein's power over the mill villages. And the Dorn family lore included vivid memories of no less than Cole Livingston Blease persuading the folks of the red hills to vote for Al Smith despite that nominee's Roman Catholic and New York identity. Nana and Dada had supported Al Smith, and they had pinned Smith campaign buttons on each of their seven boys, most prominently Bryan Dorn, then twelve years old. The congressman reckoned that he could dissuade his people from anti-Catholicism as effectively in 1960 as his extended family had in 1928—especially if Jack Kennedy would be discreet in civil rights rhetoric during appearances in South Carolina.[7]

Much earlier and much louder in his support of JFK in 1960 was his junior colleague in the South Carolina delegation, Congressman Robert Witherspoon Hemphill of the Fifth District (textile-producing central piedmont south of Charlotte, including Rock Hill, York, Lancaster, and Congressman Hemphill's own hometown, Chester). Hemphill, also an Army Air Corps man in the Good War, was a bear of a fellow with a face as broad as his shoulders. Although Hemphill was an attorney raised by an attorney, there was nothing *petit bourgeois* about him, and he fit in well with his millworker constituency. More publicly than any other South Carolina congressman, Hemphill stumped the state for JFK in the primary season and in the national election. In truth, Bryan Dorn was less supportive of Kennedy than he himself recalled, at least in early public statements. Despite his personal support and his own shrewd calculations, he was, in fact, reserved,

---

[6] Joseph Lyon (Lowenstein Mills) to WJBD, 17 August 1959; Leon Lowenstein to WJBD, retrospective, 28 June 1963, with enclosure, *Anderson Daily Mail*; retrospective, WJBD to Lowenstein, 15 July 1963, WJBD/SCPC.

[7] Tindall, *Emergence of New South*, 248–53. Cf. WJBD, *OTP*, 188; 1960 Presidential Campaign, Robert Witherspoon Hemphill Papers (hereinafter RWH), SCPC.

putting most public effort into the period *after* late summer 1960, when Congress took its traditional five-week break; that was after Kennedy had secured the nomination and his own platform at the convention in Los Angeles. The Barratt House Labor Day barbeque marked the closing of the congressional break, and on that occasion Bryan Dorn was loud and proud in support of Jack Kennedy, as he remained throughout the fall season. He constantly reassured constituents not to worry about Roman Catholicism, to trust the decorated veteran's anti-Communism, and not to expect any serious action on behalf of civil rights, all "talking points" approved by the JFK campaign handlers. By contrast, Bob Hemphill was four-square behind the Irishman, emphasizing the Populistic legacy of the still-remembered New Deal, a stance taken also by senior US Senator Olin Johnston. Even so, Kennedy remembered and rewarded Dorn as gratefully as he did Senator Johnston and Congressmen Hemphill, since most of the South Carolina delegation was either noncommittal, or in the case of junior US Senator Strom Thurmond, hostile. Indeed, Thurmond later announced that he had voted for Richard Nixon in 1960 despite a self-professed identity as "rambunctious Democrat."[8]

Kennedy was wise to reward all helpers, even if some, like Bryan Dorn, came on late. Indeed, late support was desperately sought. The race was painfully close, and little South Carolina's eight electoral votes were needed and appreciated, based as they were on a winning margin of only 8,000 people. That close win in the state was traceable to black voters in the Charleston, Columbia, and Greenville metropolitan areas *but also* to Hemphill's and Dorn's districts among the working-class whites—areas where most black men and women were not permitted to vote in the 1960 elections. By contrast, the white wards of urban areas and the suburban wards of college-educated folk in Greenville, Rock Hill, and Spartanburg went overwhelmingly for Nixon. The black citizen's allegiance to JFK cut across class lines, but among white people, the college-educated bourgeois class went overwhelmingly Republican. Thus, a class divide opened up between working-class—that is, millhands—and the service sector among white folk. For the briefest time, there was in 1961 the old Populistic alliance between black and working-class white. However, the rapidly growing educated white town

---

[8] 1960 Presidential Campaign, RWH/SCPC; 1960 Presidential Campaign, especially DNC memoranda, WJBD/SCPC; Sorensen, *Kennedy*, 127, 187; Tindall, *Disruption of the Solid South*, 42, 55–62; Bass and Thompson, *Ol' Strom*, 189–90.

folk were in their own Republican wing; and they, and thus the Republicans, bid fair to outvote Democrats in all subsequent elections.[9]

In any case, as Bryan Dorn reflected on the hard-fought campaign for president, he realized and acknowledged that Jack Kennedy was, in the horse-racing term, "much the best" for substantive—but slow-paced—progressive politics among all the presidents that he had seen in his political life. Not only was it going to be easier working with JFK than with Nixon, it was going to be easier than working with Eisenhower or Truman. He wrote out a memorandum in June and sent it to Kennedy, urging "the old Jim Farley technique" of personal visits and personal favors, bold plans, high energy, and activism, but all of it always tempered with willingness to compromise. He included the old chestnut useful both for New Frontier domestic policy and for foreign policy: "We cannot always sell a philosophy, but we can sell a personality." And he really believed in Kennedy's personality.[10]

The congressman had a new secretary, and around him he built his most effective staff, one whose attention to constituent service and whose personal loyalty to Bryan Dorn became legendary. Mack Gerald Fleming, recently from Clemson College and still fulfilling Army Reserve weekend and summertime obligations, was a personal favorite largely because he was so personable. A native of Seneca, "Rock" was son of a millworker at Abney Mills and could afford Clemson only with scholarships based on need, academics (applied chemistry for textile engineering), and Reserve Officer Training Corps (ROTC). He could kick back and talk idly and unhurriedly about Clemson football (he had managed the team, earning a letter and joining the Block C Club) or fishing holes, but he could also spring into the most intensive action as soon as need be. He not only fit in, but in gentlemanly way pursued and attracted assistant Libby McClellan, marrying her in 1963 and making the family-like office still more closely knit.[11]

In this period, Bryan Dorn's energies were at least as great as ever before in his life, and all of those energies were concentrated on being a congressman in the New Frontier. He spent all day and much of each evening

---

[9] Tindall, *Disruption*, 55–62; Edgar, *South Carolina*, 538–44; Bass and Thompson, *Ol' Strom*, 189–90; correspondence, WJBD with Lowenstein, Lura Self, Gordon McCabe, and Hemphill, telegram to Kennedy, 5 November 1960, WJBD/SCPC; Presidential Campaign Folders, 1960, RWH/SCPC; WJBD, "John F. Kennedy," *Congressional Record*, vol. 109, pt. 18, 88th Cong., 1st sess., 4 December 1963, 23504.

[10] WJBD, "Memorandum to President," 14 June 1961, WJBD/SCPC.

[11] Mack Gerald Fleming folders, 1961–1967, WJBD/SCPC.

politicking, and he expected his staff to keep up with him in the frantic pace. As before, Bryan Dorn set a goal of answering every personal letter from a constituent within twenty-four hours. Now, with Rock Fleming and assistants Shirley O'Neal, Libby McClellan Fleming, and Jane McGowan, he really did get most mail answered within twenty-four hours of its receipt. The congressman even went to newly appointed postmaster J. Edward Day to find out the most direct first-class air routes for getting mail to all points in the Third District.[12]

All of his staff helpers over the years were knowledgeable and helpful, but with "Rock Fleming and the girls," Bryan Dorn, and to some extent even Millie Dorn and Nana, began to relax more about constituent service, because they trusted the staff to the utmost. For instance, once Millie Dorn had upbraided a male assistant when she overheard him responding to a constituent request by announcing confidently, "I will get it done for you." On that occasion, Millie Dorn had let the assistant know that it was the congressman who did things for his constituents—and these assistants needed to report their doings in the correct light of their lesser roles. Actually, it was fortunate that it was Millie and not Nana who had overheard the offending phrase. No such admonition ever went out to Mack Fleming or to Shirley O'Neal or to Jane McGowan, for all of them understood their places and their duties from the first day in the DC and in the Greenwood offices.[13]

To serve these constituents, Bryan Dorn as usual intended to work across the aisle with Republican congressmen who needed their own tariffs and quotas and their own waterway projects. As to the vital committee assignments, in an era when committee chairmen really were feudal lords, Dorn had moved up in the Veterans Administration Committee—and, more importantly, he and the chairman, Tiger Teague, became even more effective as a tem than beforehand. Democratic successes in the 1960 elections also gave him a seat on the Committee on Education and Labor, an interesting assignment because the chair was the redoubtable civil rights activist from Harlem, the Rev. Adam Clayton Powell Jr. —a man of large

---

[12] Retrospectives: WJBD to John D. Swygert, 30 April 1966; Lura Self to WJBD, 8 April 1966; Addison Carwile to WJBD, 18 April 1966; Jessie E. Morris to WJBD, 9 April 1966, WJBD/SCPC.

[13] WJBD to Nana (Pearl Dorn), 24 March 1960; interviews: Steve Griffith with Herb Hartsook and Roper (25 September 2013) and Griffith with Hartsook and Roper (31 January 2012) JHR/SCPC.

parts suspected of loose dealing with lobbyists, if not absolute corruption, but a man congressmen had to cooperate with to get anything done. Dorn, for his part, made connections with Powell through their shared Baptist beliefs and their many shared concerns for teachers and students (and above all, their shared schooling in the Board of Education of Sam Rayburn). Ever the polite student of Nana and Dada and ever the dutiful Sunday school student, Dorn was as carefully respectful of the most prominent African American in Congress as he was of the most prominent white Texans.[14]

Yet Dorn wanted an additional committee assignment, one where he could do more for Duke Power, to include blocking Trotter Shoals in order to open up the Middleton site. He wanted to get himself onto the Public Works Committee. Besides the waterway projects, that committee, chaired by New York's Charles Anthony Buckley (who had served since 1935), was also in charge of the lucrative interstate highway system appropriations. It would take some time, but with coordinated help from Buckley, Sam Rayburn, and John McCormack, Dorn was able to remain as ranking member of Tiger Teague's VA committee and serve on Adam Clayton Powell's Committee on Education and Labor but also join Buckley's Public Works Committee in 1963.[15]

Powerful interests wanted to block Duke's proposed plant, especially the Georgia, North Carolina, and South Carolina electrical cooperatives, who would rather buy federally generated electrical power than Duke-generated power. Federally generated power was cheap, and the spread between the cooperative's legal asking price and its legal cost was great—a greater spread than it would be if the private Duke Power supplied the electricity for the cooperatives. And these electrical cooperatives could speak through the dominant US Senators Olin Johnston and Georgia's Richard Russell. However, it was actually Buckley's committee that was writing and

---

[14] Appointments, *Congressional Record*, vol. 109, pt. 1, 88th Cong., 1st sess., 17 January 1963; folder, Committee on Education and Labor, 1962–1972; corr., the Rev. Adam Clayton Powell, 1961–1972, WJBD/SCPC; Thomas A. Johnson, "A Man of Many Roles (Powell obit.)," *New York Times*, 5 April 1972, 1; Charles V. Hamilton, *Adam Clayton Powell, Jr.: A Political Biography for an American Dilemma*.

[15] Interview, Steve Griffith with Roper and Hartsook (25 September 2013), JHR/SCPC; Committee on Veterans Affairs, ranking, *Congressional Record*, vol. 107, pt. 2, 87th Cong., 1st sess., 30 January–24 February 1961, 1791; appointments, Committee on Public Works; Committee on Veterans Administration, *Congressional Record*, vol. 109, pt. 1, 88th Cong., 1st sess., 17 January 1963, 565; "Charles Anthony Buckley," Congressional Biographical Directory, s.v.

reporting (or *not writing and not reporting*) the money bills concerning waterworks and waterways; even the two powerful senators and the influential electrical cooperatives were dependent on the Committee on Public Works. Thus, Dorn's new seat on Public Works gave him the room to maneuver and thus to speed up or slow down such projects, which meant time to maneuver to develop something that might appeal to all interested and involved entities.[16]

Besides the complexities of waterway and power plants on the Savannah River, there were increasingly complicated politics with an administration that boldly spoke about big and active government. Bryan Dorn's long settled and highly successful tactics were to decry big spending in general but to ensure that his Third District got every possible nickel of appropriation—which could only be done by horse trading with other congressmen who needed their own nickels of appropriation, until the cumulative process made William Jennings Bryan Dorn very much part of *tax and spend, tax and spend, elect and elect*, exactly like his fellow Populistic New Deal legislators. Much of this could be declared to be defense spending, and much of it was, and that part of Bryan Dorn's anti-Communism always squared neatly with Jack Kennedy's anti-Communism in the militaristic Keynesianism that both men had favored since meeting in Congress in 1947. All the same, there were moments when rhetoric and voting record collided, and at those moments Bryan Dorn always returned to the Populistic side of his identity. The congressman complained about "wild socialistic programs" as Kennedy Democrats began pressing his fiscal agenda; but item by item, that actual agenda included generous increases in Social Security pensions, VA services, and interstate highway construction, all things important to Third District constituents—and all "wild socialistic programs" supported by Dorn for his people.[17]

---

[16] Interview, Steve Griffith with Roper and Hartsook (25 September 2013), JHR/SCPC; on Russell, "Massacre at Savannah River (carton with edit.), *Charlotte Observer*, 19 October 1962, op. ed.; Mack Fleming to John Hicks (Duke Power), 24 October 1962, WJBD/SCPC.

[17] WJBD to George Gage, 3 February 1961, and correspondence with Dr. Thomas Parker, 1961, especially February 1961; "ammunition" from Association of American Physicians and Surgeons, WJBD to Dr. Phillip L. Bates, 4 December 1961; WJBD to Etta M. Dorn (State Department of Education), 14 August 1961; WJBD to Robert D. Anderson (Manpower Development and Training), 19 February 1962; William B. Finlayson to WJBD, 7 March 1961 (nurse practitioner training funds); Ernest Frederick Hollings to WJBD (federal school lunch program), 26 February 1962; folders, Federally

However, the Kennedy administration also pressed for expanded medical care for the poor and for the elderly, generally calling the former Medicaid and the latter Medicare. Such proposals brought Dr. Thomas Parker into action, and the Greenville doctor sometimes wrote three letters a day to Bryan Dorn. Parker, prominent among up-country physicians and with some national recognition in his profession (becoming president of the Association of American Physicians and Surgeons in 1964), was right wing by birthright and by household environment. His father, Thomas Fleming Parker, was an important founding member of the extremist John Birch Society, and Dorn knew of this lineage, intending to ride with Dr. Parker as an anti-Communist in foreign affairs while avoiding extremist positions on social and political issues domestically (something he truly believed, but also something pounded home by Leon Lowenstein and others in the classes).[18]

But on the specific issues of Medicaid and Medicare, Dr. Parker represented what Bryan Dorn called the "powerful bloc" of organized physicians who opposed extending benefits to the masses. Early and often, Dorn observed to close friends and in his own notes that the "powerful bloc" simply could not be resisted on the specific legislation concerning health care benefits. Dr. Parker almost weekly reminded the congressman about his promises to stop such programs originally proposed by Theodore Roosevelt. In addition to Dorn's pragmatic recognition of the power relationship with "the doctors' bloc," he and Thomas Parker seemed genuinely to like each other. For all that, Dr. Parker and his pressure group of organized physicians pushed and pulled the congressman into voting that was inconsistent with his other policies and practices. Although Dorn needed only small funds to run his campaigns for office, he often stated that he could not legislate anything if opposed by certain interest blocs, especially the American Medical Association (AMA) and other organizations of politically active physicians—and particularly Dr. Parker's Association of American Physicians and Surgeons.[19]

Impacted Deficiency Appropriations for SC, March 1961, WJBD/SCPC; WJBD, remarks (2 hours), *Congressional Record*, vol. 107, pt. 5, 87th Cong., 1st sess., 18 April 1961, 6174–79; .

[18] Correspondence, Thomas Parker, 1961–1974; WJBD to Dr. Phillip L. Bates, 4 December 1961; Leon Lowenstein, 1961–1974 especially retrospective, 28 June 1963, WJBD/SCPC; "Dr. Thomas Parker," *Charleston News & Courier*, 11 July 1987, 9-A.

[19] WJBD to George Gage, 3 February 1961; correspondence, WJBD with Dr. Thomas Parker, February 1961, WJBD/SCPC.

Dorn spoke against such federal assistance for medical expenses, and he placed in the *Congressional Record Appendix* for 1961 alone more than a dozen editorials and speeches reflecting the AMA point of view. Thus, Dorn broke ranks with other Populistic New Deal congressmen by early and loudly and always opposing Medicare and Medicaid. In his correspondence, he sometimes even "agreed" with Dr. Parker that most of the New Deal was a mistake, especially Social Security, protection of worker safety, and any minimum wages. Too, he talked loudly about a coalition of Midwestern Republicans and conservative Southern Democrats who could give a "rough time" to Kennedy's "wild programs." This much was popular talk among warm correspondents; but when it came time to vote, Dorn voted reliably as a Populistic New Deal progressive with the singular (if whopping) exception of health care.[20]

Yet he was still the man of the people, and he was stung by the letter he received from Douglas A. Baumgardner of Anderson, who described himself as a lowly clerk and "longtime friend and supporter of yours and one that helped to defeat a great Congressman Butler B. Hare, to elected [*sic*] you." This friend and supporter, self-described as poor and living on a pension, said bluntly that he was "much disappointed in the way you have voted twice recently to defeat measures that would help poor people." Continuing, the pensioner reminded the congressman, "You are elected by the people, to serve the best interests of all the people." And now, Baumgardner told him, this anti-liberal talk was "betraying the trust of the good working people."[21]

Awakened by the stinging words, Dorn wrote back reminding his longtime supporter that he had campaigned for Jack Kennedy, and more importantly, "I am tremendously interested in how working people feel about things up here." He said that he had always supported Social Security, always worked to reduce the full-retirement starting point from age sixty-five to age sixty-two, always opposed foreign aid that took away from social benefits like schools and roads for the people of the Third District, and always resisted free trade and so-styled reciprocal trade in favor of fair trade with quotas and tariffs. Indeed, Dorn said truthfully, "I spent more than an hour with the president on this problem. I urged him to save the jobs of our textile people by keeping these cheap foreign goods out of our country." And

---

[20] WJBD to George Gage, 3 February 1961, and correspondence with Dr. Thomas Parker, February 1961, WJBD/SCPC; *Congressional Record* Appendix, vol. 107, pt. A, 87th Cong., 1st sess., 1 January 1961–31 December 1961, s.v.

[21] Douglas A. Baumgardner to WJBD, 25 March 1961, WJBD/SCPC.

lastly, he reported accurately, "I believe a bill will pass before long increasing the minimum wage" and thus helping all the still-working clerks and millhands in Baumgardner's red hills. That was not the first time, and would hardly be the last, that a plain-folk Populist from down home took his congressman to task and elicited an apology, a restatement of principles, and a defensive turn in which he voted in response to majority will. Whatever the pressures and fears brought from organized blocs of doctors and lobbyists for conservative causes, the man *of the people* could always be reined in *by the people*, especially the Baumgardners who had put him into the Cannon Building offices in the first place in 1946.[22]

The upshot was that the right-wing Americans for Conservative Action (ACA) always rated him C-plus, around 78, grading him "down" because of his support for big-spending Populistic New Deal Southern-focused programs. And, by like sign, Humphrey's neo-abolitionist Americans for Democratic Action (ADA) always rated him close to 0 because of his tepid rhetoric and weak support for an aggressive civil rights agenda. With no real contradiction, he could refer to himself as liberal, speaking of New Deal "safety net" issues *and* as conservative, speaking of civil rights issues. Dr. Parker and his bloc, uninterested in civil rights and at peace with other aspects of the safety net, always protested to the ACA that Dorn deserved much higher grades, while John Bolt Culbertson, indeed Hubert Horatio Humphrey himself, and other allies from fair-deal days protested the low ADA grades because of his reliable support for the safety net (and because they believed him that he was still like Brooks Hays, a man who wanted a slowly arriving rather than a never-arriving day of racial justice and equality). Again, the congressman insisted that Jack Kennedy was in fact exactly *where Dorn himself voted*. Many Dixie congressmen agreed with Dorn's assessment. Indeed, historian George Brown Tindall gently chided the Kennedyites: They "avoided antagonizing Southerners with any action beyond a strong civil rights plank."[23]

---

[22] Baumgardner to WJBD, 25 March 1961; WJBD to Baumgardner, 30 March 1961; folder "Social Security," 1961, at least a half-inch thick, promises to constituents to lower age for eligibility for social security to age 62; WJBD/SCPC; see also 1959–1969, John Bolt Culbertson Papers, SCPC, hereinafter JBC/SCPC.

[23] Correspondence, Parker, 1961–1966. Cf. Clint McCall to WJBD, 20 June 1952, and reply, WJBD to McCall, 24 June 1952, WJBD/SCPC; quotation, Tindall, *Disruption*, 42.

The New Frontier seemed to be picking up a momentum of its own, beyond the needs of a loose coalition of rural white Southerners and Northern urban labor, and it was civil rights, regardless of JFK's actual intentionality, that provided much of the momentum. A more active, if not aggressive, civil rights stance suggested problems for Bryan Dorn in national policies with JFK. Too, there was personal sadness and extreme political discomfiture when Sam Rayburn became ill and left Congress in mid-November of 1961. The congressman's relationship with new speaker John McCormack of Massachusetts was ever cordial and efficient, but it lacked the ingenious *pizzazz* that had come in Mr. Sam's Board of Education room. Then, the people around JFK circulated press stories in the *New York Times* and in the *Wall Street Journal* that Dorn and some other recalcitrant foot-draggers on civil rights issues would soon be "purged" from the Kennedy ranks in Congress. To that specific point of an FDR-style purge, President Kennedy (who surely had approved the "leak" to the liberal press) knew exactly how to deal with Populistic New Deal Southerners: "I remember him pushing through a crowded White House reception last winter [1962] to assure Mrs. Dorn and me the stories in the *New York Times* and the *Wall Street Journal* were untrue about me being placed on his purge list. He assured me I was on no purge list of his—that we might differ on certain issues but we would always be friends."[24]

JFK's gesture at the reception was carefully conceived public theater, as was Bryan Dorn's staged recounting of it. However, it also reflected what Bryan Dorn and Jack Kennedy both knew quite well as students of modern history, namely, that FDR's purge had been a political catastrophe, one that subsequently hamstrung Roosevelt's social programs, most of which were delayed until after World War II, and some of them delayed until Kennedy brought them forward again. The congressman calculated that he needed the alliance with his president, and the president assured Dorn that he needed continued support from Southern representatives like Dorn.[25]

In fact, it was education and Clemson College, the two things most dear to Dada's son, that pushed both Bryan Dorn and Jack Kennedy into a

---

[24] On McCormack efficiency, WJBD to Lindley Beckworth, with McCormack procedural note enclosed, 28 September 1962, and WJBD to Beckworth, 8 October 1962: "when the heat was on...the speaker helped us"; Bedkworth to WJBD, 9 October 1962: "Speaker McCormack, you are a friend indeed"; WJBD, "John F. Kennedy."

[25] Corr., Beckwith, September 1962, WJBDSCPC; Dunn, *Roosevelt's Purge;* Sorensen, *Kennedy,* 471, 501.

progressive civil rights stance that gladdened JFK's liberal supporters and established a sea change in the congressman's own record. Much as had been the case in Little Rock, demagogic governors belied the counsel of moderation from Brooks Hays (still on the scene, in the White House talking to Jack and Bobby Kennedy, in the governor's councils talking to Ross Barnett and George Corley Wallace).

There was a series of university integration events, starting in September of 1962 in Oxford, Mississippi, and concluding in July 1963 in Tuscaloosa, Alabama. Squarely in between was Clemson College and the integration event of January 1963. At Oxford, President Kennedy and quite a number of reasonably well-informed officials were expecting that the quiet university would bring James Meredith into its student fold with little incident. Like many university centers, Ole Miss was actually regarded in the state as liberal, at least in the classic sense of tolerating dissent and encouraging discussion about all things, to include racial relationships. And Governor Ross Barnett had been heretofore quiet on such issues, often speaking convincingly about the need for order and progress. However, when the last legal appeals were exhausted and it came time for James Meredith to matriculate, Governor Barnett, like Orval Faubus before him, suddenly and unexpectedly emerged as a champion of segregation who encouraged massive resistance, to include demonstrating mobs on the campus. With Governor Barnett heatedly denouncing integration, crowds gathered at Oxford and made violent demonstrations, wrecking much of the campus and causing two deaths, both brought off "execution style," suggesting the Ku Klux Klan. Jack and Bobby Kennedy continued to bargain with Ross Barnett, even talking with him about a theatrical "principled surrender" in which federal marshals would tap their holstered guns as if the governor were in physical danger before he "reluctantly stepped aside." By the end of September, Jack and Bobby Kennedy had had enough of such negotiation and they brought in the military—the 503rd Military Police backed up by a Tennessee naval medical unit accustomed to "battlefield wounds" and the federalized Mississippi National Guard. The Kennedys thus enforced integration with no more efforts to make Barnett look good or otherwise for his voters.[26]

---

[26] Sorensen, *Kennedy,* 483–88; Claude Sitton, "3000 Troops Put Down Mississippi Rioting and Seize 200 as Negro Attends Classes," *New York Times Special Edition*, 1 October 1962, 1; tapping holsters for show, interview, David Sansing (October 1986), JHR/SCPC; "The civil rights movement in America," Chancellor's Symposium, 1985,

The coming showdown at the University of Alabama loomed on the horizon, likely for summer session of 1963, and Clemson College became the next sequential piece in the unfolding series of higher-institution crises. It was obvious even in fall of 1962 that Governor George Corley Wallace intended to make a scene at his state university, even if it involved violence and property damages. South Carolina and Clemson were ciphers: demographically, the state was poor, black, and backward, much as were Alabama, Mississippi, and Arkansas. Arkansas, as noted, had accomplished integration of its university and graduate and professional centers quietly and successfully. However, as also noted, at the high school level Arkansas's governor, Orval Faubus, had reversed his previous course of moderation and encouraged willful and violent resistance, producing one year of federally forced integration for a few students, followed by a year of closing Little Rock's public schools. Mississippi's leaders by contrast had cost its people hundreds of physical injuries, two deaths, and continuing damage to the reputation of the University of Mississippi. South Carolina could go any of those routes, and none of the routes looked good.

There were some differences about South Carolina, however, and Congressman Dorn played his proper and fitting role in what became a happy story of integration. The applicant was Harvey Bernard Gantt, Charleston native and successful student of engineering at Iowa State University. Originally trained at Burke High School in Charleston, Gantt was thus in a line of activist scholars who went on to do important things in civil rights in the country. He came to this campaign with background and training as well as determination and support. His attempted transfer was set for spring term, commencing in late January 1963. Governor Fritz Hollings, on the way out, could have passed the entire problem over to his elected successor, Donald Russell, the austere and scholarly former president of the University of South Carolina. Instead, Hollings called in veteran newspaper reporters and their publishers and told them frankly that college integration was coming, because all legal ways of keeping Gantt out had been exhausted. He bluntly told the pressmen in private that it was up to them to start preparing their readers for the coming of integration at Clemson College. With that background work, he then gave a series of addresses and public statements in which he reminded sandlappers that the Supreme Court was the "fact of the land" even if one resented its claim to be the "law of the land." Hollings said

---

Oxford, MS; "The civil rights movement in Mississippi," Porter L. Fortune Symposium, 2010; Eagles, ed., *The Civil Rights Movement.*

in many places, "This should be done with dignity. It must be done with law and order." With cooperation from editors and publishers as well as frontline reporters, Fritz Hollings did a superb job of preparing resentful people for the inevitable.[27]

But others worked away as well. In Columbia, the oft-maligned but always efficient "Barnwell Ring" of Solomon Blatt and "Bishop" Edgar Brown cooperated with powerful veteran senator Marion Gressette—he who once proudly chaired the Segregation Committee of the Segregation Sessions—to set a tone of peaceful cooperation among all elected and appointed state officials. President Robert C. Edwards at Clemson never stood taller or with more dignity as he prepared his student body and his alumni for the coming of Harvey Bernard Gantt. Among the classes, Leon Lowenstein and Jim Self made clear their support for peaceful integration; and Bernard Claude Inabinet, himself a onetime Clemson footballer, insisted that his Tigers integrate in a classy way without destroying his alma mater. No less than building magnate Charlie Daniel, at a watermelon festival in the low country's remote Walterboro, studiedly and effectively prepared a hard-drinking crowd of the white masses for an integration of Clemson that he described as inevitable—*and right.*[28]

Meanwhile, Jack and Bobby Kennedy and all their people had learned important lessons about bringing enough force soon enough and also about which politicians to trust. As for Bryan Dorn, he was already telling constituents that Clemson was to be integrated and that the process must go smoothly and peacefully. However, on 24 January 1962, Dorn was surprised to receive a personal telephone call from the White House. It was his friend—and "classmate" from the House of Representatives Class of 1947—President Kennedy. If that telephone call was recorded like other Kennedy calls, the presidential librarians have not located it or made it available. But the congressman took notes. He said that, as always, Jack Kennedy was gracious and friendly and reported himself only to be in need of reassurance

---

[27] Clemson College folders, 1960–1962, Ernest Frederick Hollings Papers, hereinafter EFH/SCPC; Ballantyne, "Art of Political Biography"; idem., "Ernest Frederick Hollings"; idem., *New Politics for Old South*; Jon Hale, "The Fight Was Instilled In Us," *South Carolina Historical Magazine,* 114/1 (January 2013): 4–28; Burke High Students, *Who Is Burke High*?; Brown, "Civil Rights Activism in Charleston"; Sorensen, *Kennedy*, 488; quoted, Bass and DeVries, *Transformation of Southern Politics*, 63.

[28] Harvey Bernard Gantt folders, Robert Cook Edwards Papers, University Archives, 1960–1964, RCE/SC/CU; Edgar Arthur Brown folders on Gantt, 1960–1964, EAB/SC/CU.

that integration at Clemson could go smoothly. There was a hint that the president, or at least one of his people, was worried about what Bryan Dorn would do. Dorn hastened to assure all concerned that he loved Clemson College, loved higher education, and intended to be part of the most successful integration of a Deep South public college campus. There was, of course, awkwardness and hurt, for Bryan Dorn realized his old friend and comrade regarded him as a potential problem not unlike Faubus and Wallace and Barnett, whose divisive and demagogic actions he disdained.[29]

Even so, he spoke enthusiastically to Jack Kennedy, and the president reminded his supporter that this particular process was just as important as the 1960 campaign. Likely, the old Army Air Corps sergeant was already "on the right page," but he saluted vigorously and made sure that he played his small but vital role the right way, as he had done in Operation Overlord, in the Battle of the Bulge, in the 1960 campaigns in the textile mills—and now at his beloved Clemson College. Clemson's integration, like those grand campaigns, likely would have been concluded successfully without Bryan Dorn, but his good work surely helped things along—and every one of those wartime and peacetime campaigns was marked by many close calls, so that everyone playing a minor role was important. Without exaggerating Dorn's role, the biographer has to mark his sense of history as a story of progress at least in this episode of the civil rights movement.[30]

By the time the golden dusk and blue light of Indian summer arrived in 1963, Dorn had found a comfortable place in his evolving relationship with President Kennedy. They were warmly avuncular, certainly a bit shallow, with each other, and it was not a deep relationship. However, the two politicians could count on each other for the things each valued highest. In particular, JFK counted on Dorn for vigorous support of the aggressive Cold War policy that the Kennedyites brought to the Caribbean, Central America, Eastern Europe, Southern Africa—and most dramatically, Southeastern Asia. As the conflict in Vietnam intensified, Jack Kennedy began to commit

---

[29] Tape recordings, JFK, 1961–1962, The Presidential Recordings, 4 vols., Miller Center Presidential Recordings Program, University of Virginia, hereinafter, PRCMC/UVa; response to telephone call, WJBD to Mr. President (JFK), 25 January 1963; notes on history, passim, especially political folders, 1962–1964; WJBD, corr. WJBD/SCPC.

[30] WJBD, Clemson reference, "John F. Kennedy"; Response to telephone call, WJBD to Mr. President (JFK), 25 January 1963; Dalberg-Acton, "Inaugural Lecture on the Study of History," 1–30; 319–42.

more money and more weapons and also ground forces. Enamored as he was of high-technology devices, Kennedy leaned on his air force F-4 Phantom jet and a host of new helicopters for reconnaissance and unique striking power; there were also the B-52 Stratofortress bombers for the kind of carpet bombing that Dorn thought could win the war. On Vietnam, Bryan Dorn had intensified his own speeches as his pro-war emotions intensified. Earlier, he said that he wanted to give aid in materiel and advice as well as some money to the South Vietnamese. However, as Ngo Dinh Diem replaced the assassinated Bao Dai as chief executive, the South Vietnamese ally seemed unable to defend itself against North Vietnam's Ho Chi Minh as the latter revolutionary gained strength from Chinese help as well as from the fifth columnist Vietcong inside the South.[31]

Dorn borrowed an old image from the Spanish Civil War to describe the position Vietnam was in. In 1936, General Emilio Mola Vidal had boasted that he had four columns of troops outside Madrid threatening the city and another column inside Madrid, destroying from within. Dorn liked the image, also employed by Ernest Hemingway in a play about the Spanish Civil War, and he spoke of fifth columnists, namely the Vietcong, operating from inside the besieged Saigon. He also occasionally spoke more darkly about fifth columnists of Communist sympathizers operating inside the US to defeat the South Vietnamese and their American supporters.

In the developing crisis, the congressman agreed with his commander in chief that there would have to be traditional ground forces, infantry and artillery, and that these must be deployed in increasing numbers in Vietnam for long years to come. As counsel Theodore Sorensen noted at the time, Kennedy "not only carried out" earlier administration commitments to South Vietnam, but compensate[d] for the political weakness of the Diem regime" by "a vast expansion of effort." All of this fit with Bryan Dorn's Cold War politics and reflected his understanding of the domino theory as he read and talked with Bonner Fellers, with Hillaire Belloc du Berrier, with the Citadel's Mark Clark, and with South Carolina's own William C. Westmoreland, commander in the field. It comported, too, with his own observa-

---

[31] Cold War commitments worldwide, JFK speeches, *"Let the Word Go Forth,"* sel. and ed. Sorensen, ch. 13; Moyar, *Triumph Forsaken;* re southeast Asian tour, WJBD to Carlos Pena Romulo, 25 August 1960; Frederick G. Dutton off-the-record memorandum to WJBD, 16 September 1963, WJBD/SCPC; JFK, Opening Statement, President's News Conference, Washington, DC, 23 March 1961; JFK, Conference of Central American Republics, San Jose, Costa Rica, 18 March 1963; Sorensen, *Kennedy*, 639–61.

tions in Southeast Asia on a trip in that year, and for that matter, it comported with opinions and attitudes expressed in the era by Hubert Humphrey, Edmund Muskie, and Walter Mondale.[32]

Too, JFK could count on Dorn to support the "New Frontier" domestic spending programs, most of which could be gathered under the umbrella of the Cold War because the defense department claimed such sprawling needs. As the president prepared for a trip to Dallas, he shared with supporters a speech (never delivered but published subsequently) in which he again "let the word go forth" that a strong economy and a strong military were inextricably linked: "We are strengthening our security as well as our economy in our recent record increases in national income and national output." Although hardly an insider in Camelot, Dorn knew of and fully appreciated the planned Dallas address with its full commitment to militaristic Keynesian political economics.[33]

To strengthen the domestic economy and to strengthen global defense, JFK agreed that there was an "essentiality of textiles" for wartime. The poor state of South Carolina could benefit from New Frontier spending. It did so directly with the expansion of training facilities at Fort Jackson and with the creation of the *John C. Calhoun* submarine, whose naming and deployment signified sandlapper involvement with the military. But there were other, much more oblique, connections that were no less real: desilting Charleston Harbor and extending the interstate highway system along the I-95 corridor through the Pee Dee and on into Beaufort, developing the I-85 corridor in the red hills, and extending the proposed I-77 interstate far south of Charlotte into mid-country South Carolina. All of these New Frontier projects obviously helped state manufacturers and state tourism, but in each case were said to let soldiers and sailors get from here to there as military strategy demanded. Dorn insisted to JFK that the USSR's Nikita Khruschev and Vietnam's Ho Chi Minh had to be fought "at the psychological time" at home as well as abroad. "Let us move forward," the congressman admon-

---

[32] JFK quoted, Sorensen, *Kennedy*, 51; correspondence with Fellers, Clark, and Belloc regarding Fellers's *Wings for Peace* and Belloc's manuscript "Background to Betrayal"; correspondence, Westmoreland, 1961–1968; "Memorandum to President," 14 June 1961; Walter Becher to WJBD, 3 October 1963; WJBD to Daniel R. Flood, 21 January 1963, WJBD/SCPC; "Dorn: Coexistence Dangerous," *Charlotte Observer*, 13 November 1963.

[33] JFK, Remarks Prepared for Delivery at Dallas Trade Mart Luncheon, 22 November 1963.

ished yet again, "with the tremendous advantage" of JFK's "salesmanship," of the "personable leader" in the Cold War—a war that was everywhere.[34]

Examples of Dorn's work for the domestic New Frontier involved two House bills he sponsored, originally enumerated HR 3000 and HR 5580. Both concerned adult basic literacy. These were things he would do anyway, but JFK had given him the perfect words and a melodramatic setting to deploy those words. In his 1962 State of the Union Address, the president demanded a "massive attack to end illiteracy," and he quoted H. G. Wells: "Civilization is a race between education and catastrophe." Kennedy then declared, "It is up to you in this Congress to determine the winner of that race." The remarks hit Dorn's home, for the Palmetto State in 1962 still counted some 20 percent of adults older than twenty-five who could not read and write beyond the most primary school level. Not surprisingly, then, high school diplomas, or their equivalent, the GED, had been earned by fewer than two-thirds of the state populace. Since his days observing Dada wrestling with underfunded schools in Saluda and then Greenwood, Bryan Dorn knew that rural Southern school districts could not find the money to pay teachers to bring adults up to a national standard of literacy—not unless they reduced expenditures on the secondary and post-secondary efforts to teach those who could read and write. Yet Dorn was a self-proclaimed states' rights Democrat, suspicious of large federal budgets for nondefense items. He was also concerned, if not anxious, about federal oversight of schools, which oversight would likely hasten the day of truly integrated schools.[35]

For all that, the congressman listened closely as Henry L. Sneed, superintendent of public schools in Florence, District One, described a "pressing" situation in his own Pee Dee region. Sneed, a onetime segregationist opposed to any federal funding, had completely changed his mind and now supported both integration with federal oversight and an expanded federal role in school budgets and directions. He described his epiphany about Dorn's bills, as amended by integrationists:

> I feel that the urgency of the intent behind this bill is such that I might waive my feeling with respect to Federal Aid. If I felt that

---

[34] WJBD, "Memorandum to President," 14 June 1961; folders, I-77, I-85, I-95, political folders, 1961–1974, WJBD/SCPC.

[35] Drafts HR 3000, HR 5580, 1962, WJBD/SCPC; JFK, Annual Message to Congress on the State of the Union, 22 January 1962, Congressional Record, vol. 108, pt. 19, 75.

> there was any possibility for South Carolina to make these funds available within the next year or so I would certainly oppose even this Federal Aid. However, I feel that the matter is so pressing with us in South Carolina that we need all the help that we can get to overcome the illiteracy of the adult population 25 years and over.[36]

That feeling of urgency in the face of need could have been spoken by Dada himself, and his son, the congressman, remained attuned to Dada's (and Nana's) schoolteacher voice. It was more politic and more relevant to quote Sneed, the sandlapper educator who was on the front lines in schools right now, than to quote the actual influences, the dead Dada or even the dead Jefferson. New Frontier money could do for the red hills and the Pee Dee and indeed all of South Carolina what the New Deal and the Fair Deal could not do, and more than that, it could do for Dorn's people what they simply could not do for themselves. Federal aid applied intelligently could ameliorate, someday eradicate, illiteracy among hard-working but unschooled millhands and farmers as the economy began to offer high-skills, and someday high-wage, employment for the underpaid and abused labor of both races. The congressman's duty was to push the Kennedy men as hard as he could to attain funding sufficient to the daunting task. But to get the task done, he would have to accept a modicum of liberal treatment, including some federal demand for integration in the adult programs. He thus "reluctantly" accepted progressive treatment of black adults as part of the price for progress in basic adult literacy. It is possible that he actually supported that aspect of progressive federal policy with a "reluctance" displayed only for his white constituency. But given his anguish over all aspects of race relations, it seems more likely that he resented federal usurpation of local prerogative. He resented even more the local poverty that was so clearly tied to poor schools for his people. Thus *reluctant* was an accurate word for the way he came to sponsorship of these two bills, however loud that sponsorship eventually became.[37]

Once Dorn entered the lists, he jousted well, speaking eloquently on the floor of the House, and more importantly lining up solid support among Republicans as well as his own Democrats to pass the bills. For their part, the Kennedy people also played their roles well, at least from a white sandlapper's point of view. Despite the president's own bold language and despite fierce-sounding federal agents, the Kennedy men, at least in South

---

[36] Henry L. Sneed to WJBD, 3 July 1963, WJBD/SCPC.
[37] Ibid.; HR 3000, HR 5580, WJBD/SCPC .

Carolina's Third District and Fifth District, always backed away from substantive racial progressivism, especially on voting rights and housing rights. It was a policy that the Kennedy men understood to pursue by order (and example) of their commander in chief in these civil rights wars.[38]

As his Bible told him, *there was nothing new under the sun*. FDR had consciously employed defense spending on behalf of Southern industry and Ike had built the interstate infrastructure ostensibly to serve military needs. What was different, however, was the speed and scope of the spending at a time when war was not hot, but officially Cold. As Bryan Dorn had memorandized his president, it was the post-Keynesian Deep South version of old Jim Farley's *tax and spend, tax and spend, elect and elect*. Only now, economic advisor Walter Heller and speechwriters Theodore Sorensen and Richard Goodwin and the president himself spoke affectingly about cutting taxes on the wealthy and on corporations without cutting spending in order to stimulate the macroeconomy. On the stump, Bryan Dorn spoke as loudly as before about wasteful spending, but he agreed in his personal correspondence with his economics advisor, wily, old Hubert Aull of Clemson, that the tax cutting and the spending—that is, the Keynesian deficit spending in times of recession and slow growth—were vital to South Carolina, especially in the Third District.[39]

From service in Congress, Bryan Dorn knew that the red-hills district could only gain appropriations if other congressmen in other districts got theirs too. Above all, he agreed with Dr. Aull and with the dead Keynes that "make work" spending, the kind that could start easily and stop easily, was needed to stimulate regional economics, but also must be stopped once growth ensued and prices rose. He accepted the demand-pull explanation of the inflation that scared him, but he was not afraid of inflation when the economy crawled (with employment beneath "full" levels). Following Keynes, through Dr. Aull, he was afraid of inflation when—and if!—the economy should start running rapidly (with "full" employment). Too, he accepted Keynes's early and rather nuanced teaching that investment, and not savings, was the link to employment, as he accepted Keynes's claim that there could actually be too much saving, and thus too much "leaking" out of

---

[38] WJBD to George W. Bowling, 23 July 1963, WJBD/SCPC; Tindall, *Disruption*, 59.

[39] Quotation, Ecclesiastes 1:9, all trans.; corr., GHA, 1960–64; Sneed to WJBD, 3 July 1963, WJBD/SCPC; retrospectives, WJBD to GHA, 8 February 1971 and GHA to W. W. McEachern, 9 December 1964, GHA/SC/CU.

the macro system. In other words, the Fair Deal for the Textile Region had been worthily replaced by the New Frontier for the Textile Region.[40]

There was the personal issue of Lyndon Baines Johnson, the big man and bigger force who could never be ignored. LBJ was no longer the main bridge from Southerners to mainstream Democrats, at least not for this Deep South congressman, or for the rest of the South Carolina delegation. Despite LBJ's historic ties with the late Sam Rayburn and his coalition of Populistic New Deal progressives, despite his ties with Southern conservative Democrats, especially Richard Russell, and despite the vice president's own militaristic defense of Cold War spending that sometimes masked domestic spending, he made little impact in this season on Bryan Dorn. In this regard, Dorn was unable to forgive what he regarded as LBJ's cruel and treacherous mistreatment of his onetime mentor Rayburn. As marked, at least once, Dorn rather plaintively begged off from pleas by textile and other people that he seek out LBJ for help. He had told them on that occasion what his actions implied throughout the period 1960 to 1963, which is that he was more comfortable working with House Democrats, Midwestern Republicans, and JFK people, albeit always minus Bobby Kennedy, than with Johnson.[41]

Perhaps this distancing from LBJ can be explained because the JFK circle emphasized Harvard and Camelot and excluded the gritty and practical-minded Populism of LBJ. But Bryan Dorn was as gritty and practical-minded a Populist as any Texan, and he had no love for Harvard or the Ivy League and no rhetorical interest at all in Camelot. For all his speechifying flourishes about Jack Kennedy, the congressman said nothing about Camelot. Always keen to smell out and respond to personal nuance in politics, he "got it" that LBJ was not in favor with the Kennedy crowd. And he could be cool and distant to the vice president if need be in front of that crowd. Yet when away from the Kennedy inner circle—which was most of the time—in this period, he deliberately kept himself distant from Johnson, even though

---

[40] Retrospective, WJBD to GHA, 8 February 1971 and GHA to W. W. McEachern, 9 December 1964, GHA/SC/CU; Frank, "The New Mandate on Defense." 50–56; Fraser, "A Lettered Numbers Man (John Kenneth Galbraith)." *Los Angeles Times*, 13 February 2005, bk. sect.; Parker, *John Kenneth Galbraith*.

[41] Textile folder, 1963; WJBD to H. C. Jones, 7 March 1960, WJBD/SCPC; betrayal of Rayburn, *Means of Ascent*, 17.

the South Carolina delegation enjoyed the vital LBJ liaison with assistant Bobby Baker, a Clemson man from Pickens County.[42]

While John McCormack remained a taciturn and uninspiring speaker of the house, there was a wonderful relationship with Majority Whip Carl Albert, who besides being a friend from that Class of 1947 revealed that he had married into a South Carolina family and therefore into Bryan Dorn's own sprawling family history. In the blue light of that golden dusk, then, Dorn felt good about Jack Kennedy, even as he felt bad about onetime friend Lyndon Johnson. During a break in the sessions, probably the late summer before Labor Day, Dorn took Nana to meet Kennedy. The two shameless charmers, Nana and JFK, charmed each other despite the age difference. Nana was thrilled with the handsome young man, and the handsome young man, as always, showed his appreciation for a fine-looking woman of any age. Conversation was spirited and enthusiastic, and later the mother and son wondered how the busy president could give them so much time from his pressing schedule. The brief visit, its official date not even recorded, reflected feelings common among the extended Dorn family in those optimistic days.[43]

Blue light and golden dusk are photographer's images that describe the kind of late afternoon light ideal for capturing a mood of comfort and reassurance and beauty. These images remind all that Dorn, in looking back at JFK, used special lenses and special lighting, perhaps to make it all better than it had been. That being said, the comments and quotations by Dorn used here are almost exclusively from the period before the assassination. JFK rode high in Dorn's estimation, and the congressman was pleased to be a part, admittedly a small part, of the Kennedy years. Writing to dyspeptic old Midwestern Republican Wint Smith, Dorn declared full optimism about the coming 1964 elections. Smith worried that New York governor Nelson Rockefeller would take the Republican nomination and that there would be a Kennedy-Rockefeller contest among Northern liberals. Dorn saw it otherwise. He was convinced that Barry Goldwater of Arizona, whom he considered a Jeffersonian liberal, would be nominated and would run against JFK,

---

[42] Correspondence, Bobby Baker, 1963; WJBD, "Memorandum to the President," 14 June 1961, WJBD/SCPC.

[43] WJBD, "John F. Kennedy"; WJBD, *OTP*, 68–69. Correspondence, WJBD and Wint Smith, 1963. See especially retrospective, WJBD to Smith, 2 December 1963, WJBD/SCPC.

whom Dorn also considered a Jeffersonian liberal. To Dorn, the foreign policy—quite hawkish—was identical, as were the civil rights—quite liberal in his view. He liked the two men and preferred Kennedy because of his macroeconomic policies. Even there, he thought that a victorious Goldwater could be reasoned with on militaristic Keynesianism by Southern Neo-Populist Progressives. Preferring Kennedy, Dorn assured Wint Smith that Jeffersonian liberals would be in good shape regardless of who won in the coming Kennedy-Goldwater contest.

Smith, genuinely fond of Bryan Dorn, was not having any of this, but he liked *hearing it* almost as much as the congressman liked *saying* it. Only the removal of the familiar Jack Kennedy and the ascent of the suddenly unfamiliar and even hostile Lyndon Baines Johnson could threaten this present good system, with its happy auguries for future politics and future personal relationships.

Chapter 9

The Great Society 1964–1968

The JFK years could not have been as golden as Bryan Dorn remembered them, but their sudden and bloody ending was a fierce and unsettling shock to his personal and political equilibrium. On 22 November 1963, Kennedy was assassinated in Dallas during a political trip entered into with hopes for a new appeal to Southern voters—hopes shared fully by Dorn and by most of his Third District supporters, who were a people personally fond of JFK and politically beholden to Kennedy's militaristic economics, which were improving employment and production in the mill villages while pumping research dollars into Clemson. In terms of Dorn's personal correspondence and his family's memories of his response to the assassination, there is no overstating the pain of the loss—or of the apprehension, if not panic, about what was coming next. Dorn grieved mightily for the loss of a favored one, and he tried not to panic over the ascendancy of LBJ, the mistrusted one. In public statements, he was cautious, guardedly optimistic about the new day. But he did not expect that new day to be a good one.

Quite early in the second session of the 88th Congress, Bryan Dorn got a letter from a man in Clemson that showed Third District distrust of Lyndon Baines Johnson, and it forecast hostilities to aspects of the Great Society then abuilding. It also outlined the congressman's own problems with the new regime, both domestically and in foreign affairs. After all, he was no more ready for the ascendancy of LBJ than his constituents. J. T. Mauldin Jr. had watched a special program on NBC television, Greenville station WFBC, and this show detailed lavish spending on the Sam Rayburn House building, soon to be the new home for Dorn himself. In his thorough and dogged way, Dorn actually visited architect George Stewart, hoping to find that NBC had its facts wrong; but on that visit he could only tease out a statement that "the figures used...were a little misleading." Dorn wrote

Mauldin, "I agree with you that more money was spent than I feel is necessary."[1]

Otherwise Mauldin's note affirmed what Bryan Dorn had told the House of Representatives and readers of the *Congressional Record* in a memorial address. The loss of JFK not only hurt, but represented a turning point in history:

> Washington will never be the same to me. President Kennedy represented an era—the era of television in politics for the first time, the era of downtown parades in open convertibles, the era of political glamour.
>
> John Fitzgerald Kennedy was an intellectual. He was brilliant. He was well-groomed, well-mannered, and cultured. He was gracious and hospitable. He loved the typical American. He was a man of humility and charm....
>
> I will miss him as long as I live.[2]

Night had fallen, the blue light had gone, and the golden dusk had completely disappeared. The new era was here, and it would be the era of Lyndon Baines Johnson, to Bryan Dorn one of the most intimidating forces he had ever encountered. LBJ, once pushed to the outer edge of JFK's charmed circle, now had redrawn the lines, with himself in the center and with many concentric circles, perhaps none of them charmed, but all of them intimidating, even threatening. At least that was the way the congressman saw it.

All the same, he was still a Democrat, and so he recorded for the piedmont mill public a hopeful statement about President Johnson. "No one," the orator declaimed for the millworkers, "ever came to this high office, in the history of the nation, better qualified or more devoted to the principles and ideals that made the nation great." Speaking to and for Democrats he then whistled up the echoes of the happy days: "Upon many occasions, President Johnson said that Franklin D. Roosevelt was his second father. I say he picked a good one."[3]

---

[1] J. T. Mauldin to WJBD, 30 June 1964; WJBD to Mauldin, 6 February 1964, WJBD/SCPC.

[2] WJBD, "John F. Kennedy," *Congressional Record*, vol. 109, pt. 18, 88th Cong., 1st sess., 4 December–12 December 1963, 23504.

[3] WJBD, "Future of the Democratic Party," *Congressional Record*, vol. 110, pt. 3, 88th Cong., 2d sess., 13 February–3 March 1964, 2965–66.

The words of praise were true but were carefully chosen. He could have taken truth serum or undergone torture and still affirmed each phrase. But *between* each phrase there were unspoken attitudes gleaned from personal history. Bryan Dorn himself never really liked FDR, especially the dying commander in chief, whom the Army Air Corps NCO had considered both out of touch and tyrannical. To choose that awesome but amoral force as "second father" was to choose political ambition over moral behavior. To say that the choice of second father was a good one was only to affirm *crooked hand, crooked glove*. Indeed, in his words for a Gastonia winter gathering, words placed in the *Congressional Record* by two grateful North Carolina congressmen, William Jennings Bryan Dorn had spoken honestly about LBJ's "devotion to the principles and ideals that made the nation great," but he had said nothing about *how* Senator Johnson, much more President Johnson, would serve those principles and what means he would employ "to pursue these ends."[4]

Despite the way Bryan Dorn had fought for a Fair Deal for textiles, and then for a New Frontier for textiles, he was appalled by LBJ's spending and his grand plans. It was partly a matter of scale, since JFK's domestic proposals were modest compared to LBJ's. President Johnson laid out a proposed budget that was about double anything FDR attempted for the domestic economy. But yet the objection was mostly about how to execute plans and how to operationalize a budget. Funds for projects should be parceled out by cross-party and interregional negotiations in Congress, discussions in which everyone who played honestly lost something but gained something, too. Such compromise was especially important in the most significant public works projects Congressman Dorn assayed, the Duke steam plant and the extensions of interstate highway routes. Negotiations were complex and reasoned and were always undertaken with essential respect for the intentions of one's trading partners in the House of Representatives. Jack Kennedy and his people understood the processes and engaged with good nature, joshing along, among, and between respected equals. Lyndon Johnson had brought a different, rougher style to the trading. Dorn considered Kennedy to be tough but fair, LBJ to be cruel, mean-spirited, unfair, and without scruples. Unlike his correspondent Mauldin, the congressman already knew all about Johnson's rise to senatorial power, a "means of ascent" that had involved combat with adversaries and even betrayal of friends and

---

[4] Ibid.; on FDR: WJBD to Folks, 11 October 1944; WJBD to Folks, 8 November 1944, WJBD/SCPC.

associates. As Dorn understood it, though he did not fully articulate it to his constituents, LBJ's domestic plans, whatever size, small or large, would be brought off by force of egoistic executive will and without regard for congressional processes.[5]

As to foreign policy, there was discussion about increasing compensation to Panama for use of the canal, and even some discussion about complete independence for Panama, with its own national sovereignty over the canal. Mauldin was Clemson Tiger blunt: "It would be ridiculous for the United States to shell out money to pay Panama any money not completely due them!" Dorn readily agreed and, in fact, restrained himself in his reply since he himself firmly believed in the switchblade-wielding confrontation in the Cold War favored in the red hills, and he considered Panama's "informal imperial" relationship with the US to be a vital part of the Cold War. Indeed, most of Dorn's faithful correspondents described the assassination of JFK as a Communist conspiracy hatched in Mexico by Cubans and encouraged by the Soviets if not, in fact, directed by Moscow. Likely, Dorn agreed with that view, even with the apocalyptic expressions of Communism as a satanic conspiracy. In his otherwise poignant tribute to the slain Kennedy, Bryan Dorn had pointedly noted that the assassin was a man trained by Cuban Communists beholden to a unified international conspiracy. Just to be sure he was not too restrained in reply, Dorn passed along to Mauldin and to other correspondents some appropriately Red-baiting and Christian fundamentalist speeches.[6]

There was the reality of power, and Bryan Dorn could feel the forces coalescing into newly configured camps despite all the talk about "unity and harmony." Many old States' Rights Democrats, most prominently Strom Thurmond and members of the Byrd Machine in Virginia, were actively negotiating with the Republican Party, especially if Arizona's Barry Goldwater was to lead a GOP largely Southern and Western in composition. Rumors abounded, with some newspaper confirmation, that no less than Ernest Frederick Hollings and William Jennings Bryan Dorn were seriously consid-

---

[5] WJBD to Wint Smith, 2 December 1963; WJBD to Mauldin, 6 February 1964; WJBD to Mauldin, 30 June 1964; on "fear of LBJ in Senate," Caro, *Means of Ascent*, 16–18; idem., *Master of the Senate*, chs. 12, 17, and 21.

[6] Mauldin to WJBD, 30 June 1964; Thomas Parker to WJBD, 7 January 1964, Parker to WJBD, 14 January 1964; WJBD to Mauldin, 6 February 1964; WJBD to Parker, 15 January 1964, WJBD/SCPC; WJBD, "John F. Kennedy."

ering a change in party affiliation. Hollings actually did meet with some GOP officials in his state, but Bryan Dorn did not. He remained as self-consciously a Democrat as Andrew Jackson. Since he had stayed firmly in the party, insisting on the label States' Rights Democrat instead of Dixiecrat in 1948 and 1949, he saw no reason to abandon William Jennings Bryan's party in 1964. All the same, the Democratic Party was now LBJ's, and Dorn had to reestablish relations that were working and functional, if not truly good. No less than textile magnate Leon Lowenstein sent a complimentary telegram to LBJ, and in his manner, Lowenstein also sent Dorn a copy of the telegram. The man who had built at least eight major facilities in upstate South Carolina urged the secretary of the Textile Congressional Group to support Johnson's plans for full employment—since it was Kennedy's, but Kennedy was killed before he could successfully push it through.[7]

Lowenstein hit home, as he generally did. Textile employment remained in the doldrums, and the congressman agreed that jobs legislation was needed, especially in its militaristic Keynesian format. The departed JFK had actually not enjoyed much success in getting legislation through Congress, while the deeply resented President Johnson was, after all, the once and future *Master of the Senate*. Accordingly, Dorn told Lowenstein that he would write a letter to President Johnson supporting the jobs bill.[8]

Thus he swore personal respect, he reaffirmed loyalty to the Democratic Party, and he also underlined his undying loyalty to his constituents on a number of local issues. One such issue was personal as well as political, for Rock Fleming wanted to leave the congressman and become the president's "advance man." In his file folders, Fleming is revealed as the consummate team player who dutifully gave out Bryan Dorn's "line" and never expressed his own opinions, exactly as he was supposed to do and be. However, a few notes between Anderson editor Wilton Hall and Fleming show that both men were concerned that Bryan Dorn was drifting away from his properly liberal moorings in 1962 and 1963. One of Hall's reporters even lamented that "he can quote [conservative senator] Goldwater backwards" and then scrawled to Fleming, "Keep him *liberal* [writer Markeson's italics]." Dorn

---

[7] Interview: Herb Hartsook (18 February 2013), JHR/SCPC; Ballantyne, "Ernest Frederick Hollings"; idem., *New Politics for Old South*, 55–66; Leon Lowenstein to WJBD, 7 January 1964 with enclosure, Lowenstein to LBJ, 6 January 1964, WJBD/SCPC.

[8] WJBD to H. Klugh Purdy, January 22, 1948; WJBD to LBJ, 10 January 1964 with enclosures on Carver; WJBD/SCPC.

understood the opportunity for Fleming, and of course he also understood that there would still be personal loyalty between the two piedmont figures no matter where Rock worked. Likely, too, the congressman hoped that Fleming could in some small way ease relations between powerful president and ambitious congressman. At any rate, it was good to have a friend so close to the new commander in chief. But it was also disconcerting to realize that one's closest associate in the office could be so attractive to a man so feared, so intimidating, and so little trusted by Bryan Dorn.[9]

The office in its way recovered quite quickly, everyone congratulating Rock Fleming on his promotion. The "girls," Jane Boroughs, Dorothy Abbot, and Libby McClellan Fleming, conducted things successfully as before, since each knew how the congressman thought and expressed himself. For Jane Boroughs, in particular, he could write the briefest phrase and she knew at once what kind of "personalized" and detailed letter to write on his behalf. There were a number of "catch phrases," and Boroughs knew them all: contingencies included gracious response to fulsome praise, respectful response to all grades and conditions of complaints and criticism (always emphasizing the congressman's delight in hearing from a constituent, especially hearing what the constituent *really* thought). And, of course, there was the large but neatly maintained pile of specific requests that the congressman had to address at once. Both Nana and wife Millie Dorn had always insisted that a MAN had to be in the office of the secretary, partly because constituents would expect that and mostly because Nana and Millie Dorn themselves expected a man in charge. Quickly, William Beacham emerged to fill the role, and everyone continued her good work apace. All concerned knew that LBJ would push much harder for his agenda, and all understood that Republican opposition would be much more effective back in South Carolina than ever before.[10]

In fact, "his people" compelled Bryan Dorn and the reconstituted team to write at once about their interests and a dispute with one arm of the federal government. But the letter also had to discuss another threat to jobs, and that part of his message had to register not support but protest. The problem was that his people, classes and masses, were ready to revolt over environmental regulations for industrial facilities in the Savannah River ba-

---

[9] Fleming folders, 1961–1963, especially, Benson Markeson to Fleming, 15 May 1961 ("keep them *liberal*"), WJBD/SCPC.

[10] Fleming folders, 1964; example of Jane Borough's work: Gene Merritt Jr. to WJBD, 9 April 1962 and Congressman's response, 9 April 1962, WJBD/SCPC.

sin. No Keynesian stimulus could make up for the jobs the district stood to lose if policies and practices changed according to the rulings by Interior department assistant John A. Carver.

Much as he liked to write letters about policies and practices, the congressman sweated over this task, which was to affirm support for one LBJ proposal but to register a complaint about LBJ's secretary of the Interior Morris K. Udall, or at least Udall's activist assistant, John A. Carver. The latter was insisting on clean industrial practices for Savannah and Saluda waterways (less dumping of raw chemical waste and more attention to whatever manufacturers put into the waterways) in the Third District, practices that could be costly for various industries and possibly even Clemson University (Dorn's preferred college had been proclaimed a university in that very year). The regulations so angered some industries that a few owner/operators spoke darkly of leaving the region, thereby throwing out of work several thousand people. On such issues, the congressman stood, as he had with Jack Kennedy, on the high ground of full employment, something that usually trumped all other concerns. At least this dispute was not about civil rights, and thus the tightrope was easier to walk. Dorn wrote,

> Mr. President:
>
> My constituents and I overwhelmingly approve of the forthright and highly capable manner in which you are handling the presidency.
>
> The enclosed [letter of protest] is only critical of the Assistant Secretary of the Interior [John A. Carver], whose actions [concerning treatment of industrial waste and waterways] for more than a year have contributed to a division among my people.
>
> I agree with you that this is a time for harmony and unity and not for strife and discord.
>
> As one who has been a loyal Democrat and who has stumped the Country time and again for the Democratic ticket, I am convinced that now is the time to promote the unity of all elements in the Democratic Party as never before. I pledge you my cooperation to that end.[11]

Lawrence O'Brien, special assistant and counsel (and soon to be very political postmaster general after the style of Jim Farley), answered for the president and reassured Third District textile people and their representa-

[11] WJBD to LBJ, 10 January 1964 with enclosures on Carver; WJBD/SCPC.

tive. Johnson's jobs bill was going to sail through both houses, and Morris Udall was going to rein in John Carver and protect the relevant industries in the river basins. The LBJ people, which included the affable red-hills native (and Clemson Tiger) Bobby Baker as major liaison, would thereby preserve at least a few thousand jobs until many more thousands could be added by the jobs bill that featured major tax cuts coupled with major government spending, much of it specific to the Third District red hills.[12] The first big challenge of working with the intimidating Lyndon Johnson had been met without personal confrontation. That much done, Bryan Dorn could deal with other problems.

The Third District had not featured a primary contest since 1950, when Bryan Dorn himself was the outsider challenging incumbent Jim Hare. Subsequently, through constituent service and attention to classes and masses, the district had become "safe," and its congressman had even been part of the team that delivered the millhands and small-time farmers to Jack Kennedy in 1960, as had been done for Adlai Stevenson in 1952 and 1956. This year of 1964 looked to be quite different. Both Anderson's Pete Griffith and Calhoun Falls' Thomas M. Tucker were loudly talking about a run against Dorn in the Democratic primary. As for delivering a presidential vote, constituent mail was easily running ten to one against LBJ, with some trying to bring forward George Corley Wallace as a segregationist Democrat and others ready to vote for Barry Goldwater and the Republicans.[13]

Ever the Democrat, Dorn was at pains to shore up Southern support for his party as well as district support for his own candidacy. His district and the entire state, as well as neighboring Georgia, seemed all but guaranteed for Goldwater. However, electoral votes in both North Carolina and Virginia were available to LBJ—but so, too, were key congressional districts available to Republican challengers in those two states. Whatever Lawrence O'Brien and his boss LBJ thought of Dorn, they knew he could win friends and influence voters in the piedmont mill communities of North Carolina and Virginia. He could orate effectively in front of any millworkers in any state (although always in piedmont regions). There were even rural and remote places in the Florida panhandle where he could be useful, and he was sent into action in all those places, even as he realized his first serious oppo-

---

[12] Laurence O'Brien to WJBD, 12 January 1964, WJBD/SCPC.

[13] Political folders, 1964, WJBD/SCPC; *Anderson Independent* (Wilton E. Hall), 10 January–28 February 1964, South Caroliniana Library.

sition at home. Dorn gave old-fashioned speeches that were one portion New Deal, one portion Baptist revival, and huge portions of 1890s Populism, complete with mistrust of the Republicans and the investment bankers who financed them.[14]

The winter address in Gastonia, North Carolina, on 15 February 1964 illustrated his strategy and was so well received that North Carolina's Basil Whitener and Horace Kornegay and Florida's D. R. (Billy) Matthews placed it in the *Congressional Record* for all Democrats—and Republicans—to see. Drawing consciously on his namesake, Dorn repeated old William Jennings Bryan language about the "party of the people" and traced the Populist elements of the Democratic Party from Jefferson through Jackson and Bryan and FDR all the way to LBJ. Gastonia's event was in the North Carolina red hills and featured piedmont barbeque, Lexington formula, and Bryan Dorn looked out at the millhands and small-time farmers and all the Baptists and talked to them as if he were in Ware Shoals. The audience responded as if they were Ware Shoals folks. Just as he had done for Harry Truman in the earliest days of the Fair Deal, Dorn was again leading cheers for the party and celebrating the president as legitimate heir to Populistic New Deal traditions. To large degree, he not only ran against bankers and Communists, but he also "ran against Hoover," despite his personal regard for the old president with whom he was a warm and admiring correspondent. Crucial to his message was the point that Lyndon Baines Johnson stood in the line of Andrew Jackson and Franklin Delano Roosevelt, and no less crucial was this ringing line: LBJ "will, with his usual decisiveness, alacrity, and energy be overwhelmingly elected in November." He made the same points on DC radio station WMAC, 630 on the A.M. dials, where other Southern Democrats, especially capital party regulars, heard him and approved.[15]

It was old-time religion as well as old-time Populism, and it resonated with the working-class white Southerners because he talked to them about pocketbook issues and ignored racial issues, a plan for his own upcoming primary contest and one he hoped LBJ would adopt in his Southern marches for 1964. He roared at the crowd against the "days of monopoly and vested

---

[14] Horace Kornegay to WJBD, 18 February 1964; D. R. Matthews to WJBD, 18 February 1964; WJBD to E. L. Forrester, 14 May 1964; and Carl Albert to WJBD, 25 July 1964, WJBD/SCPC.

[15] WJBD, "The Future of the Democratic Party," *Congressional Record*, vol. 110, pt. 3, 88th Cong., 2d sess., 13 February–3 March 1964, 2965–66; Matthews to WJBD, 18 February 1964, WJBD/SCPC.

interests" and he roared for President Johnson, who "championed the underprivileged and carried the banner of the typical American." He did not even whisper anything about racial justice, such as the proposed Voting Rights Bill and the proposed Civil Rights Bill, but neither did he say a single "code word" about black people. It was how he still understood Jack Kennedy, and how he continued to describe the late president, with nothing of Camelot and Harvard and instead huge doses of the frontier Jacksonians Thomas Hart Benton and Sam Houston and William Jennings Bryan, whom JFK had written about in *Profiles in Courage*. As always beforehand, those Populistic New Deal progressives put little faith in free markets and still distrusted investment bankers, especially large international financial institutions; as always beforehand, such Populistic New Deal progressives wanted to preserve as much of the rural life as they could, and were anxious to use a powerful central government to interfere in monopolistic markets in order to save small farms, small businesses, and the large but threatened large textile industry. "In your Democratic Congress, with a Democratic president, the future of the textile industry can be assured and will remain stable," he opined there and also in other mill towns in North Carolina and Virginia.[16]

The other side of his updated Fair Deal for Textiles campaign was to recruit private industry and thereby provide job opportunities in his district, where things were improved since the Eisenhower years but still straitened. To do that, he worked hard with corporate recruiters and local business people (to include bankers like C. Douglas Wilson and Mac MacEachern of Greenville and W. W. "Hootie" Johnson of Columbia) to lure General Cable to Greenwood County, and all of this was in the same brief and cold month of February. General Cable, incorporated in New Jersey in 1927, made the list of *Fortune* magazine's successful (and very *large*) companies. It had a complex legal and economic relationship with General Telephone, and it made the most of its revenues by providing cable made from copper, aluminum, and optical fiber for that telephone company in remote and rural areas such as the Third District. Its immediate needs were for relatively low-skilled labor to do final assembly of cables and then pack them for shipment on train and truck. There was also hope for more high-skilled jobs—and corresponding high wages—since General Cable also provided the control

---

[16] Kennedy, *Profiles in Courage*, 50–100; 151; WJBD, "JFK: A Memorial," *Congressional Record*, vol. 109, pt. 18, 88th Cong., 1st sess., 4 December–12 December 1963, 23504.

and commerce cable for the Minuteman Missile systems at various air force bases. At the very least, the newcomer firm might need some Clemson engineers as well as a host of currently unemployed assembly-line people and packers and loaders for the rail and truck depots.[17]

Far larger than General Cable was Duke Power Company, and Dorn persisted in his long-running efforts to help the utility giant build a dam and establish a steam power plant on the Middleton River in Anderson County. The proposed plant would provide electricity through his red hills and part of the sand hills. Onetime campaign manager Steve Griffith had become general counsel for Duke Power and was thus privy to the utility's objectives and goals. Griffith explained the plans, both big-picture and particular. Without violating confidence and without seeking special favors, Griffith and Dorn thereby functioned in the traditional South Carolina system where politics and business were dominated by interlocking families. Duke Power, already the major force in North Carolina's piedmont, intended to extend its base of commercial and residential customers by following Interstate 85 from Greensboro through Charlotte and Spartanburg and then down into Anderson and the contiguous red hills, thereby serving the most rapidly growing enterprises in the two Carolinas as well as serving the most rapidly growing metropolitan areas of the two Carolinas. Griffith also reiterated for his cousin that the proposed federal dam and artificial lake at Trotters Shoals would keep Duke Power from coming to Anderson County, regardless of various studies that purported to show there was enough waterpower to support all the projects.[18]

Water projects were very much part of the Populistic New Deal, and no less a Populistic New Dealer than Olin Dewitt Talmadge Johnston was the father of the proposed Trotters Shoals federal dam, with its cooperative arrangement for cheap electricity and its artificial lake for recreation. It seemed odd to people to oppose the Trotters Shoals dam when Dorn had celebrated the earlier coming of the Hartwell Reservoir and other waterways projects, especially those proposed by Midwestern and Western Republicans. It took a moment to explain, and the master politician knew quite well how little

---

[17] WJBD to Wingate H. Lucas, 3 February 1964, with enclosure, WJBD/SCPC; Standard & Poor, *Standard Listed Stock Reports*, 10 December1963, vol. 30, no. 236, 958; "General Cable," *Greenwood Index*, 10 February 1964, 1; retrospective, WJBD to Harold Cooley, 13 January 1965, WJBD/SCPC.

[18] Interview: Griffith with Roper and Hartsook (25 September 2013); WJBD, retrospective statement on Keowee Toxaway, 10 May 1967, WJBD/SCPC.

patience people had for long newspaper explanations or elaborate lectures at public meetings, especially his beloved barbeques. For all that, Bryan Dorn was convinced that many more jobs and better electricity service were to come from the Duke Power proposal, and thus he bent to the task of explaining why he wanted the Duke Steam Plant and not the federal project—and why people could not have both. He talked at barbeque rallies, but he also sent a personally signed note to the teachers in Anderson County, many of whom remembered Dada and most of whom he had met at least once:

> Education and Opportunity in Anderson County
>
> Taxes from the Duke Steam Plant alone could double the salary of every teacher in Anderson County and improve all school facilities. An abundance of cheap electricity, thus generated, could attract other industry, creating greater opportunity for our school graduates.
>
> Should you re-elect me to Congress, I will continue my efforts to locate the Duke Steam Plant in Anderson County and expand our tax base and economy through free enterprise development of our natural resources.[19]

For other audiences, he explained carefully that his people could not have both the Duke Steam Plant *and* the Trotters Shoals dam and lake. Duke Power engineers were not convinced that there was enough water force for both dams, and frankly they did not want to compete with federal or public-cooperative electricity. It was hard to be more Populistic than Olin Johnston, but Dorn gave it a marvelous try. The Populists in the 1890s and in the 1960s had emphasized the countryside and production, preferring tangible products like cotton lint or corn or timber and their manufactured derivatives to leisure activities like boating or recreational fishing (as distinguished from a man rowing out in his own boat and fishing for family food). Dorn could point to his early days as cotton farmer and his continuing operations in beef cattle and timber as proof that he was a producing man. He also reminded all audiences that he otherwise supported the electrical cooperatives, and, in fact, relied on them for power and light at his farm and in his home on Callison Road. *Did y'all want rich lawyers and their sons to drive powerboats and ski on an artificial lake that you paid for while you used electricity paid for by your own taxes? Or did y'all want thousands of good-paying jobs at a*

[19] WJBD, retrospective statement on Keowee Toxaway, 10 May 1967, campaign letter marked (Anderson County) teachers, 20 May 1964, WJBD/SCPC.

steam plant while Duke Power laid out at a minimum $1 million in taxes, mostly for schools and roads in Anderson County? Dorn could make this argument in town-square meetings, at church basement covered-dish suppers, and at barbeques. He also placed a statement in the *Congressional Record* and sent tear sheets out to every soul who lived, moved, or had his being in the Third Congressional District.[20]

LBJ was much closer to Olin Johnston than to Bryan Dorn, but he was entirely too clever to tip his hand and show which of these Populistic New Dealers he was going to support, especially since he had reason to believe that Dorn might just win this tussle. Otherwise, Dorn took pains to make sure that Lawrence O'Brien, Bobby Baker, and other LBJ people knew how hard the congressman was working for the president's reelection, and in particular how he had turned down overtures from George Wallace for help and had kept his distance from the Southern Republican Party then rapidly abuilding.[21]

Mayor Thomas M. Tucker of Calhoun Falls persuaded Anderson's Pete Griffith that he could make the most effective run against Bryan Dorn, taking as his issues Trotters Shoals and Johnson's proposals for Medicare, Medicaid, and other strengthening of the welfare "safety net." To all of that, Mayor Tucker could add a heavy seasoning of Olin Johnston racist diatribe, associating Dorn with those who were "too liberal on race." The *Anderson Independent*, intensely loyal to Olin D. Johnston and for long years now a family foe as well as political foe to Bryan Dorn, pumped for Tucker in the primary set for mid-June. Unlike the Second, Fifth, and Sixth districts, however, no significant Republican candidates registered in the Third that winter; whoever won between Tucker and Dorn would be unopposed in November. While it was annoying to the congressman to have the *Anderson Independent* working against him, and even more annoying to hear that cousin Strom Thurmond had tried hard to find Republican opposition to run against him in November, the threat of Tucker winning was never a serious one. The much larger television and newspaper outlets in Greenville, Spartanburg, and Columbia were immediately on Bryan Dorn's side. And

[20] A. M. Doolittle (Duke employee, Anderson) to WJBD, n.d. (January 1962), Sam Rayburn folder; L. L. Lesesne to WJBD, 8 December 1962; WJBD, "Duke Steam Plant," *Congressional Record.*, vol. 110, pt. 8, 88th Cong., 2d sess., 4 May–18 May 1964, 10456–57.

[21] WJBD to LBJ, with enclosures, 10 January 1964; correspondence with Lawrence O'Brien, summer 1964, WJBD/SCPC.

the congressman and his staff, now led by Bill Beacham (and still mightily assisted by Rock Fleming in the White House), made effective use of the power of the incumbent to do favors for people, especially in Anderson and the communities where it seemed that everybody was a Clemson Tiger. No one was a better Clemson Tiger than Bryan Dorn, and President R. C. Edwards had long worked closely with him on Great Society funding for the university.[22]

At the national level, the Clemson man Bobby Baker and Postmaster Lawrence O'Brien did indeed function for and with Bryan Dorn, as he had hoped and planned; that is, they behaved like old Jim Farley. Personal feelings about LBJ were no more important than personal feelings about FDR as long as major campaign men could help out. Indeed, the congressman had little to do personally with his president in these days, a most unusual circumstance for the powerful and personalistic—and always deeply involved—Lyndon Johnson. In the June primary voting, Bryan Dorn swamped Thomas M. Tucker, winning all counties and gaining some 70 percent of the vote. By contrast, Columbia's Albert William Watson, running as a Goldwater Democrat in the Second District, was unopposed in the primary but was punished (denial of major committee assignments and loss of seniority) in the House because of his active support of Goldwater. Meanwhile, old friends John L. McMillan in the Pee Dee Sixth District and Robert Hemphill in the piedmont Fifth District faced primary opposition, but McMillan and Hemphill won with almost two-thirds of the votes. Of the congressional candidates, only Albert Watson had adopted the Olin Johnston strategy of baiting the races, and it was not immediately clear that voters still responded to such racist demagoguery. The rest of the South Carolina delegation, like Dorn himself, had said next to nothing about race but had instead focused on pocketbook issues and promises of FDR-type support for the state's ailing industries and small-time farms.[23]

---

[22] *Greenwood Index*, June issues, 1964, South Caroliniana Library; correspondence, Walter Brown (Spartanburg radio, television, and newspaper), April–June 1964; notice of Clemson grants, 1964–1968, WJBD to RCE, especially WJBD to RCE, 20 June 1966; retrospective, RCE to WJBD, 12 April 1966, WJBD/SCPC.

[23] Jorden, "1964," *The Primary State*, s.v.; *Supplemental Report of the Secretary of State to the General Assembly of South Carolina* (Columbia, SC: State Printing, 1964), 1–64; WJBD to Don Rickert, 16 June 1964 re Olin Johnston and Wilton Hall; flyer, "Strom Thurmond Urges Conservative Democrats to Join Republican Party," n.d. (September) 1964, WJBD/SCPC.

With the district primary concluded, Bryan Dorn returned to the capital to face the most substantive piece of civil rights legislation since Emancipation itself. The Civil Rights Bill of 1964 was quite different from the act passed in 1957. It can be recalled that in 1957, LBJ, Master of the Senate, had personally amended the Eisenhower bill so as to draw out the sting of federal enforcement, rendering the subsequent Civil Rights Act an important statement of ideals *but with little practicable way to enforce most of its provisions*. Now, as president, LBJ was bound in his determination that his own Civil Rights Act would not be one so amended; his act would include enforcement by the Civil Rights Division of the Justice Department, with specific authorization for affirmative action to seek redress. President Kennedy's term "affirmative action" had little meaning in practice, but President Johnson made crystal clear his personal resolution to enforce the law vigorously. Most important, no one trying to defend civil rights had to prove *intent*—something damnably hard to prove since only Jesus knew "what was in a man." Instead, data collected to show effect and result were prima facie cases in point of evidence that a person had suffered discrimination because of race. For Johnson's proposals and practices, *effect*—something easily documented—was necessary and sufficient to produce strong executive action.[24]

Like other Southerners, Bryan Dorn had been amused when his old friend, the cagey Virginia segregationist Judge Howard Worth Smith, had added to the bill's language the category "sex," so that the proposed bill would also protect civil rights for women as well as black citizens. Surely, the wily old Keeper of the Rules for US Congress—signatory to the Southern Manifesto and veteran foe of all civil rights legislation—had inserted a "poison pill" that would cause people to vote against the entire proposal. Now the important section 703 (a) about employment said that it was unlawful for an employer to "fail or refuse to hire or to discharge any individual, or otherwise to discriminate against any individual with respect to his compensation, terms, conditions or privileges of employment, because of such individual's race, color, religion, sex, or national origin." This section would be marked as Title VII, and that title was destined to be the federal hammer for women as well as black people in disputes about hiring, firing, promotion, and other job-place issues.[25]

---

[24] John 2:25, KJV; Caro, *Means of Ascent*, xvi, 125; Clark, "Sexual Harassment."

[25] PL 88: 352, NARA General Records, 2 July 1964, Identifier 299891; Clark, "Sexual Harassment."

The self styled feminist attorney Martha Wright Griffiths, congresswoman from Michigan's 17th District, took Judge Smith at his literal word and led a successful effort to include *sex* (later it would be called *gender*) in the final bill. The ironies and comedies available in politics were rich indeed, for Congressman Smith's "poison pill" became an integral part of a truly progressive piece of civil rights legislation, and Judge Smith subsequently took credit for incorporating important provisions in honor of activist Alice Paul. As the Bible-reading Congressman Dorn had to note, with all this discussion about intent and effect, only Our Lord and Savior could know what was in *Judge Smith's heart*. All that Congressman Dorn knew in his own heart was that LBJ and a newly energized Democratic Party were certainly turning his Third District world upside down. Bryan Dorn wrote to constituents that black people and women deserved "equal protection" but that the Civil Rights Act of 1964 was a "really bad" law that usurped states' prerogatives.[26]

In light of President Johnson's vigorous and activist push for civil rights, it seemed obvious that a confrontation with Congressman Dorn was bound to happen. The tactic of ignoring Lyndon Johnson and working instead with Bobby Baker or Larry O'Brien seemed unlikely to endure. "Everyone knew"—or at least William Jennings Bryan Dorn knew—that the president would eventually give the congressman "the treatment." This was the dreaded "laying on of hands," in which the six-foot-four intimidator with the probing eyes took one by the lapels and leaned in close and offered help, all the while implying threats that were powerfully suggested by the sheer physical force of the "treatment."

The Third District congressman's moment came in August, and it was much as advertised. LBJ made no bones about the fact that Dorn needed him a lot more than he needed Dorn. "I will and can do more for you," Johnson said in the moment of laying on hands and leaning in close, "than Charlie Halleck" (minority leader from Indiana who often voted with Dorn on social issues and who rolled logs with him on pocketbook issues such as waterways and military bases).[27]

---

[26] Clark, "Sexual Harassment"; "two really bad Civil Rights bills" example, retrospective, WJBD to F. G. Scurry, 29 April 1966, WJBD/SCPC; George, *Martha W. Griffiths*; Dierenfeld, *Keeper of the Rules*; Brauer, "Women, Activists, Southern Congressmen, and...Title VII," 37, 50, 55–56; "Martha Wright Griffith" and "Howard Worth Smith," *Biographical Directory of US Congress*, s.v.

[27] WJBD, Memorandum to files, plural copies, 12 August 1964, WJBD/SCPC; Caro, *The Years of Lyndon Johnson*, 3 vols., especially photographs of "the treatment."

With the Democratic convention and the Republican convention both approaching in August, and with no question that LBJ was to face Barry Goldwater, the president stepped up the pressure for his Great Society legislation, with particular emphasis on the War on Poverty. He also sent more troops into Vietnam and publicly advocated and executed a more aggressive foreign policy in Southeast Asia, though insisting he would be more responsible than Goldwater and would never use nuclear weapons in the conflict. On most of these things, Dorn agreed, as a militant Cold Warrior who wanted victory in South Vietnam and a Populistic New Dealer who wanted South Carolinians to get federal funds for roads and dams, federal help for schoolteachers, and increases in veterans' benefits as well as increases in Social Security payments.[28]

However, his friend Dr. Thomas Parker of Greenville made it clear that the AMA would work hard against any congressman who supported Medicare—and Dr. Parker was now the sitting national president of the American Society of Physicians and Surgeons as well as a loud member of the AMA bloc. Thus, Dorn worked with powerful Ways and Means chairman Wilbur J. Mills to "decouple" Medicare from the Social Security improvement bill, so that Dorn and others could vote "aye" for improving Social Security coverage while voting "nay" on Medicare. And although Dorn was angling for some help for his district in the omnibus Appalachian programs, he was not voting for the War on Poverty as such. Too, he had reached his limits on what he could support for civil rights legislation and was trying hard not to talk about the Civil Rights Bill, which he had voted against, or the forthcoming Voting Rights Bill, which he opposed. This was exactly his successful strategy with Jack Kennedy, and Dorn hoped it could work as well with Lyndon Johnson.[29]

In reality, it was *not* working. Dorn learned so on 5 August as congressmen gathered for picture-taking day before the last big votes prior to adjournment for the Democratic National Convention in Atlantic City, New Jersey. House Speaker John McCormack asked to meet with him at 2:00 P.M. that day, and his tone in asking was troubling. Lately, McCor-

---

[28] On "safety net": WJBD to Douglas A. Baumgardner, 30 March 1961, Jessie E. Morris to WJBD, 19 April 1966, and staff compilation of WJBD votes on Social Security issues and VA pension issues, Oliver Meadow to WJBD, 23 May 1966, WJBD/SCPC.

[29] WJBD to Thomas Parker, 7 August and 10 August 1968; staff compilation of WJBD votes on Social Security issues and VA pension issues, Oliver Meadow to WJBD, 23 May 1966, WJBD/SCPC.

mack had been behaving very differently from his old days when he was majority leader and Sam Rayburn's sidekick. All Southern congressmen knew that the Johnson team was pushing hard on the entire War on Poverty, intending to run on it as a major plank in the party platform. As he had confided to retired Kansas congressman Wint Smith, Dorn noted that "we are being outvoted on every Conservative issue due to a lot of pressure on those who can be pressured." When he approached the Speaker in his lobby, Dorn knew there would be a discussion about the War on Poverty, or, as he called it, the poverty bill. And the old boxer intended to show that he was decidedly *not* among "those who [could] be pressured."[30]

Even so, McCormack was still the man who had been so charmed by Nana on a recent visit to the capital, and he always behaved as one who seemed genuinely fond of Dorn. He was still the man whose "fine cigars" Dorn "loved to smell." Dorn recorded that McCormack "called me to one side and we met alone on one of the window seats in the Speaker's Lobby." Dorn was not surprised that McCormack was counting votes on the poverty bill and wanted his vote. McCormack was hardly surprised when Dorn said he would vote against the it. "I was rather shocked," Dorn recorded, "when he suggested that I have business out of town and not vote on the poverty bill rather than vote against the bill...he said just don't be here...be missing" [Dorn's ellipses]. Given Dorn's pride in faithful attendance at major votes and his anger with congressmen who missed such votes, he was less shocked by strong-arm tactics (Sam Rayburn had been a lot scarier in confrontations in his dank basement Board of Education) than by the mere suggestion of deliberately missing a vote. Although burning with anger at the idea of running from a fight by hiding, Dorn kept his cool, politely declined, and went back to his offices—the ones in the expensive new building named for McCormack's predecessor, Sam Rayburn.[31]

After the picture-taking session concluded about 6:30 P.M., Dorn was called over for a personal conference in private with Lyndon Johnson. In rather legalistic fashion, he carefully listened to everything and then wrote it all down in a signed and stamped memorandum in his offices. "The President said to the Congressman at about 6:30 P.M. that the poverty bill was his bill and meant much to him personally. Said that his prestige was at stake

---

[30] WJBD to Wint Smith, 24 July 1964; WJBD, Memorandum to Files, 12 August 1964, WJBD/SCPC.

[31] WJBD, Memorandum to files, 12 August 1964; interview: Dorn with Joseph Wide, n.d. (late 1970s, transcribed, 1993), WJBD/SCPC.

not only in the country but throughout the world as he was in the midst of the Viet Nam crisis. He said it would be a terrible blow to him world-wide if his own bill was rejected by the House at the height of the Viet Nam crisis." Again, the president noted his personal dislike for Congressman Halleck and declared that this Congress would not "rub his nose in the dirt before Charlie Halleck." Johnson added with emphasis "that I had a choice between him and Halleck. Then he made the startling suggestion that if I couldn't vote for his Poverty Bill just don't vote at all—get lost or have a speech somewhere...just be absent." There it was *again*, the "startling suggestion" that he run away from the conflict as if he were afraid—or worse, as if he did not care. LBJ was uninterested in the way that Bryan Dorn had repeatedly made attendance and transparent voting a matter of personal honor as well as a matter of practical politics.[32]

Dorn took his leave, politely but stiffly, and stewed over the pressure tactics for a full week. He attended the roll call vote and voted against the poverty bill as he had planned. It passed handily, by a vote of 286 to 184, with plenty of Southern Democrat and Northern Republican support. On the week's anniversary of the confrontations, he formally dictated his memorandum to Mack Fleming. At that moment, despite impending new duties (with LBJ himself) for the Clemson man, Dorn trusted Rock Fleming much more than he did Bill Beacham or "the girls." The reserve officer, now holder of the JD from American University, recorded things as if taking an affidavit, with Dorn speaking of himself in third person as congressman, and the two of them carefully recording the time of day for the document, 5:30 P.M. on Wednesday, 12 August 1964. The two placed a copy in the Rayburn congressional offices, formally sent a copy to Millie Dorn, and placed another copy in the Greenwood congressional offices in the Federal Building back home. He and Fleming carefully noted that there were copies and where those copies were. Both men wanted these notes saved for posterity. Both men knew that LBJ pressure could surely get a lot more intense than what they recorded in this one instant. Fleming did not then reveal how deeply sympathetic he was to LBJ on the principle of the legislation, and not just because of his evolving relationship with the president.[33]

---

[32] WJBD, Memorandum to files, 12 August 1964; on attendance, WJBD to Thomas Parker, 7 August 1964, WJBD, SCPC.

[33] WJBD to Thomas Parker, 10 August 1964; WJBD, Memorandum to files, 12 August 1964, WJBD/SCPC.

The congressman's struggles in the summer of 1964 are interesting, the more so because he so carefully preserved records of those struggles. The records show that he discovered himself, in the end, to be "one of those who can be pressured." He joined the LBJ team, campaigning vigorously (the only way he knew how to campaign in that day) and campaigning also for the Great Society legislation, especially those aspects concerned with the dramatically expanded "safety net," and also with veterans' rights, waterways and the interstate highway system, and federal aid to education. The Third District, only the northwestern Blue Ridge of which could be called Appalachian, became completely Appalachian for purposes of significant federal funding for all manner of things. Despite his vote against the poverty bill, the War on Poverty was waged in Dorn's district since he supported President Johnson and the Great Society. Because he was now soldiering in the War on Poverty, his vote against the poverty bill was forgiven, if not forgotten. Also, he was forgiven the vote against the Civil Rights Bill, and he was allowed to resist on constitutional grounds the much more important legislation, the forthcoming Voting Rights Bill. However, and most tellingly, he was expected to live with the reality of the Voting Rights Act once it passed; that is, Dorn was expected to seek black votes in the 1966 campaign and those campaigns coming thereafter. The greatest change was the most inevitable: Bobby Baker and Larry O'Brien remained important conduits, for he was no more part of LBJ's inner circle than he had been part of JFK's inner circle. But for any number of things, he was to come straight to the president, and he must be prepared for the president to come straight to him on certain occasions. With LBJ, you got it all, not only the "treatment," but a very complicated and quite egoistic friend who took personal interest in what you were "up to."[34]

The presidential election that fall not only was a stomping, but one that isolated the Deep South states and Goldwater's own Arizona. Johnson-Humphrey garnered 486 electoral votes in forty-four states and rolled up more than 42 million popular votes. Goldwater-Miller, by contrast, gained 52 electoral votes from only six states and attracted some 27 million popular votes. In terms of its lopsidedness, all data put the race in the top six in all

[34] W. Henry Cone to WJBD, 25 November 1964; LBJ to WJBD, 14 April 1965; retrospective: WJBD to Wellaman Johnson, 10 September 1966; WJBD to Roger Milliken, 2 September 1966; WJBD to Walter Harper, 2 May 1966; correspondence with Leon Lowenstein, especially WJBD to Lowenstein, 26 May 1966; on "Negro" constituents, Lura Self to WJBD, 8 April 1966, WJBD/SCPC.

categories (popular vote, electoral vote, number of states carried, percent of vote) among presidential races. In South Carolina, very few white people voted for LBJ, especially in the Third District, where folk showed the ability to split their ticket. Bryan Dorn hastened to send President and Mrs. Johnson a telegram: "Your victory was greatest in the history of the United States. Mrs. Dorn joins me in congratulations and best wishes always. We are proud of you and your magnificent family." The way he included the wives and the families made the whole thing more Southern and more personal. Calling it "the greatest in the history of the United States" was incorrect with regard to statistics, but certainly acceptable in terms of the congressman's dutiful compliment to the egoist at the moment of triumph. The Dorn family received back warm thanks for their own part in the campaign as well as eager pledges of support to work together for a Great Society, to include the mill villages of Third District red hills.[35]

Tangible things happened at once with regard to the coalition of textile interests, now openly calling itself the Informal Textile Group. Leon Lowenstein made clear his own delight in these election results, and also made clear his own expectations of protection against foreign competition in textiles. Somewhat surprisingly, Hubert Aull, now retired from Clemson and serving Mac McEachern's South Carolina National Bank (SCN) as a paid consulting economist, agreed to join LBJ's National Advisory Committee for Southern Regional Manpower Development and Training. It was a whopper of a title that promised whopping Great Society benefits for red-hills employment. Doc Aull, always heretofore proud of being nonpartisan (though obviously intensely engaged in political discussions across party lines) was given to understand by no less than McEachern himself that joining the National Advisory Committee was encouraged by the full Informal Textile Group—and *expected* by his new employer, SCN Bank.[36]

With regard to the coming debate and roll call vote on voting rights, Bryan Dorn enjoyed LBJ's tacit permission to "vote ag'in'" because of constitutional scruples. The final vote was set for 9 July 1966, safely after Mayor Tucker was banished in the primary and safely after the time that Strom Thurmond and others gave up the idea of finding someone to register and run as Republican in the following November for Third District congress-

---

[35] Tom Wicker, "Johnson Swamps Goldwater," *New York Times Special Edition,* 4 November 1964, 1; WJBD to the President, n.d. (3 November 1964), telegram; LBJ to Congressman Dorn, 3 November 1964, WJBD/SCPC.

[36] GHA to W. W. McEachern, 9 December 1964, GHA/SC/CU.

man. John McCormack sent everyone the word: the Voting Rights Bills would win by a stomping majority, and Southerners could speak and vote as they liked on the occasion without affecting the outcome. So informed, the speechifying by the Southern congressmen became long and frankly tedious, and on this occasion Bryan Dorn, usually a fine speaker, was also long and frankly tedious.[37]

His most memorable misconduct concerned McCormick County, the heavily black and still largely unindustrialized land of ancestors and relatives—and a place where he owned timberland. The county had a "reading requirement," which meant that aspirant voters had to read a selected part of the Constitution and explain what it meant to the voting registrar. Dorn noted that the registrar was authorized to read aloud the section of his choice to the aspirant registrants who were illiterate—and many of both races in the county were reading at no more than the fourth grade level. As statistics redundantly showed, white people (even those who were functionally illiterate) passed the test on reading the Constitution, and black citizens (even those few with college degrees) *did not.* The University of South Carolina's political science scholar Donald Lionel Fowler talked often about this with Democratic leaders, especially Bryan Dorn, and he published a book showing that McCormick County had almost no black people voting despite their preponderance in the population; indeed, it was more black than white and the seventh blackest county in the state. Fowler wrote in a study, "In areas of high percent of Negro population, the racial factor dominated the voting behavior of the whites." That is, the McCormick whites voted in self-consciously racist fashion responding to racist appeals, while the black majority generally could not vote at all.[38]

With a straight face and squared shoulders, Congressman Dorn insisted that it was a matter "not of race but of reading." Yet he also said that he was concerned that black would "not vote," but instead "be voted" by nefarious interests. In this same period, he noted to friends his dismay that his friend Secretary of State Dean Rusk, a native Georgian, had given his blonde daughter's hand in marriage to a black man, and he also noted that a

---

[37] Remarks, *Congressional Record*, vol. 111, pt. 12, 89th Cong., 1st sess., 9 July 1966, 16260–86; Fowler, *Presidential Voting in South Carolina*, 122; Fowler to WJBD, retrospective, presentation of *Presidential Voting* book, 20 November 1967 and 4 December 1967, WJBD/SCPC.

[38] WJBD remarks, *Congressional Record*, vol. 111, pt. 12, 89th Cong., 1st sess., July 9, 1966, 16268–70; Fowler to WJBD, retrospective, WJBD/SCPC.

black female graduate of the University of Georgia had married a white boy from a "good family in South Georgia." In thinking about these things, this racial mixing that dominated the correspondence of his constituents, he showed in private correspondence that he was as upset by miscegenation as was any other white racist, regardless of the "growth and advancement" that his minister and others saw in him on the racial issue. In fact, as he spoke, he had in mind the "neophyte" voting by the first black people who had voted in South Carolina between 1868 and 1898. This period he characterized as a time of decline and despair for the "beloved Southland," and he worried aloud on the floor and in his private correspondence that voting by large numbers of black voters—those who lacked the intelligence to vote, but would instead "be voted"—would produce much more miscegenation. For his congressional audience, he emphasized again: "There is a vast difference between voting and being voted."[39]

The votes came in as John McCormack had counted them, Voting Rights became law, and now Bryan Dorn had to fulfill his part of the pledge: now, he had to *live with* and *work with* the reality of black people voting. Besides fulfilling his part of the bargain in this surrender, Dorn was fulfilling what even his cousin Strom Thurmond had to fulfill: from 1966 onward, black men and women were his *voting* constituents, a qualitative change from his earlier understanding that Third District black people were his constituents and deserved services—help with veterans' benefits, help with Social Security payments, help with issues in the armed forces (all services rendered superbly by the staff led by Bill Beacham *and the girls*) because they lived there. But starting in 1966, black citizens would be allowed to vote by virtue of the awesome power of the federal government, and the remote areas of McCormick and Edgefield and Greenwood and Seneca and soon Aiken and North Augusta would feature entire wards that looked like Burnet Maybank's black wards in the rural low country beyond Charleston. In his district, black individuals comprised close to 30 percent of eligible voters, and it was quite obvious that "these neophyte voters" *fully intended to vote*, as historian Vann Woodward put it. These neophyte votes would be Democratic, for sure, but not necessarily for *any* Democrat. There was a new color scheme, and there were now no Yellow Dog Democrats, black or white.

---

[39] WJBD, remarks, loc. cit.; WJBD to Sam F. Reeder, 2 October 1967; RCE to WJBD, "The Brown Case," n.d., 1958, WJBD/SCPC.

Bryan Dorn would have to *ask* for black votes in the same personal way he sought votes from millhands and white small-time farmers and *bidness* folk.[40]

Indeed C. Vann Woodward, known to Dorn for his work for the NAACP in the hated Brown decision, (especially the initial decision rendered by Dorn's enemy Waties Waring, the jurist whose very name Dorn could not say without spitting contempt) had famously defended the "neophyte voters" among black freedmen in the period 1868 to 1898, insisting with considerable evidence that the black men had voted rationally and effectively for good government. Later, black scholars Hanes Walton Jr., Josephine A. V. Allen, Sherman C. Puckett, and Donald R. Deskins Jr. quantitatively tested Vann Woodward's "optimistic" insistence that the newly enfranchised or neophyte voters would show "maturity" and "wisdom" and would engage in virtually no corruption. Looking at the voting between 1868 and 1898, the research team found maturity, wisdom, and virtually no corruption among voters. Looking at the Burnet Maybank territory inland from Charleston after 1947, the Walton team again found maturity, wisdom, and virtually no corruption. They then predicted, as did the avowedly liberal integrationist Woodward, that black people could vote in Bryan Dorn's Third District with the same maturity, wisdom, and virtually without corruption.[41]

In seeking the votes of black constituents, then, Bryan Dorn would have to approach these neophytes not as simple and childlike and easily corruptible but rather as informed and concerned voters—and above all as people who were going to vote now that the Ku Klux Klan could not easily kill them and now that their votes could not be easily pitched out the window. While the essay by Woodward and the study by the black team may seem to state the obvious, recall that States' Rights Democrats, *to include Bryan Dorn*, had declared their profound concerns about immaturity, unwisdom, and corruption—as well as their outrage at Burnet Maybank and his black voting wards. Recall, too, that long after Bryan Dorn's death, Republican politicians in the Deep South would continue to insist that immaturity, unwisdom, and corruption were reasons to withdraw the protection of the Voting

---

[40] Phrase and concept, Woodward, *Burden of Southern History (3d rev. ed.*, 2008), 98, 99, 100.

[41] Walton Jr., Allen, Puckett, and Deskins Jr; "Woodward's New Intellectual Stream," 153–88. Cf. WJBD, "two really bad Civil Rights bills" example, retrospective, WJBD to F. G. Scurry, 29 April 1966; Negro Committee of South Carolina to WJBD, 22 June 1948, WJBD/SCPC.

Rights Act from the black folk in the six affected former Confederate states.[42]

In other words, the black scholars tested exactly those things politicians such as Bryan Dorn had said beforehand about the dangers of letting black people vote. Looking at all Deep South states, but with special focus on neighboring Georgia, Walton and his team found the black Georgia voters voted their interests intelligently and supported candidates who proffered special plans to serve those interests. They found no hint of corruption in the voting processes. Moving to data covering all the states of the former Confederacy, the Walton team found the same evidence of neophyte voters behaving just like the veteran white voters. Dorn had rejected such logic before, especially as he had read Woodward's essays and research done for and with the NAACP. But now, by his actions, Congressman Dorn conceded Woodward's point as it was reaffirmed by the team of black scholars. He would have to seek these votes. And in doing so, he would have to approach black citizens differently than before.[43]

It would redefine Bryan Dorn, because some white people would never be able to forgive him, and he would have to work hard to recalibrate his voting support, trying to make the additional black support counterbalance the loss of racist whites who could not accept the new day. For example, a white Edgefield veteran wrote to thank Bryan Dorn for help with his pension, but also declared that he "hated LBJ and your support for negroes" and would not vote for Democrats again. Some political scientists estimated that a politician in the Third District who sought black votes would need to gain more than 90 percent of the black people eligible to vote while expecting to lose at least 60 percent of the white vote. Always saying to the Drane brothers and to John Bolt Culbertson and to Dr. Bennie Mays and even Modjeska Simkins that he supported full civil rights *in the long run*, he now had to face the fact that the long run was, in fact, completed. *The day was here*. Those folk called on him at once to stand up and be counted. He immediately went

---

[42] Walton Jr., et al., "Woodward's New Intellectual Stream," 153–88. Interview, James Burrows Edwards (9 August 2011), JHR/SCPC; WJBD, remarks, Voting Rights, *Congressional Record*, vol. 111, pt.12, 89th Cong., 1st sess., 9 July 1966, 16268–70; Roper, "Voting Rights Act"; interviews: staffers, Justice Department (1983), JHR/SHC.

[43] Walton et al., "Woodward's New Intellectual Stream," 172–76; 185; Roper, *C. Vann Woodward* ,193–200 ; Roper, *The Magnificent Mays*, 245–46; retrospective, James O. Sheppard Sr. to WJBD, 6 May 1966, WJBD/SCPC.

to work. Some journalists called him "the New Bryan Dorn," and he accepted the sobriquet, especially in the memoirs he was working on.[44]

There was a request that black Pennsylvania congressman Robert Nix, a graduate of South Carolina State College, receive an honorary degree and more substantively, that Nix's son Robert Nix Jr. become a district judge. Dorn worked to get the honorary degree for Nix *pere*, and he worked with Attorney General Nicholas Katzenbach for the district judgeship for Nix *fils*. He worked as hard, and as effectively, for the black Robert Nix Jr. as he had for his white colleague Robert Hemphill. Yet there was still more. It meant not just praising Bennie Mays as a great man from Greenwood, but actually *conferring* with the Morehouse College president on issues that included voting rights and opportunities for education and housing. However late a start Dorn got in being a man who worked on behalf of black constituents, he became quite good at it once he started. The Bennie Mays family was so grateful for the congressman's hard work that he was selected as one of the pallbearers for his black friend's funeral. Most gratifying was a letter from his longtime religious counselor, the Rev. James Bowers of the hometown Greenwood Baptist Church. Speaking specifically to issues of race, the Reverend Bowers thanked God for "your progress and inner growth." The praise from family friend and counselor was echoed by an Episcopal priest in North Augusta who barely knew the congressman but who thanked Dorn for "improv[ing] the image of Democrats" in the district.[45]

All of this "new" approach to race relations was important for the well-being of the congressman and for the well-being of his Third District. Given the large numbers of black men and women voting in statewide elections, such things were no less important for the long dreamed-of runs for governor and then US senator.

---

[44] Correspondence, WJBD with Drane, 1945, 1946, 1963, especially W. Bryan Drane to WJBD, 6 May 1963 (retrospective) and WJBD to Drane, 13 May 1963 (retrospective), WJBD/SCPC; Roper, *The Magnificent Mays*, 245–46; Herbert Hartsook, remarks, "The Art of Political Biography," 22 January 2013; WJBD, *OTP*, ch. 7, especially 190.

[45] WJBD to Nicholas de B. Katzenbach, 26 July 1966; the Rev. N. C. Nix Sr. to WJBD, 22 July 1966; the Rev. James A. Bowers to WJBD, retrospective, 21 November 1966, and Fr. David Corbin Streett to WJBD, retrospective, 9 November 1966, WJBD/SCPC.

Any plans for the US Senate became moot the following April. Bryan Dorn and everyone else with ambitions knew that Strom Thurmond was safely in the Senate for as long as he wanted (which turned out to be until 2003, long after his one hundredth birthday). It was Olin Johnston who seemed likely to vacate his seat due to a protracted fight with a slowly growing cancer. Yet few, certainly not Dorn, were prepared for Senator Johnston's very sudden death on 18 April 1965. One who was prepared was Governor Donald Russell. Russell conferred with Lieutenant Governor Robert Evander McNair and arranged a clever deal: Russell would resign as the governor, McNair would succeed him, and then the new governor would appoint the former governor to the Senate vacancy. Donald Russell would serve in the US Senate for a few months and *then* run for the full six-year term in 1966 as a "seasoned incumbent." But all of this reckoned without the irrepressible and equally ambitious Ernest Frederick Hollings, who had so skillfully managed much of the peaceful integration of Clemson College (albeit an integration actually concluded by the equally skillful management of Governor Donald Russell). Too, the handsome Charlestonian with the classic features had demonstrated acumen in luring high-wage industries to the Palmetto State, and that work was remembered fondly by those who hoped to diversify as well as grow the economy.[46]

Hollings knew that the South Carolina public (or publics) would dislike Russell's seemingly clever little ploy—especially if reminded constantly about it by Hollings. He discreetly consulted many, including the shrewd Hubert Aull, on the issues and the approaches and then announced his candidacy for 1966. In doing so, he pointed to two things, the first positive, the second negative. First, he touted his progressive record as the governor, especially for racial harmony and for economic growth. But second, he hammered the negative, that is, the "political self-appointment" that his successor Russell had committed. Hollings won the Democratic primary handily, survived a close race with the Republican Marshall Parker of Greenwood, and then became a successful US senator, in his progressive way as invincible as Strom Thurmond was in his traditionalist way. While this series of events was unfolding, Bryan Dorn was forced to stay on the sidelines of the Senate race. The congressman had to salute Hollings's political acumen, had to

[46] Bass and DeVries, *Transformation*, 261; Bass, *Ol' Strom*, 221–22 ; Ballantyne, *New Politics in the Old South,* 60–63; Hollings to GHA, 17 February 1966, GHA/SC/CU.

wonder at Russell's political miscalculations, and in any case had to give up on ever running for either South Carolina seat in the US Senate.[47]

Once fully committed to the Great Society, now to include support for civil rights legislation and support for black voters in McCormick and Edgefield counties, Bryan Dorn was unopposed for the 1966 primary, but the November general election would feature serious Republican opposition. Cousin Thurmond persuaded John T. "Bud" Grisso of the selfsame red hills to run as a Republican for Dorn's seat, and Thurmond's many admirers and allies provided the money for the campaign, although fundraising in those days for congressional districts only ran into the thousands and not the millions of dollars. Now LBJ's help really was needed, and it was assuredly true that the president could do more for him than Charlie Halleck. The stream of Great Society grants to local communities was stepped up, with Larry O'Brien and Bobby Baker and the president himself making sure that Congressman Dorn received maximum credit and publicity over each grant, whether a half-million dollars for Clemson University or a new post office building in Calhoun Falls or a few thousand dollars for a planning grant in Walhalla.

For all that, Bryan Dorn was frankly scared. He confided in longtime House colleague L. Mendel Rivers, and Rivers returned favors long due from past campaigns of his own. Rivers wrote to the classes, especially Jim Self Jr., C. Douglas Wilson, Robert Stevens, and Roger Milliken and told them that Bryan Dorn *needed them* to get out the vote among the masses; that is, those loyal millworkers needed to be reminded to vote in the November general election rather than in the accustomed summertime primary elections. The classes immediately swung into action, working with WSPA and WFBC radio and television broadcasting stations and with the *Greenville News* and the *Columbia State*. Every good thing Bryan Dorn did received maximum coverage, and commentators reminded listeners and readers of the "threat" posed by Bud Grisso (that is, the threat of the loss of congressional patronage for the district).[48]

---

[47] Bass and DeVries, *Transformation*, 261; Ballantyne, *New Politics in the Old South,* 64–68; Jordan, "1966," *The Primary State*, s.v.; Hollings to GHA, 17 February 1966, GHA/SC/CU.

[48] Correspondence, Walter Brown, B. H. Peace, Wayne Freeman, W. D. Workman, October to November 1966; L. Mendel Rivers to TEXTILE MAN (form letter) and to WJBD, 22 October 1966; Mrs. L. P. Jones to WJBD, 9 April 1966; John W. Glenn to WJBD, 22 April 1966; WJBD to RCE, retrospective, 1 July 1967; and espe-

One thing Dorn was doing, however, could not be publicized in its fullness. As noted, the long-running Savannah River projects—since 1952 there had been more than eleven proposed federal hydroelectric dams with lakes and the Duke steam plant and the Mead paper mill—were not only competing for the waterways, but were literally bumping into each other as legislative proposals. In the late summer, Dorn entered into the most complicated, vexing, but also most hopeful set of negotiations about the same sites on the Savannah River since 1952. To review, both Mead and Duke private enterprises were unwilling to build dams and sites if a number of federal projects flooded some potential sites and also altered the speed and volume of the river's flow sufficiently to interfere with the needs of a hydroelectric plant, a nuclear generator, and a paper manufacturer. For that reason, Dorn had gotten himself appointed to the Public Works Committee to block the long-proposed federal project at Trotters Shoals and to work for approval of the Duke and Mead proposals at Middleton Shoals. At the same time, the electrical cooperatives of North Carolina and Georgia were opposed to Duke Power generating and selling electricity in the upper valley of the Savannah River. After much discussion, the South Carolina electrical cooperative had withdrawn its opposition to Duke, but the much larger and politically better-heeled North Carolina and Georgia cooperatives remained in opposition. For Dorn, there was always and in all cases room for compromise, and nowhere more so than here. Yet, in order to negotiate the concessions between each party, he needed to conduct discussions away from the glare of public scrutiny during the middle of a general election, especially since the greatest demand for the Trotters Shoals federal project now came from the venerable Strom Thurmond and Bud Grisso, the new contender whom the senior senator sponsored for Dorn's district seat.[49]

On 19 July 1966, Bryan Dorn convened counsel from Duke Power, the North Carolina electrical cooperatives, and the Georgia cooperatives in his offices in the Sam Rayburn Building. The attorneys present were his own cousin, Steve Griffith, for Duke Power and Walter Harrison for the bi-state power cooperative of North Carolina and Georgia. Not attending were

---

cially WJBD to Lawrence O'Brien with specific requests for publicity, 27 August 1966; Martin D. Watkins to WJBD, 15 June 1966, WJBD/SCPC.

[49] Interview: Steve Griffith with Herb Hartsook and Roper, (25 September 2013), JHR/SCPC; WJBD, Keeowee-Toxaway Statement for the Federal Power Commission, 16 August 1966 and WJBD, "Keeoway [*sic*] Toxaway Statement," n.d., 1967, WJBD/SCPC.

counsel or lobbyists from the South Carolina electrical cooperatives, which were no longer in opposition to anything, or Mead, whose leaders were unwilling to discuss plans for a paper mill at this time. Bryan Dorn had talked and talked and had listened and listened to his cousin and with Harrison one-on-one, but he had never gotten everyone into one set of offices. Now that Harrison and Griffith were there together, he left the room briefly, returning with two press releases, both dated for that very evening. One of them stated that Duke Power had withdrawn any objections to the Trotters Shoals project and that the Bi-State Power Commission had withdrawn any objections to the steam plant at Keeowee Toxaway and to a retaining wall for a nuclear generator at Middleton Shoals. It was labeled "Positive Alternative." The other press release said that each of the contesting parties had chosen to "block progress toward cheap electricity" and thus "thwart" job creation along the Savannah River.[50]

The "Positive Alternative" was well known to each counsel in discussions alone with Congressman Dorn, but the two counsels had never revealed *to each other* a willingness to make this compromise. Bryan Dorn told the two men that he had Edgar Brown's assurance of enabling legislation from the South Carolina General Assembly and that John McCormack would work with this section of the Public Works Waterways, Rivers, and Harbors omnibus bill due out the third week of October. He also assured them that the redoubtable US Senators Strom Thurmond and Richard Russell were prepared for this compromise. In fact, the latter statement was pure speculation on the congressman's part. Finally, he said that Lyndon Johnson himself wanted this legislation and would sign it with due publicity and fanfare in November, a statement that was completely true. Like most such things, it sounds simple, and one wonders why no one got all parties into one room before 19 July 1966. Even so, it does not sound easy, and decades later one still wonders at the sheer gall of speaking on behalf of Thurmond and Russell, since each senator was publicly in favor of Trotters Shoals and opposed to the Middleton Shoals and Keeowee-Toxaway projects. At any rate, Harrison and Griffith accepted for their people. The "Positive Alternative" press release went forward.[51]

---

[50] WJBD, "Positive Alternative, 19 July 1966"; description of blocking progress, not actual release, "Keeoway [*sic*] Toxaway Statement," n.d. 1967, WJBD/SCPC.

[51] Interview: Steve Griffith with Hartsook and Roper (25 September 2013), JHR/SCPC.

Senator Richard Russell came over and was the epitome of the gracious Solon, announcing grandly that he had always wanted to hear "this very good news you all have brought us." In one of the few moments of petty behavior he permitted himself, Bryan Dorn sent cousin Steve Griffith over to give the news to Strom Thurmond, who exploded in white-hot anger, not particularly at the deal itself as at the very idea of such negotiations going on in his absence—and a mere congressman speaking for him. Steve Griffith remembers that Strom Thurmond was livid and "cussed like a sailor." But that was only in front of Griffith, himself a cousin and friend of Thurmond's. In front of other folk, Senator Thurmond was nothing if not a most adroit politician, and he quickly recovered and hurried over to shake hands all round and announce his own long-running support for exactly such a compromise.[52]

From that day, everything fell into place. On 20 October 1966, George Fallon of Maryland, chairman of the House Committee on Public Works, duly presented a full Committee's Bill for Construction, Repair, and Preservation of Certain Public Works on Rivers and Harbors for Navigation, Flood Control, and for Other Purposes. That omnibus package included a lengthy portion, Section 109, concerning Savannah River projects, one part authorizing Duke Power to develop Middleton Shoals, another authorizing Duke Power to develop Keowee Toxaway and to seek Atomic Energy Commission permission to build a nuclear reactor, and a third authorizing federal funds for the Trotters Shoals dam, lake, and hydroelectric plant first dreamed of by the late Olin Johnston. Representative Fallon's bill passed, was reconciled with a related US senate bill enthusiastically supported by Richard Russell and Strom Thurmond, and Lyndon Johnson signed Public Law 89-789 that selfsame November. Among many other things, the omnibus bill took away Bud Grisso's most telling critique, namely, that Congressman Dorn was preventing the popular Trotters Shoals projects from happening. In later years, both Thurmond and Russell would have dams and lakes named for them in the area, as was fully appropriate. Eventually there would be a bridge named for Bryan Dorn, but it has been quite clear that he did not *want* anything named for him. Instead, he wanted "a billion dollars" for his red hills (his estimate, possibly low, of the money Duke Power spent in the area on its projects) and he wanted the votes. Far from being modest, this consummate congressional politician considered that he had gotten eve-

---

[52] Ibid. Cf. "Keeoway [*sic*] Toxaway Statement," n.d. 1967, which omits the Thurmond and Russell episodes, WJBD/SCPC.

rything he could possibly ask for—and exactly on time for the general election.[53]

Otherwise, Bryan Dorn campaigned as if he were again the outsider, as he had been in 1950. He even absented himself often from DC, although he was careful never to miss a roll call vote, and of course he was always present for Committee on Public Works discussions about the Savannah River or about interstate highways. In this season, many congressmen were up for election in contests that looked hot and contentious, especially in the South, with its rapidly growing Republican Party. Accordingly, John McCormack and the Republican minority leader, Gerald Ford, arranged to bring House sessions to an end in late October (conveniently *after* Fallon's omnibus waterways bill was approved) so that all representatives could have maximum time for campaigning back home. Dorn conducted barbeques as before, but more of them—having commenced in late spring, he continued hosting in the "old Virginia way" on into November itself. He hosted district postmasters for a memorable occasion at Barratt House in mid-June, and his Labor Day session featured as much music and speechifying and handshaking as if Dada were still on the scene.[54]

The classes also sponsored barbeque rallies in each mill village, and Mayor John Glenn of Anderson said what many local officials were saying: "You can rest assured that the people of Anderson will be informed." He worked with veterans groups—Disabled American Veterans, the American Legion, the VFW, and those less formally organized—and Tiger Teague sent out a flyer reminding all veterans what a particular Army Air Corps veteran had done for them in 1966, reminding them that their congressman was now number two in seniority on the VA committee and was also the chair of the vital pensions subcommittee. Teachers, ever the darlings of the

---

[53] WJBD, "Keeoway [*sic*] Toxaway" Statement, n.d., 1967; Edgar Arthur Brown to WJBD, 25 July 1966, WJBD/SCPC. PL 89-789 signed, *Congressional Record*, vol. 112, 89th Cong., 2d sess., 7 November 1966, 28902; discussions, loc. cit., 20 October 1966, 28181–901.

[54] WJBD to A. P. Brown (timber), 20 May 1966; Alex M. Quattlebaum (building contractors and carpenters) to WJBD, 15 June 1966; Richard H. Lange (municipal bonds trader) to WJBD, 20 May 1966; WJBD to Constituents (personalized template) for barbeque, 18 May 1966; WJBD to (individualized constituents; form letter), 18 October 1966 barbeque, WJBD/SCPC; Sydnor, *Gentlemen Freeholders*.

Dorn family, were courted, and librarians received local funding, state funding, and federal funding as well as special attention.[55]

Always one to walk great distances, especially when fueled by nervous energy, Bryan Dorn went all over the district, parked his Plymouth, and walked around shaking hands. His white suits, always resplendent, were so impressive that fellow Congressmen L. H. Fountain and Wayne Hays inquired where he was buying them—and Bob Stevens of J. P. Stevens ordered up a supply of special dress shirts, all with the right-sized neck, 18 inches, the right sleeve longer than the left, and of course all prominently made in the red hills plants. When the votes were counted, Bud Grisso had been routed despite Strom Thurmond's help. In fact, Bryan Dorn won nearly two-thirds of the voters, both in his traditional wards and in the new ones added for Aiken County. Anderson attorney Charles Wellborn spoke for many when he announced, "I do not desert the party because of some position of the National [Democratic] Party," namely civil rights. Indeed, Wellborn went on to add that his representative was "the moderate, reasonable minded man who recognizes that we all have a new day facing us, calling for men of some tolerance and wisdom along with a bit of humor." And Lura Self, matriarch of the most important mill family in Greenwood, sent a note that she and her son Jim Jr. (heir to the Greenwood mills) "were urging Negroes to remember their friend Bryan Dorn." With the "neophyte voters," however, the white classes likely were less important than Bryan Dorn himself. He visited influential ministers and kept himself on the friendly side of civil rights leaders Bennie Mays, Modjeska Simpkins, Maceo Nance, and members of the Nix family (who, it will be recalled, "owed" him at least one favor).[56]

---

[55] WJBD to Thomas G. Morris (DAV), 16 June 1966; Walter Brown to WJBD, 2 September 1966; Estell P. Walker (State Library Board) to WJBD, 17 May 1966; WJBD to George H. Mahan (Teague statistics on VA), 30 April 1966; WJBD to J. W. Dellastatious (Teacher Education Deductions), 27 August 1966; Oliver Meadows (Teague secretary) to District Voters re WJBD, 23 May 1966; WJBD to Wellaman Johnson (Abney Mills), 10 September 1966; WJBD to Roger Milliken, list attached, 2 September 1966; Robert T. Stevens to Rivers, 31 October 1966; WJBD to Constituents, 18 May 1966; Rivers to WJBD (list of supporters), 27 October 1966, WJBD/SCPC.

[56] Supplemental Report of the Secretary of State to the General Assembly of South Carolina, Reports and Resolutions of South Carolina to the General Assembly of the State of South Carolina. Vol. 2, ed. Watson (Columbia, SC: R. L. Bryan, 1967), 17. RCE to WJBD, 12 April 1966; Charles Welborn to WJBD, 8 April 1966; Lura Self to WJBD, 8 April 1966; WJBD to Helen Ludwig (Aiken County), 8 August 1966; L. H. Fountain to WJBD, 31 July 1968 and Wayne Hays to WJBD, 23 July 1968 (M. Stein &

Back in his offices, Bryan Dorn put up new pictures of Lyndon Johnson and of Vice President Hubert Humphrey posed with him. To drive home the point about his Great Society bona fides, he also displayed a signed picture of Sargent Shriver, director of the Office of Economic Opportunity. He sent Strom Thurmond sincere congratulations on his own victory over Greenville Democrat Bradley Morrah, whom Dorn had supported in what he knew would be a vain effort. Indeed, Republicans had done very well in congressional races, and the Democratic majority was slimmed down considerably. His cousin Thurmond graciously accepted and as graciously congratulated Dorn, illustrating again that Thurmond would never under any circumstances make political enemies by holding grudges about campaigns, or about lawmaking legerdemain. Besides another kind note from his longtime minister, the Reverend Bowers, Dorn was pleased with a letter from Anderson's John Rouse, who opined that a new day was dawning in a New South, one to be marked by racial tolerance with Dorn himself leading "us back into the mainstream of American life." Clemson's Bob Edwards was characteristically gracious and humble, as if he himself had not had anything to do with Dorn's big victory. Surprisingly humble, at least in a letter, was none other than Lyndon Johnson himself: the president welcomed back a supporter of the Great Society—and a supporter of the great build-up of troops and bombing in Vietnam. In all the box of well-wishes, there were two letters that portended a different future: Verna Forrest of Johnston scored her congressman for being "too liberal," especially on race, and Corbett B. Anderson of Anderson wrote ominously that "'us racists and bigots' [*sic*] may completely turn the tide against you" in 1968 and thereafter.[57]

The immediate issue of contention for the powerful president and the strengthened minority of Republicans in the House of Representatives in-

---

Co., 1823 M Street NW, Washington); WJBD to Robert T. Stevens, 18 April 1966; retrospective, WJBD to Chris (Duke Power) McGuire, 17 May 1967; WJBD to City of Anderson, 4 August 1966; (Lawrence O'Brien) to All Managers (form letter personalized), 4 October 1966, WJBD/SCPC.

[57] The Rev. James Bowers to WJBD, 21 November 1966; exchange, Strom Thurmond and WJBD, 28 November 1966; LBJ to WJBD, (n.d.) November, 1966; RCE to WJBD, retrospective, n.d. (January) 1967; LBJ to WJBD, (n.d.) November, 1966; John D. Rouse to WJBD, 12 January 1967; Verna Forrest to WJBD, 30 November 1966; Corbett B. Anderson to WJBD, 10 November 1966; WJBD to Hubert Horatio Humphrey, 1 December 1967, WJBD/SCPC.

volved a proposal by LBJ for a surtax on income that was progressively skewed against higher incomes but also hitting the more prosperous range of America's large middle class. Johnson wanted the surtax because of Keynesian economics: after a long period of expansion and after employment was "full," continued deficit spending would lead to inflation, according to most economists of the day. LBJ was blunt: he intended to fight and win the war in Vietnam *and* the War on Poverty, but both were expensive, and he could not pay for both without a tax hike—unless he "paid" through demand-pull inflation that could be ruinous. Indeed, inflation had climbed from an "acceptable" 1.5 percent per year to a current 3.5 percent, with dire projections if taxes were not raised (or if government spending were not cut). The issue was a perfect rally cry for emboldened if not quite empowered Republicans: they could compel LBJ to slow down spending on Vietnam (as their liberals wanted), or they could compel LBJ to slow down spending on the War on Poverty (as their conservatives wanted). John McCormack tried to round up the votes, but it was a tough sale, especially for his own conservative Democrats, who wanted to curtail the War on Poverty, and for his own anti-war Democrats, who wanted to cut spending on Vietnam and eventually leave the conflict. Liberal Democrats in the day were evenly split, with many following Hubert Humphrey in taking a hawkish position on Vietnam and an aggressive position on antipoverty "wars." In other words, in 1967, the term liberal did not automatically signal anti-war, nor did the term conservative automatically signal pro-war. On the issues of the day, Bryan Dorn, hawkish on Vietnam, seeking black votes, and aggressive for Appalachian regional programs and other Great Society programs, was solidly in place with liberals of both parties and all regions—despite or even because the American definition of liberal was not then what it became.[58]

Whatever confusion existed about political labels inside and between the two parties was nothing compared to the personal confusion of identity visited on Bryan Dorn in the winter of 1967. Nana was failing in her health. Brother Watson and his wife, Kate Dorn, gave maximum attention to Nana, and Bryan and Millie and their children visited often. There was the wonderful counselor, the Rev. Jim Bowers. But the fact remained that the most powerful and overwhelming female figure in Bryan Dorn's life was losing the fight to the ravages of her body much as she had earlier lost the fight to dementia. On 15 March, Bryan Dorn walked away from the tempestuous de-

---

[58] Remarks and votes on surtax, *Congressional Record*, vol. 113, pt. 23, 90th Cong., 1st sess., 1–9 November 1967, 30689–2116.

bates among the factions and the personalities and went home with his family to bury Pearl Griffith Dorn. He was devastated, and it was hard on his wife, Millie, especially since he responded to his grief by plunging into the vexsome details of this complicated surtax. He intended to deal with his grief by working too hard to notice it. Ever Nana's son, Bryan did his homework on fiscal policy, and he honed his elocution for the debates and discussions back in House chambers.[59]

As usual, Dorn consulted Clemson's Hubert Aull, emeritus from the classroom but active with the classes as consultant to South Carolina National Bank. He also consulted the much more prominent figure Herbert Stein of the Brookings Institute. True to his understanding, Congressman Dorn spoke as a Keynesian in Congress, giving an almost textbook "naïve Keynesian" description of inflation and demand-pull. He said that the economy had expanded for eighty-one consecutive months and inflation had more than doubled during a time of deficit spending, with more deficit spending projected for an increasingly expensive war in Vietnam and an increasingly expensive War on Poverty. He reminded all concerned that they had enthusiastically voted for tax cuts in 1962, 1964, and 1965 because of stubbornly low employment and low rates of economic growth—votes that were true to Keynesian "stimulus" policy. Now it was time, he said, "to raise [taxes] to slow the economy to a more moderate and maintainable pace." He recommended to fellow congressmen Herbert Stein's analysis for laymen, done in the then-popular slick magazine *The Reporter* (which, like Dorn of 1967 to 1969, was hawkish on foreign policy and progressive on social policy). To be sure that fellow congressmen (and constituents among the masses and the classes) got the point, he placed Stein's essay into the *Congressional Record*.[60]

In fact, the surtax proposal was a hard one to push through despite a solid Democratic majority and despite yeomen labor by Speaker McCormack, Whip Hale Boggs, and powerful committee chairs Wilbur Mills and Wayne Hays. Opposed was an ad hoc and curious alliance of anti-war people, some who were opposed to the Great Society, and others with some

---

[59] Nancy Huffman (administrative assistant) to Ed Bryan, March 15, 1967; WJBD to Kate Dorn, retrospective, 28 April 1967, WJBD/SCPC.

[60] WJBD, remarks, *Congressional Record*, vol. 113, pt. 23, 90th Cong., 1st sess., 3 November 1967, 31091–92; and WJBD, remarks, loc. cit., 8 November 1967, 31849; Stein, "Tax Policy," *The Reporter*, November 1967, clipping, WJBD/SCPC; GHA, editorial files, 1965–1974, *Anderson Independent*, GHA/SC/CU.

personalized anger at LBJ. Some genuinely wanted to force spending cuts by denying tax revenues; others in both parties hoped to embarrass LBJ. Neither party members, nor faction members, nor even like personalities were voting in immediately recognizable blocs. At last, Senator Everett Dirksen, Republican of Illinois and a past master at such compromise, put together a proposal to cut domestic spending by $4 billion while imposing a surtax that would bring in $4 billion. Consulting with Hubert Aull, Dorn realized that the proposal, attractive as it stood, flew in the face of Keynesian policy *since it produced no surplus*. In fact, it preserved a sizable deficit in the middle of rapid and prolonged expansion of the gross domestic product. However, Democrats and Republicans across the broad middle jumped at the proposal, and McCormack gave the word to vote for it, as Dorn dutifully did. He and everyone else recorded as speaking on the floor that November missed something important in their Keynesian analysis: the Vietnam War was costing far more than the Johnson administration acknowledged, so that the deficit was bound to grow much faster than officially projected, especially with a plan that officially retained a deficit by exactly balancing new proposed taxing with new proposed spending. Dorn cast his vote in some discomfort, knowing that inflation was on the way—but considerably underestimating how severe a problem it was going to be.[61]

Nevertheless, it was not the intricacies of fiscal policy that doomed the once indestructible Lyndon Baines Johnson—and considerably "complicated up" the political life of the Third District congressman. It was instead the one thing that Bryan Dorn never saw coming: opposition to the Vietnamese War. Dorn had never paused to question the war in Southeast Asia. The Cold War was his congressional reality, anti-Communism was his trademark, and fighting the proxy Communist forces of the Russians and the Chinese was an assumed fact and a presumed duty for him. Besides the ideology of it all, he was doubly and trebly committed to militaristic Keynesianism that made the federal government the first purchaser and the prime demander of goods and services, especially textile products, related to the army and the navy. No less a neo-abolitionist liberal than Hubert Horatio Humphrey combined social progressivism with vigorous and militaristic an-

---

[61] Remarks and votes on surtax and Dirksen amended proposal, *Congressional Record*, vol. 113, pt. 23, 90th Cong., 1st sess., 1–9 November 1967, 30689–2116; Stein, "Tax Policy" clipping, WJBD/SCPC; hidden cost of Vietnamese War, GHA to WJBD, 8 February 1971 retrospective, GHA/SC/CU; Caro, *The Passage of Power*.

ti-Communism. Even the pacifist Bennie Mays from his own backyard had reluctantly supported the Korean War. That Bennie Mays, and above all Jack Kennedy's very brothers, would suddenly began protesting the war in Vietnam was beyond Dorn's immediate understanding. Indeed, some of his first and loudest speeches concerning Vietnam were essentially attacks against Republicans![62]

In January of 1968, the North Vietnamese launched the ambitious Tet Offensive, so named for the New Year holiday when infantry movements began. Forces coordinated by General Vo Nguyen Giap rolled forward, with twin movements by North Vietnamese troops marching southward and South Vietnamese Communist Vietcong attacking from inside the borders. General Giap's forces and the Vietcong pressed all the way to Saigon, briefly causing US personnel to abandon State Department and military offices. General William C. Westmoreland, who had been asking for more troops, combined his South Vietnamese troops with hundreds of thousands of US forces, and together they reversed the Tet Offensive by February 26. Westmoreland reclaimed military control, if not political support, in all of South Vietnam. The Spartanburg native told Bryan Dorn and other hawkish congressmen that the fight was like the Battle of the Bulge, that is, a dramatic recovery by US forces after an initial and bloody setback. Dorn was pleased with that analogy from his own military background, and he was pleased that LBJ was building US ground forces toward 500,000 effectives while launching massive air force strikes along the 17th parallel that marked the newly reinforced border between North and South. Indeed, Dorn was so enthusiastic about the war's progress that he took an essay written by an Easley High School junior, Martha Sue Hudgens, and published her words in the *Congressional Record.* He also proudly displayed her hand-drawn cartoon that illustrated the falling dominoes theory that he had presented to Hudgens and fellow Easley students in their high school auditorium.[63]

---

[62] Speech, Young Democrats, Wade Hampton Hotel, Columbia, 17 September 1966; Speech, Young Democrats, Lexington County, 17 September 1966; Speech and Press Release, "Moderation," Columbia Lions Club, Wade Hampton Hotel, 30 October 1967; "All Evil Cannot Be Blamed on the Federal Government," address, Annual Truckers Night, Augusta, GA, 22 May 1967; Oconee County High School Speech, n.d., March 1967, Speeches Folders, 1966–1967, WJBD/SCPC.

[63] "Tet Offensive," *New York Times,* 31 January 1988, 1, retrospective; WJBD, speech outline, n.d., 1967, Easley High School, Political Speeches, 1966–1968; WJBD to Martha Sue Hudgens, 4 April 1967; Hudgens illustration, n.d. 1967, WJBD/SCPC.

Bryan Dorn was chagrined to see that most Americans outside of his Third District regarded the Tet Offensive as a defining military *defeat* for the US, a bloody conflict that cost more than 4,000 American lives in a few weeks. Even at Clemson and the University of South Carolina, there were some students protesting the war and citing Tet as a reason for withdrawal. Officials at both universities assured Dorn that such student opinion was decidedly in the minority, and another visit to Vietnam convinced the congressman that the policy was morally right and that the strategy was doable. Despite his personal beliefs, Dorn had to acknowledge that Johnson was losing ground in the Senate and even in the relatively hawkish House. He marked it as odd more than ominous when the New Hampshire presidential primary included among the contestants Senator Eugene McCarthy, an intellectual from Minnesota with whom Dorn had often conferred concerning agricultural issues and manufacturing issues. Dorn and most Democrats and Republicans sincerely liked McCarthy but simply did not regard him as energetic or aggressive enough to be president (or even a serious contender for the office).[64]

Nor was Dorn worried when LBJ declined to register himself as a candidate in New Hampshire and thus refused to "run" in the primary, relying instead on the local operatives to work on his behalf with Larry O'Brien. These developed a special pledge card explaining how to write-in LBJ's name; it had a perforated section that could be detached and mailed to campaign headquarters in New Hampshire. That section of the pledge card said, "As an expression of your support, this card will be forwarded to President Johnson." The cards were distributed to potential voters at about the same time as the early reports of the Tet Offensive, and their label "pledge" seemed an especially ironic description since LBJ had himself "pledged" an early and successful end to the war. The cards were a "public relations disaster" as the *Manchester Union Leader* judged them, and Senator Eugene McCarthy said of them, "[It is] a Texas-style branding party" and "an intrusion into a free democratic process not altogether inconsistent with the way the Johnson administration is operating."[65]

On 12 March, the polls showed that McCarthy had scored 41.9 percent of the votes cast, when early predictions projected barely 20 percent for him. The president won this primary, gaining some 49.6 percent of votes

---

[64] WJBD to Bennett Rose, 28 February 1968, WJBD/SCPC.

[65] Retrospective from morgue, "McCarthy Stuns the President," *Manchester Union Leader*, 3 May 2011, 1.

with the pledge-card write-in, but no one considered the result a "win" for LBJ—especially since the margin of victory was only some 200 votes in the small field of participants. Since LBJ had not been officially listed on the ballot, he could not control the New Hampshire delegates to the summer convention; thus, twenty of the twenty-four delegates subsequently declared for Eugene McCarthy. Only three days later, New York senator Robert Fitzgerald Kennedy sent a telegram to every member of Congress:

> I want you to know before my public announcement that I have decided to seek the Democratic Presidential nomination. Running in harmony with Senator McCarthy, I shall campaign not in opposition to any person but in support of a new policy of hope and reconciliation at home, in Vietnam, and around the world. Fully aware of the deep divisions already present in the Party, I earnestly seek your thoughtful consideration and support.[66]

Moments after the mass telegraph was delivered, Robert Kennedy announced his candidacy in the same Senate room where his brother Jack Kennedy had made his announcement. Dorn responded formally and politely that he was "grateful for your consideration and kindness to let us know in advance." No fan of RFK, Dorn actually thought that the "deep divisions" were more caused by the New York senator than by President Johnson. Nor could he find much "hope and reconciliation" in the opposition to Johnson, whose Great Society Dorn not only supported now for his own region but celebrated for the entire nation. Thinking back to the sharp and acerbic criticism laid on Harry Truman, Bryan Dorn still considered that the attacks on LBJ had become more personalized, even obscene, and were largely undeserved. He often noted with shock a bumper sticker that he had found in Texas: "Lee Harvey Oswald, Where Are You Now That We Really Need You?" Moreover, Dorn was dismayed to see the racist edge of much anti-LBJ rhetoric, especially since he remained convinced that a new day of moderation in race relations was dawning in his region. Before he had actually digested public opinion polls that showed Americans increasingly uneasy about the war or that showed LBJ's falling poll numbers, he was quite shocked to learn that the intimidating Texan was himself intimidated, stepping down and declining to run in the next election, an announcement made on 31 March. Worse for Dorn, in that same announcement, LBJ declared a cessation of saturation bombing in Vietnam and the beginning of peace talks

[66] Ibid.; RFK to WJBD, 15 March 1968, WJBD/SCPC.

to be conducted in Paris. Dorn continued to blame Republicans for failure to support the war, and he tried to demonstrate that anti-war Democrats were not in tune or in touch with majority American opinion.[67]

Trying to recover his political balance, Dorn got in touch with Hubert Humphrey to assure the vice president of his support in the fall. He noted his close cooperation with Robert E. McNair, and said that McNair could run as a "place-holding Favorite Son" in the coming Chicago convention and then instruct delegates to vote for Humphrey. In reality, though, Humphrey could not easily enter any major primary contests at this relatively late date, and would have to employ strategies somewhat like Dorn's suggestion since he would need to gain uncommitted convention delegate votes. Ever the optimist, Humphrey had earlier assured Dorn that a rematch with Republican Bud Grisso in November was nothing to fear, because Dorn was himself "invincible" in the Third District.[68]

Yet Bryan Dorn was not feeling particularly *invincible*, especially after the abdication of the mighty intimidator Lyndon Baines Johnson, who in a few years had moved from being the congressman's nemesis and threat to being someone he pitied. His reading of Machiavelli reminded him yet again that for all a politician's machinations, it was Fortuna's sudden turning of the wheel that often made or unmade a king. He would never use the term Fortuna at a barbeque, but his people certainly understood about good and bad luck with regard to timing in football, farming, and politics. Those same people expected anyone—coach, farmer, congressman—who was victim of bad luck to get up and get back into the fight quickly.[69]

---

[67] WJBD to RFK, 4 April 1968; Tom Wicker, "Johnson Says He Won't Run," *New York Times*, 31 March 1968, 1; "Johnson Halts North Vietnam Raids; Bids Hanoi Join Peace Talks," *New York Times*, 31 March 1968, 1; WJBD, speeches: Chesterfield Young Democrats, 22 February 1966; Sertoma Club, Greenville, 22 February 1966; Wade Hampton High School, Greenville, 25 February 1966; Jefferson-Jackson Day, Raleigh, NC, 26 February 1966; Oconee County High School, n.d., March 1967; "All Evil Cannot Be Blamed on the Federal Government," Augusta Traffic Club, Annual Truckers Night, 21 May 1967; Oswald decal, John M. Bailey to WJBD, 11 August 1967, WJBD/SCPC.

[68] WJBD to Hubert Horatio Humphrey, n.d. (April) 1968; H. H. H. to WJBD, 31 December 1967, WJBD/SCPC.

[69] Machiavelli, *The Prince* (2007 trans.), ed. and trans., Constantine, ch. 9; ch. 33; see Benner, *Be Like the Fox*, especially 285–88.

Chapter 10

After LBJ
1968–1973

The dynasties were over. Perhaps they never really existed, but in the chaotic months between mid-March 1968 and the inauguration of Richard Milhous Nixon, Bryan Dorn became convinced that there would be no more FDRs in the White House, no more Edgar Browns in the South Carolina Senate, no more Sol Blatts in the South Carolina House. There would be no more Sam Rayburns in the US House, and no more Tiger Teagues, or any other long-lived tigers, running the congressional committees.[1] And the place of longevity and prestige, the US Senate, was now forever closed to him. As powerful, effective, and often unprincipled as Lyndon Johnson had been, he had become president through the oddest of circumstances, had mastered all he surveyed for a season, but finally had established no dynasty and then, too, was gone—remembered more for tales of his excesses than for his substantive accomplishments. The period after LBJ marked a new phase in US and in South Carolina political life, at least as far as William Jennings Bryan Dorn understood it.

This new phase of rapidly shifting social coalitions, ad hoc alliances among partisan factions, and temporarily coalesced business interests, all emphasizing compromise and close study and adroit adjustments, was actually quite well suited to Bryan Dorn's temperament. He was, in many ways, the ideal congressman for the new realities. It was indeed *After LBJ*, but perhaps more so it was a belated understanding that this epoch was *After FDR*. Lyndon Johnson was simply the most prominent and most colorful of those attempting to build his own dynasty in the model of the departed Roosevelt. In this final phase of his office-holding career, William Jennings Bryan Dorn would demonstrate the most remarkable skills in getting things done for the people in his red hills. Yet he would lunge for the governorship, a

---

[1] Longevity and committees: WJBD, *OTP*, 234–38; WJBD, address, n.p., outline and notes, 4 December 1967, Speeches Folder; Robert M. Vance to WJBD, 7 December 1967; interview: WJBD with Joe Wider, n.d. (transcribed, 1993), WJBD/SCPC..

position that in South Carolina was constitutionally designed to allow a person to do remarkably little *other than* preach and teach from a bully pulpit. Only partly recognizing his own genius for one sphere of politics, he exhausted political and moral energies attempting to gain office in another sphere where little practicable could be accomplished. Too, he overestimated his own talents for preaching and teaching from the bully pulpit. For all his rapid growth in terms of understanding civil rights, he was, more than any other man in this era, the *progressive manqué*, one among many who too late saw that the old abolitionist "arc of the moral universe is long, but it bends toward justice"—and who then did too little in chasing after that arc and the justice toward which it bent.[2]

James Sloan, piedmont boy, army veteran, and family friend who had become a Harvard MBA and economics scholar, sent his onetime congressman a note after a dining club of Harvard and Radcliffe scholars had hosted a dinner and speech for Dorn in Cambridge. Sloan wryly marked it: "There is no more exciting story in American politics than that of a Southerner who comes to have a 'national view' without losing his regional charm and rural vigor." It was the image that Sloan and his clubbable friends at Harvard and Radcliffe had formed after a theatrical dinner speech by Bryan Dorn that featured full white suit, full Roman oratory, and deepest Baptist confessional. The scholars so gathered had been dreading redneck anti-intellectualism and unthinking racism. Those were never Dorn's attributes, but the low expectations of the audience were overmatched by the speechifying acumen taught long ago by Emma Andrews of the Shepp Foundation, nurtured by Nana, and fervently practiced behind Jim Self's textile mill. Like his model Sam Rayburn, Bryan Dorn was still the lonely country boy anxious to please the city visitor. More than that, though, would be needed for the overwhelming challenges of this period after LBJ.[3]

As he worried about Hubert Humphrey and the challenges of the presidential race in 1968, and as he worried about a reenergized Bud Grisso seeking his own seat in the US Congress, Bryan Dorn was working overtime with Governor Robert E. McNair, a Great Society figure who had cooperated with Dorn and with what remained of the "Barnwell Ring" to build roads

[2] Theodore Parker, "Of Justice and the Conscience," 1857; Commager, *Theodore Parker*, 197–213; Martin Luther King Jr., "Out of the Long Night," *Gospel Messenger*, 8 February 1958, 14.

[3] James Sloan to WJBD, 10 November 1967, WJBD/SCPC; Rayburn quote, WJBD, *OTP*, 4.

and schools in South Carolina while also attempting to develop a self consciously progressive "national view" about civil rights for the Palmetto State. In Dorn's judgment, Governor McNair was superb, especially at using the bully pulpit of the governor's office to say the right things and set the right example for issues of civil rights. As noted, Bryan Dorn had suggested to McNair and Humphrey that the congressman come to Chicago in August and place the governor's name in nomination as Favorite Son—a holding device until the full delegation could be given over to Humphrey. Dorn and McNair were completely in support of Humphrey but were worried about the logistics since it was almost impossible for the vice president to get his own name on the ballot in most of the primary states—all of which would make the convention a time of important negotiation.[4]

But more than anything else, Bryan Dorn's lateness to discern the bending moral arc was apparent as he tried to help Governor McNair. Regardless of McNair's own qualities of commitment to full civil rights, his top administrators had performed badly, even viciously, in several instances. While the governor had inherited some top departmental executives—or in some cases, had seen them get elected without his involvement—the fact remained that the heads of the State Law Enforcement Division (SLED) and the South Carolina Army National Guard (SCARNG) and the South Carolina Highway Patrol (SCHP) answered to the people *through* the state's chief executive. Thus Governor McNair was in public view and in reality ultimately responsible for anything bad done by those agencies.

Indeed, on 7 February in that fateful year of 1968, SLED, SCARNG, and SCHP each had performed abysmally in a crisis at historically black South Carolina State College in Orangeburg. There, some 200 college demonstrators had protested segregation at a local bowling alley—a segregation probably illegal under the Civil Rights Act of 1964, and in any case a painful reminder of the low regard white authority had for young black scholars in Orangeburg at State College and at the private historically black Claflin College also in town. By most accounts, demonstrators at the bowling alley were peaceful and orderly. Although sources of their grievances were complex, the main issues were segregation at the bowling alley and grossly inadequate funding for State College. On the evening of the 7 Feb-

---

[4] Robert E. McNair to WJBD, 9 October 1967; WJBD to McNair, 28 July 1967; WJBD to McNair, 3 August 1967; WJBD to John M. Bailey, 28 March 1968; L. Mendel Rivers to WJBD, 19 June 1968; WJBD to Hubert Horatio Humphrey, 16 April 1968; WJBD to John West, 1 May 1968, WJBD/SCPC.

ruary demonstration, a scuffle started involving some police officials, and the first person injured, apparently by rock or bricks or other thrown objects, was officer David Sheally. On that evening, the local officials made some arrests, Officer Sheally was attended to, and students dispersed to the campus.[5]

On the following day, 8 February, many more students massed, this time on campus. Although still orderly and peaceful, the hundreds of students built a bonfire on a vacant lot adjoining campus (students regarded the lot as part of the campus; authorities insisted it was *off campus*). Meanwhile, SLED agents and highway patrol personnel and SCARNG units were brought in to maintain order. Despite the demeanor of the demonstrating crowd, all law enforcement officials were armed with live ammunition because of the violence the previous evening. The law enforcement officials moved in to put out the bonfire and disperse the crowd. There were shouts and some rock throwing and brick throwing, and for a period of eight to ten seconds (a long time when live ammunition is involved), numerous armed officials opened fire on the demonstrating crowd. No students fired weapons, and indeed no weapons were even found among students. Three students were killed outright, and twenty-eight were injured or wounded, including a pregnant woman who subsequently suffered a miscarriage. Some students may have been shot on the vacant lot, but most were shot as they fled the lot and entered the campus proper.[6]

At least a score of wounded students spent the evening in the college infirmary; otherwise, hundreds of students huddled in the relative safety of their dormitories. Law enforcement officials declared that campus order was restored, as it seemed to be, at least to the eye. Governor McNair supported SLED, the highway patrol, and the SCARNG (all agencies of the executive office), and he insisted for some months that all shooting had occurred off campus (that is, confined to the vacant lot). Also, he continued for some time to exaggerate the "arms" of the demonstrators, only a few of whom threw bricks or rocks and none of whom had guns. He ignored the fact that many wounds were in the back and some even in the bottoms of feet, indicating that demonstrators were *running away from the scene* rather than to-

---

[5] Bass and Nelson, *The Orangeburg Massacre* (1970. rev. ed. 2003); Bass, "Documenting the Orangeburg Massacre," reviewing the press coverage; Shuler, *Bone and Blood*; Roper, "The Orangeburg Massacre: Experience & History" posted on 4 December 2013 by Kate Moore, SCPC Capital Blog.

[6] Bass and Nelson, *The Orangeburg Massacre*; Jack Bass to Herbert Hartsook, 2 December 2013, JHR/SCPC; Orangeburg/SC State College folders, John Drummond Papers/SCPC.

ward law officials. University of South Carolina journalism students covering the "Governor's Beat" also were told by Press Secretary Wayne Seal that demonstrators were armed and dangerous and were not on the campus. Black people at once called the incident the Orangeburg Massacre, and most white people, especially Governor McNair and his ally Congressman Dorn, called it the Orangeburg Riot. To his credit, Governor McNair did authorize Lieutenant Governor John Carl West to begin serious investigation into the root causes of the disturbances. And to his own credit, Bryan Dorn made a careful study of the reports drawn up by John West, by Mayor Lester L. Bates of Columbia, and by Don Fowler, the scholar newly named executive director of the South Carolina Democratic Party.[7]

But before these studies were published and distributed, the congressman had issued a ringing endorsement of Governor McNair, the SCARNG, and SLED—and he continued to lay blame for the riot on black students, specifying Martin Luther King Jr. as the prime example of civil unrest and thus the prime agitator in any racial disputes. In winter of 1968, no reminders about the Nobel Peace Prize Dr. King had earned and no words from respected friends such as John Bolt Culbertson or Bennie Mays could budge Dorn from his criticisms of King. Indeed, the congressman continued to absolve white law officials even after mastering the documents and developing an otherwise more nuanced view of the roots of racial unrest over education. Only some forceful and wise words in private from respected Greenwood friend Assemblyman John Drummond moved Dorn to a position sympathetic to the State College demonstrators—and that position did not emerge during 1968; it would take Bryan Dorn almost a full year to speak reasonably about the massacre.[8]

When student Cleveland Sellers was arrested and eventually sentenced for a long imprisonment—the only person so convicted despite evidence that he was merely a peaceful demonstrator—Bryan Dorn was loud and frequent in his remonstrations against Sellers and other such "agitators." In such fulminations, he dutifully sounded the tocsin of "national views" on civil rights

---

[7] West, "Report on South Carolina State College," 1968; WJBD to John C. West, 1 May 1968; Lester Bates, "Report on Negro Students...and Columbia"; WJBD to Robert Moot, 10 March 1968; WJBD to Franchot A. Brown (legal scholar of racial unrest), 2 April 1968, WJBD/SCPC; 1968 folders, John Drummond Papers, SCPC, hereinafter JD/SCPC; Roper, "The Orangeburg Massacre: Experience & History," 4 December 2013, A Capital Blog, SCPC.

[8] WJBD statement, "Governor McNair and SC State Riot," *Congressional Record*, vol. 113, 90th Cong., 2d sess.

and supported the Great Society civil rights, but otherwise continued to describe Martin Luther King Jr. as a dangerous agitator. In that winter and early spring, he exhausted his considerable oratorical skills attacking Cleveland Sellers and Martin Luther King Jr. As before, he grouped black and white campus demonstrators together as agitators responsible for violence and property damage at universities and colleges.[9]

He was thus mortified when Martin Luther King Jr. was assassinated in Memphis during Easter season on 4 April 1968. Of course, he could say that he had expressed his concern that immoderate language and race hatred had brought about the assassination, but he was redundantly on record as *blaming Dr. King himself* for much of that immoderate language and race hatred. No serious student of Dr. King's career can make such unfounded claims of that exhaustively documented life of prophecy. There was nothing to do but be quiet while congressmen and others gave eulogies—be publicly quiet and privately assure Bennie Mays and Modjeska Simkins and John Bolt Culbertson that he was belatedly recognizing the good that Dr. King had done. An especially poignant statement came from his friend Bennie Mays, whose words were placed in the *Congressional Record* by Texas Senator Ralph Yarbrough. In this season, Dorn quietly arranged with veteran black politico Isaiah DeQuincey Newman to hire Luther James Battiste III to help with his messages to the black community, especially in Columbia. On the issue of Martin Luther King Jr., Dorn faced a long and a slow climb back to respectability among black citizens, and indeed among any reasonable people. Many Southern politicians were making that slow and awkward climb with him at the time, proof that the general public was much more quickly getting itself into line with the moral arc of the universe than was the South Carolina delegation.[10]

---

[9] MLK Jr.: WJBD to Moot, 10 March 1968; WJBD, address, n.p., "Support LBJ in Vietnam," 19 September 1967; WJBD to Donald Lionel Fowler, 20 November 1967; WJBD, address, "Moderation," n.p., 4 December 1967; Thomas Pope to WJBD, 8 December 1967; and WJBD to Elaine Mayo Paul, 5 December 1967, WJBD/SCPC; WJBD statement, "Governor McNair and SC State Riot"; Roper, "The Orangeburg Massacre."

[10] Battiste statement, 25 September 2013, quoted Hartsook (25 September 2013), JHR/SCPC; correspondence, Battiste and Isaiah DeQuincey Newman, ID Newman Papers/SCPC (hereinafter IDN/SCPC); retrospective, 1980, Luther James Battiste III Papers, SCPC (hereinafter LJB/SCPC); Roper, *Magnificent Mays*, 265;statements, MLK Jr. memorials, *Congressional Record*, vol. 113, 90 Cong., 2d. sess., 27 May 1968, especially Yarbrough insertion, appendix E 4653.

Particularly galling was that Humphrey rival Robert Francis Kennedy delivered one of the most poignant of the many memorial tributes to Dr. King—and did so in heroic and peacemaking circumstances in a ghetto in Indianapolis. Besides calming a crowd, Kennedy had quoted Aeschylus, getting most of the words right from memory and getting everything right in that moment of the arc's bending:

> Even in our sleep, pain that cannot forget
> Falls drop by drop upon the heart,
>   And in our own despair
>   Against our will,
> Comes wisdom through the awful grace of God.[11]

Whatever his evolving opinion about the slain King, Bryan Dorn preferred Bennie Mays's Baptist reformist words in eulogy—but the orator Dorn had to salute the orator RFK. In any case, candidate Humphrey himself, Dorn's clear preference for president, was at least on record redundantly as a friend and admirer of Dr. King, and Dorn could turn his attentions to working with McNair, Humphrey, and Great Society Democrats in the House to get things done for constituents. Among other tasks, Dorn succeeded in getting no fewer than twenty black businessmen special low-interest SBA loans for building up firms, and opportunities, for the much-oppressed black community of Orangeburg. He also continued to discuss the coming Chicago Democratic Convention, worried that either Gene McCarthy or Bobby Kennedy might come into those sessions with such momentum that he could carry away the nomination.[12]

Even as contenders and campaigners and everyone else in politics grappled with the meaning of Dr. King's career and his assassination, urban riots broke out. On 28 May, Bryan Dorn drove his Plymouth "up Seventh Street after the riots." To crusty old retired Republican Wint Smith of Kansas, Dorn confided, "it looked exactly like a lot of towns in Germany and France after a bombardment." He was more bemused than frightened by these riots. But mere days later, before he could even formulate an acceptable public

---

[11] R. W. Apple Jr., "Kennedy Appeals for Nonviolence," *New York Times*, 5 April 1968, 33. Cf. Aeschylus, *Agamemnon*, trans. Gilbert Murray, lines 1178–343.

[12] Retrospective, McNair to WJBD, 13 September 1968; WJBD to John M. Bailey, 28 March 1968; L. Mendel Rivers to WJBD, 19 June 1968; WJBD to Hubert Horatio Humphrey, 16 April 1968; WJBD to John West, 1 May 1968, WJBD/SCPC; 1968 folders, JD/SCPC; retrospective, Battiste, 1980, LJB/SCPC.

expression for truly interracial audiences, came the news that Robert Kennedy himself had been slain.[13]

On 4 June, RFK, narrowly winner over Gene McCarthy in the California primary, was shot in Los Angeles at the moment of his political triumph. When he died soon thereafter, Tom Wicker wrote a piece for the *New York Times* that summarized feelings, at least among Democrats: "A Pall Over Politics." There certainly was a pall hanging over Bryan Dorn, who considered that American discussion about politicians had reached the point that cursing and then killing rivals were almost the same act. He repeated what he said often in luncheon and dinner and barbeque addresses: "Too many negativists have no plans" and "*Hate LBJ* scapegoaters...poison the political climate." Senator Edward M. Kennedy, someone that Bryan judged to be a very conventional politician willing to work patiently inside the legislature to get things done, moved the congressman profoundly when he spoke a family, and a politician's, eulogy for yet another Democrat and yet another Kennedy:

> My brother need not be idealized, or enlarged in death beyond what he was in life; to be remembered simply as a good and decent man, who saw wrong and tried to right it, saw suffering and tried to heal it, saw war and tried to stop it.
> I quote him:
> *Some men see things as they are and ask why*
> *I dream things that never were and say, why not?*[14]

The discontent and violence in the nation's cities and college campuses—even at the relatively conservative and quiet Clemson and University of South Carolina—were not found in the villages and towns of Bryan Dorn's Third District. There was respite from the pangs of unemployment and there was at least temporary racial peace as blacks in McCormick and Edgefield began voting and began "neophyte" testing of what it actually meant to be an equal citizen. The remainder of his district was so overwhelmingly white that the majority population could for the nonce virtually

---

[13] Gladwin Hill, "Kennedy Is Dead, Victim of Assassin," *New York Times Special Edition*, 4 June 1968, 1.

[14] Tom Wicker, "A Pall Over Politics," *New York Times Special Edition*, 4 June 1968, 1; WJBD, address, n.p., 5 December 1967; Harlan E. McClure to WJBD, 15 December 1967, quoting WJBD; EMK statement, 1967 WJBD/SCPC; interview: Steve Griffith with Hartsook and Roper (24 September 2013), JHR/SCPC.

ignore black aspirations, at least as such aspirations were manifest in Pickens and Pendleton, Seneca and Calhoun Falls. Almost every week that summer and fall, Congressman Dorn could issue some sort of press release about a sugarplum for his communities: a National Guard Armory in Johnston, construction along Trotters Shoals, additional workers hired in mills to meet the army's heavy demands for textile products, a new postal station in Oconee, an army-sanctioned Junior ROTC program for Seneca High School, prominent visits and statements by Ford Shepherd of Mead Paper Company and that firm's interest in building a plant in Abbeville County—and above all, continuing news about Duke Power's nuclear reactors and need for skilled workers.

All the same, Dorn declared great anxiety about Bud Grisso's second general election challenge. He absented himself often from Congress in order to appear in person before his constituents. When J. Howard Morton declared candidacy as an Independent, complaining that Dorn and Grisso were "too liberal," Dorn's people told him Morton would hurt the Republican nominee (and thereby help the sitting congressman), but Dorn stepped up his efforts all the same. In that context, he and Millie Dorn made a decision, largely political but quite personal too. In the newly emerging society of recreational drugs and other dangerous "play" among teenagers, the couple fretted about teenaged life in the DC suburbs of McLean. Of special concern was daughter Brianna Dorn's high school. Since Greenwood in that era was changing far more slowly than McLean, Millie Dorn took the children to Barratt House for good, and Bryan came home each weekend. The Dorn family was no longer resident in McLean, and so the congressman had to relinquish his official connections to the adored Old Dominion of Virginia, though of course his rhetorical and emotional connections remained strong. As recounted by staff members, the move to Greenwood made congressional life more hectic. Much that had been done on weekends in DC now had to be done "on the fly" Fridays and Sundays. Each Friday, as a veteran staffer recounted, "We gathered up all the mail and all the papers and studies and we sprinted—and I mean it was a sprint!—to a cab to get to the airport for home."[15]

At Greenwood High School, Brianna prepared herself to be in the early waves of female enrollees at the once completely male Clemson University. At the time, Clemson was also a goal for her younger sisters, Olivia and

---

[15] Interview: Steve Griffith with Hartsook and Roper (1 February 2012) and Ed Poliakoff and staffer, quoted, "In Their Own Words," 2012 audio display, SCPC.

Debbie. For their parts, Dorn's sons, Jennings and Johnson entered fully into the youth athletic leagues in football and basketball that fed the successful Greenwood High School teams of legendary Coach Pinky Babb. Life for Millie Dorn was particularly challenging since she was not only raising the children in a difficult era without much help, but she was also first in line to help out with the masses in Greenwood while still expected to return to DC for formal occasions with the classes and their lobbyists. "Mrs. Dorn entertains in Greenwood," the congressman acknowledged more in wonder than gratitude, "and comes back here to entertain too."[16]

Given the intensity of the congressional campaigning, Bryan Dorn eschewed the tumultuous convention in Chicago, where his candidate Humphrey was successfully nominated—but in such unruly and even violent circumstances that the onetime Happy Warrior entered the fall campaign badly wounded (and considerably saddened) as he contested against the largely reinvented Richard Milhous Nixon. The latter spoke grandly about many things: a special but undisclosed way to leave Vietnam, an end to the hated military draft, a Southern Strategy prominently featuring Dorn cousin Strom Thurmond, and above all an intentionality to "bring us all together again" after the urban riots and campus protests. It seemed unlikely that supporters of the late Robert Kennedy would get on board with Humphrey at all, and even the milder anti-war figure Eugene McCarthy offered only the most lukewarm of endorsements for the ticket.

Far removed from such left-wing disputes, many Democrats in South Carolina planned to split their ticket again, voting for Nixon while continuing to support Congressmen McMillan, Rivers, Getty—and, of course, Dorn. The Dorns were deeply concerned about the neighboring Fourth District: what would the Greenville and Spartanburg educated middle class do now that the Populistic New Deal progressive Robert Thomas Ashmore was retired? So, agreeing with his wife, the shrewd former journalist Millie, Bryan Dorn put effort into helping new Democratic candidate James R. Mann (much experienced in the South Carolina General Assembly) against Republican nominee Charles Bradshaw. Bradshaw was new to politics but was well known as Wofford College football star and regional business entrepreneur, a cofounder of the Hardee's chain of hamburger restaurants.

Then Bryan Dorn showed how perfectly attuned his ears were to his own district—and how tone-deaf he could be to the rest of the world beyond

[16] WJBD to Robert W. Hambrook, 16 September 1968; restrospective, WJBD to Jane Howle, 29 January 1971, WJBD/SCPC.

Ware Shoals. He confounded continuing youthful support for the war (still double the approval among those older than thirty-nine years old) with widespread disgust about the way Mayor Daley handled the anti-war protestors. In the *Congressional Record*, he placed a statement praising Mayor Richard Daley for his conduct at the Chicago convention—and he sent a perfectly sincere, in its way innocent, note to Daley: "You are the most popular figure in American history." True enough for Honea Path and Anderson and Edgefield, the words badly described the rest of the Republic. By contrast, on the evening of 25 August, that bellwether of liberal consensus, the *CBS Evening News with Walter Cronkite*, featured commentator Eric Sevareid, who said, "The city of Chicago runs the city of Prague a close second right now as the world's least attractive tourist attraction. The Russian soldiers in Prague may feel slightly more frustrated than the Democratic Party delegates, the reporters, and hangers-on in Chicago, but the Russians, at least, have tanks in which to travel from A to B." Similar anti-Daley language was popularly employed in the commercially successful photojournalism of *Life* magazine.[17]

The upshot of the upheavals was that Bryan Dorn swept back into office, winning 66.1 percent of Third District votes, while his friend James R. Mann swamped Bradshaw by 61 percent to a mere 38.8 percent for the hamburger entrepreneur in the Fourth District. However, Richard Nixon easily carried South Carolina electoral votes as sandlappers split their tickets. And the South Carolina delegation reflected a portent for the future: Second District Goldwater Democrat Albert Watson had become a full-fledged Republican and a very loud racist demagogue, and he easily won reelection, doing especially well in the affluent Arcadia Lakes suburbs of Columbia.[18]

More than anything else, the future political story was cousin Strom Thurmond. The senior senator was honored among the Nixonites, largely

---

[17] WJBD to Richard Daley, 11 September 1968; Daley to WJBD, 21 October 1968; James R. Mann to WJBD, 29 January 1969, WJBD/SCPC; WJBD, "Chicago," *Congressional Record*, vol. 114, Pt. 20, 90th Cong., 2d sess., 5 September 1968, 25853; *CBS Evening News with Walter Cronkite*, 25 August 1968 tape, WSPA, Spartanburg; *Life*, 23 August 1968, entire issue; Mueller, *War, Presidents, and Public Opinion*, 72–98; George Gallup, "Approval/Disapproval," *Gallup Opinion Polls*, Vietnam by age groups, August 1968.

[18] WJBD to F. A. Kennedy, 4 September 1968; Mann to WJBD, 29 January 1969, WJBD/SCPC; Harrison Jenkins, "On the Record," *Columbia State*, 3 April 1968, A 14; *Supplemental Report of Secretary of State to General Assembly of South Carolina, Reports and Resolutions of the General Assembly of South Carolina*, ed. Inez Watson, 1969.

because he had successfully kept South Carolina's many George Wallace admirers inside the Republican Party. Unlike previous presidential elections, South Carolina did not join the other Deep South states, the remainder of whom voted for Wallace. Thus, Nixon "owed" Senator Thurmond, who promised substantive change in the Supreme Court, having already led a successful trashing of the effort by lame duck LBJ to make the avowed liberal Abe Fortas the high court's Chief Justice. In the autumn weeks before the election, LBJ had given up on Fortas's nomination and withdrew it. It was the first time that a sitting associate justice was denied ascent to chief justice—and the first time the US Senate had rejected a presidential nomination for chief justice. President Nixon would be able to name his own chief justice, and Senator Thurmond was in unique position to influence that process. Dorn supported Fortas publicly, although the prerogative was in the Senate, and he could have ducked the issue. Fortas's defeat he took hard, especially as reinforced by constituents such as "a Newberrian," who praised Senator Thurmond and scolded his congressman over the issue: "Proclaiming Liberalism is no substitute for Good Government."[19]

Otherwise, Democrats retained control of John McCormack's House, with a big margin of 248 to 192—but Dorn and everyone else had to acknowledge that the Massachusetts representative with the wonderful cigars was worn out and his party riven by disputing factions. In fact, liberal Morris K. Udall, congressman from Arizona's Southern district, a veteran representative best known for environmental activism, led a rebellion against McCormack featuring anti-war Democrats who put forward the former NBA basketball player Udall for speaker. Dorn liked Morris Udall almost as much as he had liked the congressman's older brother Stewart, but he supported McCormack partly because of the speaker's hawkish stance on Vietnam (Dorn noted correctly that support for the war had actually *risen* between August 1968 and January 1970, especially among those *under thirty* years of age, half of whom supported it). Mostly, however, Dorn considered that the Irishman had earned his oats in leadership while Udall was largely untested. In unprecedented secret voting about an unprecedented challenge inside a powerful majority party, McCormack prevailed. Having won and

---

[19] Tindall, *Disruption of Solid South*, 69–70; Bass and Thompson, *Ol' Strom*, 223–33; Abraham, *Justices, Presidents, and Senators*, 197–270; A. Newberrian to WJBD, 28 June 1968, WJBD/SCPC.

once again organized the majority, the House speaker now presided over shifting coalitions as the energized Nixon took office.[20]

Even before Richard Nixon delivered his Inaugural Address, Bryan Dorn actively worked with Bryce Harlow, assistant to the president-elect in charge of transition, and with South Carolinians Fred Dent, Harry Dent, and J. Fred Buzhardt, all figures well known in the textile world but newly important in the transformed DC landscape. He quickly extracted from postmaster-general designee Winton M. Blount a promise "to be certain I have your recommendations and have perhaps discussed with you personally" before appointing postmasters. More important, Blount promised to move slowly on Nixon's proposal to make the US Post Office essentially a private enterprise sanctioned by the federal government. Any privatization of the Post Office was a serious threat to Southern Democrats, not only endangering service in remote and low-populated rural communities but also damaging the long-established local patronage and party loyalty of the institution. Dorn, following the lead of Senator Tom Watson, was a powerful advocate of the Post Office and was personally loyal to postmasters Jim Farley of the New Deal days and to Larry O'Brien of the Great Society. He was determined to work with Nixon's man Blount to preserve the Post Office as a constituent service and as a congressman's patronage.[21]

Along with telegraphs of support for new Vice President Spiro T. Agnew and new President Richard Nixon, Dorn hurriedly arranged a conference about Japanese textile wages with Buzhardt, both Dents, the classes, and Harold Whitecomb of the American Textile Manufacturers Institute (ATMI). Dorn presented data showing that Japanese wages throughout the era of the 1960s were relatively *lower* with regard to South Carolina textile wages than during the Eisenhower recessions. While Japanese wages had risen, so had South Carolina wages, and thus the *spread* in compensation for textile labor had actually gotten worse. It was still low wage competition,

---

[20] *Congressional Record*, vol. 115, pt. 1, 9lst Cong., 1st sess., 3 January 1969; Nelson, "Irish Identity Politics: The Reinvention of Speaker John W. McCormack," 7–34; Gordon, "John W. McCormack and the Roosevelt Era," PhD diss., Boston University, 1976; Carson and Johnson, *The Life and Times of Morris K. Udall*; Richard Madden, "Rep. Udall Seeking McCormack Post as House Speaker," *New York Times*, 2 January 1969, 1; Marjorie Hunter, "McCormack Stops Udall Challenge in 178–58 Secret Vote," *New York Times*, 3 January 1969, 1.

[21] Bryce N. Harlow to WJBD, 12 January 1969; WJBD to Winton Blount, 1 February 1969, WJBD/SCPC.

"unfair," and it still hurt piedmont millworkers even in good times. He and the classes gathered there reminded everyone about Nixon's promises to textile executives in Charlotte during the recently concluded campaign.[22]

Over on his own side of the congressional aisle, Bryan Dorn leaned on his friend Wilbur Mills, chair of Ways and Means Committee, to ensure that freshman representative James R. Mann had a proper seat on the House Judiciary Committee. Mann had requested this, but vital to Dorn was the fact that someone from the South Carolina delegation needed to be on that committee. Not unrelated to his request for the seat for Mann were complicated arrangements to obtain an honorary degree form Clemson for Mills. These arrangements were eventually successful, thanks largely to Dorn's persistence and to his long friendship with Robert C. Edwards. And Jimmy Mann was soon writing a note of gratitude to his senior in the South Carolina delegation, declaring that he owed the prized appointment "due in large measure to the influence and to the respect which the members of the Ways and Means Committee have for your opinion."[23]

Thus Bryan Dorn prepared himself to work with another Republican administration, this one led by yet another of that 1947 class of war veterans who had come with him to the House of Representatives. He had more in common with Nixon than most Democrats, and he was convinced that Nixon was an Eisenhower engineer, that is, one fully committed to efficiently building and maintaining the liberals' architectural blueprints. Strom Thurmond had the president's ear, but Nixon would certainly need some of those 248 Democratic representatives to pass his agenda, most of which sounded in the bright early winter of 1969 remarkably *liberal.* At least for Dorn, Nixon's progressive potentiality was nowhere more apparent than in his behavior concerning race relations. Southern Strategy or not, Congress had now set in motion substantive civil rights programs, and J. Stanley Pottinger, Nixon's director of the civil rights division, immediately convinced staffers and civil

---

[22] Mann to WJBD, 29 January 1969; WJBD to Wilbur Mills, 30 December 1968; WJBD to Harold Whitecomb with statistics enclosed, wages 1959–1969, 24 January 1969, WJBD telegram, n.d. (November 1968) to R. M. Nixon, WJBD telegram n.d. (November 1968) to Spiro Agnew; WJBD to Charlotte Textile Club, 11 November 1968, WJBD/SCPC; Mueller, *War, Presidents, and Public Opinion*, 72–98; George Gallup, "Approval/Disapproval by Age," *Gallup Polls*, August 1968, October 1968, February 1969.

[23] Correspondence with R. C. E. and Wilbur Mills, summer 1968, especially WJBD to Mills, 2 July 1968; WJBD to Mills, 30 December 1968; James R. Mann to WJBD, 29 January 1969, WJBD/SCPC.

rights activists that Nixon's people intended to enforce the full measure of the Voting Rights Act of 1965 and the Civil Rights Act of 1964.[24]

Furthermore, Nixon's people promised to strengthen the "safety net," as folk were beginning to call the unemployment stipends and the medical benefits for the poor and the elderly. The president even set in motion increases in the food stamps, the training, and the special low-interest loans and outright grants-in-aid that LBJ had developed in the Third District, but, of course, also in all impoverished areas. Perhaps most heartwarming was the way President Nixon promised to clean up the environment, especially the polluted waterways. Dorn was cosponsoring legislation that provided generous business tax credits for firms that spent money cleaning up the environment, and he had been recently recognized at Duke University by environmentalists for his efforts in Congress on behalf of clean air and clean water. Though a later era would laugh bitterly at the concept, Bryan Dorn considered himself an environmentalist with specific regard to the Savannah River system, and above all in his hope to supplant "dirty" coal with "clean" coal (that is, treated or "scrubbed" coal) and with nuclear power. For Dorn, as he hoped for Nixon, Duke's two nuclear plants and the two private utility reactors in Aiken were only the start of a thorough commitment to nuclear energy, with electricity "too cheap to meter."[25]

It developed, then, that Dorn's transition from LBJ to Nixon was a remarkably smooth affair, at least for the sessions of the 91st Congress. On the horizon, however, problems loomed, primarily macroeconomic and thus fiscal. Neither LBJ nor Nixon was forthright about the cost of the Vietnamese War, and so each president ran large deficits that became apparent only later, since their budget documents dealt only with projected and planned expenses that seemed to balance (much of war spending was "off budget"). In this period, Congress became aware how ineffective was the LBJ surtax that Bryan Dorn had supported at some political risk. That surtax, designed

[24] Interviews: Staffers of House Judiciary Committee, 22 March 1983, JHR/SHC; Roper, "Essay on the Voting Rights Extension Act."

[25] Commencement address, Linwood Holton, 13 May 2012, Emory & Henry College, Emory, VA, Earl G. Hunt Collections, Kelly Library, EHC; WJBD, Press Release, Air and Water Improvement Tax Credit, 11 July 1966, WJBD, address, "Southern Water Resources and Pollution Control," Duke University, 6 April 1967, Speeches folder, 1966-67; Steve Griffith to WJBD, 28 May 1968; correspondence with SC Wildlife Federation re endangered species: Paul V. Shea to WJBD, 12 July 1968, and John A. May, 1965–1968; WJBD to Martin Labar, 21 September 1968, WJBD/SCPC; Farmer, "A Collision of Cultures," 40–49; Frederickson, *Cold War Dixie*.

to restore balance between spending and taxing by raising some taxes, was *smaller than* the dramatic increases in government expenditures in the war effort in Vietnam. As Hubert Aull had predicted, such continuing fiscal deficits during a time of economic growth were generating a rise in the general level of prices, that is, inflation. Dorn preferred serious cuts in expenditures plus new taxes to fix the inflationary problem that was thus revealed to be greater than feared. But yet for the time being, Dorn *vote by vote* supported policies that wise Dr. Aull told him were going to result in inflation.[26]

In May of 1970, Speaker McCormack, smarting over continued dissension in his large and increasingly unwieldy majority party, declared that in 1970 he would not seek the speakership and would not even seek his own district seat. This abdication cleared the way for Carl Albert. The diminutive Oklahoman, also from the Class of 1947, and one with energy and pragmatism acceptable to all Democratic factions, was able to move from majority leader to speaker when Congress convened in 1971. Much legislation went forward, especially concerning clean air and clean water, as well as protections for textiles, and Minority Leader Gerald Ford of Michigan proved cooperative and useful in such law-crafting. The VA committee expanded benefits to Vietnam era veterans, a key goal for Third District veterans, and Bryan Dorn became fascinated with the idea of a new medical college in Columbia that could work in conjunction with the VA hospital there, taking as his model such an arrangement sponsored successfully by Tennessee Republican Jimmy Quillen for East Tennessee State University and the Mountain Home VA facility, both in Johnson City. In his way, Dorn bided his time, helping Quillen and quietly building support for a much larger project to come to his home state—and a project for once involving the University of South Carolina instead of his adored Clemson. Dorn had climbed steadily in the Public Works Committee and was now ranking member; South Carolina projects thus abounded, both for waterways and for interstate highways. He received full credit for this work not only among his own constituents but also among South Carolinians who lived and worked in other districts.[27]

---

[26] WJBD to Mr. All Textile People, n.d., 1970 form letter; Robert C. Jackson to WJBD, 3 March 1969; WJBD to Jennings Dorn, 9 March 1971; G. W. (Jerry) Vaughan to WJBD, 14 February 1969, WJBD/SCPC; retrospective, WJBD to GHA, 8 February 1971, and GHA, retrospective, "Weasel Words," *Anderson Independent*, 6 August 1971, GHA/SC/CU.

[27] Marjorie Hunter, "House Democrats Elect Albert Their Leader," *New York Times*, 30 May 1970, 1; Olin E. Teague to WJBD, 11 August 1968; James H. Quillen to

Even so, Dorn saw and heard but missed the significance of a trend in public opinion. In the South Carolina delegation, he and Mendel Rivers were the most prominent supporters of the Vietnamese War, and here he enjoyed support among his people. He knew, too, from polls and from his travels to high schools that youth supported the war more than did those aged thirty to forty-nine, and much more so than those older than forty-nine (opposite of prevailing wisdom then and now, Dorn's observation was borne out by Gallup Polls). But ever since the increase in casualties, *all support* for the war had waned among all age groups, though it waned less among the youth he visited than among others. Public opinion was changing quite rapidly, and Rivers and Dorn were increasingly out of step with the developing popular consensus. For instance, Martha Sue Hudgens, onetime essayist and onetime cartoonist supporting the war at Easley High School, sent him a polite note. Once, she had declared that a "boy next door" had died for a glorious cause, and once, she had believed that "falling dominoes" would, one by one, topple all free countries in their turn, finally knocking over the US. At the time that she drew her cartoon for the pleased congressman, most youth, well over 50 percent, had fully supported the war. Now, however, Martha Sue had married and was living in Greenville: she regretted her statement permanently registered in the *Congressional Record* because now she wanted all the boys to come home—and she did not want her own children ever to go to Vietnam. By summer of 1968, only 45 percent of youth supported the war effort, only 39 percent of the middle-aged supported it, and only 27 percent of seniors supported it. Nixon's promises about ending the war had raised his personal approval in all age categories above 50 percent, with youth again more favorable than other age groupings. Dorn was certainly correct that *most youth in his state* disagreed with his family friend Martha Sue, but he missed the all-important *trend*, the fact of broadly decreasing support for the war, especially when compared to the days of 1965.[28]

WJBD, 28 July 1967 and WJBD to J. H. Q., 2 August 1967; Press Release, Mountain Home, 28 June 1967, and retrospective, speech, Columbia, VA, 12 May 1971, speeches, 1967–1971, WJBD/SCPC.

[28] Martha Sue Hudgens to WJBD, 16 Feburary 1967; Hudgens to WJBD, n.d., winter, 1969/1970, WJBD/SCPC; George Gallup, "Approval/Disapproval of Vietnam Policy," *Public Opinion Polls*, 1968; Mueller, *War, Presidents, and Public Opinion*, 72–98.

When Democrats gathered at Barratt House on Labor Day in 1970, Bryan Dorn was assured of an easy win in ten weeks over H. Grady Ballard, the Republican nominee.

Much looked good for his party, especially prospects for a huge Democratic majority in Congress. Everywhere he traveled, all over South Carolina but also in Virginia, he delivered the message that a firm Democratic majority could translate into Democratic control of congressional committees, and thereby *progressive* or liberal legislation (*Great Society* was a term suddenly unacceptable and thus unused, but both *liberal* and *progressive* were favorable words "of the people" in 1970). Such liberal legislation was said to be highly practical, with important benefits for those districts that sent Democrats to DC. The message was well received. He was, however, extremely worried about the gubernatorial race that pitted popular Lieutenant Governor John Carl West against Republican Albert William Watson, who was leaving Congress in order to run. In addition to his long-lived passion for his party, Dorn needed West to win—and to win the right way—because of the veteran congressman's own personal ambitions. In 1974, Dorn intended to fulfill his boyhood dream of running for governor himself. In any case, Dorn liked and admired John West, especially for his studious and methodical approach to the vexing challenges posed by South Carolina's racism. It was West as much as anybody who had taught the state's politicians the new language, in which the old term *Negro* soon disappeared, replaced by *black* and occasionally by *African American*. Dorn, ever Nana's self-conscious orator, quickly and thoroughly adapted to the new language, saying *black* and *African American* and no longer using the word *Negro*.[29]

Yet by summer's end, a once-large West lead had all but evaporated, and Dorn and others thought the slump had less to do with Watson's appeal than with missteps by John West himself. The veteran Charleston journalist Hugh Gibson noted dyspeptically that West had "blown" the advantage of "a long head start," and was now "sweating on the hustings." Press Secretary and campaign veteran Philip G. Grose, himself "beating the drums" and "sweating on the hustings," unhappily agreed, as did state Democratic Party

---

[29] WJBD, *OTP*, 6–7, 238–40; WJBD, Speeches Folders, summer 1970, September/October 1970; John Carl West, "Report on South Carolina State College," 1968, WJBD/SCPC; Roper, blog, "Race and SCPC Records," SCPC website, December 2013, printout, 2014, JHR/SCPC.

chair Don Fowler, who had polling data to back up the anecdotal observations.[30]

It seemed that the slump could be traced to two especially charged racist moments, one in early winter, the other in late summer. The first, in the Pee Dee region, showed Watson at his worst, even by his own "aggressively, racially oriented" standards of practice—but West had failed to capitalize on and exploit the Republican's negrophobic gaffes. The second, in early July, featured the normally thoughtful and calm lieutenant governor suddenly announcing with a shout that the US Supreme Court mandate for busing was "senseless and stupid"; unexpectedly, West called for a "major fight" against all desegregation. The latter statement, so uncharacteristic of West's entire career, had delighted Republican Party chairman Ray Harris, who announced that West was "the biggest political phony" in the state—and it had dismayed NAACP field secretary Isaac Williams, who said it was "designed to appease white bigots and racists." Things had to be fixed, and quickly, this very September.[31]

As for that gubernatorial race, Watson chose a hard-edged racist appeal at a moment when surveys by Don Fowler and observations by journalists Hugh Gibson, Wayne Freeman, and Jack Bass showed most white South Carolinians dramatically changing their views about race. It was certainly the case that few among white people supported Supreme Court-mandated busing to achieve racial balance. And there was special displeasure with the ruling that Darlington County integrate mid-school year. But the days of violent resistance to the Supreme Court decisions were supposed to have expired with the peaceful integration of Clemson. Nevertheless, in January of 1970, Frank Best, supported by the Ku Klux Klan, though likely not himself a member, had organized white parents to form a boycott of the schools, keeping their own children at home and massing in protest at the Lamar High School as school buses brought in the black pupils. Best invited politicians to come to Lamar, especially the gubernatorial candidates. Only Watson accepted, and in a "Sunday speech" on 22 February at the Lamar football stadium, Watson praised the boycott and said, "I've been called a racist, a

[30] Gibson quoted, Grose quoted, Grose, *Looking for Utopia*, 152.

[31] Interview, John C. West with Jack Bass, 1972, cited by Grose, *Looking for Utopia*, 153 and 321; Bass, "John C. West of South Carolina," unpublished ms., John C. West Papers, SCPC; James F. Clyburn, memoirs ms., copy in possession of Herbert L. Hartsook; Clyburn, *Blessed Experiences: Genuinely Southern, Proudly Black* (Columbia: University of South Carolina Press, 1914).

bigot and a buzzard, but I intend to tell it like it is." He wound up the peroration, "I will stand up and take a stand and tell people where I stand as regards freedom of choice. God bless anyone who is interested in their children. I will stand with them and applaud them."[32]

The "stand" taken on freedom of choice became a marching mob on 12 March as more than 200 people, some armed with clubs and chains, confronted law enforcement agents at Lamar High School. Dispersed that day with minimal violence, the mob returned on 13 March as the buses arrived. They menaced the teenagers riding in the buses, and, only moments after students had gotten inside the school, the mob charged the buses, damaging all of them and completely overturning two. Ensuing violence between demonstrators and law enforcement was a frightening thing for South Carolinians to behold. Thankfully, no one was killed. Fairly or unfairly, Watson's long heritage of racist haranguing was connected directly to the violent scenes of 12 March and 13 March 1970. President Nixon expressed his outrage at the treatment of the black students, and federal officials did their best to protect the black students and community. Important Republican state leaders like journalist Bill Workman and Charleston assemblymen Jim Edwards and Tommy Harnett reaffirmed their own principled stands for peaceful and orderly enforcement of law—and these leaders insisted that Watson's mid-January Sunday speech had nothing to do with the mob actions in mid-March. Anecdotal evidence plus polling data, however, showed that *black people definitely connected Watson with the mob violence.* The Darlington NAACP president, Arthur Stanley, told Philip Grose: "You might as well say that Watson poured gasoline on the fire." Yet West did not aggressively seek black votes in the instance, and instead attempted to condemn violence *and* the Supreme Court at the same time. Dorn and others agreed it was a missed opportunity and worried that West was suddenly stumbling and fumbling on integration and education, despite the careful and nuanced studies he authorized and despite his measured and thoughtful words in private conversations.[33]

---

[32] Grose, *Looking for Utopia*, 152–53; Bass, *Ol' Strom*, 252–53; Bass, "Strom Thurmond," Art of Political Biography, 22 January 2013.

[33] Grose, *Looking for Utopia*, 151–52; "Lamar School Re-opens without Violence but Little Attendance," *Darlington News and Press*, 12 March 1970, 1; O. L. Warr, "Background on Handling of Lamar Incident," *Charleston News & Courier*, 12 March 1970, 1; notes, 1970, John Drummond Papers/SCPC.

Then on 8 July, West went on record with the Associated Press about Nixon Justice Department lawsuits to force compliance with integration in the several remaining "noncompliant" school districts: "South Carolina will not accept federal school integration without an all-out legal fight." To other journalists, he said, the state "must continue to fight to prevent the massive disruption of our public school system threatened by the actions of the federal government." These statements not only countered his own record, but countered the actual policies of the man who was still governor, Robert Evander McNair. The sitting governor was scathing in private criticism of West. To his credit, West recognized his own mistakes and made things right with Governor McNair. More relevant, he made things right with the "neophyte" black electorate. Fowler, the party chair himself, traveled the state alongside I. DeQuincey (Deek) Newman, the onetime NAACP field secretary. Black Masonic Lodges, evangelical black churches, black business leaders, and black political aspirants—respectively represented by I. P. Stanback, Billy Fleming, Luther Battiste, and Deek Newman—worked to repair the damage and to get out the black vote for West. John Roy Harper, supported by young James Clyburn and Thomas Broadwater, created the United Citizens Party (UCP) in protest against West and his veteran black supporters, but the UCP drew few votes and angered veteran black politicos. Clyburn, who later credited Bryan Dorn for wise advice in the moment, chose to make his own apologies to the elders and was admitted back into the fold of the state's mainstream Democrats. It was understood that Clyburn would receive an unprecedented executive appointment if West became governor. Indeed, Clyburn was appointed commissioner of Human Affairs by West, a Dorn-inspired arrangement that came to fruition.[34]

It was against that backdrop that Bryan Dorn and others gathered for pig-picking and string-band music and politicking at Barratt House, with greatest concentration on West's problems with Watson. That event and all subsequent Barratt House gatherings were interracial. Bryan Dorn and his party followed the statistical observation by Don Fowler that Democrats would need to get almost all black votes while seeking earnestly for at least two-fifths of white votes in order to win. Thereafter, West ran true to form, with no more racist missteps, and he profited therefrom. West attained a big

---

[34] Grose, *Looking for Utopia*, 153–58; interview, Clyburn with Grose, 11 October 2005, Grose Papers/SCPC; Clyburn, *Blessed Experiences*; "John West," editorial, *Florence Morning News*, 25 September 1970, op. ed.; "John West Governor," *Columbia Record*, 11 November 1970, 1.

black turnout but also gained white voters who had earlier supported George Wallace, winning by 28,000 votes, or some 53.2 percent of all voters. Across the aisle, Republicans in the state seemed to learn from Watson's experiences. In a post-election meeting, Strom Thurmond, who was himself very careful nowadays how he spoke about black people, agreed with a speaker who said, "Well, it means you can't win any longer just by cussin' the niggers." Thurmond's shrewd advisor Harry Dent not only cooperated across party lines with Dorn but also cooperated with black business and educational leaders, and Dent persuaded the Republican senator to add to his staff Thomas Moss, son of a sharecropper and an activist for black voting rights. In the face of such dramatic changes, the "new" Bryan Dorn duly marked it that both political parties were themselves new—and the new party with the black voting constituency was his own Democratic Party.[35]

As to the Third District, Dorn beat Ballard overwhelmingly, taking 75.2 percent of all votes cast and winning 60,708 to 19,981. His fellows in the South Carolina delegation did as expected, with the Second District's Floyd Spence being the only Republican. Spence was elected to fill the seat vacated by Albert Watson, the gubernatorial candidate. Of importance to Dorn was the fact that Spence was moderate on race, practical-minded about cooperating with Democrats in DC and back home, and focused on issues of education and roads. Perhaps Nixon in his State of the Union address to the joint session of the 91st Congress was prophetic in sounding themes both conciliatory and (to Dorn) liberal:

> It is no longer enough to live and let live. Now we must live and help live.
>
> How we seize the opportunities I have described today will determine not only our future, but the future of peace and freedom in this world in the last third of the century.
>
> May God give us the wisdom, the strength and, above all, the idealism to be worthy of that challenge, so that America can fulfill its destiny of being the world's best hope for liberty, for opportunity, for progress and peace for all peoples.[36]

---

[35] Supplemental Report of the Secretary of State to the General Assembly, Reports and Resolutions of the South Carolina General Assembly, vol. 2, 1971, ed. Watson (Columbia: State of SC, 1971).

[36] Ibid.; Nixon quoted, *Congressional Record*, vol. 116, pt. 1, 91st Cong., 2d sess., 22 January 1971.

How carefully Bryan Dorn planned the gubernatorial campaign of 1974. By 1971, even as he joyfully attended the inaugural ball for his candidate John Carl West, he and Millie and the family and friends were setting things up for the 1974 race. There was still to come another congressional session with Richard Nixon, 1971, followed by another district general election, 1972, followed by a final congressional session, 1973 to 1974 that would be dedicated to doing things to win a Democratic primary in summer 1974. And then there would be the general election in November of 1974, one that would likely feature a very electable Republican opponent. In between was also one more presidential campaign, one for which the congressman hoped for a candidate in the mold of Estes Kefauver or Hubert Humphrey. Indeed, Humphrey was very much a viable candidate until a big loss in the California primary. Also attractive to Southern hawks and Populistic New Dealers was Henry "Scoop" Jackson of Washington state. Dorn loved Ted Kennedy, and could happily work with him, but also there were Sargent Shriver and Edmund Muskie and Morris Udall and any number of good young Southern Populistic progressive New Dealers, not least Robert E. McNair, whom others considered discredited by the Orangeburg Massacre. Dorn was troubled only by the anti-war forces with whom he vigorously disagreed. He did not then judge anti-war activists to be a genuine force in the "party of the people."[37]

In any case, Millie Dorn, cousins, friends, and certainly the seventh child of Nana and Dada, never underestimated the work involved in the gubernatorial race three years hence. They always knew it would be hard. There was already forming a gauntlet of aspirant Democrats for the party primary in 1974, possibly to include General William Childs Westmoreland, a hero to the congressman (and in 1974 with no declared party affiliation). There was one personal development that Bryan Dorn did not reveal until later: for all his genius as a congressman, he was ready to leave Congress. As

---

[37] WJBD, *OTP*, 6–7; 254–58; WJBD, "Future of the Democratic Party," *Congressional Record*, vol. 110, pt. 3, 88th Cong., 2d sess., 13 February 1964; 3 March 1964, 2865–66; Sargent Shriver to WJBD, 27 February 1967 (color portrait for office), WJBD to Hubert Humphrey, 1 December 1967; HHH to WJBD, 31 December 1967 (color portrait for office) and WJBD-HHH, 16 April 1968; WJBD to Robert Evander McNair (hereinafter REM), 27 July 1967; REM to WJBD, 8 October1967; REM to WJBD, 13 September 1968; WJBD to Robert Moot, 10 March 1968; WJBD to REM, 9 July 1968, WJBD/SCPC.

he told cousin Steve Griffith and brother Watson Dorn, he had seen congressmen become "old and irrelevant," and he wanted "no part of that."[38]

In his own delegation, he had watched dear friend Lucius Mendel Rivers of the First District drink too much and begin to lose his focus. And he had watched John Lanneau McMillan of the Pee Dee Sixth District exhaust his once considerable energies fighting "Home Rule" for the largely black District of Columbia until he began to neglect the Great Pee Dee, especially the many black voters there, eventually losing a primary election in the very district "Johnny Mac" himself had once made "safe for incumbents." And he had watched the once magisterial Robert Thomas Ashmore of the populous and progressive Fourth District lose energy and enthusiasm before stepping aside—and then he had also watched Ashmore try vainly to find *something to do* in Washington thereafter (an unsuccessful, almost pitiable campaign in which Bryan Dorn and the classes of the Textile Group had pitched in to help, finally resolved with a sinecure in the Council of Government in Greenville, an agency Ashmore had voted *against* when he had served in Congress).[39]

As to the surging Republicans, he had watched Albert Watson of the rich and prestigious midlands Second District lose his head to racist rhetoric, but perhaps more tellingly, Watson had failed his white constituents as a Goldwater Democrat and then as a Republican who was not on Nixon's team. More than one frustrated Columbia citizen wrote Dorn for certain constituent services because "the incumbent" (Watson) would not answer them. While Watson had been defeated for governor because of racist demagoguery, Dorn judged that his friendly foe had been losing votes in his congressional district by failing to provide constituent services to voters of either race. In other words, everyone on the Dorn team knew from redundant examples that the best way to be reelected or to win the next highest seat was

---

[38] Interviews: Steve Griffith with Roper and Herb Hartsook (25 September 2013); and Griffith with Watson Dorn (28 February 2012), JHR/SCPC.

[39] Rivers: Rivers, Eastman, and Rivers, *Me and Mendel*, 175; Drew Pearson and Jack Anderson, "Hard Drinking, Hard Traveling Rep. Mendel Rivers, the King of Junketeers," Washington Merry Go Round column (Bell McClure Syndicate), 8 January 1968; interview: Bud Ferillo with Roper and Hartsook (7 November 2013), JHR/SCPC; McMillan: obit. "Johnny Mac Dies at 81," *Sumter Daily Item*, 4 September 1979, 11A; Ashmore employment, WJBD to Harold Whitecomb (American Textile Manufacturers Institute), 24 January 1969, and Robert C. Jackson (American Textile Manufacturers Institute) to WJBD, 3 March 1969, WJBD/SCPC; Council of Government folders, 1964–1968; COG folders, 1979, John T. Ashmore Papers, SCPC.

to serve your constituents faithfully and sincerely and never let flag one's efforts on their behalf.[40]

Back in Congress, with Carl Albert directing a big Democratic majority party, Bryan Dorn came to terms with reforms that gave the committee chairs less power than they once wielded. He still did not fully comprehend the power of the gathering revolt against the Vietnamese War. For his district, the latter would not matter a great deal, and, in fact, his hawkish position was basically true to that of his voting constituents of both races and all age groupings. However, congressional unrest over foreign policy, combined with weakening power of committee chairmen, did make it slower and sometimes messier to get bills considered on the floor. All the same, he worked with his fellow representatives across party lines and across other lines to develop the Savannah River waterways and to extend the interstate highway system, especially the I-77 route from Charlotte to Columbia. The VA committee increased education benefits for Vietnam veterans, and medical services were dramatically improved.

As for Public Works, Bryan Dorn drafted legislation that allowed Sumter's Williams Brice family to bequeath a huge estate gift, essentially untaxed, to expand the University of South Carolina football stadium and to improve nursing instruction at USC. It took joint action with the US Senate to get the bill approved, and none other than Massachusetts senator Edward M. Kennedy was presiding pro tempore when Congressman Dorn brought the bill over for consideration by the upper chamber. Kennedy graciously gave his friend the floor to get the bill approved in special action by the Senate. As local historian Ruth J. Edens marked it, "It took an act of Congress" to expand the USC stadium, and the catalyst for the effort was none other than Clemson devotee Bryan Dorn. The handsomely rebuilt and enlarged stadium was renamed in ceremonies on 9 September 1972.[41]

Also important to USC was the issue of a medical university in Columbia that would be sponsored by the university but closely connected to the dramatically expanded VA hospital four miles east of the main campus. As noted, it was Tennessee Republican Jimmy Quillen who had given Dorn the

[40] Watson, racism, Bass, *Ol' Strom*, 150–60; Watson constituents, correspondence with WJBD, 1967–1968, especially Charles E. Lee to WJBD, 31 July 1968, WJBD/SCPC.

[41] Edens, *It Took an Act of Congress*; Williams Brice Stadium folders, 1971, WJBD/SCPC.

concept of tying an existing VA facility to a new university medical school. The medical students could benefit from seeing first-hand some of the great advances in treatment of wounds and other trauma, while the VA facility could benefit from association with university research scholars. The two institutions in concert could create a whole far larger than the mere arithmetic sums of the parts involved. Popular among the congressmen and the VA officials (and popular among veterans who were treated), the proposal met some resistance back in the Palmetto State. The existing Medical University of South Carolina in Charleston, one of the oldest medical colleges in the US and an institution proud of serving the entire state, was the epicenter of resistance. In particular, Dr. James Burrows Edwards, dental surgeon and Republican assemblyman, spoke for many who were concerned that there was not enough funding for *one* top-drawer medical university, *let alone two*. And now USC in Columbia, with little history of medical instruction and services, would compete for the state funding. However, Dorn and bipartisan supporters noted the federal funding available through the VA, they noted the state's dramatically increasing population and dramatically increasing total wealth, and above all, the old Army Air Corpsman and friends noted the desperate need for such services among South Carolina veterans. This campaign, which became public in 1971 to 1972, would take coordinated state, federal, and university action for some five years and was the kind of slowly evolving and complicated legislation that Bryan Dorn was particularly good at.[42]

As for President Nixon, he signed these public works and VA projects readily enough, but Congressman Dorn was dissatisfied with other things. *Vietnamization*, Nixon's wartime strategy of transferring the brunt of the battlefield fighting to South Vietnamese from American troops, was suspect to him. To be sure, there was a powerful air force bombing assault designed to force the North Vietnamese to the negotiating table, but the carpet-bombing and the training of South Vietnamese troops were done in tandem with a massive draw-down of US troops, unacceptable to one who wanted an all-out effort for victory and not a truce. However, even the hawks had to

---

[42] Interview, James Burrows Edwards (8 August 2011), JHR/SCPC; WJBD to JHQ, 2 August 1967; USC School of Medicine folders, 1977–1976, WJBD/SCPC.

concede that in current political context, they flew closer to Nixon concerning the war than to any viable alternative.[43]

Closest to home, the entire Textile Group was convinced that the Nixon Republicans by 1971 and thereafter were not helping their industry in trade negotiations and were indeed hurting textiles. Once again, there were economists talking about free trade and wielding theory whose end result was closing some mills while sending tens of thousand of millhands into "short time" working status. Perhaps most perplexing were two of Nixon's major fiscal decisions. He imposed wage and price controls despite assurances that he would not, and despite a recently published column by his chief economist, Paul McCracken, in which the chairman of the Council of Economic Advisors not only critiqued cogently the problems with wage and price control but went on record opposed to them. At any rate, Dr. Aull, and for that matter the dead Dr. Keynes, still held sway for Bryan Dorn, who believed that inflationary pressures would have to be met by deep cuts in government spending and by increases in taxes. Most perplexing of all, Nixon removed the US from the gold standard for international exchange, a move consistent with the fact that the US dollar, not gold, was actually the unit of exchange in all transactions. Rather than seek Dr. Aull's counsel on this move (and rather than review his own reading of Keynes), Bryan Dorn simply opposed it. It was the campaign season, and he had to realize that he would be campaigning against Nixon in November 1972 just as surely as he would be campaigning against Roy Etheridge, the Nixon man selected by the Republicans to contest for the Third District seat. The Republicans, as his namesake had repeated again and again, were standing on the manure spreader, and they had to be resisted forthwith.[44]

Yet during the Nixon era, it was surprising where Bryan Dorn took his loudest stand—and his longest stand. Making his peace with the legacy of the late Dr. King, along with the Voting Rights Act of 1965, entailed Dorn making his peace with full-scale integration, especially of that institution

---

[43] Nixon, "Vietnamization," 3 November 1969, Public Papers of the Presidents of the US, Nixon, 1969, 901–909; George Gallup, Approval/Disapproval of Vietnam, table, 1969–1972, Mueller, *War, Presidents, and Public Opinion*, 98.

[44] Textile Group folders, 1971–1973; WJBD, "Mills Close," 3 March 1971, and other textile speeches, speeches folder, 1971; (on gold) WJBD to Otto E. Passmore, 18 June 1968; (on wage and price controls) WJBD to Harry Cheek, 14 September 1968, WJBD/SCPC; Grayson, *Confessions of a Price Controller*; Paul McCracken, "No Price Controls," *Washington Post* op. ed., 28 July 1971; Yergin and Stanislaw, *The Commanding Heights*, 60–64.

most important to the Dorns and Griffiths and the Colemans, that is, the public school. The issue foremost in integrating schools in 1970 and 1971 was court-mandated busing to bring a true representation of the races into the classroom. He had to confess that his own father, Dada, had spent money busing black children far distances to *keep them segregated*, and now Dada's descendants were going to have to spend money busing black children distances to integrate them. It was an expensive process in a time of tight budgets, and only federal money could enable the strapped South Carolina school districts to accomplish this integration mandate that Dorn now conceded was not only court-approved and legal but *moral*. Yet Nixon was cleverly campaigning against busing with his right hand while his left hand, his own judges and Justice Department officials, put busing into effect. Suddenly, in this crazy era, there was loud and legislated resistance to busing from self-professed Liberal Integrationists, led by Michigan Democrat Robert Paul Griffin. Of course, this legislation was supported by Senators Hollings and Thurmond, but it also included Liberal Integrationists Senator Hugh Scott of Pennsylvania and Senate Majority Leader Michael Joseph Mansfield of Montana. This large alliance was offering a compromise bill that would effectively resist busing in *Northern* schools.[45]

Dorn would have none of it. In particular, a jointly proposed bill, sponsored and supported by Northern liberals, would make it illegal for a school district to use federal funds to bus children. Yet the US Supreme Court said that the selfsame district was required to bus the children. The upshot was that much-needed federal money would be withheld from South Carolina school districts while a clear and powerful federal mandate required the districts to spend money on busing. The only logical consequence was that the school districts would have to cut something from other lines in their budgets. In a public school system, cutting something almost always entailed firing someone, often the youngest teachers. The hypocrisy was an issue, but a greater issue was the sheer arithmetic of the proposed law and the damage it would do to the poorest of his people—not only his black constituents in McCormick and Edgefield but also his millworkers in the struggling textile villages. Forever the Jeffersonian, Dorn insisted, as he had since he was a

---

[45] Robert Allen, "Forced Busing of Children vs. US Constitution," *Anderson Daily Mail*, 20 September 1971, op. ed.; Lee Bandy, "School Aid Banned From Busing," *Columbia State*, 4 November 1971, 1.; Robert Paul Griffith, Michael Mansfield, Hugh Scott, remarks, HR # 13387 and Senate Bill 5541, *Congressional Record*, vol. 118 pt. 5, 92d Cong., 2d sess., 24 February 1972, 5490–500.

Shepp Foundation Fellow, that only a good education could lift people out of poverty. And now the poorest would be penalized by direct congressional action sponsored by representatives in the richest states. Combining the practicality of the feedstore man with the moral zeal of John the Baptist, Congressman Dorn self-consciously quoted Abraham Lincoln as he demanded the ending of the "dual system" of schools and called actively for busing to be enforced and to be funded by the federal government: "This indeed should be one Nation indivisible with liberty and justice for all."[46]

The logic was sound, but Bryan Dorn stood alone in the South Carolina delegation and indeed alone among Deep South congressmen. Dorn won some support from frontline journalist Lee Bandy in Columbia and from Wane Freeman's editorial board in the *Greenville News*. He also won surprising support from veteran civil rights journalist Carl T. Rowan writing in the *Washington Evening Star*, "Let us salute those House members who did not cave in to the passions over busing that rage in their districts." And the ever fervent Baptist Sunday school teacher was supported in his prayer breakfast meetings at the Calvary Baptist Church in DC and also the hometown church presided over by the Rev. James Bowers—not for the political issue, but because churchgoers in both cities admired his courage on the moral issue. In terms of effectiveness politically, he had the full support of Governor John C. West and of a plurality of Southern governors who understood Dorn's practical point about budgets in their poorest school districts.[47]

---

[46] "Dorn: Little Effect on Abbeville Schools," *Abbeville Press and Banner*, 23 March 1972, 2; WJBD, remarks, Congressional Record, vol. 118, pt 5, 92d Cong., 2d sess., 24 February 1972, 5492–93; WJBD, remarks, *Congressional Record*, vol. 118, pt. 6, 92d Cong., 2d sess., 8 March 1972, 7562.

[47] "Ethridge Says Dorn Sides with 'South-Haters,'" *Greenwood Index*, 17 May 1972, 1; "Education Bill Stalled Over Busing," *Anderson Independent*, 8 May 1972, 3B; Lee Bandy, "Dorn: Anti-Busing Package Unfair to Southern States," *Columbia State*, 9 April 1972, 6B; "Little Effect on Abbeville Schools," *Abbeville Press and Banner*, 23 March 1972, 2; Bass, quoted, Grose, *Looking for Utopia*, 153; (Freeman) "House Bill Will Not Work," *Greenville News*, 10 November 1971, op. ed., B1; Paul Clancy, retrospective, "Three Capitals" (op. ed. column), *Charlotte Observer*, 29 March 1974, B1; Lee Bandy, "Anti-Busing Package Unfair to Southern States," *Columbia State*, 9 April 1972, 6B.; "Baptist Preacher (Wade Burton) Commends (Dorn) School Position," *Greenwood Index-Journal*, 8 March 1972, 28; Gene Goldenberg, "Senate Reverses Itself on School Busing," *Greenville News*, 1 March 1972, 1; "Southern Governors Feel US Should Pay for Busing," *Anderson Independent*, 12 November 1971, 1; Carl T. Rowan, "Let Us Salute," op. ed. column, *Washington Evening Star*, 10 November 1971, A21.

Dorn lost the floor vote among Northerners and Southerners, the legislation passed, and many pieces of the congressman's mail smoked with vocal complaints. The behavior of Northern liberals on the issue exasperated him. They were responding to popular opinion (styled "Second Look" in the day), but to Dorn they were betraying principles they themselves long espoused. In any case, back home a clear majority continued to support him, if not fully on this issue, then on all other issues. That most sensitive barometer of district public opinion insisted, "Most of my people would oppose a dual school system even if it were possible to reincarnate this relic of the past." And, in his patented way, he soon fell to, working with Midwestern Republicans and with Southern Democrats and above all with Governor West to find some ways to ease financial and racial pressures on the already burdened school districts. Jack Bass, Lee Bandy, Wayne Freeman, and other journalists covering the issues agreed then and later that the old speechifier in the tailored white suits had never stood more courageously, or more alone, on an issue of social justice.[48] Theirs is a judgment that the biographer looking back four decades can only salute.

The Barratt House gathering on Labor Day in 1972 reflected "the best of times and the worst of times." For the national party, Bryan Dorn and the Democratic Party regulars were faced with the candidacy of George McGovern, someone whose platform they could not support at all. McGovern the man, Dorn liked much: the South Dakotan was a decorated air force veteran and longtime ally on waterways projects and farm legislation. But the "prairie Populist" and the red-hills Populist had always parted company on foreign policy, and nowhere more spectacularly than in 1972 concerning Vietnam. Worse, for Dorn, McGovern was making the entire platform essentially about peace in Vietnam, with little practical consideration of the deepening woes of the textile industry, the odd inequalities of wage and

---

[48] "Education Bill Stalled Over Busing," *Anderson Independent*, 8 May 1972, 3B; Lee Bandy, "Dorn: Anti-Busing Package Unfair to Southern States," *Columbia State*, 9 April 1972, 6B; "Little Effect on Abbeville Schools," *Abbeville Press and Banner*, 23 March 1972, 2; Bass, quoted, Grose, *Looking for Utopia*, 153; (Freeman) "House Bill Will Not Work," *Greenville News*, 10 November 1971, op. ed., B1; Paul Clancy, retrospective, "Three Capitals" (op. ed. column), *Charlotte Observer*, 29 March 1974, B1; "Baptist Preacher [Wade Burton] Commends [Dorn] School Position," *Greenwood Index-Journal*, 8 March 1972, 28; Gene Goldenberg, "Senate Reverses Itself on School Busing," *Greenville News*, 1 March 1972, 1; White and Langer, "Confessions of a 'Second Look' Liberal."

price controls, or the unfinished business of the civil rights agenda. Fairly or not, Dorn judged McGovern to be a one-issue candidate, and he had chosen the issue on which Dorn could never agree with him. Indeed, the South Dakotan had proposed cutting $31 million from the defense budget, in today's terms some $167, 810,000, a reduction that Hubert Humphrey had said "cut into the very muscle of our defense." Still worse, McGovern seemed to be star-crossed; he could not deliver his convention acceptance speech until most Americans were in bed, and his choice for vice president, Missouri's Thomas Eagleton, was compelled to withdraw after eighteen days because of public outrage over his onetime treatment for bipolar disorder.[49]

As always, Bryan Dorn was careful in his words, knowing that South Carolinians were going to split votes. He disagreed with McGovern most agreeably and he noted his ability to work with the Richard Nixon administration. In the nick of time, President Nixon imposed a tax on imports, and the tariff seemed to help Dorn's Textile Group politically if not economically. Roy Ethridge's attacks on busing, personalized in focus on Bryan Dorn, may have pushed some black people to the polls to vote for their congressman without gaining the Republican challenger much support from supposedly anti-busing millworkers. At least in this season, Dorn was convinced that the preponderance of Third District millworkers could live with busing (especially since it was accomplished for them in relatively high quality county-wide combined schools).[50]

When all votes were tallied, Dorn had one of his most remarkable victories, 75 percent of voters at a moment when his party's presidential electors could only take Massachusetts and the District of Columbia. To be sure, Nixon had no coattails in this election: venerable Kansas Republican Robert

---

[49] Quotation, Charles Dickens, *A Tale of Two Cities*, 1; R. W. Apple Jr., "McGovern Enters the Race Pledging Troop Withdrawal," *New York Times*, 18 January 1971, 1; Humphrey quote and data, David S. Broder, "Nixon Wins Landslide Victory," *Washington Post*, 8 November 1972, 1; Friedman Inflation Calculator, Consumer Price Index, 1790–1975, statistics from *Historical Statistics of the United States* (Washington, DC: USGPO, 1975); 1975–2016, *Statistical Abstracts of the United States* (Washington, DC: USGPO, 2017); Adam Clymer, "Thomas F. Eagleton, 71, a Running Mate for 18 Days, Dies," *New York Times* obit., 5 March 2002; Lawrence K. Altman, "Hasty and Ruinous 1972 Pick Colors Today's Hunt for a No. 2," *New York Times*, 23 July 2012, 1.

[50] "Southern Governors Feel US Should Pay for Busing," *Anderson Independent*, 12 November 1971, 1; WJBD, *OTP*, 249–50; Douglas A. Irwin, "The Nixon Shock After Forty Years: The Import Surcharge Record," *World Trade Review*, 12/1 (January 2013): 29–56.

Dole marked it ruefully as a "personal triumph for Mr. Nixon and not a party triumph." The *Washington Post* headlines shouting the Nixon "landslide" also shouted that the Democrats controlled the House and the Senate. It was, then, a bad year for Democrats in the presidential election but a good year in House elections.

As noted, some claim that Dorn's District Three was always safe for him. For all that, Frank Jordan produced data showing that over the years after World War II it was more risky for incumbents than were other districts. Certainly, too, Democratic congressmen throughout the South were oftentimes changing to the Republican Party or suffering defeat to Republicans or to various iterations of New Democrats. It seems obvious that Bryan Dorn had made his district safe for himself by his decades of effective constituent service—*the lack of which had cost him once in 1948.* It is possible that the personal devotion of "the people" in the Third District—something redundantly testified to in his correspondence and something noted by his shrewd successor, Congressman Butler Carson Derrick Jr.—preserved some votes among constituents otherwise angered by his stand on busing. Dorn himself thought that his constituents had evolved and liberalized on such issues, much as he himself had evolved and liberalized. At any rate, it is noteworthy that he boldly defended busing at a time when Midwestern districts "safe" for Liberal Integrationists were attacking busing.[51]

---

[51] Robert Dole quoted, David Broder, "Nixon Wins Landslide Victory; Democrats Hold Senate, House," *Washington Post*, 8 November 1972, 1; and *Supplemental Report of the Secretary of State to the General Assembly of South Carolina, Reports and Resolutions of the General Assembly, 1973,* ed. Watson; Jordan, *The Primary State*; Derrick, remarks, "Art of Political Biography."

Chapter 11

The Mills Are Closing

1973–2005

South Carolina politics was always about race and families. Scholars knew that, and Bryan Dorn had read their books. Of course, he had learned that just by living where he did in the era. He was convinced by his correspondence and by his close listening to the plain folk back home that a new day really had come, that the millworkers were integrated in the factories now and integrating in their schools, integrating in their army units and integrating on their football teams, and generally ready now for genuine integration everywhere. As noted, when he had spoken against a bill designed to reverse court-mandated busing, he did so out of deep conviction, but also because he was convinced that his people believed as he did. Now he was being called on that vote. It was 29 March1974, the site was Greenville—out of his district and thereby crucial to his hopes to be governor. A "hostile questioner" demanded to know how *dare* he vote against this congressional measure. It was time to tell what he really thought and say what he really believed.[1]

Dorn stood tall, squared his shoulders, and said the truth, the whole truth about race, perhaps for the first time in such a setting in front of so many professing racists:

> Do you think we're going back to the days when the bus went around and picked up the black children and took them to school and came back and picked up the white children? Those days are gone forever. My children ride the bus 10 miles each way to school, and they go to a good consolidated high school, and it's part of a child's education these days to go to school with children of different races and differ-

---

[1] Paul Clancy, retrospective, "Three Capitals" (op. ed. column), *Charlotte Observer*, 29 March 1974, B1; Key with Heard, "South Carolina: The Politics of Color," *Southern Politics in State and Nation,* 130–55; Phillips, "The Central Theme of Southern History"; Roper, *U.B. Phillips: A Southern Mind*, 1–4; ch. 7; 167.

> ent colors and learn it's one small world we live in and that we've got to get along with Chinese and Japanese and people from all countries. My father used to be school superintendent in Greenwood County and I remember when he consolidated the schools, and it ended classism in Greenwood County. And busing might end another kind of "ism."[2]

According to Jack Bass and Paul Clancey, two newspapermen who were there, the hostile questioner sullenly hushed and did not heckle thereafter, and otherwise the crowd seemed to accept it. Bass noted something else: the incident received remarkably little attention in the press; Clancey's piece was published in a feature for Northern eyes that emphasized the change in speech in an "old time Southern mossback." Bass told the incident and placed it in a widely read textbook years later, but no one printed his observations in a newspaper at the time. Polls of the day indicated that most South Carolina voters considered themselves to be "more liberal" than Bryan Dorn on issues of race and other issues too. After years of being careful not to offend right-wing sensibilities, especially *racist* right-wing sensibilities, Bryan Dorn had to worry about not sounding liberal enough. In any case, this segment of the Greenville gathering included a generous portion of textile workers, and he never had troubles with a crowd of working-class people—even in those days when some of the millhands and small-time farmers had been secret Ku Kluxers. Always, they saluted him for what he was, and they counted on him to help them with their VA and Social Security benefits and the myriad things that an active veteran congressman could fix for them.[3]

But the gubernatorial race of 1974 did have its own challenges. For it, Bryan Dorn had borrowed some $300,000, the equivalent of $1.377 million in today's currency. In his baker's dozen congressional races, he had occasionally borrowed the equivalent of $15,000 in current spending power, but generally family and friends had walked places with him and some of the textile classes had sponsored barbeque gatherings. His congressional campaigns were never expensive, even in an era when political races generally were inexpensive; indeed the greatest expenditure was the energy spent on letter writing and speechifying months and even a full year before the many

---

[2] Quoted, Bass and Poole, *The Palmetto State*, 148–49; Clancey, "Northerners Backslide on Busing," *Detroit Free Press*, 29 March 1974, 29A.

[3] Carl Stepp, newspaper polls on SC liberalism, "Who Will Get Ravenel Votes?" *Charlotte Observer*, 3 November 1974, 27A.

walking tours of a fall season. It was very different running for governor in a new era of television "messaging." Especially for a man who had to be reminded to send in a "touched up" photograph for use by the Columbia television station WIS.[4]

There was quite a crowd jostling for position among the Democrats seeking the governorship. There were two barbeque restaurateurs, one riding a white horse and the other a bicycle on their campaigns. The former was Columbia's Lloyd Maurice Bessinger, a melodramatic segregationist who dressed in white and flew Confederate flags and rode a white horse. A mark of the year's relative progressivism is that the Piggie Park proprietor was regarded as a complete anomaly, so much so that his own brother, also a barbeque pitmaster, did not support him. Bessinger's competing barbeque foe was Milton Dukes of Summerville, an ordained Baptist minister and idealist of the New Deal Populistic days who rode his bicycle throughout the low country promising to reform the insurance industry.[5]

Equally idealistic but with more complex proposals were Dorn's erstwhile friend from the Greenville NAACP, John Bolt Culbertson, and Florence's Eugene Noel (Nick) Ziegler. Culbertson, then styled "the bravest white man in South Carolina," enjoyed a generally favorable press and was personally liked by most folk but did not seem to be a likely winner since he had never won statewide political office. By contrast, Ziegler was a onetime assemblyman, successful in both South Carolina House and Senate. In the recent 1972 race for US Senate, Ziegler had tangled with no less than J. Strom Thurmond. He had lost convincingly, but losing to the invincible senator was no disgrace and not necessarily political death. Ziegler was a savant of the arts and author of books about Pee Dee history, gardening, and his beloved Episcopal church. Graduate of the University of the South, he had earned a law degree at Harvard and then served with distinction in naval officer ranks in World War II both in Atlantic and Pacific theaters. Like Culbertson, Ziegler often went before the bar to fight against the powerful and the entrenched on issues of race and gender, and like Culbertson he sometimes won in court what he lost on the hustings. For instance, Ziegler

---

[4] Note, n.d., fall 1974, media invited (Ed Poliakoff?), 1974 campaign folders, WJBD/SCPC.

[5] John Monk, "Lloyd Maurice Bessinger," *Columbia State*, 24 February 2014, B1; "Candidate Dukes Rides Bicycle," *Spartanburg Herald-Journal*, 19 June 1974, B8.

won a case about gender discrimination and he won a major lawsuit against powerful tobacco manufacturers.[6]

Far ahead of these, and likely ahead of Dorn, was veteran assemblyman Earle E. Morris Jr., longtime head of the state Democratic Party, brilliant fundraiser, and John West's lieutenant governor. A Pickens native and Clemson man, Morris was from the very heart of Bryan Dorn's own territory, and his politics were much the same, right down to seeking macroeconomic advice from his old professor Hubert Aull. There were precedents for popular lieutenant governors "ascending" to the governor's chair, but his recent divorce hurt Morris in this very traditionalist state. With Morris's support weakening, a more important rival seemed to be William Childs Westmoreland. "Westy," supreme commander of forces in Vietnam during the period when Bryan Dorn (though not many other people) was convinced the US was "winning," had moved to Charleston, had received an honorary doctor of law degree from the University of South Carolina (facilitated through Dorn), and now stood ready to become governor by acclamation. Since 1973, rumors abounded that the general was available to the Democrats, although he had made no statements about party identification.[7]

In fact, the most important rival was none of these and was not immediately obvious as a threat. This was Charles "Pug" Ravenel, Charleston native with a revered Charleston name who had quarterbacked the Bishop England Catholic High School football team in Charleston, then quarterbacked Harvard, earned an MBA there, and subsequently made a fortune on Wall Street. Hollywood handsome with a self-consciously Kennedyesque haircut and Camelot style, Ravenel had returned to Charleston in 1972 and established the firm Ravenel, Dawson, and Hastie Inc., an investment house dedicated to "assembling investment partnerships to purchase and hold undeveloped land." The financier intended to become the Reform Governor of the twentieth century. Initially, Dorn did not take this candidacy seriously since the congressman generally acknowledged only those with a political record inside South Carolina.[8]

---

[6] 1974 campaign folders, John Bolt Culbertson Papers; Hartsook, "Nick Ziegler," exhibit and blog remembrance, 9 October 2012; 1974 campaign folders, Eugene Noel Ziegler Papers, SCPC; Ziegler, *When Conscience and Power Meet.*

[7] William Childs Westmoreland Papers, 1974, SCPC, hereinafter WCW/SCPC; interview: Herbert Hartsook (28 September 2015), JHR/SCPC.

[8] Ravenel campaign, interview: Bud Ferillo with Roper and Herb Hartsook, 8 November 2013, JHR/SCPC; Charles Ravenel Papers, 1972–1976, SCPC, hereinafter

Among Republicans there was a happy buzz of rumors producing much confusion. Briefly, J. Strom Thurmond was rumored to be planning a campaign for a second term as governor, featuring his young wife, Nancy Moore Thurmond, as First Lady—or perhaps even featuring Nancy Moore as Governor Strom Thurmond's appointive US senator replacing Senator Strom Thurmond. As these rumors dissipated, General Westmoreland revealed himself to be a Republican, and it was assumed that he would win the Republican primary handily, thus becoming the first serious Republican candidate for governor in the twentieth century. Little noticed amongst the discussions about the Thurmond family and Westy was the announcement by James Burrows Edwards that he would seek the Republican nomination. Edwards, a distinguished dental surgeon with ten years of service in the General Assembly and with quiet but substantive fundraising experience, actually enjoyed considerable black support in the low country because of his longstanding racial integrationism. Dr. Edwards's racial progressivism went back long decades: he had always served black patients right alongside white patients, and he had sponsored black physicians and surgeons for statewide offices and honors. But his announcement of candidacy in fall of 1974 was back-page news compared to speculation about Senator Thurmond and discussions about General Westmoreland.[9]

When the 93rd Congress convened, Bryan Dorn became chairman of the VA committee, and he remained the ranking member of the Public Works Committee. Although he was anxious to run for governor, he delayed an announcement until November so that he could focus his own and media attention on the construction at the Columbia VA Hospital and the development there of the school of medicine associated with the University of South Carolina. Many congressmen in January 1973 were talking about "dirty tricks" played by Nixon against McGovern, with heavy discussions about impeachment, but the South Carolinian initially paid little attention to these discussions. As he noted then and later, "McGovern never had a chance," and Nixon "did not need to cheat," but was elected overwhelmingly by the people. Even so, *Washington Post* journalists Bob Woodward and Carl

---

CR/SCPC; interview: John Carl West with Herbert Hartsook, 10 July 1997, John Carl West Papers, hereinafter, JCW/SCPC.

[9] Bass with Thompson, *Ol' Strom*, 235–39; Garry Clifford, "With His Young Wife's Help," *People Magazine*, 10/22 (27 November 1978); interview: James Burrows Edwards with Roper, 8 August 2012, JHR/SCPC.

Bernstein amassed considerable evidence of Nixon's people spying on Democratic candidates and illegally raising and hiding huge sums of money for the 1972 campaign. Since operatives for the Committee to Reelect the President (CREEP) were convicted of breaking into Democratic Party headquarters at the Watergate Hotel, the various scandals—spying, rumor mongering, illegal fundraising, secret spending—were grouped together loosely as Nixon's Watergate scandal.[10] Compounding Watergate scandals was an unrelated and separate Justice Department investigation into the vice president, begun when Spiro Agnew was governor of Maryland. As noted, Dorn liked Agnew, found him a complicated man—after all, he had done racially progressive things in Baltimore County and then in the state of Maryland—and agreed with him about a hawkish stand in Vietnam. On the other hand, Agnew did not comport himself as Dorn thought a politician should in his treatment of opponents during the debates. As more and more evidence of Agnew's personal corruption began to emerge, Dorn distanced himself. There was a fair amount of evidence that Agnew took bribes not only in Maryland as a state politician but also while sitting vice president. Too, he apparently had evaded paying taxes, and the congressman was one who routinely turned over his full IRS statement to public scrutiny and urged that all officeholders do so. On 10 October 1973, Agnew resigned, and Dorn thought this resignation for the best, since he judged that Agnew's misdeeds were completely independent of anything Nixon did—and especially since the deeply respected Gerald Rudolph Ford, longtime House minority leader, was willing to step in to be the vice president. Dorn, while ambivalent about Agnew's actual guilt, was glad to see Ford come and considered that this good and decent man could assist President Nixon mightily in doing things, most of which the congressman fully supported.[11]

---

[10] Alfred E. Lewis, "5 Held in Plot to Bug Democrats' Office Here," *Washington Post*, 18 June 1972, A1 (contributions by Bob Woodward and Carl Bernstein et al.); Woodward and Bernstein, "Bug Suspect Got Campaign Funds," *Washington Post*, 1 August 1972, Al; Woodward and Bernstein, "Mitchell Controlled Secret GOP Funds," *Washington Post*, 29 September 1972, Al; Woodward and Bernstein, "FBI Finds Nixon Aides Sabotaged Democrats," *Washington Post*, 10 October 1972, Al; Woodward and Bernstein, *All the Presidents' Men*; idem., *The Final Days*; WJBD, *OTP*, 252; Woodward, comp. and ed., *Responses of Presidents to Charges of Misconduct*, x–xii; 349–53.

[11] Witcover, *White Knight*; James N. Naughton, "Agnew Quits Vice Presidency," *New York Times*, 10 October 1973, 1; Cannon, *Time and Chance*; James N. Naughton and Adam Clymer, "Gerald Rudolph Ford, 38th President, Dies," *New York Times* obit., 27

Nevertheless, Dorn's view was hardly shared by many. Investigations into the Watergate scandal continued. Prodded by journalists and by popular pressure from citizens, as well as responding to unique opportunities during the winter of 1974, congressmen and senators took up the myriad issues involving Nixon's deeds and misdeeds. On 9 May 1974, Peter Wallace Rodino of New Jersey's Tenth District, and sixty-four-year-old chair of the House Judiciary Committee, began formal hearings. Other committees were also investigating, but if Rodino's committee reported out Articles of Impeachment, and if those articles were accepted by the House, then the US Senate would try the case as presented by the representatives. Dorn was a longtime friend of Rodino, but the piedmont farmer was always skeptical of Watergate's importance and dubious about the motives of Nixon's opponents.[12]

Many veteran Democrats thought that the overwhelmingly Democratic House and solidly Democratic Senate had an ideal opportunity to regain power in all branches of government—and their aspirations angered Dorn despite his love for his party. His friend Allen Drury, Millie Johnson's onetime writing partner, had convinced the congressman at the end of World War II that the *Washington Post* was a highly politicized organ of the left wing of the Democratic Party and not a fair newspaper at all. He realized that many journalists, politicians, and average citizens thought that Nixon and Agnew were corrupt and merited punishment, but Dorn said that judgment was overly harsh. Generally, Dorn considered that a number of issues not truly germane to the 1972 presidential campaign were clouding judgments about Nixon's actions: the slow and bloody disengagement from Vietnam, the emerging revelations about how expensive the long war had actually been, the *New York Times* publication of the Pentagon Papers that showed patterns of systematic government lying about Vietnam, unhappiness over wage and price controls, worries about inflation, and concern about loss of manufacturing jobs. For his part, Bryan Dorn defended Nixon, personally visited the president to assure him of his support, and began a speaking tour in which he "defended politicians" generally and called for a return to patriotism and support for public servants. This is not the place to judge in some final sense Nixon's guilt or innocence, but only to mark it that Bry-

---

December 2006; WJBD, IRS statement and statement of personal wealth, 1973, enclosure, WJBD to Clerk of House of Representatives, WJBD/SCPC.

[12] Michael T. Kaufman, "Peter W. Rodino Dies at 96 [*sic*]; Led House Inquiry on Nixon," *New York Times*, 8 May 2005, obit.; "Rodino," *Congressional Biographical Directory*, s.v.

an Dorn then and thereafter disagreed with the majority of both houses, with majority public opinion (in which Nixon fell to 24 percent approval that summer), and with the measured assessment provided by a team of distinguished historians headed by Yale University's C[omer] Vann Woodward. Although Bryan Dorn now accepted Vann Woodward's explanation of Jim Crow, he did not accept the historian's explanation of Nixon's "presidential misconduct."[13]

In November of 1973, Bryan Dorn notified Speaker Carl Albert that he was not seeking reelection in 1974 in order that he could run for governor. Speaker Albert and Majority Leader Tip O'Neill would need to talk with other Democratic leaders to make the tentative assignments for committee chairmanships and memberships for the 94th Congress. More to the point, he sent in his notice to Robert Strauss and Lawrence O'Brien of the Democratic National Committee and to Don Fowler of the South Carolina Democratic Party. His old friend Fowler remarked that the Republicans could not seem to find a candidate but the Democrats had too many. Bryan Dorn assured all concerned that attorney Butler Carson Derrick Jr., Johnston native and assemblyman representing Edgefield from 1969 to 1974, stood ready to serve as Third District congressman—and that Derrick would be reliably within the traditions of the Populistic New Deal Southerners.[14]

Congressman Dorn had disagreements with President Nixon through the years, and the fights were the same ones he had had with every sitting president, save Jack Kennedy. He wanted strong and specific quotas on imported apparel and other trade restrictions to protect the textile industry. Although Nixon had imposed generalized reduction of imports late in 1972 during the election campaign, Dorn was concerned that "unless the Nixon administration rigidly enforces the agreements, the U.S. will be outfoxed, out-traded and sabotaged again by the Japanese." The other fight was also one he had

[13] Drury (with Mildred Johnson), *A Senate Journal*; Drury, *Advise and Consent*; Drury, *Anna Hastings*, Irvin Rare Book Collection, Hollings Library, USC; WJBD to Sarah Jamison Bailey, 24 February 1961, re Mildred Johnson and Allan Drury, WJBD/SCPC; WJBD, *OTP*, 251–52; Nixon approval ratings, 1974, Gallup Historical Presidential Job Approval Statistics, *Gallup Historical Statistics and Trends*, IRSS/UNC; Woodward, comp. and ed., *Responses of Presidents*, introd. and 349–53; Roper, *C. Vann Woodward*, 263–67; 339n.

[14] Butler Carson Derrick Jr., remarks, "The Art of Political Biography," 22 January 2012, SCPC; Butler Carson Derrick Papers, 1974–1975, SCPC; Debbie Dorn to WJBD and Millie Johnson Dorn, 10 March 1975, WJBD/SCPC.

with all presidents, again excepting Jack Kennedy. There were proposals to cut VA benefits, in this case some $160 million from allocations for Vietnam-era veterans with disabilities. In 2016 dollars, the cut amounted to more than $932,500,000. Also, President Nixon had impounded funds appropriated by Congress for I-77 as it extended from Charlotte to Columbia; it was a pet project of Dorn's, and of course he disavowed any ability of the president to impound—or otherwise prevent the spending of—funds duly appropriated by the House of Representatives. As was obvious from his career, the sitting chairman of the VA and the ranking member of Public Works Committee intended to expand, not contract, highway building just as much as he intended to expand and not contract disability and educational benefits, with particular focus on Vietnam-era veterans. As he marked it, some friends from time to time said in print that he was too desperately needed in the US House of Representatives to run for governor, and he marked the compliment ruefully since he was bound in determination to run for governor and did not need friends providing reasons to vote against him.[15]

Things became hectic indeed, for he spent the period from February to November in 1974 engaging in major struggles in DC while attempting a full statewide campaign, especially one featuring television—when he was past master only of campaigning face-to-face and barbeque to barbeque in the Third District. He accepted some advice, reluctantly laying aside his signature white suits because they made him look like "the Political Good Humor man, all dressed in white." He hired J. Crawford Cook, the first in a paid professional campaign staff, and Cook supervised television taping, much of which went badly. Dorn, always delighted to be around people and almost feasting on avuncular small talk with strangers, yet hated posing for photographs and hated still more posing for taping. Away from actual constituents, dealing with a camera, he became wooden and almost withdrawn. One otherwise sympathetic archivist noted, "The Congressman always looked miserable in his posed pictures, almost like he was smelling something offensive."[16]

---

[15] WJBD, *OTP*, 255, quoted, 249; Friedman Inflation Calculator Consumer Price Index statistics, 1974–1975 from *Historical Statistics of the United States* (Washington, DC: USGPO, 1975); 1975–2012, *Statistical Abstracts of the United States* (Washington, DC: USGPO, 2017).

[16] WJBD, *OTP*, 259; WJBD, Campaign Files, 1974, WJBD/SCPC; Herbert Hartsook to Roper, 19 December 2013, JHR/SCPC.

As for the crowded field of candidates who were back in South Carolina full time, there were some legal questions about residency for General Westmoreland and for Pug Ravenel. The South Carolina Constitution declared,

> No person shall be eligible to the office of Governor who denies the existence of the Supreme Being; and who on the date of such election has not attained the age of thirty years; and who shall not have been a citizen of the United States and a citizen and resident of this State for five years next preceding the day of election. No person while Governor shall hold any office or other commission (except in the militia) under the authority of this State, or of any other power.

It had never before been an issue. General Westmoreland, active in the US Army more recently than five years, had claimed South Carolina residency and had paid taxes in the state in the time period. Attorney General Daniel R. McLeod decided not to rule on any question concerning Westy's status. State Republican Party chairman Kenneth Powell said, "I just wish the Democratic Attorney General would come out with an opinion that a four-star general who has paid taxes in this state, been born here, and has family here is not a resident. That would suit me just fine."[17]

There were similar issues of residency for Pug Ravenel, who had been active on Wall Street for fifteen years and had paid taxes in New York. He had declared residency and established a land development business in Charleston, but only recently. By the time of the election, his business and residential occupancy in Charleston would each amount to some two and a half years, well short of the five consecutive years required. Bryan Dorn initially paid little attention to the issue for Ravenel; he considered military service in Vietnam quite different from trading stocks on Wall Street, and he considered that Westmoreland had done other things (early declaration of residency, paying taxes) that Ravenel had not done. Thus, Dorn saw no inconsistency in his understanding of Westmoreland's eligibility and his understanding of Ravenel's ineligibility. Nor did he see any ironic parallel between Ravenel's situation and his own youthful entry into politics when there had been controversy about twenty-four-year-old Dorn's eligibility for the House in the General Assembly. In any case, he did not mark it that

---

[17] See WJBD, *OTP*, 259; South Carolina Constitution, Article IV, Section 2, Office of Governor; "Gen. Westmoreland Runs for Gov. of SC," (UPI), Lodi, CA *News Sentinel*, 13 March 1974, 5; Westmoreland Folder, 1974, C. Kenneth Powell Papers, SCPC.

Ravenel was a serious candidate for the Democratic nomination. Whatever the merits of Ravenel's case for residency, Dorn took his eye off the ball concerning Ravenel's appeal to the public, especially college-educated youth.[18]

Whether prepared for the legal considerations or not, Ravenel was certainly prepared to take his case directly to the people—and through television. He ran a very effective television advertisement in which he sat comfortably and naturally in the shade of a live oak in Magnolia Gardens and said simply, "South Carolina is my home." The Dorn people belatedly saw how effective the advertisements were, and they tried to intervene and impress on Ravenel the legal issues. Steve Griffith, general counsel for Duke Power and intensely interested in cousin Bryan Dorn's campaign, urged the congressman to file a protest against Ravenel's candidacy at once. Griffith has recalled that Dorn declined, stating that the campaign was going to be "fun" and also expressing doubt in March of 1974 that Ravenel could ever be the kind of opponent that Earle Morris already was. Governor John West recalled a meeting with Ravenel in which the sitting chief executive expressed his doubts about the Charlestonian's eligibility but declined to issue an opinion and instead referred him to "the best lawyer I could think of," Harry M. Lightsey. He noted years later in an interview that Lightsey called West back to tell him that he had proffered an opinion that "I don't think your friend wanted to hear," namely, that the Supreme Court on appeal would rule against his eligibility.[19]

However, Ravenel persisted and approached South Carolina Attorney General McLeod, who advised that the would-be candidate seek an opinion from the Circuit Court. He did, and Judge John Grimball ruled that Ravenel was fully eligible to run. Judge Grimball also declared that Ravenel had been born a resident and had done nothing to "lose his residency" by being educated out of state. Grimball did not say so specifically, but he seemed to give credence to Ravenel's claim that his years of working for financiers Donaldson, Lufkin, and Jenrette, Inc., in New York were part of an educational experience during which time he had never lost his residency. Two issues are

---

[18] WJBD, OTP, 259–60; interviews: Steve Griffith with Hartsook and Roper (31 January 2012); Herbert Hartsook to Roper, 19 December 2013; and notes, Eldred E. Prince, remarks, Phi Alpha Theta Conference on Election of 1974, Coastal Carolina University, 2 December 2014, JHR/SCPC.

[19] Interview: Steve Griffith with Hartsook and Roper (31 January 2012) and Bud Ferillo with Hartsook and Roper (8 November 2013), JHR/SCPC; interview: West with Hartsook (10 July 1997), JCW/SCPC; Campaign, Charles Ravenel Papers, SCPC (hereinafter CR/SCPC).

important with regard to Judge Grimball's ruling: first, a Circuit Court judge could always be overruled on appeal to the State Supreme Court, and second, the South Carolina Constitution declared that such issues could be settled at the time of the general election rather than at the time of filing for the primary election. In other words, the State Supreme Court could overturn Judge Grimball's ruling after the primary, even in mid-August. Each of those points would reemerge.[20]

Another controversy involved timing, namely, *when* to schedule the Democratic primary. When Dorn first borrowed money and began notifying people of his intentions, he thought that the primary would be held on 11 June. However, the General Assembly was wrestling with several issues concerning representation and apportionment, and whatever they finally decided would have to be approved by the Justice Department because of the Voting Rights Act of 1965—and because of demonstrated decades of racist abuse against black citizens attempting to vote. It became obvious that the General Assembly would not be through with its work in time for an 11 June primary. The money concerned Dorn, for he noted, "There is a lot of difference in planning a campaign to end on July 16 rather than June 11." The larger concern, however, was the looming vote on the impeachment of Richard Nixon. Dorn, as one of the few defenders of the president, stood to lose votes either way, "no matter what decision I made." With regret, he marked it that "the state legislature was in a position to make or break candidates, based on the primary date they set."[21]

The candidate most likely to be "made" by a late primary date was Pug Ravenel. Dorn kept a clipping from an observer, probably Charleston newspaperman Hugh Gibson, "the roving reporter," who said, "Ravenel won't make it off the launching pad in a June primary. But he might make it all the way to the governor's office if he has the gift of an additional ten weeks or so in which to campaign." Indeed, the state senate set the date for 16 July, and the congressman unhappily recorded polling data in early June that showed Dorn himself with 24 percent approval, Earle Morris with 20 percent, and "newcomer" Ravenel with 13 percent approval. But such data also

[20] See WJBD, *OTP*, 260; "No Appeal Planned by McClane," *Sumter Daily Item*, 1 May 1974, 1B; "Despite Years of Absence, Court Rules Ravenel 'Remained SC Resident'; Can Run for Office," (AP) *Danville Register*, 30 April 1974, 12; South Carolina Constitution, Article IV, Section 2 Office of Governor; interview, West with Hartsook (10 July 1997), JCW/SCPC.

[21] Quoted, WJBD, *OTP*, 260–61.

showed a real trend of increasing support for Ravenel. Dorn also noted his displeasure when told "more and more people replied, 'I'm voting for the TV man,'" a reference to the brilliant advertising spots for the "telegenic" Ravenel placed in stations broadcasting from Greenville, Columbia, and Charleston.[22]

As the 16 July primary loomed ever nearer, as "the TV man" gained more and more support, as Earle Morris gained more and more support, the lame-duck congressman faced a daunting set of facts about representing South Carolina in 1974. Textile unemployment was growing, not only amongst his millworker masses but amongst middle management and even amongst some properly listed in the textile classes. The two Carolinas were now the most industrialized states in the US—and most such industrial employment was *not* textile. The educational reforms of Governors Russell through West, all assisted mightily by federal money swept in by Congressman Dorn, had laid the groundwork for a different kind of economic structure, one built on high-wage, high-skills manufacturing, racially integrated, well educated, nonunionized, and materially well-off, closing in on national norms for income, wealth, savings, educational levels, and health (specifically, around 75 percent of national norms, where once each marker had stood close to 50 percent). Yet textiles remained the major player in Dorn's own district and was thus a major factor throughout much of South Carolina. Indeed, in 1973, more people worked in the textile industry in South Carolina than in any previous year. The Recession of 1973 to 1975 was later officially dated by the NBER to start in November of 1973 when employment and growth reached its peak in the first year of Nixon's reelection. Whoever was measuring, it was well underway by the following summer when the Democratic primary was attempted.[23]

---

[22] Hugh Gibson quoted, WJBD, *OTP*, 261; Gibson paraphrased, interview, West with Hartsook (10 June 1997), JCW/SCPC.

[23] Donald Schunk and Douglas Woodward, *A Profile of the Diversified South Carolina Economy, 1970–2000* (Columbia: Darla Moore School of Business at University of South Carolina, 2000); Valerie Personick, "Industrial Output and Employment at the End of the Century," *Monthly Labor Review* (September 1987): 36; Robert J. Gordon, "The Response of Wages and Prices to the First Two Years of Contraction," *Brookings Papers on Economic Activity*, vol. 3 (fall/winter 1973): 765–79. Edmund Ravenel Roper Sr., my father, was a textile executive and conversant with the circle of Textile Classes, including Peace, MacEachern, Inabinet, and Lowenstein; he lost his position in the Recession, as did a number of regional Textile Classes, some of whom were studied by Dr.

The representative as usual was displeased with professional economists talking about "natural rates of unemployment" and "mild inflation" and "moderate contraction." What Dorn saw was mills closing, unemployment approaching Eisenhower levels in his own district, inflation at 10 percent and rising, and the Index of Consumer Confidence at a post-World War II low of 58 percent. With hindsight, he himself realized years later something that no one could quite see then: this "mild" Recession from 1973 to 1975 was, in fact, a major structural change in which textile manufacturing began its long (and initially rather graceful) exit from the Palmetto State and the Tar Heel State. Other manufacturing jobs replaced millwork, and service jobs emerged in the cities in education, allied health care, government, and (Ravenel's specialty) investment banking and finance. As state textile employment fell from 158,000 to 155,500 workers, Dorn and the Textile Group thought in terms of the three Eisenhower recessions. When those three downturns were at last over, textile employment had again rocketed upward under Jack Kennedy, finally attaining its remarkable peak during the beginning of Nixon's second term. Dorn and the Textile Group in Congress and the textile classes back in the state Chamber of Commerce and the state Development Board were sure that the usual import restrictions based on the complicated apparatus of quotas and special exemptions would restore the whole economy—and textile employment would press toward 165,000. In fact, such employment would drop and drop and drop, reaching 137,300 by the end of 1974. From that year, textile employment would continue to drop until its virtual disappearance in the new century that William Jennings Bryan Dorn welcomed in as a private citizen back on his farmland. But he knew none of this in the first year of the Recession, Dr. Aull did not even suspect it, and the congressman worked feverishly with the Textile Group across party lines and across regional lines to restore textiles while he watched his polling numbers fall as rapidly as Richard Nixon's.[24]

Robert Hopkins and Dr. Thomas Till of the business and economics department at St. Andrews Presbyterian College.

[24] Schunk and Woodward, loc. cit., 6, figure 1; Kimberly Zeuli, "Communitiy Resilience in Southern Mill Towns," *Federal Reserve Bank of Richmond Bulletin*, 9 May 2012; Mark Mittlehauser, "Employment Trends, Textile and Apparel, 1975–2005," *Monthly Labor Review*, August 1997, 24, 25; US Dept. of Labor. Bur. of Labor Statistics, *Employment, Hours and Earnings* (winter 1984) vol. 2, 784; Victor Zarnowitz and Geoffrey H. Moore, "Recession and Recovery, 1973–1976," *NBER Explorations in Economic Research*, 4/4 (winter, 1977) 1–87.

Brother Watson Dorn and cousin Steve Griffith, Assemblyman John Drummond, aspirant congressman Butler Derrick, and journalists Jack Bass, Hugh Gibson, Lee Bandy, and Paul Clancey all marveled at the 1974 primary races. *Nothing was as it had been.* In the Republican contest, attracting fewer than 35,000 voters, General Westmoreland was handily defeated by the unassuming and vastly underrated Dr. Edwards. Edwards garnered 20,177 votes, or 57.7 percent of the total. Moreover, after taking the victory, Dr. Edwards graciously went to friends and associates to raise money to help the disgruntled four-star general pay off some $15,000 of campaign debts. Had the situation been reversed, it seems unlikely that the general would have expended time and energy to help Dr. Edwards with any debts. More to the point, Jim Edwards showed in all phases of the campaign, particularly the weeks after his triumph, the kind of disinterested professionalism and the kind of fence-mending that would be required of a governor. Nor was he working only for his personal political goals. He was a major, perhaps the major, factor in building a strong and effective Republican Party in his state, and his work in the summer of 1974 was vital and valuable in such a mission. For the nonce, he quietly raised money for the coming November contests—in which registered Democrats would outnumber registered Republicans by approximately ten to one—and he watched intently as the majority Democrats gave him talking points and demonstrated various vulnerabilities in their protracted interparty struggles.[25]

As for the congressman's part of the summer campaigns, he kept long hours even by his own standards, estimating that he was either legislating or campaigning a minimum of fourteen hours every day. Much of the time, he enjoyed himself, especially the long road trips down country roads with various friends and allies. In particular, he had fun with I. DeQuincey (Deek) Newman, the veteran NAACP official who was helping him seek and gain black votes, especially in the rural low country. The two Baptists enjoyed their stories and their friends and their liquor as much as any other members of that denomination, and they had a grand time driving around on the campaigns. Deek Newman often assured Congressman Dorn that he would easily gain 70 percent of black votes in the primary alone. The two did not realize that this estimate was based on older black church members and was a spectacular miscalculation of younger black voters, many of whom ap-

[25] State Elections Commission, *SC Elections Report, 1974* (Columbia: SC State Elections Commission, 1975); interview: James Burrows Edwards (9 August 2012), JHR/SCPC.

peared energized for the primary. Despite the good, hard work, and despite the obvious affection shown for the "Congressman of the People," Bass and Gibson and Clancy noted how little impact Dorn was having on urban voters, especially young ones of either race; and brother Watson and cousin Steve noted how unwilling the congressman and his wife, Millie Dorn, were to delegate authority to other campaign workers. Friends and professionals began to fear disaster even as the Dorns soldiered on happily in the old routines with the old friends and allies.[26]

On 16 July, when 307,929 of some 450,000 registered Democrats actually voted, Pug Ravenel narrowly edged Bryan Dorn, 107,345 to 105,743, or by percentage of votes, 33.6 to 33.1. Dorn for his part was excited to put distance between himself and Earle Morris, whom he persistently regarded as the greater practical threat in the race. Morris gathered 80,242 votes, or some 25.2 percent of all votes cast. Maurice Bessinger barely registered despite (or in 1974 perhaps because of) his old-time racist, almost circus appeal, taking a mere 7,883 votes, or 2.5 percent. Gaining even fewer votes were, respectively, "the bravest white man in the state" John Bolt Culbertson, 4,187 and 1.3 percent; and Milton Dukes, 2,529 or 0.8 percent. To Dorn, it was all good. Surely the fine piedmont folk who supported his old friend Earle Morris would hurry to his side; surely, too, "stay at home" Democrats, somewhere between 40,000 and 100,000 voters, would come out and vote in the well-publicized, clear-cut, two-man contest. Surely, then, the "newcomer" could be banished in the runoff, which was scheduled for 30 July.[27]

The "newcomer" had made his own calculations. Marvin Chernoff, onetime campaign manager for Hubert Humphrey, helped Ravenel develop a television-based campaign that targeted the citizenry of the metropolitan areas, Greenville, Charleston, and Columbia. Originally planning to spend around $300,000, Ravenel eventually spent something north of a half-million dollars, much more than what was spent by his six competitors. With Chernoff's guidance, Ravenel perfected short, sharp television images emphasizing his newness to the political scene, his youth and energy, and a bit vaguely, his progressivism. Implied though never said was the fact of Dorn's

---

[26] WJBD, *OTP*, 261–62; 1974 Primary Folders, WJBD, SCPC; 1974 Primary Folders, Charles Ravenel Papers, SCPC.

[27] State Elections Commission, loc. cit.; Elections Series, 16 June 1974, Democratic Party of South Carolina, SCPC, hereinafter DPSC/SCPC.

age, his long years of political service, and his association with Washington politics, all things noted negatively by pollsters, especially as expressed by young, affluent, and well-educated people. Too, South Carolina's population was expanding dramatically—it would more than double between the Census of 1960 and the Census of 2000—and much of the increased population were out-of-staters who had moved south, thus themselves "newcomers." Ravenel made special (and highly successful) appeal to the many newcomer voters. In other words, with hindsight, it is obvious that Bryan Dorn's strengths, especially in the midst of Vietnam war-weariness and Watergate corruption, were his *weaknesses* in the eyes of many voters throughout the state. And conversely, what Dorn regarded as Ravenel's weaknesses—his newcomer status and lack of experience, his non-record in politics, even his lengthy absence from South Carolina—were strengths in the eyes of many voters.[28]

And so Bryan Dorn flew to DC to support Nixon and to support what remained of the Indochina military efforts and to negotiate on behalf of textile jobs. In each case, he still thought things were winnable, both in Vietnam and in Ware Shoals. The former was at least debatable, but the latter was becoming clear to everyone else: Ware Shoals was not the issue, but rather Greenville, Charleston, and Columbia. Then he flew back to South Carolina to drive the back roads and go to the textile mills at shift changes and speak to high school crowds and Rotary Clubs and Lions Clubs and otherwise campaign as always, with an emphasis on small towns. Ravenel put just as much energy into his campaign, but all of it was aimed at the bright future of the non-textile and non-farming, generally non-industrial service sectors of three cities. On 30 July, candidate Ravenel built up an immediate lead as urban wards reported in votes for him. Dorn expected as much, and was pleased to see the piedmont rural wards going his way. But Ravenel's strategy was clearly the superior one, and the runoff was not close at all. More than 341,000 people voted, an increase of nearly 11 percent above the 16 July primary. The Morris people, if they voted at all, did not come in a great bloc over to Dorn, and the stay-at-homes must have come out in full force for Ravenel. Ravenel took 186,985, or 54.8 percent of votes cast; Dorn mustered only 154,187, or 45.19 percent. For the first time,

[28] Interview: Bud Ferillo with Roper and Herbert Hartsook (8 November 2013), JHR/SCPC; 1974 Primary Campaign folders, CR/SCPC; 1974 Primary Campaign folders, especially flyer, WJBD, Democratic Barbeque Planned, Barratt House, WJBD/SCPC.

Congressman Dorn knew exactly what Congressman Butler Black Hare had felt in 1942 when Hare was "the tired old guy" with balding pate and his opponent was the young fellow with no record at all. Remembering as much, Dorn also knew how to behave in such a loss. When the evening was still young, Bryan Dorn went to Pug Ravenel's headquarters in Columbia and grandly shook hands and offered full support in November, reminding the nominee that there would be a "superb" Labor Day weekend barbeque to kick off the general campaign at Barratt House, and that Pug Ravenel would be the featured dignitary there.[29]

Congressman Dorn was now not only a lame duck but a lame duck with no prospects for any office (certainly not the governorship). As a congressman, lame duck or otherwise, he needed to hurry back to DC for more voting on military affairs, public works impoundments—and above all, impeachment hearings. On the very day that he absorbed his overwhelming defeat, he learned from staffers the major *New York Times* headline of the day: "House Committee, 21 to 17, Adopts Impeachment Articles Charging President Defied Its Subpoena." Now everything was ready for a trial of the executive involving both legislative houses. Such a thing had not happened since Andrew Johnson was impeached and then survived his trial in 1866. Now that the House committee had acted, Dorn was quite beside himself: no more doubtful than beforehand about Nixon's fitness to remain president, he could count votes well enough to see how likely it was that Nixon would be convicted and removed. He needed to get back to DC. But he paused to see reporters, all long time friends, and make a statement: "There's one thing about the Democratic Party of South Carolina that I learned years ago—we stay together. I will support Mr. Ravenel in November. He just licked me and that's all. I'm going to do everything I can for him."[30]

Back in DC, things were quite evolved. Nixon was on the way out. He was candidly *with* only a few trusted advisors, mostly Henry Kissinger, who leaked out word that the president, usually so sharp and incisive, was rambling and vague. White House Chief of Staff Alexander Meigs Haig Jr.,

---

[29] Democratic Run-off Primary, 30 July 1974, State Elections Commission, loc. cit.; "Defeated Candidate and Wife," AP photograph and caption, *Aiken Standard*, 31 July 1974, 1.; "tired old guy," interview: Steve Griffith with Roper and Hartsook (31 January 2012), JHR/SCPC.

[30] James M. Naughton, "House Committee 21 to 17 Adopts Impeachment Article," *New York Times*, 31 July 1974, 1; "Article III Passed by Panel," *Washington Post*, 31 July 1974, 1; "Judiciary Committee," *Washington Post*, 31 July 1974, A 20; WJBD quoted, "Ravenel and West Air November Plans," *Aiken Standard*, 31 July 1974, 1.

decorated veteran and once second in command in the US Army, was performing the role of going between Nixon and Republican leaders and apparently working to help Nixon resign with dignity. The good Gerald Rudolph Ford, himself appointed vice president and not elected, was prepared to step in and restore order and decency. Negotiations went forward, none of them involving Bryan Dorn in any substantive way, and the congressman and his staff listened to rumors much as did everyone on Capitol Hill. Then, on the evening of 8 August, President Nixon asked to meet with a "small group" of legislators, which the congressman remembered as including Senators John Stennis of Mississippi, Barry Goldwater of Arizona, Harry Byrd of Virginia, Jesse Helms of North Carolina, and Strom Thurmond of South Carolina. The only representatives he remembered, and the only Democrats he remembered, were his old VA chair Tiger Teague of Texas and Dorn himself. Given the importance of the meeting and Dorn's odd angle of perspective as participant/observer but not as major player in the proceedings, it seems worthwhile inserting almost all that he said about the meeting:

> It was obvious that Nixon was terribly upset when he came in. Everything he had hoped for and achieved was slipping away. As he walked into the Cabinet Room, we stood and applauded. He gave us a forced smile. It was very awkward and he had trouble getting started. He said, 'This will be the last time I am going to sit in the Cabinet Room." He laughed out loud several times for no apparent reason—a kind of uncontrolled, ghoulish laugh. Then he told us about his early years in college athletics. He said the only reason he made the football team as a freshman was that only eleven men tried out. He talked about always having to work harder than everyone else. He mentioned one game which he played with a broken ankle and told us how he always fought hard and had never given up on anything. Then he told us he didn't want to resign the presidency. "My personal inclination is to fight to the finish. Every inch of me says to fight." His family had urged him to fight to the end. When he made references to his family he had to stop. It seemed like ages to me. It was quiet as death in that room. Several times he fought hard to continue at all.
>
> After an interval he said that he would resign in the interest of the country. He said he realized that the impeachment hearings and the Senate trial would last perhaps eight months. During that time the country would have a part-time president and a Senate focused on the trial. He felt he had to consider what was best for the nation and the cause of freedom. He told us that he recognized that we had stood by him for a strong national defense, and he appreciated what we had done. Then he told us that our support had made possible the with-

> drawal of troops from Vietnam with honor and the return of our POWs from North Vietnam.
>
> At the conclusion of his talk, he expressed hope that he had not let us—his friends—down. Then he broke down. As he left his chair, he staggered or tripped and his aides grabbed his arms to steady him for a few steps. He left with a bowed head, while we stood and applauded. Most of those present were in tears. It was sadder than attending my mother's funeral. Jesse Helms, who sat next to me, commented several times as though to himself, "Bless his heart, bless his heart."[31]

Part of Dorn's strong reaction was personal: Nixon too was part of his Class of 1947 in the postwar House of Representatives. Early, late, and in the middle of the impeachment hearings, Bryan Dorn always insisted in public and private that Richard Nixon was "one of my favorite Presidents." Although he never "rated" them as such, he left firm opinions about all the other executives, and from those notes it seems clear that JFK was his favorite and Nixon a close second. He admired what Nixon had accomplished, including the opening of ties to China and the way he made liberal Democratic policies work efficiently. Part of his reaction was his need for institutional stability, both for himself and for his people. His studies and reflections on the Civil War were unusual for a Southerner, in that he deeply regretted the war's coming at all, quoting often from Georgia's Alexander Stephens, vice president of the Confederate States of America who worked, if not schemed, often to end the fighting early. He also quoted often from Henry Grady, the Atlanta newspaperman who urged a New South based on industrial development, racial harmony (albeit with segregation), and peace with Northerners. Even more unusual for a Southerner of his era was his pleasure that slavery ended and that Abraham Lincoln had established a better government than ever envisioned by Thomas Jefferson. His constant use of Lincoln's phrases, especially "of the people, by the people, and for the people" was quite calculated. Indeed, *of the people* became the title of his memoir.[32] But there was something else: Nixon was not the only sitting of-

---

[31] Quoted, WJBD, *OTP*, 252–54; Woodward and Bernstein, *Final Days*; Cannon, *Time and Chance*; John Herbers, "Nixon Resigns," *New York Times*, 9 August 1974, 1; Anthony Ripley, "Ford Will Take Office," *New York Times*, 9 August 1974, 1.

[32] Christmas address, n.d., (1960s) quoting Henry Grady, copy in possession of Steve Griffith; WJBD to Georgia Craven, 26 August 1966; Robert G. Stephens Jr. to WJBD, 9 June 1961, WJBD/SCPC.

ficeholder of whom Dorn could write, "everything he had hoped for and achieved was slipping away."[33]

In September, suddenly it was Pug Ravenel who faced the prospect of watching hopes and achievements slipping away. As marked, Circuit Court Judge Grimball's ruling was subject to review by the State Supreme Court, and an appeal of Grimball's ruling was filed to that body. The appeal noted that Ravenel had paid taxes and listed himself as a resident only two consecutive years, and it declared extreme doubts about the "out of state educational experience" of fifteen years making a fortune for Wall Street financiers Donaldson, Lufkin, and Jenrette. The appeal was filed by "Friendly" Ben Dekle, a country and western disc jockey for Cayce radio station WCAY.[34]

Friendly Ben was a Dorn original, if not a tall-tale character worthy of good stories and bad literature. He waxed philosophic on the airwaves in between playing the popular country and western music so loved by Bryan Dorn's constituents in the mill villages and on the small farms—and so cornball and disconnected for the urban and well-educated youth who were Pug Ravenel's followers. Besides a steady stream of banter about common sense and hard work, Friendly Ben Dekle had dreamed up the Chitlin Strut for the community of Salley in Aiken County in 1966. The Chitlin Strut was Deep South and deep country, and it was also interracial, since both black and white people liked chitterlings (chitlins)—but as Friendly Ben wryly noted, sometimes sophisticated people lacked the "guts" to admit they liked them. The event went off that year, with some 1,000 people eating chitlins and showing off dance steps. Thereafter, it was scheduled for each Saturday after Thanksgiving, with black and white people getting into long lines and "shaking it" and otherwise strutting. Dorn went to the event when he could and sent regrets when he could not; he made it in 1973 and a few months later on 16 March did the strut with Friendly Ben and sang country songs at the Salley School at a Democratic Party gathering. Friendly Ben's support in person and his kindly "unpolitical and nonpartisan" words over the country airways were important to Dorn. In the fullness of time, Friendly Ben went the way of many a rural personality in the country South, being discovered in *flagrante delicto* in his car with another man's wife and shot dead, along with her, by the enraged husband in 1978. But this violent end was completely unsuspected in 1974 when the avuncular disc jockey was

---

33 WJBD, *OTP*, 252–54.
34 Ibid., 265.

"spinning stacks of wax" while waxing philosophic about hard times and good living.[35]

This one, this Friendly Ben Dekle, hired attorney Eugene C. Griffith Sr. of Newberry to argue the case before the State Supreme Court. As marked, the Griffiths were also Welsh cousins linked up with the Dorns in educational, church, and political endeavors. Eugene Griffith was a first cousin, a former state senator, and a former judge. Griffith's father had been a prominent judge on the State Supreme Court, had established a successful law firm in Newberry with Colie Blease's distinguished brother, the jurist Eugene, and, as marked, had extended a $500 donation (in twenty-first-century spending power, $5,800 or more) for Bryan Dorn's first run for the US Congress. This branch of the family produced a number of successful attorneys and judges, including Steve Griffith Jr., who left South Carolina courts to become general counsel for Duke Power. On 24 September, the State Supreme Court heard the arguments and responded in the way that Governor West and attorney Harry Lightsey had warned Ravenel: the court ruled that Ravenel did not meet the constitutional requirements of residency, being a resident less than five years "next," indeed less than three years "next."[36]

Ravenel did have contingent plans in case the state court decided as it did: he attempted a petition to call the state General Assembly, then in its normal recess, into special session to change the residency requirements. However, Lieutenant Governor Brantley Harvey, presiding over the state senate, and Rex Carter, House speaker, were uninterested in doing such an extraordinary piece of work; and in fact were unsympathetic, being themselves gubernatorial candidates in the fast-shifting and fluid scene. More important, Governor John Carl West refused to cooperate and did not ask the General Assembly to reconvene. Governor West called Bryan Dorn to tell him, "You may be back in the race." State party chairman Don Fowler elected to call a convention in Columbia, with candidates former governor Robert McNair, House Speaker Rex Carter, Lieutenant Governor Brantley

---

[35] "Salley School," 1974 Primary Campaign, 16 March, WJBD/SCPC; "Bond Posted in Lexington Murder Case," *Charleston News and Courier*, 24 February 1978, 7; "Ben Dekle," obit., *Cairo* (GA) *Messenger*, 17 February 1978, 1.; "Salley Gets Ready for 48th Annual Chitlin Strut," *Aiken Standard*, 15 November 2013, 1; website Salley2@pbt.comm.net accessed 23 December 2013; YouTube *AugustaChronicleTV*, produced by Sarah Caldwell youtube.com/watch?v=kmnjckSr5yE4, accessed 23 December 2013.

[36] "Ravenel Ruled Ineligible," *Aiken Standard*, 24 September 1974, C12.

Harvey, US Congressman James R. Mann, state Senator Richard W. Riley, and Dorn. Since Fowler considered Ravenel ineligible, the Charlestonian was not listed as an eligible candidate. Nevertheless, Ravenel announced that he would appeal to the US Supreme Court and would remain a candidate until that body ruled. It was understood that Ravenel would not be eligible for the convention, but that he would continue campaigning independently of the formal state party organization until the final court ruling.[37]

One thing Bryan Dorn and most of the veterans remembered was the debacle of the 1952 "Barnwell Ring" senatorial nomination after Burnet Maybank's sudden death over the Labor Day weekend. As noted, Edgar Brown was named as the Democratic Party nominee for Maybank's US Senate seat, but Strom Thurmond, then briefly out of office, had launched his own "write-in" campaign and then overwhelmed the organized party with his victory. With the 1952 morass in memory, Fowler called a public Democratic Party Convention for 30 September in Columbia. No one wanted a convention that seemed to be closed and otherwise "rigged" in some way and thus set apart from the people. By its nature, the convention, not being a popular and statewide primary election, would always have some tincture of organized party machination, but Don Fowler made it as open and as public as he could, and there were certainly candidates aplenty in the offering.[38]

In these sessions, it was Richard "Dick" Riley, self-professed liberal attorney and ten-year veteran of the General Assembly, who posed the greatest threat for Dorn. The Riley family of Greenville was another political family, and one with important connections to and with the Dorns. Edward Patterson (Ted) Riley, the patriarch, was also a World War II veteran and American Legion figure as well as a former chair of the state's Democratic Party. He was long-time friends with Bryan Dorn, and, in fact, had worked to ensure a high status in the American Legion for his Greenwood friend. *Riley pere* was a moderate on race relations in the days of Jim Crow, and his profile was much like Bryan Dorn's, that is, moderate segregationist until 1965 and thereafter a moderate integrationist. Ted Riley had supported Bryan Dorn in the primary. *Riley fils*, however, was always progressive on issues

---

[37] "Pug Ravenel's Loss May be Dorn's Gain," *Gastonia Gazette*, 24 September 1974, 3A; interview: John Carl West with Herb Hartsook (10 July 1997), 63–68; "Candidates Doing Fancy Stepping in Final Days," *Aiken Standard*, 29 October 1974, 18.

[38] South Carolina Democratic Party Papers, 30 September 1974 Convention, SCDP/SCPC; interview: John Carl West with Herb Hartsook (10 July 1997), 63–68; "Candidates Doing Fancy Steps," *Aiken Standard*, 29 October 1974, 18.

racial and moved easily inside the world of the modern civil rights moment. Dick Riley had supported Pug Ravenel in the primary. Now he sensed a unique opportunity, much as had young Pug Ravenel and young Bryan Dorn in other contexts and in other places. Briefly, Dick Riley thought he had the requisite convention delegate votes, despite "the well-organized Dorn forces" with their "telephone bank" and longtime "contacts." Two ballots were chaotic and inconclusive, with Riley tantalizingly close to winning. However, as everyone kept negotiating between balloting, Bryan Dorn gained the unexpected support of the Chesterfield delegates, and Riley claims that such support put Dorn above 50 percent. Indeed, on the third ballot Dorn had the Chesterfield vote, had the overall majority, and thus was officially nominated by the Democratic Party to run against Jim Edwards—in nine weeks! As for Dick Riley, he recalled being "mad as hell" with the result, but he hurried to offer full support for Bryan Dorn, and, in fact, he did give very useful support in the truncated campaign that remained.[39]

The congressman, institutionalist and party man, was quite uncomfortable despite his long and fervently held dreams. He made it clear that should Ravenel win on appeal to the US Supreme Court, he would step aside at once. By contrast, Governor West and legal experts, especially the Griffiths, Eugene C. Griffith Sr. and Steve C. Griffith Jr., were reminding him that the US Supreme Court did not have any precedents for overruling any state on this kind of issue about residency. Whenever the US Supreme Court heard the case, each Griffith said, they would refuse to overturn the South Carolina Supreme Court, and then Ravenel would have to accept that he was ineligible this year. Meantime, Dr. Edwards was pursuing the governorship with the same dogged and gritty and methodical approach that had brought down the four-star general. Indeed, Dr. Edwards was looking pretty good to Republicans and to many disaffected Democrats. And to confound things still further for Democrats, Peggy Jennings registered as an Independent candidate, serving those who did not want to be Republicans but felt in some way abandoned by the "party of the people." As the congressman put it flatly, "It was a mess."[40]

---

[39] Interview: John Carl West with Herb Hartsook (10 July 1997), 63–68; interview: Richard Riley with Jack Bass (19 December 1986), 15, and interview: Riley with Bass (22 December 1986), 22, SCPC; WJBD, *OTP*, 267.

[40] Interview: Steve Griffith with Herb Hartsook (31 January 2012); interview: James Burrows Edwards (8 August 2012), JHR/SCPC; 1974 Campaign, October, SCDP/SCPC; WJBD quoted, *OTP*, 267.

On 21 October, the US Supreme Court upheld the South Carolina State Supreme Court, and Ravenel's appeal was denied. Now there were barely two weeks to get the 450,000 registered Democrats into the race against Dr. Edwards. The energy that Ravenel and his campaign staff had put into enthusiasm for their own campaign was almost instantly converted into energy-sapping bitterness. Ravenel and campaign man Bud Ferillo spent much time, then and decades later, speculating on who "really filed" for Friendly Ben Deckle and what attorney really "helped" Eugene C. Griffith Sr. Bud Furillo, energetic anti-war activist and Ravenel campaign wizard, continued to suspect Millie Dorn as the impetus for the appeal of Judge Grimball's ruling. As he insisted in 2013, this kind of legal case was "well beyond the legal competence" of Eugene C. Griffith Sr. No amount of training in the law or practice of the law could move the Charlestonians Ferillo and Ravenel to grant that there was competence in attorneys from the small-town piedmont. As for endorsement—the kind of thing done so grandly and quickly by Congressman Dorn in Columbia on 30 July as soon as most ward boxes had been counted up—Ravenel was first reluctant and then petulant. He finally told his people to vote for Bryan Dorn by "writing in" the name Dorn—the idea being that vote counters could then see how many people voting for Dorn were *really for* Ravenel. If it sounds confusing even to read today, conceive what it sounded like to voters in the *final two weeks* of the campaign.[41]

All such disputes drew attention away from the task at hand, which was mounting a campaign against a Republican who had been steadily and effectively running with a singular focus on the governor's chair since July. It was no less a television campaign for Edwards than it had been for Ravenel, and Bryan Dorn was not developing any skills for television. Here were the issues for which the congressman stood: racial Liberalism; dramatic improvement in the schools, with special emphasis on technical education at the state's post-secondary technical colleges (not community colleges); building of better secondary roads to link up with the dramatically extended interstate system of roads; final and full development of the School of Medicine of the University of South Carolina in conjunction with much-expanded services at the VA Center campus east of the main university; and further development

[41] "Pug Ravenel's Loss May be Dorn's Gain," *Gastonia Gazette*, 24 September 1974, 3A; interview: John Carl West with Herb Hartsook (10 July 1997), 63–68; "Candidates Doing Fancy Stepping in Final Days," *Aiken Standard*, 29 October 1974, 18; notes, Prince, remarks, "Election of 1974," 2 December 2014, JHR/SCPC.

of the Savannah River branches and tributaries. Those were Dr. Edwards's issues too. In the structure of South Carolina's General Assembly, it would be the state senators and the state representatives who would actually *do* these things, and the governor would be the bully pulpit urging the assemblymen on—but the governor also must, as John Carl West had mastered, work quietly with the legislative denizens. Although Bryan Dorn had done that for years as a deeply involved US congressman, so, too, had Dr. Edwards as a deeply involved state senator. For the first time, and for the last recorded time to date, it was a race among progressives, with the Republican and the Democratic candidates trying to convince the electorate that each was "as liberal" as the voters—at least "as liberal" as the voters said they were in various polls in 1974.[42]

One thing Dr. Edwards had learned from Pug Ravenel: television advertisements should be targeted to city viewers, and indeed the city voters were going to determine the outcome. The surgeon traveled the state, and he shook hands and ate barbeque at many an out-of-the-way place, but he poured his money into television advertisements aimed with a rifle's scope at what Frank Holleman called "Ravenel supporters...young, affluent, well-educated, many immigrants [that is, immigrants from New Jersey or Ohio]." Bryan Dorn understood the demographic, and he wanted those votes too, but he was still at his best walking the dusty back roads and meeting people in person at Baptist churches and at high school stadiums and field houses and, above all, at picnic grounds at the mill villages that still had plants operating at least two shifts.[43]

In stump speeches, Bryan Dorn could always attack an issue without attacking a man, could argue vigorously and then bound across the stage to pump the hand of the opponent and shout out, "That was great! God Bless you, Friend!" Only Jim Hare had ever disliked him, and that was only for a season. As Dr. Edwards noted long years later, most people liked Bryan Dorn, especially his opponents. On television, however, attacking an issue was a matter of style, and the closely focused faces made such attacks personal at times—in ways they really were not. Dorn was simply bad at it. Edwards, although noted by journalist Carl Stepp as "tone deaf" on issues of

---

[42] South Carolina Democratic Party Papers, 30 September 1974, Convention, SCDP/SCPC; interview: John Carl West with Herb Hartsook (10 July 1997) 63–68; "Candidates Doing Fancy Steps," *Aiken Standard*, 29 October 1974, 18.

[43] Carl Stepp, "Issues, Style Divide Dorn, Edwards," *Charlotte Observer*, 3 November 1974, 3B.

welfare, was comfortable and kindly and studied and respectful. He was fully acceptable. He recalled how "some of Bryan's staff" had made a television commercial that attacked the Republicans on issues of welfare and civil rights: during a late debate on television in Augusta (Dorn territory if there ever were!), Jim Edwards directly challenged the congressman on the nature of the advertisement. Dorn apologized at once, and Dr. Edwards "hit the issue hard" thereafter.[44]

Still later, at another televised debate, everyone sat listening to questions, and the congressman looked stiff and uncomfortable; at last he leaned down and gave his ankle a good, satisfying scratch. On a stand in the sunlight at Salley or Honea Path, it would have seemed natural, even folksy. On television, it was a disaster. As Congressman Butler Carson Derrick recalls it, "I said, oh, no, Bryan, oh no!" The distinguished professional, the dental surgeon, sat alongside a man who was literally a "scratch-ankle farmer"—and both wanted to occupy the governor's chair. On still another televised occasion, Bryan Dorn listened to a complicated question, frowned, and looked over at Jim Edwards: "I dunno, you take that one, Doc!" To a man self-identified as the farmer he was, representing the millhands for what they were, the world of careful negotiation over fine points and the many special exchanges between folk, the tedious building of relationships over decades, all that was replaced by instant messages—messages that had to be "delivered" with subtle facial expressions and clothing and hair style and not the grand gestures of the Baptist evangelizer in a village square. It was hardly something that Dr. Edwards had mastered, but he worked doggedly at it, and he bested his opponent at it during those few televised minutes, making a lasting impression.[45]

Jimmy Carter, governor of Georgia and a rising star among still another group of "New" Democrats in the South, traveled South Carolina, supporting Dorn and talking about the corruption of the Nixon administration, thus trying to link Edwards to the corrupt presidency. But Edwards was simply not part of Nixon in any way, and Bryan Dorn did not like the strategy since *he still liked Nixon*. In fact, any mention of "tired" and "same old" politics seemed to help Edwards and to hurt Dorn. The fact that on television Dorn often looked distracted and tired and out of place only added to

---

[44] Ibid.; interview: James Burrows Edwards (8 August 2011), JHR/SCPC.

[45] Butler Carson Derrick Jr., remarks, "Art of Political Biography," 22 January 2013, SCPC; interview: Steve C. Griffith Jr. and Watson Dorn (1 February 2012) JHR/SCPC.

the effect, the very effect whose opposite—youth, vigor, energy, freshness, even brashness and innocence—had helped Pug Ravenel in the first place. The state Democratic Party was trying to spend $100,000 for Dorn's campaign, and individuals were sought to match that amount, but Bryan and Millie Dorn had long ago expected to make up any shortfall with their own money, hence the $300,000 that they eventually borrowed in total to cover the primary, the primary runoff, and the general election. Dr. Edwards raised more, but most important, every nickel he spent on television paid him back well. By contrast, Bryan Dorn's television advertising was not money well spent. The *Charlotte Observer*'s Carl Stepp marked it that Dorn "seemed sharper" and had the more "remarkable memory" and above all a "deeper attachment to people" than Dr. Edwards. Significantly, newspaperman Stepp noted that these were impressions from following the two men around the state for a month, creating a different impression altogether than the television spots.[46]

As it came time to vote, the Republican campaign official Ken Allen introduced what was almost the only non-progressive element into the long campaign: Allen announced that the state GOP would place "Ballot Security Teams" at each polling place to make sure there were "tough poll watches" and thus no cheating by black voters. Once again, there were those nagging concerns about misbehavior by the "neophyte voters" among the black citizens. It was a dim harbinger of such Republican efforts in heavily black polling places in the coming century and an unhappy reminder of Democratic misbehavior intimidating black voters in McCormick and Edgefield and other Dorn territories in previous decades. Howard Covington was one black official who claimed that such tactics "slowed down voting in some black precincts," but he could produce no evidence of any voters who gave up and went away. For his part, Jim Edwards was having none of such talk or tactics, and Deek Newman reported nothing significant in the way of racist bullying at the polls. As for black voting, Edwards was quite sure he got the black votes in Charleston, and Dorn was quite sure he got the black votes in the piedmont and in Columbia, and both men seem to be correct, given

---

[46] William Cotterall, "'Bind Wounds,' Carter Tells SC Democrats," *Charlottes Observer*, 3 November 1974, 3C; "Dorn Lists $73,000 of Funds," *Aiken Standard*, 29 October 1974, 1; Stepp, "Issues, Style Divide Dorn, Edwards," *Charlotte Observer*, 3 November 1974, 3B; Broder, *Changing of the Guard.*

post-election polling results and votes in the most heavily black-populated wards of the two regions.[47]

More significant to Congressman Dorn was an article on the business page of the *Charlotte Observer* reporting something he and every member of the Textile Group already knew all too well: "Greenwood Mills Join Other Firms in Cutback." He knew, too, that Jim Edwards and the Charlestonians were themselves reeling from defense department cutbacks for the navy. Whoever won this race was going to wrestle with unemployment in textiles and military sectors during this continuing "mild recession." Each candidate said that education was the answer—better training in secondary schools, improved adult education to include technical retraining of sailors and soldiers and millworkers, and better training of the teachers at every level of schooling. Whoever became governor, Congressman Dorn would have a few lame-duck congressional weeks of feverish activity with the lame-duck but strongly Democratic majority on behalf of jobs and schools and veterans. He had already decided that those weeks would be transitional, probably to make a transition into being governor, possibly to make a transition into being a spokesman and figure preparing for the 1978 gubernatorial campaign.[48]

James Burrows Edwards won. Congressman Dorn congratulated the governor-elect, and he made it clear that he fully intended to bring Mille Johnson Dorn to the governor's inauguration and evening inaugural ball. The vote had been damnably close. Jim Edwards swamped Bryan Dorn in Greenville, Spartanburg, and Columbia. Better than two out of three city dwellers in those areas went for Edwards. Bryan Dorn did get some votes in Charleston, but the clear majority went for the local surgeon. The Third District was as loyal to Bryan Dorn as ever before, and the congressman took the rural counties there by around 66 percent of voters. Even outside his own district, he completely dominated six rural counties and won the majority of counties overall. However, the normally reliable Anderson, on the way to being a

---

[47] Carl Stepp, "GOP in SC Plans Tough Poll Watch," *Charlotte Observer*, 1 November 1974, 1; Howard Covington quoted, "Edwards Victor in Close Contest," *Charlotte Observer*, 5 November 1974, 1B, 10B; SC Elections Commission, *Supplemental Report to the General Assembly of South Carolina*, ed. Risher (Columbia: SC Elections Commission 1975).

[48] Carl Stepp, "GOP in SC Plans Tough Poll Watch," *Charlotte Observer*, 1 November 1974, 1; Howard Covington quoted, "Edwards Victor in Close Contest," *Charlotte Observer*, 5 November 1974, 1B, 10B.

metropolitan sector in its own right, was majority Edwards. Statewide turnout was heavy, more than 529,000, reflecting an actual contest in the general election. Peggy Jennings picked up more than 1,000 Independent protest votes, and an agglomeration of nonparty write-ins amounted to 5,528. Much of the Ravenel vote did not stay home, and very few of them wrote-in. Instead, a huge bloc, perhaps a majority, of the Ravenel voters went Republican, and Edwards benefited from the Ravenel strength in urban areas, just as he suffered from the Ravenel weakness in the countryside. It was really an urban/country split, and in this new era, winning the urban areas elected one. As George Tindall showed conclusively, urban South Carolina was ready to go Republican in state as well as national elections. Final tally was 266,338 to 248,861.[49]

In 1949 Bryan Dorn had last felt this sensation as he made his way through the congressional offices. He behaved now as he had then, tending to the business of the Third District and of the Democratic Party. Now, as then, he was in no sense retiring from politics but already planning the next campaign, the one in 1978 for governor. There were a few differences. As a veteran and a committee chair, he enjoyed some prerogatives. He paid the value of his office desk and chair in 2256 Rayburn Building and collected that furniture for Barratt House. Oliver Meadows of the VA sent him his name plate *Chairman Bryan Dorn* for a souvenir. The congressman sat for his portrait to be displayed in the Veterans Affairs Committee Room. It is a good portrait, and doubtless the artist had to loosen up his subject to attain the effect. And despite the years of ambivalent tensions between the two gentlemen, Strom Thurmond made a charming speech of tribute to his cousin, placed it in the *Congressional Record*, and sent over the tear sheet.[50]

A different kind of tribute came his way, one ultimately more important, given his ongoing relationships with the people of South Carolina and their Democratic Party: Oliver Meadows sent him a personal note, "We will not be giving special attention to new South Carolina cases unless you

---

[49] SC Elections Commission, *Supplemental Report to the General Assembly*, ed. Risher (1975); Carl Stepp, "Edwards Victor in Close Contest," *Charlotte Observer*, 6 November 1974, 1; Southern urban areas did not act "like Yankee cities," Tindall, *Disruption*, quoted 57; see also 55–60.

[50] WJBD to W. Pat Jennings, 9 December 1974; Oliver Meadows to WJBD, 8 January 1974; Ray Roberts to WJBD, 3 January 1975; John A. Blatnik to WJBD, 14 December 1974; Strom Thurmond to WJBD, 18 December 1974, with *Cong. Record* tear sheet, WJBD/SCPC.

let us know that you have a special interest." Indeed, there was still much of such detailed work to do. Gerald Ford wanted Nelson Aldrich Rockefeller for his vice president. For a South Carolina Populist, self-conscious heir to the "Great Commoner" William Jennings Bryan, the very name *Rockefeller*, Northeastern and indeed New York monopolist of oil, was the symbol of all that was evil in "unrestrained capitalism." But Bryan Dorn, the lame-duck congressman, was also an institutionalist, and years of baiting New York liberals on various issues had only been another form of charming theater. He spoke forcefully and favorably in testimony for Rockefeller during confirmation debates that actually ran right up against the Christmas holidays. Rockefeller wrote Dorn, "That was a wonderful statement you made in my behalf...I deeply appreciate it."[51]

Whatever else, in those bleak midwinter days, he reaffirmed his devotion—and consummate skills—to the "art and craft of legislating, of making law and policy," in the House of Representatives. Louis Stokes of Ohio, the first black congressman from the Buckeye State, still needed help on a supplemental appropriation bill for Title IX expenditures for education for minorities. Dorn gave the help at once, and Stokes responded with the ultimate tribute from a professional politician: "It is good to be able to depend on you when it counts." And his red-hills people still depended on him, as he and the exhausted staff tended to a bushel barrel full of continuing requests to speed up visa applications, straighten out veterans' benefits, explain pension benefits, and help with waterways and other projects. Dorn was still a cattle farmer and a timberman, and so was Spartanburg television man Walter Brown, who demanded, and of course got, *very* last minute help on a price-parity program in which heifers were bought by the federal government and then donated to people in poor countries.[52]

Tidying up a few more such details, Dorn turned over the keys to the Rayburn Building Offices, made arrangements to sell the McLean house in the beloved Commonwealth, and then drove the Plymouth southward to Barratt House—on stretches of interstate he himself had legislated for. One

---

[51] Oliver Meadows to WJBD, 8 January 1975; Nelson Aldrich Rockefeller to WJBD, 26 December 1974, WJBD/SCPC.

[52] Weber, *Politics as a Vocation*, trans., Augenmass, 268; Louis Stokes to WJBD, 4 December 1974; Walter Brown to WJBD, 16 December 1974; two folders, 1974 Congress and Post Office Matters, 1974, WJBD/SCPC;

thing was sure: a lost election after three different decades of successes did not diminish his "calling" for politics.[53]

An early order of business was to pay off debt from the campaign. Neither the party nor individuals had come through as hoped for in the gubernatorial election, and thus Bryan and Millie Dorn had done what they had dreaded (but planned for), which was to borrow up to their established limit of personal debt for the campaign, some $300,000. Selling the substantial home in McLean, selling off some timber, selling off some beef cattle, realizing revenues from the normal operations of the farm and timberland attached to Barratt House and the land in McCormick County, all these actions would pay off the entire debt over a period of time. But family and friends wanted to help their old benefactor pay off the campaign debts long before then. Friends organized a barbeque benefit at Barratt House, publicized in the *Greenville News*, and the fundraising apparently helped. According to his records, conscientiously publicized each season as if he were still a member of Congress (something not required of representatives, but something Dorn had always advocated), by 1976 his major debt was mortgage on Barratt House and mortgage on farmland, and the total of those notes amounted to less than half of the real assets. When it was all over, the expensive campaign had not hurt his family financially. Even so, he determined that for the 1978 campaign, he was going to limit spending, setting and keeping a limit of $50,000.[54]

As he prepared for another run at the governorship, Bryan Dorn found inspiration not from Virginia but from Georgia. Jimmy Carter, progressive governor, was different in kind from the Atlanta progressives like Roy Hartsfield or Ivan Allen. In fact, he was different even from Augusta's progressive Carl Sanders, well known to Bryan Dorn because of his piedmont heritage and because of his public school reforms as governor of Georgia from 1963 to 1967. Indeed, when Sanders attempted to return as Georgia governor in 1970, he lost to Jimmy Carter, who offered a more pragmatic, engineer-based approach to problems that emphasized recognizing limits and working with relatively small budgets. In addition, Carter, at least in the 1970 campaign, took the gains of the civil rights movement as givens in a

---

[53] Weber, loc. cit., trans. Gerth and Mills, 126.

[54] *Greenville News* clipping on WJBD fundraiser, n.d. (1975); WJBD to Pat Jennings, 1960–1975, enclosure IRS statements; WJBD, IRS Statements, 1975–1979, WJBD/SCPC; WJBD, *OTP*, 269.

"New South" rather than as a continuing neo-abolitionist mission. Working across racial lines and emphasizing practicality and common sense inside a progressive Southern Baptist theology of helping all men, Jimmy Carter to Bryan Dorn seemed a younger version of his own beloved pastor Jim Bowers—and also of his longtime associate and inspiration Brooks Hays. In any case, Jimmy Carter brought forward yet another iteration of a New South politics, one yet again supposedly more progressive than its predecessors. Summing up the complexities, Bryan Dorn described Carter as a kind of New Deal Southerner, but without the proclivities for big spending. Most significantly, Carter was fully at peace with the results of the civil rights movement. Especially important was that Bennie Mays, of Greenwood County and Morehouse College, sent word that Jimmy Carter was a white Southerner who could be counted upon—exactly the status that the "new" Bryan Dorn had finally earned with Louis Stokes and other black congressmen. Among other things, the term *liberal* was seldom used in his case, but instead the term *progressive* was consciously deployed.[55]

This Carter was also important to Dick Riley, one who still sometimes called himself liberal, and Riley was integral to the 1976 presidential campaign in South Carolina. Carter won the Deep South handily in his race with Gerald Ford, and Riley (far more so than Dorn) was a major factor in securing a big winning margin in South Carolina. By 1978, Riley was in excellent position to run for governor in the Democratic primary, especially since Pug Ravenel, the cause of such excitement in 1974, was now a candidate for US Senate, taking on none other than Strom Thurmond. Former congressman Bryan Dorn and sitting lieutenant governor, Brantley Harvey, seasoned veterans of state politics, were joined in opposition to Riley by Tom Turnipseed, a one-term state senator and one notorious for colorful and unpredictable actions and ideology.[56]

In fact, Bryan Dorn thought that Turnipseed could provide him a unique way to win the Democratic Party primary, set for 13 June 1978. He intended for Turnipseed to draw attention to himself, attacking both Riley and Harvey and leaving the piedmont farmer as the last standing man of

---

[55] Cook, Carl Sanders; Broder, *Changing of the Guard*; Roper, *Magnificent Mays*, 284–305; WJBD, OTP, 268.

[56] Retrospectives: Tom Turnipseed, "King Day at the Dome," *Columbia State*, 18 January 2009, op. ed.; "What Lee Atwater Learned and the Lessons for his Protégé," *Washington Post*, 16 April 1991, A19; Carter, *From George Wallace to Newt Gingrich*, 69; Frye Gaillard, "Laments on the Demise of Tom Turnipseed," *Southern Changes*, 4/4 (1982) 31.

common sense. Turnipseed, a native of Mobile, Alabama, had been educated at the University of North Carolina and then had earned a law degree there before coming to Columbia in 1966. At that time a rabid segregationist, Turnipseed established the South Carolina Independent School Association, an educational accreditation association for private schools, many of which could be very properly styled "segregation academies." In 1968, Turnipseed had been a vigorous supporter of George Wallace for president, but in 1970 he, with as much enthusiasm, joined the Americans for Democratic Action (ADA) and began espousing civil rights, even using the term "liberal" to describe himself. As a 1970s liberal, Turnipseed became a colorful and quotable advocate for fundamental reform, and in 1976 he was elected to the state senate. He also became active on local radio stations, including Friendly Ben Dekle's country station WCAY. As state senator, the segregationist turned ADA liberal brought some country musicians and disc jockeys onto the legislative floor to sing with him about high gas prices. By the time of the gubernatorial campaign, Turnipseed was a bona fide character, one who named both Jesse Jackson and George Wallace as good friends, and one who could be counted on for interesting copy for the newspaper and interesting talk for the radio.[57]

As in 1974, each man thus spoke as some kind of progressive, making no racist assertions but, in fact, seeking black votes. Riley had the genuine progressive pedigree and the more consistently progressive career. By contrast, Dorn and Harvey presented themselves as they were, that is, moderates who had *evolved* into progressive positions on racial matters. Turnipseed could make the discussions go even farther toward reformism with his unique speeches and presentations. In a peculiarly Baptist kind of confessional, he emphasized his own "reactionary Wallace days" as an "unreconstructed Southerner" and then described a transformation into reformist and liberal activism thereafter: the "redeemed soul," sometimes an effective trope, if genuine. Schools were emphasized even more than had been the case in the 1974 elections, and each Democratic candidate was trying to show himself to be the most dedicated to full educational reform—and each was candid that such full reform cost money and would involve raising taxes. Riley was quite precise in his descriptions of how to improve schools, and he also offered specific remedies for indigent health care in the state. On the latter such issues, both Harvey and Dorn were too much beholden to the chamber of commerce publicists to talk frankly about fundamental needs for reform in

---

[57] WJBD, *OTP*, 268–69.

a poor state—especially since, as Dorn often noted, any talk of health care brought immediate opposition from the powerful bloc of doctors' votes, the one group Dorn never intended to cross on any major issue. Turnipseed kept things interesting and was "angry and shrill" in denouncing Harvey and Riley, whom he knew well from the state senate. However, as the *Charlotte Observer*'s Frye Gailliard (who had known Turnipseed from childhood days in Mobile) noted, "Even some of the people who agreed with him wished he'd go away." And in mid-May, Turnipseed did "go away," at least as far away as dropping out of the race.[58]

The Democratic primary was scheduled for 13 June, and Dorn campaigned for it much as he had beforehand, walking and walking and meeting people in all the out-of-the-way places. He tried to win voters in the cities, but he knew it was almost hopeless. As Dorn noted, Turnipseed's "dropping out of the race changed the campaign at the last minute." Dorn had plans as specific as Riley and Harvey, but he could not articulate them in a way to gain any real attention except in his own rural red hills. Riley dominated cities and Harvey dominated the country precincts except for Bryan Dorn's stronghold in the Saluda Valley. The three-way portion of the race thus ended with Harvey taking 142,785 votes (37.5 percent), Riley 125,184 (32.9 percent), and Dorn a mere 112,743 (29.6 percent). Somewhat surprising was Bryan Dorn's actions and announcements shortly after he learned that he was eliminated. "Harvey set the pace," said the UPI wire service report, "but Riley has received the endorsement of former Rep. William Jennings Bryan Dorn."[59]

It was important news, for whatever else, Bryan Dorn's supporters were a loyal lot, and surely 50,000 or more of them would vote according to his endorsement. Lieutenant Governor Harvey all but exploded. "After the endorsement," reported the UPI wire service, "Harvey charged that the Carter administration pressured Dorn to back Riley, the president's South Carolina campaign manager in 1976." Yet it seems unlikely. The campaign correspondence and the recollections of newspaper personnel who followed the race do not reveal Carter to be much of an influence in such things by midsummer 1978, a time when his approval rating had sunk to 39 percent (and his disapproval rating had risen to 44 percent) because of high inflation, unemployment, and the frustrations of expensive gasoline and other power

---

[58] Gaillard, "Laments on the Demise," 31.

[59] "Democratic Primaries," *Valley* (TX) *Morning Star*, 25 June 1978, 32; "Big Names Are Big Losers," *Salina* (KS) *Journal*, 28 June 1978, 32.

sources (and the public's unhappiness with Carter's proposed solutions of conservation based on puritanical self-sacrifice by consumers). More likely is what Bryan Dorn himself said then and repeated: he was profoundly concerned about losing ground in education, and Dick Riley had the record and the real plans for fundamental educational reform. Too, in a land where family relations (along with race) were always foremost, the Rileys and the Dorns had a piedmont personal history going back to 1946. And, in the Machiavellian perspective, Dorn "owed" Riley—*and not Harvey*—for the strong support the Greenville attorney provided in 1974. In the world of "seeing and hearing," "loyalty and scrupulousness" were *sine qua non*, and in this instant Bryan Dorn was seen to be loyal and scrupulous for the populace to see—regardless of what Brantley Harvey was "feeling."[60]

By whatever route Dorn came to Riley's side, he campaigned vigorously once he got there. He insisted that Riley walk with him around the Third District and other rural areas in the state. This walking was a challenge for Riley because of a spinal ailment that he suffered (while in the US Navy he had contracted a tropical disease that attacked his spinal cord "like daggers"). He could not stand upright, had trouble sitting, and had to sleep in a fetal position—and walking not only looked awkward but *hurt*. All the same, Riley gamely followed Bryan Dorn around, shaking hands and meeting the folk, and they responded to his own genuineness as much as to their man Dorn. On the runoff day of 27 June, Riley won 180,882 (53.3 percent) to Harvey's 158,655 (46.7 percent). Riley won everywhere but was especially dominant in the Third District, and surely a sizable portion of the additional 355,698 voters that the Greenville attorney gained in the two weeks runoff campaign must have been Dorn supporters. Riley immediately and often thereafter thanked Dorn and went on record that he "owed much of his strong showing in the runoff to former Rep. W. J. Bryan Dorn."[61]

---

[60] Harvey quoted, "Democratic Primaries," *Valley* (TX) *Morning Star*, 25 June 1978, 32; 1978 Primary Campaign folders, WJBD/SCPC; 1978 Primary Campaign, SCDP/SCPC; WJBD, *OTP*, 255; interview: Richard Riley with Jack Bass (22 December 1986); "Carter Approval/Disapproval Ratings, August, 1978" Cable News Network/USA Today Gallup Poll, Roper Center, University of Connecticut, 2001; Machiavelli, *Essential Writings*, ed. and trans. Constantine, 70; corr. with Riley family members, 1946–1974, WJBD/SCPC.

[61] Riley quoted, "Big Names Are Big Losers," *Salina (KS) Journal*, 28 June 1978, 26; interview: Richard Riley with Jack Bass (22 December 1986), 20, 32, Richard Riley Papers/SCPC.

As for the general election, the Republican nominee, Edward Lunn Young, was simply waxed by Riley, 384,898 to 236,947, or 62.3 percent to 37.7 percent. Although Governor Edwards had been a solid achiever who worked across party lines in office—as he had reached across party lines in seeking office—he had established no precedent, and many political scientists and newspapermen described his 1974 election as a "fluke," pointing to the chaos among Democrats in 1974 and to Young's abysmal showing in 1978. More likely, Edwards was simply the right candidate at one moment and Riley the right candidate for another moment. State voters were overwhelmingly registered as Democrats throughout the decade of the 1970s, but they showed facility in splitting tickets in each instance that it suited them. Riley noted then and later that in the state senate, his voting record was "identical to Jim Edwards's."[62]

Riley also said that it was past time for the governor to succeed himself. Dorn agreed and supported the campaign for the change even though it definitively ended his own gubernatorial ambitions. Dorn agreed with Governor Riley that Edwards—and all his Democratic predecessors—had been "a lame duck the day he was elected." Moreover, both piedmont politicians agreed that "the power of the governor going back to the people for their approval is very, very forceful." Riley thus pushed for a constitutional amendment allowing the governor to succeed himself, and the people responded in the popular vote, passing the amendment in November of 1980. In the 1982 Democratic primary contests, no one in the party opposed the popular reformist. As for the general election, the journalist and intellectual William D. Workman owned the Republican nomination, but the erstwhile candidate again lost, taking less than 30 percent of the votes, and carrying not a single county in the state. Dorn was happily involved, but understood that Riley did not *need* his help (or anybody else's) in this cause. Because of his two consecutive terms, Governor Riley brought long-lived reforms to the structures of South Carolina offices, with commendable improvements in the public schools. In the world of what might have been, it is hard to imag-

---

[62] Edwards "fluke," "Big Names are Big Losers," *Salina* (KS) *Journal*, 28 June 1978, 26; interview: James Burrows Edwards with Roper (8 August 2011), JHR/SCPC; quotations, interview: Richard Riley with Jack Bass (22 December 1986) 17, 18, Richard Riley Papers/SCPC; WJBD, *OTP*, 240, 255, 258.

ine Bryan Dorn accomplishing the substantive reforms that Richard Wilson Riley brought forth.[63]

Thus, the governorship would never be Dorn's. There remained the even more futile dream of becoming US senator, despite the overwhelming popularity of Strom Thurmond—and despite his cousin's firm determination to serve until death. Even so, the dream died hard. In 1978, this same year that Dick Riley swept all before him on behalf of substantive reform in education and indigent health care, the seventy-five-year-old Thurmond had faced a challenge from the *wunderkind* Charles "Pug" Ravenel. Excitement still surrounded the Charlestonian, who at age forty looked barely thirty, and who still sounded the tocsin of change and reform, with echoes redolent in the same urban areas that he had won in the 1974 primary. Somehow, Bryan Dorn thought that Thurmond might lose—and he thought that Ravenel might subsequently disappoint constituents because he had never held an office and because he would know neither the "slow boring through hardwood" of law-crafting, nor the thousand tedious details of serving constituents. With such whimsical contingencies, Bryan Dorn in 1978 convinced himself that perhaps 1984 could be his chance for the US Senate.[64]

Whatever Dorn might think about Pug Ravenel, there were many progressive ribbons pinned to the Charlestonian's lance, and he enjoyed popularity and respect outside the Deep South. *Time* magazine in particular ran articles all but pumping for Ravenel, and Jack Bass has recalled how progressives almost everywhere all but hungered for Thurmond's defeat. Yet Thurmond was primed for the contest, sometimes attacking his young opponent with surprising vigor and even viciousness—especially when Ravenel at a New York fundraiser was quoted to the effect that he was "embarrassed to be from South Carolina" and would prefer to serve as "third Senator from New York." Thurmond spoke often of Ravenel as "another New York liberal," and by the time of October, Ravenel's negative ratings (the percentage of disapproved), which had been under 20 percent, had ballooned to more than 40 percent. In the general election itself, the rejuvenated Thurmond won

---

[63] Supplemental report to South Carolina General Assembly, *Reports and Resolutions of the South Carolina General Assembly*, ed. Risher (1981); South Carolina Elections Commission, *Report on Elections*, 1982 (Columbia, SC: Elections Commission, 1982), 54; Edgar, *South Carolina*, 553, 583; Broder, *Changing of the Guard*.

[64] Bass and Thompson, *Ol' Strom*, 290–92; Bass and DeVries, *Transformation*; Tindall, *Disruption*, 71; WJBD, *OTP*, 255.

easily, 351,733 (55.6 percent) to Ravenel's 281,119 (44.4 percent). George Tindall noted, as did Jack Bass, that Thurmond showed strength in the cities among youth, regardless of what logic might suggest. Most significantly, the seventy-five-year-old made it quite clear he intended to serve in the US Senate longer than anyone, perhaps into his 100th year. Dorn was thus defeated for 1984 as surely as Ravenel was defeated in 1978. Indeed, Dorn's aspirations in retrospect look almost comical.[65]

Yet Dorn knew that he was not dead politically in South Carolina, but only blocked from holding office. He knew about how party politics worked from the inside, and he determined to be a mover and shaker completely behind the scenes, or at least as much behind the scenes as one would be serving as chairman of the Democratic Party. The research-oriented Don Fowler was hinting about stepping down, and Dorn thought this was the moment to take over. Dorn did know his history, and he could easily see a nightmare in which the Democrats of the 1980s swapped places with the Republicans of the 1880s: a party with a national base and with a black constituency, one incapable of electing anyone to statewide office and able to elect people only in areas with overwhelming black voting strength. He also remembered his youth, and he found a Republican nightmare, one in which the Republican Party swapped places with the Jim Crow Democrats, becoming the "Party of White People" and so completely in charge of statewide offices that personalities and corruption dominated. Only a strong and vibrant interracial Democratic Party could prevent the coming—or really the return/reversal—of the twin nightmares. Bryan Dorn thought he knew how to work with black politicians, especially Deek Newman and the up-and-coming James Clyburn, to create such an interracial union with the veteran white Democrats left over from the old days of progressive New Deal Populism.[66]

---

[65] South Carolina Elections Commission, Report on Elections, 1978 (Columbia, SC: Elections Commission, 1979), 54; Supplemental Report to South Carolina General Assembly, Reports and Resolutions of the South Carolina General Assembly, vol. 2, ed. Risher; Bass and Thompson, Ol' Strom, 290–92; Tindall, Disruption, 66–71; "South Carolina Quarterback Sneak," Time, 14 October 1974; retrospective: "Get Ready: McCain Surrounded by GOP Thugs," *Daily Kos*, 23 May 2008, 24; "Ravenel Challenges Thurmond," *Sumter Daily Item*, 28 July 1978, 18; WJBD, OTP, 255.

[66] "Dorn Wants Party Chairmanship," *Aiken Standard*, 23 January 1980, 6A; Party Convention, 12 April 1980, SCDP/SCPC; SCDP folders, 1980, WJBD/SCPC; Earl Black, quoted, Lee Bandy, "Long Time Congressman Had Progressive Streak," *Columbia*

In early winter 1980, Bryan Dorn began his work among the local party officials, the county clerks and the county sheriffs and the circuit judges and the state senators and state representatives and above all the county party delegates who would go to the state convention scheduled for Columbia on 12 April. He told all of them about the "need to rebuild from the grassroots level," and he noted politely what most of them knew all too well, which was that the finances of the party were a wreck, with poor tracking systems for budget items and no organized fundraising statewide. When the party delegates actually convened, Bryan Dorn was easily elected. He went to work at once, clearing out three veteran office staffers and instituting a "blind audit" system for all expenses and revenues. And as for fundraising, there remained the classes of the Textile Group. While the children of the masses some time ago had abandoned the mill as a place to seek work, the mill owners still expected and got congressional preference on trade and tariffs and other restrictions, and the classes continued to put money forward, as much for Dorn Democrats as for Republicans. For his part, Bryan Dorn loved the work, hosting barbeques and traveling the state speaking to Lions Clubs and Pilot Clubs and American Legion gatherings, still the bull of the woods in the small-town gathering places. All of it was important to Jim Clyburn, who eventually won election as US congressman from the heavily black Sixth District, but also to Butler Derrick, Dorn's shrewd and able successor in the Third District, and Governor Dick Riley, who, as noted, had persuaded the General Assembly in that very year of 1980 to enact a change in the state constitution so that a governor could succeed himself. It was also vitally important to all the town and county clerks, circuit judges, county sheriffs, and others for whom Congressman Dorn had long worked. Now, in the interracial South Carolina Democratic Party, these strictly local officials needed the funds he raised and the structures he provided them.[67]

Without claiming more than can be claimed for a party chairman, Bryan Dorn was certainly a major reason that the South Carolina Democratic Party remained viable among white voters throughout the 1980s when other Deep South Democratic Parties were becoming all-black affairs. And be-

---

State, August 19, 2005, A1; Earl Black, *Southern Governors and Civil Rights: Racial Segregation as a Campaign Issue in the Second Reconstruction*.

[67] Remarks, Luther Batiste, interview: Herb Hartsook (18 February 2013); James Clyburn, memoirs manuscript, quoted in text, Herb Hartsook to Roper, (n.d.) October 2013, JHR/SCPC; Convention folder, 12 April 1980, SCDP/SCPC SCDP folders, 1980, WJBD/SCPC; "Democratic Party Staff Resigns [Marcia Duffy, Betsy Rader, and Mildred Johnson] Because of Dorn," *Spartanburg Herald Journal*, 23 July 1980, 8.

cause the South Carolina Republican Party featured such moderates as Jim Edwards and Greenville's Carroll Campbell, who worked effectively and pragmatically across party, class, and racial lines, there was throughout the decade a vital and viable two-party system in the Palmetto State. Besides helping to reorganize the Democratic Party, Bryan Dorn began teaching political science courses at the University of South Carolina at Spartanburg (today's USC Upstate) and at Greenwood's Lander College, where his daughter Brianna attained her degree. Earl Black of Rice University and Jack Bass and partner Walter DeVries noted Dorn's role in the development of the party in the decade, as did David Broder of the *Washington Post*, who featured the progressive beneficiaries of Dorn's organization, namely, Dick Riley and Jim Clyburn.[68]

Particularly gratifying to him was his Southern Baptist faith. By no means the "main currents" in South Carolina politics, his racial progressivism was still a powerful tributary in the time. Replacing the beloved Rev. Jim Bowers as his pastor in Greenwood was the Rev. Tony Hopkins, who also became a fast friend and one who counted on the old congressman to lead Sunday school discussions. There were a gracious plenty of Baptist Republicans in the old-home church, and the Rev. Hopkins noted with admiration that his parishioner "did not use his church to practice politics."[69]

In March of 1984, Dorn's friend, the much-admired Benjamin Elijah Mays, president emeritus of Morehouse College and president emeritus of the Atlanta School Board, died. Bryan Dorn was a pallbearer in the ceremonies both at Morehouse and in Greenwood, and he was the architect of fundraising efforts among both private individuals and state assemblymen to get a historical marker for Mays in the old Rambo section of Greenwood County, and to get a museum built that featured the modest frame house where Mays was born and recorded speeches that the crusading educator had delivered. Loy Sartin, curator of the Benjamin Elijah Mays Museum, has noted how vital Bryan Dorn's fundraising and publicity efforts were for the institution. It was difficult to set up monuments to a civil rights activist in a

---

[68] Earl Black, *Politics and Society in the South*; Broder, *Changing of the Guard*; Bass and DeVries, *Transformation*; clippings, 1980–1984, SCDP/SCPC.

[69] Tony Hopkins quoted, Carolyn Click, "Man of the People," *Columbia State*, 19 August 2005, 1.

state still given over to ancestor worship of various Confederate officers and leaders of Jim Crow days, but Dorn did vital work in the tasks.[70]

On 14 August 1983, Bryan Dorn was driving in the late afternoon on US 378 in Lexington County after a campaign speech on behalf of US Senator Fritz Hollings. In the intense glare of the early evening summer sun, he lost his bearings and collided with a car driven by an eighteen-year-old from West Columbia who survived with minor injuries. There were obvious head injuries, and officers arriving on the scene reported that Mr. Dorn was "a little nostalgic," though otherwise alert and making good sense as they talked with him. Treated at Columbia's Baptist Hospital, he was transferred to Providence Hospital and released in a few days. He was confined to a wheelchair, which was just about the only way he could be physically restrained from doing the farm labor that he still thrived on. A year later, he decided to resign as chairman of the Democratic Party, though Barratt House would remain a center for party barbeques and other political and civic gatherings. He and Millie slowed down a little, since he needed to travel in a special handicapped-accessible van. The two began tending the history and the biography of their lives and turned over a treasure trove of personal and party and congressional papers to the South Caroliniana Library at the University of South Carolina. In these twilight days, Democratic Party officials celebrated his career. He was elected chairman emeritus of the party, the first person so honored, and in 1987 the South Carolina state legislature commissioned and hung a portrait of him in the State House. The South Carolina Educational Television, SCETV, which he had supported since the Great Society days of LBJ, produced a special about his career.[71]

In one sense, the car crash ended his political career. He was never again a real force, either behind the scenes or in in the forefront. For all that, he remained a student of politics, with focus on South Carolina's political economy, conceding that textiles were a lost cause for employment but still hopeful about nuclear energy, especially at the five facilities of du Pont, generally called Savannah River Plant (SRP), both for cheap energy and for high-wage employment in the Augusta-Aiken area (sometimes called its

---

[70] Roper, *Magnificent Mays*, 284–308; Benjamin Elijah Mays Commemoration, 5 September 2012, Benjamin Elijah Mays Museum, Greenwood, SC; Loy Sartin to Roper, 12 August 2012 and 10 September 2012, JHR/SCPC.

[71] "Dorn Injured in Car Accident," *Charleston News and Courier*, 14 August 1983, 17A.

own special region by economic historians) of his old district. He was saddened to see the rapid decline of the SRP as an employer after the 1980s, the rapid decline of non-textile industrial jobs throughout the 1990s, and difficulties in the public schools after the bright hopes and substantive accomplishments of Dick Riley. In what must have seemed a story of "shirt sleeves to shirt sleeves," he kept track of the increasing relative poverty in McCormick, Edgefield, Abbeville, and his own Greenwood, even as he reveled in the growing prosperity of Aiken-Augusta and Anderson.[72]

He took solace in the fact that his successor, Butler Carson Derrick of Edgefield, was also a progressive Southern Populist who sweated over these employment problems as much as had Bryan Dorn. In particular, he was glad that Congressman Derrick was true on interracialism—vital in the minority/majority counties of McCormick and Edgefield—and true to the rural factory folk; even though the mills were locked up and abandoned, the rural counties of the Third District remained heavily dependent on some kind of industry for employment. Like Congressman Dorn, Congressman Derrick made the district "safe" for Democrats by providing close attention to constituent needs. And when Derrick voluntarily stepped down in 1994, it became a Republican territory (the first statewide victory for Lindsey Graham) suggesting again that it was close attention to constituent service and not habit that had made the Third District so "safe" for so long for Populistic Democrats.[73]

Bryan and Millie Dorn took delight in their children as they grew and flourished, and soon there were grandchildren growing and flourishing, eventually seven. Daughter Brianna married Bruce Lawrence and remained in Greenwood, where she was a frequent visitor to the Barratt House and always willing to help visitors understand the unique history of the place. Brother Watson continued as a small-town attorney and major figure in the Baptist Sunday school at First Baptist Church and also as marvelous raconteur of family and regional doings. Daughter Olivia earned a degree in mass communications and journalism at USC, became active in the SCETV, and attained local note as a television journalist; she married Jim Kennedy of Northfield, Minnesota. Son Johnson Griffith became an ordained Baptist

---

[72] Frederickson, *Cold War Dixie*, 123–46; Schunk and Woodward, "A Profile of the Diversified South Carolina Economy," 65.

[73] Butler Derrick, remarks, "Art of Political Biography"; Butler Carson Derrick Jr. Papers, 1974–1994, BCD/SCPC; Adam Bernstein, "Butler Derrick," obit., *Washington Post*, 6 May 2014; and "Butler Derrick" obit., *Aiken Standard*, 7 May 2014, 1.

minister with the same evangelical zeal and progressivism as his Sunday-school-teaching father and had the unique pleasure of baptizing sister Olivia; he was married to Sharon Dorn. Son Jennings married Anne and moved to St. Louis, Missouri; they produced a grandson named for the congressman, William Jennings Bryan Dorn III. Daughter Debbie Griffith moved to nearby Anderson, also in the Third District, while brother Charlie moved to San Jose and sister Gracie moved to Columbia. Cousin Steve Griffith Jr., of the Griffith lawyering cousins, retired from Duke Power and restored an historic home in Prosperity. Steve Griffith enjoyed meeting with Watson Dorn and the children, especially Brianna and Johnson and Olivia, and sharing tales about Dorn's political career and about local history and local politics. The entire family helped Bryan and Millie Dorn gather papers and photographs and taped interviews and other artifacts for archiving at the South Carolina Political Collections of USC, and the old Clemson Tiger Steve Griffith even became president of the University of South Caroliniana Society.[74]

On 2 July 1990, Mildred Johnson Dorn died, and Bryan Dorn lost his love and his best friend. For her tombstone, he had engraved:

Journalist

Covered US Congress for US News and World Report

Editor

Political Advisor

Wife Mother Grandmother[75]

The leave-taking of Millie Johnson Dorn left Bryan Dorn sad and a little lonely, but he soldiered on another fifteen years, keeping an active schedule of speaking and meeting people in American Legion, Baptist, state Democratic, and local history sessions. He met with archivist Herb Hartsook and added valuable personal papers to his collection, especially bringing forward material documenting the South Carolina Democratic Party. One thing the archivist noted of the old congressman was that the raconteuring spirit remained, but the old passions were dulled; in various interview sessions both formal and informal, Bryan Dorn could not be drawn out

---

[74] "Olivia Dorn-Kennedy obituary," Blythewood Funeral Home notice, Herb Hartsook to Jack Roper, 17 December 2013, JHR/SCPC.

[75] Tombstone rubbing, Bethel United Methodist Church, Greenwood, JHR/SCPC.

to make critical remarks about his old political foes, or even particularly meaningful remarks about them. For all that, the many written sources are enhanced by the sound of his red-hills voice and the images of the orator, collected and made available by Hartsook and his team.[76]

On 19 August 2005, his heart failed, and William Jennings Bryan Dorn joined his wife and Dada and Nana and other departed family members in the Bethel United Methodist Cemetery in the ancestral Greenwood. He was buried with full military honors, but the commemoration was by no means a formal ritual. Pastor Tony Hopkins officiated, allowing plenty of good old-time storytelling as appropriate, especially from brother Watson Dorn, cousin Steve Griffith Jr., and Baptist minister son Johnson Dorn. Columbia's state newspaper, then still the daily of record for South Carolina, featured front-page photographs and two remembrances, one by Carolyn Click and the other by veteran political observer Lee Bandy. Carolyn Click entitled her piece "Man of the People" and Lee Bandy entitled his, "Longtime Congressman Had Progressive Streak." For a part of the piedmont dominated by small-time farmers and millhands, it called up Populistic memories almost forgotten by 2005. A popular man of these people in the red hills and cotton fields could indeed be true to his own—and still be a progressive.[77]

---

[76] Interview: Herb Hartsook with Roper and students Mark Robertson and Matthew Wilkinson (18 February 2013), JHR/SCPC.

[77] Carolyn Click, "Man of the People Honored," *Columbia State*, 19 August 2005, Al; Lee Bandy, "Long-time Congressman Had Progressive Streak," *Columbia State*, 19 August 2005, A1.

Postlude

The Latch String Is Always Out

People in the red hills have a lot of sayings, all generally Southern, but some *sui generis*. The phrase "The latchstring is always out" is likely rural as much as red hills or even generally Southern. It refers to a time when doors had latches that locked them shut, but the latches also had a string. The string could be hung outside the door through a hole, and a visitor could pull the latchstring down, lifting the latch up and thereby opening the door. Long after the system disappeared, the concept lingered, and folk said, *The latchstring is always out,* meaning that one could drop in any time to visit, with the strong implication that you did not even need to knock, but simply open the door and come in. Bryan Dorn used the phrase, and in his era it probably made as much sense in the rural Midwest as it did in the red hills. During much of his youth, even into middle-aged years, the idea of locking a door was foreign and odd. As he noted in his memoirs, Greenwood County was marked by long periods of loneliness, and a visitor was a welcomed diversion. Whatever age he attained, Bryan Dorn kept using the phrase, intending to say that he wanted company—probably more at the end in 2005 than even in the 1920s, when he would practice speeches alongside the roadway and look anxiously for some traveling soul to come by the farm place.

By any measure of personality type, William Jennings Bryan Dorn was an extrovert, one who drew energy from others and who hungered to be around folk. Although a bright fellow who thought deeply, he did not like to spend solitary time in contemplation, but would get up and go find someone to talk with, doing much of his thinking in the middle of conversation. Such personality traits are garden variety among politicians, and the red-hills expression of it is only a regional expression of something that marks American politicians no matter where they are from. Another trait of his was that he liked solving problems, *especially your problems.* It came in handy on a farm, where something is always breaking or otherwise causing a problem, and if nothing needed fixing on your farm, there were always your neighbors. Working alongside someone to fix your problem was especially gratifying. It brought an almost physical pleasure.

From earliest childhood, probably even infancy, Bryan Dorn wanted to please, first and forever the beautiful Nana. And almost as much, the handsome Dada. Whenever he could please some stranger, the gratifying emotions were profound, as if the stranger were, in fact, Nana. The physical act of helping had to be narrated, and if the task were humdrum, as most tasks are, the narration could be intensified, marked with jokes and melodrama. Some constituent asking for help with a delayed Social Security check was much like a wandering stranger who might stop along the Callison Road at Barratt House and ask directions. The stranger would get directions, as the constituent would get service, but along with it came something in the order of a Sufi tale narrated in the dialect of the red hills. Most Southerners reading these words are likely growing impatient, since everything described is perfectly normal and as taken for granted as humidity, dew, mosquitoes—and the need for tea to be achingly sweet and Bible phrases to be ready to hand. Most non-Southerners reading these words are likely growing even more impatient, since they have seen and heard everything described and it all seems like so much self-conscious posing, so much tedious play-acting, above all so much insincere *talk. I just have to hug your neck* could not mean anything, and no one going on and on about *come by any time* actually wants you to come by any time.

In the same way, it likely strains credulity to offer the picture of Bryan Dorn reading constituent mail, as is done in the prelude, "Please help us." The knowing citizen, especially nowadays in the red hills, cannot fathom unemployed or underemployed people writing letters in longhand to a congressman—and certainly cannot fathom the congressman literally taking off his jacket and rolling up his sleeves and *doing* something about the correspondent's problem. But in 1958, William Jennings Bryan Dorn wanted to help his friends and neighbors, and especially about their jobs. He took pains to write responses, dictated with precision to his staff, all of whom were as anxious to please the Third District folk as he was. Even and especially if he disagreed with whatever they offered in the way of an opinion, he kept going over the letter until he could find something to agree with, and when he found it, he could say with a perfectly straight face, I agree with *almost* everything you say. He let the writer know that he knew what they were talking about, that he took it seriously as a problem, and that problems could be solved. In the depths of the three Eisenhower recessions, he often called on the classes, those businessmen who owned the mills and managed the firms and controlled credit, and asked generally—and sometimes quite specifically—about job openings. Then he would press the classes, whether it was Jim Self Sr. or Jim Self Jr. or BC Inabinet or Bubba Abney, to hire Miss Lura or Mrs. Becknell or Pete and Sallie Lou's boy Phil. He would, of course, listen to the classes about the problems they had, and he could promise legislation, sometimes quite specific, sometimes quite detailed and convoluted, to help them in what they needed. Everybody needed help, *and Bryan Dorn needed to help everybody.*

In assessing him, then, the biographer cannot ask what Bryan Dorn would have done as governor or senator. By his own standard—the will of the people expressed after he had talked with them and walked with them—state governor was not his role to play and US senator was not his role to play. Burnet Maybank beat him for the latter office, and for governor, Pug Ravenel beat him twice, and then Doc Jim Edwards and Dick Riley and Brantley Harvey also beat him. The rejections hurt, but he certainly accepted the verdicts. The people remembered him as a great congressman, and the biographer has found evidence that Third District citizens were more than willing to send a congressman away if he did not serve them. The years since Butler Carson Derrick retired have shown that the people of the red hills are also more than willing to change political parties. In other words, as noted, incumbents found the Third District less "safe" than any other district in the state. So, too, have Democrats found the Third District no more "safe" than any other district in the state. The people, then, judged Bryan Dorn as a congressman, and the biographer must judge him as a congressman, the role chosen for him by the people and the role he served with most natural spirit and learned expertise

In ascending order, there were three huge social issues that he dealt with as congressman: public works, veterans' affairs, and civil rights. On the Public Works Committee, Dorn was at his most professional and his most courtly in getting things done for South Carolinians, especially the Savannah River projects and the interstate highway projects. Such projects came easily to every congressman, for no district could afford to do the expensive construction work with its own resources, and thus every representative sought federal monies for things he or she needed. What distinguished the congressman from the Third District was his effectiveness in working across party lines and his effectiveness in working across regional borders. In all such cases—especially those involving projects like the St. Lawrence Seaway or Rocky Mountain water projects—he did his homework carefully and voted both from knowledge about what representatives wanted (and were willing to "trade" or "pair votes" or otherwise "roll logs" on behalf of South Carolina) and from a careful study of the environmental impact of such projects.

Dorn's passion for nuclear energy now seems misspent because of the recent era's devaluation of atomic energy, but the broader point is that in his time, he consciously worked as an environmentalist decades before others expressed such concerns, so much so that his efforts were recognized by environmentalists at Duke University. In that passion for the environment—

and working before economic models were developed by scholars such as Gordon Tullock or James Buchanan—he always measured the "trade-off" between clean air and clear water on the one hand and cheap energy and jobs on the other hand. In his days of service, he was as responsible as anyone for transforming Aiken County from a place of middling farmland and a place for tourists to ride horses and play golf into a dynamic and quite progressive—and prospering and racially harmonious—community because of the Savannah River Plant (SRP). That his era miscalculated the costs and benefits of nuclear energy is a shared fault of his, but the more important issue, now largely missing from such related debates, is his constant weighing of the inevitable balance between economic needs and environmental needs, always done (and again, before formal models for such measurements were created) with a statesman's sense that it was not an either/or contest between one want and the other, but rather a series of artfully spun and artfully maintained trade-offs.

As to veterans, Dorn always approached the needs of veterans and their families as a grunt and a gun bunny and never as a privileged officer. Likely, his own failure to become an officer and fly jet planes as a professional lent a poignancy to his efforts. He understood what Nana understood, that is, that soldiers and sailors give up something—at the very least, years of their lives when other people are establishing careers, usually doing so by training in educational institutions. Son of educators, he alone among the offspring missed the college education and had to teach himself, which he did remarkably well. He was bound in determination that other soldiers who were in service during "normal" college years have the federal help to regain those lost years of study and training. He understood that entire families made sacrifices, although not always as extremely as the Dorns did during World War II, and that such sacrifices had earned each family member the right to receive help, especially educational benefits. Bryan Dorn's correspondence betrays an almost physical want in helping a surviving daughter of a combat veteran gain full college benefits—especially if, like Nana, she intended to become a teacher.

Working with veterans, he also understood from personal observation how many unseen wounds were laid on someone in service. Long before anyone had the term "post traumatic stress disorder," Corporal Dorn and American Legionnaire Dorn understood that some emotional wounds labeled "non-service connected" (the *NSC* term he pathologically hated) were, in fact, as directly tied to the years of service as were legs lost or hearing impaired. He worked like a Trojan alongside Tiger Teague to force the Eisenhower people, and all people thereafter, to treat the veterans for NSC disabilities. In 2007, the once-magnificent Walter Reed Hospital was found guilty of neglect and abuse of Iraqi and Afghanistan war survivors, and the facility was eventually closed in disgrace for the institution and its staff. Bryan Dorn was by then two years gone, but one could hear him thundering from his grave in Greenwood County his impassioned protests at the very idea of shortchanging medical care for gobs and grunts.

Related to that demand for the best care for military personnel was his once-controversial concept, borrowed from Tennessee Republican Jimmy Quillen, that new schools of medicine should be established alongside existing VA hospitals, thereby allowing a healthy symbiotic relationship between the staff at the VA, the patients at the VA, and the teaching doctors and the practicing students at the school of medicine. Both East Tennessee State University and Mountain Home VA flourished because of this plan proffered by the Republican and pushed through by the Democrat, and in the flourishing each institution spun out benefits to civilians who were treated in the light of the research and practices there. By the same token, the VA facility now named for Bryan Dorn in Columbia, rather than being closed, became a fine one, and a new school of medicine at the University of South Carolina developed the same symbiosis with the same benefits to the veterans—which included, in his own late years, none other than Bryan Dorn himself—and with "spin-off" benefits for civilians.

By far the greatest issue for Southern politicians, especially in the Deep South rural districts, was the moral challenge posed by the civil rights movement. A signer of the Southern Manifesto and an apologist for Jim Crow in 1956, Bryan Dorn was a moderate segregationist between 1943 and 1969. As such, he was as often a practical problem for those seeking legislation to bring justice as were those who actively demonstrated the most hateful and violent resistance. Following Brooks Hays, he attempted a failed Baptist conception of gradually evolving racial brotherhood based on local acceptance by the white racists involved. Only using the "N-word" once in a personal correspondence for which he was punished by his entire women's adult Sunday school class back in Greenwood, Bryan Dorn was careful in how he talked to and about black people, carefully and precisely pronouncing the word *Negro* until general acceptance of the term *black,* after which time he adopted the term *black*. More substantively, he made sure that black veterans got their fully deserved benefits and that black Social Security retirees got their full benefits, and he even worked to try to do the impossible, that is, to make segregated schools the full equal of integrated schools. Friends with Bennie Mays and Modjeska Simkins and John Bolt Culbertson and Deek Newman, Dorn was often hurt when black people and white progressives grouped him with his cousin Strom Thurmond and others who so consciously used racist appeals.

Because of Lyndon Johnson, a galling irony given his personal dislike for the Texan, Bryan Dorn was jerked into the civil rights movement and fell into line with the rapidly "bending arc of moral history." But when he turned toward the bending arc, he was true to Baptist training and did not deviate again from the moral compass. For civil rights, he achieved a complete submersion and a complete transformation. His son, the Baptist preacher Johnson Dorn, recalled the congressman taking the five children in his Plymouth to a Klan rally. Dousing the lights and shushing the children, the congressman rolled down the windows and let his children hear some of his constituents in Greenwood County cuss him and talk about killing him because of his Liberal Integrationism. His mail dripped with vehemence from onetime friends, but he became quite bold, even confrontational, on issues of civil rights. When one family friend wrote asking where she could find a Ku Klux chapter to send money to, he told her he did not know—but he asked that if she found them that she please tell him so he could report them to the FBI.

More important to him was what he found while driving around with Deek Newman on the back roads in a losing gubernatorial campaign: he found that his people were ready for integration, at least at some levels. True to the concepts of a "small 'd' Democrat," Bryan Dorn at last found the progressive streak in most of his constituents, and he responded to it despite the regressive racism in some of his loudest constituents. On the vital issue of his post-World War II days, the civil rights movement, Bryan Dorn came late, but he did come, and nothing mattered more to his people or to the march of history. His speech on behalf of busing was not only remarkable for its oratorical exuberance and its lasting message, it was remarkable because he delivered it so completely alone amongst the Deep South congressmen and especially among the South Carolina delegation. Even more remarkable than his speech on the floor of the US House was his related speech on the curbside in Greenville in response to a hostile questioner. In each case, he spoke without notes, with words he believed God gave him, and he spoke well. Most important to him, and to us, is that his people accepted both speeches, the one in Congress and the one in Greenville. He lost that particular vote and he lost that gubernatorial vote, but his people, both races, won on both occasions.

As noted, Willliam Jennings Bryan Dorn was not given to solitary reflection. He ate breakfast with Bible study groups, and he ate lunch with the classes, who brought him their demands for legislation. Then he went through his mail, the beloved letters from the masses, to see what demands they had for legislation. Then he walked the hallways looking for congressmen and staffers to talk with about shared problems. He loved this, and he lived for it.

Few things made him as happy or as fulfilled as drafting a complex piece of legislation, a piece that had to suit a Northeastern liberal and a Midwestern conservative without running off his fellow Southerners. He loved going to Sam Rayburn's Board of Education, something dreaded by others, even if Mr. Sam were pushing him to do something he did not want to do, because Mr. Sam was solving a problem and if you helped him, why, he would sure see to it that you got help with your problem. Like the great majority of long-serving congressmen, William Jennings Bryan Dorn lived to write specific legislation as he lived to go by and jawbone a government worker on behalf of some constituent.

Like the great majority of long-serving congressmen, William Jennings Bryan Dorn dreamed up no new dreams, offered no bracing visions, did very little on a grand scale. He focused on the tedious and mechanical and repetitive parts of law crafting and policy implementation. When political scientists looked at Fritz Hollings, they saw the governor with the vision for integrated public schools and the senator with the vision for resolving hunger in America; they saw the classic model of the politician who painted in broad strokes and used a huge canvas and dreamed large dreams. When they looked at James F. Byrnes, they saw a statesman who occupied many offices: they saw one always focused on "grand issues." And yet both Byrnes and the much more progressive Hollings are unnoted for attention to detail, especially the details of service to individual communities and constituents.

When the same political scientists looked at Bryan Dorn, they saw a man who took on tasks and made things work and accepted the guidance of others who painted and dreamed. He was in the parlance, not really an Issue man and not really a Policy man, but a Process man. The various quotes from Machiavelli and from Max Weber have to do with getting law enacted and making the written laws work, and he understood Machiavelli and Weber with a depth and a subtlety not matched by many intellectuals and scholars. In some of the photographs, we students of the past see Bryan Dorn as he was: note the photograph in Figure 5, where he is with a group of Anderson public schoolteachers; note the photograph in Figure 3, where he sits at a table in his Greenwood Federal Building Offices while the town manager and local plant managers point fingers at him and talk about unfair Japanese competition. In those and other settings, Bryan Dorn has left the latchstring out. In those moments, the great speechifier is not talking, but listening. His blue eyes are peeled to take you in, and his big ears are cocked to hear you. When he does talk, he will give you back your own words, served up with an anecdote about your grandfather and an analogy to boxing or football. And he will tell you, meaning it sincerely, *he is just so happy that you came to see him* and *just so happy that he can help you.*

Bryan Dorn had great faith in his own people, and that faith extended to the black people in his district, the folk who made up the majority population in McCormick and Edgefield counties. From 1946 to 1968, he listened and listened and then put words from Thomas Jefferson and Abraham Lincoln around things he heard white people saying about black people. He was in that time a moderate segregationist, in red-hills parlance, *run of the mill* and *cut from the cloth*. He kept his own counsel on his actual belief that God had made us all equal and that Jesus had died for justice and that economic opportunity could never come without racial integration. Brother Brooks Hays, the Baptist minister and Arkansas congressman, had said it just right after all, and in ways that did not contradict Machiavelli or Weber: when the folk realize the time is right, they will find the way to justice. Certainly, in the depths of violent responses to every black call for justice, his words rang hollow about going slow and waiting for the local people to find the way to justice. In the long run, we are all dead, said Lord Keynes, whose prescriptions for full employment Dorn followed through Dr. Hubert Aull. Sometimes black constituents—to say nothing of students of history reading through the speeches and correspondence half a century later—must have wondered if all of us would be dead before Bryan Dorn's white people could find their way to justice. They and we coming later must occasionally wonder why it was so hard for Dorn to make the connection between Keynes's words about the macroeconomy and Dr. King's call for justice now.

And yet in 1969, he was convinced his people had found their way there. The millhands and small-time farmers and mom-and-pop *bidness* folk were ready for racial justice, starting first with their own children and grandchildren riding school buses to attend integrated schools. In 1971, on the floor of Congress, and in 1974, while running for governor, the congressman had to go on the record one way or the other on the issue of busing to achieve racial balance. Dada had said he ended "classism" by busing the children in the county to consolidated schools that served rich and poor, common and classes—and Dada's son said he was going to end racism by busing the children in the same county to consolidated schools that served black and white. Both Dada and his son Bryan Dorn knew quite well that merely integrating classes and merely integrating races in a schoolroom would not end any kind of "-ism," but each knew that such integration was quite a start. He said that the common folk, the salt of the earth, the people in the Third District, had gotten there, and indeed some popular opinion polls showed that in 1974 his people loved him but found him "less liberal" than they themselves were.

This notion that he sensed in 1969 was sharpened into a perception, even a policy that was operational and actionable and remained so until his car crash took him from active political engagement. He used his oratorical skills to go out there on behalf of busing to integrate schools when even some self-professed Liberal Integrationists from the rest of the country were busy figuring out ways not to put their own children in school desks next to black children. When the "hash man" heard Bryan Dorn in the period 1971 to 1983, he had to stop stirring the hash because the moderate segregationist was declaring that now was the time, come at last, to integrate and to offer real opportunity to everyone.

This least original, this most complaisant, this one most determined to get the crowd on his side, insisted that his own people had been stirred to accept justice, justice now and not in some incredibly distant vanishing point when we are all dead. From that conviction, achieved in 1969 and acted on with alacrity thereafter, William Jennings Bryan Dorn followed the progressivism of his own people and helped to rebuild the "party of the people," the Democrats recast in South Carolina as the same old hickory nut Jacksonians and the same speechifying Jeffersonians but with the hard-eyed practicality and *git 'er done* common sense of Abraham Lincoln, even of Alexander Hamilton.

The moment did not last forever, but while serving out his last congressional term and while chairing the party, Bryan Dorn stepped to the front of his own fast-running folk and led. The election of 1974 was remarkable in that the three candidates who dominated the talk and the action from July on to November, Pug Ravenel, Dr. Jim Edwards, and Congressman Dorn, all spoke as progressives, especially on issues of race and with particular focus on schools and other opportunities. In that moment of "forgotten alternatives," each man vigorously sought black votes and each man straightforwardly told people of his own race and class that a new day was here, and that the new day was good. In those complicated three-way discussions, Bryan Dorn lost twice to Pug Ravenel and once to Dr. Edwards, but his people did not lose. In that same twilight, he lost to Dick Riley, but his people did not lose. When he stepped off stage and worked behind the scenes, Dick Riley and Jim Clyburn and Butler Derrick and others got things done for his people—and that was all he wanted. A mark of his own wounding by the car crash and a mark of his vital importance is the long slide away from what was achieved in the language of that race involving Edwards, Ravenel, and Dorn. No one after 1983 would note South Carolina as a place of enlightenment and progressive thought and action about race relations, the environment, job training, or education at any level from pre-K to graduate school.

Interesting as he is to study, Willliam Jennings Bryan Dorn cannot be called great. He can, however, be noted for his significance for a congressional district during a transitional period of time. And he can be saluted for his faith in his people and for his patience in waiting for them to come around to the march for justice. Dorn's career is instructive, especially in moments when congressional politics seems most frustrating for its combinations of nastiness and ineffectiveness. He got things done, and done well, and his long congressional career reminds us that the people have a great potential. The deep progressive spirit in the folk of the red hills has expressed itself before and will express itself again.

The man of the people and the "party of the people" responded to the people at their best, and Bryan Dorn left written and recorded documents to remind us that there have been moments of progress. It is not the case, as sometimes claimed even by good scholars, that South Carolina voters and the politicians they elect are perpetual "bottom-feeders" who advance nowhere and who are slaves to family ties and to racial prejudices. Family ties are always there, and racial prejudices never entirely go away, but families can be worked with and racism can be ameliorated. As the great historian Edward Halleck Carr noted, progress exists, but it does not move in an unrelievedly straight line. There are moments, as there were at the end of Bryan Dorn's life, and certainly continuing into the second decade of the twenty-first century, when the march of history hits a plateau. The congressman's papers and the party chairman's papers document a moment or two of substantive advance. And the same documents remind us that in the future it could be better.

Epigraph

Government of the people

by the people

for the people

Source: "Bliss Copy" of "Gettysburg Address." Colonel Alexander Bliss arranged for Lincoln to make a copy of the address. The original speech was hard to read because he had made corrections and had written on both sides of it. The last known copy written by Lincoln and signed by him and dated by him, it is on display at the Lincoln Room Lincoln Room of the White House. Dorn liked to look at the copy.

Bibliography

William Jennings Bryan Dorn

Books

With Scott Derks. *Dorn: Of the People, A Political Way of Life*. Columbia, SC: Sandlapper/Bruccoli Press, 1988.

Selected Articles and Speeches

"In His Own Words: Recorded Speeches of William Jennings Bryan Dorn." Preserved at South Carolina Political Collections, Ernest Frederick Hollings Library, the University of South Carolina.

Primary Sources

Manuscript and Archival Collections

Emory & Henry College Archives, Emory & Henry College, Emory, VA.

Brooks Hays Address Earl G. Hunt Papers

White Topper Files

National Archives and Records Administration, Southeast Region, Atlanta, GA.

Presidential Archives, the Citadel, Military College of South Carolina, Charleston, Mark Wayne Clark Papers.

Special Collections of Clemson University, Clemson, South Carolina.

Edgar Allan Brown Papers

George Hubert Aull Papers

Earle E. Morris Jr. Papers

Ernest Frederick Hollings Library of University of South Carolina

Allen Drury, *Anna Hastings, The Story of a Washington Newspaperperson*

George Eliot, *Daniel Deronda*.

Romulo, Carlos Pena. *I Saw the Fall of the Philippines*. Garden City, NY: Doubleday, Doran & Co., 1943.

Seversky, Alexander Procafieff de. *Air Power: Key to Survival With a Prologue on the Lesson of Korea*. New York: Simon & Schuster, 1950.

Irvin Department of Rare Books and Special Collections

Legal Law Library of University of South Carolina

General Assembly Reports and Resolutions

South Carolina Political Collections

William Jennings Bryan Dorn Papers

Interviews
Watson Dorn and Steve Griffith (2006)
James Burrows Edwards (2011)
Steve Griffith and Herb Hartsook (2012)
Steve Griffith and Watson Dorn (2012)
Bud Ferillo and Herb Hartsook (2013)
Steve Griffith and Herb Hartsook (2013)

South Carolina Political Collection, Hollings Library, University of South Carolina
John T. Ashmore Papers
Joseph Raleigh Bryson Papers
John Drummond Papers
James Burrows Edwards Papers
Robert Witherspoon Hemphill Papers
Olin DeWitt Talmadge Johnston Papers
Richter Hermann Moore, Jr. Papers
University of South Carolina Young Democratic Students
States' Rights Democratic Club of the University of South Carolina
South Carolina Democratic Party Papers
George Bell Timmerman Papers
South Carolina State Department of Archives and History
Manuscript Collections, Columbia, South Carolina
Clarendon County Board of Education Records
Governor William Ellerbe Papers
South Carolina Department of Human and Health Resources

South Carolina State Library, Columbia
Acts and Joint Resolutions of the General Assembly of the State of South Carolina
South Caroliniana Library
University of South Carolina, Columbia, South Carolina
James Allen Hoyt, "The Phoenix Riot," Kosmos Club
Daniel Rogers McLeod Papers
Elison Durant Smith Papers
Watson Family Papers
Harry LeGare Watson Papers
Harry LeGare Watson Phoenix Day Book, 1900–1901.

Southern Historical Collection
University of North Carolina Library, Chapel Hill
Frank Porter Graham Papers
Jonathan Worth Daniels Papers

Morris Randolph Mitchell Papers
National Association for the Advancement of Colored People Board of Directors, 1950–1955.
North Carolina Council on Interracial Cooperation
North Carolina Council on Human Relations Records
Penn School Papers
John Herbert Roper Papers

Southern Oral History Program
Interview with Harvey E. Beech
Interview with Dallas Blanchard

West Virginia Archives and History, Charleston, WV
Elizabeth Kee Papers
Keenotes Files

Newspapers
Abbeville Press and Banner
Aiken Press and Banner
Anderson Independent
Atlanta Constitution
Charleston News and Courier
Charlotte Observer
Columbia Record
Columbia State
Danville Register
Edgefield Advertiser
Edgefield Chronicle
Greenville News
Greenville Piedmont
Greenwood Index
Greenwood Index and Journal
New York Times
Philadelphia Inquirer
Pittsburgh Courier
Spartanburg Herald Journal
Sumter Daily Item
Washington Post

Secondary Sources

Abraham, Henry Julian. *Justices, Presidents, and Senators, A Political History of Appointments to the Supreme Court*. London: Rowan and Littlefield, 2008.

Aeschylus. *Agamemnon*. Edited and translated by Gilbert Murray. London: George Allen and Unwin, 1920.

Albert, Carl Bert. *Little Giant: The Life and Times of Speaker Carl Albert*. Norman: University of Oklahoma Press, 1990.

Ambrose, Stephen E. *Eisenhower, Vol. 2: The President*. New York: Simon & Schuster, 1983.

____. *Nixon, Vol. 1: The Education of a Politician, 1913–1962*. New York: Simon & Schuster, 1987.

American National Biography. Edited by John A. Garratty and Martin C. Carnes. New York: Oxford University Press, 1999.

Apple, R. W. Jr. "Kennedy Appeals for Nonviolence." *New York Times* (5 April 1968): 33.

Arendt, Hannah. *The Origins of Totalitarianism*. 1951. Revised edition. New York Harcourt Harvest Book, 1984.

Aristotle. *Collected Works*. Edited and translated by W. D. Ross. London and Oxford: Clarendon Press, 1908.

____. *Politics*. Edited and translated by Benjamin Jowett. New York: Random House Modern Library, 1943.

Associated Press. "Text of Vishinsky Speech to U.N. General Assembly Meeting," *Washington Post* (19 September 1947): 2.

Atto, William J. "Brooks Hays and the New Deal." *Arkansas Historical Quarterly* 60 (Summer 2008): 167–86.

Baker, James Thomas. *Brooks Hays*. Macon, GA: Mercer University Press, 1989.

Baker, Ray Stannard. *Following the Color Line: An Account of Negro Citizenship in the American Democracy*, 1904. Reprint. Edited by Maurice Filler. Williamstown, MA: Corner House, 1973.

Ballantyne, David T. "Ernest Frederick Hollings." PhD dissertation. Cambridge University, 2014.

____. *New Politics in the Old South; Ernest F. Hollings in the Civil Rights Era*. Columbia: University of South Carolina Press, 2016.

Barron, Robert G. "Challenge and Change: William Jennings Bryan Dorn and the Cold War." MA thesis, University of South Carolina, Columbia, 1994.

Bass, Jack. "Documenting the Orangeburg Massacre." *Nieman Reports: Journalism and Black America* (Fall 2003).

Bass, Jack and Jack Nelson. *The Orangeburg Massacre*. Revised edition. Macon, GA: Mercer University Press, 2003.

Bass, Jack and W. Scott Poole. *The Palmetto State: The Making of Modern South Carolina*. Columbia: University of South Carolina Press, 2009.

Bass, Jack and Marilyn W. Thompson. *Ol' Strom: An Unauthorized Biography of Strom Thurmond*. Atlanta: Longstreet, 1998.

___. *Strom: The Complicated Personal and Political Life of Strom Thurmond.* New York: Perseus Group BBS, 2006.

Bass, Jack and Walter De Vries. *Transformation of Southern Politics: Social Change and Political Consequences Since 1945.* Athens: University of Georgia Press, 1995.

Basso, Joseph Hamilton. *Mainstream.* New York: Ayer, 1940.

Beeman, Richard. *Plain, Honest Men, the Making of the American Constitution.* New York: Random House, 2009.

Belloc du Berrier, Hilaire. *Background to Betrayal: The Tragedy of Vietnam.* Americanist Library Series. Boston and Los Angeles: Western Islands, 1965.

Benner, Erica. *Be Like the Fox: Machiavelli in His World.* New York: W. W. Norton, 2017.

Berry, Mary Frances. "Brown Out?" *The Lost Promise of Civil Rights. Democracy.* 6 (2007): 85–92.

Biographical Directory of the Senate of the State of South Carolina, 1776–1964. Columbia, SC: South Carolina Archives, 1964.

Black, Earl and Merle Black. *Politics and Society in the South.* Cambridge, MA, and London: Harvard University Press, 1987.

Blake, Nelson Morehouse and Richard Spencer Palmer. *The Vaughn Bible Class, Calvary Baptist Church, Washington, D.C.: A Fifty-Year History.* Franklin Center, PA: Franklin Press, 1940.

Branch, Taylor. *Parting the Waters: America in the King Years, 1954–1963.* New York: Simon & Schuster, 1988.

Brauer, Carl. "Women Activists, Southern Conservatives, and the Prohibition of Sex Discrimination in Title VII of the 1964 Civil Rights Bill." *Journal of Southern History* 49 (1983): 37–56.

Brinkley, David. *David Brinkley, a Memoir.* New York: Alfred A. Knopf Borzoi Books, 1995.

Brock, Clifton. "Americans for Democratic Action: A Study of Liberal Frustration with Postwar United States." MA thesis, Tallahassee: Florida State University, 1961.

___. *Americans for Democratic Action: Its Role in National Politics.* Reprint. New York: Praeger, 1985.

Broder, David S. *Changing of the Guard: Power and Leadership in America.* New York: Simon & Schuster, 1980.

Brown, Millicent Ellison. "Civil Rights Activism in Charleston, 1940–1970." PhD dissertation. Tallahassee: Florida State University, 1997.

Brown, Richard Maxwell. *Strain of Violence: Historical Studies of American Violence and Vigilantism.* New York: Oxford University Press, 1975.

Burke High Students. *Who Is Burke High? The History of Burke High School Family.* Charleston: South Carolina Humanities Society, 2010.

Burns, James McGregor. *Roosevelt, Vol. 2: Soldier of Freedom, 1940–1945*. New York: Harcourt, 1970.

Cannon, James Monroe III. *Time and Chance: Gerald Ford's Appointment with History*. New York: HarperCollins, 1974.

Capturing the Future: Earl Warren and Supreme Court History. Edited by Bernard Schwartz. New York and London: Oxford University Press, 1998.

Carlton, David. *Mill and Town in South Carolina, 1880–1920*. Baton Rouge: Louisiana State University Press, 1982.

Caro, Robert A. "Johnson's Dream; Obama's Speech." *New York Times* (27 August 2008).

___. *Means of Ascent*. New York: Alfred A. Knopf, 1991.

___. *Master of the Senate*. New York: Alfred A. Knopf, 2003;

___. *The Passage of Power*. New York: Alfred A. Knopf, 2013.

___. *The Years of Lyndon Johnson, 4 vols. The Path to Power*. New York: Alfred Knopf, 1982.

Carpenter, JoAnn Decker. "Olin D. Johnston, the New Deal, and the Politics of Class in South Carolina, 1934–1938." PhD dissertation. Atlanta: Emory University, 1987.

Carr, Edward Hallett. *What Is History?* Regius Lectures of Cambridge University. New York: Cambridge University Press, 1961.

Carter, Dan T. *From George Wallace to Newt Gingrich: Race in the Conservative Counter-revolution*. Baton Rouge: Louisiana State University Press, 1996.

___. *Scottsboro: A Tragedy of the American South*. London: Oxford University Press, 1969.

Carter, Jimmy. *An Hour before Daylight: Memories of a Rural Boyhood*. New York: Simon & Schuster, 2001.

Casey, Steven. *Selling the Korean War: Propaganda, Politics, and Public Opinion*. New York: Oxford University Press, 2008.

Casey, Steven and William Stueck. "Reflections on the MacArthur Controversy at Sixty." *Historically Speaking* (April 2011): 37–40.

Chappell, David. *A Stone of Hope*. Chapel Hill: University of North Carolina Press, 2003.

Cherny, Robert W. *A Righteous Cause: The Life of William Jennings Bryan*. Norman: University of Oklahoma Press, 1994.

The Civil Rights Movement. Chancellor's Symposium, 1985. Edited by Charles W. Eagles. Jackson, MS: University Press of Mississippi, 1986.

The Civil Rights Movement in Mississippi. Porter L. Fortune Symposium, 2010. Edited by Ted Ownby. Jackson: University Press of Mississippi, 2011.

Clark, Charles S. *Sexual Harassment: Men and Women in Workplace Power Struggle*. Washington, DC: Congressional Quarterly, 1991.

Clark, Kenneth Bancroft. *Prejudice and Your Child*. Boston: Beacon Press, 1951.

Clark, Thomas Dionysius. *The Rural Press and the New South*. Walter Lynwood Fleming Lectures. 1947. Reprint. Westport, CT: Greenwood Press, 1970.

___. *The Southern Country Editor*. Southern Classics Series. Edited by John G. Sproat. 1948. Reprint. Columbia: University of South Carolina Press, 1991.

Cleaver, Eldridge. *Soul on Ice*. New York: McGraw-Hill, 1968.

Clyburn, James E. *Blessed Experiences: Genuinely Southern, Proudly Black*. Columbia: University of South Carolina Press, 2014.

Commager, Henry Steele. *The American Mind*. New Haven, CT: Yale University Press, 1950.

___. *Theodore Parker*. Boston: Little, Brown, 1936.

Controversies in Minority Voting: The Voting Rights Act in Perspective. Edited by Bernard N. Grofman and Chandler Davidson. Washington, DC: Brookings Institution Press, 1992.

Converse, Philip E., Warren E. Miller, Donald E. Stokes, and Angus Campbell. *The American Voter*. University of Michigan Survey Research Center Series, 1956. Chicago: University of Chicago Press, 1960.

Cook, James F. *Carl Sanders, Spokesman of the New South*. Macon, GA: Mercer University Press, 1993.

___. *Carl Vinson, Patriarch of the Armed Forces*. Macon, GA: Mercer University Press, 2004.

Croly, Herbert David. *The Promise of American Life*. 1909. Princeton, NJ: Princeton University Press. 2014.

C. Vann Woodward: A Southern Historian and His Critics. Edited by John Herbert Roper Sr. 1997. Revised edition. Athens and London: University of Georgia Press, 2011.

Dalberg-Acton, John Emerich Edward. "Inaugual Lecture on the Study of History." Cambridge, 11 June 1895. *Lectures on Modern History*. London: Macmillan, 1906.

Dallek, Robert. *Camelot's Court: Inside the Kennedy White House*. New York: HarperCollins, 2013.

Damer, T. Edward. *Attacking Faulty Reasoning: A Practical Guide to Fallacy-Free Arguments*. Boston: Wadsworth, 2012.

Davis, David Brion. *The Problem of Slavery in the Age of Revolution*. New York: Cornell University Press, 1975. Culture, 2000.

Day, John Kyle. "The Fall of a Southern Moderate: Congressman Brooks Hays and the Election of 1958." *Arkansas Historical Quarterly* 59 (Autumn 2000): 241–64.

"Demagogue McCarthy; Does He Deserve Well of the Republic?" *Time* 48/17 (22 October 1951): 20–23.

Dierenfield, Bruce J. *Keeper of the Rules: Congressman Howard W. Smith*. Charlottesville: University Press of Virginia, 1987.

Drury, Allen. *A Senate Journal, 1943–1945*. Illustrations by Joseph Papin. New York: McGraw-Hill, 1963.

Duffy, John J., Jr. "Charleston—The People and the Place at the Start of the Twentieth Century." *St. Andrews Review* (n.d., 197?): 43–53.

Dunn, Susan. *Roosevelt's Purge: How FDR Sought to Change the Democratic Party.* Cambridge: Belknap Press of Harvard University Press, 2010.

Dykeman, Wilma and James Stokely. *Seeds of Southern Change: The Life of Will Alexander.* Chicago: University of Chicago Press, 1962.

Edens, Ruth J. *It Took an Act of Congress: Martha Williams Brice Bequest for the Williams Brice Stadium of the University of South Carolina.* N.P., 1995.

Edgar, Walter B. *South Carolina: A History.* Columbia: University of South Carolina Press, 1998.

Edmonds, Bobby F. *The Making of McCormick County.* McCormick, SC: Cedar Hill, 1999.

The Essential Writings of Machiavelli. Edited and translated by Peter Constantine. New York: Random House Modern Library, 2007.

Exploring the Unknown: Selected Documents in the History of the Civil Space Program. 3 volumes. Edited by John M. Logsdon, Linda J. Lear, Jannelle Warren-Findley, and Ray Warren Hall. Washington, DC: NASA Special Publications, 1995.

Farmer, James Oscar. "A Collision of Cultures: Aiken, South Carolina, Meets the Nuclear Age." *Proceedings of the South Carolina Historical Association* (1995): 40–49.

Forster, Arnold and Benjamin R. Epstein. *Danger on the Right.* Anti-Defamation League of B'nai B'rith. New York: Random House, 1961.

Fortenay, Charles L. *Estes Kefauver: A Biography.* Knoxville: University of Tennessee Press, 1980.

Fowler, Donald Lionel. *Presidential Voting in South Carolina, 1948–1964.* Columbia: University of South Carolina Bureau of Government Research and Service, 1966.

Fowler, Glenn. "Edward W. Barrett, 79, Ex-Journalism Dean, Dies." *New York Times* obituary (25 October 1989).

Frank, Barney. "The New Mandate on Defense." *Democracy* 27 (Winter 2013): 50–56.

Frederickson, Kari. *Cold War Dixie: Militarization and Modernization in the American South.* Athens: University of Georgia Press, 2013.

Gaddis, John Lewis. *George F. Kennan: An American Life.* London: Penguin, 2011.

Gates, Henry Louis, Jr. "After the Revolution." *New Yorker* (29 April and 6 May 1996): 59–61.

———. "Thirteen Ways of Looking at a Black Man." *New Yorker* (23 October 1995): 56–65.

George, Emily. *Martha W. Griffiths.* Washington, DC: University Press of America, 1982.

George, Henry. *Progress and Poverty: An Inquiry into the Cause of Industrial Depression and of Increase of Want with Increase of Wealth: The Remedy.* 1890. Reprint. New York: Robert Schalkenbach Foundation, 1942.

Goluboff, Risa. *The Lost Promise of Civil Rights*. Cambridge and London: Harvard University Press, 2007.

Gona, Ophelia DeLaine. *Dawn of Desegregation: J. A. De Laine and Briggs v. Eliot*. Columbia: University of South Carolina Press, 2011.

Goodale, Gregory. *Sonic Persuasion: Reading Sound in the Recorded Age*. Studies in Sensory History Series. Urbana and London: University of Illinois Press, 2011.

Gordon, Lester J. "John McCormack and the Roosevelt Era." PhD dissertation. Boston: Boston University, 1976.

Gorman, John Bruce. *Kefauver: A Political Biography*. New York and London: Oxford University Press, 1971.

Gunther, John. *The Riddle of MacArthur: Japan, Korea, and the Far East*. New York: Harper & Brothers, 1951.

Haile, Cantey. "Gold Mining." *South Carolina Encyclopedia*. Edited by Walter Edgar. Columbia: University of South Carolina Press for South Carolina Humanities Council, 2006.

Harlan, Louis Round. *Separate and Unequal: Public School Campains and Racism in the Southern Seaboard States, 1901–1915*. Chapel Hill: University of North Carolina Press, 2000.

Harrell, David Edwin. *All Things Are Possible: The Healing and Charismatic Revivals in Modern America*. Bloomington: Indiana University Press, 1975.

Hawk, Emory Q. *Economic History of the South*. Edited by Carl Wittke. Prentice-Hall History Series. New York: Prentice-Hall, 1934.

___. *The Road to Serfdom: Texts and Documents*. Edited by Bruce Caldwell. 1941. Revised edition. Chicago: University of Chicago Press, 2007.

Hays, Brooks. *A Hotbed of Tranquility: My Life in Five Worlds*. New York: Macmillan, 1968.

___. *Politics Is My Parish*. Baton Rouge: Louisiana State University Press, 1981.

___. *A Southern Moderate Speaks*. Chapel Hill: University of North Carolina Press, 1959.

___. *The World: A Christian's Workshop*. Nashville, TN: Broadman, 1958.

Hemingway, Ernest. *The Fifth Column; a Play*. New York: Samuel French, 1937.

Hollis, Daniel Walker. "Cotton Ed Smith: Showman or Statesman?" *South Carolina Historical Magazine* 71/4 (October 1970): 235–56.

Hoover, John Edgar. "These Fighters Against Youth Crime Need Your Help!" *Readers Digest* (April 1961).

Hull, Cordell. *Memoirs of Cord Hull*. Edited by Andrew Henry Thomas Berding. New York: Macmillan, 1948.

Hume, David. *An Enquiry Concerning the Human Understanding and Concerning the Principles of Morals*. 1777. Edited by L. A. Selby-Bigge. Revised. Oxford: Oxford University Clarendon Press, 1902.

Humphrey, Hubert Horatio. *The Education of a Public Man: My Life and Politics*. Garden City, NY: Doubleday, 1976.

Huss, John. *Senator for the South: A Biography of Olin D. Johnston*. Garden City, NY: Doubleday, 1961.

Irwin, Douglas A. "The Nixon Shock after Forty Years: The Import Surcharge Revolution." *World Trade Review* 12/1 (July 2013): 29–56.

Jones, George E. "Austin Charges Vishinsky Falsified." *New York Times* (21 September 1947).

Jordan, David M. *FDR, Dewey, and the Election of 1944*. Bloomington: Indiana University Press, 2011.

Jordan, Frank E., Jr. *The Primary State: A History of the Democratic Party in South Carolina*. Columbia, SC: R. L. Bryan, 1968.

Jordan, Terry G. and Mattii Kaups. *The American Backwoods Frontier: An Ethical and Ecological Interpretation*. Creating the North American Landscape Series. Edited by Gregory Conniff, Bonnie Loyd, and David Schuyler. Baltimore, MD: Johns Hopkins University Press, 1989.

Jorden, William. "Soviet Fires Earth Satellite into Space." *New York Times Special Edition* (5 October 1957).

Kaplan, Fred. *Nineteen Fifty Nine: The Year Everything Changed*. Hoboken, NJ, and New York: John Wiley, 2009.

Kaplowitz, Stan. "Using Aggregate Voting Data to Measure Presidential Coattail Effect." *Public Opinion Quarterly* 35/3 (Summer 2013): 415–19.

Kazin, Michael. *A Godly Hero: The Life of William Jennings Bryan*. New York: Alfred A. Knopf, 2006.

Kelsey, George Dennis Sale. "Social Thought of Contemporary Southern Baptists." PhD dissertation. New Haven, CT: Yale University, 1946.

———. *Social Ethics among Southern Baptists, 1917–1969*. Lanham, MD: Scarecrow Press, 1977.

Kennedy, John Fitzgerald. "New England and the South." *Atlantic* 97/1 (January 1954): 32–36.

Key, Valdimer Orlando, Jr., and Alexander Heard. "South Carolina: The Politics of Color." *Southern Politics in State and Nation*. 1949. New York: Knopf Borzoi Books, 1950.

———. *Southern Politics in State and Nation*. New York: Alfred A. Knopf, 1949.

Keynes, John Maynard. *Collected Works of John Maynard Keynes*. 29 volumes. London: Palgrave Macmillan, 1982.

King, Martin Luther, Jr. "Out of the Long Night." *The Gospel Messenger* (8 February 1958): 14.

Kirby Page, Social Evangelist: The Autobiography of a Twentieth Century Prophet for Peace. Edited by Harold Edward Fey. New York: Fellowship Press, 1975.

Klein, Katharine. "The Sacrifices of the American Textile Industry and the Common Good." MA thesis. Columbia: University of South Carolina, 2012.

Kluger, Richard. *Simple Justice: The History of Brown v. Board of Education and Black America's Struggle for Equality*. 1977. Reprint. New York: Random House, 2004.

Koestler, Arthur. "Appalling Alternatives." *Saturday Review of Literature* 34/1 (6 January 1951): 19–21, 94.

Kuhn, Ferdinand, Jr. "Russia Asks U.N. for Action Against 'War Propagandists' Leading U.S. 'Warmongers.'" *Washington Post* (19 September 1947).

Lander, Ernest M. *The Textile Industry in Antebellum South Carolina*. Baton Rouge: Louisiana State University Press, 1969.

Lawrence, David. "Question of the Parent in Aid to Education." *Cincinnati Enquirer* (4 March 1961).

Lawrence, Jerome and Robert Edwin Lee. *Inherit the Wind*. New York: Samuel French, 1955.

A Legacy of Leadership: Governors and American History. Edited by Clayton McClure Brooks. Philadelphia: University of Pennsylvania Press, 2013.

Lewis, Tom. *Divided Highways. Building the Interstate Highways, Transforming American Life*. Ithaca, NY, and London: Cornell University Press, 2013.

Lilla, Mark. "*The Reactionary Mind* by Corey Robin [review]." *New York Review of Books* 59/1 (12 January 2012): 12–17.

Llewellyn Lloyd, Richard D. Vivian. *How Green Was My Valley*. New York: Edition for Armed Services, 1940.

Lloyd, Lewis E. *Tariffs: The Case for Protection*. New York: Devin-Adair, 1955.

Marcantonio, Vito. *I Vote My Conscience: Debates, Speeches, and Writings of Vito Marcantonio*. Edited by Annette Rubinstein. 1956. Reprint. New York: Calendo Institute of City University of New York, 2002.

Martin, John Bartlow. *Adlai Stevenson of Illinois: The Life of Adlai E Stevenson*. Garden City, NY: Doubleday, 1976.

McMath, Robert C. "The History of the Present." In *The Ongoing Burden of Southern History: Politics and Identity in the Twenty-First-Century South*. Edited by Angie Maxwell, Todd Shields, and Jeannie Whayne. Making the Modern South Series. Edited by David Goldfield. Baton Rouge: Louisiana State University Press, 2012.

Meyer, Gerald. *Vito Marcantonio: Radical Politician, 1902–1954*. Albany: State University of New York Press, 1989.

Middleton, Earl Matthews and Joy W. Barnes. *Knowing Who I Am: A Black Entrepreneur's Struggle and Success in the American South*. Columbia: University of South Carolina Press, 2008.

Miller, Anthony Bary. "Piedmont Politician: The Early Political Career of Olin D. Johnston, 1894–1941." PhD dissertation. University of North Carolina, 1976.

Mills, Charles Wright. *The Power Elite*. New York: Oxford University Press, 1956.

Mitchell, Broadus. *The Rise of the Cotton Mills in the South*. Columbia: University of South Carolina Press, 2001.

Moore, Barrington. *Social Origins of Dictatorship and Democracy: Lord and Peasant in the Making of the Modern World*. Boston: Beacon Press, 1966.

Moore, Hight C. *On Duty for God and Country*. Nashville, TN: Broadman Press, 1943.

Moore, John Hammond. *South Carolina Newspapers*. Columbia: University of South Carolina Press, 1988.

Morris, Willie. *North toward Home*. Boston: Houghton Mifflin, 1967.

Mosca, Gaetano. *The Ruling Class*. Edited and translated by Hannah D. Kahn. 1896. Reprint. New York: McGraw-Hill paper, 1939.

Moyar, Mark. *Triumph Forsaken: The Vietnam War, 1954–1965*. New York and London: Cambridge University Press, 2009.

"Mr. Sound Government—Senator Edgar A. Brown." *South Carolina Magazine* (February 1958).

Mueller, John E. *War, Presidents, and Public Opinion*. New York: John Wiley, 1973.

Myers, Andrew. "The Blinding of Isaac Woodard." *Proceedings of the South Carolina Historical Association* (2004): 63–73.

Myrdal, Karl Gunnar, Richard Sterner, and Arnold Rose. *An American Dilemma*. 2 volumes. New York: McGraw-Hill, 1944.

Nelson, Garrison. "Irish Identity Politics: The Reinvention of Speaker John W. McCormack of Boston." *New England Journal of Public Policy*. 15 (Fall/Winter 1999/2000): 7–34.

Nevins, Joseph Allan. "At the Roots of Democracy." Review of *Age of Jackson*. *New York Times Book Review*. (16 September 1945): 1.

Nixon, Richard Milhous. *The Memoirs of Richard Nixon*. New York: Simon & Schuster, 1978.

Noll, Mark. *God and Race in American Politics*. Princeton, NJ, and Oxford: Princeton University Press, 2008.

Odum, Howard Washington. *Southern Regions of the United States*. Chapel Hill: University of North Carolina Press, 1936.

"Of the People." *South Carolina Historical Magazine*. 90/4 (1989): 329–30.

Parker, Theodore. *Ten Sermons of Religion*. Boston: Crosby, Nichols, and Company, 1857.

Parrington, Vernon Louis. *Main Currents in American Thought*. 3 volumes. New York: Harcourt Brace, 1927.

Peabody, Robert L. *The Ford-Halleck Minority Leadership Contest*. New York: McGraw-Hill, 1966.

Pearson, Alex Philmore. "Olin Earl Teague and the Veterans Administration." PhD dissertation. College Station: Texas A&M University, 1977.

Peterson, Merrill Daniel. *The Jefferson Image in the American Mind.* Charlottesville: University Press of Virginia, 1960.

Phillips, Kevin Price. *The Politics of Rich and Poor: Wealth and the Electorate in the Reagan Aftermath.* New York: Random House, 1990.

Plumer, Bradford. "Rick Santorum: A Brief History of the 'Some of My Best Friends' Defense." *The New Republic* (16 June 2011).

Price, Reynolds. Interview with Terri Gross. NPR: "Fresh Air" (19 June 2006).

Rivers, Margaret Middleton, Margaret M. R. Eastman, and Lucius Mendel Rivers Jr. *Me and Mendel.* Charleston, SC: History Press, 2007.

Rivoli, Pietra. *The Travels of a T-Shirt in the Global Economy: An Economist Examines the Markets, Power, and Politics of World Trade.* Hoboken, NJ: John Wiley & Sons, 2005.

Robin, Corey. *The Reactionary Mind: Conservatism from Edmund Burke to Sarah Palin.* New York: Oxford University Press, 2011.

Romulo, Carlos Pena. *I Walked with Heroes.* New York: Holt, Rinehart & Winston, 1961.

Roper, John Herbert, Sr. *C. Vann Woodward, Southerner.* 1987. Revised edition. Athens and London: University of Georgia Press, 2011.

___. "Essay on the Voting Rights Extension Act." *Phylon* 45 (1984): 188–96.

___. *The Magnificent Mays: A Biography of Benjamin Elijah Mays.* Columbia and London: University of South Carolina Press, 2012.

___. *Paul Green, Playwright of the Real South.* Athens and London: University of Georgia Press, 2003.

Schlesinger, Arthur Meier, Jr. *The Age of Jackson.* Boston: Little, Brown, 1945.

"The Secular Masque." *Poems by John Dryden.* London: J. M. Dent, Everyman's Library (1949): 282–85.

Sen, Amartya. "The Boundaries of Justice; David Hume and Our World." *The New Republic* 242/4915 (29 December 2011): 23–26.

___. *The Idea of Justice.* Cambridge, MA: Harvard University Press, 2011.

Shaffer, Alan L. *Vito Marcantonio: Radical in Congress.* Syracuse, NY: Syracuse University Press, 1960.

Shuler, Jack. *Blood and Bone: Truth and Reconciliation in a Southern Town.* Columbia: University of South Carolina Press, 2012.

Simkins, Frances Butler. *Pitchfork Ben Tillman, South Carolinian.* Southern Biography Series. Edited by Fred C. Cole and Wendell Holmes Stephenson. Baton Rouge: Louisiana State University Press, 1946.

Simon, Bryant. *A Fabric of Defeat: The Politics of South Carolina Millhands, 1910–1948.* Chapel Hill: University of North Carolina Press, 1998.

Sitton, Claude. "3000 Troops Put Down Mississippi Rioting and Seize 200 as Negro Attends Classes." *New York Times Special Edition*, October 1, 1962, p. 1.

Skaggs, Marvin Lucien. *North Carolina Border Disputes Involving Her Southern Line*. James Sprunt Studies in History and Political Science. Chapel Hill: University of North Carolina Press, 1941.

Smith, Marie. "Easter Parade Stretches." *Washington Post* (2 April 1961): 1.

Sorensen, Theodore C. *Kennedy*. New York: Harper & Row, 1965.

Stephens, Lester D. "Centers of Creation: John Perkins Barratt's Biogeological Theory of Racial Origins." *Journal of Southern History* 80/2 (May 2014).

Stueck, William. *The Korean War: An International History*. Princeton, NJ, and London: Princeton University Press, 1995.

Sweet, William Warren. *The Baptists, 1783–1830: A Collection of Source Materials*. New York: Henry Holt, 1931.

___. *Methodism in American History*. New York: Methodists Book Concern, 1933.

___. *The Presbyterians, 1783–1842: A Collection of Source Materials*. 1936. Reprint. New York: Cooper Square, 1964.

___. *Religion in the Development of American Culture, 1765–1840*. New York: Scribner, 1952.

Sydnor, Charles Sackett. *Gentlemen Freeholders: Political Practices in Washington's Virginia*. Chapel Hill: University of North Carolina Press, 1952.

Talmadge, Herman Eugene. *Talmadge: A Political Legacy, a Politician's Life: A Memoir by Herman E. Talmadge*. Edited by Mark Royden Winchell. Atlanta: Peachtree, 1987.

Tanenhaus, Sam. "Strategist and Scourge." *The New Republic*. 242/4915: 26–32.

Tate, Allen. *Selected Poems by Allen Tate*. New York: Charles Scribner's Sons, 1937.

Terrill, Tom E. *The Tariff, Politics, and American Foreign Policy, 1874–1901*. Contributions in American History No. 31. Westport, CT: Greenwood Company, 1973.

"Text of Address by Austin." *New York Times*. (21 September 1947): 44.

Thomas, Evan. *Ike's Bluff: President Eisenhower's Secret Battle to Save the World*. New York: Little, Brown, 2012.

Tindall, George Brown. *The Emergence of the New South, 1913–1945*. History of the South Series. Edited by Ellis Merton Coulter and Wendell Holmes Stephenson. Baton Rouge: Louisiana State University Press, 1969.

Varay, Jarad. "How the IMF Got Its Keynesian Groove Back." *The New Republic* (2 December 2011).

"Vital Local Issues." *Life*. 44/16 (1959): 32–33.

Von Hayek, Friedrich A. *The Collected Works of F. A. Hayek*. Chicago: University of Chicago Press, 1989–2012.

Walker, Donald Edwin. "The Congressional Career of Clare Eugene Hoffman, 1935–1963." PhD dissertation. East Lansing: Michigan State University, 1982.

Walton, Hanes, Jr., Josephine A. V. Allen, Sherman C. Puckett, and Donald R. Deskins Jr. "Woodward's New Intellectual Stream: The Enfranchisement of the Freed Slave Population." In *The Ongoing Burden of Southern History; Politics and Identity in the Twenty-First-Century South*. Edited by Angie Maxwell, Todd Shields, and Jeannie Whayne. Making the Modern South Series. Edited by David Goldfield. Baton Rouge: Louisiana State University Press, 2012.

Watson, Glen P. "How the Space Act Came to Be." Typescript. NASA Historical Reference Collection. NASA Headquarters, Washington, DC.

Weber, Max. *Politics as a Vocation*. Translated by Hans Heinrich Gerth and Charles Wright Mills. 1965. Reprint. Philadelphia: Fortress, 1972.

White, Theodore H. and Howard J. Langer. "Confessions of a Second Look Liberal." *Society* 20 (July/August 1983): 56–63.

White, Walter Francis. *Rope and Faggot: A Biography of Judge Lynch*. 1929. Reprint. South Bend, IN, and London: University of Notre Dame Press, 2001.

William Faulkner: Letters and Fiction. Edited by James Gray Watson. Austin: University of Texas Press, 1987.

Williams, Daniel K. "The Christian Right's Partisan Commitment." *Historically Speaking* (April 2011): 7–9.

___. *God's Own Party: The Making of the Christian Right*. New York: Oxford University Press, 2010.

Williamson, Joel Roudolphe. *A Rage for Order: Black-White Relations in the American South Since Emancipation*. New York and Oxford: Oxford University Press, 1986.

___. *The Crucible of Race: Black-White Relations in the American South Since Emancipation*. New York: Oxford University Press, 1984.

Wines, William A. *Ethics, Law and Business*. New York and London: Routledge, 2006.

Witcover, Jules Joseph. *White Knight: The Rise of Spiro Agnew*. New York: Random House, 1972.

Wolomine, Barbara A. *Constantino Brumidi, Artist of the Capitol*. Washington, DC: USGPO, 1998.

Womack, Steven Douglas. "Charles A. Halleck and the New Frontier: Political Opposition through the Madisonian Model." PhD dissertation. Ball State University, 1980.

Woodward, Comer Vann. *Responses of Presidents to Charges of Misconduct*. New York: Delacorte, 1974.

___. *The Strange Career of Jim Crow*. 1955. 5th revised edition. New York: Oxford University Press, 1999.

Woodward, Robert and Carl Bernstein. *The Final Days*. New York: Simon & Schuster, 1976.

Workman, William D., Jr. *The Bishop of Barnwell*. Columbia, SC: R. L. Bryan, 1963.

Wright, Gavin. *Old South, New South: Revolutions in the Southern Economy Since the Civil War.* New York: Basic Books, 1986.

Wyatt-Brown, Bertram. *Southern Honor: Ethics and Behavior in the Old South.* New York: Oxford University Press, 1986.

___. *Honor and Violence in the Old South.* New York: Oxford University Press, 1986.

Yarbrough, Tinsley E. *A Passion for Justice: J. Waties Waring and Civil Rights.* New York: Oxford University Press, 1987.

Ziegler, Eugene Noel. *When Conscience Meets Power.* Columbia: University of South Carolina Press, 2008.

Index